Lecture Notes in Computer Science   14653

Founding Editors

Gerhard Goos
Juris Hartmanis

The series Lecture Notes in Computer Science (LNCS), including its subseries Lecture Notes in Artificial Intelligence (LNAI) and Lecture Notes in Bioinformatics (LNBI), has established itself as a medium for the publication of new developments in computer science and information technology research, teaching, and education.

LNCS enjoys close cooperation with the computer science R & D community, the series counts many renowned academics among its volume editors and paper authors, and collaborates with prestigious societies. Its mission is to serve this international community by providing an invaluable service, mainly focused on the publication of conference and workshop proceedings and postproceedings. LNCS commenced publication in 1973.

Marc Joye · Gregor Leander
Editors

Advances in Cryptology – EUROCRYPT 2024

43rd Annual International Conference on the Theory
and Applications of Cryptographic Techniques
Zurich, Switzerland, May 26–30, 2024
Proceedings, Part III

 Springer

Editors
Marc Joye 🆔
Zama
Paris, France

Gregor Leander 🆔
Ruhr University Bochum
Bochum, Germany

ISSN 0302-9743   ISSN 1611-3349 (electronic)
Lecture Notes in Computer Science
ISBN 978-3-031-58733-7   ISBN 978-3-031-58734-4 (eBook)
https://doi.org/10.1007/978-3-031-58734-4

This Springer imprint is published by the registered company Springer Nature Switzerland AG
The registered company address is: Gewerbestrasse 11, 6330 Cham, Switzerland

Paper in this product is recyclable.

Preface

EUROCRYPT 2024 is the 43rd Annual International Conference on the Theory and Applications of Cryptographic Techniques. It was held in Zurich, Switzerland, during May 26–30, 2024. EUROCRYPT is an annual conference organized by the International Association for Cryptologic Research (IACR).

EUROCRYPT 2024 received 501 submissions, out of which 469 formally went to the review process. Every submission was assigned in a double blind way to three program committee members and, in some cases, one or two extra reviewers were added. The IACR version of the HotCRP software was used for the whole review process. In total, 1436 reviews were produced and 5200+ comments were made during the whole process. After a first round, 290 papers were pre-selected by the program committee to enter the second round. These remaining papers were offered a rebuttal to answer questions and requests for clarification from the reviewers. After several weeks of subsequent discussions, the committee ultimately selected 105 papers for acceptance.

The program committee was made up of 110 top cryptography researchers, all expert in their respective fields. For some papers, external sub-referees were appointed by the committee members. We warmly thank all the committee members and their sub-referees for the hard work in the peer review and their active participation in the discussions. We greatly benefited from the help of the area chairs: Shweta Agrawal for "Public Key Primitives with Advanced Functionalities", Serge Fehr for "Theoretical Foundations", Pierre-Alain Fouque for "Secure and Efficient Implementation, Cryptographic Engineering, and Real-World Cryptography", María Naya-Plasencia for "Symmetric Cryptology", Claudio Orlandi for "Multi-Party Computation and Zero-Knowledge", and Daniel Wichs for "Classic Public Key Cryptography". They each led the discussions and the paper selection in their respective area. The previous program chairs for IACR flagship conferences were also very helpful; in particular, we are grateful to Carmit Hazay and Martijn Stam for sharing their experience with EUROCRYPT 2023.

The IACR aims to support open and reproducible research within the field of cryptography. For the first time for a flagship conference, authors of accepted papers were invited to submit artifacts associated with their papers, such as software or datasets, for review, in a collaborative process between authors and the artifact review committee. We thank Martin Albrecht for having accepted to chair the artifact committee.

Three papers were awarded this year. The Best Paper Awards went to Pierrick Dartois, Antonin Leroux, Damien Robert and Benjamin Wesolowski for their paper "SQIsignHD: New Dimensions in Cryptography" and to Itai Dinur for his paper "Tight Indistinguishability Bounds for the XOR of Independent Random Permutations by Fourier Analysis". The Early-Career Best Paper Award was given to Maria Corte-Real Santos, Jonathan Komada Eriksen, Michael Meyer, and Krijn Reijnders for their paper "AprèsSQI: Extra Fast Verification for SQIsign Using Extension-Field Signing".

In addition to the contributed papers, EUROCRYPT 2024 featured two invited talks: "Cryptography in the Wild" by Kenny Paterson and "An Attack Became a Tool: Isogeny-based Cryptography 2.0" by Wouter Castryck. The conference also included a panel discussion on the future of publications; the panel was moderated by Anne Canteaut. The traditional rump session featuring short and entertaining presentations was held on Wednesday 29th.

Several people were key to the success of the conference. Our two general chairs, Julia Hesse and Thyla van der Merwe, did a fantastic job with the overall organization of EUROCRYPT 2024. Kevin McCurley ensured everything went smoothly with the review software and in the collection of the final papers. The conference relied on sponsors to help ensure student participation and reduce costs. We gratefully acknowledge the financial support of (in alphabetical order): Apple, AWS, CASA, City of Zürich, Concordium, Cosmian, Ethereum Foundation, Fair Math, Google, Huawei, IBM, Input/Output, NTT Research, SandboxAQ, Swiss National Science Foundation, Starkware, TII, Zama, and ZISC.

May 2024

Marc Joye
Gregor Leander

Organization

General Co-chairs

Thyla van der Merwe   Google, Switzerland
Julia Hesse   IBM Research Zurich, Switzerland

Program Co-chairs

Marc Joye   Zama, France
Gregor Leander   Ruhr-University Bochum, Germany

Area Chairs

Shweta Agrawal   IIT Madras, India
Serge Fehr   CWI Amsterdam and Leiden University,
       The Netherlands
Pierre-Alain Fouque   Université de Rennes, CNRS and Inria, France
María Naya-Plasencia   Inria, France
Claudio Orlandi   Aarhus University, Denmark
Daniel Wichs   Northeastern University and NTT Research, USA

Program Committee

Martin R. Albrecht   King's College London and SandboxAQ, UK
Diego F. Aranha   Aarhus University, Denmark
Nuttapong Attrapadung   AIST, Japan
Christof Beierle   RUB, Germany
Sonia Belaïd   CryptoExperts, France
Tim Beyne   KU Leuven, Belgium
Olivier Blazy   Ecole Polytechnique, France
Jeremiah Blocki   Purdue University, USA
Alexandra Boldyreva   Georgia Tech University, USA
Xavier Bonnetain   Inria, France
Jonathan Bootle   IBM Research Europe – Zurich, Switzerland
Christina Boura   University of Versailles, France

Stanislaw Jarecki	UC Irvine, USA
Jérémy Jean	ANSSI, France
Bhavana Kanukurthi	Indian Institute of Science, India
Shuichi Katsumata	PQShield LTD, UK, and AIST, Japan
Ilan Komargodski	Hebrew University of Jerusalem and NTT Research, Israel
Yashvanth Kondi	Aarhus University, Denmark
Venkata Koppula	IIT Delhi, India
Fabien Laguillaumie	Université de Montpellier, LIRMM, France
Wei-Kai Lin	University of Virginia, USA
Jiahui Liu	The University of Texas at Austin, USA
Chen-Da Liu-Zhang	HSLU and Web3 Foundation, Switzerland
Mark Manulis	Universität der Bundeswehr, Munich, Germany
Bart Mennink	Radboud University, The Netherlands
Pratyay Mukherjee	Supra Research, USA
Ruben Niederhagen	Academia Sinica, Taiwan, and University of Southern Denmark, Denmark
Svetla Nikova	KU Leuven, Belgium, and University of Bergen, Norway
Ryo Nishimaki	NTT Social Informatics Laboratories, Japan
Anca Nitulescu	Protocol Labs, France
Ariel Nof	Bar Ilan University, Israel
Kaisa Nyberg	Aalto University, Finland
Jiaxin Pan	University of Kassel, Germany and NTNU, Norway
Omer Paneth	Tel Aviv University, Israel
Arpita Patra	Indian Institute of Science, India
Duong Hieu Phan	Telecom Paris, France
Raphael C.-W. Phan	Monash University, Malaysia
Stjepan Picek	Radboud University, The Netherlands
Thomas Pornin	NCC Group, Canada
Manoj Prabhakaran	IIT Bombay, India
Carla Ràfols	Universitat Pompeu Fabra, Spain
Divya Ravi	Aarhus University, Denmark
Doreen Riepel	UC San Diego, USA
Matthieu Rivain	CryptoExperts, France
Mélissa Rossi	ANSSI, France
Adeline Roux-Langlois	CNRS, GREYC, France
Andy Rupp	University of Luxembourg, Luxembourg, and KASTEL SRL, Germany
Alessandra Scafuro	NC State University, USA
Peter Scholl	Aarhus University, Denmark

André Schrottenloher	Inria, Université de Rennes, IRISA, France
Peter Schwabe	MPI-SP, Germany, and Radboud University, The Netherlands
Yannick Seurin	Ledger, France
Mark Simkin	Ethereum Foundation, Denmark
Pratik Soni	University of Utah, USA
Akshayaram Srinivasan	University of Toronto, Canada
Damien Stehlé	CryptoLab, France
Siwei Sun	Chinese Academy of Sciences, China
Berk Sunar	Worcester Polytechnic Institute, USA
Yosuke Todo	NTT Social Informatics Laboratories, Japan
Junichi Tomida	NTT Social Informatics Laboratories, Japan
Serge Vaudenay	EPFL, Switzerland
Frederik Vercauteren	KU Leuven, Belgium
Ivan Visconti	University of Salerno, Italy
David Wu	UT Austin, USA
Mark Zhandry	NTT Research, USA

External Reviewers

Marius A. Aardal	Augustin Bariant
Aysajan Abdin	Cruz Barnum
Ittai Abraham	Khashayar Barooti
Damiano Abram	James Bartusek
Hamza Abusalah	Balthazar Bauer
Anasuya Acharya	Amit Behera
Léo Ackermann	Shalev Ben-David
Amit Agarwal	Shany Ben-David
Ahmet Agirtas	Omri Ben-Eliezer
Prabhanjan Ananth	Loris Bergerat
Yoshinoro Aono	Ward Beullens
Ananya Appan	Varsha Bhat
Nicolas Aragon	Ritam Bhaumik
Arasu Arun	Kaartik Bhushan
Gennaro Avitabile	Alexander Bienstock
Renas Bacho	Alexander Block
Youngjin Bae	Erica Blum
David Balbas	Jan Bobolz
Marshall Ball	Nicolas Bon
Fabio Banfi	Charlotte Bonte
Zhenzhen Bao	Carl Bootland
Manuel Barbosa	Joppe Bos

Katharina Boudgoust
Alexandre Bouez
Clemence Bouvier
Cyril Bouvier
Pedro Branco
Nicholas Brandt
Lennart Braun
Alessio Caminata
Matteo Campanelli
Sébastien Canard
Kevin Carrier
Ignacio Cascudo
Gaëtan Cassiers
Guilhem Castagnos
Wouter Castryck
Pierre-Louis Cayrel
André Chailloux
Debasmita Chakraborty
Hubert Chan
Anirudh Chandramouli
Rahul Chatterjee
Rohit Chatterjee
Mingjie Chen
Yanlin Chen
Yilei Chen
Yu Long Chen
Jesús-Javier Chi-Domínguez
Ilaria Chillotti
Hyeongmin Choe
Wonseok Choi
Wutichai Chongchitmate
Arka Ra Choudhuri
Hao Chung
Kai-Min Chung
Michele Ciampi
Sebastian Clermont
Benoît Cogliati
Daniel Collins
Brice Colombier
Sandro Coretti
Alain Couvreur
Daniele Cozzo
Wei Dai
Quang Dao
Debajyoti Das

Sourav Das
Pratish Datta
Emma Dauterman
Gareth T. Davies
Leo de Castro
Thomas De Cnudde
Paola de Perthuis
Giovanni Deligios
Cyprien Delpech de Saint Guilhem
Rafael del Pino
Amit Deo
Julien Devevey
Siemen Dhooghe
Zijing Di
Emanuele Di Giandomenico
Christoph Dobraunig
Rafael Dowsley
Leo Ducas
Jesko Dujmovic
Betül Durak
Avijit Dutta
Christoph Egger
Martin Ekera
Felix Engelmann
Simon Erfurth
Reo Eriguchi
Jonathan Komada Eriksen
Hülya Evkan
Thibauld Feneuil
Giacomo Fenzi
Rex Fernando
Valerie Fetzer
Rune Fiedler
Ben Fisch
Matthias Fitzi
Nils Fleischhacker
Pouyan Forghani
Boris Fouotsa
Cody Freitag
Sapir Freizeit
Daniele Friolo
Paul Frixons
Margot Funk
Phillip Gajland
Daniel Gardham

Rachit Garg
Francois Garillot
Gayathri Garimella
John Gaspoz
Robin Geelen
Paul Gerhart
Diana Ghinea
Satrajit Ghosh
Ashrujit Ghoshol
Emanuele Giunta
Kristian Gjøsteen
Aarushi Goel
Evangelos Gkoumas
Eli Goldin
Rishab Goyal
Adam Groce
Ziyi Guan
Zichen Gui
Antonio Guimaraes
Felix Günther
Kanav Gupta
Nirupam Gupta
Kamil Doruk Gur
Hosein Hadipour
Mohammad Hajiabadi
Ghaith Hammouri
Guillaume Hanrot
Keisuke Hara
Patrick Harasser
Dominik Hartmann
Keitaro Hashimoto
Rachelle Heim
Nadia Heninger
Alexandra Henzinger
Julius Hermelink
Julia Hesse
Hans Heum
Shuichi Hirahara
Taiga Hiroka
Marc Houben
James Hsin-Yu Chiang
Kai Hu
Yungcong Hu
Tao Huang
Zhenyu Huang

Loïs Huguenin-Dumittan
James Hulett
Atsunori Ichikawa
Akiko Inoue
Tetsu Iwata
Joseph Jaeger
Jonas Janneck
Dirmanto Jap
Samuel Jaques
Ruta Jawale
Corentin Jeudy
Ashwin Jha
Dan Jones
Philipp Jovanovic
Bernhard Jungk
Fatih Kaleoglu
Chethan Kamath
Jiayi Kang
Minsik Kang
Julia Kastner
Hannah Keller
Qiao Kexin
Mustafa Khairallah
Dmitry Khovratovich
Ryo Kikuchi
Jiseung Kim
Elena Kirshanova
Fuyuki Kitagawa
Michael Klooß
Christian Knabenhans
Lisa Kohl
Sebastian Kolby
Dimitris Kolonelos
Chelsea Komlo
Anders Konring
Nishat Koti
Mukul Kulkarni
Protik Kumar Paul
Simran Kumari
Norman Lahr
Russell W. F. Lai
Baptiste Lambin
Oleksandra Lapiha
Eysa Lee
Joohee Lee

Jooyoung Lee
Seunghoon Lee
Ryan Lehmkuhl
Tancrède Lepoint
Matthieu Lequesne
Andrea Lesavourey
Baiyu Li
Shun Li
Xingjian Li
Zengpeng Li
Xiao Liang
Chuanwei Lin
Fuchun Lin
Yao-Ting Lin
Fukang Liu
Peiyuan Liu
Qipeng Liu
Patrick Longa
Julian Loss
Paul Lou
George Lu
Steve Lu
Zhenghao Lu
Reinhard Lüftenegger
Vadim Lyubashevsky
Fermi Ma
Varun Madathil
Christian Majenz
Giulio Malavolta
Mary Maller
Nathan Manohar
Mario Marhuenda Beltrán
Ange Martinelli
Elisaweta Masserova
Takahiro Matsuda
Christian Matt
Noam Mazor
Pierrick Méaux
Jeremias Mechler
Jonas Meers
Willi Meier
Kelsey Melissaris
Nikolas Melissaris
Michael Meyer
Pierre Meyer

Charles Meyer-Hilfiger
Peihan Miao
Chohong Min
Brice Minaud
Kazuhiko Minematsu
Tomoyuki Morimae
Hiraku Morita
Mahnush Movahedi
Anne Mueller
Michael Naehrig
Marcel Nageler
Vineet Nair
Yusuke Naito
Varun Narayanan
Hugo Nartz
Shafik Nassar
Patrick Neumann
Lucien K. L. Ng
Ruth Ng
Dinh Duy Nguyen
Jérôme Nguyen
Khoa Nguyen
Ky Nguyen
Ngoc Khanh Nguyen
Phong Nguyen
Phuong Hoa Nguyen
Thi Thu Quyen Nguyen
Viet-Sang Nguyen
Georgio Nicolas
Guilhem Niot
Julian Nowakowski
Koji Nuida
Sabine Oechsner
Kazuma Ohara
Olya Ohrimenko
Jean-Baptiste Orfila
Astrid Ottenhues
Rasmus Pagh
Arghya Pal
Tapas Pal
Mahak Pancholi
Omkant Pandey
Lorenz Panny
Jai Hyun Park
Nikitas Paslis

Alain Passelègue
Rutvik Patel
Shravani Patil
Sikhar Patranabis
Robi Pedersen
Alice Pellet-Mary
Hilder V. L. Pereira
Guilherme Perin
Léo Perrin
Thomas Peters
Richard Petri
Krzysztof Pietrzak
Benny Pinkas
Guru-Vamsi Policharla
Eamonn Postlethwaite
Thomas Prest
Ludo Pulles
Kirthivaasan Puniamurthy
Luowen Qian
Kexin Qiao
Xianrui Qin
Willy Quach
Rahul Rachuri
Rajeev Raghunath
Ahmadreza Rahimi
Markus Raiber
Justin Raizes
Bhavish Raj Gopal
Sailaja Rajanala
Hugues Randriam
Rishabh Ranjan
Shahram Rasoolzadeh
Christian Rechberger
Michael Reichle
Krijn Reijnders
Jean-René Reinhard
Bhaskar Roberts
Andrei Romashchenko
Maxime Roméas
Franck Rondepierre
Schuyler Rosefield
Mike Rosulek
Dragos Rotaru
Yann Rotella
Lior Rotem

Lawrence Roy
Ittai Rubinstein
Luigi Russo
Keegan Ryan
Sayandeep Saha
Yusuke Sakai
Matteo Salvino
Simona Samardjiska
Olga Sanina
Antonio Sanso
Giacomo Santato
Paolo Santini
Maria Corte-Real Santos
Roozbeh Sarenche
Pratik Sarkar
Yu Sasaki
Rahul Satish
Sarah Scheffler
Dominique Schröder
Jacob Schuldt
Mark Schultz-Wu
Gregor Seiler
Sruthi Sekar
Nicolas Sendrier
Akash Shah
Laura Shea
Yixin Shen
Yu Shen
Omri Shmueli
Ferdinand Sibleyras
Janno Siim
Tjerand Silde
Jaspal Singh
Nitin Singh
Rohit Sinha
Luisa Siniscalchi
Naomi Sirkin
Daniel Slamanig
Daniel Smith-Tone
Yifan Song
Yongsoo Song
Eduardo Soria-Vazquez
Nick Spooner
Mahesh Sreekumar Rajasree
Sriram Sridhar

Srivatsan Sridhar
Lukas Stennes
Gilad Stern
Marc Stöttinger
Bing Sun
Ling Sun
Ajith Suresh
Elias Suvanto
Jakub Szefer
Akira Takahashi
Abdullah Talayhan
Abdul Rahman Taleb
Suprita Talnikar
Tianxin Tang
Samuel Tap
Stefano Tessaro
Jean-Pierre Tillich
Ivan Tjuawinata
Patrick Towa
Kazunari Tozawa
Bénédikt Tran
Daniel Tschudi
Yiannis Tselekounis
Ida Tucker
Nirvan Tyagi
LaKyah Tyner
Rei Ueno
Gilles Van Assche
Wessel Van Woerden
Nikhil Vanjani
Marloes Venema
Michiel Verbauwhede
Javier Verbel
Tanner Verber
Damien Vergnaud
Fernando Virdia
Damian Vizár
Benedikt Wagner
Roman Walch
Julian Wälde

Alexandre Wallet
Chenghong Wang
Mingyuan Wang
Qingju Wang
Xunhua Wang
Yuyu Wang
Alice Wanner
Fiona Weber
Christian Weinert
Weiqiangg Wen
Chenkai Weng
Ivy K. Y. Woo
Lichao Wu
Keita Xagawa
Aayush Yadav
Anshu Yadav
Saikumar Yadugiri
Shota Yamada
Takashi Yamakawa
Hailun Yan
Yibin Yang
Kevin Yeo
Eylon Yogev
Yang Yu
Chen Yuan
Mohammad Zaheri
Gabriel Zaid
Riccardo Zanotto
Arantxa Zapico
Maryam Zarezadeh
Greg Zaverucha
Marcin Zawada
Runzhi Zeng
Tina Zhang
Yinuo Zhang
Yupeng Zhang
Yuxi Zheng
Mingxun Zhou
Chenzhi Zhu

Contents – Part III

AI and Blockchain

Polynomial Time Cryptanalytic Extraction of Neural Network Models 3
    Isaac A. Canales-Martínez, Jorge Chávez-Saab, Anna Hambitzer,
    Francisco Rodríguez-Henríquez, Nitin Satpute, and Adi Shamir

Ordering Transactions with Bounded Unfairness: Definitions, Complexity
and Constructions ....,,, ... 34
    Aggelos Kiayias Nikos Leonardos, and Yu Shen

Asymptotically Optimal Message Dissemination with Applications
to Blockchains 64
    Chen-Da Liu-Zhang, Christian Matt, and Søren Eller Thomsen

Proof-of-Work-Based Consensus in Expected-Constant Time 96
    Juan Garay, Aggelos Kiayias, and Yu Shen

**Secure and Efficient Implementation, Cryptographic Engineering,
and Real-World Cryptography**

A Holistic Security Analysis of Monero Transactions 129
    Cas Cremers, Julian Loss, and Benedikt Wagner

Algorithms for Matrix Code and Alternating Trilinear Form Equivalences
via New Isomorphism Invariants 160
    Anand Kumar Narayanan, Youming Qiao, and Gang Tang

Generalized Feistel Ciphers for Efficient Prime Field Masking 188
    Lorenzo Grassi, Loïc Masure, Pierrick Méaux, Thorben Moos,
    and François-Xavier Standaert

A Novel Framework for Explainable Leakage Assessment 221
    Si Gao and Elisabeth Oswald

Integrating Causality in Messaging Channels 251
    Shan Chen and Marc Fischlin

Symmetric Signcryption and E2EE Group Messaging in Keybase 283
    Joseph Jaeger, Akshaya Kumar, and Igors Stepanovs

Theoretical Foundations (I/II)

Trapdoor Memory-Hard Functions 315
  Benedikt Auerbach, Christoph U. Günther, and Krzysztof Pietrzak

Probabilistically Checkable Arguments for All NP 345
  Shany Ben-David

The Complexity of Algebraic Algorithms for LWE 375
  Matthias Johann Steiner

Pauli Manipulation Detection Codes and Applications to Quantum
Communication over Adversarial Channels 404
  Thiago Bergamaschi

Certified Everlasting Secure Collusion-Resistant Functional Encryption,
and More 434
  *Taiga Hiroka, Fuyuki Kitagawa, Tomoyuki Morimae, Ryo Nishimaki,
  Tapas Pal, and Takashi Yamakawa*

Early Stopping for Any Number of Corruptions 457
  Julian Loss and Jesper Buus Nielsen

Author Index 489

AI and Blockchain

Polynomial Time Cryptanalytic Extraction of Neural Network Models

Isaac A. Canales-Martínez[2], Jorge Chávez-Saab[2], Anna Hambitzer[2], Francisco Rodríguez-Henríquez[2], Nitin Satpute[2], and Adi Shamir[1]

[1] Weizmann Institute, Rehovot, Israel
adi.shamir@weizmann.ac.il

[2] Cryptography Research Center, Technology Innovation Institute, Abu Dhabi, UAE
{isaac.canales,jorge.saab,anna.hambitzer,
francisco.rodriguez,nitin.satpute}@tii.ae

Abstract Billions of dollars and countless GPU hours are currently spent on training Deep Neural Networks (DNNs) for a variety of tasks. Thus, it is essential to determine the difficulty of extracting all the parameters of such neural networks when given access to their black-box implementations. Many versions of this problem have been studied over the last 30 years, and the best current attack on ReLU-based deep neural networks was presented at Crypto'20 by Carlini, Jagielski, and Mironov. It resembles a differential chosen plaintext attack on a cryptosystem, which has a secret key embedded in its black-box implementation and requires a polynomial number of queries but an exponential amount of time (as a function of the number of neurons).

In this paper, we improve this attack by developing several new techniques that enable us to extract with arbitrarily high precision all the real-valued parameters of a ReLU-based DNN using a polynomial number of queries *and* a polynomial amount of time. We demonstrate its practical efficiency by applying it to a full-sized neural network for classifying the CIFAR10 dataset, which has 3072 inputs, 8 hidden layers with 256 neurons each, and about 1.2 million neuronal parameters. An attack following the approach by Carlini et al. requires an exhaustive search over 2^{256} possibilities. Our attack replaces this with our new techniques, which require only 30 min on a 256-core computer.

Keywords: ReLU-Based Deep Neural Networks · Neural Network Extraction · Polynomial Query and Polynomial Time Differential Attack

1 Introduction

In this paper, we consider the problem of extracting all the weights and biases of a Deep Neural Network (DNN), which is queried as a black box to obtain the outputs corresponding to carefully chosen inputs. This is a long-standing open problem that was first addressed by cryptographers and mathematicians in the

M. Joye and G. Leander (Eds.): EUROCRYPT 2024, LNCS 14653, pp. 3–33, 2024.
https://doi.org/10.1007/978-3-031-58734-4_1

early nineties of the last century [3,8], and then was followed up one decade later by an adversarial reverse-engineering attack presented by Lowd and Meck in [12]. More recently, since around 2016, this problem has enjoyed a steady stream of new ideas by research groups from both industry and academia [2,9,14,17,19], culminating with an algorithm that Carlini, Jagielski and Mironov presented at Crypto 2020 [5], which in the general case, requires a polynomial number of queries but an exponential amount of time. Due to this time complexity, their algorithm was practically demonstrated only on some toy examples in which the layers of the showcased networks (beyond the first hidden layer, which is usually easy to extract) contain at most a few tens of neurons.

The main obstacle that made the Carlini et al. algorithm exponential in time was their inability to determine one bit of information (namely, a $\pm$ sign) about each neuron in the DNN. This hindrance forced them to use exhaustive search over all the possible sign combinations in each layer, which is prohibitively expensive for any realistic network whose width is more than a few tens of neurons. Our main contribution in this paper is to show how to efficiently find these signs by a new chosen input attack, which we call *neuron wiggling*, as well as two other methods that target the first two hidden layers and the last one. Our techniques resemble a combination of first-order and second-order differential cryptanalysis, in which we use a chosen input attack to slightly change the inputs to the DNN in a small number of carefully chosen directions and observe both the slope and the curvature produced in the output of the network as a result of these input changes. However, it differs from standard differential attacks on digital cryptosystems by using real-valued inputs and outputs rather than bit strings.

We demonstrate the practical applicability of our algorithm by performing a sign-recovery attack on a DNN trained to recognize the standard CIFAR10 classes. This DNN has 3072 inputs, 8 hidden layers, 256 neurons per hidden layer, and about 1.2 million weights. Our techniques replaced the exhaustive search over 2^{256} possible combinations of neuronal signs carried out by Carlini et al. in each layer by a new algorithm which requires only 32 min on a 256-core computer to find all the 8×256 neuronal signs in the 8 layers of the network.

Our model of deep neural networks is essentially the same as the one used by Carlini et al. We assume that the network is fully connected (with no skip connections), with r hidden layers of varying width in which each neuron consists of an affine mapping followed by Rectified Linear Units (ReLU) activation functions, and as in [5], we know the number of layers and neurons per layer. For the sake of simplicity in the analysis of our algorithm, we assume that all the network weights are real numbers, that arithmetic operations over real numbers (both by the network and by the attacker) are carried out with infinite precision in unit time, and that the attacker can perform arbitrarily small changes in the inputs of the network and observe their corresponding outputs with arbitrarily high precision. In practice, it was sufficient to use standard 64-bit floating point arithmetic to extract the full-sized CIFAR10 network, but higher precision may be required to attack considerably deeper networks due to the possible accumulation of rounding errors throughout our computations. However, since our algorithm uses only polynomially many arithmetic operations, we expect the asymptotic number of bits of precision to also grow only polynomially with the size of the network.

In our attack (as well as the one by Carlini et al.), it is essential to assume that the activation function is ReLU-like since we concentrate on the behavior of the network in the vicinity of *critical points*, which are defined as inputs in whose tiny vicinity exactly one ReLU input in one of the layers changes sign. Regardless of the complexity of the network, we expect the network's output to abruptly change its behavior as a result of this ReLU transition, which makes this event noticeable when we observe the network's outputs. Such abrupt changes are also visible when we apply a smooth softmax function to the logits, and thus, our attack can use outputs which are either the logits produced by the last linear layer or their softmax values (which translate the logits into a probability distribution over the possible classes). We can generalize the attack to any other type of activation function that looks like a piecewise linear function (with possibly more than one sharp bend), such as a leaky ReLU, but not to smooth activation functions such as a sigmoid which have no critical points. Our attack can be applied without modifications to convolutional networks since they can be described as a special form of a fully connected network.

While our analysis and experiments support our claim of efficiency in the extraction of the weights of large networks, there are several important caveats. First of all, fully connected networks have certain symmetries which make it impossible to extract the exact form of the original network, but only a functionally equivalent form. For example, we can reorder the neurons of any layer and adjust the weights accordingly, we can merge two neurons that have exactly the same weights and biases, we can eliminate any neuron whose output is multiplied by a weight of zero by all the next layer neurons, or we can multiply all the weights (including the bias) of a particular neuron by some positive constant c while multiplying all the weights which multiply the output of that neuron in the next layer neurons by c^{-1}; all these changes do not change the input/output behavior of the network, and thus they are invisible to any black-box attack. In addition, there could be some unlucky events, which we do not expect to encounter but which will cause our attack to fail. For example, there could be neurons whose values before the ReLU almost never change sign, and thus our bounded number of queries will fail to detect any critical point for them.[1] Finally, during the attack, we may fail to solve some systems of linear equations if their determinant is exactly zero, but even the slightest change in the real-valued entries in such a matrix should eliminate the problem. We thus have to qualify

---

[1] We refer to these neurons as almost always-on/off neurons and note that the almost perfectly linear behavior of such neurons will be simply absorbed by the linear mappings in the next layer, which will result in a very close approximation of the original neural network. In practice, in our networks, always-on neurons were only encountered immediately after random initialization. After training, however, this kind of neuron was never encountered, but we did find instances of always-off neurons.

our assertion that our attack always succeeds, in the same way that most crypt-analytic attacks on cryptosystems are in fact heuristics that are not guaranteed to succeed in some particularly unlucky situations.

It is important to note that when the attacker is only given an (adversarially chosen) collection of known inputs along with their corresponding outputs, then a famous result of Blum and Rivest back in 1993 [3] shows that just to decide whether there exists a 2 layer 3 neuron DNN on n inputs which is consistent with the provided pairs is NP-complete. However, in our case, the attacker can apply a chosen input attack, and thus he is not likely to suffer from this particular complexity barrier.

1.1   Our Contributions

Building on the work of [5], we present a black-box attack that permits the recovery of a functionally equivalent model of a deep neural network that uses ReLU activation functions. In contrast with the approach presented in [5], our attack has polynomial time complexity in terms of the number of neurons in the DNN, and can thus be applied (in principle) to arbitrarily deep and wide neural networks. In addition, we can easily deal with many types of expanding neural networks, where [5] struggles.

To make this possible, we develop three new sign recovery techniques. The first one, called *SOE*, is based on solving a system of linear equations derived from observed first derivative values. The *Neuron Wiggle* method applies differences in the input to maximally change the value of the neuron of interest. These changes propagate to the output and a statistical analysis of the output variations allows recovery of the sign. Finally, the *Last Hidden Layer* technique is applicable only to the last layer in the network and employs second-order derivatives to construct a different system of linear equations whose solution simultaneously yields the signs of all the neurons in this layer.

We showcase our findings with a practical sign-recovery attack against a 3072-input network with 8 hidden layers and $d = 256$ neurons per hidden layer for classifying the CIFAR10 dataset.

1.2   Overview of Our Attack

Our attack follows the same strategy as the one presented in [5] by Carlini et al. Namely, we recover the parameters (i.e., weights and bias of each neuron) for the first hidden layer and "peel off" that layer. Thus, the attack now reduces to extracting the parameters of a DNN with one less hidden layer. We then recover the parameters for the second layer, peel it off, and continue in this fashion until the last hidden layer. Finally, the parameters for the output layer[2] are obtained. After peeling off the first hidden layer, however, we no longer have full control

---

[2] By the output layer, we mean the very last layer of the DNN. We assume that this layer is linear in the sense that it doesn't contain ReLUs. The output layer is not counted as a hidden layer of the DNN.

of the input to the second layer since the first layer is not an invertible mapping (e.g., no negative numbers can be output by its ReLUs). This lack of control over the input to the layer is also true for all subsequent hidden layers.

Recovering the parameters of each hidden layer is done in two steps. First, for each neuron, we recover some multiple of its weights and bias. The sign of this unknown multiplicative factor is called the *sign for the neuron*. In the second step, we find the signs for all the neurons in the current layer; we need them to find the actual mapping represented by this layer in order to peel it off and proceed to the next layer. Recovering signs is essential because multiplication by a positive constant is a symmetry of the network, but multiplication by a negative constant is not a symmetry due to the nonlinear behavior of the ReLU.

To find the multiple of the parameters, we use the same techniques as in [5, Sections 4.2 and 4.3.2]. To recover the sign for the neurons in the general case, Carlini et al. had to use exhaustive search over all the sign combinations in all the neurons in the current layer, which required an exponential amount of time. In this work, we introduce three new polynomial-time techniques.

System of Equations (*SOE*). As pointed out in [5], in networks that are contractive enough, we essentially have full control over the inputs to any of the layers, and the signs can be easily recovered one by one through a method they propose, which we refer to as *Freeze*. Here, we present an alternative method called *SOE*, which recovers the signs for all neurons simultaneously by solving a system of equations. Not only is it more efficient in terms of oracle queries, but also in time complexity since it solves a single system of equations whereas *Freeze* would need to solve one system of equations per neuron. Both *Freeze* and *SOE* are significantly simpler and more efficient than the methods we describe next but are heavily limited by the contraction requirement and typically are only applicable to the first few layers.

Neuron Wiggle. Practically, most neural networks do not have contractive-enough hidden layers. The attack in [5] uses, in this case, a more general technique that determines the signs by exhaustive search while requiring a polynomial number of oracle queries. As our main result, we present the *Neuron Wiggle* technique, which is polynomial in both, time and queries to the oracle. This is the method of choice for most of the layers in both, contractive or expansive networks. In this method, we choose a *wiggle* (i.e., a small change in a carefully chosen direction) in the input to the network that makes the input to the ReLU for some targeted neurons experience a large change, while all the other neurons in the network are expected to experience much smaller changes. This makes it possible to recover the sign for the targeted neuron, since if the input to that neuron's ReLU is negative, the effect of the large change will be blocked, while if the input to the ReLU is positive, this change will propagate through this ReLU and the subsequent layers, and eventually cause a change at the output. By choosing a critical point and wiggling in two opposite directions, we can detect the direction where the larger output change is present, thereby recovering the sign. However, some critical points may lead to a wrong decision on the sign, and thus, we have to repeat it at multiple unrelated inputs to gather reliable statistical evidence for which wiggles are blocked and which ones go through the ReLU. It is important to note that even without knowing the neuron's sign, the attacker can easily aggregate all the experiments that are on the same active/inactive side of the ReLU, and then he can use the statistical difference between these two clusters to determine which cluster is on the active and which cluster is on the inactive side of the ReLU.

In our practical attacks, accumulating statistical evidence from 200 input points was sufficient to recover the correct sign for each neuron, except possibly in the last hidden layer. The main problem in the last hidden layer is that there is no randomization present in the function computing the output. That means if the weight that connects a particular neuron to the output is considerably smaller than the others, almost no amount of wiggling of the corresponding neuron will get through to the output. We thus used the neuron wiggle technique to successfully attack all but the first and last hidden layers of a CIFAR10 network with 256 neurons per layer.

Last Hidden Layer. Here, we develop a specialized technique to reliably deal with the last layer, which exploits exactly the same property that made the neuron wiggling technique less reliable for this layer (namely, the fact that there is a fixed linear mapping that maps the outputs of these neurons to the final output). This allows us to construct arbitrarily many linear equations in the coefficients of this fixed output function by exploring multiple unrelated inputs to the DNN, and their unique solution simultaneously yields the unknown signs for all the last layer neurons. This method has lower time and query complexity than Neuron Wiggle, but its applicability is limited to the last layer.

Organization

The remainder of this paper is organized as follows. In Sect. 2, we present a brief summary of the state of the art on DNN parameter extraction in the black-box model. In Sect. 3, we present several basic definitions, and assumptions, and state the problem to solve. We complete that section by giving an overview of the approach by Carlini et al. before presenting our own sign-recovery techniques in Sect. 4. All the practical attacks carried out in this work are presented in Sect. 5. The concluding remarks are drawn in Sect. 6.

2   Related Work

Model extraction in the context of DNNs aims to obtain its architecture, the weights, and biases associated with each neuron in the network and, occasionally, the network's training hyperparameters. Although early work can be traced back to Fefferman [8] (who proved in 1994 that perfect knowledge of the output of a sigmoid-based network uniquely specifies its architecture and neurons' weights, and also proved that two neural networks with the same input-output map are isomorphic up to trivial equivalences), followed by Lowd and Meek in 2005 [12], the most important body of literature on this topic has been published since

2016, when Tramèr et al. studied the problem of functional equivalence for the case of multi-class logistic regression and the multi-layer perceptron. Since then, many attacks have been presented considering different attack scenarios and security models [5, 6, 12, 13, 15, 16] (see also [14] for a comprehensive survey).

As discussed in Sect. 1, in this paper, we are primarily interested in a security model where the only interaction the attacker has with the DNN is submitting queries to it and observing the corresponding outputs (e.g., accessing it as a web service). Therefore, the attacker does not have access to the software or the hardware where the network has been deployed, which rules out side-channel and/or fault injection attacks as the ones reported in [2, 10]. Furthermore, the main goal of our attack is to recover a functionally equivalent model of the network. Such precision is normally out of reach for the hardware attacks described in [10].

The state-of-the-art black-box model extraction has been traditionally centered around DNNs with ReLU activation functions. In the beginning, it was thought that the most effective way of extracting the model of the networks was through oracle calls that revealed information about the gradients. In [13], this approach was theoretically analyzed and implemented to attack networks with one hidden layer. An improvement of this work followed quickly afterward in [9], offering significant improvements to the functional equivalence of the extracted model but still constrained to attacks dealing with relatively modest one-layer DNNs and relying on the unrealistic help of an oracle that leaked the gradients.

Almost simultaneously, Rolnick and Körding presented in [17] an approach that, by only observing the output of the network, was theoretically capable of extracting the parameters of deeper networks. However, in practice, the algorithm in [17] only worked for two-layer networks. Meanwhile, a similar strategy was theoretically analyzed in [6]. A follow-up work by Carlini et al. was presented in [5]. In this paper, the authors presented important technical improvements and devised novel techniques that allowed them to obtain a much higher precision in the neuron's parameters extraction while using remarkably fewer oracle calls than the previous methods reported in [9, 17] (cf. [5, Table 1]). However impressive the high precision results obtained by the authors, they only managed to deal with neural networks of no more than three hidden layers and with a relatively modest number of a few tens of neurons beyond the first layer. The main reason the approach presented in [5] could not scale up well for larger and deeper networks was that the weights of the neurons could only be obtained up to a constant of unknown sign. Indeed, finding the sign for the neurons had a prohibitively exponential cost in time and has remained until now as one of the two main obstacles towards extracting deeper and larger neural networks. The second obstacle, also acknowledged by the authors of [5], is that of dealing with so-called expansive neural networks, i.e., networks where the number of neurons in a given inner layer is larger than the number of inputs to that layer.

3 Preliminaries

3.1 Basic Definitions and Notation

Informally, a neural network is a collection of connected nodes called *neurons*. Neurons are arranged in *layers* and are connected to those in the previous and the next layer. Every neuron has a *weight* associated with each incoming connection and a *bias*. We present next several important formal definitions by closely following the definitions and notation given in [5].

Definition 1. *An* r-deep neural network *is a function* $f : \mathcal{X} \to \mathcal{Y}$ *composed of alternating linear layers* f_i *and a non-linear activation function* σ *acting component-wise:*

$$f = f_{r+1} \circ \sigma \circ \cdots \circ \sigma \circ f_2 \circ \sigma \circ f_1.$$

We focus our study on Deep Neural Networks (DNN) over the real numbers. Then, $\mathcal{X} = \mathbb{R}^{d_0}$ and $\mathcal{Y} = \mathbb{R}^{d_{r+1}}$, where d_0 and d_{r+1} are positive integers. As in [5], we only consider neural networks using the ReLU activation function $\sigma : x \mapsto \max(x, 0)$.

Definition 2. *The* i-th fully connected layer *of a neural network is a function* $f_i : \mathbb{R}^{d_{i-1}} \to \mathbb{R}^{d_i}$ *given by the affine transformation*

$$f_i(x) = A^{(i)}x + b^{(i)},$$

where $A^{(i)} \in \mathbb{R}^{d_i \times d_{i-1}}$ *is the* weight matrix, $b^{(i)} \in \mathbb{R}^{d_i}$ *is the* bias vector *of the* i-th layer *and* d_{i-1}, d_i *are positive integers.*

Layers in neural networks often have more structure than just a matrix-vector multiplication as above (e.g., convolutional layers). However, they may admit a description as a special form of a fully connected layer. We call a network *fully connected* if all its layers are fully connected. The first r layers are the *hidden layers*, and layer $r + 1$ is the *output layer*.

Definition 3. *A* neuron *is a function determined by the corresponding weight matrix and activation function. Particularly, the* j-th neuron of layer i *is the function* η *given by*

$$\eta(x) = \sigma(A_j^{(i)}x + b_j^{(i)}),$$

where $A_j^{(i)}$ *and* $b_j^{(i)}$ *denote, respectively, the* j-th row of $A^{(i)}$ *and* j-th coordinate of $b^{(i)}$.

Definition 4. *Let* $\ell = d_{i-1}$ *and* $A_j^{(i)}$ *be described as* $(a_1, a_2, \ldots, a_\ell)$. *The* signature *of the* j-th neuron in layer i *is the tuple*

$$\left(\frac{a_1}{a_1} = 1, \frac{a_2}{a_1}, \ldots, \frac{a_\ell}{a_1} \right). \tag{1}$$

Definition 5. *Let $\mathcal{V}(\eta; x)$ denote the value that neuron η takes with $x \in \mathcal{X}$ before applying σ. If $\mathcal{V}(\eta; x) > 0$ then η is* active. *When $\mathcal{V}(\eta; x) = 0$, η is* critical, *and we call x a* critical point *for η[3]. Otherwise, it is* inactive. *The state of η on input x (i.e., active, inactive, or critical) is denoted by $\mathcal{S}(\eta; x)$.*

Definition 6. *Let $x \in \mathcal{X}$. The* linear neighbourhood *of x is the set*

$$\{u \in \mathcal{X} \mid \mathcal{S}(\eta; x) = \mathcal{S}(\eta; u) \text{ for all neurons } \eta \text{ in the network }\}.$$

Definition 7. *The* architecture *of a fully connected neural network is described by specifying its number of layers along with the dimension d_i (i.e., number of neurons) of each layer $i = 1, \cdots, r + 1$. We say that d_0 is the dimension of the inputs to the neural network, whereas d_{r+1} gives the number of outputs of the network. A neural network has $N = \sum_{i=1}^{r} d_i$ neurons.*

As in [5], we specify the architecture of a neural network by enumerating the dimensions of its layers. For example, the eight-hidden-layer network for classifying the CIFAR10 dataset showcased in this paper has the architecture

$$3072 - 256^{(8)} - 10.$$

Let F_i denote the function that computes the first i layers of the DNN after the ReLUs, i.e., $F_i = \sigma \circ f_i \circ \cdots \circ \sigma \circ f_1$. By definition, all neurons remain in the same state when evaluating the DNN with an input in the linear neighborhood of $x \in \mathcal{X}$. Following the explanation in [5], for any such point x', we have that

$$F_i(x') = I^{(i)}(A^{(i)} \cdots (I^{(2)}(A^{(2)}(I^{(1)}(A^{(1)}x' + b^{(1)})) + b^{(2)}) \cdots + b^{(i)})$$
$$= I^{(i)}A^{(i)} \cdots I^{(2)}A^{(2)}I^{(1)}A^{(1)}x' + \beta$$
$$= \Gamma x' + \beta,$$

where $I^{(j)}$ are $0 - 1$ diagonal matrices with a 0 on the diagonal's k-th entry when neuron k at layer j is inactive and 1 on the diagonal's k-th entry when that neuron is active. That is, in the linear neighborhood of an input x, we can "collapse" the action of various contiguous layers into an affine transformation. If we make a change Δ to the input, we can observe the corresponding change in the value of the neurons:

$$F_i(x + \Delta) - F_i(x) = \Gamma(x + \Delta) + \beta - (\Gamma(x) + \beta) = \Gamma\Delta.$$

This Δ must be such that $x + \Delta$ is in the linear neighborhood of x.

Assume that we fully know the first $i - 1$ layers, and we are currently recovering layer i. Let F_{i-1} and G_{i+1} represent, respectively, the fully recovered and non-recovered part of the DNN, i.e.,

$$f = \underbrace{f_{r+1} \circ \sigma \circ \cdots \circ \sigma \circ f_{i+1}}_{G_{i+1}} \circ \sigma \circ f_i \circ \underbrace{\sigma \circ f_{i-1} \circ \cdots \circ \sigma \circ f_1}_{F_{i-1}}.$$

---

[3] Carlini et al.'s "critical point" is "being critical" in our definition. Carlini et al.'s "witness for a neuron being at a critical point" is "a critical point" in our definition.

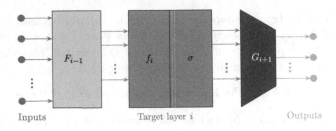

Fig. 1. Representation of the DNN according to the recovered part F_{i-1}, current target layer i and unknown part G_{i+1}.

Then, the neural network can be depicted as in Fig. 1. Furthermore, if we restrict inputs x' to be in the linear neighbourhood of x, we can collapse F_{i-1} and G_{i+1} as

$$F_{i-1}(x') = F_x^{(i-1)}x' + b_x^{(i-1)} \quad \text{and} \quad G_{i+1}(x') = G_x^{(i+1)}x' + b_x^{(i+1)},$$

respectively. We use the subscript in the collapsed matrices and bias vectors to indicate that they are defined in the linear neighborhood of x.

Definition 8. *We call the j-th row of $G_x^{(i+1)}$* the output coefficients *for the j-th output of the DNN.*

3.2   Problem Statement and Assumptions

The parameters θ of a DNN f_θ are the concrete assignments to the weights and biases. Following the setting in [5], in a *model parameter extraction attack*, an attacker generates queries x to an oracle $\mathcal{O}$ which returns $f_\theta(x)$. The goal of the attacker is to obtain a set of parameters $\hat{\theta}$ such that $f_{\hat{\theta}}(x)$ is as similar as possible to $f_\theta(x)$.

We focus on the attack presented in [5]. As mentioned in Subsect. 1.2, Carlini et al.'s attack recovers the parameters layer by layer in two steps. The first one finds multiples of the parameters, particularly the signatures of the neurons as defined in Eq. 1. Since the signature consists of ratios of pairs of weights, negating all these weights simultaneously will preserve the signature but nonlinearly change the outputs of this neuron's ReLU. Consequently, before we can peel off a layer of neurons, we have to determine for each one of its neurons separately whether the weights and biases are one possible vector of values or its negated vector. That is, we must get a sign of that neuron's weight. The second step recovers these signs for all neurons in the current layer. In this paper, we specifically focus our attention on the latter half, which was the exponential-time bottleneck in [5], under the assumption that the signatures are already known.

The following are the assumptions we have regarding the oracle and the capabilities of the attacker:

- **Knowledge of the architecture.**
- **Full-domain inputs.** We can feed arbitrary inputs from $\mathcal{X} = \mathbb{R}^{d_0}$.
- **Complete outputs.** We receive outputs directly from f without further processing.
- **Fully connected network and ReLU activations.** The network is fully connected, and all activation functions are the ReLU function.
- **Fully precise computations.** All computations are done with infinite-precision arithmetic.
- **Signature availability and uniqueness.** We have access to the signature of each neuron. Also, we assume that no two signatures are the same.

All but the last one are also assumptions in [5]. Regarding full precision, we remark that computations by both the oracle and the attacker enjoy this characteristic. Carlini et al. assume single-output DNNs. However, we allow for multiple outputs, which enhances the performance of our techniques and is incidentally also more realistic. Knowledge of the architecture is required to apply a full attack employing the methods in [5] with our sign recovery techniques.

3.3 Carlini et al.'s Differential Attack

We now present a high-level description of the techniques by Carlini et al. [5].

Finding Critical Points. To discover critical points, Carlini et al. analyze the function induced by a DNN when an input x_1 is linearly transformed into another input x_2. For the sake of simplicity and without loss of generality, we will assume in the following that the network has a single output. Let $x_1, x_2 \in \mathbb{R}^{d_0}$ and $\mu : [0, 1] \to \mathbb{R}^{d_0}$ defined as

$$\mu : \lambda \mapsto x_1 + \lambda(x_2 - x_1)$$

be the linear transformation of x_1 into x_2. This induces an output function on the DNN,

$$f^*(\lambda) := f(\mu(\lambda)),$$

which is a piecewise linear function with first-order discontinuities precisely when one of the neurons is toggling between active/inactive states. As shown in Fig. 2, we can identify the first-order discontinuities and revert the mapping μ to recover the point at which the line from x_1 to x_2 intersects a boundary between linear neighborhoods, which is a critical point for some neuron.

In practice, it suffices to measure the slope of the graph in Fig. 2 at different points and extrapolate to find the critical point, all while checking that there are no other abrupt changes in behavior in-between. We refer to [4, appendix C].

At this point, we do not yet know to which layer each critical point belongs, but by sampling enough pairs x_1, x_2 we expect to eventually find multiple critical points for every neuron in the network.

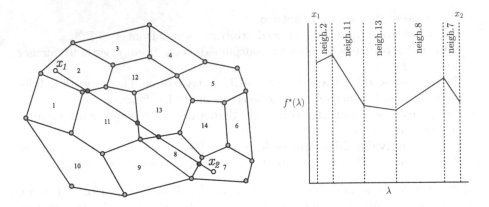

Fig. 2. The input space can be partitioned into linear neighborhoods, and the output function displays abrupt changes in behavior when moving across their borders.

Finding Signatures. The input to the DNN is also the input to the first hidden layer, and we have full control over it. Let η be a neuron with weights $(a_1, \ldots, a_\ell)$. Given $x^* \in \mathbb{R}^{d_0}$ a critical point for η, we can query $\alpha_{i,-} = \frac{\partial f}{\partial e_i}(x^* - \varepsilon e_i)$ and $\alpha_{i,+} = \frac{\partial f}{\partial e_i}(x^* + \varepsilon e_i)$, where $\{e_i\}_{i=1}^{d_0}$ is the canonical basis of $\mathbb{R}^{d_0}$ and ε is a small real number. Since x^* is a critical point, only either $\alpha_{i,-}$ or $\alpha_{i,+}$ will have η in its active state assuming that ε is sufficiently small so that no other neuron toggles. The difference $\alpha_{i,+} - \alpha_{i,-}$ contains the gradient information moving from the input coordinate i through neuron η and to the output; the gradient information through all other neurons cancel out. In other words, this difference is a multiple of a_i given by the other layers of the DNN. Dividing out by another coordinate eliminates the multiplicative factor, i.e., $(\alpha_{i,+} - \alpha_{i,-})/(\alpha_{k,+} - \alpha_{k,-}) = a_i/a_k$. If we fix $k = 1$, the signature (1) is recovered. We denote by $\hat{A}_j^{(i)}$ the signature of the j-th neuron in layer i and $\hat{A}^{(i)}$ the matrix whose j-th row is $\hat{A}_j^{(i)}$. Critical points for the same neuron in the target layer 1 will yield the same signature, while critical points for neurons in other layers will generate different signatures. This allows us to decide which signatures correspond to a layer-1 neuron (i.e., those signatures appearing with repetitions). See [5] for details on this.

After peeling off layers, we can also determine if a signature corresponds to a neuron in the current target layer by observing repetitions. However, starting from layer 2 we no longer have full control of the layer's input, and applying the method above is not possible (we cannot change one coordinate at a time). To overcome this, in layer $i > 1$, we sample $d_i + 1$ directions $\delta_k \sim \mathcal{N}(0, \varepsilon I_{d_0}) \in \mathbb{R}^{d_0}$, and let $\{y_k\} = \{\partial^2 f(x^*)/\partial \delta_1 \partial \delta_k\}_{k=1}^{d_i}$ and $h_k = F_{i-1}(x^* + \delta_k)$. The signature is then given by the vector a such that $\langle h_k, a \rangle = y_k$. This, however, yields partial signatures (since the ReLUs in the previous layer set negative values to zero). Different critical points for the same neuron yield different partial signatures. Each partial signature will yield a different set of coordinates and with enough partial signatures, we can reconstruct the full one.

Finding Signs Using the Freezing Method. We now consider the problem of finding the signs of a given layer. If the network is not expanding, this problem is easy for the first hidden layer. Indeed, for target neuron k in layer i, we can find a wiggle Δ_k in the input space that produces a wiggle $\pm e_k$ in the first hidden layer, where $e_k \in \mathbb{R}^{d_i}$ is a basis vector in the k-th direction, by solving a system of d_1 equations in d_0 variables given by the first layer's weight matrix. For any x in the input space, the outputs of the neural network at x and $x + \Delta_k$ will be equal if the k-th neuron is inactive in the linear neighborhood of x (since the k-th neuron is suppressed by the ReLU whereas all other neurons remain unchanged by construction), and will be different otherwise. We refer to this simple sign-recovery technique as *Freeze*.

There are some scenarios where the same method can be applied to deeper layers. Note that in the linear neighborhood of any input x, the mapping from the d_0-dimensional input space to the space of values entering layer i is an affine mapping since there are no ReLUs that flip from active to inactive or vice versa. The rank of this mapping determines in how many linearly independent directions we can slightly perturb the inputs to layer i when we consider arbitrary perturbations of the input x. If the rank is high enough, we can still expect to find preimages for each of the basis vectors and can apply the *Freeze* method.

In general, however, our ability to change the inputs to a deep hidden layer is severely limited, since about half of the neurons in each layer are expected to be suppressed, and thus, the rank of the affine mapping decreases as we move deeper into the network. This issue is pointed out in [5], where it is claimed that the *Freeze* method can only be applied in networks that are *"sufficiently contracting"* (that is, layer size should decrease by roughly a factor of 2 in each layer in order to compensate for the rank loss). In networks that are not sufficiently contractive, Carlini et al. use instead the much more expensive technique of exhaustive search over all the possible sign combinations (as described in [5, Section 4.4]) that is exponential in time, which makes their attack feasible only for toy examples of non-contracting networks.

4   Our New Sign-Recovery Techniques

As just mentioned, the diminishing control over the inputs to a layer is a significant problem that makes sign recovery in deeper layers harder. To better understand our proposed solutions, we first describe this problem in greater detail.

Let $x \in \mathbb{R}^{d_0}$ be an input to the DNN. Recall that $F_x^{(i-1)}$ and $G_x^{(i+1)}$ are the collapsed matrices for x corresponding to the already recovered and unknown part of the DNN, respectively.

Definition 9. *The space of control for layer i around input x, denoted by $V_x^{(i-1)}$, is the range of the linear transformation $F_x^{(i-1)}$. The dimension of this space is called the number of degrees of freedom for layer i with input x and is denoted by $d_x^{(i-1)}$.*

The space of control is the vector space containing all possible small changes at the input to layer i and, by the definition, $d_x^{(i-1)} = \mathrm{rank}(F_x^{(i-1)})$. Due to the ReLUs in layers 1 to $i-1$ making neurons inactive, for a fixed x, the number of degrees of freedom remains equal or decreases with increasing i. To see this, consider an input x making half of the d neurons in layer 1 be active. The matrix $F_x^{(1)}$ would then have rank $d/2$, and particularly, the rows corresponding to inactive neurons are the zero vector. If layer two has $d' < d/2$ active neurons (with the same input x), the matrix $F_x^{(2)}$ has rank d', and therefore the number of degrees of freedom is also d'. Now, if $d' \geq d/2$, $F_x^{(2)}$ has rank $d/2$ (since the rank of $F_x^{(1)}$ cannot be increased when multiplied by another matrix). We have the same situation for the subsequent layers: the rank can never be increased once it has decreased. In fact, the number of degrees of freedom at layer i is typically determined by the minimum number of active neurons per layer among all layers 1 to $i-1$, but in some cases, it can be strictly smaller.

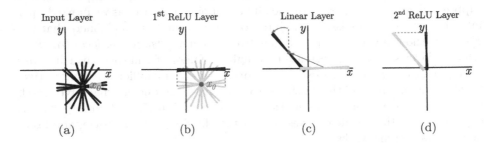

Fig. 3. Intuition for the space of control (Definition 9). Consider a network with 2-dimensional input and two hidden layers with two neurons in each. (a) For the first hidden layer, the space of control is the full 2-dimensional space. We can move around the input x_0 in any direction. (b) After the first hidden layer, if one ReLU is positive and the other negative, we lose one dimension of control. (c) The linear transformation in the second layer will rotate, translate, and scale the space of control. (d) Therefore, after the ReLU's in the second layer (if again one is positive and one is negative), we are still left with a one-dimensional space of control. Note that with no rotation, the space of control collapses into a point after these two hidden layers.

Consider a DNN with input dimension d and the same width d in all its hidden layers. Assume further that each neuron has probability $1/2$ of being active. Initially, the number of degrees of freedom is equal to the dimension d of the input to the DNN. Then, the first hidden layer will have, on average, half of its neurons active, which drops the number of degrees of freedom at the input of layer 2 to $d/2$. We can think of the ReLU's projecting the space of control onto a space determined by the active neurons. One may think that half of those $d/2$ degrees of freedom will again be lost in the second layer due to the fact that half of its ReLU's will be inactive, ending with $d/4$ degrees of freedom. However, before going to the ReLUs on that layer, the space of control for layer 2 is typically rotated by $A^{(2)}$. This rotation may make many coordinates survive the projection of the ReLUs in the second layer. We may still lose some degrees of freedom, but not as many as half of them in each successive layer. Due to this effect of the linear transformation, the number of degrees of freedom will typically stabilize after the first few layers. Figure 3 depicts this phenomenon in a two-dimensional space, and Table 2 shows the average number of active neurons and the average number of degrees of freedom in the 8 successive hidden layers of the actual CIFAR10 network we attack.

We now describe our methods for sign recovery with the loss of degrees of freedom in mind. Recall that in the context of the attack, when recovering the signs for layer i, we fully know F_{i-1}, we know f_i up to a sign per neuron, and G_{i+1} is completely unknown. To simplify our notation, we may drop the subscript x from the collapsed matrices, space of control, and number of degrees of freedom if x is clear by the context.

4.1   SOE Sign-Recovery

We first describe a method for sign recovery in cases where the number of degrees of freedom is sufficiently large. We refer to the method as SOE since it relies on solving a System Of Equations. This method is superficially similar to *Freeze*, but uses different equations and a different set of variables (in the case of [5], the variables referred to the direction we have to follow in input space to freeze all the neurons except the targeted one, while in our SOE technique the variables refer to the coefficients of the output function G_{i+1} at some randomly selected point x). Our technique is more efficient in both its query and time complexities since Carlini et al. had to solve a different system of equations for each targeted neuron, while in our SOE technique, one system of linear equations can simultaneously provide the signs of all the neurons in the current layer.

We assume without loss of generality that the network has a single output (additional outputs can be simply ignored).

As before, let $I_x^{(i)}$ be the matrix representing the ReLU at layer i on input x. The equation for the change in output under an arbitrary sequence of changes in input Δ_k, can then be written as

$$f(x + \Delta_k) - f(x) = G_x^{(i+1)} I_x^{(i)} A^{(i)} F_x^{(i-1)} \Delta_k.$$

Let $y_k = A^{(i)} F_x^{(i-1)} \Delta_k$ and $c = G_x^{(i+1)} I_x^{(i)}$. If the left-hand side is observed to take values z_k through direct queries, the equation can be rewritten as

$$c \cdot y_k = z_k,$$

which can be regarded as a system of equations where c is a vector of variables. Because of the ReLU, if neuron j is inactive on input x we will necessarily have $c_j = 0$, so after obtaining d_i equations, we can solve the system and determine which neurons are inactive around x and hence the appropriate choice of signs for the current layer.

Remark 1. In the context of the attack, we can only recover y_k up to a global scaling of each entry (including possibly a sign flip), but this results in a system of equations where the solution has the same set of variables vanishing.

Oracle Calls/Time. This method is optimal in terms of queries since it only requires $d_i + 1$ queries to solve a layer of size d_i (namely, it must query $f(x)$ and $f(x + \Delta_k)$ for d_i values of k). Once the queries have been performed, the time complexity of the attack comes from solving a system of equations, which can be done in $\mathcal{O}(d_i^3)$ with standard methods.

Limitations. Each choice of Δ_k produces a new equation, so we attempt to gather more equations until the system is uniquely solvable. However, the equations that are obtained may not all be linearly independent. In fact, since the y_k all lay in $A^{(i)}(V_x^{(i-1)})$, we will only obtain enough linearly independent equations if $d_x^{(i-1)} \geq d_i$. This is likely to be the case if the layer size is steadily contracting by a factor of 2, but there is an important exception for the first two hidden layers. Indeed, as long as the network is not expanding, the linear map corresponding to the first hidden layer can usually be inverted. This makes it easy to find an x at which all first-layer neurons are active and hence $d_x^{(1)} = d_1 \geq d_2$. Therefore, the method applies straightforwardly for the first two hidden layers on the sole condition of non-expansiveness and is likely to succeed in subsequent layers only if they each contract by a factor close to 2.

4.2 *Neuron Wiggle* Sign-Recovery

The method presented here does not have the strict constraints on the network's architecture as the one above, since its performance gradually degrades as the number of degrees of freedom diminishes, whereas in SOE the system of equations abruptly changes from solvable to unsolvable.

Definition 10. *A* wiggle *at layer* i *is a vector* $\delta \in \mathbb{R}^{d_{i-1}}$ *of differences in the value of the neurons in that layer.*

Recall that the recovered weight matrix for layer i is $\hat{A}^{(i)} \in \mathbb{R}^{d_i \times d_{i-1}}$ and let its k-th row be $\hat{A}_k^{(i)}$. For a wiggle δ at layer i, neuron $k \in \{1, \ldots, d_i\}$ in that layer changes its value by $e_k = \langle \hat{A}_k^{(i)}, \delta \rangle$. Consider one output of the DNN and let $(c_1, \ldots, c_{d_i})$ be its corresponding vector of output coefficients (i.e., its corresponding row vector in $G^{(i+1)}$). If we "push" the differences e_k through the remaining layers, the difference in the output is

$$\sum_{k \in I} c_k e_k, \tag{2}$$

where I contains the indices of all active neurons at layer i. We want to recover the sign of neuron j. If this neuron is active, the output difference contains the contribution of e_j. If the neuron is inactive, the ReLU "blocks" e_j and it does not contribute. When $c_j e_j$ is sufficiently large, we can detect whether it is present in (2) and use this information to recover the sign of the neuron. This is best achieved when δ is a wiggle that maximizes the change in value for that neuron, i.e., $\|A^{(i)} \delta\|_\infty = |e_j|$. The crucial property we use here is that maximizing the *size* of the wiggle produced by a linear expression does not require knowledge of its sign - if we negate the expression we get a wiggle of the same size but in the opposite direction. We now show how to compute such a maximal wiggle and how to recover the target neuron's sign.

Compute Target Neuron Wiggle. Let $\delta \in \mathbb{R}^{d_{i-1}}$ be parallel to $\hat{A}_j^{(i)}$ (i.e., all coordinates of δ have either the same or opposite sign to the corresponding coordinate of $\hat{A}_j^{(i)}$). Then, all summands in the dot product $\langle \hat{A}_j^{(i)}, \delta \rangle$ have the same sign. If no other row of $\hat{A}^{(i)}$ is a multiple of $\hat{A}_j^{(i)}$, with very high probability $|\langle \hat{A}_j^{(i)}, \delta \rangle| > |\langle \hat{A}_k^{(i)}, \delta \rangle|$, for all $k \neq j$. That means $\|\hat{A}^{(i)} \delta\|_\infty = |\langle \hat{A}_j^{(i)}, \delta \rangle|$. Hence, the change of value for neuron j can be maximized if the wiggle is parallel to $\hat{A}_j^{(i)}$.

Recall that $V^{(i-1)}$ is the space of control for layer i given an input x. We project $\hat{A}_j^{(i)}$ onto $V^{(i-1)}$ and get δ by scaling this projection to have a sufficiently small norm $\varepsilon^{(i-1)}$; see Fig. 4. Finally, we get the input difference $\Delta \in \mathbb{R}^{d_o}$ that generates δ by finding a pre-image of δ under $F^{(i-1)}$.

Recover Target Neuron Sign. We want to recover the sign for η_j, the j-th neuron in layer i. Let x^* be a critical point for η_j and let $\Delta \in \mathbb{R}^{d_o}$ generate the wiggle δ (at layer i) that maximizes the change in value for that neuron. Assume the sign of η_j to be positive. Then, the signs of the recovered weights $\hat{A}_j^{(i)}$ are the same as those of the real weights $A_j^{(i)}$. This implies that also the coordinates of δ have the same sign as those of $A_j^{(i)}$ and $e_k = \langle A_k^{(i)}, \delta \rangle$ has a positive value. Assume the DNN has a single output. Since x^* is a critical point for η_j, evaluating the DNN at $x^* + \Delta$ makes η_j active, thus

$$f(x^* + \Delta) - f(x^*) = c_j e_j + \sum_{k \in I \setminus \{j\}} c_k e_k,$$

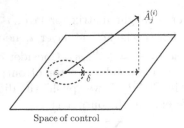

Space of control

Fig. 4. Computing a wiggle that maximizes the change in the target neuron.

where I contains the indices of all active neurons at layer i. It is necessary that Δ changes the state of neuron η_j only. Evaluating at $x^* - \Delta$ makes the wiggle δ have opposite signs to those in $A_j^{(i)}$. Then, all differences e_k also have opposite signs (compared to evaluating at $x^* + \Delta$). In this case, η_j becomes inactive and we have that

$$f(x^* - \Delta) - f(x^*) = - \sum_{k \in I \setminus \{j\}} c_k e_k.$$

Now assume that η_j has a negative sign. Then, the wiggle δ will have opposite signs to those in $A_j^{(i)}$ and following a similar analysis as above, we get that

$$f(x^* + \Delta) - f(x^*) = - \sum_{k \in I \setminus \{j\}} c_k e_k$$

and

$$f(x^* - \Delta) - f(x^*) = c_j e_j + \sum_{k \in I \setminus \{j\}} c_k e_k.$$

So, in order to find the sign we need to distinguish whether $c_j e_j$ contributes to the output difference with $x^* + \Delta$ or $x^* - \Delta$.

Let $L = f(x^* - \Delta) - f(x^*)$ and $R = f(x^* + \Delta) - f(x^*)$ denote, respectively, the output difference to the left and right of x^*. We decide $c_j e_j$ appears on the left, i.e., the sign of the neuron is -1, if $|L| > |R|$. Otherwise, we decide the sign to be $+1$. Since $c_j e_j \neq 0$, it is not possible that $|L| = |R|$.

If $c_j e_j$ and $\sum_k c_k e_k$ have the same sign, then $|c_j e_j + \sum_k c_k e_k| > |- \sum_k c_k e_k|$ always holds and the decision on the sign is also always correct. If $c_j e_j$ and $\sum_k c_k e_k$ have opposite signs, however, an incorrect decision may occur. This wrong decision happens when $|- \sum_k c_k e_k| > |c_j e_j + \sum_k c_k e_k|$. Then, it is necessary that $|c_j e_j| > 2|\sum_k c_k e_k|$ to make a correct decision.

Recall that a given input to the DNN defines a particular matrix $G^{(i+1)}$. That is, different inputs define different coefficients for the output of the DNN. We refer to this fact as *output randomization* and exploit it to overcome the problem of making a wrong sign decision. We find s different critical points for neuron η_j; each point defines different output coefficients. We expect that the majority of these points define coefficients such that $c_j e_j$ and $\sum_k c_k e_k$ fulfill the conditions for making a correct decision. For each critical point, we compute the wiggle δ, its corresponding input difference Δ, and make the choice for the sign. Let s_- and s_+ denote, respectively, the number of critical points for which the sign is chosen to be -1 and $+1$. Also, let the *confidence level* α for -1 be s_-/s and s_+/s for $+1$. Then, decide the sign to be -1 if $s_- > s_+$ and its confidence level is greater than a threshold α_0. If $s_+ > s_-$ and its confidence level is greater than α_0, decide $+1$. Otherwise, no decision on the sign is made. When the latter happens, we may try to recover the sign with additional critical points.

In our experiments in Sect. 5, very few wrong signs were initially produced by testing 200 critical points for each neuron in the CIFAR10 network; all of them were known to be problematic due to their low confidence level, and they are all fixable by testing more critical points. Note that as the number of neurons in the network increases, we expect the neuron wiggling technique to get even better since in higher dimensions vectors tend to be more orthogonal to each other, and thus the ratio between the sizes of the wiggles in the targeted neuron and in other neurons should increase.

So far, we assumed a single output for the DNN. When it has multiple outputs, we can use the Euclidean norm over the vector of outputs to compare L and R, which is beneficial for this method. This is because each critical point randomizes the coefficients of multiple outputs, and the probability of multiple outputs having simultaneously "bad" coefficients (which may lead to wrong decisions) is lower.

Oracle Calls/Time. Recall that layer i has d_i neurons. To recover the sign of a single neuron, for s critical points, we compute Δ and compare L with R. Computing Δ requires no oracle queries: it only requires linear algebra operations to find a critical point x^*, project $\hat{A}_j^{(i)}$ onto $V^{(i-1)}$ and find Δ. Particularly, matrix multiplications and matrix inversions. The size of the matrices involved is given by the number of inputs d_0 and the number of neurons d_i. So, the time complexity is $\mathcal{O}(d^3)$ operations, where $d = \max(d_0, d_i)$. Comparing L with R requires querying the oracle on x^*, $x^* - \Delta$ and $x^* + \Delta$. Computing $L = \|f(x^* - \Delta) - f(x^*)\|$ and $R = \|f(x^* + \Delta) - f(x^*)\|$ requires $\mathcal{O}(d_{r+1})$ operations, where d_{r+1} is the number of outputs of the DNN. Thus, we require $3s$ queries and $\mathcal{O}(sd^3)$ operations for a single neuron. In total, we require $3sd_i$ queries and $\mathcal{O}(sd_id^3)$ operations to recover the sign of all neurons in layer i.

Appendix A contains a back-of-the-envelope estimation of the signal-to-noise ratio for each critical point we test, showing that even in expansive networks we only require a relatively small number of experiments s to make a good guess.

Limitations. We can think of c_je_j as a signal and $\sum_k c_ke_k$ as noise. We have seen that when the signs of the signal and the noise are different, we may wrongly decide the sign of a neuron. This happens when the signal is not big enough compared to the noise. Particularly, if the number of neurons in layer i is too large compared to the degrees of freedom (for a particular input x), the signal may be really weak with respect to the noise. That means this technique may not work with DNNs which have at least one hidden layer with a large expansion factor compared to the smallest hidden layer or the number of inputs. However, we had no trouble recovering the signs when several successive hidden layers had twice the number of neurons compared to the dimension of the input space.

Also, this method may not be suitable for DNNs with a small number of neurons in the target layer. The probability of two random vectors being perpendicular decreases in low-dimensional spaces. Therefore, the wiggle for the target neuron may produce a sensibly large change for other neurons as well (those with weight vectors somewhat parallel to that of the target neuron). In this situation, the contribution of the other neurons may counteract that of the target neuron.

Finally, this method leverages *output randomization*. There is no output randomization when recovering the last hidden layer. If there are neurons in that layer with bad (constant) output coefficients, their corresponding sign will always be incorrectly recovered. The method in the next section exploits this lack of output randomization to recover the signs in the last hidden layer.

4.3 *Last Hidden Layer* Sign-Recovery

The method presented here recovers the sign of neurons in the last hidden layer. The output of the DNN is produced by the affine transformation f_{r+1} *without* subsequent ReLUs. Therefore, in layer r (the last hidden layer), the matrix $G^{(r+1)}$ is the same for any input x. This means all inputs define the same output coefficients; equivalently, there is no output randomization for that layer. We use this fact to recover the signs of the neurons. The output coefficients are recovered via second derivatives, thus, this method resembles a second-order differential cryptanalysis.

Assume that the DNN has a single output and let $c_1, \ldots, c_{d_r}$ be its output coefficients. Also, let x be an input to the DNN and $y^{(i)}$ be the output of layer i after the ReLUs, i.e., $y^{(i)} = F_i(x)$. The output of the DNN is given by

$$f(x) = c_1 y_1^{(r)} + \cdots + c_{d_r} y_{d_r}^{(r)} + b^{(r+1)}, \tag{3}$$

where $y_k^{(r)}$ is the k-th coordinate of $y^{(r)}$ and $b^{(r+1)}$ is the bias of the output layer.

With the recovered matrix $\hat{A}^{(r)}$, we can compute the value that neuron k in layer r takes before the ReLU, i.e., $e_k = \langle \hat{A}_k^{(r)}, y^{(r-1)} \rangle$, but we do not know its sign s_k. Let us consider both options. Exactly one of e_k or $-e_k$ will be positive, and the other will be negative; the latter would be blocked by the ReLU. So, $\sigma(e_k, -e_k)$ is either $(e_k, 0)$ or $(0, -e_k)$, depending on whether $e_k > 0$ or $e_k < 0$, respectively. We know the value e_k, so we can compute $\sigma(e_k, -e_k)$. Let us write $(\hat{y}_{k+}^{(r)}, \hat{y}_{k-}^{(r)}) = \sigma(e_k, -e_k)$. Now, finding s_k is equivalent to deciding whether the real value $y_k^{(r)}$ of the neuron after the ReLU is $\hat{y}_{k+}^{(r)}$ or $\hat{y}_{k-}^{(r)}$. The contribution to $f(x)$ in Eq. 3 is $c_k \hat{y}_{k+}^{(r)}$ when $s_k = +1$, otherwise, it is $c_k \hat{y}_{k-}^{(r)}$. Then, that equation can be rewritten as

$$f(x) = \sum_{k=1}^{d_r} c_k \left(s_k \hat{y}_{k+}^{(r)} + (1 - s_1)\hat{y}_{k-}^{(r)} \right) + b^{(r+1)}.$$

So, we take random inputs x, construct a system of linear equations, and solve for the unknowns s_k and $b^{(r+1)}$. We must choose at least $d_r + 1$ random inputs for the system to have a unique solution.

The output coefficients c_k can be obtained through a second derivative; the latter represents the change in the slope of the function. Figure 5 depicts that the second derivative of the ReLU function σ is the same at a critical point regardless of the sign of its input.

(a) $\sigma(y)$ (b) $\sigma(-y)$

Fig. 5. Second derivative $c = \frac{\sigma(y+\epsilon) - 2\sigma(y) + \sigma(y-\epsilon)}{\epsilon^2}$ for the ReLU function σ.

Let x^* be a critical point for neuron k in layer i and Δ be a small-norm vector in the linear neighborhood of x^*. Then,

$$f(x^* + \Delta) - 2f(x^*) + f(x^* - \Delta) = \pm \langle F_k^{(i)}, \Delta \rangle c_k,$$

where $F_k^{(i)}$ is the k-th row of the matrix $F^{(i)}$ defined by x^* when collpasing layers 1 to i. The sign above is $+$ when $x + \Delta$ activates the neuron, and it is $-$ otherwise. If Δ is parallel to $F_k^{(i)}$, $\langle F_k^{(i)}, \Delta \rangle > 0$ and the neuron is active with $x + \Delta$. Then, dividing the quantity above by $\langle F_k^{(i)}, \Delta \rangle$ yields the coefficient. When recovering the sign, we do not have access to the real $F^{(i)}$, but we know $\hat{F}^{(i)} = \hat{A}^{(i)} F^{(i-1)}$. To get the coefficient of neuron k, we choose Δ as $\hat{F}_k^{(i)}$ scaled to have a sufficiently small norm. Getting the output coefficient of a neuron can be done for any hidden layer. It is only in the last one that the coefficients remain constant for different points x^*.

Oracle Calls/Time. First, for each neuron, we find a critical point and compute the output coefficient. This requires 3 oracle queries and linear algebra operations with time complexity $\mathcal{O}(d^3)$, where $d = \max(d_0, d_r)$. That is $3d_r$ queries and time complexity $\mathcal{O}(d_r d^3)$ for all d_r neurons. Then, constructing the system of equations requires also $\mathcal{O}(d^3)$ operations (to compute the values $\hat{y}_{k-}^{(r)}$ and $\hat{y}_{k+}^{(r)}$ for $d_r + 1$ points) and $d_r + 1$ queries. Finally, solving the system of equations requires $\mathcal{O}(d_r^3)$ operations and no queries. In total, we require $4d_r + 1$ queries, and the time complexity is $\mathcal{O}(d_r d^3)$ operations.

Limitations. This technique requires the output coefficients to be constant. This only happens in the last hidden layer. Therefore, this method is applicable to that layer only.

5   Practical Sign Recovery Attacks

This section presents the experimental results of our proposed sign recovery techniques from Sect. 4. We first do a set of preliminary experiments on "well-behaved" unitary balanced neural networks of varying sizes (Subsect. 5.2), before we recover the real-world CIFAR10 network (Subsect. 5.3).

Our software implementation is available in https://github.com/Crypto-TII/deti.

We have executed the majority of our experiments on a DGX A100 server on a 40 GiB GPU. However, our experiments are not GPU intensive and will run with similar runtimes on most personal computers.

5.1   Implementation Caveats

Infinite Numerical Precision. The assumption of infinite numerical precision cannot be upheld practically, as conventional deep learning packages such as TensorFlow [1] only offer a maximal backend floating point precision of 64 bits. This practical limitation will influence all of our techniques: At infinite numerical precision, we could create an infinitesimal wiggle to be sure that we stay within the linear region of the neural network, but the limited floating point precision forces us to create a wiggle of sufficient magnitude, and this larger-magnitude wiggle, in turn, can accidentally toggle one of the other neurons. This requires us to perform a linearity check, which leads to additional oracle queries (see [4, appendix C]).

The limited floating point precision also means that the small uncertainties in our recovered weights will propagate to larger errors in our prediction of neuron values at deeper layers. For both *SOE* and the *Last Hidden Layer* method, this means that the system of equations we recover can have slightly imprecise coefficients, and variables that should be exactly zero may instead resolve to a relatively small value. For all of the networks we studied, we found it sufficient to declare a small threshold for what should be considered a zero, but this line will get increasingly blurry with deeper networks.

Neuron Wiggle: **Confidence-Level** α. The neuron wiggle is a statistical method, and in all following experiments we use $s = 200$ samples per neuron sign recovery. The sign recovery result for each neuron has a certain confidence level $\alpha \in (0.5, 1.0]$. A confidence level of $\alpha = 1.0$ ($\alpha \approx 0.5$) means absolute certainty (low certainty) in the recovered sign. The vast majority of signs is recovered **correctly** ($\checkmark$), even if $\alpha \approx 0.5$. However, a very small number of signs is recovered **incorrectly** ($\times$). We consider decisions with a confidence level below a cut-off value α_0 to be **borderline** and re-analyze the neurons with $\alpha \leq \alpha_0$ after updating the signs for all neurons with high confidence level $\alpha > \alpha_0$. The cut-off value α_0 is chosen adaptively so that the neurons with the least-confident 10% of all sign-recoveries are reanalyzed (Fig. 6(a)).

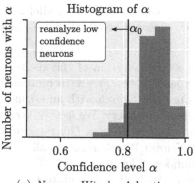

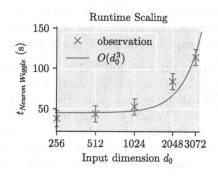

(a) *Neuron Wiggle*: Adaptive α_0.

(b) *Neuron Wiggle*: Runtime scaling.

Fig. 6. (a) illustrates that we reanalyze borderline neurons with low confidence level $\alpha < \alpha_0$ as explained in *Neuron Wiggle* Confidence-level α. (b) shows the approximately cubic runtime scaling with the neural network input dimension investigated in Results on d_0-256$^{(8)}$-10.

5.2 Unitary Balanced Neural Networks

We start with experiments on a set of "well-behaved" toy networks of varying sizes before tackling a "real-world" CIFAR10 network in the following section.

Methodology. Training small networks is sometimes done on artificial datasets, such as random data in [5]. Instead of training on random data, we purposefully create "well-behaved" networks with the following characteristics: The weights of each neuron are given by a unit vector chosen uniformly at random. The bias of each neuron is chosen such that it has a 50% probability of being active. Using our unitary balanced networks, we avoid anomalies originating from the non-deterministic neural network training on random data.

Results on 784-128-1. The largest network presented in [5] is the 784-128-1 network with around 100k parameters. Using *Freeze* the time complexity for the sign recovery can be estimated as $\mathcal{O}(d_i d^3) = 128 \times 784^3 = 2^{35}$. If *Exhaustive Search* would have to be used, the time complexity for the sign recovery can be estimated as $\mathcal{O}(2^{d_i}) = 2^{128}$. While [5] can still recover the 784-128-1 network in "under an hour", deeper networks with multiple hidden layers are untractable due to the sign recovery with exhaustive search. We can recover the signs of all neurons in the 128 neuron-wide hidden layer with either *SOE* in about (6.77 ± 0.04) s, or alternatively, the *Last Hidden Layer* technique in about (18.6 ± 0.05) seconds. In our implementations of *SOE* and *Last Hidden Layer*, parallelization and further speed-up are trivially achievable. Note that although the complexities of the two methods are similar, the execution time of *Last Hidden Layer* is mainly determined by the time it takes the algorithm to find the output coefficients, which is in turn dominated by the cost of finding critical points. Since these searches are independent, they can be done in parallel with a linear speedup factor. On the other hand, *SOE* does not require critical points, which explains the slight gap in performance.

Results on 100-200$^{(3)}$-10. This network is a larger version of the 10-20-20-1 network presented in [5]. As this network is expansive, the *Freeze* technique and *SOE* cannot be used, and before our work *Exhaustive Search* with an estimated cost of 2^{200} would have had to be employed for sign recovery. We use the *Neuron Wiggle* technique in hidden layers 1 and 2, and the *Last Hidden Layer* technique in hidden layer 3. In hidden layer 1 and 2 the *Neuron Wiggle* recovers all neuron signs correctly, even the ones with a low confidence level $\alpha \approx 0.5$. The (per-layer parallelizable) execution time per neuron is (16.3 ± 0.4) second, respectively (18.8 ± 0.5) s. The *Last Hidden Layer* technique recovers hidden layer 3 in a total execution time of (35.8 ± 0.2) s.

Results on d_0-256$^{(8)}$-10. Before moving on to our "actual" CIFAR10 network $(3072\text{-}256^{(8)}\text{-}10)$, we investigate the runtime scaling on unitary balanced networks with varying input dimensions $d_0 = \{256, 512, 1024, 2048, 3072\}$. According to our time order complexity estimation, we expect a cubic scaling of the runtime $\sim \mathcal{O}(sd_id^3)$ with the input dimension $d = \max(d_0, d_i)$. For each network d_0-256$^{(8)}$-10, we recover a subset of neurons in hidden layer three. Figure 6(b) shows an approximately cubic scaling with the shortest sign recovery time of 37 s for $d_0 = 256$, and the longest sign recovery time of 114 s for $d_0 = 3072$.

5.3   CIFAR10 Neural Network

The CIFAR10 Dataset. CIFAR10 is one of the typical benchmarking datasets in visual deep learning. It contains a balanced ten-class subset of the 80 Million Tiny Images [18]. Each of the ten classes (e.g., airplane, cat, and frog) contains 32×32 pixel RGB images, totaling 50,000 training and 10,000 test images.

Our CIFAR10 Model. Table 1 gives a detailed description of our CIFAR10 model. On the CIFAR10 dataset, we perform a standard rescaling of the pixel values from $0 \ldots 255$ to $0 \ldots 1$. For our model training, we choose typical settings (the optimizer is stochastic gradient descent with a momentum of 0.9; the loss is sparse categorical crossentropy; batch size 64), similar to [11]. Our eight-hidden-layer model shows CIFAR10 test accuracies within the expected range: Typical test accuracies for densely connected neural networks with pure ReLU activation functions are around ≈ 0.53 [11]. We note that better test accuracies are achieved using more advanced neural network architectures–beyond densely connected layers with pure ReLU activation functions. The current state of the art, Google Research's so-called vision transformer (ViT-H/14), achieves 0.995 test accuracy on CIFAR10 [7, Table 2].

Table 1. Description of our CIFAR10 model. Each image of the CIFAR10 dataset has $32 \times 32 = 1024$ pixels per RGB channel. Accordingly, our model has $3 \times 1024 = 3072$ input neurons. Further, it has 10 output neurons, one for each class in CIFAR10. We arbitrarily chose 256 neurons in each hidden layer. Our 8-hidden-layer CIFAR10 model with around 1.25M parameters is the largest model we analyze in this manuscript.

model	acc. CIFAR10	#(hidden layers)	#(hidden neurons)	parameters
$3072 - 256^{(8)} - 10$	0.5249	8	2048	1,249,802

Note: Column 'model' shows the model configuration with the number of neurons in the (input layer, hidden layers$^{\#(\text{hidden layers})}$, output layer); 'acc. CIFAR10' shows the evaluation accuracy of the model on the 10,000 CIFAR10 test images; '#(hidden layers)' shows the number of hidden layers; '#(hidden neurons)' shows the total number of hidden layer neurons; 'parameters' shows the total number of model weights and biases.

As mentioned previously, the *space of control* is essential for the sign recovery, and here we provide the experimental analysis for our $3072-256^{(8)}-10$ CIFAR10 model. Table 2 shows that after a sharp initial drop, the space of control stabilizes in the deeper layers. This supports our intuition from Fig. 3 that a dramatic fall in the space of control is prevented by the affine transformations.

Table 2. The average number of ReLUs on their positive side in each hidden layer of our $3072 - 256^{(8)} - 10$ CIFAR10 model for 10k random inputs, as well as the rank of a linearized representation $\mathcal{M}$ of the network up to the respective layer.

i: Layer ID	1	2	3	4	5	6	7	8
#(ON ReLUs)	127 ± 8	80 ± 8	72 ± 8	74 ± 6	82 ± 6	95 ± 6	99 ± 7	100 ± 10
rank($F^{(i)}$)	127 ± 8	80 ± 8	71 ± 7	68 ± 6	68 ± 6	68 ± 6	68 ± 6	68 ± 6

We analyzed our CIFAR10 network using our *SOE* (hidden layers 1 and 2), *Last Hidden Layer* (last hidden layer), and *Neuron Wiggle* (hidden layer three to penultimate) sign recovery techniques.

Results with SOE and Last Layer Technique. Table 3 shows the results of the sign recovery with the *SOE* and *Last Hidden Layer* techniques on our CIFAR10 model. Since these methods are algebraic, all neuron signs can be recovered successfully. We collect a system of equations as described in Subsect. 4.1 (*SOE*) and Subsect. 4.3 (*Last Hidden Layer*). For *SOE*, we collect one equation per hidden layer neuron (in total 256). Each equation $k = 1, \ldots, 256$ contains the model output difference $f(x + \Delta_k) - f(x)$, and therefore, a total of $256 + 1$ oracle calls are necessary. Even in our non-optimized implementation, the runtimes are well below thirty seconds for the CIFAR10 model. For the *Last Hidden Layer* technique, we collect one equation per hidden layer neuron (in total 256) and one equation per output neuron bias (in total 10).

Table 3. Results of the sign recovery with the *SOE* and *Last Hidden Layer* techniques on our $3072 - 256^{(8)} - 10$ CIFAR10 model. Each hidden layer contains 256 neurons. All neuron signs can be recovered successfully ($\checkmark$).

SOE				Last Hidden Layer			
layer ID	$\checkmark$	queries	runtime	layer ID	$\checkmark$	queries	runtime
1,2	256	256+1	(16 ± 1) s	8	256	256+10	(189 ± 40) s

Column 'queries' contains the number of oracle queries. The runtime is the total execution time for recovering all neuron signs in seconds. For both, *SOE* and *Last Hidden Layer*, these execution times can be significantly reduced further by parallelizing the implementation.

Results with the Neuron Wiggle Technique. Table 4 shows the results of the sign recovery with the *Neuron Wiggle* technique on our CIFAR10 model.

Each neuron sign was recovered using 200 critical points. We find criticals point for each target neuron by starting from a randomly chosen input image from the CIFAR10 dataset. As detailed in Sect. 5.1, the neuron wiggle technique is statistical. We reanalyze borderline neurons with a low confidence level $\alpha \leq \alpha_0$.

Detailed neuron-by-neuron results for hidden layer 7 (of 8) are shown in Sect. B. The mean sign recovery time per neuron in the relevant layers with layer IDs $2, \ldots, 8$ is $\bar{t}_{total} = (234 \pm 44)$ s. Note that the sign recovery of the 256 neurons within the same hidden layer can be parallelized. Therefore, a parallelized implementation of our sign recovery algorithm on a suitable 256-core computer would take around 4 min per layer and a total of about 32 min for the 8-hidden layer DNN.

Compared to our preliminary experiments on the unitary balanced networks, the sign recovery time for the comparable-size CIFAR10 model is almost twice as long. A more detailed analysis in Appendix B shows that the increased execution time is due to finding critical points: in the actual CIFAR10 network, it takes around 130 s, while it only took 10 s in the unitary balanced network. Notable differences to the unitary balanced network are a smaller *space of control* and the existence of *always-off* or *almost-always-off* neurons, which makes finding critical points more challenging.

Table 4. Results of the sign recovery with the *Neuron Wiggle* method on hidden layers 1, ..., 8 of our CIFAR10 model 3072-256$^{(8)}$-10. Each hidden layer contains 256 neurons. The vast majority is evaluated **correctly** ($\checkmark$), even at a low confidence level ($\alpha \approx 0.5$). <u>256</u> highlights the cases where all neurons are analyzed correctly, even those with low confidence level α. Borderline neurons with a low confidence level ($\alpha \leq \alpha_0$) are re-evaluated. The column **fixable** contains the borderline neurons with wrongly recovered signs ($\times$) and low confidence level. Zero **incorrect** decisions ($\times$) were made with a high confidence level ($\alpha > \alpha_0$).

layerID	α_0 (adaptive)	**correct** ($\alpha > 0.5$) and $\checkmark$	**fixable** ($\alpha \leq \alpha_0$) and $\times$	**incorrect** ($\alpha > \alpha_0$) and $\times$	runtime
1	0.79	255/256	1/256	0/256	1121 s
2	0.67	254/256	2/256	0/256	185 s
3	0.71	<u>256/256</u>	<u>0/256</u>	0/256	219 s
4	0.74	<u>256/256</u>	<u>0/256</u>	0/256	295 s
5	0.74	<u>256/256</u>	<u>0/256</u>	0/256	201 s
6	0.75	<u>256/256</u>	<u>0/256</u>	0/256	269 s
7	0.70	253/256	3/256	0/256	234 s
8	0.77	252/256	4/256	0/256	384 s

Note that our other two sign recovery techniques are faster for hidden layers 1, 2, and 8, and we only show the neuron wiggle timing for these layers for the sake of completeness. The column 'runtime' refers to the mean runtime per neuron in the target layer, where the signs of all the neurons in the same layer can be extracted in parallel on a multicore computer.

6 Conclusions

In this paper, we presented the first polynomial-time algorithm for extracting the parameters of ReLU-based DNNs from their black-box implementation. We also demonstrated the practical efficiency of our sign recovery by applying it to a deep network for classifying CIFAR10 images. We used SOE ($i = 1, 2$, (16 ± 1) s per layer), Neuron Wiggling ($i = 3 \ldots 7$, (234 ± 44) s per layer) and Last Hidden Layer ($i = 8$, (189 ± 40) s). The total required time is about 30 min. We also demonstrated its applicability to several layer deep, expanding networks whose width was much larger than the number of inputs (where all the previous techniques based on solving systems of linear equations failed). Among the many problems left open are:

1. Developing countermeasures and countercountermeasures for our attack.
2. Dealing with the case in which only the class decisions are provided rather than the exact logits.
3. Dealing with more modern machine learning architectures such as transformers.
4. Dealing with discrete domains such as texts in LLMs where derivatives are not well defined.

Disclosure of Interests. The authors have no competing interests to declare that are relevant to the content of this article.

A The Expected Signal-to-Noise Ratio of Neuron Wiggle in Unitary Balanced Networks

In this appendix, we perform an approximate back-of-the-envelope analysis of the relative sizes of the signal and the noise for unitary balanced networks, in which each neuron is a randomly chosen unit vector in n-dimensional space. Since both the signal and the noise are equally affected by the size of the wiggle, we can assume that at the input to the current layer i, the wiggle is a unit vector in the direction of the targeted neuron (which is WLOG the first among n neurons in this layer). Since the dot product of two random unit vectors is about $\pm\frac{1}{\sqrt{n}}$, the neuronal wiggles in the input to the ReLU's in the current layer looks like $(1, \pm\frac{1}{\sqrt{n}}, \ldots, \pm\frac{1}{\sqrt{n}})$. Assuming that half the ReLU's will be on their negative side, we have to compare the norm of this vector in two cases: When the first entry remains 1 (due to its associated ReLU being positive) and half the other entries are zeroed, and when the first entry is replaced by 0 (due to its associated ReLU being negative) and half the other entries are zeroed. It is easy to see that the norm of the wiggle vector at the output of the ReLU's will be about $\sqrt{1.5} = 1.22$ in the first case, and about $\sqrt{0.5} = 0.71$ in the second case. This almost 2:1 ratio between the expected norms is likely to persist through the remaining $d - i$ layers, making it easy to distinguish between the two distributions with a small number of experiments which have access only to the output wiggles.

To model the case in which the attacker has only d degrees of freedom at the input to layer i, assume that in the desired wiggle $(\pm\frac{1}{\sqrt{n}}, \ldots, \pm\frac{1}{\sqrt{n}})$, the attacker can optimally choose only the first d entries, while the remaining $n - d$ entries are zeroed. This will reduce the wiggle $\|\langle u, \delta \rangle\|$ of the targetted neuron from 1 to about $\sqrt{d/n}$ while keeping the norm of the noise essentially unchanged. This represents a very gradual deterioration in the signal-to-noise ratio as d decreases, and explains the success of our experiments on expanding networks with three consecutive layers of 200 neurons while the network had only 100 inputs.

B   Detailed Results for CIFAR10

See Table 5.

Table 5. Detailed neuron-by-neuron results for hidden layer 7 (of 8) in the CIFAR10 model 3072-256$^{(8)}$-10. For each neuron, 200 critical points were analyzed for the sign recovery, yielding $s_\pm$ negative and positive sign votes with confidence level α. The time to find critical points is $t_{\text{crit.}}$, and the execution time for the wiggle sign recovery itself is t_{wiggle} (the total time $t_{\text{total}} = t_{\text{crit.}} + t_{\text{wiggle}}$ had a mean of (234 ± 49) s). We highlight the three cases where the sign recovery gave an initially incorrect result (✗). Since they were all charactrized with very low confidence level α, we could identify and fix them with additional experiments.

neuronID	real sign	s_-	s_+	α	correct	$t_{\text{crit.}}$	t_{wiggle}	t_{total}
neuron 0	−	−:165	+:35	0.82	✓	135	84	221
neuron 1	+	−:0	+:200	1.00	✓	130	83	213
neuron 2	−	−:198	+:2	0.99	✓	138	83	224
neuron 3	−	−:176	+:24	0.88	✓	131	83	216
neuron 4	−	−:161	+:39	0.81	✓	132	83	217
neuron 5	+	−:0	+:200	1.00	✓	128	83	213
neuron 6	−	−:193	+:7	0.96	✓	130	84	216
neuron 7	+	−:14	+:186	0.93	✓	148	83	232
neuron 8	−	−:200	+:0	1.00	✓	128	83	213
neuron 9	−	−:125	+:75	0.62	✓	174	83	258
neuron 10	−	−:200	+:0	1.00	✓	129	83	213
neuron 11	−	−:195	+:5	0.97	✓	137	83	223
neuron 12	−	−:199	+:1	0.99	✓	128	83	214
neuron 13	−	−:194	+:6	0.97	✓	133	83	218
neuron 14	+	−:1	+:199	0.99	✓	132	83	216
neuron 15	+	−:3	+:197	0.98	✓	139	83	227
...	...	...	...	...	...	...	...	...
neuron 95	+	−:108	+:92	0.54	✗	276	83	364
...	...	...	...	...	...	...	...	...
neuron 109	+	−:105	+:95	0.53	✗	496	83	581
...	...	...	...	...	...	...	...	...
neuron 116	+	−:2	+:198	0.99	✓	152	83	239
neuron 117	−	−:87	+:113	0.56	✗	302	83	390
neuron 118	+	−:1	+:199	0.99	✓	134	83	219
...	...	...	...	...	...	...	...	...
neuron 251	−	−:184	+:16	0.92	✓	153	83	237
neuron 252	−	−:200	+:0	1.00	✓	135	84	222
neuron 253	−	−:200	+:0	1.00	✓	132	83	217
neuron 254	−	−:200	+:0	1.00	✓	132	83	218
neuron 255	−	−:195	+:5	0.97	✓	132	84	218

References

1. Abadi, M., et al.: Tensorflow: a system for large-scale machine learning. In: 12th USENIX Symposium on Operating Systems Design and Implementation (OSDI 16), pp. 265–283 (2016)
2. Batina, L., Bhasin, S., Jap, D., Picek, S.: CSI NN: reverse engineering of neural network architectures through electromagnetic side channel. In: Heninger, N., Traynor, P. (eds.) 28th USENIX Security Symposium, USENIX Security 2019, Santa Clara, CA, USA, August 14-16, 2019, pp. 515–532. USENIX Association (2019)
3. Blum, A.L., Rivest, R.L.: Training a 3-node neural network is NP-complete. In: Hanson, S.J., Remmele, W., Rivest, R.L. (eds.) Machine Learning: From Theory to Applications. LNCS, vol. 661, pp. 9–28. Springer, Heidelberg (1993). https://doi.org/10.1007/3-540-56483-7_20
4. Canales-Martínez, I.A., et al.: Polynomial time cryptanalytic extraction of neural network models. Cryptology ePrint Archive (2023)
5. Carlini, N., Jagielski, M., Mironov, I.: Cryptanalytic extraction of neural network models. In: Micciancio, D., Ristenpart, T. (eds.) CRYPTO 2020. LNCS, vol. 12172, pp. 189–218. Springer, Cham (2020). https://doi.org/10.1007/978-3-030-56877-1_7
6. Daniely, A., Granot, E.: An exact poly-time membership-queries algorithm for extraction a three-layer relu network. CoRR **abs/2105.09673** (2021). https://arxiv.org/abs/2105.09673
7. Dosovitskiy, A., et al.: An image is worth 16x16 words: transformers for image recognition at scale. arXiv preprint arXiv:2010.11929 (2020)
8. Fefferman, C.: Reconstructing a neural net from its output. Revista Matemática Iberoamericana **10**(3), 507–555 (1994). http://eudml.org/doc/39464
9. Jagielski, M., Carlini, N., Berthelot, D., Kurakin, A., Papernot, N.: High accuracy and high fidelity extraction of neural networks. In: 29th USENIX Security Symposium (USENIX Security 20), pp. 1345–1362 (2020)
10. Joud, R., Moëllic, P.A., Pontié, S., Rigaud, J.B.: A practical introduction to side-channel extraction of deep neural network parameters. In: Buhan, I., Schneider, T. (eds.) CARDIS 2022. LNCS, vol. 13820, pp. 45–65. Springer, Cham (2022). https://doi.org/10.1007/978-3-031-25319-5_3
11. Lin, Z., Memisevic, R., Konda, K.: How far can we go without convolution: improving fully-connected networks. arXiv preprint arXiv:1511.02580 (2015)
12. Lowd, D., Meek, C.: Adversarial learning. In: Grossman, R., Bayardo, R.J., Bennett, K.P. (eds.) Proceedings of the Eleventh ACM SIGKDD International Conference on Knowledge Discovery and Data Mining, Chicago, Illinois, USA, August 21–24, 2005. pp. 641–647. ACM (2005)
13. Milli, S., Schmidt, L., Dragan, A.D., Hardt, M.: Model reconstruction from model explanations. In: danah boyd, Morgenstern, J.H. (eds.) Proceedings of the Conference on Fairness, Accountability, and Transparency, FAT* 2019, Atlanta, GA, USA, January 29–31, 2019. pp. 1–9. ACM (2019)
14. Oliynyk, D., Mayer, R., Rauber, A.: I know what you trained last summer: a survey on stealing machine learning models and defences. ACM Comput. Surv. **55**(14s), 1–41 (2023)
15. Papernot, N., McDaniel, P.D., Goodfellow, I.J., Jha, S., Celik, Z.B., Swami, A.: Practical black-box attacks against machine learning. In: Karri, R., Sinanoglu, O., Sadeghi, A., Yi, X. (eds.) Proceedings of the 2017 ACM on Asia Conference on Computer and Communications Security, AsiaCCS 2017, Abu Dhabi, United Arab Emirates, April 2–6, 2017. pp. 506–519. ACM (2017)

16. Reith, R.N., Schneider, T., Tkachenko, O.: Efficiently stealing your machine learning models. In: Cavallaro, L., Kinder, J., Domingo-Ferrer, J. (eds.) Proceedings of the 18th ACM Workshop on Privacy in the Electronic Society, WPES@CCS 2019, London, UK, November 11, 2019, pp. 198–210. ACM (2019)

17. Rolnick, D., Körding, K.P.: Reverse-engineering deep relu networks. In: Proceedings of the 37th International Conference on Machine Learning, ICML 2020, 13–18 July 2020, Virtual Event. Proceedings of Machine Learning Research, vol. 119, pp. 8178–8187. PMLR (2020)

18. Torralba, A., Fergus, R., Freeman, W.T.: 80 million tiny images: a large data set for nonparametric object and scene recognition. IEEE Trans. Pattern Anal. Mach. Intell. **30**(11), 1958–1970 (2008)

19. Tramèr, F., Zhang, F., Juels, A., Reiter, M.K., Ristenpart, T.: Stealing machine learning models via prediction APIs. In: 25th USENIX Security Symposium (USENIX Security 16), pp. 601–618 (2016)

Ordering Transactions with Bounded Unfairness: Definitions, Complexity and Constructions

Aggelos Kiayias[1], Nikos Leonardos[2], and Yu Shen[3(✉)] (iD)

[1] University of Edinburgh and IOG, Edinburgh, UK
aggelos.kiayias@ed.ac.uk
[2] National and Kapodistrian University of Athens, Athens, Greece
[3] University of Edinburgh, Edinburgh, UK

Abstract. An important consideration in the context of distributed ledger protocols is fairness in terms of transaction ordering. Recent work [Crypto 2020] revealed a connection of (receiver) order fairness to social choice theory and related impossibility results arising from the Condorcet paradox. As a result of the impossibility, various relaxations of order fairness were proposed in prior works. Given that distributed ledger protocols, especially those processing smart contracts, must serialize the input transactions, a natural objective is to minimize the distance (in terms of number of transactions) between any pair of unfairly ordered transactions in the output ledger — a concept we call *bounded unfairness*. In state machine replication (SMR) parlance this asks for minimizing the number of unfair state updates occurring before the processing of any request. This unfairness minimization objective gives rise to a natural class of parametric order fairness definitions that has not been studied before. As we observe, previous realizable relaxations of order fairness do not yield good unfairness bounds.

Achieving optimal order fairness in the sense of bounded unfairness turns out to be connected to the graph theoretic properties of the underlying transaction dependency graph and specifically the *bandwidth* metric of strongly connected components in this graph. This gives rise to a specific instance of the definition that we call "directed bandwidth order-fairness" which we show that it captures the best possible that any ledger protocol can achieve in terms of bounding unfairness. We prove ordering transactions in this fashion is NP-hard and non-approximable for any constant ratio. Towards realizing the property, we put forth a new distributed ledger protocol called Taxis that achieves directed bandwidth order-fairness. We present two variations, one that matches the property perfectly but (necessarily) lacks in performance and liveness, and another that achieves liveness and better complexity while offering a slightly relaxed version of the property. Finally, we comment on applications of our work to social choice, a direction which we believe to be of independent interest.

© International Association for Cryptologic Research 2024
M. Joye and G. Leander (Eds.): EUROCRYPT 2024, LNCS 14653, pp. 34–63, 2024.
https://doi.org/10.1007/978-3-031-58734-4_2

1 Introduction

The development of blockchain protocols, starting with the Bitcoin blockchain [30], lead to increased interest in a classic problem in distributed systems — the state-machine replication (SMR) problem, cf. [34]. In SMR, the task of executing a state machine is assigned to a set of processors, and in the Byzantine fault tolerant version of the problem, processing requests should proceed unhindered by the actions of faulty nodes, even if such nodes arbitrarily deviate from the protocol in a coordinated manner.

A special case of state machine replication is the problem of ledger consensus, cf. [18–20,32], that requires the joint maintenance of a ledger of transactions so that two fundamental properties are being met: (i) consistency, i.e., the ledger of settled transactions is growing monotonically, (ii) liveness, i.e., the ledger of transactions incorporates new transactions in a timely manner. A third property related to the order of transactions has received much less attention in analysis work. In the original SMR abstraction of [34], while proper ordering of transactions is required, the *fairness* of this order is not explored.

The formal investigation of fairness in the context of ordering transactions was initiated with the elegant results of [25], which introduced it formally as "order-fairness" and pointed to an inherent impossibility to attain it in the distributed setting that relates to the Condorcet paradox. In a nutshell, (receiver) order-fairness posits that whenever two transactions tx and tx' are received in this order by most nodes in the system, then they should not be ordered differently in the ledger they maintain. The Condorcet paradox kicks in when cycles in the receiving order of three or more transactions exist across the nodes. In such case, it turns out that there may be no output transaction order that satisfies order-fairness. This motivates relaxations of order-fairness that enable protocols to circumvent the impossibility and realize them in a distributed setting.

There are two principal approaches in relaxing fairness. The first one relies on a concept of time that can apply across all participants. In approximate order fairness [25], fair ordering in the output applies only to appropriately "spaced apart" transactions across all nodes. In timed-relative fairness, cf. [27,37], if a transaction tx is received by *all* honest parties prior to tx', then tx must be sequenced before tx'. There are two obvious disadvantages of this approach to fairness: first, it requires reference to some shared notion of time. Second, it gives up on a lot of transactions whose propagation patterns somewhat overlap; in many applications however (e.g., front running mitigation) it is exactly for such transactions that fair ordering is needed.

The second principal approach, block order fairness [25], gives up on assigning a unique sequence number to all transactions in the output ledger. Transactions can be batched together in the same "block" in which case the system can be said to refrain from actually ordering them. Block order fairness has the advantage that it can be defined without referring to any shared notion of time and thus it can apply to transactions that are submitted concurrently and even apply to asynchronous execution environments. However, given that many distributed ledger applications require a total ordering of the output, it leaves open the question how far apart transactions may end up when finally serialized.

Motivated by the above, we set out to investigate the natural objective of minimizing the number of unfairly ordered transactions preceding for any transaction in the serialized output of a distributed ledger. This objective, similar to block order fairness, needs no shared notion of time to be meaningful, but it also translates to an eminently practical guarantee in the SMR setting that block order fairness lacks: the system will strive to minimize the number of (inevitable) unfair state updates that happen before the processing of any transaction.

To illustrate the importance of bounded unfairness with an example, consider a simple automated market maker (AMM) where it maintains a constant product $XY = C$ for swapping two tokens X and Y (Y is the native token) and one transaction can only sell a fixed number of tokens. When the market loses confidence in X, every stakeholder would like to sell X to minimize her loss. Consider an AMM state (X_0, Y_0) (i.e., $X_0 Y_0 = C$) and a number k of stakeholders $s_0, s_1, \ldots, s_{k-1}$, each one selling an amount of $\Delta = \delta X_0$ tokens at times $t_0 < t_1 < \cdots < t_{k-1}$, respectively. At time t_i, the AMM state has slipped to the point $(X_0 + i\Delta, C/(X_0 + i\Delta)) = ((1 + i\delta)X_0, Y_0/(1 + i\delta))$ and the exchange rate for stakeholder i should be $(Y_0/X_0)/[(1 + i\delta)(1 + (i + 1)\delta)]$. In particular, an unfair ordering $(s_1, s_2, \ldots, s_{k-1}, s_0)$, will result in stakeholder s_0 transacting with exchange rate $(Y_0/X_0)/[(1 + k\delta)(1 + (k + 1)\delta)]$ instead of $(Y_0/X_0)/(1 + \delta)$. It follows the exchange rate becomes worse proportionally to $1/k^2$ when $k - 1$ unfair state updates take place, thus keeping the number of unfair state updates at the minimum possible value (as bounded unfairness strives to do) is in the best interest of the users, protecting them from the effects of unfair slippage.

1.1 Our Results

We introduce a new class of (receiver) order fairness definitions – *bounded unfairness*. In SMR protocols all input transactions are eventually sequenced following an ordering σ which assigns a unique index to each transaction. Our definition is parameterized by a threshold φ and a bound B; each party that runs the protocol has an "input profile" which ranks all received transactions according to the order they were received. For two transactions $\mathtt{tx}, \mathtt{tx}'$, we say that $\mathtt{tx} \prec^\varphi \mathtt{tx}'$ if φ fraction of input profiles present $\mathtt{tx}$ before $\mathtt{tx}'$. Given any two such transactions, the output ordering σ should satisfy $\sigma(\mathtt{tx}) - \sigma(\mathtt{tx}') \leq B$. I.e., $\mathtt{tx}$ cannot be serialized more than B positions later compared to $\mathtt{tx}'$.

Observe that (φ, B)-fairness matches standard order fairness for the case of $B = 0$ while for any choice $B > 0$ it relaxes it. The relaxation allows transactions $\mathtt{tx} \prec^\varphi \mathtt{tx}'$ to be "unfairly" sequenced as $(\mathtt{tx}', \ldots, \mathtt{tx})$ with $\mathtt{tx}'$ coming at most B positions earlier. Given the unrealizability of fairness for $B = 0$, the obvious question to ask here is for what values of B it is possible to realize the property and what is the smallest possible choice for it.

In order to minimize B, we allow it to be a function of the parties' input profiles and the given pair of transactions. The input profiles define a transaction dependency graph G which includes an edge $(\mathtt{tx}, \mathtt{tx}')$ if and only if $\mathtt{tx} \prec^\varphi \mathtt{tx}'$.

Given this, we observe that the problem of (φ, B) fairness relates to the concept of *graph bandwidth* over G, cf. [21]. The bandwidth problem asks for a vertex ordering $\sigma : V \rightarrow \mathbb{N}$ that minimizes the *maximum difference* $\sigma(u) - \sigma(v)$ across all edges $(u, v) \in E$. We call this the *directed bandwidth* as it aims at minimizing the length of the "backward edges" in G, i.e., those that violate fairness. We instantiate the bound B using the directed bandwidth of the strongly connected component (SCC) that contains the two transactions, or 0 if no such SCC exists.

Our first result regarding our new definition that bases fairness on directed bandwidth establishes that it is the best possible we can hope for in terms of minimizing unfair state updates preceding any transaction. Indeed, we prove that for any protocol that serializes the transactions there can be SCCs in the dependency graph within which two transactions *must* be ordered spaced apart by as many positions as the directed bandwidth of the SCC. Any function B that beats this bound is unrealizable!

Our second result regarding fairness based on directed bandwidth investigates the complexity of the problem. By adapting previous results for the bandwidth problem over undirected graphs, we prove that the directed bandwidth problem is NP-hard and non approximable for any constant ratio. Armed with this result, we prove that any protocol that realizes our order fairness property optimally also solves directed bandwidth, i.e., it solves an NP-hard problem. We also prove upper and lower bounds for the maximum directed bandwidth across all graphs; this result establishes the worst-case that is to be expected in terms of serializing the transactions with bounded unfairness. In particular we show that in the worst-case directed bandwidth equals $n - \Theta(\log n)$ where n is the number of transactions. Given the above, a natural question is how previous relaxations of order fairness fare w.r.t. bounding unfairness. We present explicit counterexamples illustrating how such previous definitions do not provide good bounds.

We then turn to investigate the inherent tension between liveness and our fairness definition. Similar to block order fairness, we first prove that it is impossible to satisfy liveness and directed-bandwidth order-fairness when the transaction delivery mechanism is asynchronous. Intuitively, the reason is that Condorcet cycles may extend indefinitely in a manner which is impossible to accommodate outputting any transaction in the cycle without breaking fairness. Given this impossibility one has to either settle for weak-liveness (transactions are included *eventually* [25]) or restrict fairness a bit more. Towards this latter target we consider a bounded delay transaction dissemination environment where each transaction is disseminated within a window of time Δ_{tx}. In this setting our core observation is that Condorcet cycles spanning a long period of time can be partitioned across the time domain in such a way that a bound on directed bandwidth of the graph can be derived. In such graphs we prove that directed bandwidth is bounded by at most 3 times the maximum number of transactions disseminated concurrently within a Δ_{tx} time window. This gives rise to a relaxed definition of our fairness notion that we call *timed directed bandwidth*.

The astute reader so far would have observed that we introduced our concept in a setting where participants are static — the relation $\mathtt{tx} \prec^\varphi \mathtt{tx'}$ which gives rise to the transaction dependency graph is based on numbers of parties who witness a particular order between the two transactions. In a permissionless environment however, e.g., such as that of Bitcoin, participants may engage with a protocol in a transient manner hence making $\prec^\varphi$ ill defined. We address this issue by recasting the relation in the permissionless setting as follows: $\mathtt{tx} \prec^\varphi \mathtt{tx'}$ means that a φ fraction of hashing power "stands behind" a particular ordering between two transactions for a minimum period of time which is specified by a security parameter.

Armed with the above definitional framework, we focus on realizing directed bandwidth fairness. We put forth Taxis, a permissionless protocol that operates in the same setting as Bitcoin. We present two variants. In $\mathsf{Taxis_{WL}}$, miners continuously submit suffixes of their transaction input profile packaged within proofs-of-work using the 2-for-1 PoW technique of [20] that are included provided they are sufficiently recent using the recency condition of [33]. In this fashion it is possible to continuously compute and expand the transaction dependency graph G on-chain for the settled set of transactions. The ledger is then created by identifying SCCs of G and calculating directed bandwidth.

Our second variation of the Taxis protocol breaks long cycles when they occur and uses the median of timestamps to determine the transaction ordering within large SCCs. This enables us to achieve liveness and *timed directed bandwidth fairness*, the relaxation of our directed bandwidth fairness definition that relaxes fairness for particularly long Condorcet cycles.

We present a full analysis of our protocols in a permissionless dynamic participation setting using the analytical toolset from [17,20]. Notably, we enhance the "typical execution" concept by lower-bounding the difficulty that φ fraction of honest parties can acquire. This lower bound makes it possible for us to show that, for a specific transaction $\mathtt{tx}$, φ fraction of honest parties can accumulate more difficulty than others (including the adversary and the rest of honest parties) during K consecutive rounds, which guarantees that parties will agree on (i) the transactions that precede $\mathtt{tx}$; and (ii) a timestamp associated with $\mathtt{tx}$. Combining these properties with our dependency graph construction rules, we conclude consistency, liveness (for Taxis) and order-fairness according to the description above.

Regarding performance, we note that $\mathsf{Taxis_{WL}}$ runs exponentially on the number of edges of the subgraph of the transaction graph that is defined by the (largest) Condorcet cycle. Recall that given the hardness and non-approximability of directed bandwidth we cannot expect a polynomial-time algorithm; furthermore, in practice, Condorcet cycles may be quite small or even not occurring at all (in non-adversarial settings), see [24], hence for practical purposes exponential dependency on their corresponding subgraph length may not be prohibitive. Furthermore, for Taxis, assuming a $\Delta_{\mathtt{tx}}$ bound on transaction dissemination, we improve the complexity to be bounded by an exponential on the size of the largest Condorcet cycle (for constant throughput environments).

We conclude with a discussion on alternative ways to relaxing order-fairness and open questions regarding the structure of transaction dependency graphs. While our concept of directed bandwidth achieves an optimal ordering of transactions in terms of bounding unfairness, there can be orthogonal considerations that highlight the multi dimensionality of the fairness problem. We also discuss issues related to dynamic participation and how our results can also translate to the permissioned setting.

As a final contribution we would like to highlight how our work can have applications to social choice theory. Typically, in social choice, the input profiles of parties (e.g., rankings of the candidates) are assumed to be finite sequences. Given such rankings, it is sought to produce an agreeable ordering with good properties. In such case, fairness captures the natural property that if candidate A is preferable by a majority of participants compared to another candidate B, then A should be ranked higher in the final ranking. In the social choice context, our result can be seen as a way to answer the social choice problem when participants have an ever evolving sequence of preferences and it is desired to combine their preferences while minimizing the violations of their preferences as much as possible. For instance, consider an infinite sequence of news items, and a dynamic population of agent-editors with distinct preferences for each one, in terms of e.g., how interesting each one is. The task is to produce a single output news feed that respects the preferences of the agent-editors as much as possible. Our results readily translate to this setting enabling the agent-editors to produce a unified news feed with the minimum possible misplacement between news items: specifically if φ fraction of agents deems item n as more interesting than item n', then n' will be placed at most B positions before n in the unified news feed.

Organization of This Paper. The rest of the paper is organized as follows. In Sect. 2, we present preliminaries on the protocol exeuction model, transaction profiles and dependency graphs. We formally define and analyze transaction order fairness in Sect. 3. In Sect. 4, we present our fair-order protocol Taxis. We discuss some future research directions that might be of independent interest in Sect. 5. A survey of related works [2,5,6,9,23–25,27,28,36,37], and a detailed description of preliminaries, protocols and proofs can be found in the full version of this paper [26].

2   Preliminaries

In this section we first briefly describe our protocol execution model, transaction diffusion mechanism and the dynamic environment. Refer to [26] for more details. We then introduce transaction profiles and dependency graphs in Sect. 2.2. They are notations crucial to the discussion of order fairness.

2.1   Protocol Execution Model

Our model follows Canetti's formulation of "real world" notion of protocol execution [7,8] for multi-party protocols. To specify the "resources" that may be available to the instances running protocol—e.g., the diffuse channel—we will follow the approach of describing them as ideal functionalities in the terminology of [8].[1]

The protocol execution proceeds in "rounds". Parties are always aware of the current round (i.e., synchronous processors); this is captured by a global clock $\mathcal{G}_{\text{CLOCK}}$ [22]. Inputs are provided by an environment program $\mathcal{Z}$ to parties that execute the protocol Π. The adversary $\mathcal{A}$ is a single entity that takes control of corrupted parties, and is both "adaptive" (i.e., $\mathcal{A}$ can take control of parties on the fly) and "rushing" ($\mathcal{A}$ is allowed to observe honest parties' actions before deciding her reaction). The hash function $H(\cdot)$ is modeled as a random oracle $\mathcal{F}_{\text{RO}}$ and abstracts parties attempting to solve "proof-of-work" [14]. Following the convention that different types of messages are diffused by their own network, we consider two diffusion functionalities — one for general messages ($\mathcal{F}_{\text{Diffuse}}$) and another for transactions (see below). For all messages except transactions, the communication is bounded-delay (a.k.a., "partial synchronous" [13,32]). I.e., there is an upper bound Δ (measured in number of rounds) and the adversary may delay the delivery of messages for up to Δ rounds.

Transaction Diffusion Model. The environment program $\mathcal{Z}$ is responsible for generating new transactions and handing them to the diffusion functionality. We consider two types of transaction diffusion functionality — $\mathcal{F}_{\text{Diffuse}}^{\text{tx,async}}$ and $\mathcal{F}_{\text{Diffuse}}^{\text{tx},\Delta_{\text{tx}}}$. The first functionality captures the asynchronous transaction diffusion, i.e., in $\mathcal{F}_{\text{Diffuse}}^{\text{tx,async}}$ the adversary can deliver a transaction tx at any time (after tx is generated by $\mathcal{Z}$). The only restriction is that $\mathcal{F}_{\text{Diffuse}}^{\text{tx,async}}$ should send all transactions to all parties eventually. The second one captures a Δ_{tx}-disseminated transaction diffusion network. Specifically, in $\mathcal{F}_{\text{Diffuse}}^{\text{tx},\Delta_{\text{tx}}}$ the adversary is forced to deliver a transaction to all the honest parties within Δ_{tx} rounds after it is learnt by at least one honest participant.

Considering the physical limits on transaction throughput, we assume that the total number of transactions will be a polynomial function of the running time of protocol execution.

Dynamic Participation. In order to describe the protocol execution in a more realistic fashion, following the treatment in [3], we classify protocol participants into different types. Especially, *alert* parties—the core set of parties to carry out the protocol—are those who have access to all the resources (random oracle, network, clock) and are synchronized with each other. We also put some restriction on the environment's power to fluctuate the number of *alert* parties [17,20]; i.e., for any window of fixed length, the increase/decrease on the number of alert parties is bounded (see [26] for more details).

State Machine Replication. State machine replication [34] is a problem that asks a set of parties accepting input logs to maintain a public data structure

---

[1] Note that these notions are used for model description only, our security proof is property-based.

that serializes the logs. This public data structure is called *ledger* in the context of ledger consensus (cf. [18,19]). Conventionally, a public ledger should satisfy two properties (we adopt $\mathcal{L}$ as the settled part of the ledger in party's view, and $\widetilde{\mathcal{L}}$ the whole ledger held by the party).

- **Consistency**: For any two honest parties $\mathsf{P}_1, \mathsf{P}_2$ reporting $\mathcal{L}_1, \mathcal{L}_2$ at rounds $\mathsf{r}_1 \leq \mathsf{r}_2$, respectively, it holds that $\mathcal{L}_1$ is a prefix of $\widetilde{\mathcal{L}}_2$.
- **Liveness**: (parameterized by $u \in \mathbb{N}$, the "wait time" parameter): If a transaction $\mathtt{tx}$ is provided to all honest parties for u consecutive rounds, then it holds that for any player P, $\mathtt{tx}$ will be in $\mathcal{L}$.

2.2 Transaction Profiles and Dependency Graphs

Let $\mathbb{T}$ denote the (finite) set of all possible transactions with elements $\mathtt{tx}$. A *transaction profile* (or "profile" for short) is a bijection $\mathsf{R} : \mathbb{T} \to [m]$ where $m = |\mathbb{T}|$. For each (honest) party P_i, its receiving transaction log forms a profile which is denoted by R_i. Consider a set of n parties $\mathcal{P}$, we write $\mathcal{R} = \langle \mathsf{R}_1, \mathsf{R}_2, \ldots, \mathsf{R}_n \rangle$ as the list of all transaction profiles. Regarding order fairness, we are interested in a serialization function F that takes an indefinte number of transaction profiles $\mathcal{R}$ as input and outputs a new profile denoted by σ, namely $\sigma = F(\mathcal{R})$.

We adopt "$\prec$" to describe the "order before" relation on $\mathbb{T} \times \mathbb{T}$. Note that this relation is (i) irreflexive (not $\mathtt{tx} \prec \mathtt{tx}$); (ii) asymmetric ($\mathtt{tx} \prec \mathtt{tx}'$ implies not $\mathtt{tx}' \prec \mathtt{tx}$) and (iii) transitive (i.e., $\mathtt{tx} \prec \mathtt{tx}'$ and $\mathtt{tx}' \prec \mathtt{tx}''$ implies $\mathtt{tx} \prec \mathtt{tx}''$). We write $\mathtt{tx} \prec_i \mathtt{tx}'$ if $\mathsf{R}_i(\mathtt{tx}) < \mathsf{R}_i(\mathtt{tx}')$; i.e. $\mathtt{tx} \prec \mathtt{tx}'$ in party P_i's profile (in other words, P_i receives transaction $\mathtt{tx}$ before $\mathtt{tx}'$). For every pair of distinct transactions $\mathtt{tx}, \mathtt{tx}'$ in $\mathbb{T}$, they are ascribed either the relations $\mathtt{tx} \prec_i \mathtt{tx}'$ or $\mathtt{tx}' \prec_i \mathtt{tx}$ in profile R_i.

In order to achieve order fairness, we are interested in the pairs of transactions such that one is received by sufficiently many parties before the other. To measure what "sufficiently many" means, we adopt $\varphi \in \mathbb{R}^+$ as the order fairness parameter. We say $\mathtt{tx} \prec_{\mathcal{R}}^{\varphi} \mathtt{tx}'$ if, for profiles $\mathcal{R}$, $\mathtt{tx} \prec \mathtt{tx}'$ holds in at least φ fraction of these profiles (when the profile set is explicit in the context we drop the subscript and simply write $\mathtt{tx} \prec^{\varphi} \mathtt{tx}'$). Note that when $\varphi \leq 1/2$, it results in a logical contradiction as both $\mathtt{tx} \prec^{\varphi} \mathtt{tx}'$ and $\mathtt{tx}' \prec^{\varphi} \mathtt{tx}$ hold. Hence, we only care about φ such that $1/2 < \varphi \leq 1$.

Transaction Timestamp Assignment. We next present a timestamp assignment function F_{ts} which is useful in the context of state machine replication problem. Note that different from the one-shot consensus where input profiles are given to parties as input in an instant, the transaction log that a party receives grows with time. Hence, we assign each transaction a timestamp to indicate when it is received. I.e., parties store transactions in pair $\langle \mathtt{tx}, \mathsf{t} \rangle$ where $\mathsf{t} \in \mathbb{N}^+$ is the time that they receive $\mathtt{tx}$. We denote the timestamp of $\mathtt{tx}$ in profile R as $\mathsf{TS}(\mathtt{tx}, \mathsf{R})$ and the list of all timestamps associated with tx in $\mathcal{R}$ as $\mathsf{TS}(\mathsf{tx})$. We call the profiles $\mathcal{R}$ Δ_{tx}-disseminated if for all transactions, the timestamps associated with them are within a Δ_{tx} time window (i.e. $\forall \mathsf{tx} \in \mathbb{T}, \max \mathsf{TS}(\mathsf{tx}) - \min \mathsf{TS}(\mathsf{tx}) \leq \Delta_{\mathsf{tx}}$).

Consider an assignment of a timestamp to each transaction, which can be represented by a function $F_{\mathsf{ts}} : \mathbb{T} \to \mathbb{N}^+$. If for profiles $\mathcal{R}$ it holds that $\forall \mathsf{tx} \in \mathbb{T}, F_{\mathsf{ts}}(\mathsf{tx}) \in \mathsf{TS}(\mathsf{tx})$, then we say F_{ts} is compliant with $\mathcal{R}$. Let $\mathbb{F}_{\mathsf{ts},\mathcal{R}}$ denote the set of all compliant F_{ts} with $\mathcal{R}$. Especially, we are interested in the mapping from each transaction to its earliest receiving time; and we denote this mapping by $F_{\mathsf{ts}}^{\min}$ (i.e., $\forall \mathsf{tx} \in \mathbb{T}, F_{\mathsf{ts}}^{\min}(\mathsf{tx}) = \min \mathsf{TS}(\mathsf{tx})$).

Transaction Dependency Graphs. Consider a list of transaction profiles $\mathcal{R} = \langle \mathsf{R}_1, \mathsf{R}_2, \ldots, \mathsf{R}_n \rangle$. An $(\mathcal{R}, \varphi)$-dependency-graph is a directed graph $G_{\mathcal{R},\varphi}$ constructed as follows. For each transaction tx_i, add a vertex v_i to $G_{\mathcal{R},\varphi}$; then, for any pair of vertices $\mathsf{tx}_i, \mathsf{tx}_j$, add an edge (v_i, v_j) if $\mathsf{tx}_i \prec^\varphi \mathsf{tx}_j$. When $\prec^\varphi$ is the majority relation (i.e., $\varphi = 1/2 + 1/m$, where m is the total number of transactions), we write $G_{\mathcal{R}}$ and call the graph $\mathcal{R}$-dependency. Note that when $\varphi > 1/2$, at most one of (i,j) and (j,i) can be added — i.e., a dependency graph is oriented.

Graph Notations. A vertex ordering of a graph $G = (V, E)$ is a bijection $\sigma : V \to [n]$ where $n = |V|$. A null graph is the unique graph having no vertices. A subgraph S of G is another graph such that $V(S) \subseteq V(G) \wedge E(S) \subseteq E(G)$ ($V(S)$ must include all endpoints of the edges in $E(S)$). Conversely, a supergraph H of G is a graph formed by adding vertices, edges, or both to G. A spanning supergraph is a supergraph by merely adding edges to the original graph.

A directed graph is strongly connected if every vertex is reachable from every other vertex. The strongly connected components are maximal subgraphs of a directed graph that are themselves strongly connected.

For a dependency graph G, we slightly abuse the notation and use transaction tx and its generated vertex v interchangeably. For instance, $(\mathsf{tx}, \mathsf{tx}')$ denotes the edge from vertex v generated by tx to vertex v' generated by tx'. And $\sigma(\mathsf{tx})$ is the same as $\sigma(v)$ where v is generated by tx.

3   Order Fairness

In this section we first give a definition of order fairness in the sense of bounded unfairness. We then connect order fairness to DIRECTEDBANDWIDTH and provide a fine-grained fair-order definition which is the best that one can expect in this setting. Next, we study this problem in the context of state machine replication and permissionless participation respectively. Due to the space limit, all proofs in this section are presented in the full version of this paper [26].

3.1   Bounded Unfairness and Serialization

An ideal fair order σ on profiles $\mathcal{R}$ follows all φ-preferences in $\mathcal{R}$. I.e., for all $\mathsf{tx} \prec^\varphi \mathsf{tx}'$ it holds $\sigma(\mathsf{tx}) < \sigma(\mathsf{tx}')$. Unfortunately, this is impossible with the existence of Condorcet cycles — φ-preferences can be cyclic and hence no σ can satisfy all of them simultaneously. To see the simplest example, fix $\varphi = 2/3$ and consider three transactions $\mathsf{tx}_1, \mathsf{tx}_2, \mathsf{tx}_3$ and three profiles $\mathsf{R}_1 = \mathsf{tx}_1 \prec \mathsf{tx}_2 \prec \mathsf{tx}_3$, $\mathsf{R}_2 = \mathsf{tx}_2 \prec \mathsf{tx}_3 \prec \mathsf{tx}_1$ and $\mathsf{R}_3 = \mathsf{tx}_3 \prec \mathsf{tx}_1 \prec \mathsf{tx}_2$. We have $\mathsf{tx}_1 \prec^\varphi \mathsf{tx}_2$, $\mathsf{tx}_2 \prec^\varphi \mathsf{tx}_3$ and $\mathsf{tx}_3 \prec^\varphi \mathsf{tx}_1$.

Note that there is a hidden constant in $\sigma(\mathsf{tx}) < \sigma(\mathsf{tx}')$ (i.e., $\sigma(\mathsf{tx}) - \sigma(\mathsf{tx}') < 0$) to indicate the position that tx' can be placed before tx. A natural relaxation on standard order fairness would be to enlarge this distance to some realizable extent. I.e., an order is fair if for all preferences $\mathsf{tx} \prec^\varphi \mathsf{tx}'$, tx' is not ordered at a position that is too earlier compared with tx. In order to acquire a fine-grained fairness notion, we are interested in upper-bounding this distance on every pair of transactions $\mathsf{tx}, \mathsf{tx}'$ in specific transaction profiles $\mathcal{R}$. Thus we define B as a function of $\mathcal{R}, \varphi, \mathsf{tx}$ and tx' and require $\sigma(\mathsf{tx}) - \sigma(\mathsf{tx}') < B$. This gives us an intuitive and parametric definition of order fairness.

Definition 1 $((\varphi, B)$-fair-order).   *A profile σ is a (φ, B)-fair-order on $\mathcal{R}$ if for all $\mathsf{tx}, \mathsf{tx}'$ such that $\mathsf{tx} \prec^\varphi_{\mathcal{R}} \mathsf{tx}'$, it holds that $\sigma(\mathsf{tx}) - \sigma(\mathsf{tx}') \leq B$ where B is a function of $\mathcal{R}, \varphi, \mathsf{tx}$ and tx'.*

(φ, B)-fair-order is unrealizable when B is a function such that there exist $\mathcal{R}$ and it holds that $\forall \sigma, \exists(\mathsf{tx}, \mathsf{tx}'), \sigma(\mathsf{tx}) - \sigma(\mathsf{tx}') > B(\mathcal{R}, \varphi, \mathsf{tx}, \mathsf{tx}')$. In other words, B is too "small" on some profiles thus no ordering could order $\mathsf{tx}, \mathsf{tx}'$ "close enough" as specified by B. On the other hand, Definition 1 is trivial when B is a function such that $\exists(\mathcal{R}, \mathsf{tx}, \mathsf{tx}'), B(\mathcal{R}, \varphi, \mathsf{tx}, \mathsf{tx}') \geq m - 1$ where m is the total number of transactions in $\mathcal{R}$ (i.e., $\mathsf{tx}, \mathsf{tx}'$ can be arranged apart for an arbitrary distance). The reason such a B is called trivial is that, intuitively, given a set of profiles, any protocol that realizes an (unfair) order with $B = m - 1$ on one transaction pair $\mathsf{tx}, \mathsf{tx}'$ can be converted into a new protocol with fair order $B' < m - 1$ on every pairs, by simply swapping $\mathsf{tx}, \mathsf{tx}'$ in the output profile[2]; moreover, as we show in Theorem 5, there exists a *practical B* which requires distance strictly less than $m - 1$ (more precisely, $m - \log m/2$) for every pair of transactions.

Serialization with Adversarial Profiles. We then consider order fairness in the presence of an adversary. Given a protocol execution, the set of honest parties $\mathcal{H}$ is well-defined and we let $h = |\mathcal{H}|$ denote the number of honest parties. We abstract the sequence of transactions received by an honest party P_i as R_i, and write $\mathcal{R}^{\mathcal{H}} = \langle \mathsf{R}_1, \mathsf{R}_2, \ldots, \mathsf{R}_h \rangle$ as the honest profiles. Regarding corrupted parties, note that they can deviate arbitrarily from the protocol thus the profile

---

[2] Notice that $B = m - 1$ on a transaction pair $\mathsf{tx}, \mathsf{tx}'$ only when $\mathsf{tx} \prec^\varphi \mathsf{tx}'$ and tx is put at the last but tx' is put at the first of the output profile. By swapping $\mathsf{tx}, \mathsf{tx}'$ we get a new order with largest unfair distance strictly smaller than $m - 1$.

abstraction does not apply to them. Instead, we model the adversarial manipulation as follows. Suppose F is a serialization function that takes an indefinite number of profiles as input and outputs a new profile, for every honest party we require that they output $\sigma = F(\mathcal{R})$ where $\mathcal{R} = \langle \mathcal{R}^{\mathcal{H}}, \mathcal{R}^{\mathcal{A}} \rangle$ and $\mathcal{R}^{\mathcal{A}}$ is some arbitrary profiles (this models the adversarial behavior). Note that for different honest parties, $\mathcal{R}^{\mathcal{A}}$ can be different to them. Thus, the following definition does not ask for agreement — i.e., honest parties could output different profiles as long as they are all fair orderings on $\mathcal{R}^{\mathcal{H}}$; it implies agreement only in the all honest setting.

Definition 2 (implementing a fair-order serialization). *Given a protocol execution, an (F, φ, B)-consistent serialization event happens if and only if for any honest party P_i, there exist profiles $\mathcal{R} = \langle \mathcal{R}^{\mathcal{H}}, \mathcal{R}^{\mathcal{A}} \rangle$ such that*

(i) $\mathcal{R}^{\mathcal{H}}$ is defined by the sequence of transactions received by honest parties;
(ii) P_i outputs $\sigma = F(\mathcal{R})$ and σ is a (φ, B)-fair-order on honest profiles $\mathcal{R}^{\mathcal{H}}$.

A protocol serializes transactions according to F with (φ, B)-order-fairness, if the (F, φ, B)-consistent serialization event happens with overwhelming probability.

Notice that, in order to implement a non-trivial fair-order serialization, the adversary should not be too powerful with respect to the fairness parameter φ. To model this we consider upper-bounding profiles in $\mathcal{R}^{\mathcal{A}}$ and we write t as its maximum number of profiles. Then we consider the threshold on t with respect to the number of honest parties h and fair-order parameter φ. For instance, dishonest majority $(t > h)$ is infeasible with any φ. This is because if the adversary could select more profiles than the honest, then $\mathcal{A}$ can completely dominate the φ-preferences. In other words, the adversary can vanish any $\mathsf{tx} \prec^{\varphi} \mathsf{tx}'$ by simply inserting profiles with the opposite order.

To see how adversarial power should be restricted in terms of the fair order parameter, we prove that when $t \geq (2\varphi - 1)h$, it becomes impossible to implement non-trivial fair-order serialization.

Theorem 1. *When $t \geq (2\varphi - 1)h$, no protocol implements non-trivial fair-order serialization.*

We say an adversary $\mathcal{A}$ is admissible with fairness parameter φ if it holds that $t < (2\varphi - 1)h$ and in Definition 2 the number of profiles in $\mathcal{R}^{\mathcal{A}}$ are upper-bounded by t. All following discussions on order fairness and transaction serialization are with respect to an admissible adversary.

3.2 Transaction Dependency Graphs

Fix φ and n transaction profiles $\mathcal{R}$, there will be a unique $(\mathcal{R}, \varphi)$-dependency-graph $G_{\mathcal{R}, \varphi}$. When $\varphi < 1/2 + 1/n$ and n is odd (i.e., the majority preference), the dependency graph will be a tournament (since all pairwise preference can be extracted). As φ increases, the graph becomes more and more sparse. While the specific edges to be removed are subject to the profiles, we show that the structure of dependency graphs depends on the fairness parameter φ, and a large φ implies graphs without cycles of small size. For instance, when $\varphi > 2/3$, no directed triangle can exist in the dependency graph; when $\varphi > 3/4$, no directed square can exist; etc. We formalize this property in Theorem 2.

Theorem 2. *For any $\varphi > 1/2$ and any profiles $\mathcal{R}$, the $(\mathcal{R}, \varphi)$-dependency-graph $G_{\mathcal{R},\varphi}$ does not contain cycles of size k for all $k < \lceil 1/(1 - \varphi) \rceil$.*

Conversely, given an oriented graph G, there exist some profiles whose dependency graph is exactly G. McGarvey [29] provides an approach to construct these profiles (with majority preference). We briefly describe McGarvey's approach here. Suppose we would like to construct a profile set $\mathcal{R}$ from an oriented graph G with m vertices. For each edge $(v_i, v_j) \in G$, add two profiles $\mathsf{R}_1, \mathsf{R}_2$ to $\mathcal{R}$ with $\mathsf{R}_1(\mathsf{tx}_i) = 1, \mathsf{R}_1(\mathsf{tx}_j) = 2, \mathsf{R}_2(\mathsf{tx}_i) = m - 1, \mathsf{R}_2(\mathsf{tx}_j) = m$ and $\mathsf{R}_1(\mathsf{tx}_k) + \mathsf{R}_2(\mathsf{tx}_k) = m + 1$ for all $k \neq i, j$ — i.e., $\mathsf{tx}_i, \mathsf{tx}_j$ are put at the head and rear of the profile respectively and the rest are in an exactly reversed order. Notice for all edge (v_i, v_j), $\mathsf{tx}_i, \mathsf{tx}_j$ are in the same order only in the two profiles constructed from them.

Dependency Graph with Adversarial Profiles. Given a protocol execution, the $(\mathcal{R}^{\mathcal{H}}, \varphi)$-dependency-graph G is unique and well-defined. We are interested in the relationship between G and dependency graphs that are constructed with adversarial profiles.

Note that parties cannot distinguish which profile is corrupted, thus for $\mathcal{R} = \langle \mathcal{R}^{\mathcal{H}}, \mathcal{R}^{\mathcal{A}} \rangle$, it is infeasible to consider the dependency graph based on preferences held by φ fraction of profiles. For instance, when φh honest parties believe $\mathsf{tx} \prec \mathsf{tx}'$, the adversary can collude with the minority and vanish this preference in $\mathcal{R}$; similarly, when $(\varphi h - 1)$ honest parties receive $\mathsf{tx} \prec \mathsf{tx}'$, the adversary can join forces with them and make this preference account for φ fraction in $\mathcal{R}$.

Fix honest profiles $\mathcal{R}^{\mathcal{H}}$, we show that for any admissible adversary $\mathcal{A}$ and any adversarial profiles $\mathcal{R}^{\mathcal{A}}$ selected by $\mathcal{A}$, it yields a dependency graph G' on $\langle \mathcal{R}^{\mathcal{H}}, \mathcal{R}^{\mathcal{A}} \rangle$ with majority preference such that all edges in G remain the same orientation in G'.

Theorem 3. *Fix φ and honest profiles $\mathcal{R}^{\mathcal{H}}$ and denote the $(\mathcal{R}^{\mathcal{H}}, \varphi)$-dependency-graph by G. For any graph $G' \in \{G_{\mathcal{R}} \mid \mathcal{R} = \langle \mathcal{R}^{\mathcal{H}}, \mathcal{R}^{\mathcal{A}} \rangle$ and $\mathcal{R}^{\mathcal{A}}$ is chosen by an admissible adversary\}, it holds that G' is a spanning supergraph of G.*

Theorem 3 shows, with admissible adversarial manipulation, the φ-preferences are "robust" among all dependency graphs. We write the set of all possible dependency graphs on $\mathcal{R} = \langle \mathcal{R}^{\mathcal{H}}, \mathcal{R}^{\mathcal{A}} \rangle$ from majority preference as $\mathbb{G}_{\mathcal{R}^{\mathcal{H}},\varphi}$. Note that when given $\mathcal{R}^{\mathcal{H}}$ and φ, the set of all possible $\mathcal{R}^{\mathcal{A}}$ is well-defined with an admissible adversary by Theorem 1.

3.3 Bounded Unfairness from Directed Bandwidth

Given honest transaction profiles $\mathcal{R}$ (with Condorcet cycles), our goal is to find an ordering that does not put tx' too early before tx when $\mathsf{tx} \prec^{\varphi} \mathsf{tx}'$. Consider a dependency graph $G \in \mathbb{G}_{\mathcal{R},\varphi}$ and a vertex ordering σ on G. Theorem 3 implies that G contains cycles (as all edges forming the cycles in $G_{\mathcal{R},\varphi}$ preserve in G), i.e., there will be back edges $(\mathtt{tx}, \mathtt{tx}')$ such that $\mathtt{tx} \prec^\varphi \mathtt{tx}'$ and $\sigma(\mathtt{tx}) > \sigma(\mathtt{tx}')$. The length of a back edge $(\mathtt{tx}, \mathtt{tx}')$ is the distance of its source and target in the ordering $\sigma(\mathtt{tx}) - \sigma(\mathtt{tx}')$. Ideally, a fair order comes with back edges of small lengths. In order to quantify how small the length of a back edge can be, we are interested in finding a vertex ordering on the dependency graph G that minimizes the maximum length of back edges. Following the similar treatment in [21] (where they consider the forward edges), we state this problem as DIRECTEDBANDWIDTH in Definition 3.

Definition 3 (Directed Bandwidth). *Given a directed graph* $G = (V, E)$, DIRECTEDBANDWIDTH *asks to find a vertex ordering* σ^* *such that* $\mathtt{DBW}(\sigma^*, G) = \min_\sigma \mathtt{DBW}(\sigma, G)$ *where*

$$\mathtt{DBW}(\sigma, G) = \max_{\substack{(u,v) \in E, \\ \sigma(u) > \sigma(v)}} \sigma(u) - \sigma(v).$$

The directed bandwidth of a graph G *is* $\mathtt{DBW}(G) = \mathtt{DBW}(\sigma^*, G)$.

Note that when G is acyclic, there exist σ which is a topological ordering on G such that no back edge exists; this has little to do with the fair-order serialization problem and $\mathtt{DBW}(G) = 0$ for an acyclic graph. We also note that $\mathtt{DBW}(G) = 0$ if G is the null graph.

Analogous to Definition 3, BANDWIDTH [10, 11, 16] is a well-known and extensively studied graph problem aiming at minimizing the quantity $\mathtt{BW}(G, \sigma) = \max_{(u,v) \in E} |\sigma(u) - \sigma(v)|$ among all vertex orderings on an undirected graph. BANDWIDTH has been proved to be both NP-hard [31] and NP-hard to approximate within any constant ratio [12] over general graphs. Further, BANDWIDTH remains NP-hard and NP-hard to approximate even on very restricted graphs like caterpillars of hair length at most 3 (a restricted tree).

Since an undirected graph can be converted to a digraph by replacing each edge with two symmetric directed edges, there is a simple reduction from BANDWIDTH to DIRECTEDBANDWIDTH and thus DIRECTEDBANDWIDTH is also NP-hard and NP-hard to approximate over general graphs. Notice that, in our context, dependency graphs are all oriented graphs. We prove that DIRECTEDBANDWIDTH remains NP-hard and NP-hard to approximate within any constant ratio over oriented graphs.

Theorem 4. DIRECTEDBANDWIDTH *is* NP-*hard and* NP-*hard to approximate within any constant ratio over oriented graphs.*

DIRECTEDBANDWIDTH can be solved trivially in factorial time ($\mathcal{O}^*(n!)$) by an exhaustive search on all possible orderings; and, unlike some vertex ordering problems that can be solved by dynamic programming or divide-and-conquer, so far there is no evidence that these techniques also applies on DIRECTEDBANDWIDTH. A recent work by Jain *et al.* [21] provides exponential algorithms to find the exact and approximate solutions to DIRECTEDBANDWIDTH. Specifically, the exact algorithm runs in $\mathcal{O}^*(3^{|V|} \cdot 2^{|E|})$ time; and in order to get an ordering with bandwidth at most $(1 + \epsilon)$ times the optimal one, an approximation algorithm runs in $\mathcal{O}^*(4^{|V|} \cdot (4/\epsilon)^{|V|})$ time. We briefly describe the exact algorithm for DIRECTEDBANDWIDTH in [26].

Largest Possible Directed Bandwidth. Since all oriented graphs can be generated by profiles, we are interested in the largest possible bandwidth on graphs with a fixed number of vertices.

Note that, given n vertices, the worst bandwidth $n-1$ can always be avoided by finding an edge (i, j) and outputting σ such that $\sigma(i) = 1$ and $\sigma(j) = n$. And, for a small constant k, we can check if a graph has bandwidth $n - k$ by checking $\mathcal{O}(n^{2k})$ vertex orderings — i.e., we select k vertices each at the head and rear of orderings and see if a back edge exists between the two sets. Unfortunately, the time complexity of this simple approach grows to factorial when $k = \Theta(n)$ hence it becomes impractical for large graphs. This raises the question whether it is possible to find a vertex ordering with directed bandwidth, e.g., $0.99n$, for any oriented graph with n vertices.

Here we give a negative answer to this question. We prove that, among all oriented graphs with n vertices there exist some tournaments with large directed bandwidth compared with n^3. In Theorem 5 we show that the above simple approach to check bandwidth will soon terminate on some graphs by considering Zarankiewicz's problem.

Theorem 5. *Let* $\mathbb{G}_n$ *denote the set of all oriented graphs with n vertices. It holds that*

$$n - 4\log n < \max_{G \in \mathbb{G}_n} \text{DBW}(G) < n - \log n/2.$$

(φ, DBW)-**fair-order.** After extracting the directed bandwidth of a graph in Definition 3, we are now ready to define fair order based on upper-bounding how much tx' can be ordered before tx when $\text{tx} \prec^{\varphi} \text{tx}'$.

Note that, given a transaction profile set $\mathcal{R}$ and its dependency graph G, we cannot simply define the upper bound as $\text{DBW}(G)$. This is because G might contain several strongly connected components and their sizes might differ a lot. Actually, the bandwidth of a graph G is the maximum bandwidth among all strongly connected components in G.

$$\text{DBW}(G) = \max\{\text{DBW}(G') : G' \text{ is a strongly connected component of } G\}.$$

Suppose there is a SCC that contains thousands of transactions and $\text{DBW}(G)$ is also in the thousands. Then, for other relatively small SCCs with, for instance, 10 transactions, an upper bound as $\text{DBW}(G)$ does not set any limitation on how they should be ordered.

---

[3] This result implies that no algorithm can guarantee finding a vertex ordering of directed bandwidth $0.99n$.

Additionally, note that when given $\mathcal{R}^{\mathcal{H}}$ and φ, a fair-order serialization should consider all possible dependency graphs $\mathbb{G}_{\mathcal{R}^{\mathcal{H}},\varphi}$ with admissible $\mathcal{R}^{\mathcal{A}}$. Theorem 3 shows that $\mathcal{A}$ may create new cycles or enlarge existing ones, but $\mathcal{A}$ cannot remove any edge that has already been there in $G_{\mathcal{R}^{\mathcal{H}},\varphi}$. Due to the above observations, we propose a fine-grained definition of order fairness (Definition 4) on top of Definition 1 by replacing the initial function with largest DBW on all possible SCCs. Specifically, for a pair of transaction $\mathtt{tx} \prec^{\varphi} \mathtt{tx}'$, if among all possible dependency graphs $\mathbb{G}_{\mathcal{R}^{\mathcal{H}},\varphi}$ there is no graph with SCC that contains $\mathtt{tx},\mathtt{tx}'$ simultaneously then the final output should follow $\mathtt{tx} \prec \mathtt{tx}'$. Otherwise, we will define the upper bound on their distance in the output by extracting all SCCs containing $\mathtt{tx},\mathtt{tx}'$ over $\mathbb{G}_{\mathcal{R}^{\mathcal{H}},\varphi}$ and find the largest possible bandwidth.

Definition 4 ((φ, DBW)-fair-order). *A profile σ is a (φ, DBW)-fair-order on $\mathcal{R}$ if for all $\mathtt{tx},\mathtt{tx}'$ such that $\mathtt{tx} \prec^{\varphi}_{\mathcal{R}} \mathtt{tx}'$, it holds that*

$$\sigma(\mathtt{tx}) - \sigma(\mathtt{tx}') \leq \max_{G \in \mathbb{G}_{\mathcal{R},\varphi}} \mathrm{DBW}\big(\mathrm{SCC}(G,\mathtt{tx},\mathtt{tx}')\big),$$

where $\mathrm{SCC}(G,\mathtt{tx},\mathtt{tx}')$ is a function that outputs an SCC in G that contains both $\mathtt{tx},\mathtt{tx}'$ if it exists, and a null graph otherwise.

Note that in an all honest setting, no $\mathcal{R}^{\mathcal{A}}$ exists, thus Definition 4 can be simplified as "$\mathtt{tx} \prec^{\varphi} \mathtt{tx}' \implies \sigma(\mathtt{tx}) - \sigma(\mathtt{tx}') \leq \mathrm{DBW}(\mathrm{SCC}(G_{\mathcal{R},\varphi},\mathtt{tx},\mathtt{tx}'))$". See below for an example where we have 8 transactions in $\mathcal{R}$ and the $(\mathcal{R},\varphi)$-dependency-graph is illustrated in Fig. 1(a). Since $\mathrm{DBW}(G_{\mathcal{R},\varphi}) = 3$, a (φ, DBW)-fair-order on $\mathcal{R}$ should satisfy $\mathtt{tx} \prec^{\varphi} \mathtt{tx}' \implies \sigma(\mathtt{tx}) - \sigma(\mathtt{tx}') \leq 3$. We provide a profile $\sigma = \mathtt{tx}_2 \prec \mathtt{tx}_3 \prec \mathtt{tx}_1 \prec \mathtt{tx}_5 \prec \mathtt{tx}_6 \prec \mathtt{tx}_8 \prec \mathtt{tx}_4 \prec \mathtt{tx}_7$ which is a fair order on $\mathcal{R}$ in Fig. 1(b). Note that only back edges are illustrated and the back edges $(5,2)$, $(4,5)$ and $(8,1)$ are of maximum length 3. Also compare with the

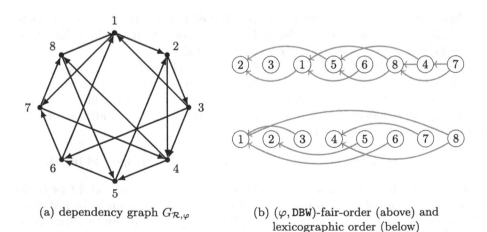

(a) dependency graph $G_{\mathcal{R},\varphi}$

(b) (φ, DBW)-fair-order (above) and lexicographic order (below)

Fig. 1. *Illustration of a dependency graph, a (φ, DBW)-fair-order and a lexicographic order on $\mathcal{R}$. Only back edges are illustrated in (b).*

lexicographic order which has a back edge of length 7 (Aequitas and Themis may output this order, see below for comparison with existing protocols).

We highlight that Definition 4 is the most precise definition that we can make on top of Definition 1 and 2. For any new definition that tries to further reduce $\max_{G \in \mathbb{G}_{\mathcal{R},\varphi}} \mathrm{DBW}(\mathrm{SCC}(G, \mathtt{tx}, \mathtt{tx}'))$ for transactions $\mathtt{tx}, \mathtt{tx}'$, there will exist some profiles $\mathcal{R}^{\mathcal{A}}$ leading to SCCs with large bandwidth which can invalidate the new definition. Refer to Sect. 5 for further discussions.

Theorem 6. *Suppose that a protocol implements (φ, B)-fairness for a function B. Then for all $\mathcal{R}$ there are $\mathtt{tx}, \mathtt{tx}'$ with $\mathtt{tx} \prec^\varphi \mathtt{tx}'$, such that B satisfies $B(\mathcal{R}, \varphi, \mathtt{tx}, \mathtt{tx}') \geq \max_{G \in \mathbb{G}_{\mathcal{R},\varphi}} \mathrm{DBW}(\mathrm{SCC}(G, \mathtt{tx}, \mathtt{tx}'))$.*

Comparison with Existing Protocols. We show that Aequitas [25], Themis [24], pompe [37] and wendy [27] fail to implement (φ, DBW)-fair-order serialization (Definition 2 and 4) even in the all honest setting. For Aequitas, the core observation here is that when an alphabetical order is adopted to order transactions within a Condorcet cycle, it is always feasible to simply manipulate the labels of transactions and produce any desired order. Next, Themis improves the transaction linearization in a Condorcet cycle to a Hamiltonian-cycle-based order. We point out that this treatment will always produce an order such that $\mathtt{tx}, \mathtt{tx}'$ are at the head and rear respectively but it holds $\mathtt{tx}' \prec^\varphi \mathtt{tx}$. Regarding pompe and wendy, note that in order to be resistant to possible adversarial manipulation, transactions are ordered by their median timestamp. Thus, we could get any desired output by constructing profiles with carefully selected timestamps.

The following two examples show how these protocols fail our fair-order serialization definition. In both examples we consider a Condorcet cycle of m transactions and denote its dependency graph as G.

Example 1 (Aequitas and Themis). Suppose $\mathtt{tx}_1 \prec^\varphi \mathtt{tx}_2$, we assign labels to transactions such that $label(\mathtt{tx}_2) < label(\mathtt{tx}_i) < label(\mathtt{tx}_1)$ for all $\mathtt{tx}_i$ other than $\mathtt{tx}_1, \mathtt{tx}_2$. Since an alphabetical order is adopted in a cycle, Aequitas will output $\sigma_{\mathsf{Aequitas}} = \mathtt{tx}_2 \prec \ldots \prec \mathtt{tx}_1$; i.e., $\sigma_{\mathsf{Aequitas}}(\mathtt{tx}_1) - \sigma_{\mathsf{Aequitas}}(\mathtt{tx}_2) = m - 1$. Note that Themis can also output $\sigma_{\mathsf{Aequitas}}$ if the transaction label is well-selected and the Hamiltonian cycle starts with $\mathtt{tx}_2$. Refer to [26] to see a detailed profile example $\mathcal{R}$ such that for all $\mathtt{tx} \prec^\varphi \mathtt{tx}'$, an output σ satisfying our definition yields $\sigma(\mathtt{tx}) - \sigma(\mathtt{tx}') \leq 1$. However, Aequitas and Themis outputs an order $\sigma_{\mathsf{Aequitas}}$ and there exist some $\mathtt{tx} \prec \mathtt{tx}'$ such that $\sigma_{\mathsf{Aequitas}}(\mathtt{tx}) - \sigma_{\mathsf{Aequitas}}(\mathtt{tx}') = m - 1$.

Example 2 (pompe and wendy). Suppose $\mathtt{tx}_1 \prec^\varphi \mathtt{tx}_2$, we assign timestamps to transactions so that the median timestamps yield $\mathsf{med}(\mathtt{tx}_2) < \mathsf{med}(\mathtt{tx}_i) < \mathsf{med}(\mathtt{tx}_1)$ for all i such that $\mathtt{tx}_i$ is a transaction other than $\mathtt{tx}_1, \mathtt{tx}_2$. Since median timestamp decides the final order, pompe and wendy will output $\sigma_{\mathsf{pompe}} = \mathtt{tx}_2 \prec \ldots \prec \mathtt{tx}_1$; i.e., $\sigma_{\mathsf{pompe}}(\mathtt{tx}_1) - \sigma_{\mathsf{pompe}}(\mathtt{tx}_2) \leq m - 1$. Refer to [26] to see a detailed profile example $\mathcal{R}$ such that for all $\mathtt{tx} \prec^\varphi \mathtt{tx}'$, an output σ satisfying our definition yields $\sigma(\mathtt{tx}) - \sigma(\mathtt{tx}') \leq \lceil m/3 \rceil$. However, pompe and wendy outputs an order σ_{pompe} on $\mathcal{R}$ and there exist $\mathtt{tx} \prec^\varphi \mathtt{tx}'$ such that $\sigma_{\mathsf{pompe}}(\mathtt{tx}) - \sigma_{\mathsf{pompe}}(\mathtt{tx}') = m - 1$.

3.4   Fairness versus Liveness

We define our fair order notions based on the *complete* transaction profiles. However, during the protocol execution parties can only learn a prefix of their profiles. In this section we discuss the inherent tension between liveness and order fairness. Specifically, we prove that it is *impossible* to satisfy all desired properties when the transaction dissemination is asynchronous (even if in the non-corrupting setting); next, we show that, when there is an upper bound on transaction diffusion, it is *possible* to have liveness with relatively weak but still useful fairness.

Fairness in an Asynchronous Network. Suppose the transaction dissemination is asynchronous — i.e. a transaction can appear at any position of a (complete) transaction profile. In order to get a complete view of the transaction set that precedes a specific transaction tx, parties may have to wait indefinitely from the first time they saw tx. Note that standard liveness is still applicable with asynchronous transaction diffusion network. We have the following dilemma: if a Condorcet cycle spans for a long period of time and part of the transactions are delivered to all participants, then these transactions should appear in the (settled) output. In such scenario, parties have to decide the order with incomplete information.

We show below that the asynchronous dissemination will inevitably lead to the failure of (φ, DBW)-order-fairness. I.e. in order to satisfy consistency and liveness, the honest parties have to output an ordering σ on $\mathcal{R}$ such that $\text{tx} \prec^\varphi \text{tx}'$ but $\sigma(\text{tx}) - \sigma(\text{tx}') = n - 1$ where n is the total number of transactions in $\mathcal{R}$.

The general proof idea is to construct two executions that are indistinguishable up to some time $t + L$ (L is the liveness parameter) so that parties have to output transactions up to time t due to liveness. However, the transaction profiles are different after time $t + L$ such that in the first execution it forms a Condorcet cycle but there is no cycle in the second. We extract the possible outputs at the end of the first execution, by carefully considering consistency and liveness conditions in both executions. We conclude that the output in the first execution must be an ordering with the worst bandwidth, which implies the failure of order fairness.

Theorem 7. *Suppose the transaction dissemination is asynchronous, there is no protocol that can achieve consistency, liveness and (φ, DBW)-order-fairness.*

One approach to solve this dilemma is to relax liveness (a.k.a. weak-liveness, cf. [25]). I.e., standard liveness holds if there is no Condorcet cycle or a cycle does not span for long time; however, the system completely loses liveness during the ongoing of a large cycle.

Definition 5 (Weak-liveness, informal). *If a transaction tx is provided to all honest parties for sufficiently many consecutive rounds, then tx will be in the (settled) ledger eventually.*

Weak-liveness is not in-line with the standard BFT SMR problem; and since Condorcet cycles can chain together thus form a cycle of infinite length, it is also difficult to measure how "weak" this relaxation is compared with the standard definition (it is subject to the largest cycle in transaction profiles). Hence, we turn to another direction towards the reconciliation — we would like to achieve standard liveness as well as slightly weaker (but still non-trivial) fairness.

Fairness with Δ_{tx}-disseminated Transactions. Suppose there exists an upper bound Δ_{tx} on transaction dissemination, i.e., if t is the earliest timestamp associated with tx, then in all honest profiles it cannot be the case $\langle tx, t' \rangle$ for $t' \geq t$. We show that the results in Theorem 7 can be mitigated in this scenario.

The core observation is, if a Condorcet cycle spans for a long period of time, we can perform partition on the set of transactions in this cycle, and these partitions correspond to a good partition on the dependency graph such that we can figure out an upper bound on the DIRECTEDBANDWIDTH problem.

The partition rule on the dependency graph goes as follows. Let T_{SCC} denote the set of all transactions in the Condorcet cycle and G_{SCC} its corresponding generated graph. Consider a timestamp assignment F_{ts} on T_{SCC} and a constant $\Delta \in \mathbb{N}^+$ such that $\Delta \geq \Delta_{tx}$. An (F_{ts}, Δ)-partition P on T_{SCC} is a set of non-empty subsets $P_1, P_2, \ldots$ such that

$$P_i = \left\{ tx \mid tx \in T_{SCC} \wedge M + (i-1)\Delta \leq F_{ts}(tx) < M + i\Delta \right\}$$

where $M = \min\{F_{ts}(tx) \mid tx \in T_{SCC}\}$ (i.e. the earliest timestamp among all transactions in T_{SCC}). Note that the union of the parts of this partition is exactly the original transaction set and the intersection of two distinct parts is empty.

An (F_{ts}, Δ)-partition on G_{SCC}, the dependency graph of T_{SCC}, is a set of non-empty subsets $V_1, V_2, \ldots$ such that V_i is a set of vertices in G_{SCC} such that all corresponding transactions are in partition P_i. Especially, consider the earliest timestamp assignment F_{ts}^{min}, transaction dissemination Δ_{tx} and its corresponding $(F_{ts}^{min}, \Delta_{tx})$-partition on G_{SCC}. The bandwidth of G_{SCC} is at most twice of the maximum number of vertices in a partition.

Theorem 8. *Consider profiles $\mathcal{R}$, their dependency graph G and a strongly connected component $G_{SCC} \in G$. Consider an $(F_{ts}^{min}, \Delta_{tx})$-partition on G_{SCC} that corresponds to the sets $V_1, V_2, \ldots,$. Then it holds that*

$$\text{DBW}(G_{SCC}) \leq 2 \max |V_i|.$$

Note that it is a non-trivial task to design a protocol that allows parties to learn the earliest timestamp of each transaction without any trusted third party[4]. Nonetheless, a protocol can, for each transaction let parties agree on a timestamp that falls in its Δ_{tx} dissemination time window; and such protocol can be resistant to an adversary that controls up to half of the total resources, which is compliant with any admissible adversary (for technical details on synthesizing

---

[4] We note that so far there is no protocol that can complete this task.

a good timestamp, see Sect. 4). Thus, we consider dependency graphs with a compliant timestamp assignment $F_{ts} \in \mathbb{F}_{ts,\mathcal{R}}$ and we allow that the specific assignment (as long as it is compliant with $\mathcal{R}$) can be chosen by the adversary.

We highlight that, in this context there exist a simple ordering trick that can provide us good bandwidth. Specifically, consider a dependency graph G and an $\mathcal{R}$-compliant timestamp assignment F_{ts}. By sorting vertices with a non-decreasing order on F_{ts} (i.e., we order u before v if $F_{ts}(u) < F_{ts}(v)$), it yields a vertex ordering with bandwidth upper bounded by three times the maximum total number of concurrent transactions in a Δ_{tx} time window (Theorem 9). We highlight that this ordering approach can be done without knowing the exact upper bound (Δ_{tx}) on transaction dissemination. Additionally, the bandwidth of this ordering is independent of the size of the Condorcet cycle — in other words, its performance is better on large cycles compared with small ones.

Theorem 9. *Consider profiles $\mathcal{R}$, its dependency graph G and a strongly connected component $G_{SCC} \in G$. Suppose $F_{ts} \in \mathbb{F}_{ts,\mathcal{R}}$ is a compliant timestamp assignment with respect to $\mathcal{R}$, and σ is a vertex ordering on G_{SCC} that orders vertices by a non-decreasing order on F_{ts}, then it holds that*

$$\mathtt{DBW}(\sigma, G_{SCC}) \leq 3 \max |V_i|.$$

Timed Directed Bandwidth. Given that Definition 4 might conflict with liveness even if the transaction dissemination is Δ_{tx}-bounded, we shall define a feasible fair order based on our observations in Theorem 8 and 9. Our technique is to extend the bandwidth function $\mathtt{DBW}$ to a timed fashion — i.e., the input dependency graph G is now accompanied with the earliest time that a transaction appears in the (honest) profile. A timed directed bandwidth function $\mathtt{TDBW}$ on a (strongly connected) graph G with timestamp assignment F_{ts}^{min} works as follows. If the earliest timestamp of two transactions are sufficiently apart from each other (i.e., the cycle is large and spans for a long time) then $\mathtt{TDBW}$ returns an upper bound as extracted in Theorem 9; otherwise it returns the directed bandwidth on graph G.

$$\mathtt{TDBW}(G) = \begin{cases} 3 \max |V_i(G)| & \textit{if } \exists(\mathtt{tx}, \mathtt{tx}') F_{ts}^{min}(\mathtt{tx}) \geq F_{ts}^{min}(\mathtt{tx}') + 3\Delta_{tx}, \\ \mathtt{DBW}(G) & \textit{otherwise.} \end{cases}$$

We are now ready to extend the $(\varphi, \mathtt{DBW})$-order-fairness (Definition 4) by replacing the bandwidth function $\mathtt{DBW}$ with the timed bandwidth function $\mathtt{TDBW}$. In this new definition, if two transactions are not within the same Condorcet cycle over all possible dependency graphs, their order in the output should follow parties' preference; if they are in the same cycle on some graphs, and all cycles are relatively small (i.e., it does not span for too long time) then their distance is upper-bounded by the largest possible bandwidth of the SCCs; and finally if some cycles do span for a long time, then we replace the upper-bound by three times the total number of concurrent transactions in a Δ_{tx} time window.

Definition 6 ((φ, TDBW)-order-fairness). *A profile σ is a (φ, TDBW)-fair-order on $\mathcal{R}$ if for all* tx, tx' *such that* tx $\prec_{\mathcal{R}}^{\varphi}$ tx', *it holds that*

$$\sigma(\text{tx}) - \sigma(\text{tx}') \leq \max_{G \in \mathbb{G}_{\mathcal{R},\varphi}} \text{TDBW}(\text{SCC}(G, \text{tx}, \text{tx}')),$$

where SCC(G, tx, tx') *is a function that outputs an SCC in G that contains both* tx, tx' *if it exists, and a null graph otherwise.*

3.5 Bounded Unfairness in a Permissionless Environment

In this section we show how to adapt our (φ, B)-order-fairness notion to a permissionless environment. We highlight that the only change we have to make in this new setting is to re-define the abstraction of profiles and the "order before by sufficiently many" notion ($\prec^{\varphi}$); all other definitions and arguments regarding order fairness could remain the same as above.

In a permissioned network, there is a one-to-one mapping from parties to profiles. This is because (honest) parties are online during the entire execution, thus profiles are exactly the abstract of their transaction logs at the end of the execution. Unfortunately, this is not the case in a permissionless environment in that parties can join and leave by their will (without notifying anyone else) and (possibly) no party can eventually hold a complete transaction profile.

Recall that in Sect. 2.1 we present a fine-grained classification on the type of participating parties. Especially, alert parties are the core participants that own all resources to run the protocol and have synchronized with each other. Under this dynamic participation model, we would like to use a profile to refer to the transaction log that an alert party holds at a specific round. In other words, we re-consider the mapping above in the permissionless setting as follows. Since there is no guarantee that an alert party P at round r will remain alert at any round other than r, we abstract the transaction log held by P at round r as a profile. Note that these profiles can be incomplete, i.e., it may only contain a few transactions $T \subseteq \mathbb{T}$ and is a mapping $T \to [m]$ where $m = |T|$. We say a profile is a (P, r)-profile, if it corresponds to the transaction log of an alert party at round r. Also note that regarding Definition 2 with an admissible adversary, the number of profiles in $\mathcal{R}^{\mathcal{A}}$ should be bounded by a round-by-round fashion — i.e., at a round r, $\mathcal{R}^{\mathcal{A}}$ can report at most $t < (2\varphi - 1)h$ profiles where h is the number of (P, r)-profiles.

Then, we re-define the notion of "order before by sufficiently many". Let t be the earliest time that at least one of tx and tx' appears in φ fraction of the (P, t)-profiles. We say tx' $\prec^{\varphi}$ tx, if during a sufficiently long period of time, say, K rounds, at least φ fraction of the (P, r)-profiles report tx' $\prec$ tx where $r \in [t, t + K)$ and P is an alert party at round r.

4 Taxis Protocol

In this section we present a new protocol Taxis and its basic building blocks. The ultimate product of Taxis is a ledger $\mathcal{L}$ providing fair transaction order. Due to the space limit, all detailed protocol description and analysis are presented in the full version of this paper [26].

Before we introduce Taxis, we present its preliminary version $\mathsf{Taxis_{WL}}$ as a direct comparison with Aequitas. $\mathsf{Taxis_{WL}}$ achieves consistency, weak-liveness and (φ, DBW)-order-fairness. Specifically, while the liveness is weak (same as Aequitas), this protocol achieves the best transaction order fairness that we can expect. Next, by adding a few simple modifications on $\mathsf{Taxis_{WL}}$, we present Taxis that reconciles the tension between liveness and fair order. The ledger of Taxis satisfies consistency, (standard) liveness and (φ, TDBW)-fair-order.

Taxis is a two-stage protocol that decouples the mining procedure of profiles and the final serialization of transactions. We will use blockchain as an intermediate information aggregator to collect profiles (i.e., transaction log) and build the ultimate ledger $\mathcal{L}$ on top of this blockchain. For simplicity, we present $\mathsf{Taxis_{WL}}$ and Taxis assuming static number of participants and discuss how to adapt them to the dynamic participation in [26].

Blockchain Notations. A block with target $T \in \mathbb{N}$ is a quadruple of the form $\mathcal{B} = \langle ctr, r, h, x \rangle$ where $ctr, r \in \mathbb{N}$, $h \in \{0,1\}$ and $x \in \{0,1\}^*$. A blockchain $\mathcal{C}$ is a (possibly empty) sequence of blocks; the rightmost block by convention is denoted by $\mathrm{head}(\mathcal{C})$ (note $\mathrm{head}(\varepsilon) = \varepsilon$). These blocks are chained in the sense that if $\mathcal{B}_{i+1} = \langle ctr, r, h, x \rangle$, then $h = H(\mathcal{B}_i)$, where $H(\cdot)$ is cryptographic hash function with output in $\{0,1\}^\kappa$. We adopt $\mathsf{TS}(\mathcal{B})$ to denote the timestamp of $\mathcal{B}$; and, slightly abusing the notations and omitting the current time $\mathbf{r}$, we will use $\mathcal{C}^{\lceil k}$ to denote the chain from pruning all blocks $\mathcal{B}$ such that $\mathsf{TS}(\mathcal{B}) \geq \mathbf{r} - k$.

2-for-1 Proof-of-Work. 2-for-1 PoW is a primitive that binds multiple PoW mining processes together by utilizing a single random oracle query. It was first proposed in [19] to improve the corruption threshold in ledger consensus. This primitive mitigates the possible attack with multiple independent mining processes, where the adversary can join forces to any one of the oracles and gain undesired advantage.

We will use 2-for-1 PoW to mine two types of blocks: ledger blocks and profile blocks. Ledger blocks form the Taxis blockchain and they will only include recent profile blocks (unlike regular blockchains, ledger blocks in Taxis will not include any transactions "directly"). Meanwhile, parties will use profile blocks to report their local profiles. We denote the mining target of ledger blocks and profile blocks by T_{LB} and T_{PB}, respectively. Taxis will maintain a constant ratio between them; for simplicity, in our presentation and analysis, we assume $T_{\mathsf{LB}} = T_{\mathsf{PB}}$.

The main goal of adopting 2-for-1 PoW to bind the mining process of these two types of blocks together, is to achieve better *chain quality*. Recall that chain quality is bad in the Bitcoin backbone protocol [19,20], where the adversary can contribute more blocks to the common prefix compared with her relative computational power. By adopting 2-for-1 PoW, Taxis guarantees that, for a sufficiently long time, φ fraction of parties mine φ fraction of the profiles (and they are all included by ledger blocks in the blockchain).

Freshness and Recency Parameter. For the sake of achieving better chain quality on profile blocks, certain changes should be made to the 2-for-1 mining procedure. Ideally, the adversary $\mathcal{A}$ should not be allowed to mine profile blocks timestamped in the very future; and, blocks should go stale as time passes by so that $\mathcal{A}$ cannot choose to withhold them to gain a sudden advantage. Analogous to the treatment in fruitchain [33], we introduce two mechanisms to help ensure the *freshness* of profile blocks. On one hand, the header of a profile block should point to the last block in the settled blockchain; this prevents the adversary from mining blocks in the very future, as an honest ledger block will introduce fresh randomness which is unpredictable for $\mathcal{A}$. On the other hand, we set a recency parameter R (in rounds) such that a profile block PB referring to a settled ledger block LB will only be valid before time $\mathsf{TS}(\mathsf{LB}) + R$ (in other words, it cannot be included by a ledger block with timestamp later than $\mathsf{TS}(\mathsf{LB}) + R$).

4.1 Taxis$_{\mathsf{WL}}$ Protocol

Mining Procedure. In every round, parties try to mine new blocks after they update their local chains according to the chain selection rule (see below for validation details). Two different block contents will be prepared: ledger block content LBContent which contains all (valid) newly seen profile blocks; and profile block content PBContent that includes the local profile of the miner. Parties then compute the Merkle root $\mathsf{st}_{\mathsf{LB}} = \mathsf{MerkleTree}(\texttt{LBContent})$ and $\mathsf{st}_{\mathsf{PB}} = \mathsf{MerkleTree}(\texttt{PBContent})$, respectively. Next, miners make a single random oracle query with the following input: ctr, a random nonce; h, the reference to previous block; h', the reference to the last block in the settled part; $\mathbf{r}$, the current timestamp; $\mathsf{st}_{\mathsf{LB}}$, the Merkle root of ledger block; and $\mathsf{st}_{\mathsf{PB}}$, the Merkle root of the profile block. They receive an ouput

$$u = H(ctr, h, h', \mathbf{r}, \mathsf{st}_{\mathsf{LB}}, \mathsf{st}_{\mathsf{PB}}).$$

If $u < T_{\mathsf{LB}}$, the party succeeds in mining a ledger block. A new block LB with content LBContent is generated and appended to the local chain. If the value of the reversed output string (which we denote by $[u]^{\mathsf{R}}$) satisfies $[u]^{\mathsf{R}} < T_{\mathsf{PB}}$, a new profile block PB is mined and will be diffused to the network.

Note that timestamp $\mathbf{r}$ is shared information in both blocks, so it is impossible to get two products with different timestamps. This prohibits the adversary from manipulating timestamp unless she completely drops from one mining procedure. For a ledger block, the reference to the settled block (h') and the Merkle root of profile blocks ($\mathsf{st}_{\mathsf{PB}}$) are dummy information and we do not care about their values, they are only useful when parties want to check their validity (see below). Similarly, for a profile block, the reference to the previous block (h) and the Merkle root of ledger blocks ($\mathsf{st}_{\mathsf{LB}}$) are dummy information.

We also highlight that there is no need for parties to include their entire transaction log in PB. A prefix of the profile can be pruned if all transactions in that prefix appear in the settled blockchain for more than K rounds (i.e., these transactions have been reported for sufficiently long time and parties agree on the set of transactions that precede them, see below for details). Note that with Δ_{tx}-disseminated transaction diffusion and liveness property of the blockchain, all transactions received by an honest party before time t is guaranteed to be in the settled blockchain within a constant time (see protocol analysis). Furthermore, if P notices that its local transaction log shares a common prefix with another profile block PB in the settled blockchain, then P can produce profile blocks with pointer to PB to indicate their common part and thus save space.

Validity Check of Chains. Recall that the Taxis blockchain is similar to that of Bitcoin's (except that Taxis includes additional 2-for-1 PoW information) and so we follow [20] regarding the validity of ledger blocks. In addition, we also need to check the validity of profile blocks. For a valid profile block PB, we require that its block header satisfies three properties: (i) PB correctly reports a reference to LB where LB is the last block after pruning the blockchain for k rounds; (ii) PB reports a timestamp that is earlier than the ledger block containing PB but no later than $\mathsf{TS}(\mathsf{LB}) + R$; and (iii) hash of PB block header is smaller than the profile block target T_{PB}. A chain $\mathcal{C}$ in Taxis is valid if $\mathcal{C}$ itself is valid and all the profile blocks included in $\mathcal{C}$ are valid.

Extracting Transaction Order. We detail how the ledger $\mathcal{L}$ is extracted in Taxis$_{\mathsf{WL}}$. Generally speaking, parties will use profile blocks in the settled part of the blockchain to build a dependency graph; then, transaction order is determined by running graph condensation and (possibly) DIRECTEDBANDWIDTH algorithm (see [26]) on all SCCs. Note that all of these computations can be done locally based on the on-chain information.

As protocol execution proceeds, local chains held by honest parties will share a long common prefix (we write k as the common prefix parameter — i.e., the rounds that parties need to prune their local chain). Protocol participants will extract a transaction pool TXPool in their common prefix by selecting those transactions that have been reported for sufficiently long time. More specifically, in order for a transaction tx to be selected, there should exist a K-time-window of tx, starting at time t such that (i) t is the timestamp of the earliest ledger block that includes a profile block PB reporting tx; and (ii) this K-time-window should be fully included in the settled blockchain — i.e., at round r a party only considers time window that starts before round $r - k - K$.

Transactions in TXPool are then added to a dependency graph G as vertices. Regarding rules to add edges, for each transaction tx we care about the profile blocks in its K-time-window: if the majority of these profile blocks report $\mathsf{tx}' \prec \mathsf{tx}$, then we add a *dotted* edge $(\mathsf{tx}', \mathsf{tx})$ to G (when tx' does not exist in G, a vertex of tx' is added). Note that a dotted edge $(\mathsf{tx}', \mathsf{tx})$ does not confirm the preference $\mathsf{tx}' \prec \mathsf{tx}$ in G. In order to count the edge in the subsequent computation, we need to wait for the K-time-window of tx' and see if the majority of those profile blocks report $\mathsf{tx} \prec \mathsf{tx}'$. When this holds, we update the dotted edge to *solid* (all the subsequent computations on G only consider solid edges). The reason for designing this two-phase edge adding rule is because, for those transaction pairs such that no φ-preference holds, the adversary might be able to report conflicting orders in the corresponding K-time-windows[5].

After constructing the dependency graph G, parties can linearize the transactions on top of G. Notice that G can be cyclic. Parties first compute the condensation graph G^* of G — i.e. each SCC is replaced by a vertex. Since G^* is acyclic, there exist source vertices (i.e., vertices without incoming edges) in G^*. Protocol participants do the following steps repeatedly. Let V_{source} denote the set of all source vertices in G^* such that for all $v \in V_{\mathsf{source}}$ all transactions in v are in TXPool (transactions that are waiting for some unconfirmed ones will never be selected in V_{source}). If V_{source} is empty then parties terminate and output the final ledger $\mathcal{L}$. Otherwise, they select $v \in V_{\mathsf{source}}$ such that the starting time of v's associated K-time-window is the earliest among V_{source} (if a vertex in G^* represents a SCC in G, we choose the earliest time window in that SCC). Then, if v represents a single vertex in G, parties append the corresponding transaction to $\mathcal{L}$ directly; otherwise, they run the DIRECTEDBANDWIDTH algorithm to extract the bandwidth-optimal order l on v_{SCC} (i.e., the component in the original graph that condenses to v in G^*) and append l to $\mathcal{L}$. After processing v, we remove it from G^* and this yields a new source vertex set V_{source}.

Taxis$_{\mathsf{WL}}$ **Ledger Properties.** With bounded dynamic participation and appropriate parameters, the ledger $\mathcal{L}$ of Taxis$_{\mathsf{WL}}$ satisfies three properties — consistency, weak-liveness and (φ, DBW)-order-fairness. Note that for consistency, a suffix of $\mathcal{L}$ should be pruned to be resistant to adversarial manipulation. Refer to the protocol anaylsis in [26] to see the detailed consistency parameter.

Theorem 10. *Assuming bounded dynamic participation, bounded network delay and honest majority, there exist protocol parameterizations such that the ledger $\mathcal{L}$ of* Taxis$_{\mathsf{WL}}$ *achieves consistency, weak-liveness and* (φ, DBW)-*order-fairness except with probability negligibly small in the security parameter.*

4.2 Taxis Protocol

We present the full Taxis protocol on top of Taxis$_{\mathsf{WL}}$ in this section. Briefly speaking, we add a fallback mechanism to order transactions that remain unconfirmed for a long time based on the beginning point of their K-time-window. Note that we only make two simple changes in the mining and order-extraction stage.

Mining Procedure. In Taxis, parties book-keep the local receiving time of transactions; and, when mining profile blocks, they additionally attach these timestamps to each transaction. All the other steps in the mining procedure remain the same. Since parties will agree on the profiles of a transaction tx in a sufficiently long time window, they will agree on the timestamp vector associated with tx as well.

---

[5] When an edge from tx' to tx exist, tx will not get confirmed into the ledger. Also note that, with overwhelming probability, solid edges will appear on those transaction pairs with φ-preference. For details, see the protocol analysis.

Extracting Transaction Order. During the order-extraction stage, a fallback mechanism is provided to deal with cycles that span for a long time. Specifically, for all unconfirmed vertices $V_{\text{unconfirmed}}$ in the condensation graph G^*, we check if there exist a vertex $v \in V_{\text{unconfirmed}}$ such that its corresponding SCC (v_{SCC}) in G contain transactions whose K-time-window begins before $\mathbf{r} - (K + k + \Delta_{\text{timeout}})^6$. Note that Δ_{timeout} is a timeout parameter that indicates the cycle spans for a long time (see protocol analysis for more details). If such v in G^* exists, we order all vertices in v_{SCC} in an increasing order based on their median timestamp. For a transaction $\mathtt{tx}$, its median timestamp $\mathsf{med}(\mathtt{tx})$ is computed on the timestamp vector associated with $\mathtt{tx}$ in its K-time-window. Note that since parties will agree on $\mathtt{tx}$'s timestamp vector, they will also agree on $\mathsf{med}(\mathtt{tx})$; and, taking the median guarantees that $\mathsf{med}(\mathtt{tx})$ falls in the Δ_{tx}-dissemination time window with $\mathtt{tx}$, thus the results in Theorem 9 applies.

In addition, when tracing the previous dependency graphs, Taxis will be able to detect those large cycles by carefully comparing the beginning point of K-time windows among all transactions in the cycle, so that it will process them using the same fallback mechanism (this guarantees consistency).

Taxis Ledger Properties. We provide a full analysis of the security of Taxis protocol with bounded dynamic participation in [26]. Specifically, we prove that the ledger $\mathcal{L}$ of Taxis satisfies three desired properties — consistency, (standard) liveness and $(\varphi, \mathtt{TDBW})$-order-fairness.

Theorem 11. *Assuming bounded dynamic participation, bounded network delay and honest majority, there exist protocol parameterizations such that the ledger $\mathcal{L}$ of Taxis achieves consistency, liveness and $(\varphi, \mathtt{TDBW})$-order-fairness except with probability negligibly small in the security parameter.*

Performance Analysis of Taxis. We detail the computation/communication complexity of the Taxis protocol. For the proof of work part and communication overhead, it requires a random oracle call per round and possibly (if a PoW is found) a message transmission with message size, worst case, linear in the security parameter plus the number of transactions that are disseminated within a sliding window of length polylogarithmic in the security parameter.

To maintain the local transaction dependency graph G, note that G can be built incrementally since all vertices and edges are extracted from the settled part of the blockchain; and, every time a vertex $\mathtt{tx}$ is added to G, the number of computational steps required (which will add the necessary edges between the vertices) is linear in the number of transactions that appear in $\mathtt{tx}$'s K-time-window, which is also of length polylogarithmic in the security parameter.

Regarding solving DIRECTEDBANDWIDTH on each SCC of the transaction dependency graph, note that while the exact algorithm from [21] consumes exponential time with respect to the number of concurrent transactions, we

---

[6] We note that two large cycles cannot run in parallel, and there is at most one vertex with multiple transactions that can pass the timeout check. Refer to protocol analysis for more details.

highlight that, in real execution, it runs in practical time for two reasons. First, a polynomial-time fallback will be triggered after a time slack of length Δ_{timeout} has passed, where Δ_{timeout} is a parameter that is of the same order of magnitude with respect to the common prefix parameter, the size of input (i.e., the number of vertices in a SCC) to DIRECTEDBANDWIDTH is therefore bounded by a polylogarithmic function of κ times the transaction throughput. On the other hand, the transaction dependency graph of a large Condorcet cycle is of good structure[7] such that we could improve the running time from $\mathcal{O}^*(3^n \cdot 2^{n^2})$ in [21] to $f(t) \cdot n^t \cdot 2^{nt}$ where t is the transaction throughput and $f(t)$ is a function that depends only on t, note that $t \ll n$. We present and analyze this algorithm in [26]. Also note that while this local computation is the most expensive step but it only needs to be performed once for each SCC throughout the entire protocol execution.

5   Discussion and Future Directions

Alternative Ways of Relaxing Order Fairness. In this paper we define transaction order fairness based on upper-bounding the positions that a transaction can be ordered before another when violating their preference. It is worth highlighting however that the graph theoretic model we put forth in Sect. 3 can accommodate a larger variety of order fairness relaxations.

For instance, one could consider the relaxation "an output profile σ should break the *least* number of φ-preferences." In the context of dependency graphs, this idea on fair order can be related to the FEEDBACKARCSET problem [4] which asks to remove a subset of edges to make the graph acyclic while keeping the subset as small as possible.

Another possible relaxation is to minimize the cumulative size of all violations. This means that instead of focusing on the maximum distance of back edges in a component, we care about their sum $\sum_{(u,v) \in E, \sigma(u) > \sigma(v)} \sigma(u) - \sigma(v)$. This definition, can be considered as the "global" variant of our order fairness notion; and, the corresponding graph problem — MINIMUMLINEARARRANGE-MENT [4] — is also well-studied.

Another flavor of fairness that can also be cast in the same context is studied in a recent work, Themis, [24], called consequent-transaction fairness, which can be viewed in our context as maximizing the number of consecutive forward edges.

Structure of Transaction Dependency Graphs. An interesting question arises with respect to $(\mathcal{R}, \varphi)$-dependency-graphs, as they were defined in Sect. 2.2. In Theorem 2 we show that, unless $\prec^\varphi$ is the majority relation, $G_{\mathcal{R},\varphi}$

---

[7] If a Condorcet cycle spans for a long time, and the time points that two transactions enter this system are sufficiently apart from each other, then the edge between these two transactions will never be selected as backward edge. For large Condorcet cycles, such type of edges account for the vast majority of all the edges. See a detailed explanation in [26].

cannot have arbitrarily small cycles. Is this also a sufficient condition? I.e., given a graph G without cycles of size less than $\lceil 1/(1 - \varphi) \rceil$, do there exist profiles $\mathcal{R}$ such that $G = G_{\mathcal{R},\varphi}$? When $\prec^\varphi$ is the majority relation, this question was answered positively for any oriented graph by McGarvey in [29] (see Subsect. 3.2). The majority case has been studied further in other works. Stearns [35] and later Erdős and Moser [15] give bounds on the required size of $\mathcal{R}$. More recently, Alon [1] looked into a more refined property of $\mathcal{R}$. We suggest the study of similar questions with respect to $G_{\mathcal{R},\varphi}$, when $1/2 < \varphi \leq 1$ as an interesting direction.

$(\varphi, \texttt{DBW})$-**fair-order.** Theorem 6 shows that $(\varphi, \texttt{DBW})$-fair-order is the best that we can expect on a Condorcet cycle SCC in terms of bounding unfairness. We note here that it is possible for some transactions $\texttt{tx}, \texttt{tx}'$ to be put even closer than the bandwidth among all bandwidth-optimal orderings. Nonetheless, there is no need to push this definition a step further (e.g., to bound the distance of any two transactions by their maximum distance among all bandwidth-optimal orderings). The reason is that Definition 4 has already been restricted enough such that only a bandwidth-optimal ordering on this SCC will satisfy it. Even if we might be able to bound the distance on some transaction pairs further it does not change the set of orderings that satisfy this definition.

Securing Order Fairness with Transient Joining. Astute readers may notice that, in Sect. 3.5, it becomes impossible to achieve order fairness in the permissionless environment if the joining pattern of alert parties is transient — i.e., no party stays alert for a long time hence no transaction order preference can persist in the network. While this problem stems from the nature of permissionless settings and is thus intrinsically impossible to solve, we provide two alternative ways to model the execution environment that can offer different trade-offs.

One route is to restrict the adversarial power on registering / de-registering parties. I.e., $\mathcal{A}$ is allowed to de-register at most τ fraction of honest parties during any time window of length K, but τ should remain sufficiently small with respect to K so that when a transaction is received by sufficiently many parties earlier than another, both could be continuously reported.

Alternatively, we could extend our dynamic participation model (Sect. 2.1) to let parties "bootstrap" to collect transactions before they become alert. Specifically, we introduce a profile as a new resource that an alert party needs in order to run the protocol. If a party P has passively listened to the protocol and obtained a sufficiently long transaction log, then P is "profile-ready." Alert parties should be those that are also profile-ready. Given this and that the environment (which controls how the population of parties fluctuates) is restricted to offer a sufficient number of alert parties, in this new setting we guarantee that all alert parties can keep reporting transaction order preference; and, this mechanism is robust against the adversarial registration and de-registration on alert parties.

Order Fairness in the Permissioned Setting. We note that $(\varphi, \mathtt{DBW})$-fair-order serialization can also be achieved with a PKI. Specifically, parties could make use of the broadcast and set consensus module in Aequitas [25] to let parties agree on a dependency graph; then, instead of alphabetically linearizing transactions in the same "block", parties use the directed bandwidth algorithm (refer to our full version [26]) to get the bandwidth-optimal order. With this additional treatment, we can adapt Taxis as a permissioned protocol that achieves consistency, weak-liveness and $(\varphi, \mathtt{DBW})$-order-fairness.

Acknowledgements. We thank the anonymous reviewers for their valuable suggestions and feedback. Yu Shen's research has been supported by Input Output (iohk.io) through their funding of the University of Edinburgh Blockchain Technology Lab.

References

1. Alon, N.: Voting paradoxes and digraphs realizations. Adv. Appl. Math. **29**(1), 126–135 (2002). https://doi.org/10.1016/S0196-8858(02)00007-6
2. Asayag, A., et al.: A fair consensus protocol for transaction ordering. In: 2018 IEEE 26th International Conference on Network Protocols, ICNP 2018, Cambridge, UK, September 25-27, 2018, pp. 55–65. IEEE Computer Society (2018). https://doi.org/10.1109/ICNP.2018.00016
3. Badertscher, C., Gazi, P., Kiayias, A., Russell, A., Zikas, V.: Ouroboros genesis: composable proof-of-stake blockchains with dynamic availability. In: Lie, D., Mannan, M., Backes, M., Wang, X. (eds.) ACM CCS 2018: 25th Conference on Computer and Communications Security, pp. 913–930. ACM Press, Toronto, ON, Canada (2018). https://doi.org/10.1145/3243734.3243848
4. Bodlaender, H.L., Fomin, F.V., Koster, A.M.C.A., Kratsch, D., Thilikos, D.M.: A note on exact algorithms for vertex ordering problems on graphs. Theory Comput. Syst. **50**(3), 420–432 (2012). https://doi.org/10.1007/s00224-011-9312-0
5. Cachin, C., Kursawe, K., Petzold, F., Shoup, V.: Secure and efficient asynchronous broadcast protocols. In: Kilian, J. (ed.) CRYPTO 2001. LNCS, vol. 2139, pp. 524–541. Springer, Heidelberg (2001). https://doi.org/10.1007/3-540-44647-8_31
6. Cachin, C., Micic, J., Steinhauer, N., Zanolini, L.: Quick order fairness. In: Eyal, I., Garay, J.A. (eds.) FC 2022: 26th International Conference on Financial Cryptography and Data Security. Lecture Notes in Computer Science, vol. 13411, pp. 316–333. Springer, Heidelberg, Germany, Grenada (2022). https://doi.org/10.1007/978-3-031-18283-9_15
7. Canetti, R.: Security and composition of multiparty cryptographic protocols. J. Cryptol. **13**(1), 143–202 (2000). https://doi.org/10.1007/s001459910006
8. Canetti, R.: Universally composable security: a new paradigm for cryptographic protocols. Cryptology ePrint Archive, Report 2000/067 (2000). https://eprint.iacr.org/2000/067
9. Chiang, J.H.y., David, B., Eyal, I., Gong, T.: FairPoS: input fairness in permissionless consensus. In: Bonneau, J., Weinberg, S.M. (eds.) 5th Conference on Advances in Financial Technologies (AFT 2023). Leibniz International Proceedings in Informatics (LIPIcs), vol. 282, pp. 10:1–10:23. Schloss Dagstuhl – Leibniz-Zentrum für Informatik, Dagstuhl, Germany (2023). https://doi.org/10.4230/LIPIcs.AFT.2023.10

10. Chinn, P.Z., Chvátalová, J., Dewdney, A.K., Gibbs, N.E.: The bandwidth problem for graphs and matrices—a survey. J. Graph Theory **6**(3), 223–254 (1982). https://doi.org/10.1002/JGT.3190060302

11. Cygan, M., Pilipczuk, M.: Faster exact bandwidth. In: Broersma, H., Erlebach, T., Friedetzky, T., Paulusma, D. (eds.) Graph-Theoretic Concepts in Computer Science, 34th International Workshop, WG 2008, Durham, UK, June 30 - July 2, 2008. Revised Papers. Lecture Notes in Computer Science, vol. 5344, pp. 101–109 (2008). https://doi.org/10.1007/978-3-540-92248-3_10

12. Dubey, C.K., Feige, U., Unger, W.: Hardness results for approximating the bandwidth. J. Comput. Syst. Sci. **77**(1), 62–90 (2011). https://doi.org/10.1016/J.JCSS.2010.06.006

13. Dwork, C., Lynch, N.A., Stockmeyer, L.J.: Consensus in the presence of partial synchrony. J. ACM **35**(2), 288–323 (1988). https://doi.org/10.1145/42282.42283

14. Dwork, C., Naor, M.: Pricing via processing or combatting junk mail. In: Brickell, E.F. (ed.) CRYPTO 1992. LNCS, vol. 740, pp. 139–147. Springer, Heidelberg (1993). https://doi.org/10.1007/3-540-48071-4_10

15. Erdős, P., Moser, L.: On the representation of directed graphs as unions of orderings. Math. Inst. Hung. Acad. Sci **9**, 125–132 (1964)

16. Feige, U.: Coping with the NP-hardness of the graph bandwidth problem. In: SWAT 2000. LNCS, vol. 1851, pp. 10–19. Springer, Heidelberg (2000). https://doi.org/10.1007/3-540-44485-X_2

17. Garay, J., Kiayias, A., Leonardos, N.: Full analysis of nakamoto consensus in bounded-delay networks. Cryptology ePrint Archive, Report 2020/277 (2020). https://eprint.iacr.org/2020/277

18. Garay, J., Kiayias, A.: SoK: a consensus taxonomy in the blockchain era. In: Jarecki, S. (ed.) CT-RSA 2020. LNCS, vol. 12006, pp. 284–318. Springer, Cham (2020). https://doi.org/10.1007/978-3-030-40186-3_13

19. Garay, J., Kiayias, A., Leonardos, N.: The bitcoin backbone protocol: analysis and applications. In: Oswald, E., Fischlin, M. (eds.) EUROCRYPT 2015. LNCS, vol. 9057, pp. 281–310. Springer, Heidelberg (2015). https://doi.org/10.1007/978-3-662-46803-6_10

20. Garay, J., Kiayias, A., Leonardos, N.: The bitcoin backbone protocol with chains of variable difficulty. In: Katz, J., Shacham, H. (eds.) CRYPTO 2017. LNCS, vol. 10401, pp. 291–323. Springer, Cham (2017). https://doi.org/10.1007/978-3-319-63688-7_10

21. Jain, P., Kanesh, L., Lochet, W., Saurabh, S., Sharma, R.: Exact and approximate digraph bandwidth. In: Chattopadhyay, A., Gastin, P. (eds.) 39th IARCS Annual Conference on Foundations of Software Technology and Theoretical Computer Science (FSTTCS 2019). Leibniz International Proceedings in Informatics (LIPIcs), vol. 150, pp. 18:1–18:15. Schloss Dagstuhl–Leibniz-Zentrum fuer Informatik, Dagstuhl, Germany (2019). https://doi.org/10.4230/LIPIcs.FSTTCS.2019.18

22. Katz, J., Maurer, U., Tackmann, B., Zikas, V.: Universally composable synchronous computation. In: Sahai, A. (ed.) TCC 2013. LNCS, vol. 7785, pp. 477–498. Springer, Heidelberg (2013). https://doi.org/10.1007/978-3-642-36594-2_27

23. Kelkar, M., Deb, S., Kannan, S.: Order-fair consensus in the permissionless setting. In: Cruz, J.P., Yanai, N. (eds.) APKC 2022: Proceedings of the 9th ACM on ASIA Public-Key Cryptography Workshop, APKC@AsiaCCS 2022, Nagasaki, Japan, 30 May 2022, pp. 3–14. ACM (2022). https://doi.org/10.1145/3494105.3526239

24. Kelkar, M., Deb, S., Long, S., Juels, A., Kannan, S.: Themis: fast, strong order-fairness in byzantine consensus. In: Proceedings of the 2023 ACM SIGSAC Conference on Computer and Communications Security, CCS 2023, Copenhagen, Denmark, November 26-30, 2023, pp. 475–489. Association for Computing Machinery, New York, NY, USA (2023). https://doi.org/10.1145/3576915.3616658
25. Kelkar, M., Zhang, F., Goldfeder, S., Juels, A.: Order-Fairness for byzantine consensus. In: Micciancio, D., Ristenpart, T. (eds.) CRYPTO 2020. LNCS, vol. 12172, pp. 451–480. Springer, Cham (2020). https://doi.org/10.1007/978-3-030-56877-1_16
26. Kiayias, A., Leonardos, N., Shen, Y.: Ordering transactions with bounded unfairness: definitions, complexity and constructions. Cryptology ePrint Archive, Report 2023/1253 (2023). https://eprint.iacr.org/2023/1253
27. Kursawe, K.: Wendy, the good little fairness widget: achieving order fairness for blockchains. In: Proceedings of the 2nd ACM Conference on Advances in Financial Technologies, pp. 25–36. AFT 2020, Association for Computing Machinery, New York, NY, USA (2020). https://doi.org/10.1145/3419614.3423263
28. Malkhi, D., Szalachowski, P.: Maximal extractable value (MEV) protection on a DAG. In: Amoussou-Guenou, Y., Kiayias, A., Verdier, M. (eds.) 4th International Conference on Blockchain Economics, Security and Protocols (Tokenomics 2022). Open Access Series in Informatics (OASIcs), vol. 110, pp. 6:1–6:17. Schloss Dagstuhl – Leibniz-Zentrum für Informatik, Dagstuhl, Germany (2023). https://doi.org/10.4230/OASIcs.Tokenomics.2022.6
29. McGarvey, D.C.: A theorem on the construction of voting paradoxes. Econometrica 21(4), 608–610 (1953). https://doi.org/10.2307/1907926
30. Nakamoto, S.: Bitcoin: a peer-to-peer electronic cash system (2008). https://bitcoin.org/bitcoin.pdf
31. Papadimitriou, C.H.: The NP-completeness of the bandwidth minimization problem. Computing 16(3), 263–270 (1976). https://doi.org/10.1007/BF02280884
32. Pass, R., Seeman, L., Shelat, A.: Analysis of the blockchain protocol in asynchronous networks. In: Coron, J.-S., Nielsen, J.B. (eds.) EUROCRYPT 2017. LNCS, vol. 10211, pp. 643–673. Springer, Cham (2017). https://doi.org/10.1007/978-3-319-56614-6_22
33. Pass, R., Shi, E.: FruitChains: a fair blockchain. In: Schiller, E.M., Schwarzmann, A.A. (eds.) 36th ACM Symposium Annual on Principles of Distributed Computing, pp. 315–324. Association for Computing Machinery, Washington, DC, USA (2017). https://doi.org/10.1145/3087801.3087809
34. Schneider, F.B.: Implementing fault-tolerant services using the state machine approach: a tutorial. ACM Comput. Surv. 22(4), 299–319 (1990). https://doi.org/10.1145/98163.98167
35. Stearns, R.: The voting problem. Am. Math. Mon. 66(9), 761–763 (1959). https://doi.org/10.1080/00029890.1959.11989405
36. Vafadar, M.A., Khabbazian, M.: Condorcet attack against fair transaction ordering. In: Bonneau, J., Weinberg, S.M. (eds.) 5th Conference on Advances in Financial Technologies (AFT 2023). Leibniz International Proceedings in Informatics (LIPIcs), vol. 282, pp. 15:1–15:21. Schloss Dagstuhl – Leibniz-Zentrum für Informatik, Dagstuhl, Germany (2023). https://doi.org/10.4230/LIPIcs.AFT.2023.15
37. Zhang, Y., Setty, S., Chen, Q., Zhou, L., Alvisi, L.: Byzantine ordered consensus without byzantine oligarchy. In: Proceedings of the 14th USENIX Conference on Operating Systems Design and Implementation. USENIX Association, USA (2020)

Asymptotically Optimal Message Dissemination with Applications to Blockchains

Chen-Da Liu-Zhang[1]([⊠])(iD), Christian Matt[2]([⊠])(iD),
and Søren Eller Thomsen[3]([⊠])(iD)

[1] Lucerne University of Applied Sciences and Arts & Web3 Foundation,
Zug, Switzerland
chen-da.liuzhang@hslu.ch
[2] Primev, Steinhausen, Switzerland
christian@primev.xyz
[3] Partisia, Aarhus, Denmark
soren.eller.thomsen@partisia.com

Abstract. Messages in large-scale networks such as blockchain systems are typically disseminated using flooding protocols, in which parties send the message to a random set of peers until it reaches all parties. Optimizing the communication complexity of such protocols and, in particular, the per-party communication complexity is of primary interest since nodes in a network are often subject to bandwidth constraints. Previous flooding protocols incur a per-party communication complexity of $\Omega(l \cdot \gamma^{-1} \cdot (\log(n) + \kappa))$ bits to disseminate an l-bit message among n parties with security parameter κ when it is guaranteed that a γ fraction of the parties remain honest. In this work, we present the first flooding protocols with a per-party communication complexity of $O(l \cdot \gamma^{-1})$ bits. We further show that this is asymptotically optimal and that our protocols can be instantiated provably securely in the usual setting for proof-of-stake blockchains.

To demonstrate that one of our new protocols is not only asymptotically optimal but also practical, we perform several probabilistic simulations to estimate the concrete complexity for given parameters. Our simulations show that our protocol significantly improves the per-party communication complexity over the state-of-the-art for practical parameters. Hence, for given bandwidth constraints, our results allow to, e.g., increase the block size, improving the overall throughput of a blockchain.

C.-D. Liu-Zhang—The work was partly done while the author was at NTT Research. Partially funded by the Hasler Foundation Project 23090, ETH Zurich Leading House RPG-072023-19 and Protocol Labs Cryptonet RFP-013.
C. Matt—The work was partly done while the author was at Concordium, Zurich, Switzerland.
S.E. Thomsen—The work was partly done while the author was at Aarhus University and afterwards at The Alexandra Institute.

M. Joye and G. Leander (Eds.): EUROCRYPT 2024, LNCS 14653, pp. 64–95, 2024.
https://doi.org/10.1007/978-3-031-58734-4_3

1   Introduction

Current blockchain protocols rely on the availability of a multicast network that allows any party to communicate with all other parties in the network, and therefore the security and efficiency of the blockchain protocol are heavily influenced by its underlying multicast network.

In typical blockchain protocols, including Bitcoin [36] and Ethereum [49], such multicast networks are efficiently implemented via a flooding protocol, which lets the sender select a set of neighbors randomly and forward the message to these parties, who will forward the messages to another randomly chosen set of neighbors and so on. For an l-bit message and n parties of which only $\gamma \cdot n$ are guaranteed to be honest, current provably secure flooding protocols that follows this design [29,33], incur $\Omega(l \cdot \gamma^{-1} \cdot (\log(n) + \kappa))$ bits of per-party communication to ensure that the message is delivered to all parties with a probability overwhelming in κ. For practical blockchain systems where messages contain large blocks (e.g., around 1MB), the incurred communication constitutes one of the main bottlenecks. As a consequence, many practical systems rely on heuristics which guarantees low bandwidth consumption rather than provable security. In fact, several works have shown such heuristic approaches to be vulnerable to practical attacks [2,25,32,45].

A trivial lower bound for the per-party communication complexity of message dissemination protocol is that for the message to reach all honest parties, some party must forward at least as many bits as the length of the message, i.e. the per-party communication must be $\Omega(l)$. This leaves a gap between the lower bounds and what current provably secure flooding protocols achieve. We bridge this gap by firstly proving that, in fact, a per-party communication complexity of $\Omega(l \cdot \gamma^{-1})$ is necessary, and secondly by providing two highly robust flooding protocols with a per-party communication that matches the lower bound. Our protocols require no setup and are practically efficient even for a small number of parties and message length. Moreover, we show how to extend our protocols to the weighted setting, where each party is assigned a positive weight of a certain resource (such as stake), and the adversary can corrupt any set of parties by accumulating any fraction of the total resource. More details follow below.

Model and Security Definition. We consider flooding protocols that allow any honest party to deliver their messages to all other parties within a certain time, but do not provide any guarantees when the sender is corrupted. This primitive suffices for most blockchain protocols [11,14,22,41,42,51].

Our results are secure for a fixed set of parties connected by point-to-point channels, and where messages sent by honest parties are eventually delivered (i.e., asynchronous channels). To compute the concrete delivery time of the overall flooding protocol, we make use of an upper bound on the channel delays.

For simplicity, our protocols are written with respect to a static adversary that can byzantinely corrupt and control *any* fraction $1 - \gamma$ (this can be, e.g., 99.9%) of the parties at the onset of the protocol. However, the protocols can be modified to the setting of delayed adaptive adversaries, with some delay between an adversary deciding to corrupt a party and gaining control over this party [33], by regularly letting the parties choose a fresh set of neighbors.

Terminology. We use the term *flooding protocol* to describe a protocol where parties can input a message, and as a result, all other parties will receive the message. We use the term *diameter* of a flooding protocol to describe the maximum number of point-to-point channels some message must pass through before delivery is guaranteed to all parties. We use the term *per-party communication* to describe the maximum number of bits any honest party must send in a flooding protocol to deliver a particular message.

1.1   Contributions

Per-party Communication Lower Bound. First, we present a new lower bound that shows that any flooding protocol that ensures delivery of a message of length l to all honest parties, assuming only γ of them remain honest, must have a per-party communication complexity of at least $\Omega(l \cdot \gamma^{-1})$ bits. Concretely, we show that there exists an adversarial strategy obeying the corruption bound that forces the initial sender of the message to send $\Omega(l \cdot \gamma^{-1})$ bits if delivery must be ensured with an overwhelming probability against this adversary.

Warm up: Optimal Flooding with a Linear Neighborhood and Constant Diameter. We then present a simple protocol ECCast[1], that requires each party to send messages to all other parties, but it achieves a constant diameter of just 2 with the asymptotically optimal per-party communication complexity. The protocol works by letting the sender of a message divide their message into n (the number of parties) different shares using an erasure-correcting code, and then send a unique share to each party. When a party receives such a share, they forward it to *all* other parties. Once a party receives sufficiently many shares, they are able to reconstruct the original message.

Theorem 1 (ECCast (Informal)). *For n parties and messages of length at least $\Omega(n \cdot (\log(n) + \kappa))$, ECCast ensures flooding with asymptotically optimal per-party communication, diameter 2, and overwhelming success probability in κ.*

Even though this protocol requires each party to send messages to all other parties, we believe that it has wide applications as it allows one to "balance" the incurred communication among parties, at the cost of doubling the diameter (over the naive protocol in which the sender directly sends the whole message to all parties). In fact, independently and concurrently with our work, Kaklamanis, Yang and Alizadeh [26] use such techniques to speed up the Hotstuff consensus protocol [51].

---

[1] ECCast from the use of Erasure-Correcting codes and each party multicasting messages to all parties.

Table 1. Comparison of flooding for messages of length l among n parties where a γ fraction of the parties is guaranteed to remain honest. We consider the maximum number of neighbors, per-party communication , and maximum distance between sender and any honest party (referenced as diameter). For ECFlood to achieve this asymptotic complexity the length of the message must be $l = \Omega((\log n + \kappa)(\log \log n + \kappa))$ and for ECCast it must be $l = \Omega(n \cdot (\log(n) + \kappa))$.

Protocol	Max. neighbors	Per-party comm.	Diameter
[29,33]	$O(\gamma^{-1} \cdot (\log(n) + \kappa))$	$O(l \cdot \gamma^{-1} \cdot (\log(n) + \kappa))$	$O(\log(n))$
ECFlood	$O(\gamma^{-1} \cdot (\log(n) + \kappa))$	$O(l \cdot \gamma^{-1})$	$O(\log(n))$
Naive	$n - 1$	$l \cdot (n - 1)$	1
ECCast	$n - 1$	$O(l \cdot \gamma^{-1})$	2

Optimal Flooding with a Logarithmic Neighborhood and Diameter. We then present the protocol ECFlood,[2] which requires each party to connect to only $O(\gamma^{-1} \cdot (\log(n) + \kappa))$ other parties and use only $O(l \cdot \gamma^{-1})$ of per-party communication.

At a high level, the protocol works by letting the sender of a message divide their message into a number of shares μ. Each of these shares will then be sent to a uniformly random subset of parties of size d. When a party receives such a share, they again forward it to a random subset of parties with size d. Once a party receives sufficiently many shares, they can reconstruct the original message.

Theorem 2 (ECFlood (informal)). *For n parties and security parameter κ, there are $\mu = O(\log(n)+\kappa)$ and $d = O(\gamma^{-1})$ such that ECFlood ensures asymptotically optimal flooding with a logarithmic diameter and an overwhelming success probability in κ, for messages of length at least $\Omega((\log(n)+\kappa) \cdot (\log(\log(n))+\kappa))$.*

Note that ECFlood shaves a factor of $\log(n) + \kappa$ the per-party communication over previous best-known constructions. This is done while keeping both the size of the neighborhood and the diameter at the same level as these previously best-known constructions. Further note that ECFlood requires no trusted setup but merely relies on an erasure-correcting code and a weak cryptographic accumulation scheme, which can be realized efficiently from standard assumptions.

We summarize the properties of ECFlood and ECCast and compare them to other flooding protocols with similar robustness in Table 1, where the "naive" protocol refers to the protocol where the sender simply sends the message to all other parties. Note that all protocols are secure for any message size; sufficiently long messages are only required for optimal communication complexity since for very short messages, the cryptographic primitives add a communication overhead.

Concrete Efficiency Evaluation of ECFlood. While the theoretical analysis of ECFlood shows that our protocol is asymptotically optimal, we use probabilistic simulations to evaluate its practical efficiency. We compare this to the efficiency

---

[2] ECFlood from the use of Erasure-Correcting codes in the flooding protocol.

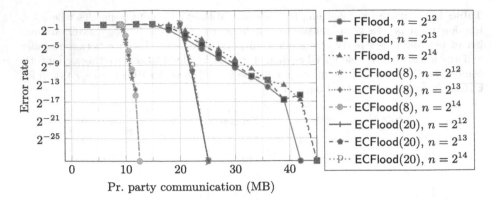

Fig. 1. The communication of ECFlood(d) (for $d \in \{8, 20\}$ where d is an internal parameter of the protocol) with a decreasing reconstruction threshold (to lower the error rate), and FFlood(k) with an increasing k (to lower the error rate). The graphs shows the percentages of the simulated executions (on the y-axis which is depicted logarithmicaly) where some party (for a different number of parties n) did not receive the message as a function of the per party communication of the protocol when the protocol sends out a message with size 1 MB , and the accumulators used in ECFlood are implemented via. a Merkle-tree with 256 bit hashes. 100000 simulations of each configuration has been executed for FFlood and for ECFlood. When a point is placed directly on the x-axis this represents the communication needed to make none of the simulations fail.

of the only approach known to be provably-secure against a byzantine adversary – namely to increase the number of parties that each party forward to make the protocol secure against a byzantine adversary.[3] The main results of our simulations are shown in Fig. 1. FFlood(k) is the protocol where each party forwards the message to k parties and the parameter k is increased in order to make the error rate drop.[4]

In the figure, two configurations of ECFlood are included where each has a neighborhood of 200 parties (which we deem to be practical for blockchains as the Bitcoin client currently allows up to 125 neighbors by default [23]). ECFlood(8) is a configuration optimized for redundancy which has a slightly higher latency than FFlood, whereas ECFlood(20) is a configuration optimized for latency. The latter configuration has a latency that is as good as the latency of FFlood.[5] It is noteworthy that while FFlood needs to increase the per-party communication to obtain a constant failure probability with an increasing number of parties the communication of ECFlood remains constant. Our simulations also show that for both configurations of ECFlood that once the per-party communication reaches a small constant factor our protocol virtually eliminates errors whereas the

---

[3] For a discussion of why other classical approaches fails in the byzantine setting see Sect. 1.3.

[4] Further details on the general setup for our simulations can be found in Sect. 8.

[5] For results about the latency see the extended version of this paper [30].

communication of FFlood needs to be increased linearly in κ to obtain an error rate of $2^{-\kappa}$. Further, to virtually eliminate errors, ECFlood needs a communication redundancy of $\sim$12 (and $\sim$25 for the latency optimized version) whereas FFlood needs a redundancy of $\geq$ 45. Hence, we conclude that our protocol is not only asymptotically optimal but offers *actual* efficiency advantages over state-of-the-art for practical parameters.

Flooding in the Weighted Setting. We also consider the setting where parties are publicly assigned a positive weight and any arbitrarily small fraction of the cumulated total weight remains under the control of honest parties. This setting immediately fits the setting of *Proof-of-Stake* protocols [11,13,14], where the stake is publicly available. There are also techniques to estimate the relative computing power in the *Proof-of-Work* setting; see [29] for an extended discussion.

We leverage the idea of emulation from [29] to make a general transformation from a flooding protocol that is secure, assuming a fraction of the parties behaves honestly, to a flooding protocol that is secure, assuming a fraction of publicly assigned weights behaves honestly. We do so by introducing the protocol Flood2WeightedFlood that reduces the task of finding a secure flooding protocol among an actual set of parties to a secure flooding protocol for an emulated set of parties. In more detail, consider n parties, let α_p denote the fraction of total weight assigned to a party p, and let the total fraction of weight given to honest parties be $\widetilde{\gamma}$. We observe that by letting each party p emulate $\lceil \alpha_p \cdot n \rceil$ parties, the fraction of honest emulated parties is at least $\widetilde{\gamma}/2$ and there are at most $2n$ emulated parties. Instantiating our protocols ECFlood and ECCast such that they are secure assuming $\widetilde{\gamma}/2$ of the emulated parties are honest, we obtain security in the weighted setting. This happens while only increasing the total communication complexity by a factor of at most 4. The per-party communication will, however, be proportional to the amount of weight each party is assigned. We note that in [29, Corollary 4], it was shown that it is inherent for the weighted setting that parties with a large fraction of weight must send more messages.

Universal Composable Security for Flooding from Delivery Guarantees. We prove a general theorem that states that any flooding protocol that guarantees delivery UC [9] realizes a flooding functionality. To do so we follow the strategy of Matt et al. [33] by letting the simulator simulate the actual protocol within itself (based on the non-secret inputs of all parties) and adjust the ideal functionality for message delivery to deliver messages according to the simulated actual protocol. Thereby, the security of the protocol is reduced to showing that no messages will be delivered late w.r.t. the delivery guarantee. Our protocols, therefore, benefit from universal composition properties, but for simplicity of presentation, we present them without the overhead of the UC model and focus only on the theorems ensuring that no messages are delivered late.

1.2 Technical Overview

As discussed above, prior works that let each party forward a message to a random subset of neighbors (see, e.g., [29,33]) need each party to connect to

$\Omega(\gamma^{-1} \cdot (\log(n) + \kappa))$ parties to ensure that the message is propagated to all parties with overwhelming probability in the security parameter κ. Intuitively, the term κ is needed to make the probability that an individual party has no honest neighbors negligible. Further, to ensure that the probability that this happens for *any party* is negligible, the additional $\log(n)$ neighbors are needed. However, for each neighbor there is only a γ chance that this neighbor is honest which is why the γ^{-1} factor is necessary.

In fact, it has been shown [28, Section 3.2, p. 6] that the probability that there is an isolated honest party for $n \to \infty$ when the number of random neighbors $d = \gamma^{-1} \cdot (\log(n \cdot \gamma) + c + o(1))$ for some constant c is given by $1 - e^{-e^c}$. It is therefore not possible to decrease the number of needed neighbors for such flooding protocols significantly. In order to further improve the communication complexity, we focus instead on investigating how much we can reduce the number of bits sent by each party.

Per-party Communication Lower Bound. We sketch our lower bound, stating that deliverying an l-bit message requires per-party communication $\Omega(l \cdot \gamma^{-1})$ bits, where γ denotes the fraction of honest parties. To show this, we describe an explicit attack that an adversary corrupting $(1 - \gamma)$ fraction of the parties can do to ensure that the sender needs to send $\Omega(l \cdot \gamma^{-1})$ bits with overwhelming probability.

The attack works as follows. Divide the set of parties into γ^{-1} subsets $C_1, \ldots, C_{\gamma^{-1}}$ of size $\gamma \cdot n$ parties each. The adversary chooses an index i uniformly at random and corrupts all parties except the sender s and the parties in C_i. Each corrupted party in any other set $C_j \neq C_i$ ignores all messages that do not come from the sender s or parties in the same set C_j. And moreover, each corrupted party also drops all messages that are sent from C_j to any other outside party $p' \notin C_j \cup \{s\}$.

Intuitively, from the point of view of the honest sender s, it is impossible to identify which C_j is honest, and therefore, *each of these sets* needs to receive full information about the whole message. Moreover, since effectively each set only receives information from the sender s (messages between different sets are ignored or dropped), then the sender needs to transmit the full message to each of these sets, and the total incurred communication is at least $\Omega(l \cdot \gamma^{-1})$.

Optimal Per-party Communication Upper Bound. From the feasibility side, we deviate from previous approaches and design our flooding protocol in two steps. First, we consider a so-called *weak* flooding protocol that ensures that for every fixed party, there is a constant probability, that this party receives the message within $O(\log n)$ steps. Secondly, we introduce a compiler that lifts a weak flooding protocol to a (strong) flooding protocol that guarantees delivery to all parties with overwhelming probability.

A Weak Flooding Protocol. Our candidate for a weak flooding protocol is the protocol FFlood(d) in which every party chooses d random neighbors and forwards each message to those.

As mentioned, [28] showed that for similar protocols, the probability that there is an isolated party for $n \to \infty$ when $d = \gamma^{-1} \cdot (\log(n \cdot \gamma) + c + o(1))$ for some constant c is given by $1 - e^{-e^c}$. This means that one needs to set $d = \Omega(\gamma^{-1} \cdot \log(n \cdot \gamma))$ to have a constant success probability for all parties to receive the message. As a consequence, the expected size of each neighborhood would be $\Omega(\gamma^{-1} \cdot \log(n \cdot \gamma))$, which is too much communication. To overcome this, a novel analysis of the protocol is required.

Obtaining a Constant Bound on the Success Probability. Similarly to [29], we first lower bound the probability of delivering a message to a specific party timely by the probability that this party is reachable within $O(\log n)$ steps from the sender in the communication graph produced by letting only the honest parties forward the message. We then observe that it is sufficient to prove that for an honest sender of a message, there is a constant probability to reach a constant fraction of all honest parties in $O(\log n)$ steps. Since the flooding is completely random, this then implies that any fixed party receives the message with constant probability within $O(\log n)$ steps.

To analyze how many honest parties can be reached in $O(\log n)$ steps, we look at a process where in the first step, the sender sends the message to d random neighbors, and at the ith step, we consider all parties at distance $i - 1$ from the sender each sending the message to d random neighbors. Within each step, we look at the parties in some arbitrary order and consider a party successful, if the d random neighbors of that party contain at least two honest parties that have not been reached, yet. If enough parties are successful, the number of honest parties reached so far increases by some constant > 1 fraction in this step, in which case we consider the step successful. This means after $O(\log n)$ successful steps, we can reach a constant fraction of all honest parties.

We now fix some constant fraction we want to reach. If the targeted constant fraction has already been reached, we can stop. Otherwise, there are enough unreached honest parties left such that for appropriately chosen d independent of n, the probability that at least two of the d neighbors are unreached and honest is at least some positive constant. We note that all constants and parameters need to be set carefully at the end to obtain the desired constant success probability. While the precise calculations are somewhat involved, we intuitively need to set $d = \Theta(\gamma^{-1})$ because when the number of corrupted parties is doubled, this halves the probability that a random neighbor is honest, which can be countered by doubling the number of neighbors.

We next fix some further constant k and look at the first k steps and the remaining ones separately. For the first k steps, we can use a simple union bound to conclude that (for carefully chosen constants) the probability that there exists an unsuccessful party in the process is bounded by a constant. Hence, we have that all the first k steps are successful with constant probability.

It remains to consider the remaining steps. Since there are $O(\log n)$ steps left, it is not sufficient to bound the success probability of each of these steps by a constant. We thus show that the failure probabilities of the remaining steps decrease as the summands in a geometric series to bound the overall failure probability by a constant. We have already established a constant success probability p for each individual party. If there are r parties involved in the current step, the expected number of newly reached honest parties in this step is $2rp$. If we could apply the Chernoff bound to obtain that the actual number is at most a $1 - \delta$ factor away from $2rp$, and thus a constant > 1, except with probability negligible in r, we could conclude the proof, using that r is increasing in every step under the assumption that previous steps are successful. Unfortunately, we cannot directly apply the Chernoff bound here because the success events of the individual parties are not independent: If the first party already reaches many fresh honest parties, there are less left for the next parties, thereby reducing their success probabilities.

We overcome this obstacle by considering a modified experiment as follows: Firstly, when a party reaches more than two fresh honest parties, we only consider two of them as reached and ignore the additional ones. It is clear that this modification can only decrease the probability that there are enough fresh parties in the current step. We then modify the experiment further by *always* adding two additional parties to the set of parties we consider "not fresh and honest". That is, whenever a party is not successful and reaches less than two fresh honest parties, we add one or two extra parties to that set. We do, however, record that this party was not successful. Note that this modification does not increase the success probabilities of any party since removing additional parties from the set of fresh and honest parties can only decrease the success probability of subsequent parties. In this new experiment, the success probabilities of the individual parties are now indeed independent and we can use the Chernoff bound as sketched before to bound the number of successful parties, which concludes the proof.

Flooding Amplification. The protocol compiler WeakFlood2Flood splits a message into a number μ of shares using erasure-correcting codes and makes use of a weak flooding protocol to distribute each of these shares independently. Since the shares are created using erasure-correcting codes, it is not necessary for each party to receive all shares to reconstruct the original message. More concretely, consider a reconstruction threshold of $\tau = \xi \cdot \mu$, with constant ξ. Using standard erasure-correcting codes (e.g., Reed-Solomon codes), this can be obtained with a share size of $O(l \cdot \tau^{-1})$, where l is the length of the original message. To achieve a flooding protocol, we then need to ensure that each party receives τ shares.

An apparent attack on such protocol would be for an adversary to try to inject "fake" shares into the set of shares honest parties try to reconstruct the message from. We prevent this by using a cryptographic accumulation scheme, to prove that a particular share is part of the original shares. Such accumulator can be implemented efficiently, e.g., using Merkle trees or signature schemes.

Flooding Amplification Security Proof. We need to show that for appropriately chosen parameters, all parties receive a constant fraction of the shares with overwhelming probability, which allows all parties to reconstruct the original message. We know that the underlying weak flooding protocol ensures that every fixed party receives each individual share with a constant probability. However, even though the honest parties behave independently for flooding the different shares, the events of receiving these shares are not independent. This is because the adversary can, e.g., decide to always deliver some share if another share is delivered, thereby correlating the events. We need to show that the adversary cannot use any correlations to reduce the delivery probability of any of the shares.

To this end, we generalize a result by Maurer, Pietrzak, and Renner [34] to more than two systems. The high-level idea is that we can split the single adversary into smaller adversaries where each of these interacts with a single instance of the weak flooding protocol. Letting the adversaries communicate with each other allows them to jointly emulate an execution of the original adversary and maintain the same advantage in preventing the delivery of the shares. We now inductively reduce the number of messages sent among the adversaries until no communication is needed as follows: The last message is not sent, and the adversary expecting it instead considers all possible messages and behaves as if it received one that maximizes the probability that the delivery guarantee in its flooding instance is violated. Note that this step requires the adversaries to be computationally unbounded, but this is not a problem since security of our weak flooding protocol holds against such adversaries (even though the amplification protocol itself depends on computational assumptions).

Considering the now independent adversaries, we have independent delivery probabilities for the individual shares and can use the Chernoff bound to show that with overwhelming probability, all parties receive sufficiently many shares to reconstruct.

1.3   Related Work

Flooding Protocols. Flooding protocols are used to implement so-called multicast networks, which allow a party to distribute a message among a set of parties within some prescribed time. Current flooding protocols (as in Bitcoin [36], Ethereum [49], etc.) are typically implemented via a forwarding mechanism, where in order for a party to distribute a message, the party simply selects a random subset of neighbors, who then forward the message to their neighbors and so on.

The security of such a protocol relies on the fact that the graph induced by the neighbor selection procedure among honest parties is connected. Kermarrec, Massoulié and Ganesh [28] showed that when choosing each neighbor with probability ρ in a setting with up to $t = (1 - \gamma) \cdot n$ corruptions (out of n parties), it is necessary that $\rho > \frac{\log(n \cdot \gamma) + \kappa}{\gamma \cdot n}$ to ensure that messages are delivered to all honest parties with overwhelming probability in κ.

Matt, Nielsen, and Thomsen [33] formally proved security of such a flooding protocol against a so-called delayed adaptive adversary (where it takes a certain delay for the adversary to gain control over a party) corrupting any fraction of the total number of parties. In a followup work [29], Liu-Zhang, Matt, Maurer, Rito, and Thomsen gave the first protocol that remains secure in the setting where all parties are publicly assigned a positive weight and the adversary can corrupt parties accumulating up to a constant fraction of the total weight. We adapt the techniques from Liu-Zhang, Matt, Maurer, Rito, and Thomsen and provide a general procedure for obtaining a flooding protocol for the weighted setting from one secure in the none weighted setting. In particular, this allows our protocols to be used in the weighted setting.

The protocols of [29,33] incur a per-party communication of $O(l \cdot \gamma^{-1} \cdot (\log(n) + \kappa))$ bits, for a message of size l.[6] In contrast, our protocols incur the (asymptotically) optimal per-party communication of $O(l \cdot \gamma^{-1})$.

Coretti, Kiayias, Moore, and Russell [12] considered the problem of designing a message diffusion mechanism based on the majority of honest stake assumption tailored specifically for the Ouroboros Praos consensus protocol [14]. However, their flooding protocol achieves a weaker guarantee in that it allows a certain set of honest parties to be eclipsed. In contrast, our work focuses on flooding protocols that guarantee delivery to all honest parties.

Another line of work seeks to improve on the efficiency of flooding protocols for blockchains by applying structured approaches and heuristics [18,44,48]. However, the behavior of these protocols under byzantine corruptions is not documented, and our focus is on provably secure protocols. We do, therefore, not comment on this line of work further.

Agreement Primitives. A significant line of work is dedicated to building broadcast and Byzantine agreement primitives for long messages for different thresholds, setups, and assumptions, starting from the work of Turpin and Coan [47]. Most works in this direction focused on achieving optimal total communication complexity $O(l \cdot n + \text{poly}(n, \kappa))$ (see, e.g., [6,20,21,37]), for sufficiently large messages. Recently, techniques similar to those we use for our ECCast protocol were used to also achieve low per-party communication in the context of agreement protocols [24,31,37,50], and information dispersal protocols [38]. In all these works, however, parties communicate to all other parties (so the neighborhood size is $n - 1$). In contrast, we provide ECFlood where each party communicates to only $O(\gamma^{-1} \cdot (\log(n) + \kappa))$ neighbors. Some recent works also improved the per-party communication of consensus protocols [7,46] using flooding.

Classic Randomized Epidemic Dissemination. Epidemic algorithms or gossip protocols were first considered for data dissemination by Demers et al. [15], and have been studied extensively since then, see e.g., [17,19,27,28] (and more).

[19] showed that if in each period of time, a rumor is forwarded to a random party, then it takes only $\log(n)$ time before the message has reached all parties (thereby the message complexity becomes $O(l \cdot n \cdot \log(n))$. [27] extended this to show that if additionally parties that have not heard about a message pull for it

---

[6] To see this for the work of Matt et al., see [33, Corollary 1, Eq (47)]. To make the failure probability negligible in κ, each party must forward to any other party with probability $\Omega\left(\frac{\log(n)+\kappa}{n \cdot \gamma}\right)$ and hence each party will expectedly have $\Omega(\gamma^{-1} \cdot (\log(n) + \kappa))$ neighbors.

(and thereby they assume that it is known that a new message is to arrive) the complexity drops to $O(l \cdot \log(\log(n)) \cdot n)$. [17] showed that by slightly "steering" the randomness based upon whether or not the most recent party already had received the message, an asymptotically optimal message complexity of $O(l \cdot n)$ can be achieved.

The big difference between this line of work and our work is that no byzantine adversary is considered and none of these protocols are proven secure against a byzantine adversary. A natural approach to obtain a protocol with reduced communication complexity would be to try to adapt the techniques of this line of work to the byzantine setting. This is however highly non-trivial.

Any protocol which allows parties to pull information from other parties faces the problem that an adversary might issue large amounts of false queries and thereby blow up the communication complexity of the protocol (this would, for example, be a problem for the anti-entropy protocol [15] and the protocol of [27]). Further, trying to detect the current state of the network and limit the number of redundant messages based upon this (by either or steering whom to send as in [17] to or how many parties to send to as in the rumor mongering of [15]) inherently has the problem of dishonest parties reporting false information. Finally, note that a very minimal requirement for a protocol to possibly guarantee the delivery of a message is that each honest party must communicate with at least one other honest party. To ensure this with an overwhelming probability in κ when a byzantine adversary controls a constant fraction of the parties each party needs at least κ connections, and if the entire message is forwarded over these channels the communication complexity already becomes $\Omega(\kappa \cdot l \cdot n)$ when sending an l bit message among n parties.

Due to the above difficulties, state-of-the-art in the byzantine setting is simply to increase the number of parties each party forwards the message to, to obtain a secure protocol (as in the protocols of [28,29,33] and FFlood which we compare our protocol to in Fig. 1). New insights are therefore needed to obtain an asymptotically optimal communication complexity in the byzantine setting. The main contribution of our work is to give an efficient protocol for the byzantine setting that achieves exactly such optimal communication complexity and per-party communication.

Miscellaneous. A line of works considered improving the number of connections per party of MPC protocols [8,10] using flooding.

Al-Bassam et al. [1] use similar techniques including Reed-Solomon codes and Merkle trees for data-availability proofs. They use more sophisticated encodings to produce short fraud proofs, which are out of scope of our paper.

2 Model and Preliminaries

2.1 Parties, Adversary and Communication Network

We consider a fixed set of n parties $\mathcal{P} = \{p_1, p_2, \ldots, p_n\}$. For simplicity, we assume an adversary that can statically corrupt a set of parties such that only a subset $\mathcal{H} \subseteq \mathcal{P}$ will behave honestly.[7] The corrupted parties are byzantine, i.e. fully controlled by the adversary and can behave in an arbitrary way. We will use h to denote a bound on the size of $\mathcal{H}$. For the remainder of the paper, we will assume that $|\mathcal{H}| \geq h$. We will use $\gamma := \frac{h}{n}$ to denote the fraction of parties guaranteed to be honest. We will use the execution semantics of UC [9] with the notion of time from TARDIS [4] when reasoning about executions of our protocol. That is no global clock is available but all parties is ensured to be activated in each time step.

We assume that all parties are connected via point-to-point channels, but our protocol does not rely on a synchrony assumption and is secure in a fully asynchronous network. We only use Δ_{NET} to quantify the delivery guarantees of our protocol (parties do not need to know this bound). This is the same as in previous works [29,33].

2.2 Primitives

Erasure Correcting Codes. In our protocols we make use of a special type of weak error-correcting code that is only able to tolerate a certain number of erasures. We refer to these as erasure-correcting codes.

Definition 1 (Erasure Correcting Code Scheme). *Let $\mu \in \mathbb{N}$ be the number of shares, and let $\varrho \in \mathbb{N}$ be the number of erasures that are to be tolerated. A pair of algorithms ζ is a (μ, ϱ)-erasure-correcting-code-scheme (abbreviated (μ, ϱ)-ECCS) if it consists of two algorithms:*

- *ζ.Enc: An encoding algorithm that takes a message $m \in \{0,1\}^*$ and produces a sequence of shares $s_1, \ldots, s_\mu$.*
- *ζ.Dec: A decoding algorithm that if a sequence of shares $s'_1, \ldots, s'_\mu$ s.t. it holds for at least $\mu - \varrho$ of them that $s'_i = s_i$ and for the remaining $s'_i = \bot$ is input, then the original message is m is returned.*

We will use the notation ζ.ShareSize(l) for a function that bounds the size of each share when a message of length l is encoded.

Standard Reed-Solomon codes [43] can be used to instantiate a (μ, ϱ)-ECCS efficiently in a straightforward manner for arbitrary message lengths. That is, to share a message m with length l into μ shares such that $\mu - \varrho$ shares can be used to reconstruct the original message, we choose the symbol size $a = \lceil \log(\mu) \rceil$ (in bits) and split the message into chunks $c_1, \ldots, c_{\lceil \frac{l}{a \cdot (\mu - \varrho)} \rceil}$ that each has size $a \cdot (\mu - \varrho)$. Because each of these chunks consists of $\mu - \varrho$ symbols, we can use Reed-Solomon encoding to for chunk c_i obtain micro shares $s'_{i,1}, \ldots s'_{i,\mu}$ where any $\mu - \varrho$ of the micro shares can be used to obtain the entire chunk c_i via. Reed-Solomon decoding. We now define shares $s_1, \ldots, s_\mu$ by letting $s_j := s'_{1,j}, \ldots, s'_{\lceil \frac{l}{a \cdot (\mu - \varrho)} \rceil, j}$.

---

[7] One can extend our protocols to handle so-called delayed adaptive adversaries, using techniques presented in [33].

Obtaining any $\mu - \varrho$ of such shares allows to reconstruct all chuncks using Reed Solomon decoding. Thereby, the original message can be reconstructed.

Let ζ be this scheme, and we will have that

$$\zeta.\texttt{ShareSize}(l) = O\Big(\frac{l}{\mu - \varrho}\Big). \tag{1}$$

This implies that the total bitlength of the shares will be $O\big(l \cdot \frac{\mu}{\mu-\varrho}\big)$. It has been shown that the encoding and decoding of such codes be done in $O(2^a \cdot a^2)$ time [16]. This means that the entire encoding and decoding for this scheme can be done in just $O(\mu^2 \cdot (\log(\mu)^2))$ time. For further comments on the practicality of this, see the extended version of this paper [30].

Weak Cryptographic Accumulators. We will in the paper make use of a *weak* version of a *static positive* accumulator. *Weak* refers to that we only require collision-freeness and correctness to hold for honestly generated accumulators, *static* refers to that we do not need the set of accumulated values to be dynamically extendable, and *positive* means that we only need to prove membership of an accumulator (in particular we do not need to prove that an element is not a part of the accumulator).

Definition 2 (Weak Static Cryptographic Accumulation Scheme). *A weak static cryptographic accumulation scheme (abbreviated WSCAS) α consists of two algorithms:*

- $\alpha.\textit{Accumulate}(\{m_1, \ldots, m_\eta\})$: *A PPT algorithm for accumulating a set of values $\{m_1, \ldots, m_\eta\}$. It returns an accumulated value z and a sequence of proofs $\pi_1, \ldots, \pi_\eta$ where π_i can be used to prove that m_i is in the accumulated value z where each $m_i \in \{0,1\}^*$.*
- $\alpha.\textit{Verify}(m, \pi, z)$: *A function that checks if a proof π proves that a message m was in the set of elements used to create the accumulated value z.*

With the following properties:

Completeness: *All honestly generated proofs are accepted by $\alpha.\textit{Verify}$.*
Collision-freeness: *No PPT adversary can find a set of values $M :=$ $\{m_1, \ldots, m_\eta\}$, a value $m' \notin M$, and a proof π such that $\alpha.\textit{Verify}(m', \pi, z) = \top$ for $z \leftarrow \alpha.\textit{Accumulate}(M)$ except with negligible probability.*

See [3] for the original formal definition of collision-freeness and [40] for an overview of accumulator constructions. We use the notation $\alpha.\texttt{AccSize}$ for a bound on the size of the accumulated value and $\alpha.\texttt{ProofSize}(\eta)$ for a function that bounds the size of each proof as a function of the number of messages accumulated η.

Because we only require collision-freeness for honestly generated accumulators, a WSCAS scheme can be efficiently instantiated using a regular signature scheme by letting the accumulated value z be the public verification key, and a proof for a message be a signature of that message. For suitable signature schemes:

$$\alpha.\texttt{AccSize} = O(\kappa) \text{ and } \alpha.\texttt{ProofSize}(\eta) = O(\kappa). \tag{2}$$

The same complexity can be achieved by basing α on RSA accumulators [5] or bilinear accumulators [39]. To avoid generating keys or a setup assumption, one can also use Merkle Trees [35] as accumulators, at the cost of slightly increasing the proof size to $\alpha.\texttt{ProofSize}(\eta) = O(\log(\eta) \cdot \kappa)$.

2.3   Flooding

A flooding protocol allows a set of parties to send messages to each other subject to certain delivery guarantees. Our definition is based on the one presented in [29] with minor differences.

Definition 3 (Flooding). *Let Π be a protocol executed by parties $\mathcal{P}$, where each party $p \in \mathcal{P}$ can input a message at any time, and as a consequence, all parties get a message as output. We say that Π is a strong Δ-flooding protocol if when a message m is input to an* honest *party at time t, then by time $t + \Delta$ there is a probability overwhelming in the security parameter κ that all other honest parties output m.*

Note that our definition allows a message sent by the adversary to be only received by a subset of honest parties. This is sufficient for most blockchain protocols [11, 14, 22, 41, 42, 51]. If total delivery from dishonest senders is required, one can simply let the honest parties re-distribute the received messages.

Preventing Denial-of-Service in a Flooding Network. As noted in [29], there exists a trivial denial-of-service attack against flooding networks because they allow to flood *any* message. An adversary can simply input a large number of arbitrary messages and as all messages must be propagated by the definition of a flooding network, this will allow an adversary to exhaust the bandwidth of honest parties. A simple solution to this is to only let honest parties forward "valid" messages (w.r.t. some validity predicate determined by upper-level protocols). A drawback of our flooding protocols is that such an approach cannot be applied naively, because shares are forwarded instead of full messages, and therefore validity checks depending on the full message cannot be performed. However, instead, one can add an extra field of data to the shares sent around by our FFlood protocol, and parties will then verify that this extra data proves that this share should be forwarded. In the context of for example proof-of-stake blockchains, such extra data can for example simply be a signature by the baker of the block and a proof that this baker is allowed to create a block. For clarity of presentation, we have left this out of our presentation as the details of such validity predicates necessarily must be determined by upper-level protocols.

2.4   Additional Notation

We use the notation $\Gamma_s^\lambda(G)$ for the set of neighbors of a party (usually the sender) s at distance at most λ in a graph G. When clear, we omit both s and G for this set and merely write Γ^λ. We write $A \xleftarrow{\$} \mathcal{D}$ to sample the value A from the distribution $\mathcal{D}$. We let $\mathcal{U}(A)$ denote the uniform distribution on a set A. We denote by $\log x$ the natural logarithm of x. For two random variables X and Y, we will write $X \preceq Y$ if Y stochastically dominates X, i.e. $\Pr[Y \geq k] \geq \Pr[X \geq k]$ for all k.

3 Per-Party Communication Lower Bound

In this section, we present and prove a new lower bound that states that any protocol must have a per-party communication of at least $\Omega(l \cdot \gamma^{-1})$ when sending a message of length l.

Theorem 3. *For any Δ, any protocol that is Δ-flooding protocol must have per party communication complexity $\Omega(l \cdot \gamma^{-1})$ when sending a message of length l.*

Proof. Let $\Delta \in \mathbb{N}$. For the sake of contradiction let us assume that there exists a protocol Π with $o(l \cdot \gamma^{-1})$ per-party communication complexity when sending a message of length l.

We select a party s as the initial sender and reason about an execution of the protocol where a message of length l is input to s against a specific adversarial strategy. Before the protocol execution starts the adversary divides the set of parties without the sender $\mathcal{P} \setminus \{s\}$ into sets $C_1, \ldots, C_{\lfloor \gamma^{-1} \rfloor}$ such that for all i we have that $C_i \geq n \cdot \gamma - 1$. At random the adversary now chooses a $j \in \{1, \ldots, \lceil \gamma^{-1} \rceil\}$ and corrupts all sets C_i where $i \neq j$. This is possible because for any z we have

$$|C_z \cup \{s\}| \geq \gamma \cdot n. \tag{3}$$

In particular, this holds for C_j, and therefore the corruption threshold is not exceeded. The adversary now lets the corrupted parties in each of the sets C_i execute the protocol Π with the following modifications:

- When a party $p \in C_i$ receives a message from a party $p' \notin C_i \cup \{s\}$, the party p ignores the message and acts as if they had not received it at all.
- Whenever the protocol dictates that a party $p \in C_i$ should send a message to party $p' \notin C_i \cup \{s\}$, the message is dropped and not send.

Now note that from the perspective of the sender, s it is impossible to distinguish which C_i is honest and which is corrupted, as it cannot be distinguished from the sender side whether a message is dropped on the sending side or the receiving side, and by Eq. (3), it could be for any i that each set C_i is actually the only set of honest. If there exists a k such that C_k has a constant probability of receiving less than l bits from the sender, then there is at least $\lfloor \gamma^{-1} \rfloor^{-1}$ probability (because the non-corrupted set where selected uniformly at random) that $k = j$ and hence the protocol would fail with a non-negligible probability. Therefore, the protocol must, with overwhelming probability, let the sender send each set of parties at least l bits as they would otherwise not be able to deliver the message to all honest parties with overwhelming probability. Therefore, with overwhelming probability at least $l \cdot \lfloor \gamma^{-1} \rfloor = \Omega(l \cdot \gamma^{-1})$ bits are sent by the sender. This contradicts that a protocol with $o(l \cdot \gamma^{-1})$ per party communication complexity exists. $\qquad \square$

4 Warm Up: Optimal Flooding with Constant Diameter and Linear Neighbors

In this section, we present our protocol ECCast and show that it is a flooding protocol with a maximum per-party communication of $O(l \cdot \gamma^{-1})$, a total communication complexity of $O(l \cdot \gamma^{-1} \cdot n)$, and a diameter of 2.

Our protocol ECCast is parameterized by an erasure correcting code scheme that shares a message into n shares and a cryptographic accumulator. When a sender wishes to send, they will share the message into n shares and send a unique share to each party. When a party receives such a share, they will forward the share they receive to *all* other parties. This will ensure that each party ends up receiving as least as many shares as there are honest parties. Therefore, the only thing that can prevent honest parties from reconstructing the original message is if they try to reconstruct from some shares that were not sent by the original sender. To prevent this, we use the cryptographic accumulator.

Protocol ECCast(ζ, α)

The protocol is parameterized by, a (n, ϱ)-ECCS ζ for some $\varrho \in \mathbb{N}$, and a cryptographic accumulator α. Each party $p_i \in \mathcal{P}$ keeps track of a set of shares received for a particular accumulator z, ReceivedShares$_i[z]$. Additionally, each party p_i keeps track of a set of received messages Received$_i$.

Initialize: Initially, each party p_i sets ReceivedShares$_i := \varnothing$, and Received$_i := \varnothing$.

Send: When p_i receives (Send, m) they share the message m into shares $\zeta.\mathsf{Enc}(m) = s_1, \ldots, s_n$. Furthermore, they obtain an accumulated value and proofs for each share and its share number $z, \pi_1, \ldots, \pi_n = \alpha.\mathsf{Accumulate}(\{(s_j, j) \mid 1 \leq j \leq n\})$. For $1 \leq j \leq n$, the party now sends $(\mathit{Forward}, s_j, j, \pi_j, z)$ to party p_j using the point-to-point channel between them. Finally, they add m to Received$_i$.

Get Messages: When p_i receives $(\mathit{GetMessages})$ they return Received$_i$.

When party p_i receives a tuple (T, s, j, π, z) over a point-to-point channel where $\alpha.\mathsf{Verify}((s, j), \pi, z) = \top$ they add (s, j) to ReceivedShares$_i[z]$. Furthermore, p_i does the two following checks:

- If $|\mathsf{ReceivedShares}_i[z]| \geq n - \varrho$, then they
  1. Obtain a sequence of shares $s_1, \ldots, s_n$ by letting $s_j = s$ if $(s, j) \in$ ReceivedShares$_i[z]$ and otherwise sets $s_j = \bot$ (i.e. if no such pair is in ReceivedShares$_i[z]$).
  2. Decode the shares and add the recovered message to the set of received messages, Received$_i := \mathsf{Received}_i \cup \{\zeta.\mathsf{Dec}(s_1, \ldots, s_n)\}$.
- If $T = \mathit{Forward}$, it is the first time they receive (T, s, j, π, z), and $j = i$, then they send $(\mathit{Receive}, s, j, \pi, z)$ to all parties over their respective point-to-point channels.

Below, we state that ECCast is flooding protocol. Due to space constraints we refer to the full version of this paper [30] for the proof.

Theorem 4. *Let $\varrho \geq n \cdot (1 - \gamma)$, let ζ be a (n, ϱ)-ECCS, and let α be a WSCAS, then the protocol ECCast(ζ, α) is a strong $(2 \cdot \Delta_{\mathrm{NET}})$-flooding protocol.*

Communication Complexity of ECCast. We now analyze the communication complexity of ECCast(ζ, α) (for ζ and α instantiated as suggested by Theorem 4) when a message of length l is input. The neighborhood of each party is n as all parties will talk to all other parties. The per-party communication is given by the size of the neighborhood times the size of the tuple sent over each point-to-point channel. As each tuple consists of a bit (*Forward* or *Receive*), a share, a sequence number of the share, an accumulator proof, and an accumulated value, we have that the communication for each party is given by

$$n \cdot (1 + \zeta.\mathsf{ShareSize} + \log(n) + \alpha.\mathsf{ProofSize} + \alpha.\mathsf{AccSize}).$$

If we instantiate the ECCS with Reed-Solomon codes, we get that the size of each share is bounded by $\zeta.\mathsf{ShareSize} = O(l \cdot (\gamma \cdot n)^{-1})$. By using an efficient WSCAS α with size of the accumulated value and proof $O(\kappa)$ (see Eq. (2)), we get that the communication of each party is bounded by

$$n \cdot (1 + O(l \cdot (\gamma \cdot n^{-1}) + \log(n) + O(\kappa) + O(\kappa)) = O(l \cdot \gamma^{-1} + n \cdot (\log(n) + \kappa)).$$

This is optimal when $l = \Omega(n \cdot (\log(n) + \kappa))$ by Theorem 3.

5 Optimal Flooding with Logarithmic Neighborhood and Diameter

We show a flooding protocol with (asymptotically) optimal communication complexity, in two steps. First, we define a weaker notion, denoted *weak flooding* and propose an instantiation of it. Then we show how to lift the security guarantees from a weak flooding protocol to achieve a full-fledged flooding protocol.

5.1 Weak Flooding

A weak flooding protocol is a flooding protocol that, instead of being guaranteed to deliver all messages to all parties, only ensures that there is a lower bound on the probability that each party receives a message.

Definition 4 (Weak Flooding). *Let Π be a protocol executed by parties $\mathcal{P}$, where each party $p \in \mathcal{P}$ can input a message at any time, and as a consequence, parties may get a message as output. We say that Π is a weak (Δ, ξ)-flooding protocol if at any time t when a message m is input to some honest party, then it must be that for any $p_i \in \mathcal{H}$*

$$\Pr[p_i \text{ receives } m \text{ at latest at time } t + \Delta] \geq \xi.$$

Protocol Description. We now describe a simple flooding protocol, in which each party samples a random set of d neighbors for some parameter d and relays all new messages to all their neighbors.

Protocol FFlood(d)

Each party $p_i \in \mathcal{P}$ keeps track of a set of relayed messages $\texttt{Relayed}_i$ which will also be used to keep track of which messages party p_i has received.

Initialize: Initially, each party p_i sets $\texttt{Relayed}_i := \varnothing$ and samples a uniform random set $N_i \subseteq \mathcal{P}, |N_i| = d$ of d neighbors.

Send: When p_i receives (*Send*, m), they forward the message to all parties in N_i. Finally, they set $\texttt{Relayed}_i := \texttt{Relayed}_i \cup \{m\}$.

Get Messages: When p_i receives (*GetMessages*), they return $\texttt{Relayed}_i$.

When party p_i receives message m on a point-to-point channel where $m \notin \texttt{Relayed}_i$, party p_i continues as if they had received (*Send*, m).

In Sect. 5.2, we provide intuition for how to prove the theorem below. Due to space constraints we refer to the full version of this paper [30] for actual proof. Note that we explicitly quantify over the number of parties n after the existential quantification of the success probability bound, to highlight that the probability is independent of the number of parties.

Theorem 5. *There exists $\xi \in (0,1]$ such that for any $n \geq 50 \cdot \gamma^{-1}$ there is a $d = O(\gamma^{-1})$ and $\Delta = O(\log(n) \cdot \Delta_{\mathrm{NET}})$ such that the protocol FFlood(d) is a weak (Δ, ξ)-flooding protocol. The security also holds against computationally unbounded adversaries.*

Previous analyses of related protocols [28,33] only considered the probability to deliver the message to *all honest parties*, and for this required $d = \Omega(\gamma^{-1} \cdot \log(\gamma \cdot n))$ to obtain a constant probability. Our analysis instead proves that $d = O(\gamma^{-1})$ is sufficient to guarantee that *any fixed party* receives the message with constant success probability.

5.2 Analysis of FFlood

In order to prove that FFlood is a weak flooding protocol, we have to prove that for any party, the probability that this party receives a specific message is constant. We do so by re-using the honest sending process from [29]. The idea of the honest sending process, is to let it mimic the communication graph induced by the sending message where only the honest parties participate in the distribution of the message, and the adversary only delivers the message on the point-to-point channels at the latest point in time possible. We will use the notation $\mathsf{HSP}(s, d, \lambda)$ to denote the honest sending process for a sender s, FFlood using degree d, and the process stopping at distance λ from the sender. See the full version of this paper [30] for the exact definition.

The following lemma relates the probability of a party being in the neighborhood of the sender in the graph produced by the honest sending process with FFlood being a weak flooding protocol. The proof is analogous to the one of [29, Lemma 5 on p. 16] and therefore omitted.

Lemma 1. *Let $\lambda \in \mathbb{N}$ be a distance, let $d \in \mathbb{N}$, and let $\Delta := \lambda \cdot \Delta_{\mathrm{NET}}$. Further, let $s_{min} \in \mathcal{H}$ and $p_{min} \in \mathcal{H}$ s.t. when $G \xleftarrow{\$} \mathsf{HSP}(s_{min}, d, \lambda)$ then $\Pr[p_{min} \in \Gamma^\lambda_{s_{min}}(G)]$ is minimized over all such $s, p \in \mathcal{H}$. If*

$$\xi \le \Pr[p_{min} \in \Gamma^\lambda_{s_{min}}(G)],$$

then $\mathsf{FFlood}(d)$ is a weak (Δ, ξ)-flooding protocol.

Next, we lower bound for any party the probability that this party is in a logarithmic neighborhood of the sender in the honest sending process.

Lemma 2. *Let $\alpha, \delta \in [0, 1]$. Further, let $\phi \in \mathbb{R}$ be an expected expansion factor, $d, k \in \mathbb{N}$, and let $\lambda := \frac{\log(\alpha \cdot |\mathcal{H}|)}{\log((1-\delta) \cdot \phi)}$. Finally, let $s \in \mathcal{H}$ and let $G \xleftarrow{\$} \mathsf{HSP}(s, d, \lambda)$. If $n \ge 11 \cdot \gamma^{-1}$, $\alpha < 1/3$,*

$$\phi \le 2 - 2(d+1) \cdot \left(\frac{11}{11 - \gamma} \cdot (1 - (1 - 3\alpha) \cdot \gamma) \right)^{d-1}, \tag{4}$$

and

$$(1 - \delta) \cdot \phi \ge \frac{3}{2}, \tag{5}$$

then for any party $p \in \mathcal{H}$

$$\Pr[p \in \Gamma^\lambda_s(G)] \ge \frac{\alpha \cdot |\mathcal{H}| - 1}{|\mathcal{H}|} \cdot \left(1 - \frac{d^k - 1}{d - 1}(d+1) \cdot \right.$$

$$\left. \left(\frac{11}{11 - \gamma} \cdot (1 - (1 - 3\alpha) \cdot \gamma) \right)^{d-1} - \frac{e^{-\frac{\delta^2 \phi \cdot ((1-\delta) \cdot \phi)^k}{20}}}{1 - e^{-\frac{\delta^2 \phi \cdot ((1-\delta) \cdot \phi)^k}{4}}} \right).$$

5.3   Flooding Amplification

We present a compiler that amplifies delivery guarantees of a weak flooding protocol to full-fledged flooding. The protocol WeakFlood2Flood is parameterized by a *weak* flooding protocol, an erasure correcting code scheme (ECCS), and a cryptographic accumulator. The idea of the protocol is that when a sender wishes to send a message, they divide the message into multiple shares using the ECCS. The sender will then send each of these shares using the weak flooding protocol. Each receiver will receive a set of shares and try to reconstruct the original message from this. Intuitively, if everybody receives sufficiently many of the original shares within the given time, then the only thing that can prevent an honest party from reconstructing the message sent by the sender is if an adversary managed to inject some "false shares" into the set of shares an honest party tries to reconstruct their message from. To prevent this from happening, the sender will create an accumulated value of all shares, and then instead of sending out only the share, they will send out the share, an accumulated value, and a proof that this share belongs to this accumulated value. On the receiving end, honest parties will group shares by the accumulated value they belong to and only try to reconstruct from shares that belong to the same accumulated value. Hence, an adversary will have to break the collision-free property of the accumulator scheme in order to inject such false shares.

It is only left to ensure that all parties receive sufficiently many of the original shares. We will ensure this by instantiating WeakFlood2Flood with a weak flooding protocol FFlood, such that each party is guaranteed to receive a constant fraction of the shares if a message is split into sufficiently many shares and set the parameters of the ECCS accordingly. For the security proof of our amplification, we need the weak flooding protocol to be secure against computationally unbounded adversaries, which is the case for the protocol we presented above, see Theorem 5.

Protocol WeakFlood2Flood(Π, ζ, α)

The protocol is parameterized by a weak flooding protocol Π, a (μ, ϱ)-ECCS ζ for some $\mu, \varrho \in \mathbb{N}$, and a cryptographic accumulator α.

Each party $p_i \in \mathcal{P}$ keeps track of a set of shares received for a particular accumulator z, ReceivedShares$_i[z]$. Additionally, each party p_i keeps track of a set of received messages Received$_i$.

Initialize: Initially, each party p_i sets ReceivedShares$_i := \varnothing$, and Received$_i := \varnothing$. Furthermore, μ independent instances $\Pi_1, \dots, \Pi_\mu$ of the weak flooding protocol are initialized.

Send: When p_i receives (Send, m) they share the message m into shares $\zeta.\mathsf{Enc}(m) = s_1, \dots, s_\mu$. Furthermore, they obtain an accumulated value and proofs for each share and its share number $(z, \pi_1, \dots, \pi_\mu) = \alpha.\mathsf{Accumulate}(\{(s_i, i) \mid 1 \leq i \leq \mu\})$. Now, the party inputs the message (s_j, π_j, z) to Π_j for $1 \leq j \leq \mu$. Finally, they add m to Received$_i$.

Get Messages: When p_i receives $(\mathit{GetMessages})$ they return Received$_i$.

When party p_i receives a tuple (s, π, z) in Π_j where $\alpha.\mathsf{Verify}((s, j), \pi, z) = \top$, they add (s, j) to ReceivedShares$_i[z]$. Furthermore, p_i checks if $|\text{ReceivedShares}_i[z]| \geq \mu - \varrho$. If that is the case, p_i ignores further messages with this accumulated value z and does the following:

1. Obtain a sequence of shares $s_1, \dots, s_\mu$ by letting $s_j = s$ if $(s, j) \in$ ReceivedShares$_i[z]$ and otherwise sets $s_j = \bot$ if no such pair is in ReceivedShares$_i[z]$.
2. Decode the shares and add the recovered message to the set of received messages, Received$_i := $ Received$_i \cup \{\zeta.\mathsf{Dec}(s_1, \dots, s_\mu)\}$.

Security of WeakFlood2Flood. We now state the theorem for the security of WeakFlood2Flood. Again, due to space constraints we refer the full version of this paper [30] for the proof.

Theorem 6. *Let $\xi \in (0,1]$, let $\Delta \in \mathbb{N}$, and let Π be a weak (Δ, ξ)-flooding protocol with security against computationally unbounded adversaries. Further, let $\delta \in (0,1]$, let $\mu \in \mathbb{N}$, let $\varrho \geq \mu \cdot (1 - (1 - \delta) \cdot \xi)$, let ζ be a (μ, ϱ)-ECCS, and let α be a WSCAS. The probability in an execution with a PPT adversary $\mathcal{A}$ that a message sent using the protocol WeakFlood2Flood(Π, ζ, α) is not delivered within time Δ to all honest parties is less than*

$$|\mathcal{H}| \cdot e^{-\frac{\delta^2 \cdot \xi \cdot \mu}{2}} + \mathrm{negl}(\kappa).$$

It is noteworthy that WeakFlood2Flood inherits the delivery guarantee of the weak flooding protocol that it is instantiated with. Next, we state a direct corollary of the above theorem, stating that for appropriate parameters, WeakFlood2Flood is a strong flooding protocol.

Corollary 1. *Let $\xi \in (0,1]$, let $\Delta \in \mathbb{N}$, and let Π be a weak (Δ, ξ)-flooding protocol. Further, let $\mu \geq 8 \cdot \frac{\log(n)+\kappa}{\xi}$, let $\varrho \geq \mu \cdot \left(1 - \frac{\xi}{2}\right)$, let ζ be a (μ, ϱ)-ECCS, and let α be a WSCAS. The protocol WeakFlood2Flood(Π, ζ, α) is a strong Δ-flooding protocol.*

Proof. We note that $|\mathcal{H}| \leq n$ and use Theorem 6 instantiated with $\delta := \frac{1}{2}$ to obtain that the probability that some honest party does not obtain a message sent by an honest party within time Δ is at most

$$|\mathcal{H}| \cdot e^{-\frac{\delta^2 \cdot \xi \cdot \mu}{2}} + \mathrm{negl}(\kappa) \leq n \cdot e^{-\log(n)-\kappa} + \mathrm{negl}(\kappa) = e^{-\kappa} + \mathrm{negl}(\kappa) \leq \mathrm{negl}(\kappa). \square$$

5.4 Communication Complexity of the Combined Protocol

We consider the combined protocol

$$\text{ECFlood}(d, \zeta, \alpha) := \text{WeakFlood2Flood}(\text{FFlood}(d), \zeta, \alpha),$$

instantiated with a (μ, ϱ)-ECCS ζ, and a WSCAS scheme α. Note that Corollary 1 and Theorem 5 imply that for $\mu \geq 8 \cdot \frac{\log(n)+\kappa}{\xi}$, $\varrho \geq \mu \cdot \left(1 - \frac{\xi}{2}\right)$, $n \geq 50 \cdot \gamma^{-1}$, $d = O(\gamma^{-1})$, and $\Delta = O(\log(n) \cdot \Delta_{\text{NET}})$, ECFlood$(d, \zeta, \alpha)$ is a strong Δ-flooding protocol.

To analyze the (per-party) communication complexity, consider the case where a single message of length l is input to an honest party. First note that the honest sender produces μ shares and sends these together with the sequence number of the share, an accumulator proof, and an accumulated value using FFlood(d). Hence, the size of each of these messages is bounded by $\zeta.\text{ShareSize}(l) + \log(\mu) + \alpha.\text{ProofSize}(\mu) + \alpha.\text{AccSize}$. The protocol FFlood$(d)$ uses a neighborhood of size d for every message and every honest party sends each message at most once to their neighbors. Furthermore, no other messages related to this message is sent by any honest party, unless the adversary breaks the collision freeness of the accumulator and manages to inject additional shares, which is only possible with negligible probability. Hence, each honest party sends at most $\mu \cdot d$ messages (except with negligible probability) and the per-party communication complexity is upper bounded by

$$\mu \cdot d \cdot (\zeta.\texttt{ShareSize}(l) + \log(\mu) + \alpha.\texttt{ProofSize}(\mu) + \alpha.\texttt{AccSize}). \qquad (6)$$

Using Reed-Solomon codes and since we can set $\varrho := \lceil \mu \cdot (1 - \frac{\xi}{2}) \rceil$, Eq. (1) implies that the share size can be bounded by

$$\zeta.\texttt{ShareSize} = O\left(\frac{l}{\mu - \varrho}\right) = O\left(\frac{l}{\mu \cdot \xi}\right) = O\left(\frac{l}{\mu}\right).$$

Furthermore, using efficient accumulators (see Eq. (2)) that have accumulator and proof sizes of $O(\kappa)$ bits, setting $\mu = O\left(\frac{\log(n)+\kappa}{\xi}\right)$, $d = O(\gamma^{-1})$, and using that ξ is just a constant, we obtain from Eq. (6) that the per-party communication complexity is bounded by

$$O\big((\log(n) + \kappa) \cdot \gamma^{-1} \cdot (l \cdot (\log(n) + \kappa)^{-1} + \log(\log(n) + \kappa) + \kappa)\big)$$
$$= O\big(\gamma^{-1} \cdot (l + (\log(n) + \kappa) \cdot (\log(\log(n)) + \kappa))\big), \qquad (7)$$

and the total communication complexity is at most n times that. For $l = \Omega\big((\log(n)+\kappa) \cdot (\log(\log(n))+\kappa)\big)$, this simplifies to $O\big(l \cdot \gamma^{-1}\big)$, which is optimal by Theorem 3.

6   Flooding in the Weighted Setting

Model. We consider the setting where parties are assigned a fraction of the total weight, and assume that the assigned weights are public. We let W_p denote the weight assigned to party p, and let $\alpha_p := \frac{W_p}{\sum_{p \in \mathcal{P}} W_p}$ i.e., the fraction of the total weight assigned to party p. The adversary can corrupt any subset of the parties such that the remaining set of honest parties together constitutes more than a $\tilde{\gamma} \in (0,1]$ fraction of the total weight. That is, $\sum_{p \in \mathcal{H}} \alpha_p \geq \tilde{\gamma}$, and all parties have a non-zero positive weight i.e. $\forall p \in \mathcal{P}, W_p > 0$.

Transformation. We provide a general transformation for a flooding protocol in the equal-weights setting to the weighted setting, leveraging ideas from [29]. The main idea of our transformation is to let each party *emulate* a number of parties in another flooding protocol. We use the same emulation function as [29] where each weighted party $p \in \mathcal{P}$ emulates $\lceil \alpha_p \cdot n \rceil$ non-weighted parties. For each party $p \in \mathcal{P}$, we define a set of parties that this party emulates as $\mathsf{E}(p) := \{p_i \mid i \in \mathbb{N} \wedge i \leq \lceil \alpha_p \cdot n \rceil\}$. Note that because all parties have a non-zero weight, all parties emulate at least one party, i.e., for any party $p \in \mathcal{P}$ we have $\mathrm{E}(p) \neq \varnothing$. For convenience, we introduce notation for the set of emulated parties, $\mathcal{P}_\mathrm{E} = \bigcup_{p \in \mathcal{P}} \mathrm{E}(p)$, the total number of emulated parties $n_\mathrm{E} = |\mathcal{P}_\mathrm{E}|$, the set of emulated parties that are emulated by honest players $\mathcal{H}_\mathrm{E} = \bigcup_{p \in \mathcal{H}} \mathrm{E}(p)$ and the number of honestly emulated parties $h_\mathrm{E} = |\mathcal{H}_\mathrm{E}|$. Following [29], we note that

$$n_\mathrm{E} = \sum_{p \in \mathcal{P}} \lceil \alpha_p \cdot n \rceil \leq \sum_{p \in \mathcal{P}} \alpha_p \cdot n + 1 = 2 \cdot n, \tag{8}$$

and

$$h_\mathrm{E} = \sum_{p \in \mathcal{H}} \lceil \alpha_p \cdot n \rceil \geq \widetilde{\gamma} \cdot n. \tag{9}$$

When defining a strong flooding protocol in Sect. 2.3, we were not explicit about the set of parties a flooding protocol has to provide guarantees for, as all of our previous flooding protocols have simply worked for the same set of assumed parties $\mathcal{P}$. Below, this will not be the case, as the flooding protocols we discuss will work for a different set of parties. Hence, we will make these sets explicit by using the phrase that "a protocol is a flooding protocol for a set of parties".

Protocol Flood2WeightedFlood(Π)

The protocol is parameterized by a protocol Π that is a flooding protocol for $\mathcal{P}_\mathrm{E}$.
Each party $p \in \mathcal{P}$ starts a process for each of their emulated parties, and lets these processes participate in the protocol Π.

Initialize: Initially, each party p initialize all of their emulated parties $\mathrm{E}(p)$ in Π.
Send: When p receives ($Send, m$) they pick $p_i \in \mathrm{E}(p)$ and forward ($Send, m$) to p_i in Π.
Get Messages: When p receives ($GetMessages$) they pick $p_i \in \mathrm{E}(p)$ forward ($GetMessages$) to p_i in Π, and return the set of messages returned to p_i.

Below we prove that if Flood2WeightedFlood is instantiated with a strong flooding protocol for n_E, then Flood2WeightedFlood will be a strong flooding protocol.

Theorem 7. *Let $\Delta \in \mathbb{N}$. If Π is a strong Δ-flooding protocol for $\mathcal{P}_\mathrm{E}$ under the assumption that at least $\widetilde{\gamma} \cdot n$ of them behaves honestly, then Flood2WeightedFlood(Π) is a strong Δ-flooding protocol for $\mathcal{P}$.*

Proof. Let m be a message that is input to some honest party at time t. Since all parties emulate at least one party, this implies that the message will also be input to some honest emulated party in Π at time t. Because Π is a strong Δ-flooding protocol for $\mathcal{P}_\mathrm{E}$ when $\widetilde{\gamma} \cdot n$ parties are honest (Eq. (9) ensures that this is actually the case), then there is an overwhelming probability in κ that all emulated parties receive m before $t + \Delta$. As each honest party emulates at least one party, this implies that all honest parties will also receive the message with a probability that is overwhelming in Π. $\square$

Realising a Strong Flooding Protocol for $\mathcal{P}_E$. It may seem like Theorem 7 allows us to easily translate the protocols presented in Sect. 5 to the weighted setting. However, even though the protocols in these sections work for any set of parties, they make channels, which are only assumed for the actual set of parties $\mathcal{P}$ and not the emulated set of parties $\mathcal{P}_E$. To use these protocols blackbox, we need to show how to establish channels between the emulated parties.

We note that channels for the emulated set of parties can easily be established from channels between the original set of parties. One way to do this is by simply prepending $(p_e, p_{e'})$ to any message that an emulated party p_e wishes to send to another emulated party p'. When a party receives such a message on a normal channel, they will take it as an input on the emulated channel between the emulated parties p_e and $p_{e'}$.

Communication Complexity Analysis. The analysis in Sect. 5.4 also applies when the protocol is transformed to work for the weighted setting because $n_E = O(n)$ (Eq. (8)) and the fraction of honest emulated parties $\frac{h_E}{n_E} = O(\widetilde{\gamma})$ (by Eqs. (8) and (9)). The only thing that changes is that all messages will have identifiers for emulated parties prepended. The size of such identifiers is bounded by $O(\log(n))$. When this is threaded through the analysis using the same parameters as in Sect. 5.4, we see that for a suitable d, ζ and α, the communication complexity of the Flood2WeightedFlood(ECFlood(d, ζ, α)) is bounded by $O(\gamma^{-1} \cdot n \cdot (l + (\log(n) + \kappa)^2))$, which is optimal when $l = \Omega((\log(n) + \kappa)^2)$. It is, however, worth noting that for our particular protocol, it is not necessary to keep the messages delivered to different emulated parties separate. In particular, Flood2WeightedFlood(ECFlood(d, ζ, α)) would have the same guarantees if any message sent from an emulated party of party p_i to an emulated party of p_j is simply delivered to *all* emulated parties of p_j. In that case, the communication complexity of Flood2WeightedFlood(ECFlood(d, ζ, α)) would be optimal under the same constraints as ECFlood(d, ζ, α).

7   Security in the UC Model

The Universal Composable (UC) model by Cannetti [9] is by many considered the golden standard for security for cryptographic protocols, because security in this model ensures that the protocol remains secure independently of the context it is deployed in. In this section, we formalize a theorem that informally says that any protocol that is a flooding protocol w.r.t. the property-based definition (Definition 3) is a UC secure implementation of a flooding network. The theorem is basically a generalization of the proof ideas that appear in [33] when proving that their flooding protocol implements the ideal functionality.

7.1 Flooding as a UC Functionality

We base our flooding functionality on the flooding functionality from [33] but do not consider pre-corrupted parties (a corruption type specific to the model of delayed adversaries used in their work) nor relay messagesas this is not needed for most blockchains protocols (see Sect. 2.3).

Functionality $\mathcal{F}^{\Delta}_{\text{Flood}}$

The functionality is parameterized by a set of parties $\mathcal{P}$ and a delivery guarantee Δ.

It keeps track of a set of messages for each party Mailbox. These sets contain the messages that each party will receive after fetching. Additionally, it keeps track of the set of parties that has been corrupted by the adversary Corrupted.

Initialize: Initially, Corrupted $:= \varnothing$ and Mailbox$[p_i] := \varnothing$ for all $p_i \in \mathcal{P}$.
Send: After receiving $(Send, m)$ from p_i it leaks $(LeakSend, p_i, m)$ to the adversary.
Get Messages: After receiving $(GetMessages)$ from p_i it outputs Mailbox$[p_i]$ to party p_i and $(LeakGet, p_i, \text{Mailbox}[p_i])$ to the adversary.
Set Message: After receiving $(SetMessage, m, p_i)$ from the adversary, the functionality sets Mailbox$[p_i] := \text{Mailbox}[p_i] \cup \{m\}$.

At any time after all parties have been initialized the functionality automatically enforces the following: For any message m that is input to an honest party p_i at some time t, it is ensured for any honest party $\forall p_j \in \mathcal{P} \setminus$ Corrupted that by time $t + \Delta$ they have received the message i.e., $m \in \text{Mailbox}[p_j]$.
The property are ensured by the functionality automatically[a] making the minimal possible additional calls with $SetMessage$.

---

[a] The global clock used to check the time ensures that the functionality is invoked at least once per time step, and therefore such automatic checks are possible.

7.2 Strong Flooding Implies UC Flooding

We are now ready to state the main result of this section. The theorem informally says that any flooding protocol that for UC executions is a strong flooding protocol (w.r.t. Definition 3) also securely implements $\mathcal{F}_{\text{Flood}}$.

Theorem 8. *Let $\Delta \in \mathbb{N}$ and let Π be a protocol. If Π is a Δ-flooding protocol, then Π securely implements $\mathcal{F}^{\Delta}_{Flood}$.*

To prove this we exploit that the functionality has no secrecy and therefore the full protocol can be simulated in black-box manner by simply forwarding the inputs that are leaked to the simulator from the functionality. We refer the reader to the full version of this paper [30] for the proof due to space constraints.

A direct corollary of Theorem 8 is that ECFlood securely implements $\mathcal{F}_{\mathsf{Flood}}^{\Delta}$.

8   Practicality of ECFlood

In Sect. 5.4, it was shown that parameters could be set such that ECFlood theoretically constitutes an asymptotically optimal flooding. We instantiated many variables to constants required by our analysis, but these are most likely not instantiated optimally, and nor are our analyses themselves optimal.

In this section, we use probabilistic simulations[8] to compare ECFlood to state-of-the-art for provably secure flooding protocols. Several additional results of our probabilistic simulations useful for guiding the instantiation of the parameters of our protocols, as well as a report on a small scale experiment[9] that indicates that the computational overhead of the WSCAS and ECCS are no hindrance for practical adoption of the protocol, can be found in the extended version of this paper [30].

8.1   Comparison to State-of-the-Art

To compare the practicality of ECFlood to existing approaches for byzantine fault-tolerant protocols, we compare it to FFlood where the number of parties each party forwards to is increased to obtain a decreasing failure probability.[10] To do so, we implemented both protocols as a probabilistic experiment among n nodes where $\frac{n}{2}$ of them behave honestly and forward any received message according to our protocol. We consider not forwarding any messages the worst-case adversarial behavior. So the remaining $\frac{n}{2}$ parties, which we consider corrupt, will not participate in forwarding any sent to them.

To ensure that the comparison does not hide any large constants, and therefore accurately depicts the performance that can be expected in practice, we compare a scenario where both protocols are to sent out a 1 megabyte message (corresponding to a Bitcoin block), and take into account the overhead of the additional nonce, erasure correcting codes, and cryptographic accumulator used in the solution for ECFlood. As previously noted, the per-party communication overhead of $\mathsf{ECFlood}(d, \zeta, \alpha)$ is upper bounded by

$$\mu \cdot d \cdot (\zeta.\mathsf{ShareSize}(l) + \log(\mu) + \kappa + \alpha.\mathsf{ProofSize}(\mu) + \alpha.\mathsf{AccSize}). \quad (10)$$

---

[8] The source code, and a description of how to run all benchmarks, can be found at https://github.com/Flooding-Research/optimal-message-dissemination-simulations.

[9] The source code is available at https://github.com/Flooding-Research/optimal-message-dissemination-prototype.

[10] For a discussion of why other classic approaches fail in the byzantine setting, see Sect. 1.3.

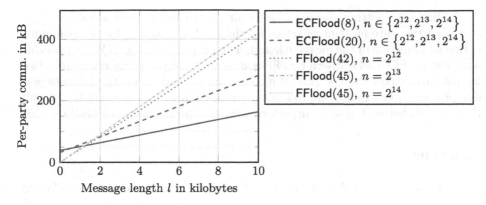

Fig. 2. Per-party communication as a function of the message length l in kilobytes with parameters chosen such that all parties receives the message for all $100\,000$ simulations. For ECFlood(8), $\mu - 25$ shares is used and the reconstruction threshold for the erasure codes is $\mu - \varrho = 16$. For ECFlood(20), $\mu = 10$ shares is used and the reconstruction threshold for the erasure codes is $\mu - \varrho = 8$.

We let ζ be instantiated with Reed-Solomon codes s.t. it is a (μ, ϱ)-ECCS, and let the accumulator α is implemented with a Merkle-tree (using 256-bit hashes). Then the per-party communication complexity in bits is upper bounded by

$$\mu \cdot d \cdot \left(\left\lceil \frac{l}{\mu - \varrho} \right\rceil + \lceil \log(\mu) \rceil + 256 \cdot \lceil \log(\mu) \rceil + 256 \right). \tag{11}$$

This calculation is included in the comparison which is presented in Fig. 1, and thereby it depicts the actual number of bits communicated in a real execution, and not only an asymptotic estimation. In the figure, two configurations of ECFlood(d) are included, where each has a neighborhood of 200 parties (which we deem to be practical for blockchains as the Bitcoin client currently allows up to 125 neighbors by default [23]). ECFlood(8) is a configuration optimized for redundancy with the number of shares $\mu = 25$ which has a slightly higher latency than FFlood, whereas ECFlood(20) is a configuration optimized for latency with the numbers of shares being $\mu = 10$. We note that the latter configuration has a latency that is as good as the latency of FFlood.[11]

If one wants to virtually eliminate errors our protocol enables a per-party communication of just ~12 MB to send out a 1 MB message, and if the latency optimized version is used each party communication will be roughly ~25 MB. FFlood which can be considered state-of-the-art, on the other hand, needs a per-party communication of $\geq$ 45 MB to eliminate delivery errors. We conclude that our protocol allows to drastically (as much as ~75%) cut the communication complexity at the cost slightly larger neighborhoods.

---

[11] For several additional simulations of how the internal parameters influences latency and the redundancy, see the extended version of this paper [30].

Additionally, setting the parameters similar to the configurations in Fig. 1 such that there are no failures across all the simulations, we plot the communication as a function of the message length using Eq. (11) in Fig. 2. We obtain that our protocol ECFlood outperforms FFlood in terms of per-party communication for messages larger than $\sim$ 2kB. With growing message sizes, the advantage of our protocol over existing approaches increases. Thus, our protocol is not only theoretically better, but also outperforms existing protocols in practical regimes.

References

1. Al-Bassam, M., Sonnino, A., Buterin, V., Khoffi, I.: Fraud and data availability proofs: detecting invalid blocks in light clients. In: Borisov, N., Diaz, C. (eds.) FC 2021. LNCS, vol. 12675, pp. 279–298. Springer, Heidelberg (2021). https://doi.org/10.1007/978-3-662-64331-0_15
2. Apostolaki, M., Zohar, A., Vanbever, L.: Hijacking bitcoin: routing attacks on cryptocurrencies. In: IEEE Symposium on Security and Privacy, pp. 375–392. IEEE (2017)
3. Barić, N., Pfitzmann, B.: Collision-free accumulators and fail-stop signature schemes without trees. In: Fumy, W. (ed.) EUROCRYPT 1997. LNCS, vol. 1233, pp. 480–494. Springer, Heidelberg (1997). https://doi.org/10.1007/3-540-69053-0_33
4. Baum, C., David, B., Dowsley, R., Nielsen, J.B., Oechsner, S.: TARDIS: a foundation of time-lock puzzles in UC. In: Canteaut, A., Standaert, F.-X. (eds.) EUROCRYPT 2021. LNCS, vol. 12698, pp. 429–459. Springer, Cham (2021). https://doi.org/10.1007/978-3-030-77883-5_15
5. Benaloh, J., de Mare, M.: One-way accumulators: a decentralized alternative to digital signatures. In: Helleseth, T. (ed.) EUROCRYPT 1993. LNCS, vol. 765, pp. 274–285. Springer, Heidelberg (1994). https://doi.org/10.1007/3-540-48285-7_24
6. Bhangale, A., Liu-Zhang, CD., Loss, J., Nayak, K.: Efficient adaptively-secure byzantine agreement for long messages. In: Agrawal, S., Lin, D. (eds.) Advances in Cryptology. ASIACRYPT 2022. LNCS, vol. 13791, pp. 504–525. Springer, Cham (2022). https://doi.org/10.1007/978-3-031-22963-3_17
7. Blum, E., Boyle, E., Cohen, R., Liu-Zhang, C.D.: Communication lower bounds for cryptographic broadcast protocols. In: Oshman, R. (ed.) 37th International Symposium on Distributed Computing (DISC 2023). Leibniz International Proceedings in Informatics (LIPIcs), vol. 281, pp. 10:1–10:19. Schloss Dagstuhl – Leibniz-Zentrum für Informatik, Dagstuhl, Germany (2023). https://doi.org/10.4230/LIPIcs.DISC.2023.10
8. Boyle, E., Goldwasser, S., Tessaro, S.: Communication locality in secure multiparty computation. In: Sahai, A. (ed.) TCC 2013. LNCS, vol. 7785, pp. 356–376. Springer, Heidelberg (2013). https://doi.org/10.1007/978-3-642-36594-2_21
9. Canetti, R.: Universally composable security. J. ACM **67**(5), 28:1-28:94 (2020)
10. Chandran, N., Chongchitmate, W., Garay, J.A., Goldwasser, S., Ostrovsky, R., Zikas, V.: The hidden graph model: communication locality and optimal resiliency with adaptive faults. In: Proceedings of the 2015 Conference on Innovations in Theoretical Computer Science, pp. 153–162 (2015)
11. Chen, J., Micali, S.: Algorand: a secure and efficient distributed ledger. Theor. Comput. Sci. **777**, 155–183 (2019)

12. Coretti, S., Kiayias, A., Moore, C., Russell, A.: The generals' scuttlebutt: Byzantine-resilient gossip protocols. In: CCS, pp. 595–608. ACM (2022)
13. Daian, P., Pass, R., Shi, E.: Snow White: robustly reconfigurable consensus and applications to provably secure proof of stake. In: Goldberg, I., Moore, T. (eds.) FC 2019. LNCS, vol. 11598, pp. 23–41. Springer, Cham (2019). https://doi.org/10.1007/978-3-030-32101-7_2
14. David, B., Gaži, P., Kiayias, A., Russell, A.: Ouroboros Praos: an adaptively-secure, semi-synchronous proof-of-stake blockchain. In: Nielsen, J.B., Rijmen, V. (eds.) EUROCRYPT 2018. LNCS, vol. 10821, pp. 66–98. Springer, Cham (2018). https://doi.org/10.1007/978-3-319-78375-8_3
15. Demers, A., et al.: Epidemic algorithms for replicated database maintenance. In: Proceedings of the Sixth Annual ACM Symposium on Principles of Distributed Computing, pp. 1–12 (1987)
16. Didier, F.: Efficient erasure decoding of Reed-Solomon codes. CoRR abs/0901.1886 (2009)
17. Doerr, B., Fouz, M.: Asymptotically optimal randomized rumor spreading. In: Aceto, L., Henzinger, M., Sgall, J. (eds.) ICALP 2011. LNCS, vol. 6756, pp. 502–513. Springer, Heidelberg (2011). https://doi.org/10.1007/978-3-642-22012-8_40
18. Fadhil, M., Owenson, G., Adda, M.: A bitcoin model for evaluation of clustering to improve propagation delay in bitcoin network. In: 2016 IEEE International Conference on Computational Science and Engineering (CSE) and IEEE International Conference on Embedded and Ubiquitous Computing (EUC) and 15th International Symposium on Distributed Computing and Applications for Business Engineering (DCABES), pp. 468–475 (2016). https://doi.org/10.1109/CSE-EUC-DCABES.2016.226
19. Feige, U., Peleg, D., Raghavan, P., Upfal, E.: Randomized broadcast in networks. Random Struct. Algorithms 1(4), 447–460 (1990)
20. Fitzi, M., Hirt, M.: Optimally efficient multi-valued byzantine agreement. In: Proceedings of the Twenty-fifth Annual ACM Symposium on Principles of Distributed Computing, pp. 163–168 (2006)
21. Ganesh, C., Patra, A.: Broadcast extensions with optimal communication and round complexity. In: Proceedings of the 2016 ACM Symposium on Principles of Distributed Computing, pp. 371–380 (2016)
22. Garay, J., Kiayias, A., Leonardos, N.: The bitcoin backbone protocol: analysis and applications. In: Oswald, E., Fischlin, M. (eds.) EUROCRYPT 2015. LNCS, vol. 9057, pp. 281–310. Springer, Heidelberg (2015). https://doi.org/10.1007/978-3-662-46803-6_10
23. Gervais, A., Ritzdorf, H., Karame, G.O., Capkun, S.: Tampering with the delivery of blocks and transactions in bitcoin. In: Proceedings of the 22nd ACM SIGSAC Conference on Computer and Communications Security, pp. 692-705. CCS 2015, Association for Computing Machinery, New York, NY, USA (2015). https://doi.org/10.1145/2810103.2813655
24. Guo, B., Lu, Y., Lu, Z., Tang, Q., Xu, J., Zhang, Z.: Speeding dumbo: pushing asynchronous BFT closer to practice. Cryptology ePrint Archive (2022)
25. Heilman, E., Kendler, A., Zohar, A., Goldberg, S.: Eclipse attacks on bitcoin's peer-to-peer network. In: USENIX Security Symposium, pp. 129–144. USENIX Association (2015)
26. Kaklamanis, I., Yang, L., Alizadeh, M.: Poster: coded broadcast for scalable leader-based BFT consensus. In: CCS, pp. 3375–3377. ACM (2022)

27. Karp, R., Schindelhauer, C., Shenker, S., Vocking, B.: Randomized rumor spreading. In: Proceedings 41st Annual Symposium on Foundations of Computer Science, pp. 565–574. IEEE (2000)
28. Kermarrec, A., Massoulié, L., Ganesh, A.J.: Probabilistic reliable dissemination in large-scale systems. IEEE Trans. Parallel Distrib. Syst. **14**(3), 248–258 (2003)
29. Liu-Zhang, C., Matt, C., Maurer, U., Rito, G., Thomsen, S.E.: Practical provably secure flooding for blockchains (2022)
30. Liu-Zhang, C.D., Matt, C., Thomsen, S.E.: Asymptotically optimal message dissemination with applications to blockchains. Cryptology ePrint Archive, Paper 2022/1723 (2022). https://eprint.iacr.org/2022/1723
31. Lu, Y., Lu, Z., Tang, Q., Wang, G.: Dumbo-MVBA: optimal multi-valued validated asynchronous byzantine agreement, revisited. In: Proceedings of the 39th Symposium on Principles of Distributed Computing, pp. 129–138 (2020)
32. Marcus, Y., Heilman, E., Goldberg, S.: Low-resource eclipse attacks on Ethereum's peer-to-peer network (2018). https://eprint.iacr.org/2018/236
33. Matt, C., Nielsen, J.B., Thomsen, S.E.: Formalizing delayed adaptive corruptions and the security of flooding networks. In: Dodis, Y., Shrimpton, T. (eds.) Advances in Cryptology - CRYPTO 2022, pp. 400–430. Springer Nature, Cham (2022). https://doi.org/10.1007/978-3-031-15979-4_14
34. Maurer, U., Pietrzak, K., Renner, R.: Indistinguishability amplification. In: Menezes, A. (ed.) CRYPTO 2007. LNCS, vol. 4622, pp. 130–149. Springer, Heidelberg (2007). https://doi.org/10.1007/978-3-540-74143-5_8
35. Merkle, R.C.: A certified digital signature. In: Brassard, G. (ed.) CRYPTO 1989. LNCS, vol. 435, pp. 218–238. Springer, New York (1990). https://doi.org/10.1007/0-387-34805-0_21
36. Nakamoto, S.: Bitcoin: a peer-to-peer electronic cash system. Decent. Bus. Rev. 21260 (2008)
37. Nayak, K., Ren, L., Shi, E., Vaidya, N.H., Xiang, Z.: Improved extension protocols for byzantine broadcast and agreement. In: DISC (2020)
38. Nazirkhanova, K., Neu, J., Tse, D.: Information dispersal with provable retrievability for rollups. arXiv preprint arXiv:2111.12323 (2021)
39. Nguyen, L.: Accumulators from bilinear pairings and applications. In: Menezes, A. (ed.) CT-RSA 2005. LNCS, vol. 3376, pp. 275–292. Springer, Heidelberg (2005). https://doi.org/10.1007/978-3-540-30574-3_19
40. Özçelik, I., Medury, S., Broaddus, J.T., Skjellum, A.: An overview of cryptographic accumulators. In: ICISSP, pp. 661–669. SCITEPRESS (2021)
41. Pass, R., Shi, E.: Fruitchains: a fair blockchain. In: PODC, pp. 315–324. ACM (2017)
42. Pass, R., Shi, E.: Thunderella: blockchains with optimistic instant confirmation. In: Nielsen, J.B., Rijmen, V. (eds.) EUROCRYPT 2018. LNCS, vol. 10821, pp. 3–33. Springer, Cham (2018). https://doi.org/10.1007/978-3-319-78375-8_1
43. Reed, I.S., Solomon, G.: Polynomial codes over certain finite fields. J. Soc. Ind. Appl. Math. **8**, 300–304 (1960)
44. Rohrer, E., Tschorsch, F.: Kadcast: a structured approach to broadcast in blockchain networks. In: AFT, pp. 199–213. ACM (2019)
45. Tran, M., Choi, I., Moon, G.J., Vu, A.V., Kang, M.S.: A stealthier partitioning attack against bitcoin peer-to-peer network. In: IEEE Symposium on Security and Privacy, pp. 894–909. IEEE (2020)
46. Tsimos, G., Loss, J., Papamanthou, C.: Gossiping for communication-efficient broadcast. In: Dodis, Y., Shrimpton, T. (eds.) Advances in Cryptology. CRYPTO

2022. LNCS, vol. 13509, pp. 439–469. Springer, Cham (2022). https://doi.org/10.1007/978-3-031-15982-4_15

47. Turpin, R., Coan, B.A.: Extending binary byzantine agreement to multivalued byzantine agreement. Inf. Process. Lett. **18**(2), 73–76 (1984)

48. Vu, H., Tewari, H.: An efficient peer-to-peer bitcoin protocol with probabilistic flooding. In: Miraz, M.H., Excell, P.S., Ware, A., Soomro, S., Ali, M. (eds.) iCETiC 2019. LNICST, vol. 285, pp. 29–45. Springer, Cham (2019). https://doi.org/10.1007/978-3-030-23943-5_3

49. Wood, G., et al.: Ethereum: a secure decentralised generalised transaction ledger. Ethereum Project Yellow Paper **151**(2014), 1–32 (2014)

50. Yang, L., Park, S.J., Alizadeh, M., Kannan, S., Tse, D.: DispersedLedger: High-Throughput byzantine consensus on variable bandwidth networks. In: 19th USENIX Symposium on Networked Systems Design and Implementation (NSDI 22), pp. 493–512 (2022)

51. Yin, M., Malkhi, D., Reiter, M.K., Golan-Gueta, G., Abraham, I.: Hotstuff: BFT consensus with linearity and responsiveness. In: PODC, pp. 347–356. ACM (2019)

Proof-of-Work-Based Consensus
in Expected-Constant Time

Juan Garay[1], Aggelos Kiayias[2], and Yu Shen[3(✉)] (iD)

[1] Texas A&M University, College Station, USA
garay@cse.tamu.edu
[2] University of Edinburgh and IOG, Edinburgh, UK
aggelos.kiayias@ed.ac.uk
[3] University of Edinburgh, Edinburgh, UK

Abstract. In the traditional consensus problem (aka Byzantine agreement), parties are required to agree on a common value despite the malicious behavior of some of them, subject to the condition that if all the honest parties start the execution with the same value, then that should be the outcome. This problem has been extensively studied by both the distributed computing and cryptographic protocols communities. With the advent of blockchains, whose main application—a distributed ledger—essentially requires that miners agree on their views, new techniques have been proposed to solve the problem, and in particular in so-called "permissionless" environments, where parties are not authenticated or have access to point-to-point channels and, further, may come and go as they please.

So far, the fastest way to achieve consensus in the proof-of-work (PoW)-based setting of Bitcoin, takes $O(\text{polylog}\kappa)$ number of rounds, where κ is the security parameter. We present the first protocol in this setting that requires **expected-constant** number of rounds. Furthermore, we show how to apply securely sequential composition in order to yield a fast distributed ledger protocol that settles *all* transactions in expected-constant time. Our result is based on a novel instantiation of "m-for-1 PoWs" on parallel chains that facilitates our basic building block, Chain-King Consensus. The techniques we use, via parallel chains, to port classical protocol design elements (such as Phase-King Consensus, super-phase sequential composition and others) into the permissionless setting may be of independent interest.

1 Introduction

Byzantine agreement (BA, aka consensus) is a classical problem introduced in [40] that asks n parties to agree on a message so that three properties are satisfied: (i) termination, (ii) agreement and (iii) validity, in a setting where any t of the parties may behave maliciously. Validity enforces the non-triviality of solutions, as it requires that if the non-faulty/"honest" parties start the execution with the same value, then that should be the output value.

© International Association for Cryptologic Research 2024
M. Joye and G. Leander (Eds.): EUROCRYPT 2024, LNCS 14653, pp. 96–125, 2024.
https://doi.org/10.1007/978-3-031-58734-4_4

BA has been classically considered in a "permissioned setting": the parties running the protocol are setup so they are able to reliably and directly communicate with each other, or have access to a public-key directory that reliably lists all their public keys. This is captured by a suitable network or *trusted setup* assumption. The "permissionless setting," on the other hand, was introduced with the development of the Bitcoin blockchain [37], and refers to an environment where parties may enter the protocol execution at will, the communication infrastructure is assumed to deliver messages without reliably identifying their origin, and the trusted setup is reduced to the existence of an unpredictable public string—the "genesis block" (which sometimes for simplicity we will just refer to as a CRS [common reference string], or "public-state setup" [25]).

BA in the permissionless setting above using proofs of work (PoW)[1] was first (formally) studied in [26]. In terms of running time, the protocols presented in [26] run in $O(\text{polylog}\kappa)$ rounds, where κ is the security parameter and address the binary input case, where the parties wish to agree on a single bit. Subsequent work improved on various aspects at the expense of stronger assumptions. For example, Andrychowicz and Dziembowski [1] offered a multi-valued BA protocol also based on PoWs (RO) but with no trusted setup, assuming in addition the existence of existentially unforgeable signatures, and with a running time proportional to the number of parties. The latter was in turn improved by Garay *et al.* [28] to $O(\text{polylog}\kappa)$ rounds, and just assuming PoWs and no trusted setup. Recently, an expected-constant-round BA protocol was introduced by Das *et al.* [13], by requiring in addition to the Andrychowicz and Dziembowski [1] assumptions the existence of *verifiable delay functions* (VDFs) [7]. Refer to Table 1 for a comparison of existing PoW-based (or "PoW-inspired") BA protocols.

Table 1. *Round complexity of PoW-based (or PoW-inspired) permissionless Byzantine agreement protocols, with their corresponding setup and cryptographic assumptions.*

Protocol	Setup and assumptions	Round complexity
[1]	RO + SIG	$O(n)$
[26]	CRS + RO	$O(\text{polylog}\kappa)$
[28]	RO	$O(\text{polylog}\kappa)$
[17]	RO + SIG + TLP	Expected $O(1)$
[13]	RO + SIG + VDF	Expected $O(1)$
This paper	CRS + RO	Expected $O(1)$

Given the above state of the art, in this work we focus on the question of solving permissionless BA in the original PoW-based blockchain model of Bitcoin with expected-constant round complexity.

---

[1] As implemented in the Bitcoin blockchain, via hash functions modeled as a *random oracle* (RO) [4].

1.1 Overview of Our Results

We present a new permissionless PoW-based multi-valued BA protocol that has expected-constant round complexity and demonstrate how it can be used to solve permissionless *state machine replication* (SMR, or, equivalently, a *distributed ledger*) [42] with fast settlement. In more detail, our results are as follows.

A new PoW-based permissionless consensus protocol. We put forth *Chain-King Consensus*—the first PoW-based permissionless consensus protocol that achieves agreement and validity in *expected-constant* time. Our construction is based on mining on parallel chains, and "emulating" a classical "phase-king" consensus protocol [6] with a randomized chain (the "chain-king") selection rule on top of the parallel chains construction. Our protocol is based on the following ideas.

First, we revisit the parallel chain technique (cf. [3,21,22]) as a method for combining multiple blockchains advancing in parallel. Our key observation is that running $m = \mathsf{polylog}(\kappa)$ parallel chains is sufficient to maintain independence via an $m \times 1^2$ PoW technique [26] (while prior work set $m = \Theta(\kappa)$ and hence at best was only able to argue "sub-independence"; see [22]). In fact, our protocol runs m independent instances of 2×1 PoWs, with the latter component being responsible for transaction processing.[3] The key property we utilize is that in a constant number of rounds, a fraction of the m parallel chains will be sufficiently advanced to offer a form of "common prefix" property (cf. [26]) with a constant probability of success.

Second, and contrary to prior work on parallel chains, we "slice" the chain progression into stages where parallel chains can cross-reference each other. In the first stage, parties converge on their views and ensure fresh randomness is introduced; in the second stage they process transactions; and in the third, they prepare for the cross referencing by the upcoming stage, after which the stages rotate indefinitely. A key property of our cross-referencing rule is the concept of a *dense chain*—a strengthening of the concepts of "chain growth" and "chain quality" [26]. Given the short length of each stage (a constant number of rounds), chain density ensures that the adversary faces difficulties to create multiple compromised chains. The key conclusion of this chain structure is *phase-oblivious agreement*, which refers to the fact that, on a large fraction of chains, the majority of input values are contributed by honest parties.

The core agreement component of our protocol follows the "phase king" approach (cf. [5,6]). The key idea of porting this protocol design technique to the permissionless setting is to map the chains in the parallel chains cluster to the roles of the different parties in the classical protocol. As a result, the king itself is one of the chains. Moreover, due to the "dilution" of adversarial power that occurs in the parallel chains setting, we can set the king deterministically to be a specific chain. This technique, which may be of independent interest, results in our "Chain-King Consensus" algorithm.

---

[2] Pronounced "m-for-1.".

[3] As in [26], the "transactions" being processed in a BA protocol are the input values being proposed by the parties.

Chain-King Consensus is one-shot, in the sense that it will provide just a single instance of agreement in the permissionless setting in expected-constant time. The natural question given such protocol is whether it is possible to apply sequential self-composition with running time remaining expected linear in the number of instances. This is a delicate task due to non-simultaneous termination (cf. [12]). We provide a round-preserving sequential composition solution that first adapts Bracha termination [8] to the permissionless setting and reduces the "termination slack" among honest parties to 1 phase. Then, we adapt the super-phase expansion technique of [12] to widen the interval between state updates from 1 phase to 4 phases. We identify a set of good properties for a sequence of phases that when they occur parties that are in different timelines can converge on the same single phase and make a unanimous decision to update their state.

A new PoW-based permissionless fast SMR protocol. Given that Chain-King Consensus is a one-shot multi-valued Byzantine agreement protocol terminating in expected constant rounds, next we show how to build a state machine replication protocol on top of its sequential composition. The resulting protocol achieves consistency and expected-constant-time liveness for *all types* of transactions (including the conflicting ones). This answers a question left open in previous work on PoW-based fast ledgers [3,22], where fast settlement of transactions was offered only for non-conflicting transactions, thus making our ledger construction the first expected-constant processing time ledger in the PoW setting. We note that fast processing of conflicting transactions can be crucial for many applications such as sequencing smart contract operations. We also describe how it is possible to "bootstrap from genesis": this essential operation permits new parties to join the protocol execution as well as facilitate third party observers who wish to connect and parse the distributed ledger in order to issue transactions or read transaction outputs.

1.2 Related Work

Round Complexity of Synchronous BA Protocols. For "classical" BA protocols with deterministic termination, it is known that $t + 1$ rounds [19] are necessary, where t denotes the upper bound on the number of corrupted parties, and matching upper bounds exist, both in the information-theoretic and cryptographic settings [16,31,35].

The linear dependency of the number of rounds on the number of corrupted parties can be circumvented by introducing randomization. Rabin [41] showed that consensus reduces to an "oblivious common coin" (OCC)—i.e., a common view of the honest parties of some public randomness. As a result, randomized protocols with linear corruption resiliency and probabilistic termination in expected-constant rounds is possible. Later on, Feldman and Micali [18] showed how to construct an OCC "from scratch" and gave the first expected-constant-time Byzantine agreement protocol, tolerating the optimal number of corrupted parties (less than 1/3 of the total number of parties), in the information-theoretic setting. In the setting where trusted private setup (i.e., a PKI) is provided, Katz and Koo [32] presented an expected-constant-round BA protocol with optimal resiliency (less than $1/2$ in the cryptographic setting).

We already mentioned that with the advent of blockchains, BA protocols that do not rely on a fixed set of participants became possible. For PoW-based BA protocols, please refer to the beginning of this section. Regarding Proof-of-Stake protocols, Algorand [11] uses *verifiable random functions* (VRFs) to self-elect parties, and agreement and validity are achieved in expected-constant time.

Regarding BA protocols based on some other assumptions, we note that in an unpublished manuscript (also mentioned in the introduction) [17], Eckey, Faust and Loss design an expected-constant-round BA protocol based on PoWs and time-lock puzzles (TLPs). Further, Das *et al.* [13] propose a BA protocol based on the much stronger primitive of *verifiable delay functions* (VDFs) that also terminate in expected-constant time.

Many PoWs from One PoW. As mentioned in the introduction, Garay, Kiayias and Leonardos [26] showed how to use a Nakamoto-style blockchain to solve BA. Achieving the optimal corruption threshold of less than $1/2$ of the participants, however, presented some challenges, which were resolved by the introduction of a technique called "2×1 PoW," which is used to compose two modes of mining, one for blocks and one for inputs. In a nutshell, in 2×1 PoW, a random oracle output is checked twice with respect to *both* its leading zeros and tailing zeros. Sufficient leading zeros implies the success of mining a block, and that's the original—i.e., Bitcoin's—approach to assess and verify whether a PoW has been produced, while sufficient *trailing* zeros imply the success of mining an input. This scheme guarantees that both mining procedures can be safely composed and the adversary is bound to its original computational power and is not able to favor one PoW operation over the other.

The 2×1 PoW primitive has found applications in many other scenarios (e.g., [39]) and its generalization—$m \times 1$ PoW—makes parallel chains possible and has been used to improve transaction throughput [3] and for accelerating transaction confirmation [22]. We note that, in the case of parallel chains existing $m \times 1$ PoW constructions cannot achieve full independence on all parallel chains. We elaborate on this in the full verision of this paper [24].

Non-simultaneous Termination and Sequential Composition. A consequence of the round complexity "acceleration" provided by randomized BA protocols is that their termination is probabilistic and not necessarily simultaneous [15]. This is problematic when this type of BA protocol is invoked by a higher-level protocol. More specifically, parties would not be able to figure out when to safely return to the higher-level protocol and start the next execution. One solution is to run randomized BA protocols for $O(\mathsf{polylog}\kappa)$ rounds where κ is the security parameter. The running time is still independent of the number of parties, and, with overwhelming probability, parties would terminate and be able to start the next execution when $O(\mathsf{polylog}\kappa)$ rounds have elapsed. A more sophisticated sequential composition approach is to employ so-called "Bracha termination" and "super-round" expansion in order to preserve an expected-constant round complexity (cf. [12]). We adapt these techniques to the permissionless setting.

Settlement Latency in State Machine Replication. Most PoW-based SMR protocols achieve liveness in a time which is a function of the security parameter, hence suffering from long transaction settlement latency. The "Ledger Combiner" approach [22] proposes a novel grade assignment function to build a virtual ledger on top of different parallel ledgers, achieving constant settlement time but only for *non-conflicting* transactions. Prism [3] also gives a PoW-based parallel chain protocol with expected-constant settlement time, but only for non-conflicting transactions. Other approaches to fast transaction settlement include Algorand's [11], which being Proof-of-Stake-based, achieves expected-constant settlement delay for all types of transactions. Finally, Momose and Ren [36] achieve expected-constant confirmation delay, assuming a PKI and VRFs.

Due to space limitations, complementary material, the detailed specification of some of the building blocks and algorithms, as well as all the proofs, are presented in the full version of this paper [24].

2   Model and Preliminaries

Our model of computation follows Canetti's formulation of "real world" notion of protocol execution [9,10] for multi-party protocols. Inputs are provided by an environment program $\mathcal{Z}$ to parties that execute the protocol Π. The adversary $\mathcal{A}$ is a single entity that takes control of corrupted parties. $\mathcal{A}$ can take control of parties on the fly (i.e., "adaptive") and is allowed to observe honest parties' actions before deciding her reaction (i.e., "rushing"). To specify the "resources" that may be available to the instances running protocol Π—for example, access to reliable point-to-point channels or a "diffuse" channel (see below)—we will follow the approach of describing them as *ideal functionalities* in the terminology of [10].

Clock, Random Oracle, Diffusion and CRS Functionalities. We divide time into discrete intervals called "rounds." Parties are always aware of the current round (i.e., synchronous processors) and this is captured by a global clock $\mathcal{G}_{\text{CLOCK}}$ [33]. By convention, the hash function H to generate PoWs is modeled as a random oracle $\mathcal{F}_{\text{RO}}$. Message dissemination is synchronous and it guarantees that all honest messages sent at the current round to be delivered to all honest parties at the beginning of the next round. This synchronous communication behavior is captured by $\mathcal{F}_{\text{DIFFUSE}}$ and the adversarial power is limited to reorder messages and let honest parties receive messages originally from $\mathcal{A}$ in two adjacent rounds by selectively choosing the receiver in the first round. Finally, we model a public-state setup by the common reference string (CRS) functionality $\mathcal{F}_{\text{CRS}}^{\mathcal{D}}$ with some distribution with sufficiently high entropy. A full specification of the above resources can be found in the full version of this paper [24].

Honest Majority. We express our honest majority condition in terms of parties' computational power, measured in particular by the number of RO queries that they are allowed per round, as opposed to by the number of parties (which are assumed to have equal computational power—cf. [26]).

Definition 1 (Honest majority). *Let h_r, t_r denote the number of honest and corrupted random oracle queries at round r respectively. For all $r \in \mathbb{N}$, it holds that $h_r > t_r$.*

To limit the adversary to make a certain number of queries to $\mathcal{F}_{\mathrm{RO}}$, we adopt the "wrapper functionality" approach (cf. [2,29,30]) $\mathcal{W}(\mathcal{F}_{\mathrm{RO}})$ that wraps the corresponding resource, thus enforcing the limited access to it.

Byzantine Agreement. We adapt the definition of the consensus problem (aka Byzantine agreement [35]) to our permissionless setting (cf. [26]). Note that here agreement implies (eventual) termination.

Definition 2 (Byzantine agreement). *A protocol Π solves Byzantine Agreement in the synchronous setting provided it satisfies the following two properties:*

- **Agreement:** *There is a round after which all honest parties return the same output if queried by the environment.*
- **Validity:** *The output returned by an honest party* P *equals the input of some party* P′ *at round 1 that is honest at the round* P*'s output is produced.*

Blockchain Notation. A block with target $T \in \mathbb{N}$ is a quadruple of the form $\mathcal{B} = \langle ctr, r, h, x \rangle$ where $ctr, r \in \mathbb{N}$, $h \in \{0,1\}$ and $x \in \{0,1\}^*$. A blockchain $\mathcal{C}$ is a (possibly empty) sequence of blocks; the rightmost block by convention is denoted by $\mathrm{head}(\mathcal{C})$ (note $\mathrm{head}(\varepsilon) = \varepsilon$). These blocks are chained in the sense that if $\mathcal{B}_{i+1} = \langle ctr, r, h, x \rangle$, then $h = H(\mathcal{B}_i)$, where $H(\cdot)$ is cryptographic hash function with output in $\{0,1\}^\kappa$. We adopt $\mathsf{TS}(\mathcal{B})$ to denote the timestamp of $\mathcal{B}$; and, slightly abusing the notations and omitting the time r, we will use $\mathcal{C}^{\lceil k}$ to denote the chain from pruning all blocks $\mathcal{B}$ such that $\mathsf{TS}(\mathcal{B}) \geq r - k$. Let $\mathbb{C} = \langle \mathcal{C}_1, \mathcal{C}_2, \ldots, \mathcal{C}_m \rangle$ denote m *parallel* chains and $\mathbb{C}_j$ the j-th chain $\mathcal{C}_j$ in $\mathbb{C}$.

Finally, we introduce some basic string notation, which will be useful when describing our multi-chain-oriented PoW mechanism. For a κ-bit string s, where κ is the security parameter, we will use s_i ($i \in [m]$) to denote the i-th bit of s, $[s]_{i \sim m}$ to denote the i-th segment after s is equally divided into m segments— i.e., $[s]_{i \sim m} = s_{[(i-1)*\kappa/m]+1}, \ldots, s_{i*\kappa/m}$. We will write $[s]^\mathsf{R}$ as the reverse of string s (i.e., by flipping all its bits), and use $[s]^\mathsf{R}_{i \sim m}$ to denote the reverse of the i-th segment.

3   Chain-King Consensus

In this section, we present our permissionless expected-constant-time Byzantine agreement protocol, which we name ChainKingConsensus[4]. We first sketch the basic protocol approach—parallel chains in Sect. 3.1 and phase-based chain-selection rule in Sect. 3.2. Then, we describe the main protocol in Sect. 3.3. We next show how to adapt the one-shot protocol execution using sequential composition in order to decide on a series of outputs in Sect. 3.4.

---

[4] Drawing from the "Phase King" approach to solve classical consensus [6].

3.1 Parallel Chains and $m \times 1$ Proofs of Work

We introduce a new approach to achieve full independence of mining on parallel chains while preserving the original simple structure. At a high level, our scheme emulates an ideal setting of m parallel oracles while bounding the security loss that such parallel mining incurs. More specifically, the protocol will run $m = \Theta(\mathsf{polylog}\kappa)$ parallel chains; note that the number of bits allocated on each chain will still be super-logarithmic in the security parameter (i.e., $\kappa/\Theta(\mathsf{polylog}\kappa) = \Omega(\mathsf{polylog}\kappa)$), and hence the protocol will allow an arbitrary number of participants. Later we will show that (i) poly-logarithmically many parallel chains suffice to achieve the desired convergence; and (ii) poly-logarithmically many bits (those will be the bits available to each of the parallel random oracle invocations) will suffice to eliminate bad events with respect to the random oracle.

Our Parallel Chain Structure. We will use $m = \Theta(\log^2 \kappa)$ parallel chains as the basic building block for ChainKingConsensus. Importantly, on each chain we will employ the 2×1 PoW technique [26] to bind the mining process of the chain with input messages (which will be used to reach consensus; details in Sect. 3.3). At a high level, this can be viewed as running m ideal parallel repetitions of a 2×1 PoW blockchain.

We will call the blocks that form the blockchains a *chain-block* (or block for short) and denote it by $\mathcal{B}$, and the application data field, which will contain consensus-related values, we will call an *input-block*, and denote it by IB. Since the protocol will run an m chain production procedure and m input-block production procedure, we will make a one-to-one correspondence between the chain-blocks and input-blocks. More precisely, the input-block produced by the i-th segment of the RO output will only be valid on the i-th parallel chain. See Fig. 1 for an illustration of the RO output and how successes on the bounded mining procedures are achieved.

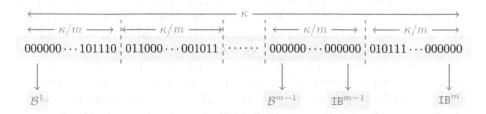

Fig. 1. *The mining process on our parallel chain. We assume that the target value is appropriately set so that at least 6 leading zeroes imply a success of the chain's block mining and at least 6 tailing zeroes blocks implies a success of the input mining. The blocks' superscript denotes on which chain they will be valid.*

We now provide details on the blocks' structure. Since the mining procedure of chain-blocks and input-blocks are bound together, they share the same block header $\langle ctr, r, h, st, h', val \rangle$, which is a concatenation of random nonce

$ctr \in \mathbb{N}$, timestamp $r \in \mathbb{N}$, previous hash reference $h \in \{0,1\}^\kappa$, block state $st \in \{0,1\}^*$ (Merkle root of content), input freshness $h' \in \{0,1\}^\kappa$, and input message $val \in \{0,1\}^*$. Note that the previous hash h is a string of κ bits, consisting of m segments of the previous block hash of length κ/m. Block state st is a concatenation of m block states; this is by convention the Merkle tree root of block content whose details we will omit for now (later on we will use Blockify to denote the procedure of generating block states). Input freshness h' is a string of κ bits and can be extracted from the (local) chain by procedure ExtractInputFreshness. We defer the details of this algorithm to Sect. 3.2 and use it in a black-box way here. The input value val is the message that is of concern to the consensus protocol. For instance, in the case of binary consensus, $val \in \{0,1\}$ and in multi-valued consensus val is a value picked from a larger input domain. Looking ahead, we note that when performing "slack" reduction and sequential composition of protocol instances, val may convey additional information (Sect. 3.4). Moreover, we remark that for all parallel chains, parties will try to mine the input-block that contains the *same* input message, hence, unlike h, st and h', in this field all values only need to appear once.

We note that as multiple mining procedures are bound together, for a valid block with respect to a particular chain, those header bits associated with other procedures become "dummy" and will only be useful when validating whether the block corresponds to a successful PoW. We now provide details about such dummy information. Regarding a valid chain-block on the i-th chain, only the nonce ctr, timestamp r, i-th segment of previous hash reference $[h]_{i \sim m}$ and i-th segment of block state $[st]_{i \sim m}$ are useful information. All other bits in h and st, along with input freshness reference h' and input message val are dummy information and they are merely used in the PoW validation[5] On a similar vein, for input-blocks that are valid on the i-th chain, only the nonce ctr, timestamp r, input message val and i-th segment of fresh randomness $[h']_{i \sim m}$ are useful information; all other bits in h', previous hash reference h and block content root st are dummy information.

We are now ready to describe the mining procedure. Given a parallel chain $\mathbb{C}$, block state st and input val, first, the protocol extracts the previous hash reference by concatenating the i-th segment of block hash computed from the tip of the i-th chain (recall that each segment is a (κ/m)-bit string). (When the chain is empty it refers to the corresponding segment in the CRS.) Next, after calling ExtractInputFreshness on $\mathbb{C}$ to obtain the input randomness, the protocol queries the random oracle and gets output u. Then, it divides u into m segments of equal length and iterates over those segments. If the original i-th segment is less than T, the protocol successfully mines a new chain-block on the i-th chain and appends it to $\mathbb{C}$. If the reverse of i-th segment is less than T, the protocol succeeds in mining an input-block and stores it locally (and will be diffused in the future). See [24] for a full description of the mining procedure.

---

[5] We note that later on (Sect. 3.2), after we introduce *phase-based* parallel chains, initial blocks in each phase will have to provide a good fresh randomness h' in order to pass the cross-chain validation check.

Basic Properties of our Parallel Chain Structure. As a warm-up, we present a preliminary analysis of our parallel chain structure. The goal is to show that, when appropriately parameterized, a constant fraction of the parallel chains will have "good" properties.

Our main analytical approach follows that in [23, 27], where the focus is on whether an execution on a *single* chain is *typical*—i.e., whether random variables related to the execution on this single chain stays close to their expected values and bad events with respect to the RO never happen. In [23] it is proved that any execution of the protocol for a number of rounds at least polylogarithmic in the security parameter, is *typical* with overwhelming probability.

Here we apply the above technique to a *constant* number of rounds and adapt it to our setting where the mining procedure of chain-blocks and input-blocks are bound together. Importantly, we are interested in the random variables expressing the total number of rounds that *at least* one honest chain-block (resp., input-block) is produced, the total number of rounds that *exactly* one honest chain-block is produced, and the total number of adversarial successes on chain-blocks (resp., input-blocks). For the sake of conciseness, here we provide an informal description of typical executions; refer to [24] for more details.

Definition 3 (Typical execution, informal). *An execution is* typical *if for any set of at least k consecutive rounds, bad events (collisions) on the RO never happen, and the following quantities stay close to their expected values:*

 (i) the number of rounds where at least *one honest chain-block (resp., input-block) is produced;*
 (ii) the number of rounds where exactly *one honest chain-block is produced;*
 (iii) the number of adversarial chain-blocks (resp., input-blocks).

Note that since in our case k is a constant, the probability that in a k-round window the execution is typical is constant due to Chernoff bounds. Hence, the probability that an execution running for $L = \mathsf{poly}(\kappa)$ rounds is typical will be negligible. Nonetheless, let us consider a constant number $\rho \in \mathbb{N}^+$ of rounds. When the protocol is appropriately parameterized, the execution running for ρ steps will be typical with constant probability. The intuition here is that, the number of windows of at least k rounds within the period of ρ rounds is $\Theta(\rho^2)$. For any constant $\beta < 1$, when the probability that a k-round time window is typical is α, then by choosing $\rho \leq \sqrt{\ln \beta / \ln \alpha}$ we get the desired convergence probability. Moreover, for the same β, ρ can be chosen as an arbitrary multiple of k.

Given the full independence of the m mining processes, we show that when the number of m parallel chains is sufficiently large, the success probability of a single execution being typical translates to the *fraction* of typical executions among the m parallel executions, yielding the following:

Theorem 1. *For any $\beta < 1$, running $m = \Theta(\log^2 \kappa)$ parallel chains as described above for a constant number ρ of rounds, results in at least a β fraction of them being typical with overwhelming probability in κ.*

3.2   From Parallel Chains to Phase Oblivious Agreement

Given that running parallel chains from the CRS enjoy good properties only when the lifetime of the execution is bounded by a constant (Theorem 1), we now show how to combine the parallel chain structure with a novel phase-based cross-chain reference scheme in order to provide fresh randomness and extend the protocol running time to any polynomial in terms of the security parameter. This gives us novel chain validation and selection rules. Moreover, we show that in each phase, the approach achieves what we call *phase oblivious agreement*, which serves as an essential building block in our ChainKingConsensus protocol.

In this section, we assume static participation where parties are always online and their number is fixed yet unknown to any protocol participant. Later on (Sect. 4.2), we elaborate on how to let new joining parties synchronize with other participants.

Protocol Phases. We divide the protocol execution time into sequential, non-overlapping phases of length ρ rounds. Note that ρ is a constant and at round i parties are in the $\lceil i/\rho \rceil$-th phase (the phase index starts at 1). As we assume synchronous processors, parties are always aware of the current round and phase numbers (they maintain local variables r and phase to store this information).

In contrast to the "conventional" longest-chain consensus rule where parties keep extending chains starting from the genesis block, in our protocol in each phase parties will build parallel chains separately, which we will denote $\mathbb{C}^{(i)}$, and the j-th chain in the i-th phase by $\mathbb{C}_j^{(i)}$. Let $\mathbb{C}$ now denote the sequence of parallel chains in each phase—i.e., $\mathbb{C} = \mathbb{C}^{(1)}, \mathbb{C}^{(2)}, \dots, \mathbb{C}^{(i)}$. In the first phase, $\mathbb{C}^{(1)}$ points to the CRS, thus the adversary starts the computation simultaneously with the honest parties. Unfortunately, the CRS is only available at the onset of the execution, and hence, naïvely, there is no method to prevent the adversary from mining into the future—e.g., when it is in phase i, he can mine blocks for phase $i+1$. If pre-mining is possible for an unbounded time, then no security guarantees can be achieved in the $(i + 1)$-th phase even if typical execution holds.

One conventional method to solve the pre-mining problem in blockchains (cf. [39]) consists of referring to a stable block with randomness that is unpredictable to the adversary (e.g., an honest block). Unfortunately, since phases here only last for a constant number of rounds, thus far there is no approach that would enable parties to explicitly agree on common unpredictable randomness in constant time (as this would directly imply full agreement on a non-trivial fact, which is our goal). Without a full agreement on common randomness, the adversary can split the honest computational power by building a chain with randomness that is acceptable by, say, half of the honest parties but that will be rejected by the rest. In such way the adversary can then split the honest computational power and thus completely break the security of the protocol.

To overcome the failure of the conventional common fresh randomness approach, we propose a new scheme called "cross-chain reference" to secure the execution on parallel chains in the second and subsequent phases. In short, cross-chain reference asks for all chains in the i-th phase to point to a large fraction of the chains in the $(i-1)$-th phase that are "dense," a property which we will elaborate on soon.

As a preparation for securing phase-based parallel chains, we first introduce the structure of a phase (see Fig. 2). A phase, consisting of ρ rounds, is further divided into three non-overlapping *stages*. A block is assigned to a specific stage based on its timestamp. The first stage, *view convergence*, consists of the first ρ_{view} rounds in a phase. It guarantees that at the end of this stage, on sufficiently many parallel chains, honest parties agree on a common prefix *obliviously* and they input some *recent* randomness so that the adversary cannot pre-compute too many blocks for the next stage. Then, the second stage, *output generation*, which consists of ρ_{output} rounds after the view convergence stage, is used to decide the output of this phase. Only input blocks that are included by chain-blocks in this stage will be considered in the decision making procedure at the end of this phase (details in Sect. 3.3). The length ρ_{output} is chosen sufficiently large so that the honest input blocks account for the majority on sufficiently many parallel chains. Finally, the last stage, *reference convergence*, consists of the last ρ_{ref} rounds. This last stage is used to secure the blocks that will be pointed by the cross-chain reference. Note that ρ_{ref} is also the upper bound on adversarial pre-mining—i.e., the adversary cannot start to mine blocks in the next phase ρ_{ref} rounds earlier than the honest parties.

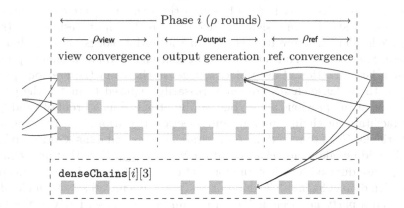

Fig. 2. *An illustration of a party* P*'s local parallel chains* $\mathbb{C}_{\mathsf{local}}$ *and dense chains* denseChains. *In order for initial blocks in phase* $i+1$ *to be valid, they should point to at least 2 dense chains in phase* i. *In this toy example, all blocks point to the first dense chain in* $\mathbb{C}_{\mathsf{local}}$ *and the third dense chain in* denseChains. *Note that the second chain is not dense.*

Dense Chains. Next, we introduce a new concept called *dense chains* which asks for the density of a chain (in terms of the number of blocks with timestamps in a given time period) and can also be used as a proof of "chain growth" (cf. [23]).

J. Garay et al.

Definition 4 (Dense chains). *A chain $\mathcal{C}$ is a (τ, s, u, v)-dense chain if for any set $S = \{p, \ldots, q\}$ of consecutive rounds such that $u \leq p < q \leq v$ and $|S| > s$, there are at least $\tau \cdot |S|$ blocks in $\mathcal{C}$ with timestamp in S. A chain $\mathcal{C}$ is a dense chain on phase i if it is a $(\tau, \rho_{\mathsf{ref}}, (i-1)\rho + \rho_{\mathsf{view}}, i \cdot \rho)$-dense chain—i.e., the chain is dense in the last two stages of the i-th phase.*

We choose the density parameter τ in such a way that when typical execution property holds on a single chain, the following two properties are guaranteed: (i) even if the adversary completely stops producing PoWs, the honest parties by themselves can produce a dense chain; and (ii) in the i-th phase, the adversary cannot come up with a dense chain before the reference convergence stage.

With foresight, the purpose of dense chains is to secure the execution of future phases, by asking parties to provide sufficiently many dense chains as a proof of having invested enough computational power before the current phase.

Cross-Chain References. Next, we elaborate on the cross-chain reference approach which we use to "link" neighboring phases (this provides unpredictability so that the adversary can only pre-mine for a bounded amount of time). At a high level, a cross-chain reference on an initial block in the j-th chain and i-th phase is a κ-bit string consisting of m pointers to m sufficiently deep blocks on chains in the $(i-1)$-th phase. These deep blocks are picked as the last blocks in the output generation stage, one on each chain. Their hashes (that is, the j-th segment of a block hash, for a block on the j-th chain) are concatenated to form the κ-bit string. We assign this reference to the input freshness h' (recall our block header structure in Sect. 3.1) in the initial blocks on each chain's i-th phase. For a cross-chain reference to be considered valid, it should point to at least a large fraction of deep blocks in *dense* chains in the previous phase[6]. However, these dense chains are not necessarily required to match the parties' own chains of the previous phase, but can be attached as a proof of validity.

To facilitate the chain validation and selection algorithm, a party P maintains local variables $\mathbb{C}_{\mathsf{local}}$ to record her own parallel chains and `denseChains` to bookkeep all valid (single) dense chains that are not in $\mathbb{C}_{\mathsf{local}}$. Note that `denseChains` and $\mathbb{C}_{\mathsf{local}}$ are diffused together. In more detail, `denseChains` is a two dimension vector with `denseChains`$[i][j]$ containing a (possibly empty) set of (single) dense chains that a party has seen as the j-th chain in i-th phase. Party P also maintains a local variable `chainBuffer` which contains all pairs of $\langle \mathbb{C}, \mathsf{denseChains} \rangle$ that P receives at the beginning of the round. Refer to Fig. 2 for an illustration of our phase-based parallel chain.

We now formalize the ExtractInputFreshness procedure (see [24]) which parties use to extract cross-chain reference and fresh randomness for input-blocks. Specifically, when this algorithm is called in the view convergence stage of the

---

[6] We cannot require the cross-chain reference to point to all the dense chains in previous phase for two reasons: (i) when typical execution fails it can be the case that neither the honest parties nor the adversary produce a dense chain; and (ii) the adversary can split parties by delivering a private adversarial dense chain to only some of them.

i-th phase ($i > 1$), it returns a κ-bit string which is a concatenation of hashes of the blocks with largest block height whose timestamp is less than $(i-1)\rho - \rho_{\text{ref}}$ on each chain. When ExtractInputFreshness is called in the output generation stage, it returns the concatenation of m hashes of the blocks that are k-rounds before the end of the view convergence stage in this phase (we will show later that k is the parameter for common prefix on typical chains). When this algorithm is called at any other time, it returns an all-zero string.

Parallel-Chain Validation Algorithm. Recall that in our protocol, we use a $m \times 1$ PoW scheme to mine m parallel chains, and, on each chain, we use 2×1 PoW to bind the mining process of chain-blocks $\mathcal{B}$ and input-blocks IB together; moreover, we divide chains into phases and introduce cross-chain reference to link neighbouring phases. Our validation rule will consider the validity of all blocks, chains (in a single phase) and the cross-chain references. Specifically, a parallel chain $\mathbb{C}$ (with its associated denseChains) will be considered valid if the following holds (refer to [24] for a full description):

– *Valid single chains.* For any $\mathcal{C} = \mathcal{B}_1, \mathcal{B}_2, \ldots, \mathcal{B}_n$ (either a $\mathbb{C}_j^{(i)}$ or in denseChains$[i][j]$), $\mathcal{C}$ should be a valid single chain. More specifically, $\mathcal{C}$ is a valid chain if (i) all blocks are the result of successful PoWs; (ii) all blocks' state st match their corresponding block content; and (iii) for all $i > 1$, $\mathcal{B}_i$ refers to the hash of $\mathcal{B}_{i-1}$. Additionally, for chains in the first phase, $\mathcal{B}_1$ should point to the CRS.
– *Valid input blocks.* For any input block IB included in $\mathcal{C}$ in the i-th phase, IB should pass the following check: (i) it reports a unique hash among all input-blocks; (ii) the timestamp of IB falls in the output generation stage; (iii) IB is a successful PoW and contains a valid input message val; and (iv) IB points to the last block on $\mathcal{C}$ with timestamp less than $(i-1)\rho + \rho_{\text{view}} - k$ (i.e., good fresh randomness).
– *Valid cross-chain reference.* In the i-th phase ($i > 1$), all initial blocks of chains in $\mathbb{C}^{(i)}$ and denseChains$[i]$ report good cross-chain reference. In order for a cross-chain reference to be good, at least a $\beta > 3/4$ fraction of hashes should match the last blocks in the output generation stage on dense chains in the $(i-1)$-th phase, either in $\mathbb{C}$ or denseChains. Note that their positions should also match—i.e., the j-th segment of reference should match a deep block in $\mathbb{C}_j^{(i-1)}$ or denseChains$[i-1][j]$.

We remark that our chain validation rule is different from that used in both the single chain validation as well as in all previous parallel-chain constructions due to its novel cross-chain reference mechanism. Specifically, starting in the second, the initial block on a single chain $\mathcal{C}$ does not directly point to the last block in the previous phase—i.e. its previous state reference h becomes dummy. As long as $\mathcal{C}$ provides a valid cross-chain reference and forms a valid single chain, $\mathcal{C}$ will be considered as valid. We note that since previous state references (the hash pointer) between neighboring phases are not continuous, the adversary is allowed to keep extending the head of the chains in the previous phase by keeping mining and inserting blocks. Moreover, as our protocol does not ask for cross-references to all previous chains, it is also possible that honest parties never hold exactly the same parallel chain.

We now provide some more intuition on these two new properties. Regarding the adversarial extension of chains from previous phases, parties will check-point their chains phase-by-phase (see the chain selection rule below), hence this does not undermine the security of online parties. Regarding the possible disagreement on a certain fraction of the parallel chains, we note that this is unavoidable. Otherwise, if parties were aware that they would achieve a full agreement on a specific phase, this would directly imply that they reach consensus (and with simultaneous termination!). Our goal is to let honest parties share parallel chains such that in each phase, they *obliviously* agree on the prefix of a large fraction of the chains.

Parallel-Chain Selection Algorithm. We now introduce the chain selection algorithm. In a nutshell, this algorithm does not update local parallel chains as a whole; rather, it updates each single chain in the current phase—i.e., after phase i has passed, $\mathbb{C}_{\text{local}}$ is check-pointed up to phase i and all chains in the previous phases will never be changed. When parties are in the first phase, they use the longest chain rule to select each single chain separately. When parties are in the i-th phase ($i > 1$), a party P processes the chains stored in `chainBuffer` as follows:

- *Filter invalid chains.* For any $\mathbb{C} \in$ `chainBuffer`, if $\mathbb{C}$ is not a valid chain, P rejects $\mathbb{C}$ immediately and removes it (as well as its associated dense chains) from `chainBuffer`.
- *Update* `denseChains` . For all $i' < i$ and $j \in [m]$, P updates `denseChains`$[i'][j]$ as follows. If there is a valid dense chain $\mathcal{C}$ as the j-th chain in phase i' (either in $\mathbb{C}$ or `denseChains`$[i'][j]$ from another party) that forks from all the chains in `denseChains`$[i' - 1][j]$ for more than ρ_{ref} rounds, P adds $\mathcal{C}$ to `denseChains`$[i' - 1][j]$ (i.e., it bookkeeps new dense chains with new cross-chain reference pointer blocks).
- *Adopt longer chains.* P uses the longest chain rule to select chains in the current phase. For any incoming chain $\mathbb{C}$, if $\text{len}(\mathbb{C}_j^{(i)}) > \text{len}(\mathcal{C})$ where $\mathcal{C}$ is the j-th chain in $\mathbb{C}_{\text{local}}^{(i)}$, then P updates $\mathcal{C}$ to $\mathbb{C}_j^{(i)}$.

Refer to [24] for a detailed description of the above rules.

Phase Oblivious Agreement. Notice that in each phase, the probability that for a large fraction of chains their execution is typical (Definition 3) is over-whelming. Further, our phase-based parallel-chain structure and density-based chain validation and selection rules guarantee that the adversary can only pre-mine for a bounded amount of time, hence "good" properties—i.e., agreement and chain quality (high enough fraction of honest blocks) on the input-blocks—hold on a large fraction of the chains in every phase. Except that as parties are not able to discern on which chains they have agreement, agreement is achieved *obliviously*, yielding the following:

Theorem 2 (Phase oblivious agreement). *There exist protocol parameterizations such that the following properties hold. Let $\beta \in (3/4, 1)$ and consider a phase i. Let $\mathbb{C}, \mathbb{C}'$ denote the parallel chains held by two honest parties P, P' at rounds r, r' after phase i (i.e., $\min\{r, r'\} > i\rho$), respectively. Then there exists a subset $S \subseteq \{1, 2, \ldots, m\}$ of size larger than $\beta \cdot m$ such that for all $j \in S$, the following two properties hold on chains $\mathcal{C} = \mathbb{C}_j^{(i)}$ and $\mathcal{C}' = \mathbb{C}_j'^{(i)}$.*

- **Agreement:** $\mathcal{C}^{\lceil \rho_{ref}} = \mathcal{C}'^{\lceil \rho_{ref}}$.
- **Honest input-block majority:** *For all input-blocks included in the output generation stage of $\mathcal{C}$ and $\mathcal{C}'$, more than half of them are produced by honest parties.*

3.3   From Phase Oblivious Agreement to Chain-King Consensus

In this section we explain how our chain-king consensus protocol can be derived from phase-based parallel chains. We present ChainKingConsensus as a multi-valued consensus protocol with input domain $V, |V| \geq 2$.[7] For simplicity we assume inputs are scalars, but the formulation can be easily adapted to any other type of input.

At a high-level chain-king consensus can be viewed as following the "phase king" approach (cf. [5,6]) with randomized king selection on top of phase-based parallel chains. The execution is based on the iteration of 3 phases. Parties will only terminate at the end of each iteration (i.e., the phase with index a multiple of 3). Two thresholds, more than one half of the number of chains ($> m/2$) and more than three-quarters ($> 3m/4$), are of interest. Importantly, a distinguished chain—the *first* chain $\mathbb{C}_1$—is identified as the *king chain*. This king chain is hard-coded in the protocol and will never change during the whole execution.

Similarly to all existing consensus protocols with probabilistic termination, in ChainKingConsensus parties might terminate at different phases. We measure the quality of non-simultaneous termination by measuring the maximum number of phases that two honest parties can terminate apart from each other:

Definition 5 (c-slack termination). *A protocol Π satisfies c-slack termination if any pair of honest parties P, P' are guaranteed to terminate Π within c phases of each other.*

Input Messages and Internal Variables. So far we have not yet specified the input messages in each phase. In (multi-valued) ChainKingConsensus, at the onset of the protocol execution, party P is activated with an input $v \in V$. P starts to mine input messages (i.e., by setting a variable val in the RO query—see Sect. 3.1) which is their current suggestion for the protocol output; P will terminate based on her local states which we will detail soon.

---

[7] We remark that our protocol is a multi-valued consensus protocol directly by construction, rather than following the common approach of first designing a binary consensus protocol and then applying the Turpin-Coan pre-processing step [43].

In addition to variable val $\in V$, P locally manages two Boolean variables lock and decide which are both initialized to false, and a three-valued variable exit $\in \{\infty, 1, 0\}$ which is initialized to ∞. In more detail:

- Variable val reflects P's suggestion on the output, and can be modified if in certain phases P receives sufficiently many different input values.
- Value lock indicates whether P will "listen" to the king-chain (see Algorithm 1 below for details) in the last phase of an iteration. It is set to true if parties are confident that all honest parties will set their val to the same value. If lock remains false at the end of an iteration, P will update her val based on her local view of the king-chain. If P has not decided at the end of an interation and lock is set to true, it is reset to false for the next iteration.
- Variable decide is used to record whether P decides on her local value val. It is set to true only when P is confident that all honest parties are going to agree on the value that she holds, and the adversary is limited to only influencing in which phase parties will terminate. When decide is set to true, val is fixed and will never change in the future (except with neglibible probability). Further, it is set to true only in the first and second phase of an iteration and is checked at the last phase to see if exit needs to be updated.
- Variable exit indicates whether P should stop querying the RO and producing blocks. When exit $= \infty$, P has not yet reached the end of the iteration when she decides, hence P keeps updating the other variables. When exit $= 1$, P have set decide to true and hence is ready to output val. However, P is not aware if other honest parties have decided, hence P keeps producing blocks with val. This will last for one iteration and then exit is set to 0. When exit $= 0$, P stops making RO queries and stops the execution of (this instance of the) protocol.

We highlight one significant difference between Chain-King Consensus and classical BA protocols. In the classical setting, parties terminate the protocol once they decide on an output. For protocols with probabilistic termination, some honest parties might terminate a few rounds after other honest parties (cf. [15]). Parties who have terminated continue to send the same message to all honest parties (cf. [18,32]), and the parties that are behind can stick to the previous message if they do not receive any new message from those parties that have already terminated. As it turns out, this strategy essentially relies on the set of participating parties being known, which does not apply the permissionless setting where parties can neither authenticate with each other nor know the source of a message. Hence, in order to let parties that are behind safely terminate, we explicitly distinguish "decide," which means parties output their local variable val, and "exit," which means parties stop (or will stop) the PoW mining process and exit the protocol. We provide more details on "mining for one more iteration" after we introduce the state update algorithm.

Phase Output Extraction. The decision made at the end of each phase is based on the input messages collected in that phase. Since we have m parallel chains, parties will extract a vector of size m. For the i-th element in the vector, it is extracted from the *median*[8] of input values that appear in the input-blocks, collected in the output generation stage (i.e., blocks with timestamps in $(i\rho - (\rho_{\mathsf{output}} + \rho_{\mathsf{ref}}), i\rho - \rho_{\mathsf{ref}}]$ in i-th phase). Note that since parties might disagree on some bounded fraction of the chains, different honest parties will extract different phase output vectors. Nevertheless, thanks to Theorem 2, two honest output vectors will share a large fraction of common elements obliviously. (See [24] for the full description of this process.)

State Update Algorithm. At the end of each phase (i.e., when local clocks reach round $i \cdot \rho$), parties run Algorithm 1 to decide whether to update their local variables or not. It generally follows the randomized phase-king algorithm approach [20], but introduces a novel king selection rule and an extra termination iteration.

Algorithm 1 StateUpdate

1: **if** $r \mod \rho \neq 0$ **then return**   ◁ Not the end of a phase
2: **if** exit $= 1$ **then**
3:     **if** phase $\mod 3 = 0$ **then** exit $\leftarrow 0$ ◁ End of "extra mining iteration"
4:     **return**
5: **end if**
6: $\vec{V} \leftarrow \mathsf{ExtractPhaseVector}(\mathbb{C}_{\mathsf{local}}, r, \mathsf{phase})$
7: Let *val* denote the most frequent element in V and c its frequency
8: **if** phase $\mod 3 = 1$ **then**   ◁ Step 1
9:     **if** $c > m/2$ **then** val $\leftarrow$ *val*
10:    **if** $c > 3m/4$ **then** decide $\leftarrow$ true, lock $\leftarrow$ true
11: **else if** phase $\mod 3 = 2$ **then**   ◁ Step 2
12:    **if** $c > m/2$ **then** val $\leftarrow$ *val*
13:    **if** $c > 3m/4$ **then** lock $\leftarrow$ true
14: **else**   ◁ Step 3
15:    **if** lock $=$ false **then** val $\leftarrow \vec{V}_1$ ◁ Refer to the king chain
16:    **if** decide $=$ true **then** exit $\leftarrow 1$
      ▷ Reset lock for the next iteration
17:    **if** decide $=$ false **and** lock $=$ true **then** lock $\leftarrow$ false
18: **end if**

We now provide a high-level overview and some intuition about the state update algorithm. In the first phase of an iteration, given phase output vector $\vec{V}$, parties first check if more than $m/2$ chains report the same value *val*. If this is the case, they set their val to *val*. Since more than $m/2$ accounts for

---

[8] We note that selecting the median as output is not the only available solution to extract the phase's output. For strong consensus we can extract the plurality (see Remark 1), and for state machine replication we introduce a more refined way to extract output from the king chain (details in Sect. 4).

the majority of the chains, if there exists such value val then it will be unique. Further, if in their local view, more than $3m/4$ of the chains report val, they set both decide and lock to true and they will decide at the end of iteration. The second phase is almost a repetition of the first one except that in this phase parties will not set decide to true.

If during the first two phases in an iteration, a party P has never seen more than $3m/4$ of the chains report the same value, P is still "confused" and its internal variable lock remains false at the end of the last phase. Under such circumstance, P will refer to the king chain and adopt the median value among the input-messages included—i.e., the first element in phase vector $\vec{V}$. Note that this is different from previous phase-king style constructions, where with deterministic termination, king rotates among $t+1$ fixed parties (where at least one of them is honest) [5,6], while with probabilistic termination, parties first broadcast their val and then run an oblivious leader election algorithm to try to agree on an honest king with constant probability [32]. In contrast, in our protocol the chain-king is *always* the first chain. Moreover, even though the adversary knows that the first chain is the king, he will not be able to focus on it due to the basic nature of parallel chains. As a result, given that the adversary's power is "diluted," parties agree obliviously with constant probability on the king-chain's value. When the honest parties get lucky, they will start the beginning of the next iteration with a unanimous value in val, which guarantees decision; if they do not, they will start the next iteration with a different val and they can hope for getting lucky with the next king chain.

Next, we elaborate on the difference between decide and exit as well as their interaction. As we mentioned earlier, even if parties have decided, they should still participate in the protocol by keeping making RO queries and diffusing blocks with their output value. This is because due to non-simultaneous termination, if parties decide in the current iteration stop from participating in the protocol, then parties that are going to decide in the next iteration would not be able to get enough information since the honest majority condition might be broken. In the classical setting, this is easily circumvented by honest parties who do not receive a message from other parties, reusing their previous message as the current input (cf. [18,32]). However, in a PoW setting the above strategy is not feasible. Therefore we distinguish the termination of deciding output and mining blocks by using two different variables decide and exit. Specifically, for any party that decides the output in i-th phase, it should first keep mining for an extra iteration (by setting exit to 1 and no longer update val, lock and decide), and then terminate and set exit to 0 at the $(i+3)$-th phase (recall that an iteration consists of 3 phases).[9] After parties set exit to 0, they output val and exit the protocol.

The ChainKingConsensus protocol. Having presented the various protocol components, we are now ready to put things together and state what the protocol achieves. During the protocol execution, parties keep updating their local

---

[9] As we show later on in Sect. 3.4, this termination gap can be reduced to 1 phase by emulating so-called "Bracha termination.".

parallel chains and mining their output suggestion. At the end of each phase, they use StateUpdate to update their consensus-related internal variables. Upon setting their exit variable to 0, parties terminate the protocol and output val. The full specification of the protocol is presented in [24].

ChainKingConsensus achieves agreement and validity in an expected-constant number of rounds, and since parties terminate at the end of neighboring phases, it satisfies 3-slack termination (cf. Definition 5). Further, when parties start the protocol with a unanimous input configuration, then they decide at the end of the third phase (except with negligible probability). If they do not start with an unanimous input, then the expected time for decision is $3/(3/4) + 3 = 7$ phases.

Theorem 3. *There exist protocol parameterizations such that* ChainKingConsensus *satisfies agreement, validity and 3-slack termination with expected-constant round complexity.*

Remark 1. ChainKingConsensus *also achieves "strong validity" (i.e., that the output equals the input of at least one honest party) if (i) we change the phase output extraction from selecting the median of input-messages to the input-message with the highest plurality; and (ii) the adversarial computational power is bounded by $t < (1 - \delta)n/(|V| - 1)$. (This matches the lower bound in [20].)*

Remark 2. We note that PoW-based *Crusader Agreement* [14] (where parties either output the same value v or $\bot$, and if they start unanimously they output that value) can be achieved in constant time. Specifically, parties run ChainKingConsensus and terminate at the end of first phase. If a party P sets her decide variable to true, P outputs val; otherwise she outputs $\bot$.

3.4 Fast Sequential Composition

The chain-king consensus protocol presented in Sect. 3.3 is *one-shot*—i.e., parties start at the same time and terminate at (possibly) different phases. This non-simultaneous termination turns out to be problematic when ChainKingConsensus is invoked by a high-level protocol, such as MPC or SMR, and where parties need to decide on a series of outputs repeatedly. Given the non-simultaneous termination situation, after the first invocation, parties would not be able to return to the calling high-level protocol synchronously, and in subsequent invocations, ChainKingConsensus does not by itself provide any security guarantees if parties start at different phases[10]. Ideally, when the same protocol is invoked multiple times, the round complexity should be preserved—i.e., for ℓ sequential invocations, the total running time should be expected $O(\ell)$ rounds.

In the classical distributed computing and cryptographic protocols literature, this is studied as the sequential composition of BA protocols, with positive results: By using so-called "Bracha termination" [8] and super-round expansion

---

[10] We note that ChainKingConsensus can tolerate adversarial pre-mining for up to $\rho_{ref} \ll \rho$ rounds, details see analysis in [24].

[12], a BA protocol with probabilistic termination can asymptotically preserve the same round complexity while continuously deciding on a series of outputs.

In this section we show how to achieve fast sequential composition of multiple instances of ChainKingConsensus by first emulating the Bracha termination strategy on parallel chains, thus enabling parties to terminate in two neighboring phases; then, for later invocations, we introduce a novel "super-phase expansion" protocol that guarantees security under non-simultaneous start while preserving the expected-constant round complexity. Note that, our "super-phase expansion" works for any slack of constant number of rounds, hence Bracha termination is in fact not necessary. Nonetheless, we will first go through this strategy since it helps to achieve a more concise and (practically) efficient result.

Bracha Termination. In our one-shot Chain-King Consensus protocol, honest parties might terminate at the end of different but adjacent iterations. We now show how to reduce this slack from one iteration (i.e., 3 phases) to one phase. The high-level idea follows Bracha's original suggestion [8], but we adapt it to the PoW setting.

We first describe this approach in the classical setting (information-theoretic and assuming $n \geq 3t + 1$). In Bracha's suggestion, as soon as a party decides on an output v or upon receiving at least $t + 1$ messages $(decide, v)$ for the same value v, it sends $(decide, v)$ to all parties. Then, upon receiving $n - t$ messages $(decide, v)$ for the same value v, a party outputs v and terminates.

We now elaborate on our early termination strategy which tries to emulate Bracha's suggestion on parallel chains. Recall that in ChainKingConsensus the input-block content is its producer's output suggestion val. Here we extend it two types of messages: either output suggestion val, or decide suggestion $(decide, val)$. We say a chain $\mathbb{C}_j^{(i)}$ decides on val if more than half of the input-blocks included in the output generation stage report $(decide, val)$ for the same val. Note that when a chain does not decide on any val, the output extraction algorithm treats all $(decide, val)$ messages the same as val.

Thus, protocol ChainKingConsensus is modified with the following additional steps: (i) When P's internal variable decide is false, P includes only val in her input-blocks; when decide is true, P mines $(decide, val)$; (ii) At the end of any phase, upon observing more than $m/2$ chains decide on val, P sets her val to val and decide to true; (iii) At the end of any phase, upon observing more than $3m/4$ chains decide on val, P sets her val to val and exit to 1; and (iv) After setting exit to 1 in the previous step, P continues to mine $(decide, val)$ for *one more phase* and then set exit to 0.

We present the new state update mechanism in [24].

Theorem 4. *There exist protocol parameterizations such that* ChainKing Consensus. *modified with the above state update algorithm satisfies agreement, validity and 1-slack termination with expected-constant round complexity.*

Slack-Tolerant Sequential composition of ChainKingConsensus. Now we present how sequential composition works in the permissionless setting. We remark that this is not a straightforward emulation of the super-round expansion technique in the classical literature as in our setting, the adversary effectively has more power in "swinging" the decision of honest parties. We elaborate on the difference between classical round expansion and our novel "super-phase expansion."

In order to perform sequential composition, our protocol should be appropriately adjusted so that we have better quality of phase-oblivious agreement. Recall that Theorem 2 holds for any constant $\beta < 1$. While in one-shot ChainKingConsensus we have protocol parameterizations such that at least three quarters of the chains will reach phase-oblivious agreement, it is possible to achieve that an arbitrary (constant) fraction of chains reach oblivious agreement. One consequence is that we will get a slow-down on the length of a phase in terms of number of rounds; the asymptotic result (i.e., expected-constant number of rounds), however, is preserved.

Furthermore, consider any $n \in \mathbb{N}^+$ consecutive phases in an execution of the protocol. If β fraction of the chains have reached oblivious agreement in one phase, then at least $[1-n(1-\beta)]$ fraction of chains reach oblivious agreement over all n phases. By appropriately choosing n and β, we get the following property: In any n consecutive phases at least three-quarters of the chains achieve phase-oblivious agreement over all phases. For example, when $\beta = 95\%$ and $n = 3$, for any 3 consecutive phases, honest parties obliviously agree on at least three quarters of the chains. As a result, we have the following corollary to Theorem 2:

Corollary 1 (Multi-phase oblivious agreement). *There exist protocol parameterizations such that the following properties hold. Consider $n \in \mathbb{N}^+$ consecutive phases $i, i+1, \ldots, i+n-1$, $i \geq 1$. Let $\mathbb{C}, \mathbb{C}'$ denote the parallel chains held by two honest parties P, P' at round r, r', respectively, after the $(i+n-1)$-th phase (i.e., $\min\{r, r'\} > (i+n-1)\rho$). Then there exists a subset $S \subseteq \{1, 2, \ldots, m\}$ of size $|S| > 3m/4$ such that for any $j \in S$ and any $k \in \{i, i+1, \ldots, i+n\}$, the following two properties hold on chains $\mathcal{C} = \mathbb{C}_j^{(k)}$ and $\mathcal{C}' = \mathbb{C}_j'^{(k)}$:*

- **Agreement.** $\mathcal{C}^{\lceil \rho_{ref}} = \mathcal{C}'^{\lceil \rho_{ref}}$.
- **Honest input-block majority.** *For all input blocks included in the output generation stage of $\mathcal{C}$ and $\mathcal{C}'$, more than half of them are produced by honest parties.*

Regarding input messages, we also require that parties attach messages indicating the index of invocations and the index and steps of iterations in their input messages. That is, a valid input message in sequential composition would be of the form "This is the i-th invocation, j-th iteration and k-th phase, and my output suggestion is *val*." We omit the details of encoding such messages. Moreover, in some "dummy" phases, parties are allowed to send dummy suggestion $\perp$ that contains no information.

Given that parties can terminate and start within two neighboring phases, our super-phase expansion (which will be adopted in the second and subsequent invocations) replaces the original (aligned) phase to four (possibly unaligned) phases "input-input-input-dummy." I.e., parties report their suggested output during the first three phases in their local view, and leave the last phase dummy. See Fig. 3 for an illustration of an aligned super-phase and an unaligned one.

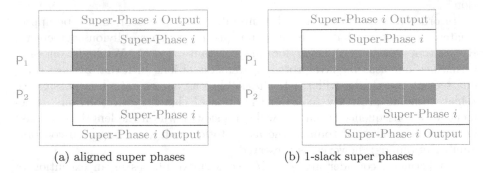

(a) aligned super phases   (b) 1-slack super phases

Fig. 3. *Illustration of the super-phase expansion and how parties extract the super-phase output.* ▉ *represents the phase where a party mines input messages with her output suggestion, and* ▨ *is the dummy phase. The i-th super phase is represented by* ☐*; and the associated phases to extract output are depicted with* ☐*.*

The decision process works as follows. When a party P reaches the end of a super-phase (in her local view), she decides an output (a vector of size m) for this super-phase based on the output of *five* previous (normal) phases (i.e., starting from one normal phase before the current super-phase (see the illustration of "Super-Phase Output" in Fig. 3). For each chain, P does the following. Recall that parties are allowed to report $\bot$. When there is a (normal) phase such that more than half of the input-blocks report $\bot$, then we say this phase reports $\bot$. Otherwise, pick the median value of all non-$\bot$ values (after sorting) as the output of this phase. The decisions are as follows: (i) When there are more than two phases that output non-$\bot$ values, output the value in the *second* phase; and (ii) when there is one phase outputting a value *val*, output *val* for this super-phase.

Next, we provide some intuition on why adding a dummy phase at the end of a super-phase is necessary. When honest parties do not start unanimously with the same value, the adversary can join forces with those late honest parties in their last phase so that the view of honest parties are not consistent (because the parties that terminate early should make a decision when other honest parties have not yet finished their current super phase). With dummy rounds, all honest parties share a consistent view under multi-phase oblivious agreement, hence guaranteeing agreement and validity.

Moreover, keeping including the output suggestion for 3 consecutive normal phases is also necessary. For a concrete example, suppose the underlying one-shot consensus protocol achieves 1-slack termination, and the honest computational power accounts for 60% of the total (i.e., the adversary owns 40%) and honest parties are equally divided into two subsets, starting from two neighbouring phases. In other words, we have parties starting and terminate early (resp., late) that accounts for 30% of computational power. Then, if parties include their output suggestion for only two phases, the adversary can refrain from mining in the first normal phase of the early parties, and join forces with the late parties in their second normal phase but inject a non-honest input. In such a case, even if parties start unanimously with v the output of this chain under multi-phase oblivious agreement will not be v (as 40% is greater than 30%), thus violating the validity property of consensus. With 3 consecutive mining normal phases, at least two of them will overlap, an adopting an output in the second non-$\perp$ phase will be safe.

We present more details on how our super-phase expansion can be adapted to c-slack termination for $c > 1$ in [24].

By adopting the 1-slack termination technique and super-phase expansion, we get the following theorem for sequential composition of ℓ invocations of ChainKingConsensus.

Theorem 5. *There exist protocol parameterizations such that the sequential composition of ℓ invocations of* ChainKingConsensus *satisfies agreement and validity on each invocation, and the round complexity is expected $O(\ell)$.*

4 Application: Fast State Machine Replication

We now show how to adapt the sequential composition approach in Sect. 3.4 to implement a state machine replication (SMR) protocol. Our resulting protocol achieves both Consistency and expected-constant-time Liveness for all types of transactions (including conflicting ones). Namely, for any transaction tx, when tx is diffused to all honest participants (miners), it takes in expectation a constant number of rounds to get settled into the immutable final ledger.

We first give our definition of SMR, and elaborate on why fast SMR protocol cannot be directly derived from the sequential composition of multi-valued Chain-King Consensus. Then, in Sect. 4.1 we propose a new method that introduces randomness to the output of the king chain and helps circumvent the above problem while preserving expected-constant settlement time for all types of transactions. Finally, in Sect. 4.2 we show how a third party observer, joining in the middle of the protocol, can catch up with honest parties and learn the state of the ledger.

SMR Background. State machine replication (SMR) is the problem of distributing the operation of a state machine across a set of replicas so that the operation of the machine is resilient to failure of a subset of the replicas. This concept was originally described in [34], and later further elaborated on by Schneider [42] where a high-level description of SMR was provided. Blockchain protocols, and in particular Bitcoin's [37] have renewed interest in SMR definitions and constructions, as they can be seen as a way to realize SMR in a setting where there is no predetermined set of replicas. This has been studied and formalized in a series of works (e.g., [23,25,38]).

We now give a concise definition of SMR. A number of n servers, a subset $\mathcal{H}$ of which is assumed to be non-faulty, maintain a log of transactions, denoted Log. The log of each server also timestamps each transaction. The notation $\mathsf{Log}_i[t]$ denotes the log of the server P_i up to time t. Furthermore, it is assumed that each server has a buffer for incoming transactions, denoted by $I_i[t]$, that are valid with respect to its view (invalid transactions are dropped). Finally, and for simplicity, assume that all well-formed transactions are admissible in the log. In SMR, the following two conditions must be satisfied:

- **Consistency:** $\forall \mathsf{P}_i, \mathsf{P}_j \in \mathcal{H}$ (where not necessarily $i \neq j$) and t, t' it holds that $\mathsf{Log}_i[t] \preceq \mathsf{Log}_j[t']$ or $\mathsf{Log}_j[t'] \preceq \mathsf{Log}_i[t]$.
- **Liveness:** There is a parameter $u \in \mathbb{N}$ for which the following holds: $(\forall \mathsf{P}_i \in \mathcal{H} : \mathsf{tx} \in I_i[t]) \implies \mathsf{tx} \in \mathsf{Log}_i[t + u]$.

Typically, the Liveness parameter u is a pre-defined value according to the protocol parameterization. It is natural to extend the notion and allow u to be a random variable with a distribution that depends on the specific parameterization. I.e., given a transaction tx appearing in all honest buffers at time t, the probability that it is included in all honest logs at time $t + u$ shares the same distribution with u. In our protocol, we achieve u with a geometric distribution, hence the time for tx to get installed in the immutable ledger is expected-constant.

Note that there are more properties of interest for SMR, such as *observability*, which is the requirement that a third party observer be capable of interpreting correctly the current state of the ledger by inspecting the logs of the servers.

4.1 From Sequential Composition to State Machine Replication

An SMR protocol accepts a batch of transactions as input. While we omit here the details on the particular form of the transactions, we note that the input domain is of exponential size. Thus, "strong validity" (i.e., the requirement that output is at least one honest input) is impossible even if the adversary only controls a tiny fraction of the computational power (cf. Remark 1). Also note that a unanimous start would rarely happen given that the adversary can collude with clients and send different or conflicting transactions to different parties. Therefore, if we follow the method from Sect. 3.3—e.g., to apply the median or plurality rule—to select the output on the king chain, as long as the adversary carefully selects the set of transactions, he can always make his input batch be selected as the output. By carefully constructing such transaction batches, the adversary will be able to indefinitely delay the confirmation of any honest transaction tx, even if tx has been provided to all honest participants.

Proof-of-Work as a Lottery. We now present a new construction that helps preventing the adversarial control described above when parties do not start unanimously. In a nutshell, when a party P is still "confused" at the end of an iteration (i.e., her internal variable lock remains false), P adopts the output of the king chain as her new input, which is the (valid) input-block reported in the first chain, with the *smallest* block hash. When the honest parties obliviously agree on the king chain (which happens with constant probability), they will refer to the same block. Notice that honest parties make more RO queries than the corrupted parties. The following lemma shows that with probability (roughly) one half, the input-block with smallest block hash is produced by an honest party.

Lemma 1. *Let $h = \mathsf{poly}(\kappa)$ and $t = \mathsf{poly}(\kappa)$ denote the number of random oracle queries made by honest and corrupted parties, respectively. Under honest majority assumption $(h > t)$, the probability that the smallest RO output is from an honest query is $1/2 - \mathsf{negl}(\kappa)$.*

Fast State Machine Replication. We are now ready describe our SMR protocol. At a high level, it can be viewed as the sequential composition of Chain-King Consensus, equipped with a new phase output extraction algorithm, described as follows. When parties are extracting output in the first and second phase of an iteration, for each chain they will output v if the majority of input-blocks is v; otherwise they will output $\perp$ (in this way, the adversary cannot let parties decide on a batch of transactions that is not an honest input in the first two stages). When they are in the third phase (i.e., that's when the "confused" parties listen to the king chain) they will output the input-block with the smallest hash value. We provide the detailed analysis in the proof of the following theorem in [24].

Theorem 6. *There exist protocol parameterizations such that the sequential composition of Chain-King Consensus with the minimum-PoW king selection rule satisfies Consistency and expected-constant Liveness.*

4.2 Bootstrapping from the Genesis Block

In this section, we focus on the *observability* property of our SMR protocol. Recall that in Sect. 3.2, we stated that a full agreement on all parallel chains in the previous phase is impossible, and parties that join at a specific phase cannot learn the previous execution by "tracing back" using cross-chain reference. Thus, it becomes challenging or even impossible for a passive observer to join the protocol in the middle of the execution. To solve this, in this section we slightly modify our Chain-King Consensus protocol and design a bootstrapping algorithm for fresh parties to synchronize state with all honest parties. Note that the design of a bootstrapping procedure to let fresh parties join is also an essential building block for protocols that support dynamic participation.

When a fresh party $\mathsf{P_{new}}$ joins, $\mathsf{P_{new}}$ has no knowledge about the protocol execution except for the CRS and global time (recall that we assume synchronous processors). To become synchronized and learn the ledger state, $\mathsf{P_{new}}$ needs to bootstrap by passively listening to the protocol. We highlight that, in order for $\mathsf{P_{new}}$ to synchronize with other honest parties (i.e., achieving phase oblivious agreement), $\mathsf{P_{new}}$ needs to run a bootstrapping procedure which lasts for a constant number of rounds (precisely ρ rounds).

In order to let fresh parties join the protocol, we modify our Chain-King Consensus protocol as follows. In the i-th phase ($i > 1$), concatenated with the consensus-related input message, parties also include the fresh randomness extracted from their local chains in the $(i-1)$-th phase. More specifically, they extract the hash of the last block in the output generation stage on each chain in the $(i-1)$-th phase of $\mathbb{C}_{\text{local}}$, assemble them as a κ-bit string and append it to the input-block content. For chains where a typical execution holds, honest parties adopt the same block hash. Next, in i-th phase, a Crusader Agreement is run on the block hash of each chain in the $(i-1)$-th phase (recall from Remark 2 that a single phase suffices to serve as a Crusader Agreement protocol). I.e., for the j-th chain with a typical execution, parties agree on a unique block hash that is the same as their local $\mathbb{C}_j^{(i-1)}$, and for other chains, all parties either output the same hash or $\perp$.

Thus, when a fresh party P_{new} joins the protocol, she first passively listens to the protocol for ρ rounds so that she observes the end of a phase, say phase i. Our chain selection rule guarantees that P_{new} has parallel chains in phase i that obliviously agree with other honest parties on more than $3m/4$ chains (recall Theorem 2). Now, P_{new} can "trace back" all the chains where typical execution holds by using the fresh randomness included in the current phase; and iterate them phase-by-phase. Specifically, when P_{new} is at the end of phase i, she runs the bootstrapping procedure (see [24] for the complete specification) to extract the hashes of dense chains in the previous phase and use them to form her local chain $\mathbb{C}_{\text{local}}^{(i-1)}$. For instance, consider the j-th chain in the $(i-1)$-th phase. If on more than $3m/4$ chains in phase i, a majority of the input blocks report fresh randomness that matches a chain $\mathcal{C} \in \mathtt{denseChains}[i-1][j]$, then P_{new} will select $\mathcal{C}$ and add it as the j-th chain in $\mathbb{C}_{\text{local}}^{(i-1)}$. If no such chain exists, P_{new} will randomly pick a chain or just leave it empty.

Note that the security of both Chain-King Consensus and Crusader Agreement only rely on the consistent view of chains where typical execution holds; hence, at the end of the joining procedure, P_{new} achieves phase oblivious agreement with all honest parties. As a result, P_{new} can reconstruct the entire execution and update her internal state to build the whole ledger.

Acknowledgements. Juan Garay's research has been supported in part by NSF grants no. 2001082 and 2055694, and by the Algorand Centres of Excellence programme managed by the Algorand Foundation. Any opinions, findings, and conclusions or recommendations expressed in this material are those of the author(s) and do not necessarily reflect the views of Algorand Foundation. He also thanks Karim Eldefrawy, Ben Terner and Vassilis Zikas for useful discussions on the topic. Yu Shen's research has been supported by Input Output (iohk.io) through their funding of the University of Edinburgh Blockchain Technology Lab.

References

1. Andrychowicz, M., Dziembowski, S.: PoW-based distributed cryptography with no trusted setup. In: Gennaro, R., Robshaw, M. (eds.) CRYPTO 2015. LNCS, vol. 9216, pp. 379–399. Springer, Heidelberg (2015). https://doi.org/10.1007/978-3-662-48000-7_19
2. Badertscher, C., Maurer, U., Tschudi, D., Zikas, V.: Bitcoin as a transaction ledger: a composable treatment. In: Katz, J., Shacham, H. (eds.) CRYPTO 2017. LNCS, vol. 10401, pp. 324–356. Springer, Cham (2017). https://doi.org/10.1007/978-3-319-63688-7_11
3. Bagaria, V.K., Kannan, S., Tse, D., Fanti, G.C., Viswanath, P.: Prism: deconstructing the blockchain to approach physical limits. In: Cavallaro, L., Kinder, J., Wang, X., Katz, J. (eds.) ACM CCS 2019: 26th Conference on Computer and Communications Security, pp. 585–602. ACM Press, London, UK (2019). https://doi.org/10.1145/3319535.3363213
4. Bellare, M., Rogaway, P.: Random oracles are practical: a paradigm for designing efficient protocols. In: Denning, D.E., Pyle, R., Ganesan, R., Sandhu, R.S., Ashby, V. (eds.) ACM CCS 93: 1st Conference on Computer and Communications Security, pp. 62–73. ACM Press, Fairfax, Virginia, USA (Nov 3–5, 1993). https://doi.org/10.1145/168588.168596
5. Berman, P., Garay, J.A.: Asymptotically optimal distributed consensus (extended abstract). In: Ausiello, G., Dezani-Ciancaglini, M., Della Rocca, S.R. (eds.) Automata, Languages and Programming, pp. 80–94. Springer Berlin Heidelberg, Berlin, Heidelberg (1989). https://doi.org/10.1007/BFB0035753
6. Berman, P., Garay, J.A., Perry, K.J.: Towards optimal distributed consensus (extended abstract). In: 30th Annual Symposium on Foundations of Computer Science, pp. 410–415. IEEE Computer Society Press, Research Triangle Park, NC, USA (Oct 30 - Nov 1, 1989). https://doi.org/10.1109/SFCS.1989.63511
7. Boneh, D., Bonneau, J., Bünz, B., Fisch, B.: Verifiable delay functions. In: Shacham, H., Boldyreva, A. (eds.) CRYPTO 2018. LNCS, vol. 10991, pp. 757–788. Springer, Cham (2018). https://doi.org/10.1007/978-3-319-96884-1_25
8. Bracha, G.: An asynchronou [(n-1)/3]-resilient consensus protocol. In: Probert, R.L., Lynch, N.A., Santoro, N. (eds.) 3rd ACM Symposium Annual on Principles of Distributed Computing, pp. 154–162. Association for Computing Machinery, Vancouver, BC, Canada (Aug 27–29, 1984). https://doi.org/10.1145/800222.806743
9. Canetti, R.: Security and composition of multiparty cryptographic protocols. J. Cryptol. **13**(1), 143–202 (2000). https://doi.org/10.1007/s001459910006
10. Canetti, R.: Universally composable security: a new paradigm for cryptographic protocols. Cryptology ePrint Archive, Report 2000/067 (2000). https://eprint.iacr.org/2000/067
11. Chen, J., Micali, S.: Algorand: a secure and efficient distributed ledger. Theoret. Comput. Sci. **777**, 155–183 (2019). https://doi.org/10.1016/J.TCS.2019.02.001
12. Cohen, R., Coretti, S., Garay, J., Zikas, V.: Probabilistic termination and composability of cryptographic protocols. In: Robshaw, M., Katz, J. (eds.) CRYPTO 2016. LNCS, vol. 9816, pp. 240–269. Springer, Heidelberg (2016). https://doi.org/10.1007/978-3-662-53015-3_9
13. Das, P., Eckey, L., Faust, S., Loss, J., Maitra, M.: Round efficient byzantine agreement from VDFs. Cryptology ePrint Archive, Report 2022/823 (2022). https://eprint.iacr.org/2022/823

14. Dolev, D.: The byzantine generals strike again. J. Algorithms **3**(1), 14–30 (1982). https://doi.org/10.1016/0196-6774(82)90004-9
15. Dolev, D., Reischuk, R., Strong, H.R.: Early stopping in byzantine agreement. J. ACM **37**(4), 720–741 (1990). https://doi.org/10.1145/96559.96565
16. Dolev, D., Strong, H.R.: Authenticated algorithms for byzantine agreement. SIAM J. Comput. **12**(4), 656–666 (1983). https://doi.org/10.1137/0212045
17. Eckey, L., Faust, S., Loss, J.: Efficient algorithms for broadcast and consensus based on proofs of work. Cryptology ePrint Archive, Report 2017/915 (2017). https://eprint.iacr.org/2017/915
18. Feldman, P., Micali, S.: Optimal algorithms for byzantine agreement. In: 20th Annual ACM Symposium on Theory of Computing, pp. 148–161. ACM Press, Chicago, IL, USA (1988). https://doi.org/10.1145/62212.62225
19. Fischer, M.J., Lynch, N.A.: A lower bound for the time to assure interactive consistency. Inf. Process. Lett. **14**(4), 183–186 (1982). https://doi.org/10.1016/0020-0190(82)90033-3
20. Fitzi, M., Garay, J.A.: Efficient player-optimal protocols for strong and differential consensus. In: Borowsky, E., Rajsbaum, S. (eds.) 22nd ACM Symposium Annual on Principles of Distributed Computing, pp. 211–220. Association for Computing Machinery, Boston, MA, USA (Jul 13–16 2003). https://doi.org/10.1145/872035.872066
21. Fitzi, M., Gaži, P., Kiayias, A., Russell, A.: Parallel chains: improving throughput and latency of blockchain protocols via parallel composition. Cryptology ePrint Archive, Report 2018/1119 (2018). https://eprint.iacr.org/2018/1119
22. Fitzi, M., Gaži, P., Kiayias, A., Russell, A.: Ledger combiners for fast settlement. In: Pass, R., Pietrzak, K. (eds.) TCC 2020. LNCS, vol. 12550, pp. 322–352. Springer, Cham (2020). https://doi.org/10.1007/978-3-030-64375-1_12
23. Garay, J., Kiayias, A., Leonardos, N.: The bitcoin backbone protocol: analysis and applications. Cryptology ePrint Archive, Report 2014/765 (2014). https://eprint.iacr.org/2014/765
24. Garay, J., Kiayias, A., Shen, Y.: Proof-of-work-based consensus in expected-constant time. Cryptology ePrint Archive, Report 2023/1663 (2023). https://eprint.iacr.org/2023/1663
25. Garay, J., Kiayias, A.: SoK: a consensus taxonomy in the blockchain era. In: Jarecki, S. (ed.) CT-RSA 2020. LNCS, vol. 12006, pp. 284–318. Springer, Cham (2020). https://doi.org/10.1007/978-3-030-40186-3_13
26. Garay, J., Kiayias, A., Leonardos, N.: The bitcoin backbone protocol: analysis and applications. In: Oswald, E., Fischlin, M. (eds.) EUROCRYPT 2015. LNCS, vol. 9057, pp. 281–310. Springer, Heidelberg (2015). https://doi.org/10.1007/978-3-662-46803-6_10
27. Garay, J., Kiayias, A., Leonardos, N.: The bitcoin backbone protocol with chains of variable difficulty. In: Katz, J., Shacham, H. (eds.) CRYPTO 2017. LNCS, vol. 10401, pp. 291–323. Springer, Cham (2017). https://doi.org/10.1007/978-3-319-63688-7_10
28. Garay, J.A., Kiayias, A., Leonardos, N., Panagiotakos, G.: Bootstrapping the blockchain, with applications to consensus and fast PKI setup. In: Abdalla, M., Dahab, R. (eds.) PKC 2018. LNCS, vol. 10770, pp. 465–495. Springer, Cham (2018). https://doi.org/10.1007/978-3-319-76581-5_16
29. Garay, J., Kiayias, A., Ostrovsky, R.M., Panagiotakos, G., Zikas, V.: Resource-restricted cryptography: revisiting MPC bounds in the proof-of-work era. In: Canteaut, A., Ishai, Y. (eds.) EUROCRYPT 2020. LNCS, vol. 12106, pp. 129–158. Springer, Cham (2020). https://doi.org/10.1007/978-3-030-45724-2_5

30. Garay, J.A., MacKenzie, P.D., Prabhakaran, M., Yang, K.: Resource fairness and composability of cryptographic protocols. J. Cryptol. **24**(4), 615–658 (2011). https://doi.org/10.1007/s00145-010-9080-z

31. Garay, J.A., Moses, Y.: Fully polynomial byzantine agreement in t+1 rounds. In: 25th Annual ACM Symposium on Theory of Computing, pp. 31–41. ACM Press, San Diego, CA, USA (1993). https://doi.org/10.1145/167088.167101

32. Katz, J., Koo, C.-Y.: On expected constant-round protocols for byzantine agreement. In: Dwork, C. (ed.) CRYPTO 2006. LNCS, vol. 4117, pp. 445–462. Springer, Heidelberg (2006). https://doi.org/10.1007/11818175_27

33. Katz, J., Maurer, U., Tackmann, B., Zikas, V.: Universally Composable Synchronous Computation. In: Sahai, A. (ed.) TCC 2013. LNCS, vol. 7785, pp. 477–498. Springer, Heidelberg (2013). https://doi.org/10.1007/978-3-642-36594-2_27

34. Lamport, L.: Time, clocks, and the ordering of events in a distributed system. Commun. ACM **21**(7), 558–565 (1978). https://doi.org/10.1145/359545.359563

35. Lamport, L., Shostak, R., Pease, M.: The byzantine generals problem. ACM Trans. Program. Lang. Syst. **4**(3), 382–401 (1982). https://doi.org/10.1145/357172.357176

36. Momose, A., Ren, L.: Constant latency in sleepy consensus. In: Yin, H., Stavrou, A., Cremers, C., Shi, E. (eds.) ACM CCS 2022: 29th Conference on Computer and Communications Security, pp. 2295–2308. ACM Press, Los Angeles, CA, USA (Nov 7 - 11 2022). https://doi.org/10.1145/3548606.3559347

37. Nakamoto, S.: Bitcoin: A peer-to-peer electronic cash system (2008). https://bitcoin.org/bitcoin.pdf

38. Pass, R., Seeman, L., Shelat, A.: Analysis of the blockchain protocol in asynchronous networks. In: Coron, J.-S., Nielsen, J.B. (eds.) EUROCRYPT 2017. LNCS, vol. 10211, pp. 643–673. Springer, Cham (2017). https://doi.org/10.1007/978-3-319-56614-6_22

39. Pass, R., Shi, E.: FruitChains: A fair blockchain. In: Schiller, E.M., Schwarzmann, A.A. (eds.) 36th ACM Symposium Annual on Principles of Distributed Computing, pp. 315–324. Association for Computing Machinery, Washington, DC, USA (2017). https://doi.org/10.1145/3087801.3087809

40. Pease, M.C., Shostak, R.E., Lamport, L.: Reaching agreement in the presence of faults. J. ACM **27**(2), 228–234 (1980). https://doi.org/10.1145/322186.322188

41. Rabin, M.O.: Randomized byzantine generals. In: 24th Annual Symposium on Foundations of Computer Science, pp. 403–409. IEEE Computer Society Press, Tucson, Arizona (Nov 7–9, 1983). https://doi.org/10.1109/SFCS.1983.48

42. Schneider, F.B.: Implementing fault-tolerant services using the state machine approach: a tutorial. ACM Comput. Surv. **22**(4), 299–319 (1990). https://doi.org/10.1145/98163.98167

43. Turpin, R., Coan, B.A.: Extending binary byzantine agreement to multivalued byzantine agreement. Inf. Process. Lett. **18**(2), 73–76 (1984). https://doi.org/10.1016/0020-0190(84)90027-9

Secure and Efficient Implementation, Cryptographic Engineering, and Real-World Cryptography

A Holistic Security Analysis of Monero Transactions

Cas Cremers[1]([✉])[iD], Julian Loss[1][iD], and Benedikt Wagner[1,2][iD]

[1] CISPA Helmholtz Center for Information Security, Saarbrücken, Germany
{cremers,loss,benedikt.wagner}@cispa.de
[2] Saarland University, Saarbrücken, Germany

Abstract. Monero is a popular cryptocurrency with strong privacy guarantees for users' transactions. At the heart of Monero's privacy claims lies a complex transaction system called RingCT, which combines several building blocks such as linkable ring signatures, homomorphic commitments, and range proofs, in a unique fashion. In this work, we provide the first rigorous security analysis for RingCT (as given in Zero to Monero, v2.0.0, 2020) in its entirety. This is in contrast to prior works that only provided security arguments for parts of RingCT.

To analyze Monero's transaction system, we introduce the first holistic security model for RingCT. We then prove the security of RingCT in our model. Our framework is modular: it allows to view RingCT as a combination of various different sub-protocols. Our modular approach has the benefit that these components can be easily updated in future versions of RingCT, with only minor modifications to our analysis.

At a technical level, we split our analysis in two parts. First, we identify which security notions for building blocks are needed to imply security for the whole system. Interestingly, we observe that existing and well-established notions (e.g., for the linkable ring signature) are insufficient. Second, we analyze all building blocks as implemented in Monero and prove that they satisfy our new notions. Here, we leverage the algebraic group model to overcome subtle problems in the analysis of the linkable ring signature component. As another technical highlight, we show that our security goals can be mapped to a suitable graph problem, which allows us to take advantage of the theory of network flows in our analysis. This new approach is also useful for proving security of other cryptocurrencies.

Keywords: Monero · RingCT · Transaction Scheme Security · Algebraic Group Model · Network Flows

1 Introduction

In the rapidly growing zoo of cryptocurrencies, Monero[1] [33,52] is among the largest and most well-known systems, with a market capitalization of about

---

[1] See https://www.getmonero.org.

© International Association for Cryptologic Research 2024
M. Joye and G. Leander (Eds.): EUROCRYPT 2024, LNCS 14653, pp. 129–159, 2024.
https://doi.org/10.1007/978-3-031-58734-4_5

three billion USD at the time of writing. One of Monero's distinguishing features is its unique transaction scheme RingCT ("Ring Confidential Transactions") which offers users a high degree of privacy for on-chain transactions. To this end, RingCT provides an efficient means of hiding how funds are transferred between users. The core property that users of a currency rely on, however, is *transaction security*. Namely, it should not be possible to spend funds twice, create money out of thin air, or steal coins from other users. To achieve transaction security, decentralized currencies require that the validity of transactions can be verified publicly, which seemingly contradicts the privacy goals of currencies like Monero.

Monero's Complexity. To achieve the challenging goal of reconciling privacy and security, RingCT combines several simpler building blocks such as linkable ring signatures, homomorphic commitments, and range proofs into a highly complex protocol. The building blocks are combined with a key derivation process in a unique way. This is in contrast to simpler currencies, e.g. Bitcoin, which merely rely on standard signatures. Unfortunately, it is not obvious at all that RingCT's complex system is indeed secure. For example, when a user Alice sends coins to a user Bob, Alice (who may be adversarial) derives new keys for Bob using Bob's long-term address. This implies that Alice has non-trivial knowledge of relations between the keys of Bob, potentially opening the door for related-key attacks. Such related-key attacks are not considered by the standard security notions of the components. Even worse, the complex nature of RingCT has led to concrete attacks [37,42,43] in the past, which were not captured by the limited prior analyses. This raises the following question:

Is Monero's transaction scheme secure?

Our Contribution. In this work, we provide the first comprehensive and holistic security analysis of RingCT. Our contributions are

- We show that RingCT as a whole achieves transaction security.
- We thereby identify which security properties of components are sufficient to imply security for the entire transaction scheme. Thus, our analysis is modular, which makes it easy to adapt to changes of RingCT in the future.
- We introduce a new proof technique which reduces a game-based security notion to a combinatorial problem of network flows. This combinatorial argument allows us to prove that no adversary can create money out of thin air. We are confident that it can be applied when analyzing other currencies as well.

Along the way, we face several technical challenges, arising from composition in the algebraic group model (AGM) [21] and the insufficiency of established security notions for building blocks. For example, we observe that the established notion of linkability for linkable ring signatures has to be strengthened significantly (see Sect. 1.2).

Due to space limitations, we refer to the full version [12] for formal details of our analysis and full proofs, and mostly give an overview here.

1.1   Our Approach: A Modular Analysis of RingCT

We provide the first rigorous security analysis of Monero's transaction system RingCT as a whole. Our framework is modular and abstracts many of the components of RingCT into stand-alone building blocks. We believe that these components naturally reflect the design ideas of RingCT, and lead to an improved understanding of the ideas at its core. In addition, this approach makes it possible to easily replace a given part of the scheme in future system updates. For example, should Monero decide to use another ring signature scheme in the future, one just needs to redo the parts of our analysis that deal with the ring signature component. Conversely, our results may also serve as guidelines for the required security properties of the components in the event of such an update.

We begin by introducing syntax and model for the desired security properties of the top-level transaction scheme (i.e., RingCT). We define a single security experiment that can be summarized as follows:

1. Whenever an honest user receives coins, they can later spend these coins. That is, an adversary can neither steal the coins that an honest user received, nor prevent the honest user from spending them.
2. An adversary can not create coins out of thin air. That is, the adversary can never spend more coins than it ever received.

In contrast to prior models for RingCT-like transaction schemes, our model is not only holistic, but also takes subtleties such as the reuse of randomness or adversarially generated keys into account.

Having defined the security properties we aim for, we then prove that our model of RingCT meets these properties. This consists of the following steps:

1. *Syntax and Security for Subcomponents.* We identify the structural components of RingCT and introduce appropriate syntax for them. Then, we define several new security notions that are tailored to the interplay of these building blocks within RingCT. For example, due to potential related-key attacks, it is necessary to define security of the ring signature component with respect to the key derivation mechanism. Thus, we require security notions that differ from well-established ones from the literature.
2. *System Level Analysis.* The next step of our analysis is to prove the security of any top-level transaction scheme that follows our syntax. Our proof is generic and only assumes that subcomponents satisfy our novel security notions. A technical highlight of our proof is the utilization of the theory of network flows. Concretely, after applying the security notions of subcomponents to extract the hidden flow of money in the system, we define a graph based on it. Then, we use further notions of subcomponents to argue that this graph constitutes a flow network. Finally, we show that no money can be created by

using the fact that every cut in such a flow network has the same flow passing through it. We are confident that this new technique is also applicable in the context of other currencies such as Bitcoin or Ethereum.

3. *Component Level Analysis.* Finally, we instantiate the components as in Monero and prove that they satisfy our security notions. Here, the biggest challenge lies with the linkable ring signature component, for which we provide an analysis in the Algebraic Group Model (AGM) [21]. We encounter several subtle issues that arise from composing different building blocks. As such, we believe that our proof sheds further light on the pitfalls of naively composing proofs in the AGM.

1.2   Technical Highlights and Findings

In this section, we give an overview of some of our findings.

Composing Extractors in the Algebraic Group Model. To show that our security notions for components imply security for the entire transaction scheme, we make use of knowledge extractors. Namely, we consider each transaction that the adversary submits to the system, and run a knowledge extractor to get the secret signing key that the adversary used to create the transaction. The existence of such an extractor should be guaranteed by our notions for the linkable ring signature components. As we extract for each submitted transaction, it is crucial that our extractor does not rewind the adversary. A common way to design such a non-rewinding extractor for a given scheme is to leverage the algebraic group model (AGM) introduced by Fuchsbauer, Kiltz, and Loss [21]. In this model, whenever an adversary submits a group element $X \in \mathbb{G}$ (e.g., as part of transaction), it also submits exponents $(\gamma_i)_i$ such that $X = \prod_i A_i^{\gamma_i}$, where $A_i \in \mathbb{G}$ are all group elements the adversary ever received. We say that $(\gamma_i)_i$ is a representation of X over basis $(A_i)_i$. A carefully crafted extractor can now use the representation to compute the secret signing key the adversary used. Unfortunately, formally defining under which conditions such an extractor has to succeed turns out to be non-trivial. The naive way of doing it would be to define an isolated notion for the linkable ring signature as follows: The adversary gets system parameters as input (including a generator $g \in \mathbb{G}$), and may output a signature and algebraic representations of all group elements over basis g, and it wins if the extractor fails to output a secret key, but the signature is valid. In fact, such an isolated approach has been used in the literature for other primitives [10,38]. However, this extractor does not compose well. Concretely, in the isolated notion, the extractor expects that all representations are over basis g. On the other hand, if we use our extractor in the wider context, i.e., in the proof of RingCT, the representations are over much more complicated bases, because the adversary receives group elements in signatures, hash values, and keys. Formally, the security game (and subsequent reductions) would have to translate all representations into a representation over basis g first. It turns out that such a translation is not compatible with our subsequent proof steps.

For example, if the adversary just forwards a signature that it obtained from a signing oracle, there is no way that we can extract a secret key from it.

The solution we opt for is to change the isolated notion for the linkable ring signature into a more involved notion resembling simulation-extractability, in which we give the adversary oracles that output signatures, hash values, and keys. We require that the extractor is able to extract a valid secret key only under certain conditions, e.g., if the adversary did not obtain the signature from an oracle. At the same time, the extractor is not allowed to share any internal state with the oracles. While this makes our extractor usable in the proof of RingCT, it substantially complicates the AGM proof of the extractor.

Notions of Linkability. In a ring signature scheme, a signer holding a secret key sk can sign a message with respect to a so-called key ring $R = (pk_1, \ldots, pk_N)$, where sk is associated with one of the public keys, say pk_{i*}. Crucially, the signature does not reveal the index i', so that the signer stays anonymous. Linkable ring signatures additionally allow to publicly identify whether two signatures have been computed using the same secret key. More precisely, they are required to satisfy a property called linkability. It states that there is an efficient algorithm Link, such Link outputs 1 on input σ, σ' (resp. 0) if and only if the signatures σ, σ' have been computed with the same (resp. different) secret key. In terms of security, no adversary should manage to compute two signatures σ, σ' using the same secret key, such that $\text{Link}(\sigma, \sigma')$ outputs 0. In other words, Link detects if two signatures are computed using the same secret key, and can not be cheated by an adversary. In RingCT, each unspent transaction output is associated to a fresh secret key, which implies that Link can detect double spending of outputs. Formally defining linkability is a non-trivial task. As already noted in [27], there are several independent notions of linkability. One of the more established notions is so-called pigeonhole linkability. It is defined in the following way: An adversary breaks pigeonhole linkability if it outputs $N + 1$ valid non-linking signatures, where all rings have size at most N. Unfortunately, pigeonhole linkability seems to be insufficient for our purposes. Concretely, suppose an adversary uses a key ring (o_1, o_2) consisting of two outputs o_1 and o_2 in two distinct valid transactions. Now, recall from our previous paragraph that we use a knowledge extractor that gives us the secret key that the adversary used. Assume this knowledge extractor returns the secret key sk_1 associated to o_1 in both cases, but the two signatures do not link. Intuitively, linkability should say that this is not possible, because the adversary used sk_1 to compute both signatures. However, pigeonhole linkability is not applicable, as we only have two signatures on rings of size two. Instead, we need a notion of linkability that is tied to our knowledge extractor, and rules out this case. More precisely, it should guarantee that if the extractor outputs the same secret key for two signatures, then the signatures link.

1.3   Related Work

In this section, we give an overview of related work.

Related Security Models. Prior to our work, security models for systems similar to RingCT have been given [18,19,35,49,56]. Notably, all of them analyze new constructions and not RingCT as it is. Further, some of these models [18,19,49,56] omit important non-trivial aspects of RingCT, e.g., adversarial key derivation. Some of them [35,49,56] do not give a security definition for the whole scheme, but instead present a set of notions, somewhat similar to the component-wise notions we present as an intermediate step. It remains unclear how these notions relate to each other and the security of the transaction scheme as a whole. We provide a more detailed discussion on these models and how they relate to our model in Sect. 5.

History of Monero. Monero's transaction scheme RingCT originates in the CryptoNote protocol [52], which is based on a linkable ring signature presented in [24]. Noether [44] introduced a way to hide transaction amounts using Pedersen commitments [45] and range proofs, and also presented a compatible new ring signature component, called MLSAG. The construction of MLSAG is mostly based on [36]. Later, MLSAG was replaced by a more concise ring signature component, called CLSAG [27], and Bulletproofs/Bulletproofs+ [7,11,26] are being used as range proofs. Bulletproofs++ [16] are investigated for potential use [46]. Overviews of Monero and its transaction system can be found in [1,33]. Prior work has studied the security of some of RingCTs's building blocks in isolation [7,26,27,45], but no rigorous security argument has been given for RingCT as a whole.

New Constructions and Functionality Enhancements. Several works presented new constructions of transaction schemes similar to RingCT. These range from efficiency and anonymity improvements [31,35,49,56] to the use of postquantum assumptions [18,19]. Also, some works modify RingCT with the motivation to increase compatibility with other protocols, e.g., second-layer protocols [40] or proof of stake consensus [39]. A variety of protocols has been designed add new functionality to the Monero ecosystem. Examples include proofs of reserve [14,15], payment channels [40,48,50], and protocols atomic swaps [28,50].

Attacks on Monero. Researchers have also studied attacks against Monero and their mitigations. These target privacy [13,17,20,32,34,41,47,53–55], centralization [9] and security aspects [37,42,43]. In terms of privacy, attacks reach from passive attacks [41,53] to active attacks [54,55], and temporal attacks [34] that make users traceable. These attacks are purely combinatorial in nature. The works [17,47] study how to mitigate such combinatorial attacks.

Related Currencies and Their Analysis. ZCash [29] is one of the most prominent privacy-focused cryptocurrencies. It is based on the Zerocash protocol [3], which comes with a cryptographic security analysis. The current protocol specification of ZCash [29] suggests that ZCash deviates from Zerocash in multiple ways. Mimblewimble [30] is a currency prototype that uses homomorphic commitments for efficiency reasons and to hide transaction amounts. In contrast to Monero's transaction scheme, Mimblewimble does not rely on ring signatures or stealth addresses. A security model and analysis of Mimblewimble has been given in [22,23].

2   Informal Overview of Monero Transactions

In this section, we give an informal overview of the Monero transaction scheme. The purpose of this is twofold. On the one hand, it should explain the complex structure of transactions for readers not familiar with Monero. On the other hand, Monero versed readers may use this section as a first introduction to our modularization. We assume familiarity with common cryptographic tools such as commitments, ring signatures, and zero-knowledge proofs.

User Addresses. Before diving into the structure of transactions, we first clarify what constitutes an address of a user, i.e., its long-term key material. Namely, each user holds a triple (ipk, ivk, isk). We call these the identity public key, identity view key, and identity signing key, respectively. While ipk serves as a public address of the user, the keys ivk and isk should remain secret and provide the following functionality:

- The identity view key ivk allows to identify payments that the user receives and decrypt the associated amounts.
- The identity signing key isk allows to spend funds, i.e., sign transactions.

Readers familiar with simpler currencies such as Bitcoin should think of isk as a secret key as in Bitcoin, and ivk as being an additional key related to privacy. Namely, leaking ivk should only compromise the privacy, but not the security of users. In the concrete implementation of Monero, the identity public key ipk contains two group elements $K_v = g^{k_v} \in \mathbb{G}$ and $K_s = g^{k_s} \in \mathbb{G}$, where isk $= k_s \in \mathbb{Z}_p$, and ivk $= k_v \in \mathbb{Z}_p$, i.e., we have ipk $= (g^{\mathsf{ivk}}, g^{\mathsf{isk}})$.

Key Concepts of Transactions. Transactions in Monero follow the widely used UTXO ("unspent transaction output") model. In this model, each transaction spends some inputs into some outputs, and all inputs are unused outputs of previous transactions. As our running example, we consider the case of a transaction with two inputs and three outputs. A transaction is visualized in Fig. 1. We refer to the sender of a transaction as Alice, and to the recipient of an output as Bob. A naive transaction (as used in other currencies) would simply contain references to the inputs, and a digital signature per input. Each output would contain the address of the receiver Bob and the amount that it is worth. In contrast, Monero uses the following core ideas:

- To hide the sender, the actual inputs are grouped with decoy inputs. Ring signatures are used for each input.
- To hide the recipient, addresses contained in outputs are rerandomized. These rerandomized addresses are also known as stealth addresses.
- Amounts contained in outputs are hidden in homomorphic commitments.

Next, we explain how these ideas are implemented in more detail.

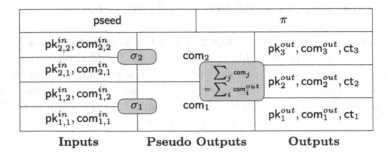

| Inputs | Pseudo Outputs | Outputs |

Fig. 1. Schematic overview of an example transaction in Monero with two inputs and three outputs. Inputs are actually references to previous outputs. Signatures σ_i connect inputs and pseudo outputs. The homomorphic property of commitments ties pseudo outputs to outputs. In addition to inputs, outputs, and signatures, a transaction also contains a public seed pseed and a range proof π.

Outputs. We start by describing what constitutes an output of a transaction, and how it is generated. Recall that in a naive transaction, an output would just be the address of the recipient and an amount. Monero hides amounts in commitments com, and recipients by using rerandomizations pk of their actual address ipk. To ensure that the recipient Bob can (1) recognize that he receives an output, and (2) use that output, the randomness for commitments and rerandomization has to be recovered by Bob. This is implemented using a Diffie-Hellman-style derivation of shared secrets: The sender Alice first includes a public seed (also called transaction public key) $\mathsf{pseed} = g^r$ in the transaction. The public seed will be used for the entire transaction, and not just for one output. Then, she derives $\mathsf{ok} = (K_v)^r$, where K_v is the view key part of Bob's identity public key $\mathsf{ipk} = (K_v, K_s)$, i.e., $\mathsf{ok} = g^{\mathsf{ivk} \cdot r}$. Thus, ok serves as a shared secret between Alice and Bob. The randomness for the rerandomization and the commitment is derived from ok and the position of the output. Namely, the first component of an output is $\mathsf{pk} = K_s \cdot g^\tau$, where the exponent $\tau \in \mathbb{Z}_p$ is deterministically derived from ok and the position of the output. The second component is a commitment $\mathsf{com} = \mathsf{Com}(\mathsf{amt}, \mathsf{cr})$, where the randomness cr is deterministically derived from ok and the position of the output. Finally, the output also contains a symmetric encryption ct of the amount amt. Most importantly, the values τ, cr, and the key for the encryption are all deterministically derived from ok and the position of the output. Let us point out the implications of this: The recipient Bob can derive the shared secret ok using his view key ivk $= k_v$ and the public seed pseed. Then, he can also derive τ and cr from ok, decrypt ct, and check whether the equations pk $= K_s \cdot g^\tau$ and com $=$ Com(amt, cr) hold. If so, Bob knows that he just received amt coins. This is possible even if isk is unknown. If isk $= k_s$ is known, then Bob can recover a secret key sk $= k_s + \tau$ for pk. This allows Bob to spend the output in a future transaction. To emphasize, ok is a shared secret between Alice and Bob, and no other party learns τ, cr, or the decryption key for ct.

Inputs. Assume Alice owns an output $o^* = (\text{pk}^*, \text{com}^*, \text{ct}^*)$ of a previous transaction. Especially, she knows the secret key sk* corresponding to pk*. Assume she wants to use this output as an input in the current transaction. A naive way for Alice to do that would be to include (a reference to) o^*, and a signature with respect to pk* to prove ownership. In order to obfuscate the link between the transaction and o^*, Monero uses a different approach. Namely, in a first step, Alice selects some random outputs $o' = (\text{pk}', \cdot, \cdot)$ of previous transactions in the system. These are not necessarily owned by Alice, and will serve as decoys. For simplicity, assume she only selects one such decoy output. Then, (references to) the outputs o^* and o' are included in the transaction. Finally, Alice does not use a standard signature, but instead she uses a ring signature for ring R $= \{\text{pk}^*, \text{pk}'\}$. This signature proves that Alice owns one of the outputs o^*, o', but does not reveal which one. However, this implies that after the transaction is accepted by the system, there has to be some mechanism that ensures that the output o^* can no longer be spent, while the decoy output o' can. We will see how to solve this later.

Homomorphic Commitments. So far, we discussed how to include outputs in transactions, and use previously received outputs as inputs for a transaction. However, we did not discuss how it is ensured that combination of inputs and outputs is valid, i.e., no money is created. In other words, we have to ensure that $\sum_j \text{amt}_j^{in} = \sum_i \text{amt}_i^{out}$, where amt_j^{in} and amt_i^{out} are the amounts encoded in inputs and outputs, respectively. To do this without revealing the amounts itself, Monero leverages homomorphic properties of the commitment scheme (i.e., the Pedersen commitment scheme). Namely, ignoring decoys for a moment, if com_j^{in} are the commitments contained in the inputs, and com_i^{out} are the commitments in the outputs, then we would ensure that $\sum_j \text{com}_j^{in} = \sum_i \text{com}_i^{out}$. Intuitively, the binding property of the commitment scheme should tell us that this equality implies the equality over the amounts that we want. However, this only holds if we avoid overflows. To do that, we ensure that the amt_j^{in} and amt_i^{out} are in a certain range. For that reason, Alice includes a range proof π in the transaction.

Pseudo Outputs. In the previous paragraph, we oversimplified our explanation. Namely, the following two obstacles remain:

- How can Alice ensure that the equation $\sum_j \mathsf{com}_j^{in} = \sum_i \mathsf{com}_i^{out}$ holds? Namely, for the Pedersen commitment, this not only requires $\sum_j \mathsf{amt}_j^{in} = \sum_i \mathsf{amt}_i^{out}$, but also $\sum_j \mathsf{cr}_j^{in} = \sum_i \mathsf{cr}_i^{out}$, where $\mathsf{com}_*^* = \mathsf{Com}(\mathsf{amt}_*^*, \mathsf{cr}_*^*)$. Given the structure of outputs, Alice has no way to ensure this.
- If we insist on the equation $\sum_j \mathsf{com}_j^{in} = \sum_i \mathsf{com}_i^{out}$, then actual inputs are distinguishable from the decoys, as they most likely do not satisfy the equation.

To get around these two problems, a level of indirection, called pseudo outputs, is used. In a nutshell, a pseudo output is just another commitment that Alice computes to connect inputs to outputs. Namely, for each of her inputs with amount amt_j^{in}, Alice computes a new commitment $\mathsf{com}_j = \mathsf{Com}(\mathsf{amt}_j^{in}, \mathsf{cr}_j)$, with freshly sampled randomness cr_j, and such that $\sum_j \mathsf{cr}_j = \sum_i \mathsf{cr}_i^{out}$. Then, instead of homomorphically checking equality between inputs and outputs, we now check equality between pseudo outputs and outputs using the equation $\sum_j \mathsf{com}_j = \sum_i \mathsf{com}_i^{out}$. This works out, because Alice now has the freedom to choose the values cr_j. In this way, we ensure that no money is created on the transition from pseudo outputs to outputs. What remains is to ensure that this also holds for the transition from inputs to pseudo outputs. To do that, for each input j, Alice needs to prove that she indeed used amt_j^{in} to compute com_j, where amt_j^{in} is the amount associated to her input $(\mathsf{pk}^*, \mathsf{com}^*, \mathsf{ct}^*)$. Recall that in our running example, this input is grouped with a decoy $(\mathsf{pk}', \mathsf{com}', \mathsf{ct}')$. We can not just insist on $\mathsf{com}^* = \mathsf{com}_j$, because this reintroduces the two problems from above. Instead, Alice could prove that $\mathsf{com}^* - \mathsf{com}_j$ or $\mathsf{com}' - \mathsf{com}_j$ is a commitment to 0. For Pedersen commitments with basis g, h, this is equivalent to proving that Alice knows some r such that $\mathsf{com}^* - \mathsf{com}_j = g^r$ or $\mathsf{com}' - \mathsf{com}_j = g^r$. Interestingly, this proof can implemented as part of the ring signature that is used: We introduce a second dimension to the public keys, and Alice signs for the ring $\mathsf{R} = \{(\mathsf{pk}^*, \mathsf{com}^* - \mathsf{com}_j), (\mathsf{pk}', \mathsf{com}' - \mathsf{com}_j)\}$ using the secret key (sk^*, r). In this way, the signature not only proves ownership of inputs, but also consistency between the amounts encoded in input and pseudo output.

Double-Spending Detection. When we discussed the structure of inputs, we claimed that ring signatures are used for each input. We already saw that this claim is just a simplification, because pseudo outputs require us to use two-dimensional ring signatures. What we did not solve yet is the problem raised in our discussion of inputs. Namely, after a transaction is accepted, the actual inputs should no longer be spendable, while the decoy outputs should be. Intuitively, if we were able to detect that two signatures are computed using the same secret key, then we could solve this problem. Namely, we force that each pk is only used once, and a transaction is only accepted if no signature conflicts with a previous one, in the above sense. Fortunately, there is a variant of ring signatures, called linkable ring signatures, that allows us to do exactly that.

More precisely, there is an algorithm $\mathsf{Link}(\sigma, \sigma')$ which outputs 1 if and only if σ and σ' were computed using the same key sk. This does not reveal which sk was used.

Summary: Transaction Generation. A user Alice can generate a transaction as follows:

1. Alice computes a public seed $\mathsf{pseed} = g^{\mathsf{sseed}}$ and includes it in the transaction.
2. Alice computes outputs. That is, for each recipient Bob with identity public key $\mathsf{ipk} = (K_v, K_s)$ that should receive amt coins, she does the following:
   (a) Derive the shared secret ok from K_v and sseed.
   (b) Using ok and the position of the output, derive commitment randomness and a rerandomization term.
   (c) Use these to compute a commitment com to amt and a rerandomization pk of K_s
   (d) Encrypt amt into a ciphertext ct using a key derived from ok.
   (e) The output is $(\mathsf{pk}, \mathsf{com}, \mathsf{ct})$.
3. For each of her inputs, Alice selects other outputs of previous transactions as decoys, and groups her actual input with these decoys.
4. For each of her inputs, Alice computes a pseudo output com_j, such that the pseudo outputs sum up to the sum of the output commitments.
5. Alice computes a range proof π showing that the amounts in output commitments and pseudo outputs do not cause overflows.
6. For each of the inputs, Alice signs the transaction using a two-dimensional linkable ring signature.

Summary: Transaction Verification. Throughout the last paragraphs, we introduced a lot of conditions that a valid transaction has to satisfy implicitly. Now, we explicitly summarize them. Namely, to verify the validity of a transaction, the following has to be checked:

1. All inputs (including the decoys) are outputs of previous transactions.
2. All signatures are valid with respect to the given rings.
3. There is no signature that links to another signature in this or a previous transaction.
4. We have $\sum_j \mathsf{com}_j = \sum_i \mathsf{com}_i^{out}$, where com_j are the pseudo outputs, and com_i^{out} are the output commitments.
5. The range proof for the commitments verifies.

3 Model for Private Transaction Schemes

In this section, we present our formal model for a private transaction scheme, such as RingCT. We first specify the components of a private transaction scheme. Then, we define how transactions are constructed using these components. Finally, we define the security of private transaction schemes.

3.1 Syntax

We introduce our syntax for private transaction schemes. A more detailed version is given in our full version [12]. Throughout, we assume that some system parameters par ← Setup(1^λ) are generated using a setup algorithm Setup. These are given implicitly to all algorithms and define certain data types. A private transaction scheme consists of several components, which we introduce below. For the informal explanation, we assume that a user Alice wants to spend coins to a user Bob.

Key Derivation Scheme. We start with the definition of a key derivation scheme KDS. This component specifies how users generate their long-term address, and how other users can then derive stealth addresses from them, i.e., keys associated to outputs in the system. Concretely, to generate its long-term address, Bob runs an algorithm GenID(par) that outputs a triple (ipk, ivk, isk). As explained in Sect. 2, the identity public key ipk serves as the public address, and the identity view key ivk and identity signing key isk are kept secret. Now, suppose Alice wants to spend coins to Bob. For that, Alice first samples a public seed pseed and a private seed sseed using an algorithm Encaps(par). Intuitively, we think of pseed as a first message in a key exchange between Alice and Bob. Alice includes pseed in the transaction such that Bob receives it. Then, she uses these seeds and Bob's address to derive a stealth address for Bob. To do that, algorithms SendDecaps and RecDecaps are used, where Alice runs SendDecaps(ipk, sseed) and Bob runs RecDecaps(ivk, pseed). As a result, both obtain a shared secret ok, called the output key. Alice now uses this shared secret in algorithm DerPK(ipk, ok, tag) to derive the public key pk, which is the stealth address. Bob uses algorithm DerSK(isk, ok, tag) to derive the corresponding secret key sk. Further, Bob can identify public keys pk that are derived for him by a further algorithm Track: if Track(ipk, ok, pk, tag) = 1, then this indicates that pk is derived for him. Here, the tag tag $\in \mathbb{N}$ is used for domain separation and ordering.

Verifiable Homomorphic Commitment Scheme. To hide the amount of a transaction while still allowing to verify consistency of inputs and outputs, a special kind of commitment scheme, and an associated proof is used. This is formalized by the notion of a verifiable homomorphic commitment scheme VHC. Namely, recall that when Alice commits to an amount she sends to Bob, then she deterministically derives the random coins cr used for the commitment from the output key ok that is shared between Alice and Bob. We model this via algorithm DerRand(ok, tag) that outputs cr. Given such random coins and an amount amt $\in \mathcal{D} \subseteq \mathbb{N}_0$, one can commit to amt using com := Com(amt, cr). Here, $\mathcal{D}$ is the set of allowed amounts. We require that Com is homomorphic in both amt and cr. Then, Alice can prove that she knows valid amounts in $\mathcal{D}$ that she committed to within one transaction. This is modeled by an algorithm PProve(stmt, witn) that takes a set of commitments as a statement stmt and the corresponding preimages as a witness witn, and outputs a proof π. The proof can then be verified for stmt by running an algorithm PVer(stmt, π).

Data Encryption Scheme. As amounts are hidden due to the use of a commitment scheme, Alice needs to communicate them privately to Bob. For that, a (symmetric) encryption scheme DE is used. It makes use of the shared secret ok as a key. We omit the details here, as they are not related to any of our security notions, but only relevant for privacy.

Key Conversion Scheme. Recall from our overview in Sect. 2 that Alice shows consistency between amounts in inputs and pseudo outputs by translating commitments in inputs and pseudo outputs into public keys used in the linkable ring signature scheme. If Alice knows the commitment randomness for two such commitments that commit to the same amount, then she can know the corresponding secret key. We formalize this process by defining a key conversion scheme KCS. Namely, Alice runs an algorithm auxpk := ConvertPublic(com, com′) to obtain an auxiliary public key auxpk from a pair of commitments com and com′, where we think of com as being part of an input, and com′ as being the pseudo output. Similarly, she can run auxsk := ConvertSecret(cr, cr′) for the associated randomness cr, cr′ to get an auxiliary secret key auxsk. The guarantee is that if com and com′ commit to the same amount with randomness cr, cr′, respectively, then auxsk is a valid secret key for auxpk, and can then be used within the linkable ring signature component.

Two-Dimensional Linkable Ring Signature Scheme. Before Alice can publish the transaction, she needs to sign it, using a variant of a ring signature scheme. Recall from our overview in Sect. 2, that this has two reasons. First, it ensures that Alice holds secret keys for one output referenced by each input. Second, in combination with the key conversion scheme, it ensures that the amounts between inputs and pseudo outputs are consistent. We formalize this as a two-dimensional linkable ring signature scheme LRS, which is given by three algorithms Sig, Ver, and Link. To sign a message m, e.g., a transaction, with respect to some key ring $R = (pk_i, auxpk_i)_{i=1}^{N}$, Alice has to know a valid pair of secret keys sk, auxsk for one of the $pk_i, auxpk_i$. Then, she can compute a signature $\sigma \leftarrow$ Sig(R, sk, auxsk, m). This signature can be verified with respect to R and m by running Ver(R, m, σ). Also, one can check whether two signatures σ, σ' were computed using the same key by running Link(σ, σ').

Generating Transactions. Suppose Alice wants to spend amt_i^{out} coins to a user with identity public key ipk_i for each $i \in [K]$. Further, suppose that Alice wants to use L inputs for that, which are outputs (pk_j^{in}, com_j^{in}) (for $j \in [L]$) of previous transactions that she owns. Because she owns them, she knows the associated amount and commitment randomness amt_j^{in}, cr_j^{in}, and the corresponding secret key sk_j. We write $Use_j = (pk_j^{in}, com_j^{in}, amt_j^{in}, cr_j^{in}, sk_j)$ for $j \in [L]$ to denote these outputs that Alice uses as inputs, along with the corresponding secret information. Finally, assume that Alice picked additional outputs (not necessarily owned by her) from previous transactions. We let Ref_j be the list of these outputs, including an entry $\mathsf{pk}_j^{in}, \mathsf{com}_j^{in}$. Now, we specify how Alice generates a transaction by defining an algorithm GenTx, which takes as inputs $(\mathsf{Use}_j)_{j=1}^{L}$, $(\mathsf{Ref}_j)_{j=1}^{L}$, and $(\mathsf{ipk}_i, \mathsf{amt}_i^{out})_{i=1}^{K}$. We formally present this algorithm in our full version [12].

Verifying Transactions. We specify how a user can verify a given transaction by defining an algorithm VerTx. As the validity of a transaction depends on the current state of the system, e.g., on previous transactions, this algorithm needs additional inputs that model this state. Concretely, we model all public seeds of previous transactions by a list PSeeds, all outputs in the system by a list Outputs, and all signatures contained in previous transactions by a list Signatures. Then, algorithm VerTx takes as input the lists PSeeds, Outputs, Signatures and a transaction Tx. We formally define this algorithm in the full version [12].

Receiving Outputs. When a transaction Tx is published, users should be able to identify outputs that they receive. For that, we define an algorithm Receive. Concretely, write $\mathsf{Tx} = (\mathsf{In}, \mathsf{Out}, \mathsf{pseed}, \pi)$ and let its outputs be $\mathsf{Out} = \left(\mathsf{pk}_i^{out}, \mathsf{com}_i^{out}, \mathsf{ct}_i, \mathsf{tag}_i\right)_{i=1}^{K}$. Then, each user with keys $\mathsf{ipk}, \mathsf{ivk}, \mathsf{isk}$ runs Receive on inputs $\mathsf{pk}_i^{out}, \mathsf{com}_i^{out}, \mathsf{ct}_i, \mathsf{tag}_i$ for each $i \in [K]$. Additionally, the user inputs pseed and its keys $\mathsf{ipk}, \mathsf{ivk}, \mathsf{isk}$. The algorithm outputs the received amount amt, and the commitment randomness and secret key cr, sk in case the amount is non-zero. The commitment randomness and secret key are then needed whenever the user wants to spend this output.

3.2 Security

In this section, we introduce our security notion for private transaction schemes like RingCT. In other words, we make explicit what we aim to prove by presenting a cryptographic security game. To define security, we introduce data structures and oracles that model the state of the world and the adversary's capabilities. For the entire section, we fix a private transaction scheme $\mathsf{PTS} = (\mathsf{LRS}, \mathsf{KDS}, \mathsf{VHC}, \mathsf{DE}, \mathsf{KCS})$ and an efficient adversary $\mathcal{A}$.

Threat Model. Before we explain the details of our security game, we provide intuition for the threat model. In our security game, the adversary is allowed to interact with honest users and a public ledger, which accepts and stores transactions whenever they are valid. The adversary can make new users appear, corrupt users, and instruct honest users to create and publish transactions. Further, the adversary can submit arbitrary transactions to the ledger. The goal of the adversary is to either create coins out of thin air, or to steal or invalidate coins from honest users. In the remainder of this section, we state the definition of this security game more precisely.

State of the World. To model the current state of the world, our game holds several data structures. First, the game should keep track of existing (honest) users, by storing identity keys and information about the outputs that these users own. For that, we introduce the following data structures.

- Identities: This list contains identity public keys ipk for users. These users are initially honest, but may later be corrupted by the adversary.
- ivk[·], isk[·]: These maps contain the identity view key ivk[ipk] and the identity signing key isk[ipk] for each ipk ∈ Identities.
- corr[·] : This map contains a value corr[ipk] ∈ {0, 1, 2} for each ipk ∈ Identities. It models the corruption state of this user, i.e., corr[ipk] = 0 by default, corr[ipk] = 1 if $\mathcal{A}$ knows ivk[ipk], and corr[ipk] = 2 if $\mathcal{A}$ knows ivk[ipk] and isk[ipk].
- Owned[·] : This map contains a list Owned[ipk] for each ipk ∈ Identities. This lists contains all outputs that user ipk owns. Additionally, it contains side information that is necessary to spend these outputs. Namely, the lists contain entries of the form (pk, com, amt, cr, sk). It is only kept consistent for users ipk with corr[ipk] < 2.

Second, the game should be able to generate and verify transactions. For that, the game has to know all previous transactions, or more precisely, previous outputs and signatures. Therefore, we introduce the following data structures.

- TXs: This list contains all transactions in the system, i.e., transactions that have been submitted and verified.
- PSeeds: This list contains all public seeds pseed that are contained in transactions in the system.
- Outputs: This list contains all outputs (pk, com) that are currently in the system. These may, for example, be part of previous transactions.
- Signatures: This list contains all signatures σ that are part of previous transactions.

Finally, we want to keep track of the amount of coins that $\mathcal{A}$ obtained from the game, and the amount of coins that it spent to honest users. This will be necessary to define security.

- received ∈ $\mathbb{N}_0$: This integer models how many coins the adversary obtained from the game, e.g., via transactions generated by honest users.
- spent ∈ $\mathbb{N}_0$: This integer models how many coins the adversary spent to the game, e.g., via transactions received by honest users.

Adversary Capabilities. The capabilities of an adversary are modeled by a set of oracles to which the adversary has access. When the adversary calls these oracles, the current state of the world may change. This means that the oracles trigger changes to the data structures discussed before. Formally, we present all oracles using pseudocode in the full version [12].

The first capability that adversary $\mathcal{A}$ has is to interact with honest users and corrupt them. It can populate the system with honest users, and we model two types of corruption. This reflects that users may store their keys in different locations. Additionally, we will see that the adversary can always generate identity public keys on its own and use them in transactions.

- NEWIDENTITY() : This oracle generates a new honest user. For that, it generates keys (ipk, ivk, isk) ← GenID(par). Then, it inserts ipk into the list Identities, and sets ivk[ipk] := ivk, isk[ipk] := ∅, corr[ipk] := 0. It returns ipk to $\mathcal{A}$.
- PARTCORR(ipk) : This oracle allows $\mathcal{A}$ to learn the identity view key of an honest user. Precisely, the oracle returns ⊥ if ipk ∉ Identities or corr[ipk] ≠ 0. Otherwise, it sets corr[ipk] := 1 and returns ivk[ipk] to $\mathcal{A}$.
- FULLCORR(ipk) : This oracle allows $\mathcal{A}$ to learn the identity signing key of an honest user. Precisely, the oracle returns ⊥ if ipk ∉ Identities or corr[ipk] ≠ 1. Otherwise, it sets corr[ipk] := 2. Then, it updates received accordingly, i.e.,

$$\text{received} := \text{received} + \sum_{(\text{pk},\text{com},\text{amt},\text{cr},\text{sk}) \in \text{Owned}[\text{ipk}]} \text{amt.}$$

It returns isk[ipk] to $\mathcal{A}$.

Recall that valid transactions are required to use outputs in the system as inputs. Thus, we need to introduce some initial supply of outputs, as otherwise there is no way to create a valid transaction. This corresponds to mining coins in the real world. In our model, we let $\mathcal{A}$ arbitrarily create new outputs by calling one of the following two oracles. Recalling that an output contains a public key and a commitment, we may allow $\mathcal{A}$ to compute the commitment on its own, or to let the game compute it. However, we need to keep track of the amount of coins that $\mathcal{A}$ spawned in this way. Therefore, if $\mathcal{A}$ submits a (potentially maliciously computed) commitment, it is only considered valid if it can be received by an honest user.

- NEWHONSRC(pk, pseed, com, tag, ct) : This oracle tries find an honest user to receive the given output. For that, it runs Receive for each user ipk ∈ Identities with corr[ipk] < 2. If for some user, the received amount is non-zero, it inserts (pk, com) into Outputs and stores the output together with the secrets necessary to spend it in the list Owned[ipk].
- NEWSRC(pk, amt, cr) : This oracle inserts (pk, com) into Outputs, where com := Com(amt, cr). It also updates received accordingly, i.e., received := received + amt.

Finally, it is clear that we should enable the adversary to put transactions on the ledger. Additionally, honest parties may publish transactions. For that, we let adversary $\mathcal{A}$ instruct honest users to generate transactions with some specified receivers. We allow $\mathcal{A}$ to determine the distribution from which the users sample decoys and coins that they spend.

- ADDADVTRANS(Tx) : This oracle first verifies the given transaction using algorithm VerTx and the current state of the system given by PSeeds, Outputs, and Signatures. If the transaction is invalid, it returns. Otherwise, it updates

TXs, PSeeds, Outputs, and Signatures accordingly, by inserting Tx into TXs, its public seed pseed into PSeeds, all its outputs (pk, com) into Outputs, and all its signatures into Signatures. It also updates the owned outputs of all honest users by running algorithm Receive for every honest user and every output of Tx, and then updating Owned accordingly. Finally, it sets spent := spent + spentnow, where spentnow is the total amount that honest users received from Tx.

- ADDHONTRANS(ipk, $(\text{ipk}_i, \text{amt}_i^{out})_{i=1}^{K}$, ISamp, RSamp) : By calling this oracle, $\mathcal{A}$ instructs an honest user with identity public key ipk to pay amt_i^{out} coins to identity public key ipk_i for each $i \in [K]$. For that, the honest user should use distribution ISamp to determine the outputs that should be used as inputs, and distribution RSamp to determine the remaining decoys. Precisely, this oracle returns if ipk $\notin$ Identities or corr[ipk] = 2. Otherwise, it generates a transaction as follows.
  1. Sample inputs to use by running $(\text{Use}_j)_{j=1}^{L} \leftarrow \text{ISamp}(\text{Owned}[\text{ipk}])$ and $(\text{Ref}_j)_{j=1}^{L} \leftarrow \text{RSamp}(\text{Owned}[\text{ipk}], (\text{Use}_j)_{j=1}^{L})$.
  2. Check validity of the inputs. Namely, each $\text{Use}_j = (\text{pk}_j, \text{com}_j, \text{amt}_j, \text{cr}_j, \text{sk}_j)$ should be in Owned[ipk], the output $(\text{pk}_j, \text{com}_j)$ contained in Use_j should be in Ref_j, and each $(\text{pk}, \text{com}) \in \text{Ref}_j$ should be in Outputs. Also, $\sum_{j=1}^{L} \text{amt}_j = \sum_{i=1}^{K} \text{amt}_i^{out}$ should hold. If one of these conditions does not hold, the oracle returns $\perp$.
  3. Generate the transaction Tx by running algorithm GenTx. If the transaction is not valid, return $\perp$. We will see later that the adversary wins the game in this case.

  Next, the oracle updates Owned[ipk] := Owned[ipk] \ $\{\text{Use}_j\}_{j \in [L]}$. It also updates Owned, TXs, PSeeds, Outputs as in oracle ADDADVTRANS. Then, it updates received accordingly, i.e., received := received + amt_i^{out} for each $i \in [K]$ with $\text{ipk}_i \notin$ Identities or corr[ipk] = 2. Finally, it returns Tx to $\mathcal{A}$.

Security Notion. Next, we define the security notion for a private transaction scheme PTS = (LRS, KDS, VHC, DE, KCS). To this end, we introduce a security game $\mathbf{UNF}_{\text{PTS}}^{\mathcal{A}}(\lambda)$ for an adversary $\mathcal{A}$. In the security game, $\mathcal{A}$ interacts with all oracles defined above. Informally, $\mathcal{A}$ breaks the security of the system, if it can create money out of thin air, or prevent honest users from spending their coins. Therefore, we say that $\mathcal{A}$ wins the security game, if at least one of the following two events occur at any point during the game:

1. Event win-create: We have spent > received.
2. Event win-steal: Adversary $\mathcal{A}$ instructs an honest user to generate a transaction using oracle ADDHONTRANS, a transaction Tx is generated accordingly, but does not verify, i.e., VerTx(PSeeds, Outputs, Signatures, Tx) = 0.

Consider a private transaction scheme PTS = (LRS, KDS, VHC, DE, KCS). For any algorithm $\mathcal{A}$ we define the game $\mathbf{UNF}_{\text{PTS}}^{\mathcal{A}}(\lambda)$ as follows:

1. Consider oracles O_{id} := (NEWIDENTITY, PARTCORR, FULLCORR), O_{src} = (NEWHONSRC, NEWSRC), and O_{tx} = (ADDADVTRANS, ADDHONTRANS) described above.

2. Run $\mathcal{A}$ with access to oracles O_{id}, O_{src}, O_{tx} on input 1^λ.
3. Output 1, if win-create $= 1$ or win-steal $= 1$. Otherwise, output 0.

We say that PTS is secure, if for every PPT algorithm $\mathcal{A}$ the following advantage is negligible:
$$\mathsf{Adv}^{\mathsf{unf}}_{\mathcal{A},\mathsf{PTS}}(\lambda) := \Pr\left[\mathbf{UNF}^{\mathcal{A}}_{\mathsf{PTS}}(\lambda) \rightarrow 1\right].$$

4   Overview of Our Analysis

In this section, we give an overview of our formal analysis of RingCT. Due to space limitations, we keep this overview informal. We encourage the interested reader to consult our full version [12] for the detailed formal analysis. Our strategy consists of three steps. First, we introduce security notions for (combinations of) the subcomponents of a private transaction scheme. Second, we show that whenever the subcomponents satisfy these notions, the security of the private transaction scheme follows generically. Third, we prove that the instantiations of subcomponents used in Monero satisfy the respective notions.

4.1   Security Notions for Components

We introduce several security notions for the subcomponents of a private transaction scheme. For each notion, we informally sketch a security game. The formal games are given in our full version [12]. We also aim to convey an intuition for why it is needed in the context of a private transaction scheme. Throughout this section, we fix a private transaction scheme $\mathsf{PTS} = (\mathsf{LRS}, \mathsf{KDS}, \mathsf{VHC}, \mathsf{DE}, \mathsf{KCS})$ and an efficient adversary $\mathcal{A}$. We assume that $\mathcal{A}$ gets the system parameters par at the beginning of each game.

Tracking Soundness. Recall that an honest user recognizes received outputs using algorithm Track. We want to ensure that when an honest user recognizes such an output (i.e., Track outputs 1), then this output can later be spent. In other words, if Track outputs 1, then a valid secret key will be derived. We capture this by the notion of tracking soundness. In the security game, $\mathcal{A}$ gets as input the keys ipk, ivk, isk of an honest user, which are generated via (ipk, ivk, isk) $\leftarrow$ GenID(par). Then, it outputs pseed, pk, tag, and the honest user runs ok $:=$ RecDecaps(ivk, pseed), $b :=$ Track(ipk, ok, pk, tag) and sk $:=$ DerSK(isk, ok, tag) as it does when trying to receive an output. The adversary $\mathcal{A}$ wins if $b = 1$ but sk is not a valid secret key for pk.

Key Spreadness. We introduce a notion that we call key spreadness. Roughly, it states that different public seeds pseed, pseed′ or different tags tag, tag′ lead to different derived keys sk, sk′. Looking ahead, this ensures that no two signatures generated by honest users link. In the security game for key spreadness, $\mathcal{A}$ gets access to an honest user's keys ipk, ivk, isk and outputs seeds pseed, pseed′ and tags tag, tag'. Then, the honest user derives keys sk and sk' via sk := DerSK(isk, RecDecaps(ivk, pseed), tag) and sk' := DerSK(isk, RecDecaps(ivk, pseed'), tag'). Finally, $\mathcal{A}$ wins this game if (pseed, tag) $\neq$ (pseed', tag') but sk = sk'.

Conversion Soundness. Recall that the key conversion scheme KCS allows to transform pairs of commitment randomness cr, cr' for commitments com, com' to the same data amt into auxiliary keys auxsk and auxpk. Intuitively, when one then uses auxsk in the ring signature and cr' in a pseudo output commitment, this should prove that one knew cr. Our notion of conversion soundness roughly states that knowing auxsk and cr' implies (via a translation algorithm) knowing cr. In other words, if conversion soundness holds, then it is enough to show that generating a valid transaction requires knowledge of auxsk and cr'. For the formal notion, we require that there is an efficient algorithm Translate, such that (any efficient) $\mathcal{A}$ wins the following game only with negligible probability. First, $\mathcal{A}$ outputs amt, cr', com, com', auxpk, auxsk. Then Translate is run given all these elements as input and outputs cr. The adversary wins the game if its input was well formed, i.e., Com(amt, cr') = com', (auxpk, auxsk) are a valid key pair, and ConvertPublic(com, com') = auxpk, but translation failed, i.e., Com(amt, cr) $\neq$ com or ConvertSecret(cr, cr') $\neq$ auxsk.

Binding Commitment. Clearly, the commitment scheme should satisfy the standard notion of binding. This ensures that an adversary can not change the amount of an output. To recall, $\mathcal{A}$ breaks binding if it outputs (amt, cr) and (amt', cr') such that (amt, cr) $\neq$ (amt', cr') and Com(amt, cr) = Com(amt', cr').

Commitment Knowledge Soundness. We introduce the notion of commitment knowledge soundness. Roughly, it states that the proofs π included in transactions are proofs of knowledge. Precisely, if an adversary generates pseudo output commitments and output commitments for a transaction along with a proof π, then the adversary must know the corresponding amt and commitment randomness cr. Looking ahead, the technical reason why we require a proof of knowledge is that we have to extract cr before we can reduce to binding in an overall proof of security. We stress the importance of being able to extract multiple times from the adversary. This is because we need to run the extractor for every submitted transaction in our overall proof. In our formal definition, we require the existence of an efficient extractor $\mathsf{Ext}_{\mathsf{VHC}}$ such that no efficient $\mathcal{A}$ wins the following game with non-negligible probability. The adversary $\mathcal{A}$ gets access to an oracle O. Whenever $\mathcal{A}$ calls O, it submits a statement stmt = $(\mathsf{com}_i)_i$ and a proof π. Then, the game runs the extractor witn $\leftarrow \mathsf{Ext}_{\mathsf{VHC}}(\mathsf{stmt}, \pi)$ to get a witness witn = $(\mathsf{amt}_i, \mathsf{cr}_i)_i$. If in any of these queries we have PVer(stmt, π) = 1, i.e., the proof verifies, and there is some i such that Com($\mathsf{amt}_i, \mathsf{cr}_i) \neq \mathsf{com}_i$, i.e., extraction failed, then $\mathcal{A}$ wins.

C. Cremers et al.

Non-slanderability. A well-established notion for linkable ring signatures is non-slanderability [27,51] (sometimes called non-frameability [2,5]). This notion states that it is not possible for an adversary to come up with a signature that links to an honest user's signature. In our setting, this means that it can not happen that an honest user computes a signature on a transaction using a valid secret key, and this transaction gets rejected because the signature links to a previous signature. However, we can not just use the standard non-slanderability notion, because the key derivation scheme KDS introduces non-trivial relations between keys. Hence, we define a game that is similar to non-slanderability, but for keys that are derived using KDS. When making signature queries, the adversary can specify the parameters with which the secret key sk is derived from an identity signing key isk. Let us now give an overview of our non-slanderability game. In this game, $\mathcal{A}$ gets access to oracles NEWIDENTITY, CORR, and SIGN. When called, oracle NEWIDENTITY generates keys $(\mathsf{ipk}, \mathsf{ivk}, \mathsf{isk}) \leftarrow \mathsf{GenID}(\mathsf{par})$ for a new honest user, and returns $(\mathsf{ipk}, \mathsf{ivk})$ to $\mathcal{A}$. The adversary $\mathcal{A}$ can corrupt any such user and learn isk by querying CORR(ipk). Further, it can ask for signatures using oracle SIGN. Here $\mathcal{A}$ submits pk, pseed, tag, R, auxsk, m. The oracle then finds an honest user with key $(\mathsf{ipk}, \mathsf{ivk}, \mathsf{isk})$ that owns pk, i.e., such that $\mathsf{Track}(\mathsf{ipk}, \mathsf{ok}, \mathsf{pk}, \mathsf{tag}) = 1$ for $\mathsf{ok} := \mathsf{RecDecaps}(\mathsf{ivk}, \mathsf{pseed})$. Then, it derives sk from ok, isk, and tag using algorithm DerSK and computes a signature $\sigma \leftarrow \mathsf{Sig}(\mathsf{R}, \mathsf{sk}, \mathsf{auxsk}, \mathsf{m})$ on the message m. This signature is returned to $\mathcal{A}$. When $\mathcal{A}$ terminates, it outputs a tuple $(\mathsf{R}^*, \mathsf{m}^*, \sigma^*)$. It wins the game, if σ^* is valid for message m^* and R^*, $\mathcal{A}$ never received a signature from SIGN by querying m^* and R^* together, and there is a non-corrupted honest user that computed a signature σ in SIGN such that $\mathsf{Link}(\sigma, \sigma^*) = 1$.

Key Onewayness. We also define a weaker notion related to non-slanderability. Namely, the adversary should not be able to come up with secret keys without corrupting a user, given access to the same oracles as in the non-slanderability game. More precisely, in the key onewayness game, $\mathcal{A}$ gets access to the same oracles as for non-slanderability, and outputs a tuple $(\mathsf{ipk}^*, \mathsf{pk}^*, \mathsf{pseed}^*, \mathsf{tag}^*, \mathsf{sk}^*)$. It wins, if $(\mathsf{pk}^*, \mathsf{sk}^*)$ are a valid key pair, ipk^* is the key of an honest and non-corrupted user, and this honest user recognizes pk^* as its key, i.e., $\mathsf{Track}(\mathsf{ipk}^*, \mathsf{ok}, \mathsf{pk}^*, \mathsf{tag}^*) = 1$ for $\mathsf{ok} := \mathsf{RecDecaps}(\mathsf{ivk}, \mathsf{pseed}^*)$, where ivk is the identity view key of this user.

Key Knowledge Soundness. If we want to use the notion of conversion soundness introduced above, we first need to extract an auxiliary secret key auxsk from an adversary submitting a transaction. Therefore, we introduce a strong property called key knowledge soundness. Roughly speaking, it states that LRS is a signature of knowledge, i.e., the adversary can only come up with a valid signature if it knows a valid secret key (sk, auxsk). Before we present the definition, let us discuss one subtlety. A natural way of defining this notion would be to allow the adversary to submit tuples $(\mathsf{R}, \mathsf{m}, \sigma)$ to an oracle O, and let this oracle try to extract suitable secret keys via an extractor in the algebraic group model. If this extraction fails, the adversary wins. While this is a good start, it is not exactly what we want. Namely, in our setting, the adversary also receives signatures from the outside, e.g., when we want to do a reduction breaking key onewayness. If the adversary simply submits these signatures to O, there is no hope that the adversary knew any secret keys. On a technical level, we would also encounter composition problems with the algebraic group model. This is because our definition defines the basis for algebraic representations that the algebraic adversary submits, and that are used by the extractor. If this basis is different when we want to apply key knowledge soundness (e.g., because the adversary received additional group elements as part of keys of honest users), then the extractor is useless. This motivates why we give additional oracles to the adversary in our notion.

We now sketch the final definition of key knowledge soundness. We require that there is an efficient extractor $\mathsf{Ext_{LRS}}$, such that no efficient adversary $\mathcal{A}$ wins the following game. Adversary $\mathcal{A}$ gets access to the same oracles NEWIDENTITY, CORR, SIGN as in the non-slanderability game. Further, it gets access to an oracle O and wins, if for at least one of its queries to O, a certain winning condition is triggered. When $\mathcal{A}$ calls O, it has to submit a triple $(\mathsf{R}, \mathsf{m}, \sigma)$ such that it never submitted R, m together to the signing oracle SIGN and obtained a signature for it, and also it has to hold that $\mathsf{Ver}(\mathsf{R}, \mathsf{m}, \sigma) = 1$, i.e., σ is a valid signature for R, m. If these conditions hold, parse R as $\mathsf{R} = (\mathsf{pk}_i, \mathsf{auxpk}_i)_i$. Then, the extractor $\mathsf{Ext_{LRS}}$ is run and outputs $(i^*, \mathsf{sk}_{i^*}, \mathsf{auxsk}_{i^*})$, which intuitively should mean that $\mathcal{A}$ used secret keys $\mathsf{sk}_{i^*}, \mathsf{auxsk}_{i^*}$ for $\mathsf{pk}_{i^*}, \mathsf{auxpk}_{i^*}$ to compute σ. The adversary wins if this extraction failed, i.e., $(\mathsf{auxpk}_{i^*}, \mathsf{auxsk}_{i^*})$ or $(\mathsf{pk}_{i^*}, \mathsf{sk}_{i^*})$ are not a valid key pair.

Knowledge Linkability. Typically, linkable ring signatures should satisfy linkability. Informally, this notion states that if one uses the same secret key to compute two signatures, then these will link. The formalization of this intuition is non-trivial. In particular, we observe that the standard formalization (sometimes called pigeonhole linkability) is not enough for our purposes (cf. Section 1.2). Instead, we need a notion that is compatible with the extractor we defined for key knowledge soundness. This is because, in some sense, the extractor already tells us which key was used to compute a signature. Motivated by this, we define knowledge linkability, which roughly rules out that the extractor extracted the same sk twice from two signatures σ, σ' that do not link. In other words, it guarantees that if the extractor extracts the same key twice, then the corresponding signatures must link. More concretely, the knowledge linkability game is similar to the key knowledge soundness game that we introduced before. The only change is the winning condition in oracle O. To describe this new winning condition, we use the notation that we used to decribe the key knowledge soundness game. With this notation, $\mathcal{A}$ wins, if it submits a triple $(\mathsf{R}, \mathsf{m}, \sigma)$ to O, subject to the same restrictions as in key knowledge soundness, and σ does not link to any signature σ' output by SIGN or submitted to O before, but a secret key associated to pk_{i*} has been used to sign before. This includes the case where the extractor identified pk_{i*} as the signing public key before.

4.2 System Level Analysis

We show that any private transaction scheme is secure, given that its subcomponents satisfy the notions introduced in the previous section. Informally, we prove the following statement.

Theorem 1 (Informal). *Let* PTS *be a private transaction scheme. Assume that the subcomponents of* PTS *satisfy all security notions introduced in Sect. 4.1. Then,* PTS *is secure.*

For the formal statement, we refer to our full version [12]. We now present the main ideas used to prove this theorem. For both this informal overview and the formal analysis, we consider the two winning conditions separately.

Honest User Can not Spend. We start with winning condition win-steal. Informally, the adversary wins via winning condition win-steal, if there is a transaction with an output o that an honest user receives, and later the honest user can not spend this output. More concretely, the adversary instructs the user to compute a transaction Tx using this output via algorithm GenTx, and then Tx is invalid, i.e., VerTx outputs 0. To bound the probability of this event, we consider the different conditions that make algorithm VerTx output 0. Write $\mathsf{Tx} = (\mathsf{In}, \mathsf{Out}, \mathsf{pseed}, \pi)$, $\mathsf{In} = (\mathsf{Ref}_j, \mathsf{com}_j, \sigma_j)_{j=1}^{L}$, and $\mathsf{Out} = \left(\mathsf{pk}_i^{out}, \mathsf{com}_i^{out}, \mathsf{ct}_i, \mathsf{tag}_i\right)_{i=1}^{K}$. The cases are as follows.

- VerTx may output 0 because the public seed pseed contained in Tx is not fresh, i.e., there is a previous transaction that has the same public seed. As pseed is generated freshly by the honest user during generation of Tx, we can rely on the entropy of pseed to rule this case out.
- VerTx may output 0 because some input contained in the transaction Tx is not a previous output. However, an honest user would never include such an input in a transaction. Thus, this case can not occur.
- VerTx may output 0 because commitments included in the transaction Tx are not valid, i.e., the proof π does not verify, or $\sum_{j=1}^{L} \mathsf{com}_j \neq \sum_{i=1}^{K} \mathsf{com}_i^{out}$. Note that all involved commitments and the proof π are computed honestly in GenTx, and it follows from the completeness of VHC that this case never happens.
- VerTx may output 0 because one of the signatures σ_j is not valid.
- VerTx may output 0 because of double spending detection. That is, it may reject the transaction because one of the signatures σ_j links to a previous signature.

For the last two cases, we observe that the secret key that is used to compute the signatures is derived from the output o, which is provided by the adversary.

Therefore, we can not use completeness properties immediately and require additional arguments. Namely, for the case of invalid signatures, we first apply the tracking soundness notion. This notion tells us that for any output $o = (\mathsf{pk}, \mathsf{com})$ that an honest user receives from an adversary, it derives a valid secret key sk such that $(\mathsf{pk}, \mathsf{sk}) \in \mathcal{KR}$. Now, we can apply completeness of LRS to argue that the signature is always valid. The case of linking signatures is a bit more challenging. Namely, we consider two sub-cases. If the signature links to a maliciously generated signature, i.e., a signature that is contained in a transaction that the adversary submitted, then the adversary breaks non-slanderability. On the other hand, if the signature links to a signature that is also generated by an honest user, then we want to use the completeness property of LRS again. Specifically, it states that signatures computed honestly using different secret keys do not link. Now, it remains to argue that an honest party does not use the same secret key twice. For that, we make use of the key spreadness notion, and the fact that public goods are not reused.

Adversary Creates Money. Consider the second winning condition win-create. Roughly, our main strategy is to define a directed graph G with weighted edges modeling the state of the system during the security game. Then, we use the security notions for building blocks to argue that this satisfies the conditions of a flow network. Recall that in such a flow network, a flow value $f(e) \geq 0$ is assigned to each edge e in the graph, such that for each vertex (except a dedicated source and sink) the incoming flow equals the outgoing flow. Then, we use the theory of network flows to conclude. We will now make this rough idea more explicit. Namely, our proof proceeds in four main steps, which are as follows:

1. We consider each transaction and extract all hidden amounts and used secret keys. More precisely, for each output and pseudo output of the transaction, we extract the hidden amount and random coins for the commitments using commitment knowledge soundness. For each signature contained in the transaction, we extract the secret key and auxiliary secret that have been used to generate the signature. This is done using key knowledge soundness. Especially, we are now able to distinguish real inputs from decoys.

2. Using the knowledge we gained in the first step, we define a directed graph $G = (V, E)$, and an assignment $f(e) \geq 0$ to each edge $e \in E$. In this graph, for each output and each transaction in the system, there is an associated vertex. Whenever an output is used in a transaction as an input, there is an edge e from the output vertex to the transaction vertex. Further, there is an edge from each transaction to all of its outputs. In addition, there are dedicated vertices s and t, where $\{s, t\} \subseteq V$. For each source output, we add an edge from s to the vertex of this output. Finally, we add an edge from each output vertex that does not have an outgoing edge yet to t. In other words, outgoing edges of s model the initial money supply of the system, while ingoing edges of t model unused outputs. In terms of edge weights $f(e)$, notice that each

edge e is incident to one[2] output vertex. We set $f(e)$ to be the amount that we extracted from this output in the first step.

3. We show that this graph G and the assignment f define a flow network. To do so, we need to prove that for each vertex v (except s and t) the incoming flow, i.e., $\sum_{e=(u,v)\in E} f(e)$, is equal to the outgoing flow, i.e., $\sum_{e=(v,w)\in E} f(e)$. For that, we distinguish transaction and output vertices:

   (a) For transaction vertices, we first show that the sum of amounts is preserved between pseudo outputs and outputs. To do that, we use the homomorphic property and the binding property of VHC. Then, we show that for each input, the amount is preserved between the input (which is the output of a previous transaction) and the associated pseudo output. For that, we first leverage conversion soundness, and then apply binding of VHC once more. Note that we can only reduce from binding because we extracted amounts and random coins for each commitment before.

   (b) Each output vertex has in-degree one by definition. Thus, as long as we can show it also has out-degree one, the flow preservation follows. The main tool to show this is knowledge linkability.

4. Now that we showed that we have a flow network, we leverage the theory of flow networks to conclude. Omitting some details, this works as follows. Recall that an st-cut in G is a partition of V into two disjoint sets of vertices V_s, V_t with $s \in V_s$ and $t \in V_t$. The value of any such st-cut is the net flow from V_s to V_t, i.e., the flow from V_s to V_t minus the flow from V_t to V_s. In our proof, we are now interested in the following st-cut. We let V_s contain s and all vertices that are controlled by honest parties, i.e., transactions that honest parties created and outputs that are owned by honest parties. We let V_t contain all other vertices, i.e., t, all transactions created by the adversary, and all outputs not owned by honest parties. For this specific cut, we can argue that its value is at most $L + \text{received} - \text{spent}$, where L is the flow from V_s to vertex t. To see that, note that the flow from V_s to V_t is at most $L + \text{received}$, because each edge with weight f from V_s to V_t which is not going into vertex t increases the value of received by f. Further, the flow from V_t to V_s is at least spent, because whenever spent is increased by f, a new edge with weight f from V_t to V_s is added to the graph.

Recall that it is our goal to argue that $\text{received} - \text{spent} \geq 0$, i.e., the adversary spent at most as much as it received. Now, our central idea is to rely on the fact that in any flow network, the value of any cut is equal to the incoming flow T of the sink vertex t. In combination with the observation above, this shows that $L + \text{received} - \text{spent} \geq T$. By definition, we have $T \geq L$, and thus $L + \text{received} - \text{spent} \geq L$. Subtracting L from both sides, we get $\text{received} - \text{spent} \geq 0$, i.e., $\text{received} \geq \text{spent}$, which means the adversary can not create coins.

---

[2] Special care needs to be taken for corruptions, but we ignore them in this informal overview.

4.3 Component Level Analysis

To conclude that Monero's transaction scheme RingCT is secure, it remains to show security of its subcomponents with respect to the notions introduced in Sect. 4.1.

Theorem 2 (Informal). *Let* PTS *be the RingCT private transaction scheme. The subcomponents of* PTS *satisfy the security notions introduced in Sect. 4.1.*

We provide the formal theorem in our full version [12].

We prove all notions based on the discrete logarithm assumption in the random oracle model. While for some of the notions (e.g., binding) standard techniques suffice, the analysis of the linkable ring signature component turns out to be the most challenging part. Here, we rely on the algebraic group model to prove key knowledge soundness, which is natural for a knowledge-based security notion. We emphasize that we do not prove the notion of commitment knowledge soundness. This notion is defined for algorithms PProve and PVer of VHC, which are implemented using Bulletproofs/Bulletproofs+ [7,11] in Monero. A detailed analysis of this would not fit the scope of this work, and we leave it as a conjecture that the schemes satisfy commitment knowledge soundness. For an analysis of Bulletproofs in a similar model the reader may consult [26].

5 Other Models for RingCT-Like Systems

While no previous work analyzes Monero's transaction scheme RingCT as it is, some previous works [18,19,35,49,56] introduce models for protocols similar to RingCT. In this section, we elaborate on the shortcomings of these models. We also encourage the reader to consult the discussion on different models in [19,35]. As our work is only about transaction security and not about privacy, we omit discussing the privacy aspects of these previous models. We assume that the reader is familiar with our overview in Sect. 2.

Fragmented Security Notions. In our work, we provide a single experiment defining security for the transaction scheme as a whole. Informally, security means that an adversary can only spend what it owns, and not steal users coins. Unfortunately, most previous models [35,49,56] do not give a single security model for that. Instead, they provide a set of notions for components. Mostly, these mimic the standard notions of a linkable ring signature scheme, e.g., non-slanderability, linkability, unforgeability, and the notions of a commitment scheme, e.g., binding. We call such a model *fragmented*. The problem of such a model is that it is not clear how the notions relate, whether they compose, and how they imply security for the entire transaction scheme. For example, in [35], it is not obvious how and why the notions of binding, balance, and non-slanderability imply security of the entire transaction scheme when combined. Comparing to our work, fragmented models are somewhat similar to the set of security notions we define for our components. For example, we also have a binding and a non-slanderability notion for the components. Arguing that such a set of notions implies the security of the entire transaction scheme is highly non-trivial, as our analysis shows.

Adversarial Outputs. Recall that in Monero, each output of a transaction corresponds to a public key pk and a commitment com. If an adversary creates a transaction spending coins to an honest user, it derives this public key pk and the commitment com based on the public seed pseed of a transaction, and the recipients identity public key ipk. As a consequence, the adversary may know relations between different outputs of the same honest user, possibly leading to related key attacks. This means that any reasonable security model has to give the adversary the ability to derive outputs for honest users. We observe that several security models in previous works [18,19,49,56] do not have this feature.

Sun et al.'s RingCT 2.0. Sun et al. introduce [49] a model for protocols similar to RingCT and give a new construction based on pairings. Their model has several shortcomings. First, by defining security via two notions called balance and non-slanderability, they obtain a fragmented model in the above sense. Second, in terms of adversarial capabilities, their model is restricted. For example, as already noted in [35], their notions do not model adversarially generated outputs (i.e., stealth addresses). Instead, they only consider honestly generated outputs, which can not be assumed in the case of Monero. Moreover, the adversary does not have the ability to submit an arbitrary transaction to the chain. Instead, it can only add transactions by calling an oracle that honestly creates the transaction. Overall, these aspects limit the expressiveness of the model significantly. Third, the authors of [49] informally claim that linkability follows from their non-slanderability notion. As explained in [35], this is not true in general. In the context of Monero, this means that there can be counterexamples in which the given non-slanderability notion holds but double spending is possible.

Yuen et al.'s RingCT 3.0. Yuen et al. [56] also provide a model for protocols similar to RingCT and give a construction based on a new ring signature scheme. In terms of security, Yuen et al. provide three notions, called unforgeability, equivalence, linkability, and non-slanderability, which is fragmented in the above sense. Similar to the model by Sun et al. [49], the adversary can only add transactions via an oracle that generates these transactions honestly, and all outputs of honest parties are derived honestly.

Lai et al.'s Omniring. Lai et al. [35] introduce a model for transaction schemes and propose a new scheme that is more efficient than Monero's current transaction scheme. Then, they give an analysis of this new scheme with respect to their notions. In their model, Lai et al. first introduce two security properties, called balance and binding. Binding is defined in a natural way, and balance is formalized via an extractor that can extract all witnesses from an adversarially generated transaction. Moreover, non-slanderability is defined as a separate notion. This leads to a fragmented model and it is not clear how these three notions relate to each other and what they mean in combination. For example, while the non-slanderability notion gives the adversary access to oracles that allow to add transactions to the system arbitrarily, this is not the case for the balance and binding notions. Also, while having an extractor seems to be close to one of the security notions we introduce for components, the extractor in [35] only has to work for a single transaction. It is not clear what happens if we run such an extractor for multiple transactions. For example, the extractor is allowed to use rewinding, leading to an exponential blowup in running time when done naively on multiple transactions. Finally, the model of Lai et al. does not capture that honest users reuse randomness within one transaction for creating the outputs.

MatRiCT and MatRiCT $^+$. In [18,19], constructions of transaction schemes based on lattice assumptions are presented. Contrary to previous works, both works provide a single experiment for security instead of giving fragmented security models. On the downside, both works [18,19] do not model adversarially generated outputs (i.e., stealth addresses). It is mentioned in Appendix C.A of [18] that stealth addresses can be added to their lattice-based scheme in an easy way. However, it is clear that not modeling stealth addresses formally completely removes the challenge of dealing with related key attacks as discussed before. Finally, both works [18,19] do not model the reuse of randomness for output generation of honest users.

6   Limitations and Future Work

In our work, we only deal with standard Monero addresses and do not consider the case of subaddresses or integrated addresses. We also do not cover multisignatures and multi-signature addresses. This work focuses on the security of Monero's transaction scheme. In particular, we do not consider the consensus layer, and we do not model privacy of the transaction scheme. We plan to elaborate a model and analysis for privacy in future work. As it is standard in the literature, we use the abstraction of a prime order group to analyze the components of Monero, while it is actually implemented over curve Ed25519 [4]. Due to the modularity of our framework, one could extend our results to the setting of Ed25519 (in the spirit of, e.g., [6]) without the need of redoing the entire analysis. We assume that transaction public keys are never reused, yet we observe the consequences for transaction proofs (see the full version [12]). Finally, we do not show that the Bulletproof/Bulletproof+ component [7,8,11,25] of the system satisfies the security notion we define for it. It has been shown in [26] that Bulletproofs satisfy a related notion. After discussion with the authors of [26], we conjecture that their proof can be extended to show that Bulletproofs satisfy our notion as well. We leave investigating all of these directions as future work.

Acknowledgments. Julian Loss and Benedikt Wagner are funded by the Deutsche Forschungsgemeinschaft (DFG, German Research Foundation) - 507237585, and by the European Union, ERC-2023-STG, Project ID: 101116713. Views and opinions expressed are however those of the author(s) only and do not necessarily reflect those of the European Union. Neither the European Union nor the granting authority can be held responsible for them.

References

1. Alonso, K.M., Joancomartí, J.H.: Monero - privacy in the blockchain. Cryptology ePrint Archive, Report 2018/535 (2018). https://eprint.iacr.org/2018/535
2. Backes, M., Döttling, N., Hanzlik, L., Kluczniak, K., Schneider, J.: Ring signatures: logarithmic-size, no setup—from standard assumptions. In: Ishai, Y., Rijmen, V. (eds.) EUROCRYPT 2019. LNCS, vol. 11478, pp. 281–311. Springer, Cham (2019). https://doi.org/10.1007/978-3-030-17659-4_10
3. Ben-Sasson, E., et al.: Zerocash: decentralized anonymous payments from bitcoin. In: 2014 IEEE Symposium on Security and Privacy, pp. 459–474. IEEE Computer Society Press (2014). https://doi.org/10.1109/SP.2014.36
4. Bernstein, D.J., Duif, N., Lange, T., Schwabe, P., Yang, B.-Y.: High-speed high-security signatures. In: Preneel, B., Takagi, T. (eds.) CHES 2011. LNCS, vol. 6917, pp. 124–142. Springer, Heidelberg (2011). https://doi.org/10.1007/978-3-642-23951-9_9
5. Beullens, W., Katsumata, S., Pintore, F.: Calamari and Falafl: logarithmic (linkable) ring signatures from isogenies and lattices. In: Moriai, S., Wang, H. (eds.) ASIACRYPT 2020. LNCS, vol. 12492, pp. 464–492. Springer, Cham (2020). https://doi.org/10.1007/978-3-030-64834-3_16
6. Brendel, J., Cremers, C., Jackson, D., Zhao, M.: The provable security of Ed25519: theory and practice. In: 2021 IEEE Symposium on Security and Privacy, pp. 1659–1676. IEEE Computer Society Press (2021). https://doi.org/10.1109/SP40001.2021.00042
7. Bünz, B., Bootle, J., Boneh, D., Poelstra, A., Wuille, P., Maxwell, G.: Bulletproofs: short proofs for confidential transactions and more. In: 2018 IEEE Symposium on Security and Privacy, pp. 315–334. IEEE Computer Society Press (2018). https://doi.org/10.1109/SP.2018.00020
8. Bünz, B., Maller, M., Mishra, P., Tyagi, N., Vesely, P.: Proofs for inner pairing products and applications. In: Tibouchi, M., Wang, H. (eds.) ASIACRYPT 2021. LNCS, vol. 13092, pp. 65–97. Springer, Cham (2021). https://doi.org/10.1007/978-3-030-92078-4_3
9. Cao, T., Yu, J., Decouchant, J., Luo, X., Verissimo, P.: Exploring the Monero peer-to-peer network. In: Bonneau, J., Heninger, N. (eds.) FC 2020. LNCS, vol. 12059, pp. 578–594. Springer, Cham (2020). https://doi.org/10.1007/978-3-030-51280-4_31
10. Chiesa, A., Hu, Y., Maller, M., Mishra, P., Vesely, N., Ward, N.: Marlin: preprocessing zkSNARKs with universal and updatable SRS. In: Canteaut, A., Ishai, Y. (eds.) EUROCRYPT 2020. LNCS, vol. 12105, pp. 738–768. Springer, Cham (2020). https://doi.org/10.1007/978-3-030-45721-1_26
11. Chung, H., Han, K., Ju, C., Kim, M., Seo, J.H.: Bulletproofs+: shorter proofs for a privacy-enhanced distributed ledger. IEEE Access **10**, 42067–42082 (2022). https://doi.org/10.1109/ACCESS.2022.3167806

12. Cremers, C., Loss, J., Wagner, B.: A holistic security analysis of Monero transactions. Cryptology ePrint Archive, Report 2023/321 (2023). https://eprint.iacr.org/2023/321
13. Deuber, D., Ronge, V., Rückert, C.: SoK: assumptions underlying cryptocurrency deanonymizations. PoPETs **2022**(3), 670–691 (2022). https://doi.org/10.56553/popets-2022-0091
14. Dutta, A., Bagad, S., Vijayakumaran, S.: MProve+: privacy enhancing proof of reserves protocol for Monero. IEEE Trans. Inf. Forensics Secur. **16**, 3900–3915 (2021). https://doi.org/10.1109/TIFS.2021.3088035
15. Dutta, A., Vijayakumaran, S.: MProve: a proof of reserves protocol for Monero exchanges. In: 2019 IEEE European Symposium on Security and Privacy Workshops, EuroS&P Workshops 2019, Stockholm, Sweden, 17-19 June 2019, pp. 330–339. IEEE (2019). https://doi.org/10.1109/EuroSPW.2019.00043
16. Eagen, L.: Bulletproofs++. Cryptology ePrint Archive, Report 2022/510 (2022). https://eprint.iacr.org/2022/510
17. Egger, C., Lai, R.W.F., Ronge, V., Woo, I.K.Y., Yin, H.H.F.: On defeating graph analysis of anonymous transactions. PoPETs **2022**(3), 538–557 (2022). https://doi.org/10.56553/popets-2022-0085
18. Esgin, M.F., Steinfeld, R., Zhao, R.K.: MatRiCT$^+$: more efficient post-quantum private blockchain payments. In: 43rd IEEE Symposium on Security and Privacy, SP 2022, San Francisco, CA, USA, 22-26 May 2022, pp. 1281–1298. IEEE (2022). https://doi.org/10.1109/SP46214.2022.9833655
19. Esgin, M.F., Zhao, R.K., Steinfeld, R., Liu, J.K., Liu, D.: MatRiCT: efficient, scalable and post-quantum blockchain confidential transactions protocol. In: Cavallaro, L., Kinder, J., Wang, X., Katz, J. (eds.) ACM CCS 2019, pp. 567–584. ACM Press (2019). https://doi.org/10.1145/3319535.3354200
20. Frost, L.: Monero developers disclose 'significant' bug in privacy algorithm. https://decrypt.co/76938/monero-developers-disclose-significant-bug-privacy-algorithm. Accessed 14 Feb 2023
21. Fuchsbauer, G., Kiltz, E., Loss, J.: The algebraic group model and its applications. In: Shacham, H., Boldyreva, A. (eds.) CRYPTO 2018. LNCS, vol. 10992, pp. 33–62. Springer, Cham (2018). https://doi.org/10.1007/978-3-319-96881-0_2
22. Fuchsbauer, G., Orrù, M.: Non-interactive Mimblewimble transactions, revisited. Cryptology ePrint Archive, Report 2022/265 (2022). https://eprint.iacr.org/2022/265
23. Fuchsbauer, G., Orrù, M., Seurin, Y.: Aggregate cash systems: a cryptographic investigation of Mimblewimble. In: Ishai, Y., Rijmen, V. (eds.) EUROCRYPT 2019. LNCS, vol. 11476, pp. 657–689. Springer, Cham (2019). https://doi.org/10.1007/978-3-030-17653-2_22
24. Fujisaki, E., Suzuki, K.: Traceable ring signature. In: Okamoto, T., Wang, X. (eds.) PKC 2007. LNCS, vol. 4450, pp. 181–200. Springer, Heidelberg (2007). https://doi.org/10.1007/978-3-540-71677-8_13
25. Ganesh, C., Orlandi, C., Pancholi, M., Takahashi, A., Tschudi, D.: Fiat-shamir bulletproofs are non-malleable (in the algebraic group model). In: Dunkelman, O., Dziembowski, S. (eds.) EUROCRYPT 2022, Part II. LNCS, vol. 13276, pp. 397–426. Springer, Heidelberg (2022). https://doi.org/10.1007/978-3-031-07085-3_14
26. Ghoshal, A., Tessaro, S.: Tight state-restoration soundness in the algebraic group model. In: Malkin, T., Peikert, C. (eds.) CRYPTO 2021. LNCS, vol. 12827, pp. 64–93. Springer, Cham (2021). https://doi.org/10.1007/978-3-030-84252-9_3

27. Goodell, B., Noether, S., Blue, A.: Concise linkable ring signatures and forgery against adversarial keys. Cryptology ePrint Archive, Paper 2019/654 (2019). https://eprint.iacr.org/2019/654, https://eprint.iacr.org/2019/654

28. Gugger, J.: Bitcoin-monero cross-chain atomic swap. Cryptology ePrint Archive, Report 2020/1126 (2020). https://eprint.iacr.org/2020/1126

29. Hopwood, D., Bowe, S., Hornby, T., Wilcox, N.: Zcash Protocol Specification, Version 2022.3.8. https://zips.z.cash/protocol/protocol.pdf. Accessed 15 Feb 2023

30. Jedusor, T.E.: Mimblewimble. https://download.wpsoftware.net/bitcoin/wizardry/mimblewimble.txt. Accessed 15 Feb 2023

31. Jivanyan, A., Feickert, A.: Lelantus spark: Secure and flexible private transactions. Cryptology ePrint Archive, Report 2021/1173 (2021). https://eprint.iacr.org/2021/1173

32. Klee, C.: Monero XMR: "Signifikanter" Privacy Bug entdeckt. https://www.btc-echo.de/schlagzeilen/monero-xmr-signifikanter-privacy-bug-entdeckt-123001/. Accessed 14 Feb 2023

33. Koe, Alonso, K.M., Noether, S.: Zero to Monero v2.0.0. https://web.getmonero.org/library/Zero-to-Monero-2-0-0.pdf (2020). Accessed 21 Nov 2022

34. Kumar, A., Fischer, C., Tople, S., Saxena, P.: A traceability analysis of Monero's blockchain. In: Foley, S.N., Gollmann, D., Snekkenes, E. (eds.) ESORICS 2017. LNCS, vol. 10493, pp. 153–173. Springer, Cham (2017). https://doi.org/10.1007/978-3-319-66399-9_9

35. Lai, R.W.F., Ronge, V., Ruffing, T., Schröder, D., Thyagarajan, S.A.K., Wang, J.: Omniring: scaling private payments without trusted setup. In: Cavallaro, L., Kinder, J., Wang, X., Katz, J. (eds.) ACM CCS 2019, pp. 31–48. ACM Press (2019). https://doi.org/10.1145/3319535.3345655

36. Liu, J.K., Wei, V.K., Wong, D.S.: Linkable spontaneous anonymous group signature for Ad Hoc groups. In: Wang, H., Pieprzyk, J., Varadharajan, V. (eds.) ACISP 2004. LNCS, vol. 3108, pp. 325–335. Springer, Heidelberg (2004). https://doi.org/10.1007/978-3-540-27800-9_28

37. luigi1111, "fluffypony" Spagni, R.: Disclosure of a Major Bug in CryptoNote Based Currencies. https://www.getmonero.org/2017/05/17/disclosure-of-a-major-bug-in-cryptonote-based-currencies.html. Accessed 14 Feb 2023

38. Maller, M., Bowe, S., Kohlweiss, M., Meiklejohn, S.: Sonic: zero-knowledge SNARKs from linear-size universal and updatable structured reference strings. In: Cavallaro, L., Kinder, J., Wang, X., Katz, J. (eds.) ACM CCS 2019, pp. 2111–2128. ACM Press (2019). https://doi.org/10.1145/3319535.3339817

39. Morais, R., Crocker, P., de Sousa, S.M.: Delegated RingCT: faster anonymous transactions. Cryptology ePrint Archive, Report 2020/1521 (2020). https://eprint.iacr.org/2020/1521

40. Moreno-Sanchez, P., Blue, A., Le, D.V., Noether, S., Goodell, B., Kate, A.: DLSAG: non-interactive refund transactions for interoperable payment channels in Monero. In: Bonneau, J., Heninger, N. (eds.) FC 2020. LNCS, vol. 12059, pp. 325–345. Springer, Cham (2020). https://doi.org/10.1007/978-3-030-51280-4_18

41. Möser, M., et al.: An empirical analysis of traceability in the Monero blockchain. PoPETs **2018**(3), 143–163 (2018). https://doi.org/10.1515/popets-2018-0025

42. Nick, J.: A Problem With Monero's RingCT. https://jonasnick.github.io/blog/2016/12/17/a-problem-with-ringct/. Accessed 14 Feb 2023

43. Nick, J.: Exploiting low order generators in one-time ring signatures. https://jonasnick.github.io/blog/2017/05/23/exploiting-low-order-generators-in-one-time-ring-signatures/. Accessed 14 Feb 2023

44. Noether, S.: Ring signature confidential transactions for Monero. Cryptology ePrint Archive, Report 2015/1098 (2015). https://eprint.iacr.org/2015/1098
45. Pedersen, T.P.: Non-interactive and information-theoretic secure verifiable secret sharing. In: Feigenbaum, J. (ed.) CRYPTO 1991. LNCS, vol. 576, pp. 129–140. Springer, Heidelberg (1992). https://doi.org/10.1007/3-540-46766-1_9
46. Project, M.: Monero-Project/Meta: List of Issues. https://github.com/monero-project/meta/issues. Accessed 11 Apr 2023
47. Ronge, V., Egger, C., Lai, R.W.F., Schröder, D., Yin, H.H.F.: Foundations of ring sampling. PoPETs **2021**(3), 265–288 (2021). https://doi.org/10.2478/popets-2021-0047
48. Sui, Z., Liu, J.K., Yu, J., Qin, X.: MoNet: a fast payment channel network for scriptless cryptocurrency Monero. In: 42nd IEEE International Conference on Distributed Computing Systems, ICDCS 2022, Bologna, Italy, July 10-13, 2022, pp. 280–290. IEEE (2022). https://doi.org/10.1109/ICDCS54860.2022.00035
49. Sun, S.-F., Au, M.H., Liu, J.K., Yuen, T.H.: RingCT 2.0: a compact accumulator-based (linkable ring signature) protocol for blockchain cryptocurrency Monero. In: Foley, S.N., Gollmann, D., Snekkenes, E. (eds.) ESORICS 2017. LNCS, vol. 10493, pp. 456–474. Springer, Cham (2017). https://doi.org/10.1007/978-3-319-66399-9_25
50. Thyagarajan, S.A.K., Malavolta, G., Schmidt, F., Schröder, D.: PayMo: Payment channels for Monero. Cryptology ePrint Archive, Report 2020/1441 (2020). https://eprint.iacr.org/2020/1441
51. Tsang, P.P., Wei, V.K.: Short linkable ring signatures for E-voting, E-cash and attestation. In: Deng, R.H., Bao, F., Pang, H.H., Zhou, J. (eds.) ISPEC 2005. LNCS, vol. 3439, pp. 48–60. Springer, Heidelberg (2005). https://doi.org/10.1007/978-3-540-31979-5_5
52. Van Saberhagen, N.: CryptoNote v2.0. https://www.bytecoin.org/old/whitepaper.pdf (2013). Accessed 21 Nov 2022
53. Vijayakumaran, S.: Analysis of CryptoNote transaction graphs using the Dulmage-Mendelsohn decomposition. Cryptology ePrint Archive, Report 2021/760 (2021). https://eprint.iacr.org/2021/760
54. Wijaya, D.A., Liu, J.K., Steinfeld, R., Liu, D.: Monero ring attack: recreating zero Mixin transaction effect. In: 17th IEEE International Conference on Trust, Security and Privacy in Computing and Communications/12th IEEE International Conference on Big Data Science And Engineering, TrustCom/BigDataSE 2018, New York, NY, USA, August 1-3, 2018, pp. 1196–1201. IEEE (2018). https://doi.org/10.1109/TrustCom/BigDataSE.2018.00165
55. Yu, J., Au, M.H.A., Veríssimo, P.J.E.: Re-thinking untraceability in the CryptoNote-style blockchain. In: Delaune, S., Jia, L. (eds.) CSF 2019 Computer Security Foundations Symposium, pp. 94–107. IEEE Computer Society Press (2019). https://doi.org/10.1109/CSF.2019.00014
56. Yuen, T.H., et al.: RingCT 3.0 for blockchain confidential transaction: shorter size and stronger security. In: Bonneau, J., Heninger, N. (eds.) FC 2020. LNCS, vol. 12059, pp. 464–483. Springer, Cham (2020). https://doi.org/10.1007/978-3-030-51280-4_25

Algorithms for Matrix Code and Alternating Trilinear Form Equivalences via New Isomorphism Invariants

Anand Kumar Narayanan[1]([✉]), Youming Qiao[2], and Gang Tang[2,3]

[1] SandboxAQ, Palo Alto, USA
anand.kumar@sandboxaq.com
[2] Centre for Quantum Software and Information, School of Computer Science, Faculty of Engineering and Information Technology, University of Technology Sydney, Ultimo, NSW, Australia
Youming.Qiao@uts.edu.au, gang.tang-1@student.uts.edu.au
[3] University of Birmingham, Birmingham, UK

Abstract. We devise algorithms for finding equivalences of trilinear forms over finite fields modulo linear group actions. Our focus is on two problems under this umbrella, *Matrix Code Equivalence* (MCE) and *Alternating Trilinear Form Equivalence* (ATFE), since their hardness is the foundation of the NIST round-1 signature candidates MEDS and ALTEQ respectively.

We present new algorithms for MCE and ATFE, which are further developments of the algorithms for polynomial isomorphism and alternating trilinear form equivalence, in particular by Bouillaguet, Fouque, and Véber (*Eurocrypt* 2013), and Beullens (*Crypto* 2023). Key ingredients in these algorithms are new easy-to-compute distinguishing invariants under the respective group actions.

For MCE, we associate new isomorphism invariants to corank-1 points of matrix codes, which lead to a birthday-type algorithm. We present empirical justifications that these isomorphism invariants are easy-to-compute and distinguishing, and provide an implementation of this algorithm. This algorithm has some implications to the security of MEDS.

The invariant function for ATFE is similar, except it is associated with lower rank points. Modulo certain assumptions on turning the invariant function into canonical forms, our algorithm for ATFE improves on the runtime of the previously best known algorithm of Beullens (*Crypto* 2023).

Finally, we present quantum variants of our classical algorithms with cubic runtime improvements.

1 Introduction

Given two objects A and B of the same type, the *equivalence problem* asks if there exists a map π such that $\pi(A) = B$. The hardness of the equivalence

M. Joye and G. Leander (Eds.): EUROCRYPT 2024, LNCS 14653, pp. 160–187, 2024.
https://doi.org/10.1007/978-3-031-58734-4_6

problem depends on the objects and how the map is defined. There are objects in the equivalence problem that were recently proposed to support public-key cryptography for quantum-resistant purposes, such as linear or matrix codes [8,13,22], alternating trilinear form [42], lattice [25,26] etc.

Linear Code Equivalence. A classical equivalence problem is the *Code Equivalence* problem, which asks whether two given linear codes are isometric, that is, whether two linear codes are the same up to permuting, and possibly scalar multiplications on, the coordinates. One digital signature scheme submitted to the NIST call for additional signatures, LESS [5], is based on the assumed hardness of this problem.

Leon [36] initiated the study of this problem and proposed an algorithm that computes a list of both codes with minimum Hamming weight and then matches them to recover the isometry. Recently, Beullens [11] improved Leon's algorithm by using collision search. Another algorithm of significance is known as the Support Splitting Algorithm (SSA) by Sendrier [40]. Its running time increases exponentially in the dimension of the hull (the intersection of a code and its dual), and it works effectively for random linear codes under permutations. When scalar multiplications are also present, SSA works when $q \leq 4$ but not $q \geq 5$. If the hull is trivial and only permutations are used, then this problem can be reduced to graph isomorphism [7].

Matrix Code Equivalence. In this work, we are interested in the equivalence problem of matrix codes, called the *Matrix Code Equivalence* (MCE) problem. A matrix code over $\mathbb{F}_q$ is a linear subspace of the space of $m \times n$ matrices over $\mathbb{F}_q$. Concerning the MCE problem, it was recently shown to be at least as hard as the Code Equivalence problem [23,31], and to be equivalent to the homogeneous version of the Quadratic Maps Linear Equivalence (QMLE) problem [31,39].

Alternating Trilinear Form Equivalence. We are also interested in another problem namely *Alternating Trilinear Form Equivalence* (ATFE), recently proposed in [42] to support a digital signature scheme. Here, the objects are alternating trilinear forms, namely a function $\phi : \mathbb{F}_q^n \times \mathbb{F}_q^n \times \mathbb{F}_q^n \to \mathbb{F}_q$ that is (1) linear in each argument, and (2) whenever two arguments are the same, ϕ evaluates to 0.

We now state the MCE and ATFE problems, which would also indicate what equivalences mean for matrix codes and alternating trilinear forms.

Definition 1 (Matrix Code Equivalence (MCE)). *Given two matrix codes $\mathcal{C}$ and $\mathcal{D}$ in $\mathrm{M}(m \times n, q)$, the problem asks whether there exist two invertible matrices $A \in \mathrm{GL}(m, q)$ and $B \in \mathrm{GL}(n, q)$ such that $\mathcal{D} = A\mathcal{C}B := \{ACB \mid C \in \mathcal{C}\}$.*

Definition 2 (Alternating Trilinear Form Equivalence (ATFE)). *Given two alternating trilinear forms $\phi, \psi : \mathbb{F}_q^n \times \mathbb{F}_q^n \times \mathbb{F}_q^n \to \mathbb{F}_q$, the problem asks whether there exists an invertible matrix $A \in \mathrm{GL}(n, q)$ such that for any $u, v, w \in \mathbb{F}_q^n$, $\phi(Au, Av, Aw) = \psi(u, v, w)$.*

MCE and ATFE: Relations and Cryptographic Uses. MCE and ATFE are shown to be polynomial-time equivalent [32] and are Tensor Isomorphism (TI)-complete [31]. Utilising the MCE and ATFE problems, two signature schemes have recently been proposed by Tang et al. [42] and Chou et al. [22]. Both schemes are based on the Goldreich–Micali–Wigderson zero-knowledge protocol for graph isomorphism [30] and the Fiat–Shamir transformation [28]. More broadly these fall into the investigations on identifying and utilising group actions in cryptography [1,19,34]. These works lead to submissions to NIST's current standardization for post-quantum signatures: MEDS [21] and ALTEQ [15]. Subsequently, various applications have been developed, including ring signatures [14,22,24] and threshold signatures [9]. Hence, it is of significance to investigate the hardness of these two problems, as it will provide insights into the selection of secure parameter sets.

1.1 Previous Works

In this section, we will briefly review some of state-of-the-art algorithms for MCE and ATFE. Algorithms for MCE and ATFE have been surveyed in [22,42], respectively. Beullens recently contributed beautiful new algorithms for ATFE in [12]. Here we explain two algorithms, one for MCE and one for ATFE, that are most relevant to us.

Leon-Like Algorithm for MCE. Leon's algorithm [36] is well-known for solving code equivalence problems in the Hamming metric. The key observation is that the equivalence preserves the Hamming weight of the codewords. Consequently, identifying the set of codewords with minimum Hamming weight within two codes can aid in revealing the equivalence or isometry between the codes. Recently, Beullens [11] improved upon this algorithm by constructing the set of codewords with a particular weight and the same multiset of entries as lists[1]. Subsequently, a collision search is conducted between the two lists to recover equivalence or isometry easily. It is natural to adapt Leon's algorithm to MCE [22]. That is, one can first build two lists of low-rank matrices in C_1 and C_2, and then do a collision search to find a matched pair of corresponding matrix codes and so recover the equivalence.

Beullens' Algorithm for ATFE. Beullens [12] currently proposed a graph-theoretic algorithm to solve ATFE problem. An alternating trilinear form ϕ can be viewed as a graph G_ϕ, where $\mathbf{v} \in \mathbb{F}_q^n$ is a vertex and $(\mathbf{u}, \mathbf{v})$ be an edge if and only if $\phi_{\mathbf{u},\mathbf{v}} = 0$. Also, a bilinear form $\phi_\mathbf{u}$ can be viewed as a matrix $M_{\phi,\mathbf{u}}$, then the rank of $\mathbf{u}$ is the rank of $M_{\phi,\mathbf{u}}$. The key observation is that the equivalence preserves the rank of the vertices in G_ϕ. Therefore, the algorithm first builds two lists of low-rank points in ϕ and ψ respectively and then finds a collision to recover the equivalence.

---

[1] In the monomial setting, Beullens considered building a set of 2-dimension subcodes with small support. This is because monomial transformation do not preserve anything beyond the hamming weight of a vector.

Gröbner Basis Approach. The MCE and ATFE problem can be solved algebraically by transforming them into a system of polynomial equations and then solving this system via Gröbner basis [22,42]. The Gröbner basis method, exhibits insensitivity to the parameter q within the system, with its efficiency contingent solely upon the values m, n and l (or n for the ATFE). Also, this approach demonstrates the high efficiency when applied to problems characterized by low dimensions.

1.2   Our Contributions

In this paper, we propose heuristic algorithms for MCE and ATFE problems. We summarize our contributions as below.

Algorithm for MCE. We present a new algorithm for MCE. Our algorithm introduces a novel invariant for matrix codes, which we call the "rank 1 associated invariant". This innovation allows us to find a collision using the birthday paradox, and it avoids the use of Gröbner basis computations. This improvement leads to an algorithm with a complexity of $O(q^{(n-2)/2} \cdot (q \cdot n^3 + n^4) \cdot (\log(q))^2)$ as described in Sect. 4.4. We provide an implementation of this algorithm, and demonstrate its practical effectiveness for small n and q (such as $n = 9$ and $q = 31$) in Sect. 4.6.

Regarding the MEDS scheme, its security is based on the hardness of the MCE problem. Although our algorithm does not yet achieve a practical break of the parameter sets proposed by MEDS, it serves to underscore that these parameters have not yet attained the target security level; see Table 1.

Table 1. Algorithms for solving the MCE problem. The data for algebraic and Leon-like algorithms are from the MEDS specification [21].

parameter set	n	q	Algebraic	Leon-like	Ours
MEDS-I	14	4093	148.1	170.68	102.59
MEDS-III	22	4093	218.41	246.95	152.55
MEDS-V	30	2039	298.82	297.77	186.57

Importantly, we note that this could be fixed easily by enlarging q. This fix should not affect the running times, and only increase the signature sizes *at most*[2] linearly in $\log(q)$. Therefore the consequence of our algorithm on MEDS should be considered as mild.

Algorithm for ATFE. We present an algorithm for the ATFE problem by introducing a new isomorphism invariant. For an alternating trilinear form ϕ and a low-rank point v, the equivalence preserves the kernel space K of v. Based on this observation, we define an isomorphism invariant as the isomorphism type

---

[2] It is 'at most', because of the use of the seed tree techniques; see [22] for more details.

of the trilinear form $\hat{\phi}$ restricted to K in the first argument, under the action of $\mathrm{GL}(K) \times \mathrm{GL}(n,q)$. We provide preliminary evidence suggesting that this isomorphism invariant can be computed efficiently, and is distinguishing. *Assuming that canonical forms for such restricted trilinear forms could also be computed efficiently*, this leads to a birthday-type algorithm, with a complexity with the dominating factor being $O(q^{k/2})$, where $O(q^k)$ is the expected number of points with the target low rank. This could be compared with the algorithms in [12] with the dominating factors being $O(q^k)$ or $O(q^{n/2})$.

It must be noted that to utilise this invariant in a birthday-type algorithm, we need canonical forms rather than merely isomorphism testing. We were not able to derive such a canonical form algorithm, though we note that while to transform an isomorphism invariant algorithm to a canonical form may not be an easy process, it is generally regarded as doable, at least from the experience from graph isomorphism [3]. Therefore, protocol designers need to take the conservative approach, namely assuming a canonical form algorithm matching the isomorphism testing algorithm running time. This was the consideration when determining the parameters of ALTEQ [15].

Quantum Speed-Up. We accelerate our algorithms for both MCE and ATFE on quantum computers by using Szegedy's quantum random walks to find collisions [41]. The runtime exponent is reduced by a factor of $2/3$, resulting in $q^{k/3}\mathsf{poly}(n, \log q)$ time quantum algorithms.

Our Algorithms as a Further Development of [12,17]. Our algorithms for MCE and ATFE follow the previous works on polynomial isomorphism and alternating trilinear form equivalence. In particular, our algorithms are a further development of the works of Bouillaguet, Fouque, and Véber [17], and Beullens [12].

In [17], algorithms for testing isomorphism of systems of quadratic forms were presented. Both algorithms rely on certain graphs associated with quadratic form systems. The first algorithm in [17] samples a list of low-rank points for each of the two input polynomial systems, and find a collision which can be used in conjunction of the hybrid Gröbner basis method [27] to recover the secret transformation. The second algorithm in [17] works for $q = 2$; it is based on birthday paradox with an isomorphism invariant obtained by examining the radius-k neighbourhood of the points in the graph.

In [12], algorithms for ATFE were presented. Two of the algorithms that are most relevant to us are as follows. (We refer the reader to [12] for a beautiful algorithm for $n = 9$.) The first algorithm follows the sampling and collision approach, with the main innovation being that for the sampling step, where Beullens uses a random walk on the graph associated with an alternating trilinear form. The second algorithm is based on the birthday paradox with isomorphism invariants. As q is large for the use of ATFE in [42], Beullens used radius-1 or -2 neighbourhoods and observed that such neighbourhood information is distinguishing.

Our algorithms for MCE and ATFE are based on the birthday paradox with isomorphism invariants (see Sect. 3). As seen from the above, previous works use isomorphism invariants that are *local* (small radius neighbourhood) on graphs associated with polynomial systems or trilinear forms. Our main technical contribution is to discover new isomorphism invariants that can be viewed as transforming the information from graphs to *global* constraints.

For example, the isomorphism invariants for MCE are obtained by associating some graphs with matrix codes. We also perform a walk on the graph (starting from a corank-1 point), but we then use the path information to transform the matrix code as a whole to obtain an isomorphism invariant. Similarly, for ATFE, the isomorphism invariants are obtained by first taking the kernel of a low-rank point. We then apply this kernel to the alternating trilinear form to obtain another (smaller) trilinear form, and use this trilinear form as an isomorphism invariant.

Paper Structure. After presenting preliminaries in Sect. 2, we present the generic algorithm framework we use in Sect. 3. We then describe the algorithm for MCE in Sect. 4, and the algorithm for ATFE in Sect. 5. Finally we present the quantum speed-ups for these algorithms in Sect. 6.

2 Preliminaries

Notations. For $n \in \mathbb{N}$, $[n] := \{1, 2, \ldots, n\}$. Let $\mathbb{F}_q$ be the finite field of q elements. We view $\mathbb{F}_q^n$ as the linear space of length-n column vectors over $\mathbb{F}_q$. Let $\mathbb{P} = \mathbb{P}(\mathbb{F}_q^n)$ be the projective space associated with the vector space $\mathbb{F}_q^n$. For a non-zero $\mathbf{u} \in \mathbb{F}_q^n$, we use $\hat{\mathbf{u}} \in \mathbb{P}$ to denote the projective line represented by $\mathbf{u}$. Let $\mathrm{GL}(n, q)$ denote the general linear group of degree n over $\mathbb{F}_q$. We use $\mathrm{M}(m \times n, q)$ to denote the space of $m \times n$ matrices over $\mathbb{F}_q$, and $\mathrm{ATF}(n, q)$ for the space of alternating trilinear forms over $\mathbb{F}_q^n$. For a finite set S, we use $s \leftarrow_R S$ to denote that s is uniformly randomly sampled from S.

Matrix Codes and Trilinear Forms. A trilinear form is a function $\phi : \mathbb{F}_q^m \times \mathbb{F}_q^n \times \mathbb{F}_q^l \to \mathbb{F}_q$ that is linear in each of its three arguments.

Definition 3 (Trilinear Form Equivalence Problem). *Given two trilinear forms* $\phi, \psi : \mathbb{F}_q^m \times \mathbb{F}_q^n \times \mathbb{F}_q^l \to \mathbb{F}_q$, *the problem asks whether there exists three matrices* $(A, B, C) \in \mathrm{GL}(m, q) \times \mathrm{GL}(n, q) \times \mathrm{GL}(l, q)$, *such that for any* $(u, v, w) \in \mathbb{F}_q^m \times \mathbb{F}_q^n \times \mathbb{F}_q^l$, $\phi(u, v, w) = \psi(A(u), B(v), C(w))$.

A $[m \times n, l]$-matrix code $\mathcal{C}$ is an l-dimensional subspace of $\mathrm{M}(m \times n, q)$. We defined matrix code equivalence in Definition 1. Matrix code equivalence reduces to trilinear form equivalence in polynomial time. This is because of the following. Let a matrix code $\mathcal{C}$ be given by an ordered linear basis $(C_1, C_2, \ldots, C_l)$, $C_k \in \mathrm{M}(m \times n, q)$, and $c_{i,j,k}$ denotes the (i, j)-entry of C_k. This gives rise to a trilinear form $\phi_{\mathcal{C}} : \mathbb{F}_q^m \times \mathbb{F}_q^n \times \mathbb{F}_q^l \to \mathbb{F}_q$, that is, $\phi_{\mathcal{C}} = \sum_{i,j,k} c_{i,j,k} u_i v_j w_k$ where $u = (u_1, \ldots, u_m)^t \in \mathbb{F}_q^m$, $v = (v_1, \ldots, v_n)^t \in \mathbb{F}_q^n$, and $w = (w_1, \ldots, w_l)^t \in \mathbb{F}_q^l$. It is straightforward to verify that two matrix codes $\mathcal{C}$ and $\mathcal{D}$ are equivalent if and only if $\phi_{\mathcal{C}}$ and $\phi_{\mathcal{D}}$ are equivalent. Furthermore, if $(A, B, C) \in \mathrm{GL}(m, q) \times \mathrm{GL}(n, q) \times \mathrm{GL}(l, q)$ sends $\phi_{\mathcal{C}}$ to $\phi_{\mathcal{D}}$, then (A, B) sends $\mathcal{C}$ to $\mathcal{D}$.

Alternating Trilinear Forms. A trilinear form $\phi : \mathbb{F}_q^n \times \mathbb{F}_q^n \times \mathbb{F}_q^n \to \mathbb{F}_q$ is alternating, if ϕ evaluates to 0 whenever two arguments are the same, e.g., $\phi(\mathbf{u}, \mathbf{u}, \mathbf{v}) = \phi(\mathbf{u}, \mathbf{v}, \mathbf{u}) = \phi(\mathbf{v}, \mathbf{u}, \mathbf{u}) = 0$ for all $\mathbf{u}, \mathbf{v} \in \mathbb{F}_q^n$. Let e_i be the ith standard basis vector and e_i^* be the corresponding dual basis which sends $\mathbf{u} = (u_1, \ldots, u_n)^t \in \mathbb{F}_q^n$ to u_i. ϕ can be represented as $\sum_{1 \le i \le j \le k \le n} c_{i,j,k} e_i^* \wedge e_j^* \wedge e_k^*$ where $\wedge$ denotes the exterior product. And $e_i^* \wedge e_j^* \wedge e_k^*$ is an alternating trilinear form which can be defined as follows:

$$(e_i^* \wedge e_j^* \wedge e_k^*)(\mathbf{u}, \mathbf{v}, \mathbf{w}) = \det \begin{bmatrix} u_i & v_i & w_i \\ u_j & v_j & w_j \\ u_k & v_k & w_k \end{bmatrix},$$

where $\mathbf{u} = (u_1, \ldots, u_n), \mathbf{v} = (v_1, \ldots, v_n), \mathbf{w} = (w_1, \ldots, w_n)$. This also implies that storing an alternating trilinear form requires $\binom{n}{3}$ field elements.

We note that the trilinear form equivalence problem differs from the alternating trilinear form equivalence problem, in that three invertible matrices are used in the former, while only one is used in the latter.

Instantiated Arguments of Trilinear Forms. Let $\phi : \mathbb{F}_q^n \times \mathbb{F}_q^n \times \mathbb{F}_q^n \to \mathbb{F}_q$ be a trilinear form and $\mathbf{u}, \mathbf{v} \in \mathbb{F}_q^n$. We use $\phi(\mathbf{u}, \star, \star)$ to denote the bilinear form obtained by instantiating the first argument of ϕ with $\mathbf{u}$. Let $\phi(\mathbf{u}, \star, \star) = \sum_{j,k} c_{j,k} y_j z_k$ then it has matrix representation $M_{\mathbf{u}} = (c_{j,k})$ with respect to standard basis $e_1, \ldots, e_n$. We use $\phi(\mathbf{u}, \mathbf{v}, \star)$ to denote the linear form obtained by instantiating the first two arguments of ϕ with $\mathbf{u}$ and $\mathbf{v}$, respectively.

Tripartite Graphs Associated with Trilinear Forms. Let $\phi \in \mathrm{TF}(\mathbb{F}_q^n)$ be a trilinear form, then we can associate ϕ with a tripartite graph $G_\phi = (U \uplus V \uplus W, E)$ where $U = V = W = \mathbb{P}(\mathbb{F}_q^n)$. To define the edge set E, let $\hat{\mathbf{u}} \in U$, $\hat{\mathbf{v}} \in V$, and $\hat{\mathbf{w}} \in W$. Then $\{\hat{\mathbf{u}}, \hat{\mathbf{v}}\} \in E$, if $\phi(\mathbf{u}, \mathbf{v}, \star)$ is the zero linear form. Similarly, $\{\hat{\mathbf{u}}, \hat{\mathbf{w}}\} \in E$, if $\phi(\mathbf{u}, \star, \mathbf{w})$ is the zero linear form. And $\{\hat{\mathbf{v}}, \hat{\mathbf{w}}\} \in E$, if $\phi(\star, \mathbf{v}, \mathbf{w})$ is the zero linear form.

Rank Distribution of Random Trilinear Forms. The following rank distribution of random trilinear forms follows from the well-known fact that the probability of a random matrix in $\mathrm{M}(n, \mathbb{F}_q)$ to be of rank $n - d$ tends to q^{-d^2} as $q \to \infty$ [10,29].

Theorem 1 ([10,29]). *Let n, d be positive integers such that $n - d$ is a non-negative number less than n. Then as $q \to \infty$, the average number of projective points with rank $n - d$ of a uniformly random trilinear form $\phi : \mathbb{F}_q^n \times \mathbb{F}_q^n \times \mathbb{F}_q^n \to \mathbb{F}_q$ tends to $q^{-d^2 + n - 1}$.*

Rank Distribution of Alternating Trilinear Forms. The following result is due to Beullens [12]; see also [14].

Theorem 2 ([12, Theorem 2]). *Let n, d be positive integers such that $n - d$ is a non-negative even number less than n. Then as $q \to \infty$, the average number of projective points with rank $n - d$ of a uniformly random alternating trilinear form $\phi \in \mathrm{ATF}(\mathbb{F}_q^n)$ tends to $q^{(-d^2 + 3d)/2 + n - 2}$.*

3   Finding Equivalences of Trilinear Forms via Invariants

We first outline the common framework of our algorithms for ATFE and TFE at a high level, following Beullens (in Sect. 5.4 of [12]). But in a departure from [12] which relies on invariants derived from graphs on projective points, we design new global invariants. The invariant functions for ATF and TF will be of the form

$$F_0 : \mathrm{TF}(\mathbb{F}_q^n) \times \mathbb{P}(\mathbb{F}_q^n) \to X_0,$$
$$F_1 : \mathrm{ATF}(\mathbb{F}_q^n) \times \mathbb{P}(\mathbb{F}_q^n) \to X_1$$

and explicitly constructed in the following sections. The subscript 0 in the function and the target set indicates that it is associated with TF. Likewise, the subscript 1 indicates association with ATF.

Invariants. To illustrate the notion of invariants, let us first name the actions underlying MCE and ATFE in the language of trilinear forms.

Definition 4 (MCE Action). *For a trilinear form* $\phi : \mathbb{F}_q^n \times \mathbb{F}_q^n \times \mathbb{F}_q^n \longrightarrow \mathbb{F}_q$ *and a triple of matrices* $(A, B, C) \in \mathrm{GL}(n, q)^3$, *define the trilinear form*

$$\phi_{A,B,C} : \mathbb{F}_q^n \times \mathbb{F}_q^n \times \mathbb{F}_q^n \longrightarrow \mathbb{F}_q$$
$$(x, y, z) \longmapsto \phi(Ax, By, Cz).$$

We design F_0 as a pairing of the trilinear form and the projective space that is invariant under twisting the trilinear form and the projective space. The trilinear form is twisted by the $\mathrm{GL}(n, q)^3$ MCE Action. The projective space is twisted by the inverse of the matrix acting on the first dimension of the trilinear form. Formally, the invariant for MCE action needs to satisfy that

$$\forall \phi \in \mathrm{TF}(\mathbb{F}_q^n), \forall \hat{\mathbf{v}} \in \mathbb{P}(\mathbb{F}_q^n), \forall (A, B, C) \in \mathrm{GL}(n, q)^3, F_0(\phi, \hat{\mathbf{v}}) = F_0(\phi_{A,B,C}, A^{-1}\hat{\mathbf{v}}).$$

Definition 5 (ATFE Action). *For a trilinear form* $\phi : \mathbb{F}_q^n \times \mathbb{F}_q^n \times \mathbb{F}_q^n \longrightarrow \mathbb{F}_q$ *and a matrix* $A \in \mathrm{GL}(n, q)$, *define the trilinear form*

$$\phi_A : \mathbb{F}_q^n \times \mathbb{F}_q^n \times \mathbb{F}_q^n \longrightarrow \mathbb{F}_q$$
$$(x, y, z) \longmapsto \phi(Ax, Ay, Az).$$

We design the function F_1 as a pairing of the trilinear form and the projective space that is invariant under twisting the trilinear form by the ATFE action and the projective space by the inverse of the matrix defining the ATFE action. Formally,

$$\forall \phi \in \mathrm{ATF}(\mathbb{F}_q^n), \forall \hat{\mathbf{v}} \in \mathbb{P}(\mathbb{F}_q^n), \forall A \in \mathrm{GL}(n, q), F_1(\phi, \hat{\mathbf{v}}) = F_1(\phi_A, A^{-1}\hat{\mathbf{v}}).$$

Distinguishing Invariant. The invariant function F_0 is called distinguishing if for all $\phi \in \mathrm{TF}(\mathbb{F}_q^n)$,

$$\Pr_{(\hat{\mathbf{v}}_1, \hat{\mathbf{v}}_2) \leftarrow_R \mathbb{P}(\mathbb{F}_q^n)^2} (F_0(\phi, \hat{\mathbf{v}}_1) \neq F_0(\phi, \hat{\mathbf{v}}_2)) \approx 1.$$

We will specify the meaning of ≈ 1 in the following. Likewise, F_1 is called distinguishing if for all $\phi \in \mathrm{ATF}(\mathbb{F}_q^n)$,

$$\Pr_{(\hat{\mathbf{v}}_1, \hat{\mathbf{v}}_2) \leftarrow_R \mathbb{P}(\mathbb{F}_q^n)^2} (F_1(\phi, \hat{\mathbf{v}}_1) \neq F_1(\phi, \hat{\mathbf{v}}_2)) \approx 1.$$

An Algorithm Template Based on Distinguishing Invariants. With such distinguishing invariant functions at hand, we have the following generic algorithm for MCE and ATFE. The version for ATFE is specified in parentheses.

To start with, recall that for a trilinear form $\phi : \mathbb{F}_q^n \times \mathbb{F}_q^n \times \mathbb{F}_q^n \to \mathbb{F}_q$ and $\mathbf{v} \in \mathbb{F}_q^n$, the rank of $\phi(\mathbf{v}, \star, \star)$ (see Sect. 2) is an invariant, which has been utilised in [12,17]. Also note that $\mathrm{rk}(\phi(\mathbf{v}, \star, \star)) = \mathrm{rk}(\phi(\lambda \mathbf{v}, \star, \star))$ for non-zero $\lambda \in \mathbb{F}_q$, so we can talk about the rank of $\phi(\hat{\mathbf{v}}, \star, \star)$ for $\hat{\mathbf{v}} \in \mathbb{P}(\mathbb{F}_q^n)$.

This rank invariant cannot be distinguished. Still, the new invariants considered in this paper are further refinements of the rank invariant, as will be seen below. In particular, the generic algorithm is parametrised by this rank R, which would be specified later depending on the specific invariants.

Input: Two equivalent (alternating) trilinear forms $\phi, \psi \in \mathrm{TF}(\mathbb{F}_q^n)$(or $\mathrm{ATF}(\mathbb{F}_q^n)$).
Output: $A, B, C \in \mathrm{GL}(n, q)$ such that $\phi_{A,B,C} = \psi$ (or $A \in \mathrm{GL}(n, q)$ such that $\phi_A = \psi$).
Algorithm

1. Pick a positive number $R \leq n$. Let

$$\mathbb{P}_{\phi, R} := \left\{ \hat{\mathbf{v}} \in \mathbb{P}(\mathbb{F}_q^n) \mid \mathrm{rk}(\phi(\hat{\mathbf{v}}, *, *)) = R \right\},$$
$$\mathbb{P}_{\psi, R} := \left\{ \hat{\mathbf{v}} \in \mathbb{P}(\mathbb{F}_q^n) \mid \mathrm{rk}(\psi(\hat{\mathbf{v}}, *, *)) = R \right\}$$

   denote the respective set of points where the trilinear forms specialize in the first dimension to give rank R matrices. Independently sample a set $L_{\phi, R}$ of $\sqrt{|\mathbb{P}_{\phi, R}|}$ points from $\mathbb{P}_{\phi, R}$ and a set $L_{\psi, R}$ of $\sqrt{|\mathbb{P}_{\psi, R}|}$ points from $\mathbb{P}_{\psi, R}$. Since ϕ and ψ are isomorphic, $\mathbb{P}_{\phi, R} = \mathbb{P}_{\psi, R}$ and we denote their cardinality as $N_R := \|\mathbb{P}_{\phi, R}\| = \|\mathbb{P}_{\psi, R}\|$. Therefore $L_{\phi, R}$ and $L_{\psi, R}$ are both $\sqrt{N_R}$-sized subsets of the same set of size N_R.

2. Apply the invariant function F_i (where $i = 0$ for MCE and $i = 1$ for ATFE) to each element in $L_{\phi, R}$ and $L_{\psi, R}$. Find a pair $(\hat{\mathbf{v}}, \hat{\mathbf{v}}')$ for which $F_i(\phi, \hat{\mathbf{v}}) = F_i(\psi, \hat{\mathbf{v}}')$, where $\hat{\mathbf{v}} \in L_{\phi, R}$ and $\hat{\mathbf{v}}' \in L_{\psi, R}$. The existence of such a pair is likely due to the birthday paradox.

3. For MCE, such a pair reveals the desired output $(A, B, C) \in \mathrm{GL}(n, q)^3$ through linear algebra, as we describe in Sect. 4. To solve the ATFE, feed the matching pair $(\hat{\mathbf{v}}, \hat{\mathbf{v}}')$ as the partial information into the Gröbner basis computation in [6,42]. This Gröbner basis computation is a heuristic that finds in polynomial time an $A \in \mathrm{GL}(n, q)$ (if it exists) such that $\phi_A = \psi$ and $A^{-1}\hat{\mathbf{v}} = \hat{\mathbf{v}}'$.

The complexity of the above algorithm parameterized by the target rank R can be estimated as

$$O\left(\sqrt{N_R} \cdot (\text{samp-cost} + \text{inv-cost}) + \text{recover-cost}\right). \qquad (1)$$

The sampling cost samp-cost refers to the cost of sampling a rank-R (projective) point, that is, a point in $\mathbb{P}_{\phi,R}$ (or equivalently in $\mathbb{P}_{\psi,R}$). And inv-cost denotes the cost of invariant computation for each point. The cost of recovering the isomorphism given a collision is denoted by recover-cost. Also note that for the invariant to be distinguishing enough in the above procedure, we need to have $\Pr_{(\hat{\mathbf{v}}_1,\hat{\mathbf{v}}_2)\leftarrow_R \mathbb{P}(\mathbb{F}_q^n)^2}(F_0(\phi,\hat{\mathbf{v}}_1) = F_0(\phi,\hat{\mathbf{v}}_2)) = O(1/N_R)$.

In the following two sections, we describe algorithms in this general framework tailored to MCE and ATFE, by describing the invariant functions and optimizing the rank R.

4   An Algorithm for Matrix Code Equivalence

In this section, we introduce an algorithm for the matrix code (or trilinear form) equivalence problem. Specifically, given two trilinear forms $\phi \in \text{TF}(\mathbb{F}_q^n)$ and $\psi \in \text{TF}(\mathbb{F}_q^n)$ that are equivalent, the algorithm computes an equivalence $(A, B, C) \in \text{GL}(n,q) \times \text{GL}(n,q) \times \text{GL}(n,q)$ between ϕ and ψ. The algorithm runs in time $O(q^{(n-2)/2} \cdot (q \cdot n^3 + n^4) \cdot (\log(q))^2)$.

4.1   The Main Idea

To instantiate the algorithm outlined in Sect. 3, the primary bottleneck is identifying invariants with sufficient distinguishing power. The main idea of the algorithm is to associate distinguishing invariants to corank-1 points, specifically for those $\hat{\mathbf{u}} \in \mathbb{P}(\mathbb{F}_q^n)$ such that the bilinear form $\phi(\mathbf{u}, \star, \star)$ is of rank $n - 1$. We shall occasionally call such projective lines as corank-1 points. Recall there is a tripartite graph $G_\phi = (U \uplus V \uplus W, E)$ associated with ϕ where $U = V = W = \mathbb{P}(\mathbb{F}_q^n)$. Each corank-1 point $\hat{\mathbf{u}} \in U$ has a unique neighbour $\hat{\mathbf{v}} \in V$, namely the one dimensional left kernel of the bilinear form $\phi(\mathbf{u}, \star, \star)$. Since $\phi(\star, \mathbf{v}, \star)$ has $\mathbf{u}$ in its left kernel, $\phi(\star, \mathbf{v}, \star)$ has co-rank at least 1. If $\phi(\star, \mathbf{v}, \star)$ is of corank-1, it has a unique neighbour $\hat{\mathbf{w}} \in W$. Repeating this procedure leads to a path on G_ϕ. We continue building this path until reaching length $3n$, collecting n points each from U, V and W. Such a path is built without ambiguity if and only if at every iteration we get a point of corank-1.

Our experiments show that for most starting points $\hat{\mathbf{u}}$, we do obtain a path of length $3n$ without ambiguity and that the vector n-tuples collected in each of the sets U, V and W are linearly independent respectively. We use these three vector tuples to transform ϕ to $\tilde{\phi}[\mathbf{u}]$ which depends only on the vectors on this path.

To make this an isomorphism invariant indexed with $\hat{\mathbf{u}}$ (instead of with $\mathbf{u}$), we need to remove the ambiguity caused by the scalar multiples, which can be done easily by locating non-zero evaluations of $\tilde{\phi}[\mathbf{u}]$ on about $3n$ inputs of the form (e_i, e_j, e_k). This gives us $\bar{\phi}[\hat{\mathbf{u}}]$ which is an invariant associated with $\hat{\mathbf{u}}$. Our experiments show that this invariant is distinguishing, i.e. different $\hat{\mathbf{u}}$ results in different $\bar{\phi}[\hat{\mathbf{u}}]$. This allows for an application of the birthday algorithm.

It is known from Theorem 1 that for a random ϕ, there exist approximately q^{n-2} corank-1 points. Thus we get an algorithm running in time $O((q^{(n/2)} + q^{(n-2)/2}) \cdot \mathsf{poly}(n, q))$ by instantiating the above invariant.

4.2   From a Vector to Three Vector Tuples

Corank-1 Points of Trilinear Forms and Paths on G_ϕ. Suppose a non-zero $\mathbf{u}_1 \in \mathbb{F}_q^n$ satisfies that $\phi(\mathbf{u}_1, \star, \star)$ is of corank-1 as a bilinear form. Consider the following steps.

1. As $\phi(\mathbf{u}_1, \star, \star)$ is of corank-1, there exists a unique $\hat{\mathbf{v}}_1 \in \mathbb{P}$ such that $\phi(\mathbf{u}_1, \mathbf{v}_1, \star)$ is the zero linear form.
2. If $\phi(\star, \mathbf{v}_1, \star)$ is of corank-1, then there exists a unique $\hat{\mathbf{w}}_1 \in \mathbb{P}$, such that $\phi(\star, \mathbf{v}_1, \mathbf{w}_1)$ is the zero linear form.
3. If $\phi(\star, \star, \mathbf{w}_1)$ is of corank-1, then there exists a unique $\hat{\mathbf{u}}_2 \in \mathbb{P}$, such that $\phi(\mathbf{u}_2, \star, \mathbf{w}_1)$ is the zero linear form.

If $\hat{\mathbf{u}}_1 \neq \hat{\mathbf{u}}_2$, then the above procedure produces a path $(\hat{\mathbf{u}}_1, \hat{\mathbf{v}}_1, \hat{\mathbf{w}}_1, \hat{\mathbf{u}}_2)$ in $G(\phi)$. We can continue the above procedure as follows.

1. Let $L_U = (u_1)$, $L_V = ()$, and $L_W = ()$.
2. For $i = 1$ to n, do the following:
   (a) Compute the unique $\hat{\mathbf{v}}_i \in \mathbb{P}(\mathbb{F}_q^n)$, such that $\phi(\mathbf{u}_i, \mathbf{v}_i, \star) = 0$.
   (b) If the corank of $\phi(\star, \mathbf{v}_i, \star)$ is not 1, or if $\mathbf{v}_i \in \mathrm{span}(L_V)$, terminate and report "Fail". Otherwise, add $\mathbf{v}_i$ to L_V.
   (c) Compute the unique $\hat{\mathbf{w}}_i \in \mathbb{P}(\mathbb{F}_q^n)$, such that $\phi(\star, \mathbf{v}_i, \mathbf{w}_i) = 0$.
   (d) If the corank of $\phi(\star, \star, \mathbf{w}_i)$ is not 1, or if $\mathbf{w}_i \in \mathrm{span}(L_W)$, terminate and report "Fail". Otherwise, add $\mathbf{w}_i$ to L_W.
   (e) If $i = n$, break.
   (f) Compute the unique $\hat{\mathbf{u}_{i+1}} \in \mathbb{P}(\mathbb{F}_q^n)$, such that $\phi(\mathbf{u}_{i+1}, \star, \mathbf{w}_i) = 0$.
   (g) If the corank of $\phi(\mathbf{u}_{i+1}, \star, \star)$ is not 1, or if $\mathbf{u}_{i+1} \in \mathrm{span}(L_U)$, terminate and report "Fail". Otherwise, add $\mathbf{u}_{i+1}$ to L_U.

If the above procedure does not return "Fail", then we obtain three vector tuples $L_U = (\mathbf{u}_1, \ldots, \mathbf{u}_n)$, $L_V = (\mathbf{v}_1, \ldots, \mathbf{v}_n)$, and $L_W = (\mathbf{w}_1, \ldots, \mathbf{w}_n)$, such that $\mathbf{u}_i$'s (resp. $\mathbf{v}_i$'s, $\mathbf{w}_i$'s) are linearly independent.

4.3   Corank-1 Invariants from Three Vector Tuples

Suppose that starting from a corank-1 $\mathbf{u}_1 \in \mathbb{F}_q^n$, we obtain three vector tuples L_U, L_V, and L_W, which are canonically associated with $\mathbf{u}_1$. We then treat L_U, L_V, and L_W as invertible matrices, that is, $L_U = \begin{bmatrix} \mathbf{u}_1 \ldots \mathbf{u}_n \end{bmatrix}^t$. Define a trilinear form $\tilde{\phi} : \mathbb{F}_q^n \times \mathbb{F}_q^n \times \mathbb{F}_q^n \to \mathbb{F}_q$ by $\tilde{\phi}(x, y, z) = \phi(L_U(x), L_V(y), L_W(z))$. This $\tilde{\phi}$ is almost an isomorphism invariant associated with $\mathbf{u}_1$ – almost because there is an ambiguity associated with the representing vectors of $\hat{\mathbf{u}}_i$, $\hat{\mathbf{v}}_j$, and $\hat{\mathbf{w}}_k$.

To remove this ambiguity, we need to study the canonical form of $\tilde{\phi}$ under the action of $\mathrm{D}(n, q) \times \mathrm{D}(n, q) \times \mathrm{D}(n, q)$, where $\mathrm{D}(n, q)$ denotes the group of invertible diagonal $n \times n$ matrices over $\mathbb{F}_q$. This can be done by carefully selecting $3n$ non-zero entries in $\tilde{\phi}$, so that the diagonal entries of the acting matrices are determined by these entries. In the following we present one choice of non-zero entries. There could be several other natural selections depending on the positions of zero entries, but we do not pursue them further as this choice is already useful enough in our practical implementation.

Consider the following entries. For any $i, j, k \geq 3$,

$$a_i := \tilde{\phi}(e_i, e_2, e_1), b_j := \tilde{\phi}(e_1, e_j, e_1), c_k := \tilde{\phi}(e_1, e_2, e_k), d_1 := \tilde{\phi}(e_1, e_2, e_1),$$
$$d_2 := \tilde{\phi}(e_2, e_3, e_5), d_3 := \tilde{\phi}(e_1, e_3, e_2), d_4 := \tilde{\phi}(e_2, e_1, e_2) \text{ are non-zero.} \quad (2)$$

In this case, we can use the action of $\mathrm{D}(n, q) \times \mathrm{D}(n, q) \times \mathrm{D}(n, q)$ to set a_i, b_j, c_k, d_1, d_2, d_3 and d_4 to be 1. More specifically, let $(F, G, H) \in \mathrm{D}(n, q) \times \mathrm{D}(n, q) \times \mathrm{D}(n, q)$, where $F = \mathrm{diag}(f_1, \ldots, f_n)$, $G = \mathrm{diag}(g_1, \ldots, g_n)$, and $H = \mathrm{diag}(h_1, \ldots, h_n)$. Then set f_i, g_j, and h_k to satisfy that, for $3 \leq i, j, k \leq n$,

$$f_1 g_2 h_1 = 1/d_1, f_i/f_1 = d_1/a_i, g_j/g_2 = d_1/b_j, h_k/h_1 = d_1/c_k,$$
$$f_2 = 1/(g_3 h_5 d_2), h_2 = 1/(f_1 g_3 d_3), g_1 = 1/(f_2 h_2 d_4). \quad (3)$$

Let $\bar{\phi} : \mathbb{F}_q^n \times \mathbb{F}_q^n \times \mathbb{F}_q^n \to \mathbb{F}_q$ be defined by $\bar{\phi}(x, y, z) = \tilde{\phi}(F(x), G(y), H(z))$. Then $\bar{\phi}(e_i, e_j, e_k) = f_i g_j h_k \tilde{\phi}(e_i, e_j, e_k)$. Therefore,

$$\bar{\phi}(e_1, e_2, e_1) = f_1 g_2 h_1 \tilde{\phi}(e_1, e_2, e_1) = 1/d_1 \cdot d_1 = 1.$$

For $i \geq 3$,

$$\bar{\phi}(e_i, e_2, e_1)$$
$$= f_i g_2 h_1 \tilde{\phi}(e_i, e_2, e_1)$$
$$= (f_i/f_1) f_1 g_2 h_1 \tilde{\phi}(e_i, e_2, e_1)$$
$$= (d_1/a_i) \cdot (1/d_1) \cdot a_i = 1.$$

Similarly, it can be verified that $\bar{\phi}(e_1, e_j, e_1) = \bar{\phi}(e_1, e_2, e_k) = 1$ for $j, k \geq 3$. Additionally, we can verify that $\bar{\phi}(e_1, e_2, e_1) = \bar{\phi}(e_2, e_3, e_5) = \bar{\phi}(e_2, e_1, e_2) = \bar{\phi}(e_1, e_3, e_2) = 1$. Furthermore, for any $i, j, k \geq 3$,

$$\bar{\phi}(e_i, e_j, e_k)$$
$$= f_i g_j h_k \tilde{\phi}(e_i, e_j, e_k)$$
$$= (f_i/f_1)(g_j/g_2)(h_k/h_1) f_1 g_2 h_1 \tilde{\phi}(e_i, e_j, e_k)$$
$$= \frac{d_1^4 \tilde{\phi}(e_i, e_j, e_k)}{a_i b_j c_k};$$

for $i = 2$ and any $j, k \geq 3$,

$$\bar{\phi}(e_2, e_j, e_k)$$
$$= f_2 g_j h_k \tilde{\phi}(e_2, e_j, e_k)$$
$$= (f_2/f_1)(g_j/g_2)(h_k/h_1) f_1 g_2 h_1 \tilde{\phi}(e_2, e_j, e_k)$$
$$= \frac{b_3 b_5 \tilde{\phi}(e_2, e_j, e_k)}{d_1 d_2 b_j c_k};$$

for $k = 2$ and any $i, j \geq 3$,

$$\bar{\phi}(e_i, e_j, e_2)$$
$$= f_i g_j h_2 \tilde{\phi}(e_i, e_j, e_2)$$
$$= (f_i/f_1)(g_j/g_2)(h_2/h_1) f_1 g_2 h_1 \tilde{\phi}(e_i, e_j, e_2)$$
$$= \frac{b_3 \tilde{\phi}(e_i, e_j, e_2)}{d_3 a_i b_j};$$

for $j = 1$ and any $i, k \geq 3$,

$$\bar{\phi}(e_i, e_1, e_k)$$
$$= f_i g_1 h_k \tilde{\phi}(e_i, e_1, e_k)$$
$$= (f_i/f_1)(g_1/g_2)(h_k/h_1) f_1 g_2 h_1 \tilde{\phi}(e_i, e_1, e_k)$$
$$= \frac{d_1^7 d_2 d_3 d_4 \tilde{\phi}(e_i, e_1, e_k)}{b_3^2 b_5 a_i c_k};$$

So $\bar{\phi}$ is completely determined by the conditions in Eq. 3.

The above suggests that $\bar{\phi}[\hat{u}_1] := \bar{\phi}$ is an isomorphism invariant associated with $\hat{u}_1 \in \mathbb{P}(\mathbb{F}_q^n)$, assuming that ϕ satisfies Eq. 2.

4.4 Description of the Algorithm

Given the above preparations, the algorithm works as follows.

Input. Two equivalent trilinear forms $\phi, \psi : \mathbb{F}_q^n \times \mathbb{F}_q^n \times \mathbb{F}_q^n \to \mathbb{F}_q$.
Output. An equivalence $(A, B, C) \in \mathrm{GL}(n, q) \times \mathrm{GL}(n, q) \times \mathrm{GL}(n, q)$.
Algorithm.
1. For ϕ, construct a list S_ϕ of $q^{(n-2)/2}$ corank-1 $\hat{u} \in \mathbb{P}$ together with the isomorphism invariant $\bar{\phi}[\hat{u}]$ as follows.
   (a) Compute one corank-1 $\hat{u} \in \mathbb{P}$ by sampling randomly $u \in \mathbb{F}_q^n$ q times.
   (b) For $\hat{u} \in \mathbb{P}$, compute three vector tuples L_U, L_V, and L_W as in Sect. 4.2.
   (c) Use L_U, L_V and L_W to transform ϕ to $\tilde{\phi}[u]$.
   (d) Use the method in Sect. 4.3 to transform $\tilde{\phi}[u]$ to $\bar{\phi}[\hat{u}]$.
2. For ψ, construct a list S_ψ of $q^{(n-2)/2}$ corank-1 $\hat{u} \in \mathbb{P}(\mathbb{F}_q^n)$ together with the isomorphism invariant $\bar{\psi}[\hat{u}]$ as above.
3. Find $\hat{u}$ from S_ϕ, and $\hat{u}'$ from S_ψ, such that $\bar{\phi}[\hat{u}]$ and $\bar{\psi}[\hat{u}']$ are the same.
4. An equivalence (A, B, C) from ϕ to ψ can be obtained by composing the transformations from ϕ to $\bar{\phi}[\hat{u}]$ and from ψ to $\bar{\psi}[\hat{u}']$.

Time Analysis of the Above Algorithm. We assume that the modular arithmetic complexity in $\mathbb{F}_q$ is in time $O((\log q)^2)$, and the number of arithmetic operations for $n \times n$ matrix computations (such as matrix multiplication and rank computation) is $O(n^3)$. As in the practical setting, n is small and matrices are dense, this should be a reasonable estimate (rather than using $O(n^\omega)$ where ω is the matrix multiplication exponent).

Step 1 is a For-loop contributing a multiplicative factor of $q^{(n-2)/2}$ to steps (a) to (d). Step (a) samples vectors in $\mathbb{F}_q^n$ and computes the ranks of the associated matrices for q times, so its complexity is $O(q \cdot (n \cdot \log(q) + n^3 \cdot (\log q)^2))$. Step (b) constructs three n-tuples of vectors. Each vector in this n-tuple is obtained by solving a system of n linear equations in n variables. So Step (b) costs $O(n \cdot n^3 \cdot (\log q)^2) = O(n^4 \cdot (\log q)^2)$. Step (c) requires $3n$ $n \times n$ matrix multiplications, so its complexity is also $O(n^4 \cdot (\log q)^2)$. For Step (d), the method in Sect. 4.3 takes $O(n^3 \cdot (\log q)^2)$ time. Taking into account of the For-loop factor, the total cost for steps 1 and (a) to (d) is $O(q^{(n-2)/2} \cdot (q \cdot n^3 + n^4) \cdot (\log(q))^2)$.

Once the two lists are constructed, finding a collision and using that to construct an isomorphism takes time $O(\log(q^{(n-2)/2}))$ as we can assume that the lists S_ϕ and S_ψ are sorted. Therefore steps 2 to 4 contribute to a running time of lower order, and the running time of the whole algorithm is $O(q^{(n-2)/2} \cdot (q \cdot n^3 + n^4) \cdot (\log(q))^2)$.

Correctness Analysis of the Above Algorithm. We assume that $\bar{\phi}[\hat{u}]$ is a distinguishing invariant of $\hat{u}$. Then by birthday paradox, the above algorithm returns $\hat{u}$ from S_ϕ, and $\hat{u}'$ from S_ψ, such that $\bar{\phi}[\hat{u}]$ and $\bar{\psi}[\hat{u}']$ are the same, with constant probability.

4.5   Heuristic Assumptions for the Invariant

We now reflect on several assumptions required for using $\bar{\phi}[\mathbf{u}_1]$ for $\mathbf{u}_1 \in \mathbb{F}_q^n$ with $\phi(\mathbf{u}_1, \star, \star)$ being of corank-1.

1. We assume that we can obtain three vector tuples L_U, L_V, L_W.
2. We assume that $\tilde{\phi}$, the trilinear form obtained after applying $L_U, L_V,$ and L_W, satisfies Eq. 2.
3. We assume that the corank-1 invariant $\bar{\phi}[\mathbf{u}_1]$ is distinguishing.

We next argue in favour of each of these heuristics.

Heuristic 1. To build the vector tuples $L_U, L_V,$ and L_W, it suffices (1) to perform a walk with corank-1 points for $3n$ successful steps, and (2) the vectors in L_U (resp. L_V, L_W) be linearly independent.

We argue for (1), by making the same assumption as in Beullens' algorithms [12], namely those points along such a walk are close to independent randomly sampled. In particular, the probability of getting a walk with corank-1 points for $3n$ steps can be estimated as follows. The probability of a corank-1 point having a corank-2 neighbour is asymptotically $O(1/q^2)$; this can be calculated following the techniques in [12]. Therefore, the probability of walking for $3n$ steps with corank-1 points is lower bounded by $1 - O(n/q^2)$, assuming points along such a walk are close to independent randomly sampled.

We argue for (2) using algebraic-geometry. To this end, consider a generic starting corank-1 vector $\mathbf{u}_1$ and think of its coordinate vector $(\mathbf{u}_{1,1}, \mathbf{u}_{1,2}, \ldots, \mathbf{u}_{1,n})$ as n indeterminates. The corank-1 assumption implies that there is a unique projective $\hat{\mathbf{v}}_1$ such that $\phi(\mathbf{u}_1, \mathbf{v}_1, *) = 0$ (that is, the zero dual vector). The coordinates of $\mathbf{v}_1$ can be expressed as some vector of polynomials in the coordinate ring of $\mathbf{u}_1$, for instance using the adjugate matrix of $\phi(\mathbf{u}_1, *, *)$. Call this vector of polynomials as $(f^{\phi}_{\mathbf{v}_1,j})_{1 \leq j \leq n} \in (\mathbb{F}_q[\mathbf{u}_{1,1}, \mathbf{u}_{1,2}, \ldots, \mathbf{u}_{1,n}])^n$. The superscript ϕ signifies that the coefficients of each $f^{\phi}_{\mathbf{v}_1,j}$ depend only on the tensor ϕ. Repeating a similar process starting with the coordinate vector $(f^{\phi}_{\mathbf{v}_1,j})_{1 \leq j \leq n}$ of $\mathbf{v}_1$, we obtain the coordinates $(f^{\phi}_{\mathbf{w}_1,j})_{1 \leq j \leq n} \in (\mathbb{F}_q[\mathbf{u}_{1,1}, \mathbf{u}_{1,2}, \ldots, \mathbf{u}_{1,n}])^n$ of $\mathbf{w}_1 \in L_W$. Note that each coordinate is a polynomial in the coordinate ring of the generic starting vector $\mathbf{u}_1$. Continuing this way, we can express each element of $L_U, L_V,$ and L_W as a vector of polynomials in the co-ordinate ring of $\mathbf{u}_1$. The vectors in L_U being linearly independent can be expressed as a polynomial condition on the coordinates of $\mathbf{u}_1$, namely the determinant of the matrix $(f^{\phi}_{\mathbf{u},j})_{\mathbf{u} \in L_U, 1 \leq j \leq n}$ vanishing. In particular, the variety of dependent L_U has co-dimension at least one, as long as the symbolic determinant $\det \left((f^{\phi}_{\mathbf{u},j})_{\mathbf{u} \in L_U, 1 \leq j \leq n} \right)$ is not identically zero. The matrix $(f^{\phi}_{\mathbf{u},j})_{\mathbf{u} \in L_U, 1 \leq j \leq n}$ depends only on ϕ. For the random choice of ϕ induced by key generation, the symbolic determinant $\det \left((f^{\phi}_{\mathbf{u},j})_{\mathbf{u} \in L_U, 1 \leq j \leq n} \right)$ is almost certainly not identically zero. Therefore, its roots, which constitutes the pathological variety of dependent L_U has co-dimension at least one. Therefore with probability at least $1 - 1/q$, we expect the co-ordinates of a random starting vector $\mathbf{u}_1$ to not be in this variety, implying that the L_U vectors are linearly independent. The probability $1 - 1/q$ is only a crude estimate. For a precise bound taking into account the structure of the polynomial, we can invoke the Schwartz–Zippel lemma or more generally the Lang–Weil bound. The Lang–Weil bound subsumes the Schwartz–Zippel lemma and gives stronger bounds in many cases where more (such as number of irreducible components, degree, smoothness, etc.) is known about the polynomial $\det \left((f^{\phi}_{\mathbf{u},j})_{\mathbf{u} \in L_U, 1 \leq j \leq n} \right)$. In either case, to unconditionally prove that a random $\mathbf{u}_1$ is not in this variety, it helps if the degree of the polynomial is not too big. Naively, the polynomial produced through expansion is of exponential degree, but this is unlikely to be optimal, as shown in the experiment part. We leave an unconditional proof of the validity of this heuristic to future work.

Heuristic 2. Here we assume that $O(n)$ entries in the transformed tensor are non-zero. Therefore, the probability of this assumption failing increases as q decreases and n increases. Note that this assumption is used only to deal with diagonal group actions, and more specialized techniques can be done to reduce the failure probability of this step.

Heuristic 3. We prove that the invariants generated by our algorithm are distinguishing with high probability, under the following well studied conjecture from [39], which we re-phrase in tensor notation. To this end, define the automorphism group of a tensor $\phi \in TF(\mathbb{F}_q)$ as the subgroup $\mathrm{Aut}(\phi) \leqslant \mathrm{GL}(n, q)^3$ such that

$$\forall (A, B, C) \in \mathrm{Aut}(\phi), \forall (x, y, z) \in \mathbb{F}_q^n, \phi(Ax, By, Cz) = \phi(x, y, z).$$

Clearly, scalar matrix triples of the form

$$\{(\lambda I_n, \mu I_n, \nu I_n) \mid \lambda\mu\nu = 1, (\lambda, \mu, \nu) \in \left(\mathbb{F}_q^{\times}\right)^3\} \leqslant \mathrm{Aut}(\phi)$$

form a subgroup of the automorphism group. We say that the automorphism group $\mathrm{Aut}(\phi)$ is trivial or equivalently that ϕ has trivial automorphism group if and only if

$$\{(\lambda I_n, \mu I_n, \nu I_n) \mid \lambda\mu\nu = 1, (\lambda, \mu, \nu) \in \left(\mathbb{F}_q^{\times}\right)^3\} = \mathrm{Aut}(\phi).$$

That is, all automorphisms are merely triples of scalar matrices.

Conjecture 1. For uniformly random $\phi \in TF(\mathbb{F}_q^n)$, with probability negligibly close to 1, the automorphism group $\mathrm{Aut}(\phi)$ is trivial.

This conjecture is stated as a "mild assumption" in [39], where the authors provide convincing theoretic and empirical evidence. In fact, this conjecture is assumed true in half of the complexity theoretic reductions in the web of problems centered around MCE ([39, Fig. 1]), that lay as the foundation for MEDS.

Consider the corank-1 invariant $\bar{\phi}[\hat{\mathbf{u}}]$ constructed at a successful completion of the first step of the algorithm. We prove in the subsequent Lemma 1 that $\bar{\phi}[\hat{\mathbf{u}}]$ is distinguishing if the isomorphism class of ϕ has a trivial automorphism group.

Lemma 1. *If $\phi \in TF(\mathbb{F}_q^n)$ has the trivial automorphism group, then the isomorphism invariant $(\phi, \hat{\mathbf{u}}) \longmapsto \bar{\phi}[\hat{\mathbf{u}}]$ determined by step 1 of the algorithm is distinguishing.*

Proof. Recall the notation in the description of the algorithm, to aid in the proof sketch. Let (L_U, L_V, L_W) and (L'_U, L'_V, L'_W) be the two vector tuples produced starting from different $\mathbf{u}$ and $\mathbf{u}'$, respectively. Let $\bar{\phi}[\hat{\mathbf{u}}]$ and $\bar{\phi}[\hat{\mathbf{u}}]$ respectively denote the images of the invariant computed by step 1 of the algorithm. If the algorithm samples two $\bar{\phi}[\hat{\mathbf{u}}]$ and $\bar{\phi}[\hat{\mathbf{u}}]$ that are the same, then the respective vector tuples (L_U, L_V, L_W) and (L'_U, L'_V, L'_W) can be composed to get a non-trivial automorphism in $\mathrm{Aut}(\phi)$. But $\phi \in TF(\mathbb{F}_q^n)$ has the trivial automorphism group, therefore $\bar{\phi}[\hat{\mathbf{u}}]$ and $\bar{\phi}[\hat{\mathbf{u}}]$ are distinct, implying the invariant is distinguishing.

The MEDS key generation algorithm chooses a ϕ uniformly at random from $TF(\mathbb{F}_q^n)$. Assuming Conjecture 1, $\mathrm{Aut}(\phi)$ is trivial with probability negligibly close to 1. Therefore, Lemma 1 applies in our setting (except possibly with negligibly small probability), implying $(\phi, \bar{\mathbf{u}}) \longmapsto \bar{\phi}[\hat{\mathbf{u}}]$ is distinguishing.

Experimental Support. We carry out experiments on Magma [16] for $n = 6$ to 10 and $q = 1021$ to verify the assumptions as above.

We examine Assumptions 1, 2, and 3 sequentially as follows. That is, for a point $\mathbf{u}$, we first verify if assumption 1 holds. If so, then we check if assumption 2 holds for $\mathbf{u}$. If both assumptions 1 and 2 hold, we call $\mathbf{u}$ an *effective point*. In Table 2, we sample 1000 points, and record the number of points failing assumption 1, and the number of points satisfying assumption 1 but failing assumption 2, as well as the number of effective points.

Finally, to verify assumption 3, we do experiments on these effective points. Our results show that for the instances in the Table 2, the isomorphism invariants corresponding to all points are pairwise distinguishable. This is expected, because each sample is generated randomly, these points are essentially distinct from one another.

Table 2. Statistics of effective points. a/b/c in the table are defined as follows: a (resp. b) is the number of points for which Assumption 1 (resp. Assumption 2) does not hold, and c is the number of effective points.

n / q	6	7	8	9	10	11	12	13	14
509	7/26/967	1/39/960	5/40/955	5/41/954	1/70/929	12/58/930	6/57/937	11/67/922	5/81/914
1021	8/10/982	5/16/979	10/20/970	4/28/968	2/18/980	1/27/972	3/31/966	2/30/968	1/29/970
2039	1/13/986	1/13/986	3/14/983	2/8/990	0/18/982	0/18/982	1/15/984	2/17/981	0/18/982
4093	1/5/994	1/7/992	1/5/994	1/7/992	0/6/994	2/6/992	0/13/987	2/11/987	0/10/990
8191	0/3/997	0/2/998	1/2/997	0/2/998	1/4/995	0/3/997	0/5/995	1/8/991	1/5/994
16381	0/0/1000	0/1/999	0/4/996	0/0/1000	0/4/996	0/1/999	0/3/997	1/4/995	0/3/997

n / q	15	16	17	18	19	20	21	22
509	1/88/911	11/99/890	6/90/904	3/119/878	3/104/893	7/99/894	6/128/866	3/116/881
1021	1/27/972	3/45/952	5/49/946	1/54/945	5/58/937	2/54/944	2/67/931	7/59/934
2039	4/18/978	1/19/980	0/28/972	2/20/978	2/25/973	2/31/967	2/29/969	2/28/970
4093	2/8/990	1/10/989	1/18/981	0/16/984	3/15/982	1/23/976	1/11/988	1/22/977
8191	1/3/996	0/4/996	1/7/992	0/4/996	1/10/989	1/9/990	0/4/996	0/8/992
16381	0/7/993	0/2/998	0/1/999	0/1/999	0/8/992	0/4/996	0/3/997	1/3/996

Note that it is enough for all but a small fraction of corank-1 $\mathbf{u}_1$ to satisfy the above. Furthermore, if some assumption is not satisfied, this would also constitute as an invariant. That is, if $\mathbf{u}_1, \ldots, \mathbf{u}_i$ in L_U becomes linearly dependent, then this number i also becomes an invariant which can be utilised. We do not attempt to deal with such cases because they rarely happen in experiments.

4.6 Experimental Results for the Algorithm

We implemented the algorithm in Sect. 4.4 in Magma [16]. We tested our implementation on a server (AMD EPYC 7532 CPU at 2.40 GHz) to solve some instances of the MCE problem. The results are given in Table 3. Our experiments demonstrate that when running ten instances, two to four of them successfully discover collisions and recover the secret matrices (A, B, C).

Because we conduct $q^{(n-2)/2}$ samplings, we cannot set q to be too large for a practical running. Therefore, we set q to be 61 or 31. As a result, the fraction of effective points is not as large as for $q = 1021$ as in Table 2. For example, in MCE-instance-1, we conducted 3721 samplings and obtained 2702 effective points. Therefore, when q is large, the success rate should increase with the number of effective points.

Table 3. Solving MCE instances

Parameter set	n	q	Number of effective points	Number of sampling times	Time (seconds)
MCE-instance-1	6	61	2702	3721	420
MCE-instance-2	7	61	20053	29062	5638
MCE-instance-3	8	61	149149	226981	100900
MCE-instance-4	9	31	64202	165870	137715

Remark 1. Following [12], a possible improvement on the sampling step (Step (a) of the algorithm in Sect. 4.4) is as follows.

Recall that in Step (a) of the algorithm in Sect. 4.4, a corank-1 point is obtained by sampling a random vector in $\mathbb{F}_q^n$ for q times. However, note that starting from a corank-1 vector $\hat{u}$, the vectors in the vector tuple L_U, if successfully built, are all corank-1. So these vectors can be utilised, instead of starting from a fresh random corank-1 vector. In general, we can walk along the path in the tripartite graph starting from a corank-1 vector until we hit a vector of corank larger than 1. This has the potential of reducing the complexity of the algorithm from $O(q^{(n-2)/2} \cdot (q \cdot n^3 + n^4) \cdot (\log(q))^2)$ to $O(q^{(n-2)/2} \cdot n^4 \cdot (\log(q))^2)$, as we would only need to sample a fresh corank-1 vector very few times during the execution of the algorithm.

One question for this approach is whether it results in a distribution close to the uniform one. To test this, we implemented the above approach. In the case of MCE-instance-1, our preliminary experimental results show that when running 6 instances, one of them successfully finds a collision and recovers the secret matrices. We leave a more careful analysis and more experiments to a future work.

5   An Algorithm for Alternating Trilinear Form Equivalence

In this section, we present our algorithm for the ATFE problem. That is, given two alternating trilinear forms $\phi \in \mathrm{ATF}(\mathbb{F}_q^n)$ and $\psi \in \mathrm{ATF}(\mathbb{F}_q^n)$, the algorithm computes an equivalence $A \in \mathrm{GL}(n, q)$ from ϕ to ψ, if such A exists.

As will be explained later, there is a component missing for implementing this algorithm for ATFE, namely the transformation of isomorphism testing procedures to canonical forms. (On the contrary, the corresponding component in our algorithm for matrix code equivalence is automatically a canonical form algorithm.) Still, as it is usually the case that an isomorphism testing algorithm can be turned into a canonical form algorithm (such as for graph isomorphism [4]), the time complexity of this algorithm is used in the parameter setup of ALTEQ [15].

Before introducing our algorithm, we review the algorithms for ATFE by Beullens [12], which inspire our algorithm.

5.1   Beullens' Algorithms for ATFE

In [12], Beullens presented some novel algorithms for ATFE. Here we describe two algorithms there that work for general n.

The first algorithm is a collision algorithm based on low-rank points based on the graph-walking sampling method. That is, suppose a random $\phi \in \text{ATF}(n, q)$ has approximately q^k-many projective points of rank r. Then for $\phi, \psi \in \text{ATF}(n, q)$ that are equivalent via $A \in \text{GL}(n, q)$, one can sample $q^{1/2 \cdot k}$-many rank-r points for ϕ, and another $q^{1/2 \cdot k}$-many rank-r points for ψ. Then by the birthday paradox, with constant probability there exists a pair of points $(\mathbf{u}, \mathbf{v})$ from these two lists, such that $A(\mathbf{u}) = \mathbf{v}$. Combined with a Gröbner basis with partial information procedure[3], this correspondence enables to recover the whole A. To sample rank-r points, Beullens invented the graph-walk sampling method, which allows for sampling e.g. corank-3 points for odd n more efficiently than directly using min-rank for relatively small q. The major cost of this approach is usually the collision step, with time complexity $q^k \cdot \text{poly}(n, \log q)$.

The second algorithm is a birthday algorithm based on isomorphism invariants. Such an algorithm was already proposed for the polynomial isomorphism problem by Bouillaguet, Fouque, and Véber in [17] for $q = 2$. Beullens observed that for radius-1 or 2 neighbours of corank-1 (for odd n) or corank-2 (for even n), the rank information should serve as a distinguishing isomorphism invariants. The major cost of this approach is the number of corank-1 or corank-2 points, so Beullens estimated the running time as $q^{n/2+c} \cdot \text{poly}(n, \log q)$.

5.2   An Algorithm for ATFE Based on a New Isomorphism Invariant

The main innovation of our algorithm for ATFE is to associate distinguishing isomorphism invariants to low-rank points.

Let $\phi : \mathbb{F}_q^n \times \mathbb{F}_q^n \times \mathbb{F}_q^n \to \mathbb{F}_q$. Suppose by Theorem 2, it is expected that there are roughly q^k many $\hat{\mathbf{u}} \in \mathbb{P}(\mathbb{F}_q^n)$, such that $\text{rk}_\phi(\hat{\mathbf{u}}) = r$. Let us *assume* that there is an easy-to-compute, distinguishing, isomorphism invariant[4] for those rank-r $\hat{\mathbf{u}}$.

---

[3] Beullens discovered that Gröbner basis with partial information still works well given (1) a correspondence between projective points, and (2) the kernel information of low-rank points.

[4] That is, a function f from low-rank points to some set S, such that $f(\hat{\mathbf{u}}) \neq f(\hat{\mathbf{v}})$ for $\hat{\mathbf{u}} \neq \hat{\mathbf{v}}$, and f is unchanged by basis changes.

Then the algorithm goes as follows: first sample $O(q^{k/2})$-many rank-r points for ϕ, and $O(q^{k/2})$-many rank-r points for ψ. For each point, compute this isomorphism invariant. Then by the birthday paradox, there exist one point $\hat{\mathbf{u}}$ from the list of ϕ, and one point $\hat{\mathbf{v}}$ from the list of ψ, such that their isomorphism invariants are the same. Finally, use Gröbner basis with partial information for $\hat{\mathbf{u}}$ and $\hat{\mathbf{v}}$ to recover the desired isomorphism.

Following Eq. 1, the running time of the above algorithm can then be estimated as

$$O(q^{k/2} \cdot (\mathsf{samp\text{-}cost} + \mathsf{inv\text{-}cost}) + \mathsf{gb\text{-}cost}),$$

where $\mathsf{samp\text{-}cost}$ denotes the sampling cost, the $\mathsf{inv\text{-}cost}$ denotes the invariant computing cost, and $\mathsf{gb\text{-}cost}$ denotes the Gröbner basis with partial information cost.

The sampling step can be achieved by either the min-rank method (Appendix A) or Beullens' graph-walking method [12]. For the min-rank method, the cost of sampling a low-rank matrix can be estimated for concrete values of n, k, and r by e.g. [6,35,44]. For the graph-walking method, the sampling cost can be estimated based on certain statistics of graphs associated with alternating trilinear forms by Beullens [12, Theorem 1].

The $\mathsf{gb\text{-}cost}$ can be estimated as $O(n^6)$ as in [12]. This is based on the hybrid Gröbner basis method with the first row known in the variable matrix. The effectiveness of this hybrid Gröbner basis method was first discovered in [27] and then utilised in [17,42]. Beullens further improved this method by noting that (1) knowing the first row up to scalar suffices, and (2) for low-rank points, the kernel information can be incorporated [12, Section 4].

The main innovation of the above algorithm is a new isomorphism invariant which we describe next.

5.3   The Isomorphism Invariant Step

Suppose $\hat{\mathbf{u}} \in \mathbb{P}(\mathbb{F}_q^n)$ satisfies that $\mathrm{rk}_\phi(\hat{\mathbf{u}}) = r$. Then $K := \ker(\phi_{\hat{\mathbf{u}}}) \leq \mathbb{F}_q^n$ is a dimension-$(n-r)$ space, also preserved by any isomorphism. This allows us to consider the trilinear form $\tilde{\phi}_{\hat{\mathbf{u}}} : K \times \mathbb{F}_q^n \times \mathbb{F}_q^n \to \mathbb{F}_q$, and it can be verified easily that the *isomorphism type* of $\tilde{\phi}_{\hat{\mathbf{u}}}$ under $\mathrm{GL}(K) \times \mathrm{GL}(n,q)$ is an isomorphism invariant.

To use the isomorphism type of $\tilde{\phi}_{\hat{\mathbf{u}}}$ in the algorithm, we need the isomorphism types are (1) easy to compute, and (2) distinguishing; that is, for different $\hat{\mathbf{u}}, \hat{\mathbf{v}} \in \mathbb{P}(\mathbb{F}_q^n)$, $\tilde{\phi}_{\hat{\mathbf{u}}}$ and $\tilde{\phi}_{\hat{\mathbf{v}}}$ are different.

To verify these, we perform the following experiment in Magma [16].

1. Sample a random $\phi \in \mathrm{ATF}(n,q)$.
2. Sample a random rank-r point $\hat{\mathbf{u}} \in \mathbb{P}(\mathbb{F}_q^n)$.
3. Sample t random rank-r points $\hat{\mathbf{v}} \in \mathbb{P}(\mathbb{F}_q^n)$. For each such point, do:
   (a) Use the Gröbner basis with partial information to decide whether $\tilde{\phi}_{\hat{\mathbf{u}}}$ and $\tilde{\phi}_{\hat{\mathbf{v}}}$ are isomorphic.

Our experiments give the following.

- For $n = 9$, $r = 4$, and $p = 3$, 10 experiments (i.e. for 10 $\hat{u}$ from 10 random alternating trilinear forms) with $t = 100$ comparisons (i.e. for 100 different $\hat{v}$ to compare with $\hat{u}$). On average, 75 out of 100 $\tilde{\phi}_{\hat{v}}$ are not isomorphic with $\tilde{\phi}_{\hat{u}}$.
- For $n = 10$, $r = 6$, and $p = 3$, 10 experiments (i.e. for 10 $\hat{u}$ from 10 random alternating trilinear forms) with $t = 100$ comparisons (i.e. for 100 different $\hat{v}$ to compare with $\hat{u}$). On average, 95 out of 100 $\tilde{\phi}_{\hat{v}}$ are not isomorphic with $\tilde{\phi}_{\hat{u}}$.

For $n = 11$, our code does not work for $n = 11$ on a laptop, due to the Gröbner basis step.

From these experiments we see that (1) the Gröbner basis with partial information algorithm is effective in practice to test isomorphism between $\tilde{\phi}_{\hat{u}}$ and $\tilde{\phi}_{\hat{v}}$, and (2) as n goes from 9 to 10, the isomorphism type of $\tilde{\phi}_{\hat{u}}$ becomes more distinguishing. These give some preliminary support that the isomorphism types of $\tilde{\phi}_{\hat{u}}$ do serve as a easy-to-compute, distinguishing, isomorphism invariant.

Note that testing isomorphism here is not enough, and canonical forms are required to serve as an isomorphism invariant. Even though to transform an isomorphism invariant algorithm to a canonical form one may not be an easy process, it is generally regarded as doable, at least from the experience from graph isomorphism [3].

5.4   Concrete Estimations of This Algorithm for **ALTEQ** Parameters

We show the improvement of our algorithm over Beullens' algorithm for a set of **ALTEQ** parameters. In [15], $n = 13$ and $q = 2^{32} - 1$ are used for the 128-bit security. In this case, Beullens' algorithm runs in time $O(q^{(n-5)/2} \cdot n^{11} + q^{n-7} \cdot n^6)$. As the major factor comes from q^{n-7}, the bit complexity is above $32 \cdot 6 = 192$. For our algorithm, using rank-$(n-5)$ points, the time complexity is estimated as $O(q^{(n-7)/2} \cdot (\mathsf{samp\text{-}cost} + \mathsf{inv\text{-}cost}) + \mathsf{gb\text{-}cost})$. The sampling cost can be estimated as in Appendix A based on [6], which is 32-bit complexity. The inv-cost and gb-cost are lower than the sampling cost. So the total bit complexity of our algorithm is $32 \cdot 3 + 32 = 128$.

6   Quantum Attacks

We lower the run time exponent of our classical algorithms for MCE and ATFE on a quantum computer by a factor of 2/3. This speed up results from deploying Szegedy type quantum random walks to find collisions, but comes at the cost of exponential quantum space requirement. Therefore, there is reason to only consider the classical algorithms to tune the parameters of the cryptosystems. We describe the quantum algorithms for ATFE in greater detail. The MCE case is analogous but a little easier, since there is no need for Gröbner basis computations.

6.1   Collision Detection Through Quantum Random Walks

The first collision detection quantum algorithms were due to Brassard, Høyer, and Tapp [18] and special to two-to-one functions, building on Grover's search [33]. Ambanis removed these restrictions and devised improved collision detection algorithms through quantum random walks, that match lower bounds [2]. Szegedy further improved these algorithms and brought them under a unified framework of quantum random walks with memory [41]. We will use Szegedy's version of quantum random walks for the quantum speedups of classical algorithms to the decision version ATFE.

We first paraphrase theorem 3 in [41], specialized to the oracle function being the identity. Let X be a finite set and $R \subset X \times X$ a binary relation with a membership tester. For a positive real number α and a uniformly random subset $H \subset X$ of size $|X|^\alpha$, let p_α denote the probability that $R \cap (H \times H)$ is non empty. There is a quantum algorithm to differentiate between the cases $p_\alpha = 0$ and $p_\alpha \geq \epsilon$ in time $\tilde{O}(|X|^\alpha + 1000\sqrt{|X|^\alpha/\epsilon})$.

Extensions of Szegedy's algorithm by Magniez, Nayak, Richter, Roland, and Santha [37,38] may be deployed to tackle the search version ATFE within the same running time. Another extension of Szegedy's algorithm is to claw finding, by Tani [43]. The claw finding formalism is convenient to phrase ATFE in and infer polynomial speed ups. Let $f : X \to Z$ and $g : Y \to Z$ be two functions between finite sets. Given oracle access to f and g, the claw finding problem is to find an $(x, y) \in X \times Y$ such that $f(x) = g(y)$, if one exists. The functions may be presented either as standard oracles or as comparison oracles. We describe the later in the quantum setting, as they suffice. A comparison oracle maps quantum states

$$|x, y, b, w\rangle \longmapsto |x, y, b \oplus [f(x) >^? g(y)], w\rangle.$$

Here, b is a bit; x and y respectively index quantum states corresponding to elements in X and Y. Fixing an ordering on Z, $[f(x) >^? g(y)]$ is a bit that is one if and only if $f(x) > g(y)$. The last register indexed by w is an ancilla for work space. For instances with X and Y of roughly the same size, Tani's algorithm finds claws on a quantum computer in time $O((|X||Y|)^{1/3})$.

In applying these quantum random walk algorithms, we will invoke generic algorithms applicable to functions on finite sets presented as an oracle. For clarity of exposition, we focus on speedups to the main exponential term and suppress incremental polynomial factors.

6.2   Solving ATFE Through Quantum Random Walks

As a warm up, we first describe quantum algorithms for ATFE that do not exploit our new invariants. Then, we build on these algorithms by incorporating the invariants to achieve the aforementioned run time exponent.

A Classical Oracle from the Gröbner Basis Attack with Partial Information. First, consider the decision version of ATFE. That is, given two alternating trilinear forms ϕ and ψ, the existence of an $A \in GL(n, q)$ such that $\psi = \phi \circ A$ is in question. Central to all our methods is a polynomial time classical algorithm to test membership in the relation set

$$R_{\phi,\psi} := \{(\hat{\mathbf{u}}, \hat{\mathbf{v}}) \in \mathbb{P}(\mathbb{F}_q^n)^2 \mid \exists A \in GL(n,q) \text{ such that } \psi = \phi \circ A \text{ and } A^{-1}\hat{\mathbf{u}} = \hat{\mathbf{v}}\}.$$

If ϕ and ψ are not isomorphic, $R_{\phi,\psi}$ is empty. A pair $(\hat{\mathbf{u}}, \hat{\mathbf{v}}) \in \mathbb{P}(\mathbb{F}_q^n)^2$ satisfying $A^{-1}\hat{\mathbf{u}} = \hat{\mathbf{v}}$ enforces n $\mathbb{F}_q$-linear constraints on A. The Gröbner basis attack with partial information in [27], augmented with these linear constraints can tell in heuristic polynomial time if the pair $(\hat{\mathbf{u}}, \hat{\mathbf{v}})$ is in $R_{\phi,\psi}$. We henceforth make the same assumptions. This polynomial time classical algorithm to test membership can be converted to a polynomial sized quantum circuit that can test membership in superposition. Further, incorporate a time out clause into the membership algorithm to make the Gröbner basis methods stop searching and declare non existence.

Invoke Szegedy's algorithm with X as $\mathbb{P}(\mathbb{F}_q^n)$, R as $R_{\phi,\psi}$, α as $1/3$ and uniformly sampling an $H \subset \mathbb{P}(\mathbb{F}_q^n)$ of size $\Theta\left(q^{n/3}\right)$. We claim that the probability gap may be taken to be $\epsilon = \Omega\left(q^{-n/3}\right)$. To prove the claim, consider two isomorphic ϕ and ψ. That is, there exists at least one $A_{\phi,\psi} \in GL(n,q)$ such that $\psi = \phi \circ A_{\phi,\psi}$. Therefore,

$$\Pr_H\left((R_{\phi,\psi} \cap (H \times H)) \neq \emptyset\right) \geq \Pr_H\left((H \cap A_{\phi,\psi}(H)) \neq \emptyset\right) \geq \Omega\left(q^{-n/3}\right),$$

proving the claim. In summary, we can tell if ϕ and ψ are isomorphic in time $q^{n/3}\text{poly}(n, \log q)$ on a quantum computer. This strategy also tackles the promise search version ATFE within the same running time, thanks to extensions of Szegedy's algorithm by Magniez, Nayak, Richter, Roland, and Santha [37,38]. An alternative is to solve ATFE by claw finding. To phrase ATFE as claw finding, independently draw uniformly random sets $X \subset \mathbb{P}(\mathbb{F}_q^n)$ and $Y \subset \mathbb{P}(\mathbb{F}_q^n)$, each of size $q^{n/2}$. Take $f : X \to \mathbb{P}(\mathbb{F}_q^n)$ as the multiplication by A^{-1} map $\mathbf{u} \longmapsto A^{-1}\mathbf{u}$ and $g : Y \to \mathbb{F}_q^n$ as the identity. The birthday paradox ensures for isomorphic ϕ and ψ that there is a solution to claw finding with constant positive probability. The algorithm for testing membership in $R_{\phi,\psi}$ from the previous subsection yields a comparison oracle. Tani's algorithm for claw finding solves ATFE in time $q^{n/3}\text{poly}(n, \log q)$.

6.3 Low-Rank Birthday Attacks on ATFE via Quantum Random Walks

We next describe how our invariant functions can be incorporated into the quantum algorithms. For $\phi \in \text{ATF}(\mathbb{F}_q^n)$ and $\hat{\mathbf{v}} \in \mathbb{P}(\mathbb{F}_q^n)$, let $\phi/\hat{\mathbf{v}}$ denote the isomorphism class of the restriction of ϕ to $\ker(\phi_{\hat{\mathbf{v}}}) \times \mathbb{F}_q^n \times \mathbb{F}_q^n$ under the $GL(\ker(\phi_{\hat{\mathbf{v}}})) \times GL(n,q)$ action. For a positive number R, let

$$S_R := \left\{(\phi, \hat{\mathbf{v}}) \in \text{ATF}(\mathbb{F}_q^n) \times \mathbb{P}(\mathbb{F}_q^n) \mid \text{rk}(\phi_{\hat{\mathbf{v}}}) = R\right\}.$$

The invariant function from Sect. 5 then takes the form

$$(\phi, \hat{\mathbf{v}}) \xmapsto{F_1} \phi/\hat{\mathbf{v}}.$$

Fix the choice of rank R and let k be the exponent such that $\|\mathbb{P}_{\phi,R}\| = q^k$. Assume that F restricted to S_R is distinguishing.

Let ϕ and ψ denote the two input trilinear forms with the existence of an $A \in \mathrm{GL}(n, \mathbb{F}_q)$ such that $\psi = \phi \circ A$ in question. Consider the relation set

$$R_{\phi,\psi}^{F_1} := \{(\mathbf{u}, \mathbf{v}) \in \mathbb{P}_{\phi,R}^2 \mid F_1(\phi, \hat{\mathbf{u}}) = F_1(\psi, \hat{\mathbf{v}})\}.$$

If ϕ and ψ are not isomorphic, then neither are their restrictions to $\ker(\phi_{\hat{\mathbf{v}}}) \times \mathbb{F}_q^n \times \mathbb{F}_q^n$, implying $R_{\phi,\psi}^{F_1}$ is empty. If ϕ and ψ are isomorphic, by the distinguishing property of F_1, with high probability, $F_1(\phi, \hat{\mathbf{u}}) = F_1(\psi, \hat{\mathbf{v}})$ if and only if $\exists A \in \mathrm{GL}(n, q)$ such that $\psi = \phi \circ A$ and $A^{-1}\hat{\mathbf{u}} = \hat{\mathbf{v}}$.

The invariance and the distinguishing property of F_1 together ensure that with high probability, a random pair $(\hat{\mathbf{u}}, \hat{\mathbf{v}}) \in R_{\phi,\psi}^{F_1}$ is a witness to the isomorphism of ϕ and ψ restricted to $\ker(\phi_{\hat{\mathbf{u}}}) \times \mathbb{F}_q^n \times \mathbb{F}_q^n$. That is, there exists an $A \in \mathrm{GL}(n, q)$ such that $\hat{\mathbf{v}} = A^{-1}\hat{\mathbf{u}}$ and A moves the restriction of ϕ to the restriction of ψ. In particular, A restricted to $\ker(\phi_{\hat{\mathbf{u}}})$ acts in the first dimension. Therefore, with $(\hat{\mathbf{u}}, \hat{\mathbf{v}})$ as the partial information, the Gröbner basis algorithm of [20, 42] becomes a heuristic polynomial time test of membership in $R_{\phi,\psi}^{F_1}$.

Invoke Szegedy's algorithm with X as $\mathbb{P}_{\phi,R}$, R as $R_{\phi,\psi}^{F_1}$, α as $1/3$ and uniformly sampling an $H \subset \mathbb{P}_{\phi,R}$ of size $\Theta\left(q^{k/3}\right)$. For isomorphic ϕ and ψ, there exists at least one $A_{\phi,\psi} \in \mathrm{GL}(n, q)$ such that $\psi = \phi \circ A_{\phi,\psi}$. Therefore, by the invariance and the distinguishing nature of F_1,

$$\Pr\left((R_{\phi,\psi}^{F_1} \cap (H \times H)) \neq \emptyset\right) \geq \Pr\left((H \cap A_{\phi,\psi}(H)) \neq \emptyset\right) \geq \Omega\left(q^{-k/3}\right),$$

proving that the probability gap may be taken to be $\epsilon = \Omega\left(q^{-k/3}\right)$. Therefore, for a rank parameter such that the sampling cost samp-cost is in polynomial time, the decision version of ATFE can be solved in $q^{k/3}\mathsf{poly}(n, \log q)$ time on a quantum computer. To tackle the promise search version ATFE within the same running time, applying the extensions of Szegedy's algorithm by Magniez, Nayak, Richter, Roland, and Santha [37, 38], the search version ATFE can also be solved in

$$q^{k/3} \cdot \mathsf{poly}(n, \log q)$$

time on a quantum computer. Curiously, it is not obvious if the claw finding formalism in Tani's algorithm can be adapted to the low-rank birthday attacks. If we can efficiently derive canonical forms in addition to testing the isomorphism class of the restriction, then Tani's algorithm apply immediately. The reason being that we can order the canonical form representatives and obtain a comparison oracle.

6.4 Low-Rank Birthday Attacks on MCE via Quantum Random Walks

Recall the notation from Sect. 4. We next phrase MCE as claw finding. Let ϕ, ψ be the two input isomorphic trilinear forms. Take X and Y as uniformly random subsets of co-rank 1 projective points, each of size $q^{n/2}$. Take f as the $\hat{u} \longmapsto \bar{\phi}[\hat{u}]$ map and g as the $\hat{u} \longmapsto \bar{\psi}[\hat{u}]$ map. The birthday paradox ensures that there is a solution to claw finding with constant positive probability. Invoking Tani's algorithm solves MCE in $q^{n/3}\text{poly}(n, \log q)$ time.

Acknowledgements. We thank the anonymous reviewers for their careful reading and helpful suggestions. Youming Qiao was partly supported by ARC DP200100950 and LP220100332. Gang Tang was partly supported by ARC LP220100332, Sydney Quantum Academy, and EPSRC grant EP/V011324/1.

A   Low-Rank Point Sampling via Min-Rank Step

The sampling step can be done by either the min-rank method, or the graph-walking method. The graph-walking method involves q, so it works best for relatively small q. When q is large, the min-rank method is more effective. To use min-rank to do sampling requires a bit of twist, so we record the idea here.

Suppose we wish to sample a rank-r point $\hat{v} \in \mathbb{P}(\mathbb{F}_q^n)$ for an alternating trilinear form ϕ, and suppose that there are q^k-many rank-r projective points for a random ϕ. To sample such points, we make a heuristic assumption that the first k coordinates of these rank-r points are in uniform random. Therefore, to sample one point, we can randomly choose the first k coordinates and then resort to the min-rank procedure.

More specifically, for $i \in [n]$, let A_i be the alternating matrix representing the bilinear form ϕ_{e_i}, where e_i is the ith standard basis vector. Let x_i, $i \in [n]$, be formal variables, and set $A = \sum_{i \in [n]} x_i A_i$. So for $i \in [1 \ldots k]$, let $x_i = \alpha_i x_1$, where $\alpha_i \in_R \mathbb{F}_q$. This gives us a min-rank instance with $n - k$ matrices of size $n \times n$.

To estimate the min-rank cost, we use the algorithm from [6]. Consider an (n, K, r) minrank instance, namely finding a rank-r matrix in a linear span of K $n \times n$ matrices. First, we need to compute the smallest b such that $b < r + 2$ and

$$\binom{n}{r}\binom{K+b-1}{b} - 1 \le \sum_{i=1}^{b}(-1)^{i+1}\binom{n}{r+i}\binom{n+i-1}{i}\binom{K+b-i-1}{b-i}.$$

Based on this b, the complexity is estimated as

$$O\left(K \cdot (r+1) \cdot \left(\binom{n}{r} \cdot \binom{K+b-1}{b}\right)^2\right).$$

For concrete values of n, $K = n - k$ and r, the above formulas allow for the estimation of the concrete security parameters.

Note that the min-rank instance above has some structural constraints due to alternating trilinear forms. As pointed out in [12], such structures should impact the min-rank algorithm from [6] adversely. Still, we use the estimates from [6] as they should serve as a lower bound. We also compare the estimates from [6] with the analysis of the Kipnis–Shamir modelling [35] in [44], and found the ones from [6] are lower.

References

1. Alamati, N., De Feo, L., Montgomery, H., Patranabis, S.: Cryptographic group actions and applications. In: Moriai, S., Wang, H. (eds.) ASIACRYPT 2020. LNCS, vol. 12492, pp. 411–439. Springer, Cham (2020). https://doi.org/10.1007/978-3-030-64834-3_14
2. Ambainis, A.: Quantum walk algorithm for element distinctness. SIAM J. Comput. **37**(1), 210–239 (2007)
3. Babai, L.: Graph isomorphism in quasipolynomial time [extended abstract]. In: Proceedings of the 48th Annual ACM SIGACT Symposium on Theory of Computing, STOC 2016, Cambridge, MA, USA, 18–21 June 2016, pp. 684–697 (2016)
4. Babai, L.: Canonical form for graphs in quasipolynomial time: preliminary report. In: Charikar, M., Cohen, E. (eds.) Proceedings of the 51st Annual ACM SIGACT Symposium on Theory of Computing, STOC 2019, Phoenix, AZ, USA, 23–26 June 2019, pp. 1237–1246. ACM (2019). https://doi.org/10.1145/3313276.3316356
5. Baldi, M., et al.: LESS: linear equivalence signature scheme (2023). https://www.less-project.com/LESS-2023-08-18.pdf
6. Bardet, M., et al.: Improvements of algebraic attacks for solving the rank decoding and MinRank problems. In: Moriai, S., Wang, H. (eds.) ASIACRYPT 2020. LNCS, vol. 12491, pp. 507–536. Springer, Cham (2020). https://doi.org/10.1007/978-3-030-64837-4_17
7. Bardet, M., Otmani, A., Saeed-Taha, M.: Permutation code equivalence is not harder than graph isomorphism when hulls are trivial. In: 2019 IEEE International Symposium on Information Theory (ISIT), pp. 2464–2468. IEEE (2019). https://doi.org/10.1109/ISIT.2019.8849855
8. Barenghi, A., Biasse, J.F., Ngo, T., Persichetti, E., Santini, P.: Advanced signature functionalities from the code equivalence problem. Int. J. Comput. Math. Comput. Syst. Theory **7**(2), 112–128 (2022)
9. Battagliola, M., Borin, G., Meneghetti, A., Persichetti, E.: Cutting the grass: threshold group action signature schemes. Cryptology ePrint Archive (2023)
10. Belsley, E.: Rates of convergence of Markov chains related to association schemes. Harvard University, Ph.D. thesis (1993)
11. Beullens, W.: Not enough LESS: an improved algorithm for solving code equivalence problems over $\mathbb{F}_q$. In: Dunkelman, O., Jacobson, Jr., M.J., O'Flynn, C. (eds.) SAC 2020. LNCS, vol. 12804, pp. 387–403. Springer, Cham (2021). https://doi.org/10.1007/978-3-030-81652-0_15
12. Beullens, W.: Graph-theoretic algorithms for the alternating trilinear form equivalence problem. In: Handschuh, H., Lysyanskaya, A. (eds.) CRYPTO 2023 - Part III. LNCS, vol. 14083, pp. 101–126. Springer, Cham (2023). https://doi.org/10.1007/978-3-031-38548-3_4
13. Biasse, J.-F., Micheli, G., Persichetti, E., Santini, P.: LESS is more: code-based signatures without syndromes. In: Nitaj, A., Youssef, A. (eds.) AFRICACRYPT 2020. LNCS, vol. 12174, pp. 45–65. Springer, Cham (2020). https://doi.org/10.1007/978-3-030-51938-4_3
14. Bläser, M., et al.: On digital signatures based on isomorphism problems: QROM security, ring signatures, and applications. Cryptology ePrint Archive, Paper 2022/1184 (2022). https://eprint.iacr.org/2022/1184
15. Bläser, M., et al.: The ALTEQ signature scheme: algorithm specifications and supporting documentation (2023). https://pqcalteq.github.io/ALTEQ_spec_2023.09.18.pdf

16. Bosma, W., Cannon, J., Playoust, C.: The Magma algebra system. I. The user language. J. Symbolic Comput. **24**(3–4), 235–265 (1997). https://doi.org/10.1006/jsco.1996.0125. Computational algebra and number theory, London (1993)
17. Bouillaguet, C., Fouque, P.-A., Véber, A.: Graph-theoretic algorithms for the "Isomorphism of Polynomials" problem. In: Johansson, T., Nguyen, P.Q. (eds.) EUROCRYPT 2013. LNCS, vol. 7881, pp. 211–227. Springer, Heidelberg (2013). https://doi.org/10.1007/978-3-642-38348-9_13
18. Brassard, G., Hoyer, P., Tapp, A.: Quantum cryptanalysis of hash and claw-free functions. In: Lucchesi, C.L., Moura, A.V. (eds.) LATIN 1998. LNCS, vol. 1380, pp. 163–169. Springer, Heidelberg (1998). https://doi.org/10.1007/BFb0054319
19. Brassard, G., Yung, M.: One-way group actions. In: Menezes, A.J., Vanstone, S.A. (eds.) CRYPTO 1990. LNCS, vol. 537, pp. 94–107. Springer, Heidelberg (1991). https://doi.org/10.1007/3-540-38424-3_7
20. Bürgisser, P., Franks, C., Garg, A., de Oliveira, R.M., Walter, M., Wigderson, A.: Efficient algorithms for tensor scaling, quantum marginals, and moment polytopes. In: 59th IEEE Annual Symposium on Foundations of Computer Science, FOCS 2018, Paris, France, 7–9 October 2018, pp. 883–897 (2018). https://doi.org/10.1109/FOCS.2018.00088
21. Chou, T., et al.: Matrix code equivalence digital signature (2023). https://www.meds-pqc.org/spec/MEDS-2023-07-26.pdf
22. Chou, T., et al.: Take your MEDS: digital signatures from matrix code equivalence. In: El Mrabet, N., De Feo, L., Duquesne, S. (eds.) AFRICACRYPT 2023. LNCS, vol. 14064, pp. 28–52. Springer, Cham (2023). https://doi.org/10.1007/978-3-031-37679-5_2
23. Couvreur, A., Debris-Alazard, T., Gaborit, P.: On the hardness of code equivalence problems in rank metric. arXiv preprint arXiv:2011.04611 (2020)
24. D'Alconzo, G., Gangemi, A.: TRIFORS: LINKable trilinear forms ring signature. Cryptology ePrint Archive (2022)
25. Ducas, L., Postlethwaite, E.W., Pulles, L.N., Woerden, W.V.: HAWK: module LIP makes lattice signatures fast, compact and simple. In: Agrawal, S., Lin, D. (eds.) ASIACRYPT 2022, vol. 13794, pp. 65–94. Springer, Cham (2022). https://doi.org/10.1007/978-3-031-22972-5_3
26. Ducas, L., van Woerden, W.: On the lattice isomorphism problem, quadratic forms, remarkable lattices, and cryptography. In: Dunkelman, O., Dziembowski, S. (eds) EUROCRYPT 2022. LNCS, vol. 13277, pp. 643–673. Springer, Cham (2022). https://doi.org/10.1007/978-3-031-07082-2_23
27. Faugère, J.-C., Perret, L.: Polynomial equivalence problems: algorithmic and theoretical aspects. In: Vaudenay, S. (ed.) EUROCRYPT 2006. LNCS, vol. 4004, pp. 30–47. Springer, Heidelberg (2006). https://doi.org/10.1007/11761679_3
28. Fiat, A., Shamir, A.: How to prove yourself: practical solutions to identification and signature problems. In: Odlyzko, A.M. (ed.) CRYPTO 1986. LNCS, vol. 263, pp. 186–194. Springer, Heidelberg (1987). https://doi.org/10.1007/3-540-47721-7_12
29. Fulman, J., Goldstein, L.: Stein's method and the rank distribution of random matrices over finite fields. Ann. Probab. **43**(3) (2015). https://doi.org/10.1214/13-aop889
30. Goldreich, O., Micali, S., Wigderson, A.: Proofs that yield nothing but their validity for all languages in NP have zero-knowledge proof systems. J. ACM **38**(3), 691–729 (1991). https://doi.org/10.1145/116825.116852
31. Grochow, J.A., Qiao, Y.: On the complexity of isomorphism problems for tensors, groups, and polynomials I: tensor isomorphism-completeness. SIAM J. Comput. **52**(2), 568–617 (2023)

32. Grochow, J.A., Qiao, Y., Tang, G.: Average-case algorithms for testing isomorphism of polynomials, algebras, and multilinear forms. J. Groups Complex. Cryptol. **14** (2022)
33. Grover, L.K.: A fast quantum mechanical algorithm for database search. In: Proceedings of the Twenty-Eighth Annual ACM Symposium on Theory of Computing, pp. 212–219 (1996)
34. Ji, Z., Qiao, Y., Song, F., Yun, A.: General linear group action on tensors: a candidate for post-quantum cryptography. In: Hofheinz, D., Rosen, A. (eds.) TCC 2019. LNCS, vol. 11891, pp. 251–281. Springer, Cham (2019). https://doi.org/10.1007/978-3-030-36030-6_11
35. Kipnis, A., Shamir, A.: Cryptanalysis of the HFE public key cryptosystem by relinearization. In: Wiener, M. (ed.) CRYPTO 1999. LNCS, vol. 1666, pp. 19–30. Springer, Heidelberg (1999). https://doi.org/10.1007/3-540-48405-1_2
36. Leon, J.: Computing automorphism groups of error-correcting codes. IEEE Trans. Inf. Theory **28**(3), 496–511 (1982)
37. Magniez, F., Nayak, A., Richter, P.C., Santha, M.: On the hitting times of quantum versus random walks. Algorithmica **63**, 91–116 (2012)
38. Magniez, F., Nayak, A., Roland, J., Santha, M.: Search via quantum walk. In: Proceedings of the Thirty-Ninth Annual ACM Symposium on Theory of Computing, pp. 575–584 (2007)
39. Reijnders, K., Samardjiska, S., Trimoska, M.: Hardness estimates of the code equivalence problem in the rank metric. Des. Codes Cryptogr. **92**, 1–30 (2024)
40. Sendrier, N.: Finding the permutation between equivalent linear codes: the support splitting algorithm. IEEE Trans. Inf. Theory **46**(4), 1193–1203 (2000)
41. Szegedy, M.: Spectra of quantized walks and a $\sqrt{\delta\epsilon}$-rule. arXiv preprint quant-ph/0401053 (2004)
42. Tang, G., Duong, D.H., Joux, A., Plantard, T., Qiao, Y., Susilo, W.: Practical post-quantum signature schemes from isomorphism problems of trilinear forms. In: Dunkelman, O., Dziembowski, S. (eds.) EUROCRYPT 2022 Part III. LNCS, vol. 13277, pp. 582–612. Springer, Cham (2022). https://doi.org/10.1007/978-3-031-07082-2_21
43. Tani, S.: Claw finding algorithms using quantum walk. Theoret. Comput. Sci. **410**(50), 5285–5297 (2009)
44. Verbel, J., Baena, J., Cabarcas, D., Perlner, R., Smith-Tone, D.: On the complexity of "Superdetermined" Minrank instances. In: Ding, J., Steinwandt, R. (eds.) PQCrypto 2019. LNCS, vol. 11505, pp. 167–186. Springer, Cham (2019). https://doi.org/10.1007/978-3-030-25510-7_10

Generalized Feistel Ciphers for Efficient Prime Field Masking

Lorenzo Grassi[1]([✉]), Loïc Masure[2], Pierrick Méaux[3], Thorben Moos[4], and François-Xavier Standaert[4]

[1] Ruhr University Bochum, Bochum, Germany
lorenzo.grassi@ruhr-uni-bochum.de
[2] LIRMM, Univ. Montpellier, CNRS, Montpellier, France
[3] Luxembourg University, Esch-sur-Alzette, Luxembourg
[4] Crypto Group, ICTEAM Institute, UCLouvain, Louvain-la-Neuve, Belgium

Abstract. A recent work from Eurocrypt 2023 suggests that prime-field masking has excellent potential to improve the efficiency vs. security tradeoff of masked implementations against side-channel attacks, especially in contexts where physical leakages show low noise. We pick up on the main open challenge that this seed result leads to, namely the design of an optimized prime cipher able to take advantage of this potential. Given the interest of tweakable block ciphers with cheap inverses in many leakage-resistant designs, we start by describing the FPM (Feistel for Prime Masking) family of tweakable block ciphers based on a generalized Feistel structure. We then propose a first instantiation of FPM, which we denote as small-pSquare. It builds on the recent observation that the square operation (which is non-linear in $\mathbb{F}_p$) can lead to masked gadgets that are more efficient than those for multiplication, and is tailored for efficient masked implementations in hardware. We analyze the mathematical security of the FPM family of ciphers and the small-pSquare instance, trying to isolate the parts of our study that can be re-used for other instances. We additionally evaluate the implementation features of small-pSquare by comparing the efficiency vs. security tradeoff of masked FPGA circuits against those of a state-of-the art binary cipher, namely SKINNY, confirming significant gains in relevant contexts.

1 Introduction

The design of symmetric cryptographic algorithms is generally oriented towards optimizing their efficiency vs. security tradeoff. For most general applications, this has led researchers to focus primarily on binary ciphers with efficient bitslice implementations, which are generally efficient in software [16] and hardware [57]. This trend has even been amplified when considering side-channel attacks, in good part due to the emergence of masking as the most popular solution to mitigate such attacks. While various types of masking schemes exist (e.g., additive [29], multiplicative [43], affine [42], polynomial [74], inner product [4], code-based [89]), the efficiency of Boolean masked implementations in

M. Joye and G. Leander (Eds.): EUROCRYPT 2024, LNCS 14653, pp. 188–220, 2024.
https://doi.org/10.1007/978-3-031-58734-4_7

software [44] and hardware [49] make it for now a default solution. As a result, ciphers optimized towards low AND complexity, enabling efficient bit-oriented implementation (e.g., bitslicing), appeared for a while as the best approach [50]. This situation is also reflected by the recent NIST Ligthweight Cryptography standardization effort, where most ciphers designed with leakage in mind (including the winner Ascon [35]) have efficient bitslice representations.[1]

While it has been shown that Boolean masking can bring high security at limited cost, it is also known to suffer from practical limitations. Among others, it is only effective in contexts where leakages are sufficiently noisy [37, 38, 73], a condition that was shown to be challenging to reach without dedicated noise generation circuitry, both in software [5, 24] and in hardware [69, 72]. Building on theoretical advances of Dziembowski et al. [41], it has then been observed that computing in groups of prime order can significantly reduce the noise requirements of masking security proofs while keeping most of the benefits of additive encodings, and even providing security gains in the context of noisy leakages (that were not covered by theoretical analysis) [67]. More precisely, Masure et al. showed at Eurocrypt 2023 that for concretely-relevant leakage functions, prime-field masking can be quite efficient by re-using simple additions and multiplication algorithms "à la ISW" [54], and that the mild performance overheads due to operating in prime fields can be largely compensated by concrete side-channel security gains. Informally, these gains can be viewed as the result of a decreased "algebraic compatibility" between the leakage functions observed in practice (which are typically close to a linear combination of bits [76]) and the field in which we mask. For example, it is well-known that observing the least significant bit of Hamming weight leakages obtained from Boolean shares leads to information about the secret independent of the number of shares [80]. Moving to prime encodings, such an attack is not directly possible anymore because partial uncertainty "diffuses" better when combining the shares.

So far, this potential advantage of prime-field masking for counteracting side-channel attacks was only demonstrated for a toy AES-like cipher. The main open challenge that we pick up in this paper is, thus, the design of a dedicated lightweight cipher optimized for prime masking to enable fair comparisons with binary ciphers which are tailored for cost-efficiency when masked.

Given the interest of Tweakable Block Ciphers (TBCs) with cheap inverse for leakage-resistant modes of operation [7, 10], we start by describing the FPM (Feistel for Prime Masking) family of tweakable block ciphers based on a generalized Feistel structure [52, 71]. Among other advantages, TBCs allow reducing the need of idealized assumptions that are hard to justify in physical security analyzes and to minimize the side-channel attack surface during tag verification (which can leak in an unbounded manner thanks to the inverse trick of [11]). The FPM family of ciphers allows tweaks of variable size including a version without tweak (i.e., a block cipher, in order to enable comparisons with generic constructions [88]). It relies on a variant of the TWEAKEY framework [56], taking advantage of the fact that for most leakage-resistant modes of operation, the

---

[1] https://csrc.nist.gov/Projects/lightweight-cryptography.

tweak is public information and requires no countermeasures (so we can actually use a simple key scheduling algorithm and a more complex, non-linear, tweak scheduling algorithm). While moving towards a first instantiation of FPM, we additionally exploit recent results from CHES 2023 which show how to obtain a secure implementation of the square operation (non-linear in $\mathbb{F}_p$) which is more efficient than a secure multiplication [27]. This provides natural incentive for designing a cipher using the square operation as only source of non-linearity, which further motivates the use of Feistel-like structures for FPM TBCs and their underlying building blocks, since the square is also non-invertible in $\mathbb{F}_p$. What then mostly remains is to choose the prime number defining the field in which we operate. Following [67], we use a Mersenne prime for efficiency reasons.[2] We set this modulus to $2^7 - 1$ in order to propose an instance tailored for secure hardware implementation, which we denote as small-pSquare.

Besides defining the FPM family of ciphers and a first instance, we provide an initial mathematical security analysis in order to select the number of cipher rounds of small-pSquare. Doing so, we try to separate the parts of the analysis that are generic (and could be re-used for other instances) from the ones that are linked to our choice of square S-box and 7-bit prime. Most importantly, we then compare masked FPGA implementations of small-pSquare and similar implementations of a binary cipher protected with Boolean masking. We use SKINNY for this purpose [6], which is a popular family of ciphers with tweakable versions that amongst other applications was used in Romulus, a finalist to NIST lightweight cryptography competition, and for which a rich literature on the construction and analysis of state-of-the-art Boolean masked implementations exist, both automated [58] and hand-made [85]. Our experiments allow us to confirm the excellent performances and significantly improved efficiency vs. (side-channel) security tradeoff for small-pSquare. We show in Sect. 6 that while unprotected small-pSquare implementations come with overheads (compared to SKINNY), these overheads vanish in the context of masked implementations where both algorithms perform similarly. As expected, small-pSquare also has significantly improved performances compared to the toy AES-like cipher considered in [67]. Furthermore, we show in Sect. 7 that for similar architectures, small-pSquare offers side-channel security levels which exceed those of masked SKINNY implementations by (at least) one order of magnitude.

We conclude the paper by discussing scopes for further research and other instances of FPM ciphers. First, considering different implementation contexts, for example mid-pSquare variants could be relevant to investigate for FPGAs with DSP blocks (e.g., with a 17-bit prime) or for ARM Cortex-like devices (e.g., with a 31-bit prime). Second, and more prospectively, big-pSquare variants (with larger primes) could be of interest conceptually due to their similarity with the different prime ciphers developed for other applications (e.g., fully-homomorphic encryption, multi-party computation, zero-knowledge proofs), in order to better understand the differences and similarities between the design goals to opti-

---

[2] Both because such prime numbers allow very efficient modular reductions and because the $x \mapsto 2x$ operation is a rotation of the bits that is free in hardware.

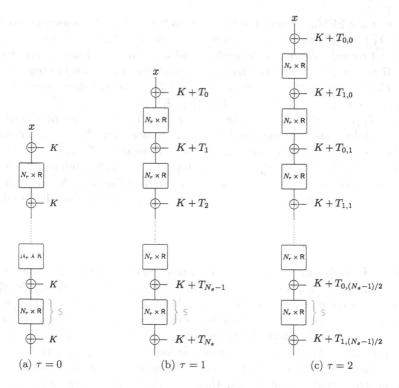

Fig. 1. High-level view of FPM (tweakable) ciphers. We use the shortcut notation $N_r \times \mathsf{R}$ to denote the application of the round R N_r times.

mize for these various applications [1–3,30,36,46], and possibly to offer stronger physical security guarantees thanks to the larger field computations [40].

2 Feistel for Prime Masking

In this section, we introduce the FPM_τ family of TBCs. We start by describing the high-level Feistel structure we use in Sect. 2.1. We then detail the internal components of this structure in Sects. 2.2 and 2.3. We conclude by summarizing the design space that this family of ciphers defines in Sect. 2.4.

2.1 High-Level Structure

Let $p \geqslant 3$ be a prime number, and let $n = 2 \cdot n' \geqslant 4$ be an integer. The high-level structure of FPM_τ TBCs is given in Fig. 1. FPM_τ ciphers take as inputs a plaintext $x \in \mathbb{F}_p^n$, a key $K \in \mathbb{F}_p^n$ and an optional tweak defined as:

$$T := \begin{cases} (T^{(1)}, T^{(2)}, \dots, T^{(\tau)}) \in \mathbb{F}_p^{\tau n} & \text{if } \tau \geqslant 1 \\ \varnothing & \text{otherwise } (\tau = 0) \end{cases}.$$

If $\tau = 0$, then FPM_0 ciphers receive no tweak input and correspond to block ciphers. FPM_τ ciphers are key alternating ciphers, where a tweakey is added every $r > 1$ rounds. We denote a single round as R, and we denote a group of N_r rounds R as a step S. A tweakey addition is performed after every step. If $\tau = 0$, the tweakey is always the master key K. If $\tau \geqslant 1$, the tweakeys are defined as $K + T_{0,0}$, $K + T_{1,0}$, ..., $K + T_{\tau-1,0}$, $K + T_{0,1}$, $K + T_{1,1}$, ..., $K + T_{\tau-1,1}$, ..., $K + T_{0,i}$, $K + T_{1,i}$, ..., $K + T_{\tau-1,i}$, where the values $T_{j,i} \in \mathbb{F}_p^n$ are produced by a tweak scheduling and are independent of the master key. If $\tau = 1$, we usually omit the first index for simplicity (i.e., we use T_i instead of $T_{0,i}$).

The rounds R : $\mathbb{F}_p^n \to \mathbb{F}_p^n$ (and the steps S) are independent of both the tweak and of the master key. The number of rounds per step N_r must at least guarantee that full diffusion is achieved in the steps. Regarding the number of steps N_s, we additionally require that if $\tau \geqslant 1$, then $N_s - 1$ must be a multiple of τ in order to guarantee that the tweak is absorbed in equal measure.

Key and Tweak Scheduling Algorithms. Since we do not claim security against related-key attacks, we opted for the simplest key scheduling algorithm, which consists of having all the subkeys equal to the master key. Note that several tweakable lightweight symmetric primitives in the literature are based on similar design choices, including SKINNY [6] (which we will use in our comparisons).

By contrast, our designs make use of a tweak scheduling algorithm. As mentioned in the introduction, this is because in many leakage-resistant modes of operation, the tweak is public and therefore does not require any protection against leakage. This context calls for operations that are cheap to implement without countermeasures (in hardware and software) while providing good cryptographic properties. Since FPM ciphers operate in prime fields, a natural candidate for this purpose is to combine a shuffling of the $\mathbb{F}_p$-words in each state with an invertible mapping of the "bits" in each $\mathbb{F}_p$-word, for example taking advantage of the fact that linear mappings in $\mathbb{F}_2$ are non-linear in $\mathbb{F}_p$. More precisely, for each $i \geqslant 0$ and for each $j \in \{0, 1, \dots, \tau - 1\}$, we define $T_{j,i}$ as:

$$T_{j,i} := \Psi_0\left(T^{(j)}_{\Pi^i(0)}\right) \| \Psi_1\left(T^{(j)}_{\Pi^i(1)}\right) \| \dots \| \Psi_{n-1}\left(T^{(j)}_{\Pi^i(n-1)}\right) \in \mathbb{F}_p^n,$$

where:

- For each $l \in \{0, 1, \dots, n-1\}$, $T_l^{(j)} \in \mathbb{F}_p$ denotes the l-th $\mathbb{F}_p$-word of $T^{(j)}$;
- Π is a shuffling of $\{0, 1, \dots, n-1\} \subseteq \mathbb{N}$ satisfying the following conditions:
  1. Π^i (where Π^i denotes the application of Π i consecutive times) is different from the identity for each $i \leqslant i'$ and a sufficiently large i';
  2. Π does not contain fix points and (if possible) two consecutive elements before the shuffling are not consecutive after it.
- For each $l \in \{0, 1, \dots, n-1\}$, $\Psi_l : \mathbb{F}_p \to \mathbb{F}_p$ is an invertible mapping.

As we are going to show in the next section, this tweak scheduling algorithm allows us to adapt the simple security arguments used in [51] to our scheme.

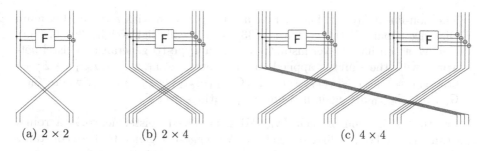

(a) 2 × 2   (b) 2 × 4   (c) 4 × 4

Fig. 2. FPM rounds. Left: $b=2$, $c=2$; middle: $b=2$, $c=4$,right: $b=4$, $c=4$.

2.2 Rounds R of FPM_τ via Type-II Generalized Feistel

Let $b, c \geqslant 2$ be positive integers such that $n = b \cdot c$ and $b = 2 \cdot b'$. The rounds R over $(\mathbb{F}_p^c)^b \equiv \mathbb{F}_p^n$ of FPM_τ ciphers are based on a Type-II generalized Feistel network structure [52,71,90]. They are defined as:

$$(x_0, x_1, \ldots, x_{b-2}, x_{b-1}) \mapsto (\mathsf{F}(x_0) + x_1, x_2, \mathsf{F}(x_2) + x_3, \ldots, \mathsf{F}(x_{b-2}) + x_{b-1}, x_0),$$

where $\mathsf{F} : \mathbb{F}_p^c \equiv \mathbb{F}_{p^c} \rightarrow \mathbb{F}_p^c \equiv \mathbb{F}_{p^c}$ is discussed in the next subsection. Such structures are characterized by two parameters: $b = 2 \cdot b' \geqslant 2$ is the number of branches in the generalized Feistel network (where each branch can carry several values in $\mathbb{F}_p$), $c \geqslant 2$ is the number of values in $\mathbb{F}_p$ of each branch, that the non-linear F function takes as input. Figure 2 illustrates three examples.

Remark: Achieving Faster Diffusion. In this paper, we limit ourselves to instances with small b values (up to 4) and to the classical Type-II generalized Feistel scheme, in which a shift is applied at the output of the non-linear layer. However, several studies have been conducted in literature to find better shuffles of the words that can achieve faster diffusion for larger b values (see for example [28,83]), which we suggest to use in place of the shift whenever applicable. Besides the minimum number of rounds necessary for achieving full diffusion, these references also provide the number of active functions F.

2.3 Function F of the Type-III Generalized Feistel

The F functions over $\mathbb{F}_p^c$ are designed to 1) be bijective (since collisions at their outputs could make the security analysis harder) and 2) ensure full non-linear diffusion. This is achieved by combining the following components:

- A first non-linear layer is instantiated via a Type-III generalized Feistel network [52,71,90] (without the shift) of the form: $(x_0, x_1, x_2, \ldots, x_{c-1}) \in \mathbb{F}_p^c \mapsto (x_0, \mathsf{G}_{0,0}(x_0) + x_1, \mathsf{G}_{1,0}(x_1) + x_2, \ldots, \mathsf{G}_{c-2,0}(x_{c-2}) + x_{c-1}) \in \mathbb{F}_p^c$, where $\mathsf{G}_{0,0}, \mathsf{G}_{1,0}, \ldots, \mathsf{G}_{c-2,0}$ are non-linear operations over $\mathbb{F}_p$.

- The non-linear layer is followed by a multiplication with a $c \times c$ Maximum Distance Separable (MDS) matrix [33, 34], typically lightweight [39, 60, 66].[3]
- Finally, a non-linear layer instantiated via a Type-III generalized Feistel network (with the shift) is applied to the state: $(x_0, x_1, x_2, \ldots, x_{c-1}) \in \mathbb{F}_p^c \mapsto (x_0, \mathsf{G}_{0,1}(x_0) + x_1, \mathsf{G}_{1,1}(x_1) + x_2, \ldots, \mathsf{G}_{c-2,1}(x_{c-2}) + x_{c-1}) \in \mathbb{F}_p^c$, where $\mathsf{G}_{0,0}$, $\mathsf{G}_{1,0}, \ldots, \mathsf{G}_{c-2,0}$ are again non-linear operations over $\mathbb{F}_p$.

Before the application of each Type-III generalized Feistel network, a round constant is added on the first element x_0. We suggest to generate these constants via bit rotations of a mathematical constant as $\pi = 3.14159\ldots \in \mathbb{R}$ rounded to a bit size that is large enough to avoid cycles for the number of cipher rounds.

We note that using a Type-III generalized Feistel network for the F functions is motivated by the fact that a potential candidate for the $\mathsf{G}_{i,j}$ functions is the square operation which is non-invertible (or other small power maps which are non-bijective in the respective field). In case the $\mathsf{G}_{i,j}$ functions are themselves bijective, a simpler alternative is to directly use SPN rounds.

We also note that since we use a bijective F, exploiting a Feistel structure for the rounds of Sect. 2.2 is not mandatory (e.g., an SPN could work there too). However, it has the advantage that the F function can be chosen without any regard for the implementation efficiency of its inverse (with or without masking), which would not be the case when used as an S-box in a typical SPN construction. Furthermore, the Feistel strategy directly enables us to obtain cheap inverses in the sense that 1) cost of decryption $\approx$ cost of encryption and 2) implementing a hardware circuit that can both encrypt and decrypt is not (significantly) more expensive than one which can only encrypt (in contrast to most standard SPN designs). In general, we believe that the high-level structure of FPM ciphers is a natural starting point given our goals. SPN-based structures would also require an additional linear layer (which may be more expensive) and it is unclear whether it would enable a reduction of the number of rounds by half (to compensate for the cost of operating on the full state in each round). Yet, investigating whether such prime SPN ciphers could potentially improve over the proposed FPM designs remains an interesting open problem.

2.4   Summary of the FPM_τ Design Space

The size of an FPM_τ cipher is determined by the number of tweaks τ, the prime integer p, the number of branches of the Type-II generalized Feistel network b and the number of input words of the F functions c. We use the notation $\mathsf{FPM}_\tau(\rho, b, c)$ for this purpose, where $\rho = \lceil \log_2(p) \rceil$. The cipher specifications additionally require to choose the functions $\mathsf{G}_{i,j} : \mathbb{F}_p \to \mathbb{F}_p$ and an MDS matrix, and to define the shuffling/mapping of the tweak scheduling algorithm and the round constants.[4] Next, we first provide high-level security arguments that justify the

---

[3] The branch number $\mathcal{B}$ of a matrix over $\mathbb{F}_p^t$ is defined as $\mathcal{B}(M) = \min_{x \in \mathbb{F}_p^t \setminus \{0\}} \{\mathrm{hw}(x) + \mathrm{hw}(M(x))\}$, where $\mathrm{hw}(\cdot)$ is denoted as the bundle weight in wide trail terminology. A matrix $M \in \mathbb{F}_p^{t \times t}$ is an MDS matrix if and only if $\mathcal{B}(M) = t + 1$.

[4] Variants where the F function uses nearly MDS matrices could be considered.

design choices of FPM ciphers in Sect. 3. We then propose a first hardware-oriented instance in Sect. 4 for which we analyze the mathematical security in Sect. 5 and the implementation efficiency & security in Sects. 6 and 7.

3 High-level Rationale and Security Arguments

We now provide a high-level rationale and security arguments for FPM_τ TBCs.

3.1 TWEAKEY Framework and LED-Like Design

FPM_τ ciphers follow the TWEAKEY framework proposed by Jean et al. [56] at Asiacrypt'14. In contrast to the majority of the TBCs following this framework (including SKINNY), we add the tweakey only every $N_r > 1$ rounds, where N_r is strictly bigger than 1. This approach is not new in the literature, as it has been already exploited in the block cipher LED [51]. Its main advantage is to allow a very simple security analysis concerning related-tweak attacks.

More precisely, since the tweaks are public, the attacker can always control them. Similar to a related-key attack [15], in a related-tweak attack the attacker encrypts (resp., decrypts) the same or different plaintext(s) (resp., ciphertexts) under several related tweaks. (Anticipating the detailed analysis of Sect. 5, we emphasize that related-tweak attacks are usually based on statistical properties and not on algebraic ones.) A possible way to avoid such attacks is to treat the tweaks exactly as the plaintexts. That is, not to make any distinction between plaintexts and tweaks. This is what is done in a sponge/duplex construction [12, 13], but it requires a larger state in order to arrange the inner part, which is not suitable in our case. Another approach to prevent related-tweak attacks is the one proposed in [51] to prevent related-key attacks. That is, adding the tweak every $N_r > 1$ rounds. The argument for $\tau = 1$ is relatively simple:

- A statistical attack as the differential one [18,19] exploits the probability distribution of a non-zero input difference leading to an output difference after a given number of rounds. The security is achieved if the probability of any differential characteristic is much smaller than the security level;
- Given $T \in \mathbb{F}_p^n$, assume for simplicity that all the T_i's $\in \mathbb{F}_p^n$ are equal to T;
- If a difference is inserted in the tweak, then every sub-tweak T_i will be active;
- Hence, it is impossible to force two consecutive steps S to be non-active (i.e., with zero input and zero output differences). That is, for every two consecutive steps S of N_r-rounds, at least one of them must be active.

Indeed, let's assume that the output difference of the i-th step S coincide with the difference in T_i. In this case, the next $i + 1$-th step S is not active, since its input difference is equal to zero. But the next tweak T_{i+1} will introduce again the difference, making the next $i+2$-th step S active. Using the number of active steps N_s (each one composed of N_r rounds), it is therefore possible to provide simple security arguments for preventing differential and other statistical attacks, which reduce to the security of the public permutation S (which is independent of the tweaks and the master key). We refer to the full version of this paper [47] for an initial analysis (based on published results) regarding the selection of the number of steps N_s independently of their internal structure.

The previous argument can be generalized for a non-trivial tweak scheduling $\mathsf{T} : \mathbb{F}_p^{\tau \cdot n} \equiv (\mathbb{F}_p^n)^\tau \to (\mathbb{F}_p^n)^*$, for example if the following properties are satisfied: 1) T is bijective, and 2) $T_{j,\cdot} \in \mathbb{F}_p^n$ is active if and only if $T^{(j)} \in \mathbb{F}_p^n$ is active. Equivalently, this second condition is satisfied if there exist τ invertible maps $\mathsf{T}_0, \mathsf{T}_1, \ldots, \mathsf{T}_{\tau-1}$ over $\mathbb{F}_p^n$ such that $T_{j,i} = \mathsf{T}_j^{i+1}(T^{(j)})$ for each $i \geqslant 0$, where $\mathsf{T}_j^{i+1} := \mathsf{T}_j \circ \mathsf{T}_j \circ \ldots \circ \mathsf{T}_j$ for i times. (We emphasize that this is not a necessary condition.) In our case, we achieve this property by defining $T_{j,\cdot}$ via a shuffle of the $\mathbb{F}_p$-words of $T^{(j)}$. (The mapping of each $\mathbb{F}_p$ does not affect this property.) A detailed argument will be given for small-pSquare with $\tau = 1, 2$ in Sect. 5.1.

We leave the question whether adding the tweakey every round could lead to improved (but harder to analyze) security as a scope for further research.

3.2   Rationale Behind the Generalized Type-II Feistel Scheme

The main motivation behind the choice of defining FPM_τ ciphers based on a generalized Feistel structure relates to the goal of having TBCs with cheap inverses that are useful in some leakage-resistant modes of operation [7,10]. This result can be achieved via 1) a Feistel or Lai-Massey scheme [45,62,84], 2) an SPN scheme with the "reflection" property like Prince [14,22,23], or 3) an SPN scheme in which every round – without the constant additions – is an involution (that is, $\mathsf{R} = \mathsf{R}^{-1}$) like Noekon [32], Khazad [82] or Iceberg [82]. Even if all options are valid from a security viewpoint, the first one comes with the least constraints on its internal components, which is desirable in our setting in order to enable these components to be selected primarily for their properties against leakage. After discarding Type-I Feistel schemes that require too many rounds for achieving full diffusion, we opted for Type-II generalized Feistel networks instead of Type-III ones. As witnessed by designs like Hight [53] or Clefia [79], they generally offer a good security vs. efficiency compromise.

3.3   Rationale and Construction of the Function F

As mentioned in Sect. 2.3, the F functions aim to ensure good non-linear diffusion while remaining bijective (in order to simplify the security analysis). For functions $\mathsf{G}_{i,j}$ over $\mathbb{F}_p$ that are themselves bijective, this could be directly obtained with two SPN rounds. Yet, and as mentioned in the introduction, one natural candidate $\mathsf{G}_{i,j}$ function is the square power map, which leads to efficient masked implementations [27]. As a result, we opted for F functions based on two rounds of a generalized Feistel network.[5] We selected the Type-III version which is more similar to SPNs in terms of their number of non-linear $\mathsf{G}_{i,j}$ functions and replaced the middle shift of the $\mathbb{F}_p$-words by an invertible linear layer in order to speed up the non-linear diffusion, an idea that resembles the one in [8].

---

[5] For instances relying on invertible $\mathsf{G}_{i,j}$ functions, we suggest using two SPN rounds.

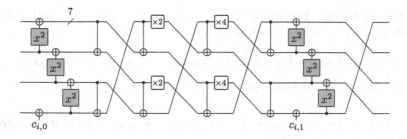

Fig. 3. F-function used in small-pSquare.

Regarding the choice of the linear layer, we opted for an MDS matrix which allows to achieve full non-linear diffusion over $\mathbb{F}_p^c$ in only two rounds. Examples include lightweight candidates [39,60,66] adapted to the prime case (where the multiplication per two can be cheap – see Footnote 2). Such MDS matrices could be replaced by any invertible matrix with a smaller branch number that allows to get full non-linear diffusion in two rounds, as the ones in [65].

Finally, the round constant additions aim to (i) differentiate the rounds (e.g., for preventing slide attacks [20,21]), (ii) break any fixed points, and (iii) break any invariant subspace [48,63,64]. Since $x \mapsto x^2$ has only two fixed points (namely, 0 and 1) and since $\mathbb{F}_p$ does not have any non-trivial subspace (as opposed to $\mathbb{F}_{2^t} \equiv \mathbb{F}_2^t$), we believe that one $\mathbb{F}_p$-constant addition before each non-linear Type-III generalized Feistel layer is sufficient. As an extra condition when using Mersenne primes, we require that the round constants do not belong to any subspace of $\mathbb{F}_2^\rho$ (where $p = 2^\rho - 1$). The choice to generate them via a bit rotation of a fixed mathematical constant like π is for efficient (hardware) implementation purposes. The mathematical constant must be chosen such that all the rotations are in $\{0, 1, \ldots, p-1\}$ where p is the prime that defines $\mathbb{F}_p$.

4 small-pSquare: a Hardware-oriented Instance

In this section, we provide the specifications of a first instance of an FPM_τ cipher. As mentioned in the introduction, its high-level rationale follows two main guidelines. First, we aim to exploit the recently proposed secure squaring gadgets from [27], which were shown to be more efficient than secure multiplications in $\mathbb{F}_p$. As a result, we use the square as power map for the $\mathsf{G}_{i,j}$ functions of Sect. 2.3. Second, we aim to enable efficient hardware implementations. As a result, we use a small Mersenne prime $p = 2^7 - 1$. We then propose to use the rounds depicted in the right part of Fig. 2, leading to a $\mathsf{FPM}_\tau(7, 4, 4)$ cipher that provides $\approx 7 \times 4 \times 4 = 112$ bits of security and we denote as small-pSquare.

We first detail the different components of the function F (depicted in Fig. 3), then finalize the specification of the tweak scheduling algorithm and conclude with the suggested number of rounds per steps and steps.

Non-Linear Layer. The non-linear layer of small-pSquare is instantiated with the following $\mathbb{F}_{2^7-1}^4 \to \mathbb{F}_{2^7-1}^4$ mapping:

$$(x_0, x_1, x_2, x_3) \mapsto \left(x_0 + x_1^2, x_1 + x_2^2, x_2 + (x_3 + c_{i,j})^2, x_3 + c_{i,j}\right) ,$$

where $c_{i,j}$ is a round constant specified thereafter.

Linear Layer. The linear layer of small-pSquare is instantiated with the invertible matrix $M \in \mathbb{F}_{2^7-1}^{4 \times 4}$ defined as:

$$M = \begin{bmatrix} 3 & 2 & 1 & 1 \\ 7 & 6 & 5 & 1 \\ 1 & 1 & 3 & 2 \\ 5 & 1 & 7 & 6 \end{bmatrix} .$$

This matrix has been introduced by Duval et al. [39] and is MDS over $\mathbb{F}_{2^7-1}$. It can be implemented as a Type-II Feistel-like construction as shown in Fig. 3, with only 8 additions and a depth of 4 (which is optimal for 8 additions). We recall that the doubling operation (i.e., $x \mapsto 2 \cdot x$) modulo a Mersenne prime is just a bit rotation, hence free in hardware and cheap in software.

Round Constants. The first 64 bits of the binary sequence of π are (in hexadecimal): $\pi_{\text{bin}64} = \text{0xC90FDAA22168C234}$. Let us denote the bit-wise rotation left via $\lll$. Then, the left F-function at round i uses the round constants:

- $c_{i,0} = (\pi_{\text{bin}64} \lll i) \bmod 2^7$,
- $c_{i,1} = (\pi_{\text{bin}64} \lll (i + 16)) \bmod 2^7$,

while the right F-function at round i uses the round constants:

- $c_{i,2} = (\pi_{\text{bin}64} \lll (i + 32)) \bmod 2^7$,
- $c_{i,3} = (\pi_{\text{bin}64} \lll (i + 48)) \bmod 2^7$.

As no sequence of 7 consecutive 1 s exists in $\pi_{\text{bin}64}$, all $c_{i,0}, c_{i,1}, c_{i,2}, c_{i,3}$'s $\in \mathbb{F}_{2^7-1}$.

Tweak Scheduling ($\tau \geqslant 1$ Only). Let Π_{16} be the shuffle of the 16 $\mathbb{F}_{2^7-1}$–words in the tweak schedule sub-tweak word permutation defined as:

$$\Pi_{16}(x_0\|x_1\|\dots\|x_{15}) = x_9\|x_5\|x_{13}\|x_{15}\|x_{12}\|x_7\|x_{14}\|x_2\|x_4\|x_6\|x_8\|x_3\|x_{10}\|x_1\|x_{11}\|x_0.$$

Π_{16} has a cycle period of 140 which is the largest we found for 16-element shuffles (and more than sufficient for our envisioned step numbers). On each $\mathbb{F}_{2^7-1}$-word, we then apply a bit-shuffle Ψ_l defined as

$$\forall l \in \{0, 1, \dots, 15\} : \qquad \Psi_l(x) = \psi_7(2^l \cdot x \bmod 2^7),$$

where the multiplication with 2^l corresponds to a shift of the bits of l positions (when working over $\mathbb{F}_2^7$), and where ψ_7 is defined as:

$$\psi_7\left(x = \sum_{i=0}^{6} x_i \cdot 2^i\right) = x_0 \cdot 2^5 + x_1 \cdot 2^3 + x_2 \cdot 2^0 + x_3 \cdot 2^4 + x_4 \cdot 2^1 + x_5 \cdot 2^6 + x_6 \cdot 2^2,$$

for each $x \in \mathbb{F}_{2^7-1}$ where $x_0, x_1, \ldots, x_6 \in \{0, 1\}$. The cycle period of ψ_7 is 12 (i.e., the maximum possible for a permutation over 7 bits). Moreover, the polynomial corresponding to ψ_7 over $\mathbb{F}_{2^7-1}$ is of degree 125 (i.e., the maximum possible) and contains 46 out of the 127 monomials possible. We refer to the full version of this paper [47] for details on ψ_7, where we also prove that the polynomial over $\mathbb{F}_{2^p-1}$ corresponding to any bit shuffling only contains monomials of odd degree.

Number of Rounds. For a security level of 112 bits and the aforementioned parameters ($p = 2^7 - 1; b = 4, c = 4$), we use $N_r = 4$ rounds per step and we use $N_s = 9$ steps for $\tau = 0$, $N_s = 16$ steps for $\tau = 1$ and $N_s = 21$ steps for $\tau = 2$. The security analysis that supports these choices is given in the next section.

5 Mathematical Security Analysis of small-pSquare

We now evaluate the security of small-pSquare against standard attack vectors, including classical and truncated differential attacks and algebraic attacks (based on interpolation, linearization, higher-order differentials and Gröbner bases). We describe the attacks having a larger impact on small-pSquare's number of rounds in the paper. Details of further attacks are presented in the full version [47].

Overview of the Attacks. As we are going to show, the main attack vector against small-pSquare is differential cryptanalysis [18,19], which we present in detail in Sect. 5.1 for the case $\tau = 0$ and the case $\tau \geq 1$ (for which we consider related-tweak differential attacks). In this last case, we exploit the strategy introduced by the LED designers and recalled in Sect. 3.1 for guaranteeing security against related tweaks. Truncated [59] and impossible differential [17] cryptanalysis as well as other statistical attacks including linear cryptanalysis [68] and boomerang attacks [87] are detailed in the full version [47]. Contrary to MPC-/FHE-/ZK-friendly schemes defined over prime fields, and similar to classical/traditional symmetric primitives, algebraic attacks are not the main threat against small-pSquare in our analysis, essentially due to the small size of the prime $p = 2^7 - 1$ and the high number of variables $n = 16$. For this reason, we discuss the degree and density of the polynomial representation of small-pSquare in Sect. 5.2, limit ourselves to linearization attacks [31] in Sect. 5.3, while we defer the description of interpolation [55], higher-order differential [59,61] and Gröbner bases based attacks to the full version of the paper [47].

We mention that in all these cases, we tried to identify concrete strategies on how to speed up the attacks by making use of related tweaks. In particular, we propose concrete ways to use related tweaks for speeding up algebraic attacks which, to the best of our knowledge, has not been thoroughly studied yet in the open literature.[6] Besides, the non-linear tweak scheduling algorithm of small-pSquare is also aimed to frustrate such improved cryptanalysis attempts.

5.1 Differential Cryptanalysis

Given pairs of inputs with some fixed input differences, differential cryptanalysis [18,19] considers the probability distribution of the corresponding output differences produced by the cryptographic primitive. Let $\Delta_I, \Delta_O \in \mathbb{F}_p^n$ be respectively the input and the output differences through a permutation P over $\mathbb{F}_p^n$. The Differential Probability (DP) of having a certain output difference Δ_O given a particular input difference Δ_I is equal to:

$$\text{Prob}_P(\Delta_I \to \Delta_O) = \frac{|\{x \in \mathbb{F}_p^n \mid P(x + \Delta_I) - P(x) = \Delta_O\}|}{p^n}.$$

In the case of iterated schemes, a cryptanalyst searches for ordered sequences of differences over any number of rounds that are called differential characteristics/trails. Assuming the independence of the rounds, the DP of a differential trail is the product of the DPs of its one-round differences.

Differential property of F. As first step, we compute the maximum differential probability of F. Since $x \mapsto x^2$ is a quadratic map, $\text{DP}_{\max}(x \mapsto x^2) = p^{-1} \approx 2^{-7}$. For our goal, we just need to compute the minimum number of active square maps in F. We can check that it corresponds to 2. Indeed, let $(x_0, x_1, x_2, x_3) \mapsto (x_0, x_0^2 + x_1, x_1^2 + x_2, x_2^2 + x_3)$ be the Feistel layer, and keep in mind that the branch of the MDS matrix M is 5. Then:

- If no square map is active in the first Feistel layer of F (hence, x_3 is the only active component), then only one output is active at its output. After the multiplication with the MDS matrix, all inputs of the second Feistel layer are active, which implies the result. A similar result holds if only one square map is active in the first Feistel layer, which corresponds to the case in which only one among $\{x_0, x_1, x_2\}$ is active. In such a case, two outputs of the first Feistel layer are active, which implies that at least 3 inputs of the second Feistel layer are active and at least 3 square maps are active for each F;
- If two inputs are active, the best scenario for the attacker occurs when the active inputs are either $\{x_0, x_3\}$ or $\{x_1, x_3\}$. In this case, exactly one square map is active in the first Feistel layer (due to the fact that x_3 does not activate any square map), and three outputs of the Feistel layer are active (due to the fact that x_0, x_1 and x_3 are not consecutive). Since the matrix is MDS, then at least two inputs are active for the second Feistel layer, which implies that at least one square map is active in the second Feistel layer. As a result, at least 2 square maps are active for each F;

---

[6] Binary schemes like AES or SHA-3/Keccak have been shown vulnerable to statistical attacks mainly, while algebraic attacks gain more popularity recently due to the raising of symmetric schemes designed for applications as MPC, FHE, and ZK. Still, symmetric schemes designed for such applications are not tweakable designs.

– If 3 or 4 inputs are active, at least two square maps are active for each F.

Overall, it directly follows that $\mathrm{DP_{max}}(x \mapsto \mathsf{F}(x)) = p^{-2} \approx 2^{-14}$.

Differential property of S. As shown in [28,83], at least four consecutive rounds of Type-II generalized Feistel network are necessary to reach full diffusion (i.e., $N_r \geq 4$). Over 4 consecutive rounds, at least 3 functions F are active (as visually illustrated in the full version [47]). As a result, by setting $N_r = 4$, it directly follows that $\mathrm{DP_{max}}(x \mapsto \mathsf{S}(x)) \leq \mathrm{DP_{max}}(x \mapsto \mathsf{S}(x))^3 \leq p^{-6} \approx 2^{-42}$.

Number of Steps for Security. Finally, we compute the minimum number of steps N_s for guaranteeing security. Due to clustering effect (that is, due to the fact that several differential characteristics can be used together for setting up the attack) and due to the possibility to exploit a Meet-in-the-Middle approach for setting up the attack, we claim that the scheme is secure if every differential characteristic has probability smaller than $2^{-2.5 \cdot \kappa} \approx 2^{-280}$ for an arbitrary factor ? 5,[7] where $\kappa = 112 = 7 \cdot 16$ is our target security level. Moreover, we conjecture that the attacker cannot skip more than 2 steps S by a simple partial key-guessing, since one step S is sufficient for achieving full diffusion.

Case: $\tau = 0$. By simple computation, we have $N_s \geq \lceil 280/42 \rceil + 2 = 7 + 2 = 9$ where 2 steps S are added for preventing partial key-guessing strategies.

Case: $\tau = 1$. Following the argument proposed by LED's designers in [51, Sect. 3] and recalled in Sect. 3.1, the attacker can choose related tweaks such that only one out of two consecutive steps S is active. As a result, it is sufficient to double the number of steps S obtained for $\tau = 0$ to guarantee security. That is, $N_s \geq 2 \cdot 7 + 2 = 16$, where we again add 2 steps S for preventing partial key-guessing.

Case: $\tau = 2$. In this case, the attacker has more freedom in the choice of the related tweaks. Still, we can adapt the previous security argument as follows. Let us consider separately the next two cases: (i) both $T^{(0)}$ and $T^{(1)}$ are active (hence, $T_{0,i}$ and $T_{1,i}$ are both active for each $i \geq 0$ due to the definition of the tweak schedule), and (ii) only one among $T^{(0)}$ and $T^{(1)}$ is active (hence, only one among $T_{0,i}$ and $T_{1,i}$ is active for each $i \geq 0$ due to the definition of the tweak schedule). In the first case, the analysis proposed for $\tau = 1$ applies, which implies that at least one among two consecutive steps S is active. In the second case, w.l.o.g., we assume that $T^{(0)}$ is active and $T^{(1)}$ is inactive. We introduce a "super-step" $\mathsf{S}^2 := \mathsf{S} \circ \mathsf{S}$ as the application of two consecutive steps S. By working as before, we can deduce at least one among two consecutive super-steps S^2 is active. Moreover, if a super-step is active, then the two steps S that compose it are active. Indeed, the fact that S^2 is active implies that $T_{0,i}$ introduces the difference in the first S. Its output difference cannot be canceled by $T_{1,i}$, which is inactive due to the tweak schedule and due to the assumption. Hence, both steps of S^2 are active. The same result applies if $T^{(1)}$ is active and $T^{(0)}$ is active.

This reasoning implies that $N_s \geq 14$ is a necessary condition for security. Yet, we have to keep in mind that the attacker can potentially skip one super-step S^2

---

[7] We take inspiration on the AES-128, which has $10 = 2.5 \cdot 4$ rounds, where 4 is the minimum number of rounds for preventing classical differential attacks.

at each side of the cipher by working with input (respectively, output) differences in the plaintexts (resp., ciphertexts) that cancel out with the ones in the tweaks, leading S^2 to be inactive. As a result, we require that $N_s \geqslant 2 \cdot 7 + 4 + 2 = 20$, where we again add 2 steps S for preventing partial key-guessing.

5.2   Degree and Density of the Polynomial Representation

In general, algebraic attacks try to take advantage of the "simple" algebraic description of a scheme for breaking it, where the simplicity can relate (among other properties) to the low degree of the encryption/decryption function, the sparsity of the polynomial representation of such functions, or a particular structure of the algebraic system generated by the cipher. The main ingredient for preventing these attacks is the minimal number of rounds such that the polynomial representations of the cipher have a sufficient degree and too many monomials for the attacks to apply with a complexity lower than 2^κ. In this section, we therefore study these two characteristics, pointing out that the encryption function of small-pSquare with a fixed key and tweak could be analyzed as a mapping over $\mathbb{F}_{p^{16}}$ for $p = 2^7 - 1$. Nevertheless, since all the operations of F are at the basis field level (squaring in $\mathbb{F}_p$), the field we consider for the cryptanalyses is $\mathbb{F}_p$, and the polynomials built by an adversary belong to $\mathbb{F}_p[x_0, \ldots, x_{15}]/(x_0^p - 1, \ldots, x_{15}^p - 1)$. Note that similar results hold in the context of related tweaks, for which the adversary can consider the same polynomials but with more variables.

Growth of the Degree. We first focus on the minimal degree that a polynomial in this representation can have, and the number of different monomials that appear in an algebraic system obtainable, after r rounds. Note that the degree in one variable is at most $p - 1$, the total degree is then at most $16(p - 1)$, and the total number of monomials is p^{16}. The degree of F is $\deg(F) = 4$. More precisely, it is 4 in three components and 2 in the last one. The degree of its inverse is $\deg(F^{-1}) = 8^2 = 2^6$. Indeed, note that the inverse of the internal function given by $(y_0, y_1, y_2, y_3) = (x_0 + x_1^2, x_1 + x_2^2, x_2 + x_3^2, x_3)$ is given by $(x_0, x_1, x_2, x_3) = (y_0 - (y_1 - (y_2 - y_3^2)^2)^2, y_1 - (y_2 - y_3^2)^2, y_2 - y_3^2, y_3)$.

In both cases (F and F^{-1}), we emphasize that one component of the internal function of F and F^{-1} has degree one only. Moreover, in the second case, we emphasize that the degree is different for each output variable, and that only one of them has actually maximum degree 8, and therefore 64 for F^{-1}. It follows that the degree of a step of r consecutive rounds S is $\deg(S) = \deg(F)^r = 2^{2 \cdot r}$, where we point out that half of the components have degree 1 at the end of the first round due to the Feistel structure. Accordingly, at round r two blocks have degree $\deg(F^{r-1}) = 2^{2 \cdot r - 2}$. Therefore the minimal degree a polynomial can have after r rounds is $2^{2 \cdot r - 3}$ until it reaches the maximum degree. Since the degree of the inverse of a Type-II Feistel scheme is equal to the degree of the Type-II Feistel scheme itself, the same bound applies for r consecutive steps S^{-1}.

Density of the Polynomial Representation. While the degree's growth is an important indicator in order to prevent algebraic attacks, another factor that plays a crucial role is the density of the polynomial representation. Indeed, various algebraic attacks depend on the number of monomials that appear in the polynomials, which implies that a scheme that admits a sparse polynomial is in general not secure against algebraic attacks even if it is of high degree.

Experimentally, we can verify the number of monomials we obtain in each of the 16 polynomials of a round, but even with simpler versions with a prime smaller than 127 it becomes too complex in practice after a few rounds. For example, even for $p = 3$, we observed by practical tests that we already get more than 2^{16} different monomials in some of the polynomials at the end of the third round. Since these experiments are quickly getting impractical, we decided instead to determine the number of rounds for which we expect each polynomial to be dense by considering the following approach. First, we determine r_m defined as the minimal number of rounds such that at least one complete monomial is present in each one of the 16 polynomials. We denote as complete monomial one monomial $x^e = \prod_{i=0}^{15} x_i^{e_i}$ such that for each $i \in [0, 15]$ it holds that $0 < e_i \leqslant p-1$ (i.e., x^e depends on all the variables). Then, we add the number of rounds such that all possible degrees in one variable can be taken, in other words we add the number of rounds sufficient to wrap over p (note that the degree in x_i inside a monomial is always between 0 and $p - 1$ since $x_i^p = x_i$ over $\mathbb{F}_p$).

We next determine a bound on r_m. First, due to the Type-II Feistel structure, after 3 rounds not every input has an impact on the 16 outputs, which implies $r_m > 3$. Then, we get an upper bound on r_m based on our experiments (the real value could be smaller, taking the upper bound is conservative). With $p = 3$ we obtain monomials depending on 10 variables in the polynomials in position 1, 2 and 3 and in positions 9, 10 and 11 by symmetry of the Type-II Feistel structure. These monomials contain all the variables from x_0 to x_7 and x_8 to x_{15} respectively. Calling X and Y monomials of this shape, we get that at round 5 there are terms of shape X+Y in the polynomials in positions 0, 1, 2, 3, 8, 9, 10 and 11, therefore giving complete monomials after passing through F due to the square operations. Since only half of the input goes through F at each round, one more round is needed to obtain these complete monomials in each position, therefore $r_m \leqslant 7$. When moving to $p = 2^7 - 1$ we can only observe more monomials (since all the ones with a coefficient multiple of 127 rather than 3 are canceled). Combined with the fact that the degree is at least 2^{2r-3} as shown before, we conclude that 5 extra rounds are sufficient to wrap around p and reach any degree in one variable. This gives us a bound of 12 rounds (equivalently, three steps S) to expect dense polynomials in the 16 positions.

5.3   Linearization Attack

Given a system of polynomial equations, one possible way to solve it is via the linearization technique which works by turning it into a system of linear equations and adding new variables that replace all the monomials in the system of degree larger than 1. The resulting linear system of equations can be solved using linear algebra if there are sufficiently many equations. Consider a system in x unknowns of degree limited by D, where the number of monomials $N(D,x)$ is given by $N(D,x) = \binom{D+x}{D}$ when $D < p$. The attack has a computational cost of $\mathcal{O}(N(D,x)^\omega)$ operations (for $2 < \omega \leqslant 3$), and a memory cost of $\mathcal{O}(N(D,x)^2)$ to store the linear equations. Depending on parameters' choices, the hybrid approach which combines exhaustive search with this resolution may lead to a reduced cost. Guessing $l < x$ variables leads to a complexity of:

$$\mathcal{O}\left(p^l \cdot N(D, x - l)^\omega\right) .$$

Case: $\tau = 0$ *(no tweak).* Since the key is composed of 16 $\mathbb{F}_{2^7-1}$-words, for any $l \in [0, 15]$ we computed that $p^l \cdot N(D, x - l)^\omega > 2^{112}$ occurs already for $D = 69$ (taking the conservative value of $\omega = 2$). Since the minimal degree follows 2^{2r-3} as shown previously (where $2^{2r-3} > 2^7 - 1$ for $r \geqslant 5$), and based on the density analysis just given, we can conclude that 3 steps S (equivalently, 12 rounds) are sufficient to prevent algebraic attacks based on linearization.

Case: $\tau \geqslant 1$ *(related tweaks).* The freedom of choosing the tweak(s) can be exploited to cancel some monomials whose coefficients depend on the tweak(s) or part of them. Similarly, the difference of two polynomials under related tweaks can be exploited to cancel monomials whose coefficients are independent of the tweaks. Moreover, the linear combinations of more polynomials under properly chosen related tweaks can be exploited to cancel monomials whose coefficients depend on the tweaks or part of them. In this last case, the attacker has to (i) set up a system of equations in which the linear combinations of the coefficients of some monomials is set to zero, and (ii) solve it (e.g., via linearization or using Gröbner bases) to find the related tweaks that satisfy such conditions.

Obviously, this procedure is not free, since one has to solve equations in the tweak variables that are dense and of high (e.g., maximum) degree. Moreover, the non-linear tweak scheduling must be taken into account as well. Based on the analysis just given (and on the results presented in the full version for attacks based on Gröbner bases [47]), it would be infeasible for the attacker to solve a system of equations (in the tweaks instead of the plaintexts) that cover more than 12 rounds (or equivalently 3 steps) of the cipher once the tweak is fully absorbed (where we remind that 12 is the minimum number of rounds for achieving full diffusion in the interpolation polynomial). For this reason, we conjecture that $12 + 4 \cdot (\tau - 1) = 8 + 4 \cdot \tau$ extra rounds (or $2 + \tau$, extra steps, which means 3 or 4 for $\tau \in \{1, 2\}$) are sufficient for preventing related-tweak algebraic attacks. We note that this conjecture does not have to be tight for the security of small-pSquare to hold, since we need a larger number of extra steps to prevent related-tweak statistical attacks (respectively, 9 and 12 for $\tau \in \{1, 2\}$).

Note on Gröbner Bases Attacks. We recall that Gröbner bases based attacks reduce to linearization attacks when (i) the attacker aims to solve equations linking the plaintexts (and the tweaks) to the ciphertexts only, with the key as only variable, and (ii) the attacker can collect enough data for linearizing the system (i.e., the best scenario for the attacker). Hence, when analyzing the security of our scheme against such attacks in the full version [47], we only consider the case in which the system of equations is set up at round level.

6   Hardware Performance Evaluation of small-pSquare

In this section we evaluate the hardware cost and performance of the small-pSquare instance in comparison to respective implementations of the SKINNY lightweight tweakable block cipher [6]. Due to its simple and efficient design, SKINNY has gained remarkable popularity in recent years, both in academia and industry, and was selected as part of the ISO/IEC 18033-7:2022 standard for tweakable block ciphers. It has been designed with efficient application of side channel countermeasures in mind, in particular masking, and is therefore ideally suited for our comparison [6]. Naturally, the general design strategy as well as the individual operations employed by the two ciphers (small-pSquare vs. SKINNY) are vastly different. At first sight, comparing two primitives with more differences than similarities may appear suboptimal to gain meaningful insights. However, in order to achieve a high level of cost-efficiency, lightweight TBCs necessarily need to be tailored to the amenities of their particular mathematical foundation. Hence, the stark differences between these primitives are a direct manifestation of their specialization to the finite fields they operate in. Only such a comparison can answer the question which mathematical setting (e.g., binary field vs. prime field masking) is preferable for constructing dedicated instances to maximize the efficiency vs. security tradeoff of protected TBC implementations.

Table 1. Cost and performance of round-based unprotected SKINNY-128 and small-pSquare hardware implementations evaluated in TSMC 65 nm technology at typical operating conditions for 100 MHz and 250 MHz clock.

Cipher	Block Size	Key Size	Tweak Size	Freq. [MHz]	Crit. Path [ns]	Area [GE]	Power [mW]	Latency [cyc/enc]
SKINNY	128	128	0	100|250	1.877155	2450.75	0.3915	40
			128	100|250	1.812617	3396.00	0.5613	48
			256	100|250	1.905185	4353.00	0.7304	56
small-pSquare	112	112	0	100	9.777720	9684.75	1.3547	36
			112	100	9.970046	10798.75	1.5424	64
			224	100	9.937350	11989.50	1.6745	84
			0	250	3.945602	12407.75	1.7942	36
			112	250	3.971674	14716.50	2.1160	64
			224	250	3.972123	16034.00	2.2392	84

small-pSquare has been designed to offer competitive performances to common binary lightweight block ciphers when masking is applied. Nevertheless, we begin by comparing its critical path delay, area, power consumption (at 100 MHz operation) and encryption latency to SKINNY-128 when both are implemented as unmasked round-based hardware circuits in Table 1. All values are post-synthesis results obtained using Synopsys Design Compiler Version O-2018.06-SP4 as a synthesis tool together with the TSMC 65 nm standard cell library at typical operating conditions for two different clock frequencies, 100 MHz and 250 MHz. The results show that regardless of the tweak size, unmasked SKINNY-128 is significantly more efficient in terms of critical path delay, area footprint and power consumption when compared to unmasked small-pSquare. The encryption latency, which directly corresponds to the number of rounds, is slightly smaller for small-pSquare without tweak compared to SKINNY-128 without tweak. However, for the tweakable variants it is larger in case of small-pSquare. We conclude that when unprotected, and hence for implementation settings where physical attacks are not a concern, small-pSquare is not fully competitive with binary lightweight ciphers in hardware. Yet, as mentioned before, this was not the primary goal of our design effort. Significantly better efficiency in unprotected hardware would have commanded different design choices that, in part, directly oppose to efficiency in masked representation.

We now focus on the more relevant comparison of secure higher-order masked hardware circuits. We have chosen to compare the small-pSquare version with $\tau = 1$ with SKINNY-128-256 for 2 up to 4 shares (i.e., first- to third-order secure designs). SKINNY-128-256 is the denotation of the SKINNY variant which receives a 128-bit plaintext, 128-bit key and 128-bit tweak (i.e., a 256-bit tweakey) as inputs and computes 48 cipher rounds for one encryption or decryption. We recall that small-pSquare with $\tau = 1$ receives a 112-bit plaintext, 112-bit key and 112-bit tweak as inputs and computes 64 cipher rounds for one encryption or decryption. To put the difference of round numbers in perspective, remember that small-pSquare is a Type-II generalized Feistel design, i.e., each round updates only half of the state. We will see in the next results that with all other factors being equal, masked small-pSquare implementations generally require fewer clock cycles per encryption (sometimes significantly) than masked SKINNY-128-256 implementations, despite the larger number of rounds of the former design.

We have scanned the literature for publicly available securely masked SKINNY- 128-256 implementations, with moderate success. The only higher-order masked hardware implementations of tweakable SKINNY-128 we could find have been published in conjunction with [78,85] as part of a study of the leakage resistance of Romulus and other Authenticated Encryption with Associated Data (AEAD) schemes that made it into the finals of NIST's Lightweight Crypto Competition. The concrete implementation is hence of the SKINNY-128-384+ variant which is used in Romulus and publicly available on GitHub.[8] Please note that the authors have not verified its security properties experimentally. However, it is based on the trivially composable HPC2 masking scheme [26] which eases the extension of gadget security to full-implementation security. We have modified this implementation slightly to make it compute SKINNY-128-256 instead of SKINNY-128-384+, which commanded small changes to the round

---

[8] https://github.com/uclcrypto/aead_modes_leveled_hw.

Table 2. Cost and performance comparison of masked SKINNY-128-256 and small-pSquare ($\tau = 1$) hardware implementations evaluated in TSMC 65 nm technology at typical operating conditions for 100 MHz and 250 MHz clock.

Cipher	Ref.	Par.	Frequ [MHz]	d	Pip.	Crit. Path [ns]	Area [GE]	Power [mW]	Latency [cyc/enc]	Random [bit/cyc]
SKINNY-128-256	[58]	128	100|250	2		1.519177	19026.75	2.8547	432/1	128
				3		1.763878	38828.75	6.2545	432/1	384
				4		1.839592	65502.00	8.9225	432/1	768
				2	✓	1.566238	58475.50	13.6144	432/9	128
				3	✓	1.801272	94611.50	21.6698	432/9	384
				4	✓	1.882408	137625.50	30.8983	432/9	768
		32	100|250	2		1.743940	9274.50	1.0755	2160/1	32
				3		1.903482	15999.00	2.0608	2160/1	96
				4		1.823993	24442.00	8.2697	2160/1	192
				2	✓	1.885406	39016.25	9.1220	2160/9	32
				3	✓	1.943746	57757.00	13.4186	2160/9	96
				4	✓	1.909085	78243.00	17.9452	2160/9	192
	[85]	128	100|250	2		3.715469	18035.75	2.5276	288/1	32
				3		3.232731	28740.75	4.1347	288/1	96
				4		3.849724	41136.75	5.9918	288/1	192
small-pSquare	[this]	112	100	2		9.845555	21714.50	2.9370	128/1	84
				3		9.854049	41982.50	5.6533	128/1	210
				4		9.852280	62587.75	8.4822	128/1	504
				2	✓	9.852014	30730.25	4.4491	128/2	168
				3	✓	9.854022	65273.00	9.2764	128/2	420
				4	✓	9.853921	101168.00	14.3426	128/2	1008
			250	2		3.857306	29438.50	3.7809	128/1	84
				3		3.861372	52073.50	6.9574	128/1	210
				4		3.907730	78441.00	10.5274	128/1	504
				2	✓	3.852503	40414.75	5.5467	128/2	168
				3	✓	3.857475	77556.50	11.0357	128/2	420
				4	✓	3.859051	121589.25	17.4111	128/2	1008
		56	100	2		9.847473	15332.25	1.9296	256/1	42
				3		9.851035	27215.75	3.4077	256/1	105
				4		9.852068	39237.50	4.9897	256/1	252
				2	✓	9.848985	20735.75	2.8794	256/2	84
				3	✓	9.941982	39958.75	5.5274	256/2	210
				4	✓	9.851659	59404.75	8.2398	256/2	504
			250	2		3.855009	20471.00	2.4330	256/1	42
				3		3.858206	34485.25	4.2527	256/1	105
				4		3.859086	48511.25	6.1763	256/1	252
				2	✓	3.858980	26823.25	3.5092	256/2	84
				3	✓	3.858999	48147.50	6.5390	256/2	210
				4	✓	3.857775	72245.00	9.9639	256/2	504

Cipher = Evaluation target, either SKINNY-128-256 or small-pSquare ($\tau = 1$).
Ref. = Reference, i.e., related publication, AGEMA is cited for automatically generated circuits.
Par. = Parallelism, i.e., size of the state that is operated on in parallel measured in bits.
Freq. = Synthesis frequency measured in Megahertz (MHz).
d = Number of shares, resulting in security order $d - 1$.
Pip. = Design is pipelined (✓) or not ( ).
Crit. Path = Critical path of the synthesized circuit measured in nanoseconds (ns).
Area = Area consumption of the synthesized circuit measured in gate equivalents (GE).
Power = Power consumption of the synthesized circuit measured in milliwatts (mW).
Latency = Latency of the synthesized circuit measured in clock cycles per encryption(s).
Random = Fresh randomness consumption measured in bits per clock cycle.

numbers and tweak schedule. Since this concrete implementation uses a specific implementation of the SKINNY 8-bit S-box that is tailored towards a certain set of optimization goals, we also wanted to include other, more general, masked SKINNY-128 implementations in our comparison. To this end we have employed the Automated Generation of Masked Hardware (AGEMA) tool published at TCHES 2022 [58] which is able to turn unprotected hardware implementations of cryptographic primitives automatically into securely masked equivalents. We have utilized the tool to autonomously generate masked implementations of SKINNY-128-256 from the source code for unprotected hardware circuits provided by the SKINNY authors on its website as source material.[9] In particular, we translated both, round-based and 32-bit serialized implementations into their masked equivalents based on the HPC2 masking scheme using the Naive processing method (see [58]), as it led to the most suitable results for a comparison. We further generated both pipelined and non-pipelined masked circuits. Given this collection of securely masked SKINNY-128-256 circuits we are now equipped for an in-depth cost and performance comparison to our prime-field TBC.

Analogously to the selected implementations of SKINNY, we created round-based and half-round-based masked hardware circuits of small-pSquare. While these implementations operate on the full state (112 bits) and half the state (56 bits) in parallel, respectively, non-linear operations are only applied to 56 and 28 bits in parallel respectively due to the Feistel structure. Hence, the half-round-based implementations compute only one F-function on a 28-bit input at a time, resulting in a similar serialization level (28 vs. 32) compared to the SKINNY equivalent. The circuits are based on the secure and composable prime-field squaring gadgets introduced in [27]. In fact, we even optimized the 4-share gadget in a way that it only needs a single register stage, using similar optimization strategies as for the 2-share and 3-share case presented by the authors of [27]. The pseudocode for the gadget is included in the full version of this paper [47]. The resulting comparison is presented in Table 2. All results are based on post-synthesis estimations obtained using Synopsys Design Compiler and TSMC 65 nm technology at typical operating conditions for two different frequencies, 100 MHz and 250 MHz. The resulting figures for the SKINNY-128-256 circuits are identical for both frequencies due to the short critical path length. The full version of this paper additionally considers the more extreme cases of 500 MHz and 1000 MHz operation [47].[10] Based on this collection of cost and performance results, we conclude that small-pSquare is indeed able to compete with SKINNY-128-256 when masked in hardware, especially at lower frequencies. The automatically generated hardware circuits of SKINNY need a rather large amount of cycles per

---

[9] https://sites.google.com/site/skinnycipher/implementation.

[10] More "extreme", because cryptographic co-processors manufactured in 65 nm technology are rarely clocked at such high frequencies. This is evident for example in research ASICs manufactured in such technology nodes, as reported in http://asic.ethz.ch/technologies/65.html. Furthermore, the vast majority of common criteria certified co-processors protected against side-channel attacks do not exceed 200-300 MHz operation (https://www.commoncriteriaportal.org/products).

round (regardless of the frequency) and are costly when pipelined. At the target frequencies considered in the table ($\leqslant 250\,\mathrm{MHz}$) SKINNY-128-256 is only consistently cheaper in terms of area when non-pipelined serialized implementations are compared. Yet, this advantage in area footprint comes at a steep price, as the encryption latency is larger by a considerable factor. Overall, considering the area/power consumption and the latency together, small-pSquare often appears preferable. This changes when very high operating frequencies are needed. Then SKINNY becomes preferable, as shown in the full version [47]. In summary, our results show that small-pSquare is indeed capable of providing competitive cost and performance results in the envisioned application settings, and even outperforms its competitor consistently when the frequency is sufficiently low.

Decryption. Our comparison focuses on encryption-only circuits. However, adding capability for decryption is trivial for small-pSquare due to the Feistel structure. The additional cost for multiplexing between addition and subtraction of F function results for the encryption and decryption process falls in the range of a few percent (depending on masking order and parallelization). Adding decryption capability to the SKINNY circuits typically requires twice the area.

Comparison to AES-prime. We note that small-pSquare is also significantly more efficient in hardware compared to AES-prime which has been introduced at Eurocrypt 2023 as the first example of a dedicated cipher for prime-field masking [67]. It shares the same block and key size as small-pSquare, but is not tweakable. Compared to AES-prime our unmasked small-pSquare with $\tau = 0$ is at least 3 times smaller. More importantly, masked small-pSquare with $\tau = 1$ is on average (over the number of shares) 5 times smaller compared to masked AES-prime despite the additional tweak input [67]. This implies that masked small-pSquare with $\tau = 0$ requires a more than 5 times smaller area footprint while also executing in fewer clock cycles under the same frequency, constituting a very notable improvement over the state of the art. In addition, we recall that all variants of small-pSquare enable efficient decryption, while AES-prime does not.

Area and Power Consumption. It is clear that the comparison of the area and power consumption in Table 2 is affected by the different block, key and tweak sizes of the analyzed primitives. Since all those size parameters are smaller for the chosen prime-field design, this fact may tilt the comparison of the implementation size to small-pSquare's advantage. However, we argue that even if normalizing all area and power figures related to small-pSquare artificially by, for example, multiplying them with the corresponding size difference factor, namely $\frac{128}{112} = \frac{8}{7}$, our conclusions would not change drastically. In order to avoid any confusion we have *not* applied any artificial normalization of our results. We would also like to mention that for cases where 112 bits of security are insufficient, increasing the security level of small-pSquare at low additional cost is possible using the trick employed by the PRINCE block cipher with whitening keys [22].

Latency vs. Frequency. small-pSquare naturally allows to trade latency in cycles for frequency in Megahertz and vice versa. The considered masked SKINNY-128-

256 implementations offer less flexibility. They always have a very short critical path but require a larger number of cycles due to the type of masked gadgets that are used. In fact, bit-wise masking, where each binary two-input non-linear gate (e.g., AND, OR, NAND, NOR) is individually replaced by a masked gadget equivalent, enables high frequency operation but requires many register stages to uphold masking security. This is because any secure masked hardware gadget computing a non-linear operation requires at least one register stage (attempts to improve this are usually based on additional specialized hardware assumptions [70,75]). Introducing a register stage for each atomic bit-level gate entails a high overhead in latency of the implementation, but also in area. While this makes masked SKINNY-128-256 well-suited for high frequency operation, it limits its performance in lower frequency and low-latency applications.

Mild Additional Constraints. We note that small-pSquare comes with a few additional constraints due to the fact that it operates in a prime field while data is usually encoded in a binary manner. It is however pretty simple to convert a vector of prime field elements into a sequence of bits, by just viewing it as a representation of an integer in basis p. For small-pSquare, the maximum value is worth $127^{16} - 1$ which can represent 111-bit values (yielding a one-bit loss in the conversion). Similarly, masking small-pSquare requires to generate uniformly random prime numbers. Rejection sampling is a viable method (with probability $1/127$ to reject a value). Using a PRNG that natively operates in $\mathbb{F}_p$ is an alternative. Eventually, small-pSquare would be best integrated in a leakage-resistant mode of operation, which should not raise specific problems since TBC-based constructions like [9] or [78] are field-agnostic. Overall, none of these minor caveats is expected to bring significant overheads.

7 Side-Channel Security Assessment of small-pSquare

Finally, we evaluate the security of our masked implementations. In particular, we experimentally assess and compare the side-channel resistance of masked small-pSquare ($\tau = 1$) and SKINNY-128-256 implementations by measuring their power consumption on an FPGA device and trying to infer the secret key from their side-channel leakage. We focus on pipelined implementations of small-pSquare and SKINNY-128-256 for 2, 3 and 4 shares. The serialized circuits constitute a scenario with lower noise, while the parallel ones help to show the differences at slightly higher noise levels, although their side-channel Signal-to-Noise Ratios (SNRs) are not drastically different. The full version of this paper additionally contains the evaluation results for the small-pSquare versions with extra register stages to enable larger maximum frequencies [47].

Setup. For our experiments we use a SAKURA-G FPGA board which houses two Spartan-6 FPGAs serving as controller and device under test, respectively. All designs are operated at 6 MHz clock frequency (for low noise) and their power consumption is measured using a PicoScope 5244D digital sampling oscilloscope at 250 MS/s sampling rate with 12-bit vertical resolution through a Tektronix CT-1 current probe (bandwidth of up to 1 GHz) placed in the power supply path of the target FPGA. Xilinx ISE Version 14.7 is used to synthesize the circuits, with default parameters except the -keep_hierarchy attribute set to yes.

Table 3. Comparative side-channel evaluation of pipelined masked SKINNY-128-256 and small-pSquare hardware implementations.

Cipher	Par.	CPR	d	mean SNR	median SNR	TVLA det. compl.	SASCA compl.
SKINNY-128-256	128	9	2	0.0023	0.0021	71 000	25 000
			3	0.0015	0.0019	811 000	362 000
			4	0.0013	0.0010	57 000 000	29 832 000
	32	45	2	0.0064	0.0048	52 000	6 000
			3	0.0026	0.0028	680 000	157 000
			4	0.0020	0.0016	48 000 000	17 169 000
small-pSquare	112	2	2	0.0021	0.0019	321 000	213 000
			3	0.0032	0.0013	8 040 000	4 002 000
			4	0.0016	0.0011	> 100 000 000	> 100 000 000
	56	4	2	0.0073	0.0031	238 000	45 000
			3	0.0030	0.0025	7 040 000	1 754 000
			4	0.0018	0.0020	> 100 000 000	> 100 000 000

Cipher = Evaluation target, either SKINNY-128-256 or small-pSquare ($\tau = 1$).
Par. = Parallelism, i.e., size of the state that is operated on in parallel measured in bits.
CPR = Cycles per round, i.e., latency of one round function computation measured in cycles.
d = Number of shares, resulting in security order $d - 1$.
mean SNR = Mean maximum SNR of all S-box/Squaring input shares in the first round.
median SNR = Median maximum SNR of all S-box/Squaring input shares in the first round.
TVLA det. compl. = Minimum number of traces to surpass the TVLA detection threshold.
SASCA compl. = Minimum number of traces to achieve key rank 1 in a SASCA key recovery.

Table 3 summarizes the evaluation results collected for the 12 different masked implementations, 6 × SKINNY-128-256 and 6 × small-pSquare. It is apparent from the mean and median side-channel SNRs computed over all first-round 8-bit S-box (SKINNY-128-256) input shares or 7-bit Squaring (small-pSquare) input shares, that the quality of observations an adversary can make of individual words processed in the circuits is quite similar in both cases (binary-field or prime-field cipher). Thus, the noise levels are not expected to significantly impact the following investigation. We have plotted one set of evaluation results in Fig. 4 for the concrete example of serialized pipelined implementations with 3 shares. For all 2-, 3- and 4-share implementations respectively, we have first measured 1 million, 10 million and 100 million traces, in a randomly interleaved sequence of measurements for fixed and for random inputs, according to the Test Vector Leakage Assessment (TVLA) methodology [77]. The resulting non-specific t-test results are illustrated in the third row of Fig. 4. The implementations satisfy the expected statistical security order in the experiments, as the smallest moment where leakage is detected is equal to the number of shares. The same holds for all evaluated circuits in Table 3. As a next step we performed exemplary key recovery attacks on the most leaking (highest SNR)

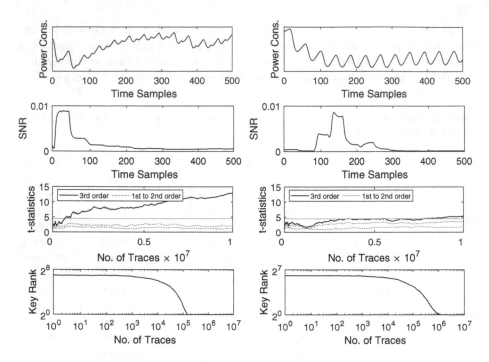

Fig. 4. Exemplary SCA results of serialized second-order masked SKINNY-128-256 (left) and small-pSquare (right) hardware implementations. From top to bottom: Sample traces, SNRs (1M traces), Fixed-vs-random t-tests (10 M traces), Profiled SASCA (1 M profiling, 10 M attack traces).

8-bit or 7-bit word respectively of the state. In order to extract the most information from the traces and reduce the effective noise level we have employed a profiled horizontal Soft-Analytical Side-Channel Attack (SASCA) [86]. In a first step all relevant intermediate values are profiled over multiple clock cycles to obtain multivariate templates. Next, a Linear Discriminant Analysis (LDA) is used to perform a linear dimensionality reduction which maximizes class separation on the profiling traces (always 1M) [81]. Finally, on the distinct attack trace set, likelihoods for all intermediate values and corresponding templates are collected separately, before a discrete probability distribution of the secret value is derived using belief propagation inside a SASCA tree graph that contains multiple intermediate computation stages of the masked S-box or squaring. These procedures are readily implemented in the publicly available SCALib library [25]. We then estimate the average rank of the correct key (over 1 000 iterations) with the probabilities obtained from all the attack traces. The results of that procedure plotted over the number of attack traces are shown in the bottom row of Fig. 4. In both the TVLA and the SASCA results it is apparent that, despite similar SNR values, successful leakage detection and key recovery require consistently significantly more traces (higher data complexity) on the small-pSquare compared to the SKINNY circuits, regardless of the concrete implementation chosen. This advantage of prime-field masking can be attributed to the "algebraic incompatibility" between physical leakage and recombination function to compute the secret from its shares. It can be observed that in case of attacks on 3- and 4-share implementations the advantage of small-pSquare is around or above one order of magnitude (slightly less in case of 2 shares). Furthermore no leakage detection or sophisticated key recovery attack succeeded on any of the 4-share implementations of small-pSquare using 100 million traces. Despite their empirical nature, we believe these results clearly emphasize the interest of efficient TBCs dedicated for prime-field masking based on established design principles (e.g., Feistel structures) while also tailoring the design to specific advantages that a given mathematical structure can lead to (e.g., using squaring as source of non-linearity in prime fields to exploit their efficient masked gadgets).

8 Summary and Open Problems

In this paper, we proposed both the FPM family of ciphers that leverages a generalized Feistel structure for prime masking and easy integration in leakage-resistant modes of operation, and the small-pSquare instance that is tailored for hardware implementations (due to its small prime) and exploits recent advances for masked squaring gadgets. Combining a hardware performance evaluation with an initial side-channel security assessment allows us to put forward the interest of this approach. small-pSquare protected with prime masking shows significantly improved (side-channel) security vs. performance tradeoffs compared to SKINNY protected with Boolean masking. Besides their concrete interest, we believe our investigations uncover new design principles for side-channel resistant implementations, leading to new challenges for further research.

Starting from more specific questions, the mathematical and physical security evaluation of small-pSquare is, as usual for new ciphers, a natural direction for deeper analyzes. Given the breadth of the FPM family, investigating other instances would be interesting as well. For example, a mid-pSquare instance with $p = 2^{31} - 1$ would be particularly well-suited for software implementations for which masking is known to be difficult to implement due to a lack of noise [5,24]. Such an instance could for example be based on the high-level structure depicted in the left part of Fig. 2 combined with the candidate F function given in Fig. 5. For modes of operation where having efficient inverses is not critical, it could also be possible to replace the generalized Feistel structure of Sect. 2.2 by an SPN one. More generally, the use of prime masking raises important theoretical questions regarding security proofs. For example, while the seed results of Dziembowski et al. provide a rationale for prime masking [41], the understanding of this approach is still far from the one of Boolean masking. Typical open problems in this respect are to improve the tightness of the security proofs and to better formalize the intuition of "algebraic incompatibility" that makes prime computations less sensitive to a lack of noise than Boolean masking.

The source code for all our small-pSquare implementations is publicly available here: https://github.com/uclcrypto/small-pSquare

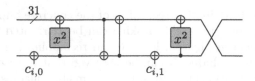

Fig. 5. Candidate F-function for a mid-pSquare instance.

Acknowledgments. Lorenzo Grassi was supported by the German Research Foundation (DFG) within the framework of the Excellence Strategy of the Federal Government and the States – EXC 2092 CaSa – 39078197. Pierrick Méaux was supported by the ERC Advanced Grant 787390. François-Xavier Standaert is a senior research associate of the Belgian Fund for Scientific Research (FNRS-F.R.S.). This work has been funded in parts by the ERC Advanced Grant 101096871. Views and opinions expressed are those of the authors only and do not necessarily reflect those of the European Union or the ERC. Neither the European Union nor the granting authority can be held responsible for them.

References

1. Albrecht, M.R., et al.: Feistel structures for MPC, and more. In: Sako, K., Schneider, S., Ryan, P.Y.A. (eds.) ESORICS 2019. LNCS, vol. 11736, pp. 151–171. Springer, Cham (2019). https://doi.org/10.1007/978-3-030-29962-0_8

2. Albrecht, M., Grassi, L., Rechberger, C., Roy, A., Tiessen, T.: MiMC: efficient encryption and cryptographic hashing with minimal multiplicative complexity. In: Cheon, J.H., Takagi, T. (eds.) ASIACRYPT 2016. LNCS, vol. 10031, pp. 191–219. Springer, Heidelberg (2016). https://doi.org/10.1007/978-3-662-53887-6_7

3. Aly, A., Ashur, T., Ben-Sasson, E., Dhooghe, S., Szepieniec, A.: Design of symmetric-key primitives for advanced cryptographic protocols. IACR Trans. Symmetric Cryptol. **2020**(3), 1–45 (2020)

4. Balasch, J., Faust, S., Gierlichs, B., Verbauwhede, I.: Theory and practice of a leakage resilient masking scheme. In: Wang, X., Sako, K. (eds.) ASIACRYPT 2012. LNCS, vol. 7658, pp. 758–775. Springer, Heidelberg (2012). https://doi.org/10.1007/978-3-642-34961-4_45

5. Battistello, A., Coron, J.-S., Prouff, E., Zeitoun, R.: Horizontal side-channel attacks and countermeasures on the ISW masking scheme. In: Gierlichs, B., Poschmann, A.Y. (eds.) CHES 2016. LNCS, vol. 9813, pp. 23–39. Springer, Heidelberg (2016). https://doi.org/10.1007/978-3-662-53140-2_2

6. Beierle, C., et al.: The SKINNY family of block ciphers and its low-latency variant MANTIS. In: Robshaw, M., Katz, J. (eds.) CRYPTO 2016. LNCS, vol. 9815, pp. 123–153. Springer, Heidelberg (2016). https://doi.org/10.1007/978-3-662-53008-5_5

7. Bellizia, D., et al.: Mode-Level vs. implementation-level physical security in symmetric cryptography. In: Micciancio, D., Ristenpart, T. (eds.) CRYPTO 2020. LNCS, vol. 12170, pp. 369–400. Springer, Cham (2020). https://doi.org/10.1007/978-3-030-56784-2_13

8. Berger, T.P., Minier, M., Thomas, G.: Extended generalized Feistel networks using matrix representation. In: Lange, T., Lauter, K., Lisoněk, P. (eds.) SAC 2013.

LNCS, vol. 8282, pp. 289–305. Springer, Heidelberg (2014). https://doi.org/10.1007/978-3-662-43414-7_15

9. Berti, F., Guo, C., Pereira, O., Peters, T., Standaert, F.-X.: TEDT, a leakage-resist AEAD mode for high physical security applications. IACR Trans. Cryptogr. Hardw. Embed. Syst. **2020**(1), 256–320 (2020)

10. Berti, F., Guo, C., Peters, T., Standaert, F.-X.: Efficient leakage-resilient MACs without idealized assumptions. In: Tibouchi, M., Wang, H. (eds.) ASIACRYPT 2021. LNCS, vol. 13091, pp. 95–123. Springer, Cham (2021). https://doi.org/10.1007/978-3-030-92075-3_4

11. Berti, F., Pereira, O., Peters, T., Standaert, F.-X.: On leakage-resilient authenticated encryption with decryption leakages. IACR Trans. Symmetric Cryptol. **2017**(3), 271–293 (2017)

12. Bertoni, G., Daemen, J., Peeters, M., Van Assche, G.: On the indifferentiability of the sponge construction. In: Smart, N. (ed.) EUROCRYPT 2008. LNCS, vol. 4965, pp. 181–197. Springer, Heidelberg (2008). https://doi.org/10.1007/978-3-540-78967-3_11

13. Bertoni, G., Daemen, J., Peeters, M., Van Assche, G.: Duplexing the sponge: single-pass authenticated encryption and other applications. In: Miri, A., Vaudenay, S. (eds.) SAC 2011. LNCS, vol. 7118, pp. 320–337. Springer, Heidelberg (2012). https://doi.org/10.1007/978-3-642-28496-0_19

14. Beyne, T., Chen,Y.L.: Provably Secure Reflection Ciphers. In: Dodis, Y., Shrimpton, T. (eds.) CRYPTO, vol. 13510. Springer, Cham (2022). https://doi.org/10.1007/978-3-031-15985-5_9

15. Biham, E.: New types of cryptanalytic attacks using related keys. J. Cryptol. **7**(4), 229–246 (1994). https://doi.org/10.1007/BF00203965

16. Biham, E.: A fast new DES implementation in software. In: Biham, E. (ed.) FSE 1997. LNCS, vol. 1267, pp. 260–272. Springer, Heidelberg (1997). https://doi.org/10.1007/BFb0052352

17. Biham, E., Biryukov, A., Shamir, A.: Cryptanalysis of skipjack reduced to 31 rounds using impossible differentials. In: Stern, J. (ed.) EUROCRYPT 1999. LNCS, vol. 1592, pp. 12–23. Springer, Heidelberg (1999). https://doi.org/10.1007/3-540-48910-X_2

18. Biham, E., Shamir, A.: Differential cryptanalysis of DES-like cryptosystems. J. Cryptol. **4**(1), 3–72 (1991). https://doi.org/10.1007/BF00630563

19. Biham, E., Shamir, A.: Differential Cryptanalysis of the Data Encryption Standard. Springer (1993). https://doi.org/10.1007/978-1-4613-9314-6

20. Biryukov, A., Wagner, D.: Slide attacks. In: Knudsen, L. (ed.) FSE 1999. LNCS, vol. 1636, pp. 245–259. Springer, Heidelberg (1999). https://doi.org/10.1007/3-540-48519-8_18

21. Biryukov, A., Wagner, D.: Advanced slide attacks. In: Preneel, B. (ed.) EUROCRYPT 2000. LNCS, vol. 1807, pp. 589–606. Springer, Heidelberg (2000). https://doi.org/10.1007/3-540-45539-6_41

22. Borghoff, J., et al.: PRINCE – a low-latency block cipher for pervasive computing applications. In: Wang, X., Sako, K. (eds.) ASIACRYPT 2012. LNCS, vol. 7658, pp. 208–225. Springer, Heidelberg (2012). https://doi.org/10.1007/978-3-642-34961-4_14

23. Božilov, D., et al.: PRINCEv2. In: Dunkelman, O., Jacobson, Jr., M.J., O'Flynn, C. (eds.) SAC 2020. LNCS, vol. 12804, pp. 483–511. Springer, Cham (2021). https://doi.org/10.1007/978-3-030-81652-0_19

24. Bronchain, O., Standaert, F.-X.: Breaking masked implementations with many shares on 32-bit software platforms or when the security order does not matter. IACR Trans. Cryptogr. Hardw. Embed. Syst. **2021**(3), 202–234 (2021)
25. Cassiers, G., Bronchain, O.: Scalib: a side-channel analysis library. J. Open Source Softw. **8**(86), 5196 (2023)
26. Cassiers, G., Grégoire, B., Levi, I., Standaert, F.-X.: Hardware private circuits: from trivial composition to full verification. IEEE Trans. Comput. **70**(10) (2021)
27. Cassiers, G., Masure, L., Momin, C., Moos, T., Standaert, F.-X.: Prime-Field masking in hardware and its soundness against low-noise SCA attacks. IACR Trans. Cryptogr. Hardw. Embed. Syst. **2023**(2), 482–518 (2023)
28. Cauchois, V., Gomez, C., Thomas, G.: General diffusion analysis: how to find optimal permutations for generalized Type-II Feistel schemes. IACR Trans. Symmetric Cryptol. **2019**(1)
29. Chari, S., Jutla, C.S., Rao, J.R., Rohatgi, P.: Towards sound approaches to counteract power-analysis attacks. In: Wiener, M. (ed.) CRYPTO 1999. LNCS, vol. 1666, pp. 398–412. Springer, Heidelberg (1999). https://doi.org/10.1007/3-540-48405-1_26
30. Cho, J., et al.: Transciphering framework for approximate homomorphic encryption. In: Tibouchi, M., Wang, H. (eds.) ASIACRYPT 2021. LNCS, vol. 13092, pp. 640–669. Springer, Cham (2021). https://doi.org/10.1007/978-3-030-92078-4_22
31. Courtois, N., Klimov, A., Patarin, J., Shamir, A.: Efficient algorithms for solving overdefined systems of multivariate polynomial equations. In: Preneel, B. (ed.) EUROCRYPT 2000. LNCS, vol. 1807, pp. 392–407. Springer, Heidelberg (2000). https://doi.org/10.1007/3-540-45539-6_27
32. Daemen, J., Peeters, M., Van Assche, G., Rijmen, V.: Nessie Proposal: NOEKEON. In: First Open NESSIE Workshop (2000)
33. Daemen, J., Rijmen, V.: The wide trail design strategy. In: Honary, B. (ed.) Cryptography and Coding 2001. LNCS, vol. 2260, pp. 222–238. Springer, Heidelberg (2001). https://doi.org/10.1007/3-540-45325-3_20
34. Daemen, J., Rijmen, V.: Security of a wide trail design. In: Menezes, A., Sarkar, P. (eds.) INDOCRYPT 2002. LNCS, vol. 2551, pp. 1–11. Springer, Heidelberg (2002). https://doi.org/10.1007/3-540-36231-2_1
35. Dobraunig, C., Eichlseder, M., Mendel, F., Schläffer, M.: Ascon v1.2: lightweight authenticated encryption and hashing. J. Cryptol. **34**(3), 1–42 (2021). https://doi.org/10.1007/s00145-021-09398-9
36. Dobraunig, C., Grassi, L., Guinet, A., Kuijsters, D.: Ciminion: symmetric encryption based on Toffoli-gates over large finite fields. In: Canteaut, A., Standaert, F.-X. (eds.) EUROCRYPT 2021. LNCS, vol. 12697, pp. 3–34. Springer, Cham (2021). https://doi.org/10.1007/978-3-030-77886-6_1
37. Duc, A., Dziembowski, S., Faust, S.: Unifying leakage models: from probing attacks to noisy leakage. In: Nguyen, P.Q., Oswald, E. (eds.) EUROCRYPT 2014. LNCS, vol. 8441, pp. 423–440. Springer, Heidelberg (2014). https://doi.org/10.1007/978-3-642-55220-5_24
38. Duc, A., Faust, S., Standaert, F.-X.: Making masking security proofs concrete. In: Oswald, E., Fischlin, M. (eds.) EUROCRYPT 2015. LNCS, vol. 9056, pp. 401–429. Springer, Heidelberg (2015). https://doi.org/10.1007/978-3-662-46800-5_16
39. Duval, S., Leurent, G.: MDS matrices with lightweight Circuits. IACR Trans. Symmetric Cryptol. **2018**(2), 48–78 (2018)
40. Dziembowski, S., Faust, S.: Leakage-resilient cryptography from the inner-product extractor. In: Lee, D.H., Wang, X. (eds.) ASIACRYPT 2011. LNCS, vol. 7073, pp.

702–721. Springer, Heidelberg (2011). https://doi.org/10.1007/978-3-642-25385-0_38

41. Dziembowski, S., Faust, S., Skórski, M.: Optimal amplification of noisy leakages. In: Kushilevitz, E., Malkin, T. (eds.) TCC 2016. LNCS, vol. 9563, pp. 291–318. Springer, Heidelberg (2016). https://doi.org/10.1007/978-3-662-49099-0_11

42. Fumaroli, G., Martinelli, A., Prouff, E., Rivain, M.: Affine masking against higher-order side channel analysis. In: Biryukov, A., Gong, G., Stinson, D.R. (eds.) SAC 2010. LNCS, vol. 6544, pp. 262–280. Springer, Heidelberg (2011). https://doi.org/10.1007/978-3-642-19574-7_18

43. Golić, J.D., Tymen, C.: Multiplicative masking and power analysis of AES. In: Kaliski, B.S., Koç, K., Paar, C. (eds.) CHES 2002. LNCS, vol. 2523, pp. 198–212. Springer, Heidelberg (2003). https://doi.org/10.1007/3-540-36400-5_16

44. Goudarzi, D., Rivain, M.: How fast can higher-order masking be in software? In: Coron, J.-S., Nielsen, J.B. (eds.) EUROCRYPT 2017. LNCS, vol. 10210, pp. 567–597. Springer, Cham (2017). https://doi.org/10.1007/978-3-319-56620-7_20

45. Grassi, L.: On generalizations of the Lai-Massey scheme. Cryptology ePrint Archive, Paper 2022/1245 (2022). https://eprint.iacr.org/2022/1245

46. Keller, N., Rosemarin, A.: Mind the middle layer: the HADES design strategy revisited. In: Canteaut, A., Standaert, F.-X. (eds.) EUROCRYPT 2021. LNCS, vol. 12697, pp. 35–63. Springer, Cham (2021). https://doi.org/10.1007/978-3-030-77886-6_2

47. Grassi, L., Masure, L., Méaux, P., Moos, T., Standaert, F.-X.: Generalized feistel ciphers for efficient prime field masking - full version. Cryptology ePrint Archive (2024)

48. Grassi, L., Rechberger, C., Rønjom, S.: Subspace trail cryptanalysis and its applications to AES. IACR Trans. Symmetric Cryptol. 2016(2)

49. Gross, H., Mangard, S., Korak, T.: An efficient side-channel protected AES implementation with arbitrary protection order. In: Handschuh, H. (ed.) CT-RSA 2017. LNCS, vol. 10159, pp. 95–112. Springer, Cham (2017). https://doi.org/10.1007/978-3-319-52153-4_6

50. Grosso, V., Leurent, G., Standaert, F.-X., Varıcı, K.: LS-Designs: Bitslice encryption for efficient masked software implementations. In: Cid, C., Rechberger, C. (eds.) FSE 2014. LNCS, vol. 8540, pp. 18–37. Springer, Heidelberg (2015). https://doi.org/10.1007/978-3-662-46706-0_2

51. Guo, J., Peyrin, T., Poschmann, A., Robshaw, M.: The LED block cipher. In: Preneel, B., Takagi, T. (eds.) CHES 2011. LNCS, vol. 6917, pp. 326–341. Springer, Heidelberg (2011). https://doi.org/10.1007/978-3-642-23951-9_22

52. Hoang, V.T., Rogaway, P.: On generalized Feistel networks. In: Rabin, T. (ed.) CRYPTO 2010. LNCS, vol. 6223, pp. 613–630. Springer, Heidelberg (2010). https://doi.org/10.1007/978-3-642-14623-7_33

53. Hong, D., et al.: HIGHT: a new block cipher suitable for low-resource device. In: Goubin, L., Matsui, M. (eds.) CHES 2006. LNCS, vol. 4249, pp. 46–59. Springer, Heidelberg (2006). https://doi.org/10.1007/11894063_4

54. Ishai, Y., Sahai, A., Wagner, D.: Private circuits: securing hardware against probing attacks. In: Boneh, D. (ed.) CRYPTO 2003. LNCS, vol. 2729, pp. 463–481. Springer, Heidelberg (2003). https://doi.org/10.1007/978-3-540-45146-4_27

55. Jakobsen, T., Knudsen, L.R.: The interpolation attack on block ciphers. In: Biham, E. (ed.) FSE 1997. LNCS, vol. 1267, pp. 28–40. Springer, Heidelberg (1997). https://doi.org/10.1007/BFb0052332

56. Jean, J., Nikolić, I., Peyrin, T.: Tweaks and keys for block ciphers: the TWEAKEY framework. In: Sarkar, P., Iwata, T. (eds.) ASIACRYPT 2014. LNCS, vol. 8874, pp. 274–288. Springer, Heidelberg (2014). https://doi.org/10.1007/978-3-662-45608-8_15

57. Kerckhof, S., Durvaux, F., Hocquet, C., Bol, D., Standaert, F.-X.: Towards green cryptography: a comparison of lightweight ciphers from the energy viewpoint. In: Prouff, E., Schaumont, P. (eds.) CHES 2012. LNCS, vol. 7428, pp. 390–407. Springer, Heidelberg (2012). https://doi.org/10.1007/978-3-642-33027-8_23

58. Knichel, D., Moradi, A., Müller, N., Sasdrich, P.: Automated generation of masked hardware. IACR Trans. Cryptogr. Hardw. Embed. Syst. **2022**(1)

59. Knudsen, L.R.: Truncated and higher order differentials. In: Preneel, B. (ed.) FSE 1994. LNCS, vol. 1008, pp. 196–211. Springer, Heidelberg (1995). https://doi.org/10.1007/3-540-60590-8_16

60. Kranz, T., Leander, G., Stoffelen, K., Wiemer, F.: Shorter Linear Straight-Line Programs for MDS Matrices. IACR Trans. Symmetric Cryptol. **2017**(4), 188–211 (2017)

61. Lai, X.: Higher Order Derivatives and Differential Cryptanalysis. In: Blahut, R.E., Costello, D.J., Maurer, U., Mittelholzer, T. (eds.) Two Sides of One Tapestry, Communications and Cryptography, vol. 276. Springer, Boston, (1994). https://doi.org/10.1007/978-1-4615-2694-0_23

62. Lai, X., Massey, J.L.: A proposal for a new block encryption standard. In: Damgård, I.B. (ed.) EUROCRYPT 1990. LNCS, vol. 473, pp. 389–404. Springer, Heidelberg (1991). https://doi.org/10.1007/3-540-46877-3_35

63. Leander, G., Abdelraheem, M.A., AlKhzaimi, H., Zenner, E.: A cryptanalysis of PRINTCIPHER: the invariant subspace attack. In: Rogaway, P. (ed.) CRYPTO 2011. LNCS, vol. 6841, pp. 206–221. Springer, Heidelberg (2011). https://doi.org/10.1007/978-3-642-22792-9_12

64. Leander, G., Minaud, B., Rønjom, S.: A generic approach to invariant subspace attacks: cryptanalysis of robin, iSCREAM and Zorro. In: Oswald, E., Fischlin, M. (eds.) EUROCRYPT 2015. LNCS, vol. 9056, pp. 254–283. Springer, Heidelberg (2015). https://doi.org/10.1007/978-3-662-46800-5_11

65. Li, C., Wang, Q.: Design of lightweight linear diffusion layers from near-MDS matrices. IACR Trans. Symmetric Cryptol. **2017**(1)

66. Liu, M., Sim, S.M.: Lightweight MDS generalized circulant matrices. In: Peyrin, T. (ed.) FSE 2016. LNCS, vol. 9783, pp. 101–120. Springer, Heidelberg (2016). https://doi.org/10.1007/978-3-662-52993-5_6

67. Masure, L., Méaux, P., Moos, T., Standaert, F.-X.: Effective and efficient masking with low noise using small-mersenne-prime ciphers. In: Hazay, C., Stam, M. (eds.) EUROCRYPT,vol. 14007. Springer, Cham (2023). https://doi.org/10.1007/978-3-031-30634-1_20

68. Matsui, M.: Linear cryptanalysis method for DES cipher. In: Helleseth, T. (ed.) EUROCRYPT 1993. LNCS, vol. 765, pp. 386–397. Springer, Heidelberg (1994). https://doi.org/10.1007/3-540-48285-7_33

69. Moos, T., Moradi, A., Richter, B.: Static power side-channel analysis of a threshold implementation prototype chip. In: Design, Automation & Test in Europe Conference & Exhibition (DATE), 2017 (2017)

70. Nagpal, R., Gigerl, B., Primas, R., Mangard, S.: Riding the waves towards generic single-cycle masking in hardware. IACR Trans. Cryptogr. Hardw. Embed. Syst. **4**(2022)

71. Nyberg, K.: Generalized feistel networks. In: Kim, K., Matsumoto, T. (eds.) ASI-ACRYPT 1996. LNCS, vol. 1163, pp. 91–104. Springer, Heidelberg (1996). https://doi.org/10.1007/BFb0034838

72. Del Pozo, S.M., Standaert, F.-X., Kamel, D., Moradi, A.: Side-channel attacks from static power: when should we care?. In: DATE (2015)

73. Prouff, E., Rivain, M.: Masking against side-channel attacks: a formal security proof. In: Johansson, T., Nguyen, P.Q. (eds.) EUROCRYPT 2013. LNCS, vol. 7881, pp. 142–159. Springer, Heidelberg (2013). https://doi.org/10.1007/978-3-642-38348-9_9

74. Roche, T., Prouff, E.: Higher-order glitch free implementation of the AES using secure multi-party computation protocols - extended version. J. Cryptogr. Eng. 2(2), 111–127 (2012). https://doi.org/10.1007/s13389-012-0033-3

75. Sasdrich, P., Bilgin, B., Hutter, M., Marson, M.E.: Low-latency hardware masking with application to AES. IACR Trans. Cryptogr. Hardw. Embed. Syst. 2020(2), 300–326 (2020)

76. Schindler, W., Lemke, K., Paar, C.: A stochastic model for differential side channel cryptanalysis. In: Rao, J.R., Sunar, B. (eds.) CHES 2005. LNCS, vol. 3659, pp. 30–46. Springer, Heidelberg (2005). https://doi.org/10.1007/11545262_3

77. Schneider, T., Moradi, A.: Leakage assessment methodology. In: Güneysu, T., Handschuh, H. (eds.) CHES 2015. LNCS, vol. 9293, pp. 495–513. Springer, Heidelberg (2015). https://doi.org/10.1007/978-3-662-48324-4_25

78. Shen, Y., Peters, T., Standaert, F.-X., Cassiers, G., Verhamme, C.: Triplex: an efficient and one-pass leakage-resistant mode of operation. IACR Trans. Cryptogr. Hardw. Embed. Syst. 2022(4), 135–162 (2022)

79. Shirai, T., Shibutani, K., Akishita, T., Moriai, S., Iwata, T.: The 128-Bit Block-cipher CLEFIA (extended abstract). In: Biryukov, A. (ed.) FSE 2007. LNCS, vol. 4593, pp. 181–195. Springer, Heidelberg (2007). https://doi.org/10.1007/978-3-540-74619-5_12

80. Standaert, F.-X.: How (not) to use Welch's T-Test in side-channel security evaluations. In: Bilgin, B., Fischer, J.-B. (eds.) CARDIS 2018. LNCS, vol. 11389, pp. 65–79. Springer, Cham (2019). https://doi.org/10.1007/978-3-030-15462-2_5

81. Standaert, F.-X., Archambeau, C.: Using subspace-based template attacks to compare and combine power and electromagnetic information leakages. In: Oswald, E., Rohatgi, P. (eds.) CHES 2008. LNCS, vol. 5154, pp. 411–425. Springer, Heidelberg (2008). https://doi.org/10.1007/978-3-540-85053-3_26

82. Standaert, F.-X., Piret, G., Rouvroy, G., Quisquater, J.-J.: FPGA implementations of the ICEBERG block cipher. Integration 40(1), 20–27 (2007)

83. Suzaki, T., Minematsu, K.: Improving the generalized feistel. In: Hong, S., Iwata, T. (eds.) FSE 2010. LNCS, vol. 6147, pp. 19–39. Springer, Heidelberg (2010). https://doi.org/10.1007/978-3-642-13858-4_2

84. Vaudenay, S.: On the Lai-Massey scheme. In: Lam, K.-Y., Okamoto, E., Xing, C. (eds.) ASIACRYPT 1999. LNCS, vol. 1716, pp. 8–19. Springer, Heidelberg (1999). https://doi.org/10.1007/978-3-540-48000-6_2

85. Verhamme, C., Cassiers, G., Standaert, F.X.: In: Buhan, I., Schneider, T. (eds.) Analyzing the Leakage Resistance of the NIST's Lightweight Crypto Competition's Finalists. CARDIS, vol. 13820. Springer, Cham (2022). https://doi.org/10.1007/978-3-031-25319-5_15

86. Veyrat-Charvillon, N., Gérard, B., Standaert, F.-X.: Soft analytical side-channel attacks. In: Sarkar, P., Iwata, T. (eds.) ASIACRYPT 2014. LNCS, vol. 8873, pp. 282–296. Springer, Heidelberg (2014). https://doi.org/10.1007/978-3-662-45611-8_15

87. Wagner, D.: The boomerang attack. In: Knudsen, L. (ed.) FSE 1999. LNCS, vol. 1636, pp. 156–170. Springer, Heidelberg (1999). https://doi.org/10.1007/3-540-48519-8_12

88. Wang, L., Guo, J., Zhang, G., Zhao, J., Gu, D.: How to build fully secure tweakable Blockciphers from classical Blockciphers. In: Cheon, J.H., Takagi, T. (eds.) ASIACRYPT 2016. LNCS, vol. 10031, pp. 455–483. Springer, Heidelberg (2016). https://doi.org/10.1007/978-3-662-53887-6_17

89. Wang, W., Méaux, P., Cassiers, G., Standaert, F.-X.: Efficient and private computations with code-based masking. IACR Trans. Cryptogr. Hardw. Embed. Syst. **2020**(2), 128–171 (2020)

90. Zheng, Y., Matsumoto, T., Imai, H.: On the construction of block ciphers provably secure and not relying on any unproved hypotheses. In: Brassard, G. (ed.) CRYPTO 1989. LNCS, vol. 435, pp. 461–480. Springer, New York (1990). https://doi.org/10.1007/0-387-34805-0_42

A Novel Framework for Explainable Leakage Assessment

Si Gao[1](✉) and Elisabeth Oswald[1,2](✉) (iD)

[1] Digital Age Research Center (D!ARC), University of Klagenfurt, Klagenfurt,
Austria
si-gao@outlook.com
[2] School of Computer Science, University of Birmingham, Birmingham, UK
sca-research@pm.me

Abstract. Schemes such as Common Criteria or FIPS 140-3 require
the assessment of cryptographic implementations with respect to side
channels at high security levels. Instead of a "penetration testing" style
approach where specific tests are carried out, FIPS 140-3 relies on non-
specific "leakage assessment" to identify potential side channel leaks in
implementations of symmetric schemes. Leakage assessment, as it is
understood today, is based on a simple leakage detection testing regime.
Leakage assessment to date, provides no evidence whether or not the
potential leakage is exploitable in a concrete attack: if a device fails the
test, (and therefore certification under the FIPS 140-3 scheme) it remains
unclear why it fails.

We propose a novel assessment regime that is based on a different
statistical rational than the existing leakage detection tests. Our statistical approach enables non-specific detection (i.e. we do not require to
specify intermediate values) whilst simultaneously generating evidence
for designing an attack vector that exploits identified leakage. We do
this via an iterative approach, based on building and comparing nested
regression models. We also provide, for the first time, concrete definitions
for concepts such as key leakage, exploitable leakage and explainable
leakage. Finally, we illustrate our novel leakage assessment framework in
the context of two open source masked software implementations on a
processor that is known to exhibit micro-architectural leakage.

1 Introduction

Security certification schemes such as the Common Criteria (CC) framework [1],
or FIPS 140 [2], mandate the evaluation of cryptographic software and hardware against side channel adversaries at high security levels. The philosophical
approach in CC schemes follows on from penetration testing: an evaluator is
tasked to identify specific side channel vulnerabilities and demonstrate exploits
via attacks. Because this approach is based on specific attacks, it comes at a
huge cost, especially if the leakage is caused by some hidden micro-architectural
effects.

© International Association for Cryptologic Research 2024
M. Joye and G. Leander (Eds.): EUROCRYPT 2024, LNCS 14653, pp. 221–250, 2024.
https://doi.org/10.1007/978-3-031-58734-4_8

In contrast, the NIST based framework FIPS 140 (now at version 3 [2]) is based on a derivative of the Test Vector Leakage Assessment (TVLA) [3]— via referencing to an associated standard ISO 17825 [4]. TVLA includes a "non-specific" test, and therefore, it can potentially identify arbitrary leaks—a huge advantage in the case of software implementations where the micro-architecture of the processor is unknown to the evaluator. TVLA utilises the simple statistical Welch's t-test[1] to ascertain if observations exhibit characteristics that depend on either data or key. For the purpose of finding general dependencies, TVLA suggests the use of a fixed-versus-random input test, which is called *non-specific detection*. In a nutshell, two sets of side channel traces are compared (one with a fixed input and one with randomly chosen inputs): if they are "different" then the device is said to have data dependent side channel leakage.

TVLA acknowledges the problem of false positives, in particular first and last round potential "leaks" may not always be exploitable (e.g. plaintext/ciphertext-based leakage). False positives are detection test outcomes that claim that there is leakage, although there is none. The common practice is then using the so-called *specific detection tests* (which are akin to "known key attacks") to confirm or refute the findings from the non-specific test. Importantly, the specific tests do not benefit from the previous non-specific test outcomes. The knowledge of time points is helpful to infer a specific test for leakage on an algorithmic level, but not if the data dependency arises from a micro-architectural component (as it interacts with data from different steps in an implementation). Thus, not much has been gained, and perhaps as a consequence, ISO 17825 does not include the specific testing regime.

1.1 The Challenge of Interpreting Non-specific Leakage Detection Outcomes

FIPS 140-3 uses a non-specific leakage detection *only* in the context of testing *symmetric* cryptographic algorithms. A previous study proposes a hybrid methodology to connect non-specific outcomes with specific tests [5], however, the approach requires *a priori* knowledge of specific intermediate states for setting up the tests. More recently non-specific leakage assessments were developed further by the introduction of a deep learning framework (DL-LA) [6]: the idea is that if a network can be trained to distinguish two sets of traces, then the network could be the "evidence" of leakage. Further sensitivity analysis on the trained network helps to determine the trace points contributing to the leakage and thus enables a similar result as TVLA—determining which (if any) trace points depend on inputs. Hence the same problem persists as before: one has to set up specific tests to confirm the leakage as exploitable in an actual attack.

There seems to be an unavoidable divide between non-specific and specific leakage detection tests: non-specific detection (per construction) is not based on

---

[1] Notice that because the Welch's t-test only captures the first central moment of a distribution, complex leakage has to be "forced into" this central moment by means of pre-processing the observations.

specific intermediate steps in the cryptographic module. The advantage of the non-specific approach is thus also its biggest drawback: because we do not test specific intermediates, it is hard to link test results to specific intermediates and therefore concrete attack vectors.

The *status quo* is thus that there is a clear desire for non-specific leakage detection as part of a leakage assessment framework, but there have been no ideas so far about how a non-specific method could produce "usefully interpretable outcomes". This *status quo* leads to three interesting research questions:

- What are useful ways of "interpreting" the outcome of a non-specific leakage detection test?
- How can we capture the idea that something is "exploitable in an attack" in a leakage detection framework?
- Can we design a leakage assessment procedure that is not only non-specific, but also delivers results that can be "interpreted" as "exploitable leakage"?

1.2   Our Contributions: An Informal Summary

Our research is situated in the context of the security evaluation of a cryptographic module (as part of a formal certification scheme) that considers side channel key-recovery attacks for symmetric cryptographic algorithms. The cryptographic module implements a symmetric cryptographic algorithm via a sequence of steps, which give rise to side channel observations. The evaluation seeks to establish if the observable side channel contains information about the secret key via statistical detection tests. In the context of a certification, the evaluator is provided with access to the device, and can supply inputs, such as plaintexts/ciphertexts and keys.

The aim of our work is to establish characteristics of the terms "explainable outcomes" and "exploitable leakage", and to map them to a concrete statistical decision making process for leakage detection that works in a non-specific manner yet delivers evidence for exploitable leakage.

As part of our contribution, we provide *novel definitions* for *key leakage*, *exploitable key leakage*, and a *explainable detection method*, together with *a concrete statistical test framework*. Our novel framework is based on iteratively building, and comparing, key-dependent nested regression models. The procedure enables us to test for key leakage, then to assess the effort of the inference step (exploitability), and finally to produce evidence for a concrete attack. We implement this framework via two algorithms, thereby representing a concrete instance of an explainable detection method. We demonstrate this framework on two open source masked software implementations (AES and ASCON) that run on a microprocessor that is known to have micro-architectural leakage.

We emphasise that our procedure is not yet another attempt to deal with the "(statistical) false positives problem of TVLA" [7]: instead, our novel framework goes beyond the original intent of TVLA (a quick and easy way to check for potential leakage) and proposes a complete method by which an evaluator can detect *arbitrary key dependencies*, for each detected key-dependent point to *decide if it is exploitable*, and if so, *deliver a concrete attack vector for specific key bytes*. Consequently, our explainable yet non-specific detection framework enables deeper understanding of observable key leakage, it enables distinguishing non-exploitable data dependency from genuine security concerns, and it enables the better interpretation of the assessment results.

Yap, Benamira and Bhasin et al. proposed a sounds similar but entirely different concept called "interpretable neural network" [8]: their work starts from some *known specific state* (e.g. one Sbox output in AES) and investigates how the network combines parts on trace ("literals") to recover this state. Our work, on the other hand, starts from non-specific detection results and shows how/if they can be exploited in certain specific attacks (i.e. finds which Sbox/combinations of Sbox-es can be attacked).

Summarising, the primary goal of our assessment framework is to explain and confirm whether a detected leak is a genuine security concern (in a non-specific setup) through demonstrating confirmatory attacks. Such attacks may not be optimal, but they can facilitate further improvements via advanced attacks (e.g. deep learning networks).

Outline. After recalling the statistical foundations of the fixed-versus-random procedure and introducing some basic notation, we explain the essential background for our novel leakage assessment framework that is based on nested model building in Sect. 2. In Sect. 3 we discuss the novel notions "key leakage","exploitable" and "explainable" and provide concrete definitions. Following on we show the construction of our non-specific detection test in Sect. 4, and define an assessment framework that has the desired qualities (i.e. outcomes which are both explainable and exploitable) in Sect. 5. We show the assessment framework in action for an implementation featuring Boolean masking applied to ASCON, and for an implementation featuring affine masking applied to AES in Sect. 7. We discuss our research in Sect. 8, whereby we consider relations to existing work, the scope and limitations of our method, and efficiency. We also briefly point out open problems and give ideas for further research.

For clarity, we provide most of our experimental trace sets through *zenodo*: interested readers can find a tutorial on how to download our trace sets and reproduce our analyses from our Github repository[2].

2 Preliminaries

For the ease of reading, we recall several basic facts about pertinent statistical tools and techniques, as well as the relevant assumptions about side channel observations. We also introduce the notation that we maintain throughout this paper, and refer to relevant related work. We keep explanations informal whenever we refer to relatively well known concepts, and introduce formalism only where it is required.

---

[2] https://github.com/sca-research/explainable-assessment.

2.1 Notation

We typeset random variables by capital letters, and their realisations by lower case letters; when we write a random variable in a set notation then we refer to multiple samples of that variable. E.g. X may be a random variable representing an input, $x = 10$ is then a realisation of X, and $\{x_{(1)}, x_{(2)}, \ldots\} = \{x\}$ refers to a set of concrete realisations of X (note that we use subscripts to indicate different realisations $x_{(i)}$).

Side channel observations are often multivariate e.g. $\mathbf{T} = (T^1, T^2, \ldots)$ refers to a random variable that represents side channel observation consisting of multiple elements. Note that we use superscripts to refer to the vector elements. Thus a set of concrete measurements is then $\{\mathbf{t}\}$, with $\mathbf{t}_{(i)} = (t_{(i)}{}^1, t_{(i)}{}^2, \ldots)$ referring to the i-th multivariate observation.

Estimates of quantities are indicated by a hat over the respective quantity, e.g. $E(X)$ is the expectation of the variable X and $\hat{E}(X)$ is the estimate of that expectation. We reserve the notation $\mathcal{N}(0, \sigma^2)$ to refer to the normal distribution with zero mean and σ^2 variance.

A secret key K is a binary string of a fixed length, which is sampled from a (uniform) distribution. We need to be able to refer to smaller portions or chunks of this key (sometimes also called subkeys in the literature) in our work, so K should also be understood as the concatenation $\|$ of such chunks $K = K_1 \| K_2 \| \ldots \| K_s$. We assume that all chunks have the same size, and the size of a chunk will be clear from the context in any concrete example.

2.2 Statistical Hypothesis Testing

The purpose of a hypothesis test is to decide, based on some gathered data, if there is enough evidence to refute a particular hypothesis, which is typically called the "null hypothesis" H_0. The alternative hypothesis H_1 is considered to be (possibly) true if the null can be refuted.

To carry out a hypothesis test, a suitable test statistic must be chosen. Assuming the distribution of the chosen test statistic is known and well understood, a statistically motivated threshold can be derived that becomes the decision criterion for the null hypothesis. Typically the line of argument is such that if the test statistic surpasses the threshold, we say that we have enough evidence to refute the null hypothesis.

2.3 Side Channel Observations

We assume that an evaluator can sample side channel observations from a cryptographic module. The module operates on some inputs and secret key, as well as internally generated randomness. In a typical evaluation context, the evaluator may supply chosen inputs and keys, and they may even control internal randomness. Our work does not require any control over the internal randomness.

We denote by $L_D(P, K)^j$ the family of (unknown) leakage functions of the cryptographic module. The function family depends on the device state, which is some unknown function[3] of the input P and the key K. Recall that a cryptographic module implements an algorithm as a sequence of steps: each step j may give rise to a different device leakage function $L_D(P, K)^j$. Thus side channel observations consist of a set of side channel traces $\{\mathbf{t}\}$, whereby a single trace of this set is a multivariate observation $\mathbf{T} = (L_D(P, K)^1 + \mathcal{N}(0, \sigma^2), L_D(P, K)^2 + \mathcal{N}(0, \sigma^2), \ldots)$. Because in our work the statistical method is applied independently to each trace point (i.e. all discussed methods are univariate), we drop the superscript in the rest of this paper.

Remark 1. Side channel observations are noisy: $\mathcal{N}(0, \sigma^2)$ is independent of the device leakage function $L_D(P, K)^j$, and we assume that observations follow a multivariate normal distribution in expectation — this assumption also underpins TVLA, Gaussian templates, linear regression analysis, etc. Despite widely used in the side-channel community, there are a few techniques that do not require this assumption, e.g. χ^2 [9] or DL-LA [6].

Pre-processing. The statistical procedures that we refer to are all univariate. By the virtue of countermeasures based on secret sharing, a single step during the computation may not leak directly on any K_s. In this case, trace points must be combined via [3,10] in an extra step to enable the application of univariate methods; also TVLA requires this extra step.

2.4 Side Channel Attacks (evaluation Context)

Previous work [11] proposes a "Detect-Map-Exploit" framework for evaluations, in which the first step is to identify "leaking trace points" with minimal assumptions. Thereafter one attempts to map these trace points to key-dependent intermediate steps (of the cryptographic algorithm), and with this knowledge the evaluator extracts and processes information (aka performs a side channel attack) from the side channel observations (with or without characterising the observations). Our method neatly fits this proposal.

The last step of the proposed evaluation framework, which is the information extraction, is based on making a statistical inference. The inference is based on relating model-based predictions and side channel observations, and a large number of strategies for this step can be found in the academic literature. We mention two common types of models. If a "standard power model" is known to be suitable for a device (e.g. the Hamming weight of a value often is a good predictor for side channel observations stemming from bus transfers in a microcontroller), then an effective method is to estimate the Pearson correlation between a set of side channel observations, and a set of (key-dependent) Hamming weight predictions. Normalised correlation estimates are then interpreted as an *a posteriori* distribution for the key (chunk). If a "standard power model" is not suitable, then an evaluator must characterise the statistical distribution of the side channel observations in order to build *a model.*

---

[3] Note that this "state" is often **not** some known state defined by the cipher's specification. In practice, various micro-architectural effects exist that make exhaustively (specific) testing on all leaking states impossibly difficult.

Model Based Attacks (template Attacks). Using a model L as a classifier for the side channel observations $\mathbf{t}$ enables to construct so called template attacks [12].

1. The **non-specific way of model building** requires the least information about the cryptographic module. It works by estimating models L for tuples of chunks of the input and key: e.g. if both the input (P) and key (K) can be divided into 2 chunks$((P_1, P_2)$ and $(K_1, K_2))$, the overall model can always be written as $L(P_1, K_1, P_2, K_2)$, where the estimating complexity (i.e. the number of all possible models) would be $|P_1| \cdot |P_2| \cdot |K_1| \cdot |K_2|$.
2. The **specific way of model building** is to include some *a priori* knowledge about the cryptographic algorithm and estimate models for an intermediate X defined by a function F, e.g. if $X = F(P_1, P_2, K_1, K_2)$, then we build models $F(Y)$, resulting in $|im(F)|$ models. Most typical attacks, e.g. attacking the AES Sbox output, follow this strategy. Note that leakage can only be captured if it truly relies on F: otherwise it will be simply discarded, even in a trivial template attack [13].
3. The **specific way of estimating model coefficients** is to even include some knowledge about the device leakage model, e.g. restricting the degree of the regression model (or the number of classes). This further reduces the number of distinct models, which leads to more efficient model building.

With a set of models the evaluator then computes the conditional probabilities $\Pr[\{\mathbf{K_i}\}|\mathbf{t}]$ (by ensuring that the cryptographic module operates on the same inputs as the learned models, and by exhaustively guessing K_i in the learned models)[4], thereby assigning each key value an *a posteriori* probability. There are many ways of estimating models, ranging from parametric Gaussian models [12], over machine learning models [15], to deep nets [16].

2.5   Regression Modelling

Let X be an n-bit discrete variable. In the following X may represent an intermediate step in the computation, or the encryption input and output, or the key. Given a set of side channel observations, we can estimate the distribution of any trace point given X. This is because any real valued function of X can be written as $L(X) = \sum_j \beta_j u_j(X)$. In this expression, the variables $u_j(X)$ are called the *explanatory variables*. They are monomials of the form $\prod_{i=0}^{n-1} x_i^{j_i}$, whereby x_i denotes the i-th bit of x and j_i denotes the i-th bit of j. The monomial with the most number of terms defines the *degree* of the model. Evaluating the regression equation at $X = x$ gives the model prediction for x. The goal of leakage modelling is to determine a function L that is "close" to the (unknown) device leakage L_D.

---

[4] A recent and comprehensive analysis of classifiers of this nature is given in [14].

Model Estimation. Estimating a regression model requires estimating the (linear) coefficients $\vec{\beta}$. The estimated model that describes the distribution of the side channel observations in dependence of X is now expressed as $\hat{L}(X) = \sum_j \hat{\beta}_j u_j(X)$ (and we evaluate it by setting $X = x$). Evidently, without any restriction on u_j, there are exactly 2^n parameters to estimate in the regression equation. A model that includes all 2^n terms is called a *full model*. However, we could also only allow certain u_j (e.g. linear terms where $HW(j) = 1$ [17,18]). This leads to the question of how to compare models in terms of their quality?

Nested Models. A special case for model comparison, that is of particular interest to us, is the case of models that are *nested*. A *restricted* model is said to be *nested* within a *full* model if it only contains a subset of the explanatory variables of the full model.

Toy example. Suppose a target state X contains 2 bits $X = (X_0 \| X_1)$. Then the full model is given by $L_f(X) = \beta_0 + \beta_1 X_0 + \beta_2 X_1 + \beta_3 X_0 X_1$ (we note that the degree of $L_f(X)$ is two). We can define a restricted model (of degree one) $L_r(X \setminus \{X_1\}) = \beta_0 + \beta_1 X_0$ (where β_2 and β_3 are restricted to be 0). Then L_f and L_r are called nested models (i.e. L_r is "nested inside" L_f).

Collapsing Variables. In many real world regression problems, variables are drawn from large sample spaces, which makes the model building computationally infeasible. The concept of collapsibility, see [19], is about restricting the included explanatory variables to a smaller space, without negatively impacting on the model building. The concept of collapsing was recently used in the side channel setting as well, see [13], and we will use this trick also in our work.

The function $Coll(X) : 2^m \to 2^n$ restricts an m-bit variable X to an n-bit space. For instance, if $X \in \{0, \ldots, 255\}$ then a collapse function that maps it to a single bit can be defined as $X \to 0$: if $X_0 = 0$, and $X \to 255$: if $X_0 = 1$. Thus the corresponding collapsed model only needs to fit two coefficients β_0 and β_1. Obviously a model that is based on collapsed input variables has a poorer predictive quality than the same model over the full input range. But in our work, we do not use models as predictors but as decision making tool about input dependency. Thus, as long as a collapse mapping preserves some input dependence, our method works.

Comparing Nested Models. Given two nested estimated models, the F-test is the suitable solution for comparison [20]. Specifically, with N measurements, if we are aiming to compare a *full* model $L_f(X) = \sum_j \beta_j u_j(X)$, $j \in J_f$ and a *restricted* model $L_r(X) = \sum_j \beta_j u_j(X)$, $j \in J_r \subset J_f$, we can construct the following hypothesis test:

- H_0: $\{u_j | j \in J_f \setminus J_r\}$ have coefficients 0 in $L_f(X)$
- H_1: $\{u_j | j \in J_f \setminus J_r\}$ have non-zero coefficients in $L_f(X)$

Informally, if the test above rejects H_0, we can conclude the missing explanatory variables have a significant contribution. Denote $z_r = \#\{J_r\}$, $z_f = \#\{J_f\}$ and the number of available measurements as N, we compute the F-statistic as

$$F = \frac{\frac{RSS_r - RSS_f}{z_f - z_r}}{\frac{RSS_f}{N - z_f}}.$$

where the *residual sum of squares* (RSS) is defined as

$$RSS = \sum_{i=1}^{N} (t_{(i)} - \hat{L}(x_{(i)}))^2$$

where $t_{(i)}/x_{(i)}$ represents the i-th observation/state.
The resulting value F follows the F distribution with $(z_f - z_r, N - z_f)$ degrees of freedom. A p-value below a statistically motivated threshold rejects the null hypothesis (i.e. the two models are equivalent) and hence suggests that at least one of the removed variables is potentially useful. Throughout this paper, we always convert the F-statistic to the corresponding p-value, then rejects the null hypothesis if the p-value is lower than the significance level α (i.e. the false positive rate). Equivalently, one can also compute a threshold for F from the null distribution and α (e.g. the 4.5 threshold in TVLA [3]), although such threshold varies alongside the degrees of freedom (i.e. the number of traces N).

Remark 2. In our work we will be often building models for collapsed input variables. An inappropriate collapse mapping can be recognised when a full model is compared with restricted models, because the individual test on the full model already fails to find any dependency. If input dependency has been reported by other techniques (e.g. TVLA), users should change the collapsing setup.

Statistical Power of Nested F-Test. The confidence in test outcomes is reflected in the percentage of false positives α (i.e. how often does the test indicate leakage although there is none) and the percentage of false negatives β_p[5] (i.e. how often does the test indicate no leakage although there is leakage).
   The parameters in any statistical test interact with each other, thus the α, the $1 - \beta_p$, the difference between the two statistical hypothesis (aka the effect size f^2), and the number of observations N, need to be considered jointly. Luckily, the F-test statistic is well understood, and there are explicit formulae for the α and β_p [20]. With these it is possible to set the decision threshold F_t for rejecting the null hypothesis:

$$F_t = Q_F(df_1, df_2, 1 - \alpha),$$

---

[5] Unfortunately the same β has been used in both statistics and linear regression models; for clarity, we denote β_p as the false positive rate.

where Q_F is the quantile function of the central F distribution. Considering the tested full model contains z_f estimated parameters, while the null model L_0 contains only one parameter, these two degrees of freedom are defined as:

$$df_1 = z_f - 1, df_2 = N - z_f.$$

The statistical power $1 - \beta_p$ can be computed as

$$\beta_p = F_{nc}(F_t, df_1, df_2, \lambda),$$
$$\lambda = f^2 \cdot (df_1 + df_2 + 1),$$

where F_{nc} is the cumulative distribution function of the non-central F distribution.

3   Characterising Exploitability and Explainability in the Context of Leakage Detection

We wish to clarify the desirable goals of a leakage assessment framework, by formalising notions such as "leakage", "exploitable", and "explainable".

3.1   Defining Leakage

The term "leakage" is often overloaded in the side channel literature. Having "leakage" can refer to having access to side channel observations, or it can refer to the assertion that some observation contains information about a secret value. We now provide a definition of the term "leakage" that we will use in this paper.

In the context of side channel evaluations we wish to determine if a cryptographic module's observable side channel (power, timing, EM) contains information about the secret cryptographic key, potentially enabling a key recovery attack. We consequently understand the term "leakage" as the presence of some key dependent behaviour in side channel observations. Because we only wish to consider "efficient adversaries" in concrete security evaluations, we say there is "key leakage" if we can efficiently[6] detect key dependency in a (finite) set of side channel observations.

Definition 1 (Key Leakage).
We assume that the evaluator has access to a finite set of side channel observations $\{t\}$, *which is obtained from a cryptographic module that performs some action with a secret value* K. *We set up the two hypotheses:*
   H_0: *there is no dependency between* $\{t\}$ *and* K.
   H_1: *there is some dependency between* $\{t\}$ *and* K.
   We say that there is ***key leakage*** *if there exists an efficient statistical test that can refute* H_0 *given* $\{t\}$.

---

[6] In practice, we expect "efficiency" to be determined by evaluation parameters, i.e. an given time/data budget.

The existence of key leakage does not yet imply that it is exploitable in a concrete attack: e.g. the key dependence could be only observable between very few keys (i.e. leakage-wise weak keys); or equivalently, the adversary has to make a too large key guess in the inference step.

Remark 3. "Key" represents the most typical side-channel key recoveries against block ciphers: for other cryptographic primitives or operation modes, depending on the context, one can expand this definition to other secret-related states.

3.2 Defining Exploitable Key Leakage

To utilise key dependency in a side channel key recovery attack, an efficient attack vector must exist. We explained before in Sect. 2 that an attack is based on making a statistical inference about the key distribution based on a set of side channel observations.

There are three factors that determine the computational complexity of an attack:

Trace complexity: In current evaluations, millions of measurements are required for hardware implementations (short traces), and tens of thousands of measurements must be obtained from software implementations.

Inference complexity: Often, the size of a key guess for a single inference is typically 8 bits, but attacks simultaneously guessing 32 bits have been reported [21].

Enumeration complexity: a side channel attack may not necessarily reveal the secret key, but it will deliver a (non-uniform) distribution for the key space, which enables to reveal the key given a plaintext-ciphertext pair. The best such effort reported in the open literature has managed to search through a key space of just under 2^{50} keys [22].

The ability to carry out the inference is **a necessary condition** for all side channel attacks. The inference step's complexity is determined by the trace and the inference complexity.

Thus, we define the property of being "exploitable" (in reference to key leakage) as the required effort to carry out the inference step.

Definition 2 (Exploitable key leakage). *Given a set of side channel observations $\{t\}$ from a cryptographic module that operates on K, we call key leakage to be* **b-exploitable** *if the complexity of the inference step in a concrete attack is bounded by $O(2^b)$.*

Remark 4. This definition for exploitable leakage implies that in the context of a specific evaluation regime the term "concrete attacks" has to be specified. For instance, in the practical examples that we will present later in this paper, we will use our method as a "replacement" for the current detection regime in ISO17825, which *only considers differential input attacks (e.g. typical DPA) at present.* Consequently, we will define **b-exploitable** in relation to DPA style attacks. Restricting attacks to DPA style attacks is perhaps a limitation of the current version of this standard, and our methodology works with it. Attacks that go beyond DPA style attacks include horizontal attacks [23], which always require knowledge of specific intermediate values. Depending on the application context, the most suitable list of specific intermediate values can be hard to find, due to restrictions on profiling (i.e. no access to random shares), hidden micro-architectural effects (i.e. software implementations) or complex hardware behaviour (e.g. all gate-level interaction within an Sbox). Thus discovering how to exploit a detected leak is still necessary, and once this has been achieved, it can potentially be incorporated into a more powerful attack vector.

3.3 Defining Explainable Key-Leakage Detection

The ultimate goal of an evaluator is to construct at least one practical attack vector. Thus we require a non-specific method that also delivers outcomes that can be "interpreted by the evaluator" so that they can derive a practical attack vector. This requirement links our research with the wider context of interpreting the outcomes of machine learning models, and a widely cited recent contribution by [24] discusses and analyses notions for "interpretable" methods such as

understandable: it is clear "what" the method achieves,
transparent: it is clear "how" the method works mathematically,
comprehensible: the output of the method can be understood by a human,
explainable: the method produces some form of evidence that enables a causal explanation for the subsequent decision making.

All notions but the last are clearly fulfilled when working with regression models assuming that evaluators have sound mathematical and computer science skills. The last notion of "explainability" requires more consideration. It challenges us to consider what is "evidence" and what is a "causal explanation". In our use case, the final goal is to produce outcomes/evidence that can be directly used to construct at least one key-recovery attack vector. If such an attack vector exists, then a device should fail an evaluation: the attack vector is the causal explanation that enables an evaluator to fail a device in an evaluation. We explained in Sect. 2.4 the concept of model-based attacks: the models are estimated based on (leaking) variables (depending on both key and plaintext bytes) in certain trace points.

Definition 3 (Explainable detection). *We call a leakage detection method* **explainable** *if it produces a list of leaking variables as evidence, alongside the associated trace points that exhibit exploitable key-leakage, both of which enable the construction of at least one concrete key-recovery attack vector.*

4 Detecting Key-Dependency via Non-specific Models

We are now ready to detail the mathematical basis for the novel approach that underpins our proposal for explainable leakage assessment. The main question is how should a non-specific detection test be configured to ensure that the found dependencies are also explainable (and therefore exploitable) without relying on some *a priori* specific intermediate states? The perhaps initially surprising answer, to this question, is to build and compare key-dependent nested models.

4.1 Detecting Key Leakage

Starting from our definition in Sect. 2, any observed leakage in leakage assessment is a function of the inputs P and the key K. To create key dependent models, we now fix the plaintext to be a constant, and thus consider a regression model for $L(K)$ (from now on we drop P as P is a constant).

Definition 4 (Key-dependent non-specific model). *Let K be an n-bit (full) secret key, we call the function*

$$L(K) = \sum_j \beta_j u_j(K), \ j \in J$$

a key-dependent non-specific leakage model for K.

If $|J| = |K| = 2^n$ (all terms of K are included, we have a degree 2^n model) then we call the corresponding model the full model, and denote this with the subscript f, i.e. $L_f(K)$ (we introduced these concepts already in Sect. 2). As the leakage function L in Sect. 3 is deterministic, with a fixed plaintext, one can easily verify that $L_f(K)$ expresses any possible key-dependent leakage. The naive model $L_0(K)$ is the model that only depends on the term β_0. The naive model is independent of the key. Leakage detection can then be framed as a hypothesis test that compares a full (i.e. "key leakage") and a restricted model ("no key leakage") using the F-test statistic (introduced in Sect. 2). If the naive model can explain the side channel observations as well as the full model, then clearly, because the naive model is completely independent of the key, there can be no information about the key in the side channel observations.

It is apparent that contemporary key sizes make building such a full model computationally infeasible, and thus we use the idea to "collapse" a full model to a smaller space whilst retaining some "salient" characteristics [13]. This is done by defining a suitable function *Coll* that maps every $j \in J$ to a $j_c \in J_c$, whereby $|J_c| << |J|$, $Coll(j) = j_c \in J_c$.

This leaves the question if working with a collapsed model is meaningful in the context of testing nested models. This question was already answered positively in [13]: if in a hypothesis test the null is rejected for a collapsed model, then it would also be rejected for the corresponding full model. Consequently we define a non-specific leakage detection test as follows.

Definition 5 (Model based Detection). *Let $L_{cf}(K) = \sum_j \beta_j u_j(K)$ denote the collapsed full model, and $L_0(K) = \beta_0$ denote the naive model (with $K \in [0, 2^n), j \in coll(J), \beta_j \in \mathbb{R}$ as before), and select a statistically motivated threshold th, together with a confidence level $0 < \alpha < 1 \in \mathbb{R}$, a statistical power*

$0 < 1 - \beta_p < 1 \in \mathbb{R}$, *an assumed effect size $f^2 \in \mathbb{R}$ and a finite set of $N \in \mathbb{N}$ side channel observations.*

The null hypothesis is defined to correspond to "no leakage", in the sense that $L_0(K)$ explains the side channel observations. The alternative hypothesis corresponds to "leakage" in the sense that $L_{cf}(K)$ is required to explain the side channel observations.

$H_0 : L_0(K) = L_{cf}(K)$, *the observations can be explained by the naive model*
$H_1 : L_0(K) \neq L_{cf}(K)$, *the observations cannot be explained by the naive model*

We reject H_0 if the F-test statistic is higher than the threshold th with confidence α, power $1 - \beta_p$ given the set of N side channel observations.

Definition 5 is the basis for our novel leakage assessment framework. It enables the detection of key dependencies in a set of side channel observations. We will refine this technique in the next section so that it satisfies the notions of exhibiting exploitable leakage, and we will embed it in an algorithm that identifies the leaking key chunks (i.e. an explainable method). Before this, we discuss important details pertaining the choice of statistical parameters and the collapsing function.

4.2 Concrete Parameter Selection in an Evaluation Setting

In the setting that is described in FIPS 140-3 (by reference to ISO17825), the security level defines the number of side channel observations that are available for leakage detection testing, e.g. $N = 10,000$ for FIPS Level 3 or $N = 100,000$ for FIPS Level 4. More traces, e.g. $N = 1,000,000$ for a higher level of security, would be aimed for in CC [1]. The effect size is typically unknown (unless some prior characterisation has taken place, which is not how the test is used in FIPS 140-3), and therefore an assumption must be made. Furthermore, when examining an implementation with a countermeasure such as masking, the traces must be processed prior to any statistical evaluation, by the so-called centred product combining technique [25] (multivariate case) or centred moment technique [10] (univariate case). This additional step does not change our discussion of the selection of the statistical parameters, it however reduces the expected effect size f^2. It is therefore very important to assume f^2 to be potentially small to capture many real world leaks.

Example 1 (Parameters for a byte-oriented implementation with 128 bit key length.). Assume that we set up a detection test for a key $K = |2^{128}| = K_1\|K_2\|\ldots\|K_{16}$. We set up the collapse function so that we represent each byte of the key with a single bit, thus the collapsed key space is of size 2^{16}. In our test we compare the collapsed full model and the null model, where $df_1 = 2^{16} - 1$ and $df_2 = N - 2^{16}$. For a small effect size $f^2 = 0.2$ [20] with $N = 655360$, $\alpha = 10^{-6}$, we have $1 - \beta_p \approx 1$, which implies that test with this configuration is very powerful [7].

5   A Novel Leakage Assessment Framework

The novel model-based leakage detection test that we formalised in Definition 5 is able to detect key leakage (as defined in Definition 1). In this section, we explain how the repeated use of model-based detection enables to determine if identified key leakage is exploitable in differential attacks, and we provide an algorithm for explainable detection by a structured manipulation of the model configuration. For easier comprehension, we provide toy examples after each step: these examples come from an eye-to-eye adoption of our proposal in a Boolean masked AES implementation. Interested readers can find more details in the full version on eprint.

5.1   Detecting Exploitable Leakage

Model-based leakage detection reveals key dependent trace points by comparing a full model (i.e. a model that incorporates the entire key) and a naive model. It is likely though that an identified trace point does not depend on the entire key, but just a part of it. We can change the restricted model in Definition 5 from the naive model to some richer (but still restricted) model to determine how much key information is required to detect a trace point as leaky. More specifically, we can parametrise the restricted models to include terms of degree at most d. Recall that the degree d is the number of terms in the largest monomial of the model, whereby the terms represent the key chunks. Thus, the degree d gives an upper bound for relevant key chunks in the inference step of a differential attack.

We configure the test defined in Definition 5 using L_{cf} and a $L_{cr,d}$ by fixing a d (the test is repeated multiple times for different values of d). If a degree-d restricted model $L_{cr,d}$ is "as good as" the full model L_{cf}, then the side channel observations can potentially be exploited in a divide-and-conquer attack using no more than $|K_i|^d$ bits of the key. With this we immediately have the following corollary.

Corollary 1. *Let H_0 represents the hypothesis where the restricted degree-d model $L_{cr,d}(K)$ can explain the leakage, whereas H_1 stands for the leakage can only be fully explained by the full model $L_{cf}(K)$. With a suitable collapse function $coll(J)$ and*

$$L_{cr,d}(K) = \sum_j \beta_j u_j(K); \ j \in coll(J), deg(u_j(K)) \leq d),$$

$$L_{cf}(K) = \sum_j \beta_j u_j(K); \ j \in coll(J)).$$

We can perform a model based detection per Definition 5. If H_0 is not rejected, and $2d \log |K_0| \leq b$, then the identified key leakage is b-exploitable.

Proof. If the restricted model of degree d is not rejected, then we know that a combination of at most d key chunks suffices to describe the leakage. Recall

---

Algorithm 1. Exploitable leakage detection: identify leakage degree

---

Require: $K = K_0 || K_1 || \ldots || K_{s-1}$, coll(J), $\{t\}$, d_m
1: Test $L_{cf}(K)$ vs. $L_0(K)$
2: **if** Not Reject **then**   ▷ Check if key dependent
3:     **return** "not a leak"
4: **else**   ▷ $L_{cf}(K)$ represents key leakage
5:     **for** $i = d_m$ to 1 **do**
6:         Test $L_{\{cf,i\}}(K)$ vs. $L_{cf}(K)$
7:             **if** Reject **then return** $d = i + 1$ ▷ Return degree d
8:         **end if**
9:     **end for**
10:     **return** $d = 1$
11: **end if**

---

that we assume that all chunks of the input and keys are of equal size, thus $|K_0| = |K_1| = |P_0| = \ldots$. We can set up a non-specific model-based attack: we can build models for tuples of the form $((P_0, K_0), (P_1, K_1), \ldots, (P_{d-1}, K_{d-1}))$ for the inference step. The computational cost for building these tuples is $|K_0|^{2d}$. The computational cost for using the tuples in the inference step is $|K_0|^d$. Thus the overall computational cost is bounded by $O(|K_0|^{2d}) = O(2^{2d \log |K_0|})$. If $2d \log |K_0| \leq b$, then the identified leakage is b-exploitable.

A repeated application of Corollary 1 leads to Algorithm 1, which finds the model of the lowest degree that is not rejected. It does so by working down from a given maximum degree d_m (determined by the evaluator's time/data budget), and checking for each lower degree if or not the respective restricted model is rejected. As soon as it finds a restricted model that is rejected, it returns the degree of the previous model.

Example 2. Assume that a cryptographic module implements a byte-wise implementation of AES-128. The evaluator "collapses" each key byte to 1 bit. As $d_m \leq s = 16$, $H_0 : L_{cf}(K)$ contains 2^{16} terms. If $H_1 : L_{cr,2}(K)$ is not rejected, then at most two bytes of the key suffice to exploit the leakage. Therefore the complexity of a divide-and-conquer attack is upper-bounded by $O(2^{4 \times 8})$.

5.2   An Explainable Detection Method

We now explain an algorithm that determines *which* key chunks are contributing to the detected leakage. We do this by narrowing down our model via placing further constraints on the restricted model. More precisely, we simultaneously restrict the degree and exclude specific terms. Algorithm 2 provides a generic description for identifying specific exploitable key chunks. It consists of two steps.

The first step is carried out in the first for loop, which removes a single chunk K_i from the key, and then checks if the corresponding restricted model is rejected. If not, then the key chunk is not important for the side channel

---

Algorithm 2. Subkey identification

Require: $K = K_0||K_1|| \ldots ||K_{s-1}$, coll(J), $\{t\}$, d
Ensure: The jointly leaking group represented by j (i.e. $\{K_i|j_i = 1\}$)
1: **for** $i = 0$ to $s - 1$ **do**   ▷ Check for not contributing subkeys
2:     $K' = K - \{K_i\}$
3:     Test $L(K')$ vs. $L(K)$
4:     **if** Not Reject **then**
5:         $K = K'$
6:     **end if**
7: **end for**
8: $l = |K|$
9: $J = [0, 1, ..., 2^l - 1]$, $J' = \emptyset$
10: Sort J with the ascending order of the Hamming Weight of $j \in J$
11: Delete any j from J if $HW(j) > d$ ▷ Restrict order to d
12: **while** J is not empty **do**
13:     $j = J[0]$, construct $u_j(K)$
14:     Test $L(u_j(K))$ vs. L_0
15:     **if** Not Reject **then**
16:         Delete j from J
17:     **else**
18:         Add j to J' ▷ $u_j(K)$ leaks
19:     **end if**
20: **end while**
21: **return** J'

---

observations, thus removed from the key. As a result of this first step, we now have a new key set K', which only consists of key chunks that are known to be relevant[7].

The second step is carried out in the while loop and it extracts each individual term from the remaining terms of K that has degree smaller than d (which is provided by Algorithm 1) and it checks whether it individually explains the side channel observations better than the naive model. If so, then an attack can be constructed based on this individual term, and the term is returned.

Example 3. Following our previous example, with the side-channel observations **t** and $d = 2$, we run the first loop (lines 1–7) in Algorithm 2. Starting from the first key byte K_0, line 3 tests if the restricted model with $K' = K_1||...||K_{15}$ (2^{15} terms) can pass the F-test comparing with the full model $L_f(K)$ (2^{16} terms). If so, K_0 can be discarded, as it does not contribute to the observed leakage. At the end of the loop, we have deleted all K_4 to K_{15}, which leaves $l = 4$ in line 8.

In theory, the observed leakage can be expressed by a function of the left 16 terms. However, since we already know the leakage only contains interaction from at most 2 key bytes, the relevant terms now are (sorted from 1 key bytes

---

[7] Recall that we apply this process independently to all trace points. Consequently, we expect that different trace points will lead to different models because different trace points correspond to different intermediate steps.

to 2 bytes, i.e. the Hamming weight of j from 1 to 2):

$$\{K_0, K_1, K_2, K_3, K_0K_1, K_0K_2, K_0K_3, K_1K_2, K_1K_3, K_2K_3\}.$$

Lines 12-18 search through this list and reports the terms that leak.

5.3   A Framework for Detection

Definition 5, Corollary 1, and Algorithm 1 and 2 are all based on the same conceptual idea of testing/comparing key-dependent models, but with increasing levels of sophistication and effort.

Definition 5 enables to test for "any" key dependency. As such it can be used as a replacement of the detection method in TVLA/ISO 17825. The computational effort for the model-based detection is comparable with that of TVLA/ISO 17825. But the application of Corollary 1 within Algorithm 1 and 2 leads to a framework that is *qualitatively* different to what any existing non-specific detection method can achieve. We are in a position to argue which of the potential leakage points are b-exploitable, and how they can be exploited.

Thus when executed in sequence, we have a framework that enables to efficiently gather increasingly sophisticated evidence regarding the behaviour of a cryptographic module: all together our methods provide a framework for the full leakage assessment of a cryptographic module. In the next sections we apply this framework to two practical examples of (open source) masked implementations.

6   Application: A Masked 32-Bit ASCON Implementation

Dietrich, Dobraunig and Mendel et al. provide a masked ASCON software implementation that "can be used as a starting point to generate device specific C/ASM implementations"[8]. Although the target platform is an ARM Cortex-M4 core (STM32F4) on ChipWhisperer CW308, the used assembly instructions are also supported by our platform[9]. We work on an ARM M3 core (NXP LPC 1313) which is running at 12 MHz. The trace set is recorded by a Picoscope 2205A running at 25 MSa/s, contains 8000 samples that covering the initial permutation (i.e. $p^a(IV||K||N)$). The authors provide a two share and a three share implementation, and they remark that for the two share implementation, extra "clearing" instructions (*MOV rd, #0*) are necessary to remove leaks that are found by TVLA.

---

[8] https://github.com/ascon/simpleserial-ascon.

[9] The authors provided various compile macros within their masked ASCON software implementation. One important option is whether the "bit-interleave" trick is applied (aka "ASCON_EXTERN_BI"). Our experiments in this section is captured when "ASCON_EXTERN_BI" is set. Note that this is not the default version: our experiments on the default version shows the same leakage can be found in a latter time point, yet related to a few different key bits (caused by the bit-interleave trick). More details can be found in the full version on eprint [26].

6.1   Leakage Detection, and Why to Dig Deep

We ported their implementation to our device, and run TVLA (with a fixed key, and fixed as well as varying plaintexts and nonce values) on their implementation without using clearing instructions. Figure 1 (left panel) shows that without the clearing instruction, TVLA reports leaks at the beginning of the encryption process (which is consistent with the authors' experiment).

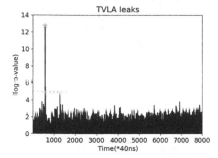 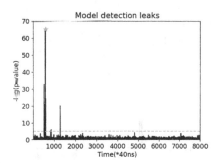

Fig. 1. TVLA vs. Model-based detection

Recall that TVLA in its' fixed-versus-random input (= varying plaintext and nonce, fixed key) setting is prone to finding plaintext-only leaks at the start of encryption processes. In the case of ASCON, the encryption starts by applying the p^a permutation to the concatenation of a (fixed) IV value, the secret key K, and the nonce N: $IV\|K\|N$. Thus, purely based on the TVLA outcome, and knowing that TVLA picks up also leakage that does not depend on the key, it would be tempting to conclude that the identified leak is an artefact that relates just the leakage of the nonce N (indeed strictly following the TVLA document, the initial $1/3$ points could be disregarded [3,4]).

We now configure our model-based detection: ASCON is based on 64-bit words, and the implementation is based on 128-bit plaintext and key. Thus we choose to collapse the two 64-bit key words into single bits, and we fix all other inputs to some constant. As a consequence, our model-based key-leakage detection achieves high statistical power with only 20k traces. Figure 1 (right panel) shows our detection finds the same leak as TVLA (the red aster), while reporting a few extra leaks at beginning of the encryption.

The outcome of the model-based detection implies that the TVLA results are not due to N alone. We can now be certain that there is key leakage. This result creates the non-trivial challenge of finding an attack vector, which we can do elegantly leveraging our novel framework.

6.2   Assessing Key Leakage: Degree Analyses

We focus on the highest leaking point (indicated in red) in Fig. 1. Following our framework, the next step is to analyse the degree of the leakage in this point.

Because there are two 64-bit key words in our collapsed model, the degree of the largest monomial in our initial model is two. Figure 2 shows the degree for all trace points. The degree of the most leaky point is in fact one, which implies that this point should lead to an attack where only one of the key words is involved.

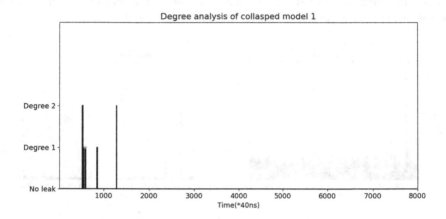

Fig. 2. Degree analysis with Collapsed model 1 (aka output from Algorithm 1)

We next use Algorithm 2 to identify which 64-bit key word contributes to the leakage in the selected point. Within each experiment, we set $\alpha = 0.01$ and reject any $-log_{10}(p - value) > 2$ (i.e. observed key dependency). As we can see in Table 1, the leakage depends on only the first collapsed key word K_0, i.e. the first 64 bit within the secret key. This key word becomes the basis for our subsequent analysis.

Table 1. Leaking key words from Algorithm 2 (masked Ascon, $d = 1$)

Key word	$-log_{10}(\text{p} - \text{value})$
K_0	66.62
K_1	1.67

6.3   Fine-Grained Analysis

Although our analysis above finds useful information, attacking a 64-bit word remains challenging in most realistic contexts. In the following, we iterate our analysis in Sect. 5 with various collapsing setups, in order to gain more fine-grained understanding of the detected leakage.

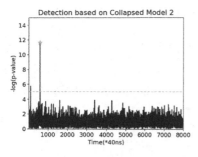 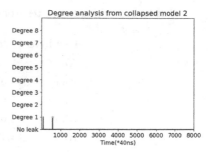

Fig. 3. Degree analysis (byte level)

Identifying the Leakage Source Within the First 64-Bit Word. Within the first 64-bit word, we further refine our analysis with a more fine-grained model. Although we know ASCON is not a byte-wise cipher, we still use a byte-wise collapsing strategy to determine if interactions between small chunks of a key word are involved in the observed leakage. The choice of byte-wise collapsing is not the only possible next step: we could also collapse to 16-bit chunks, or to 32-bit chunks, or to 4-bit chunks. Our choice is simply a trade-off between the profiling effort and the type of model that we can build.

The collapsing strategy implies that the key word K_0 can take 2^8 different values, and the key word K_1 is set to zero. As a consequence, we can stick with the parameters for configuring the test that we derived in the previous examples, and proceed with a data set containing only 20k traces. We re-run the initial detection (and identify once more the same leaky point as before, see the left panel of Fig. 3), and we also re-run the degree analysis. This time, because we represent our key word as eight bytes, the degree of the largest possible monomial is eight. Figure 3 shows the result of the degree analysis: our target point has degree $d = 1$. This means that the leakage in this point does not depend on the interaction between key bytes; key bytes contribute independently to the leakage. This information enables us to conclude that we have b-exploitable leakage for a very realistic values of b.

We run Algorithm 2 once more, which leads to Table 2. Clearly, in Table 2, the lower four bytes significantly contribute to the leakage (they lead to p-values lower than $\alpha = 0.01$). This fits neatly to the 32-bit architecture of the processor.

Identifying the Leakage Source Within the First Byte. We now refine the model further in order to determine how a single byte of the key contributes exactly to the leakage. We pick the first key byte for the analysis: we do not collapse this byte, but allow all possible values to occur; we fix all other inputs to zero, and collect another trace set. Because we do not use any collapsing on the first byte, we now need a larger trace set (200k traces, adapting the analysis in Sect. 4.2). We confirm that the leakage is still detected (first step of the framework), and we perform the degree analysis for the bit level model. It shows that the degree is still one, which implies that the key bits are contributing

Table 2. Leaking key bytes from Algorithm 2 (masked ASCON)

Key bytes	$-log_{10}(\text{p} - \text{value})$
$K_{0,0}$	3.82
$K_{0,1}$	4.67
$K_{0,2}$	4.97
$K_{0,3}$	4.62
$K_{0,4}$	1.12
$K_{0,5}$	0.76
$K_{0,6}$	0.61
$K_{0,7}$	0.48

independently to the leakage. We only show the output of Algorithm 2 in Table 3, which shows that the lowest key bits have the higher contributions. This gives us enough to construct a concrete attack vector.

Table 3. Leaking key bits from Algorithm 2 (masked ASCON)

Key bits	$-log_{10}(\text{p} - \text{value})$
k_0	3.16
k_1	5.71
k_2	2.23
k_3	1.23
k_4	0.81
k_5	1.77
k_6	1.97
k_7	1.70

6.4   Constructing a Concrete Attack Vector

We wish to demonstrate a differential attack (DPA style), and thus we need to confirm that the key also interacts with the nonce (the nonce provides the differential input). Following our previous discussion, our goal is now to find out if the lowest four key bits interact with any part of the nonce. Mindful of space, we cut to the chase: we collapse the lowest 4-bit chunk of the key to a single bit, and set the remaining key to zero. We consider the nonce to consist of 4-bit chunks and collapse each chunk in the first nonce word to a single bit, and set the second nonce word to zero.

We perform key-leakage detection (which is successful in the same point as before), re-run the degree analysis, and then we perform Algorithm 2 to find out how key and nonce contribute to the leakage. Table 4 shows that the joint leakage between nonce and key leads to considerably higher test results than just the key itself. The fact that there is joint leakage between (a small part of) the nonce and (a small part of) the key enables the construction of a differential attack, with a very small inference complexity.

Table 4. Significant key and nonce interactions as determined by Algorithm 2 (masked ASCON)

(key, nonce)	$-log_{10}(p-value)$
$K_{0,0..3}$	6.35
$(K_{0,0..3}, N_{0,0..3})$	15.76
$(K_{0,0..3}, N_{0,4..7})$	10.72
$(K_{0,0..3}, N_{0,8..11})$	10.08
$(K_{0,0..3}, N_{0,12..15})$	20.62
$(K_{0,0..3}, N_{0,20..23})$	26.64
$(K_{0,0..3}, N_{0,24..31})$	28.99

For the concrete attack we choose the pair $(K_{0,0..3}, N_{0,0..3})$ as our attack target (other choices are possible). Thus we assume the attacker attempts to recover the lowest four key bits, using the fact that the adversary has knowledge of the nonce values. The attacker thus builds non-specific templates for all values of $(K_{0,0..3}, N_{0,0..3})$ (thus there are 256 templates that need to be built; the time point for profiling is known from the leakage detection step). In the attack, the adversary does a standard template-based attack to recover the lowest four key bits. Figure 4 shows how the rank of the correct key decreases as the number of attack traces increases. The correct key guess can be found within 600k attack traces (600k traces were used for training).

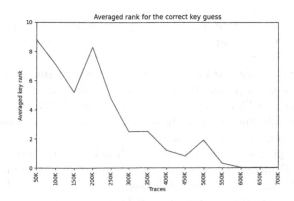

Fig. 4. Evolution of the key rank for attack on ASCON

Remark 5. We attempted a range of "natural attack vectors" arising directly from the algorithmic description and the Assembly code: targeting e.g. intermediate steps after the first round, but none of these targets lead to a successful attack. This is in fact consistent with the authors' patch: *MOV rd, #0* merely "clears" some micro-architecture, which suggests the leakage must arise from the micro-architecture.

7   Application: An Affine Masked 32-Bit AES Implementation

We now analyse the affine masking implementation from ANSSI [27]. We run this implementation on the same ARM M3 core (NXP LPC 1313). The target core is running at 12 MHz. The trace set is recorded by a Picoscope 2205A running at 100 MSa/s, and we directly focus on (a part of) the first round Sbox computations, which leads to about 1500 points per trace. We turn off shuffling in their implementation: shuffling only scales the effort of an attack, but it does not change the nature of the attack strategy. Confirming the analysis of ANSSI, we did not find any leak with 1st order TVLA on the raw traces (i.e. no 1st order univariate leak). This implies we must apply preprocessing on the trace set (see Sect. 2.3 for a brief reminder on preprocessing).

Remark 6. Our cryptographic module features a three stage pipeline. Consequently, each trace point in a side channel observation depends on three instructions which are simultaneously "in flight". The parallel nature of the processor implies that masked values and masks might be simultaneously computed on. Thus there could be key leakage due to parallel computations, and there could be key leakage due to sequential computations. We study both situations in turn using the canonical trace preprocessing functions, which are also used in TVLA.

7.1   Assessing Key Leakage Due to Parallelism

We preprocesses the traces by computing $t^{j'} = \left(t^j - \bar{t^j}\right)^2$ ($\bar{t^j}$ stands for the mean value of the observations at time j). Because the implementation is byte oriented, we use the same collapsing parameters and strategy as Sects. 4.2 and 5.

We initially perform a test for key leakage and identify multiple leaking points in the preprocessed trace set; the outcomes are akin to those obtained from TVLA. In contrast to TVLA, and its adoption in ISO17825, our framework now offers the ability to further analyse the identified points and ultimately construct (without undue overhead) an attack vector.

To do so we proceed as follows. For each point on the preprocessed trace, we adapt the full model from Definition 5 to find the maximum degree of the potential key leakage (we perform a leakage degree analysis). Figure 5 (upper half) shows that most leaking points have leakage degree two ($d = 2$). Because we represent the key as independent bytes, this analysis implies that the leakage

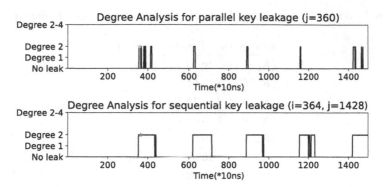

Fig. 5. Model degree analysis for affine masking (Color figure online)

Table 5. Leaking key pairs of bytes from Algorithm 2 (affine masking, parallel leakage)

Key bytes	$-log_{10}(\text{p} - \text{value})$
(K_0, K_1)	20.29
(K_0, K_2)	4.62
(K_1, K_2)	14.41
(K_0, K_3)	31.09
(K_1, K_3)	6.26
(K_2, K_3)	8.59

points depend on $d = 2$ key bytes. This implies that there is $32-$exploitable key leakage ($b = 32$) (remember that this is an upper bound, and we will reveal an attack vector with a lower complexity).

We further pick one of these points (index 360, red asterisk in Fig. 5) and run Algorithm 2 to identify the exact key byte combination, which leads to the outcomes in Table 5. As we are focusing on one single point, we simply set $\alpha = 0.01$ and reject any $-log_{10}(\text{p} - \text{value}) > 2$.

Table 5 shows that there are a number of good candidates. The pair that has the highest $-log(p - value)$ is the pair (K_0, K_3). This key pair leads to a concrete attack vector that has been reported in previous work [13], where the authors stated there is a collision attack on this particular implementation (left plot, Fig. 2 in [13]).

7.2   Assessing Key Leakage Due to Sequential Processing

The sequential processing of shares can be "undone" by creating joint distributions via the multiplication of trace points. The canonical preprocessing method is then based on computing $t'^r = \left(t^i - \bar{t^i}\right)\left(t^j - \bar{t^j}\right)$. We select the point at index ($j = 1428$) and run our leakage detection method to reveal key leakage for the entire trace (from $i = 0$ to $i = 1499$). The outcomes are akin to running TVLA,

Table 6. Leaking key pairs from Algorithm 2, sequential leakage of affine masking.

Key bytes	$-log_{10}(p-value)$
(K_0, K_4)	46.23
(K_1, K_4)	6.61
(K_2, K_4)	4.15
(K_3, K_4)	5.18
(K_0, K_5)	10.62
(K_0, K_6)	10.60
(K_0, K_7)	10.52

but we can proceed within our framework to determine a concrete attack vector. To do so, we determine the leakage degree for each of the (preprocessed) trace points.

Figure 5 (lower half) shows a combination of two key bytes suffices to describe most points on trace. This implies that the inference step is below $O(2^{32})$ bound, and thus we conclude that this is $32-$exploitable key leakage ($b = 32$).

We then select point 364 (blue asterisk in Fig. 5) as our target ($i = 364$), use Algorithm 2 to identify the key bytes that can describe the leakage, which leads to Table 6. Similar to the parallel case, we set $\alpha = 0.01$ here. The table shows that the key pair (K_0, K_4) is the best candidate for constructing a concrete attack vector. Like in the parallel case, this attack vector has been reported before in [13] (i.e. Section 4, Fig. 2).

8   Discussion

8.1   Applications to Other Types of Implementations

We provide two detailed application use cases for our technique, which show how to adapt the analysis to suit different ciphers and their resulting implementations. The two ciphers follow different construction principles and lead to different types of implementations even on the same platform. The AES cipher is byte-oriented and leads to a fully byte oriented implementation on our 32-bit platform. The ASCON cipher is word oriented, but the non-linear component is a 5-bit function. Thus some part of the ASCON cipher are mapped to the native 32-bit instructions of the processor, and some are implemented in a more bit wise fashion. These architectural differences have no impact on the principle of our analysis, they only guide the choices that we make to collapse the inputs in order to facilitate trace efficiency. The analysis of hardware implementations is akin to those of software implementations: the architecture of the implementation will guide analysis, and we expect that only the number of traces must increase. This will impact the effect size f^2 and thus the configuration of the test, we advice considering [7] to determine which (normalised) effect size to use.

Our work thus provides evidence that implementations of similar byte oriented ciphers, or ciphers based on permutations are compatible with our detection framework.

8.2   Importance of Explainability in Leakage Assessment

Although rarely prioritised in the academic literature, explainability plays a critical role in adopting evaluation schemes like FIPS 140-3/ISO 17825. For instance, any fixed-versus-random plaintext test will report trace points that depend only on the plaintext. But the plaintext contains no information about the secret key. Thus, both TVLA [3] and ISO 17825 [4] have an exemption clause: only the middle $\frac{1}{3}$ of the side-channel trace is considered. The hope is, the plaintext dependent leakage will vanish in the middle part of the trace. As a result all leaks in the beginning rounds will be excluded, even if they are potentially exploitable, as we demonstrate in our ASCON example.

Our approach does not need such an "exemption clause" because all detected leaks are key dependent and our framework produces evidence that enables to reason about exploitability and explainability.

We also wish to emphasise that other existing specific tests/attacks (e.g. NICV [28] or ρ [29]) are unlikely to find the leaks from our examples either. This is because we identify leaks that are based on combinations of key and plaintext that are likely due to the micro-architecture. They cannot be explained based on (architectural states) that arise from the algorithmic description itself, not even from an Assembly representation. Even worse, micro-architectural effects do not neatly carry over from one version of a micro-processor to another (not even for similar models from the same manufacturer, see [30]), and therefore an evaluator is unlikely to know which effects are present in advance. Our new framework is currently the only method to systematically and effectively identify such leaks.

8.3   Complexity of Our Approach

Data Complexity. The largest model to build is L_{cf}, which suggests the data complexity (i.e. the number of available traces) should be at least $O(2^s)$ (where s is the number of collapsed key chunks). Our analyses in Sect. 7 uses $2^{16}*10$ traces, which is around the same level of TVLA for hardware masking $N = 10^6$. Our analysis of ASCON is based on differently sized models, ranging from two to eight explanatory variables, all over a collapsed space, leading to trace requirements between 20k to 200k traces; which are clearly below what TVLA requires.

Time Complexity. The largest computational effort comes from the application of Corollary 1, where our analysis attempts to determine the degree d through comparing different regression models. Assuming N traces were recorded for an implementation with s collapsed key chunks, building a model with degree d takes $O(C^2N)$ elementary arithmetic operations $(C = \binom{s}{d})$.

In our AES experiments, we set $s = 16$ and $d = 4$, which gives $C = 1820$. This means the complexity for regression models is bounded by 2^{41}. If the underlying cipher has higher key size (e.g. AES-256) or smaller key chunks, one can always iteratively build more fine-grained models like our ASCON example in Sect. 6: as the regression models never exceed 256 terms ($s = 8$), the time complexity is around 2^{31}.

8.4 Extension to Other Model Building Methods and Inherently Multivariate Methods

Our work heavily uses existing statistical machinery for comparing nested regression models. The reason for this is that for such models an adequate comparison method exists: i.e. a formal statistical test exists, that can be correctly configured by an evaluator, so that the evaluator can derive the necessary number of side channel observation that they must gather. Such a comparison method currently only exists for nested regression models, and thus for now we must leave it as an open research question to extend our idea beyond nested regression models (e.g. machine learning or deep learning models). This implies that also the extension to inherently multivariate technique remains an open problem.

8.5 Optimal vs. Confirmatory Attack Vectors

Our method can reveal multiple attack vectors, with different data/time complexity. Since our primary goal is verifying a detected leak is exploitable in attacks, the "optimality" of the recovered attack vectors becomes out of our scope. However, once the attack vectors are known, it is possible to turn them into a more (trace) efficient attack. For instance, better profiling techniques can be incorporated into the very final step when an attack is carried out. It may also be possible to incorporate identified micro-architectural leakage into some horizontal attack vector. Both of these possibilities are interesting questions for further research.

Acknowledgments. Si Gao was funded in part by National Key R&D Program of China (No. 2022YFB3103800) and the ERC via the grant SEAL (Project Reference 725042). Elisabeth Oswald was funded in part by the ERC via the grant SEAL (Project Reference 725042).

References

1. Common Criteria: The Common Criteria for Information Technology Security Evaluation (2017). https://www.commoncriteriaportal.org/cc/
2. Information Technology Laboratory,NIST: Security Requirements for Cryptographic Modules. https://nvlpubs.nist.gov/nistpubs/FIPS/NIST.FIPS.140-3.pdf
3. Gilbert Goodwill, B.J., Jaffe, J., Rohatgi, P., et al.: A testing methodology for side-channel resistance validation. In: NIST Non-invasive Attack Testing Workshop. **7**, 115–136 (2011)
4. ISO/IEC: Testing methods for the mitigation of non-invasive attack classes against cryptographic modules (2016). https://www.iso.org/obp/ui/#iso:std:iso-iec:17825:ed-1:v1:en

5. Roy, D.B., Bhasin, S., Guilley, S., Heuser, A., Patranabis, S., Mukhopadhyay, D.: CC meets FIPS: a hybrid test methodology for first order side channel analysis. IEEE Trans. Comput. **68**(3), 347–361 (2019)
6. Moos, T., Wegener, F., Moradi, A.: DL-LA: deep learning leakage assessment. A modern roadmap for SCA evaluations. IACR Trans. Cryptogr. Hardw. Embed. Syst. **2021**(3) 552–598 (2021)
7. Whitnall, C., Oswald, E.: A critical analysis of ISO 17825 ('testing methods for the mitigation of non-invasive attack classes against cryptographic modules'). In: Advances in Cryptology - ASIACRYPT 2019 - 25th International Conference on the Theory and Application of Cryptology and Information Security, Kobe, Japan, 8-12 December 2019, Proceedings, Part III, pp. 256–284 (2019)
8. Yap, T., Benamira, A., Bhasin, S., Peyrin, T.: Peek into the black-box: interpretable neural network using SAT equations in side-channel analysis. IACR Trans. Cryptogr. Hardw. Embed. Syst. **2023**(2), 24–53 (2023)
9. Moradi, A., Richter, B., Schneider, T., Standaert, F.: Leakage detection with the x2-Test. IACR Trans. Cryptogr. Hardw. Embed. Syst. **2018**(1), 209–237 (2018)
10. Schneider, T., Moradi, A.: Leakage assessment methodology. In: Güneysu, T., Handschuh, H. (eds.) CHES 2015. LNCS, vol. 9293, pp. 495–513. Springer, Heidelberg (2015). https://doi.org/10.1007/978-3-662-48324-4_25
11. Azouaoui, M., et al.: A systematic appraisal of side channel evaluation strategies. In: van der Merwe, T., Mitchell, C., Mehrnezhad, M. (eds.) SSR 2020. LNCS, vol. 12529, pp. 46–66. Springer, Cham (2020). https://doi.org/10.1007/978-3-030-64357-7_3
12. Chari, S., Rao, J.R., Rohatgi, P.: Template attacks. In: Cryptographic Hardware and Embedded Systems - CHES 2002, 4th International Workshop, Redwood Shores, CA, USA, August 13-15, 2002, Revised Papers, pp. 13–28 (2002)
13. Gao, S., Oswald, E.: A novel completeness test for leakage models and its application to side channel attacks and responsibly engineered simulators. In: Dunkelman, O., Dziembowski, S., eds.: Advances in Cryptology - EUROCRYPT 2022 - 41st Annual International Conference on the Theory and Applications of Cryptographic Techniques, Trondheim, Norway, May 30 - June 3, 2022, Proceedings, Part III, vol. 13277. LNCS, pp. 254–283. Springer, Cham (2022). https://doi.org/10.1007/978-3-031-07082-2_10
14. Picek, S., Heuser, A., Guilley, S.: Template attack versus Bayes classifier. J. Cryptogr. Eng. **7**(4), 343–351 (2017)
15. Picek, S., et al.: Side-channel analysis and machine learning: a practical perspective. In: 2017 International Joint Conference on Neural Networks, IJCNN 2017, Anchorage, AK, USA, May 14-19, 2017, pp. 4095–4102. IEEE (2017)
16. Prouff, E., Strullu, R., Benadjila, R., Cagli, E., Dumas, C.: Study of deep learning techniques for side-channel analysis and introduction to ASCAD database. IACR Cryptol. ePrint Arch. **53**, 1–45 (2018)
17. Doget, J., Prouff, E., Rivain, M., Standaert, F.: Univariate side channel attacks and leakage modeling. J. Cryptogr. Eng. **1**(2), 123–144 (2011)
18. Schindler, W., Lemke, K., Paar, C.: A stochastic model for differential side channel cryptanalysis. In: Rao, J.R., Sunar, B. (eds.) CHES 2005. LNCS, vol. 3659, pp. 30–46. Springer, Heidelberg (2005). https://doi.org/10.1007/11545262_3
19. Huitfeldt, A., Stensrud, M.J., Suzuki, E.: On the collapsibility of measures of effect in the counterfactual causal framework. Emerg. Themes Epidemiol. **16**(1), 1 (2019)
20. Cohen, J.: CHAPTER 9 - F tests of variance proportions in multiple regression/correlation analysis. In: Cohen, J., (ed.) Statistical Power Analysis for the Behavioral Sciences, pp. 407 – 453. Academic Press (1977)

21. Mather, L., Oswald, E., Whitnall, C.: Multi-target DPA attacks: pushing DPA beyond the limits of a desktop computer. In: Sarkar, P., Iwata, T. (eds.) ASIACRYPT 2014. LNCS, vol. 8873, pp. 243–261. Springer, Heidelberg (2014). https://doi.org/10.1007/978-3-662-45611-8_13
22. Longo, J., Martin, D.P., Mather, L., Oswald, E., Sach, B., Stam, M.: How low can you go? Using side-channel data to enhance brute-force key recovery. IACR Cryptol. ePrint Arch. 609 (2016)
23. Veyrat-Charvillon, N., Gérard, B., Standaert, F.-X.: Soft analytical side-channel attacks. In: Sarkar, P., Iwata, T. (eds.) ASIACRYPT 2014. LNCS, vol. 8873, pp. 282–296. Springer, Heidelberg (2014). https://doi.org/10.1007/978-3-662-45611-8_15
24. Arrieta, A.B., et al.: Explainable artificial intelligence (XAI): concepts, taxonomies, opportunities and challenges toward responsible AI. Inf. Fusion 58, 82–115 (2019)
25. Chari, Suresh, Jutla, Charanjit S.., Rao, Josyula R.., Rohatgi, Pankaj: Towards sound approaches to counteract power-analysis attacks. In: Wiener, Michael (ed.) CRYPTO 1999. LNCS, vol. 1666, pp. 398–412. Springer, Heidelberg (1999). https://doi.org/10.1007/3-540-48405-1_26
26. Gao, S., Oswald, E.: A novel framework for explainable leakage assessment. Cryptology ePrint Archive, Paper 2022/182 (2022). https://eprint.iacr.org/2022/182
27. Benadjila, R., Khati, L., Prouff, E., Thillard, A.: Hardened Library for AES-128 encryption/decryption on ARM Cortex M4 Achitecture. https://github.com/ANSSI-FR/SecAESSTM32
28. Bhasin, S., Danger, J., Guilley, S., Najm, Z.: Side-channel leakage and trace compression using normalized inter-class variance. In: Lee, R.B., Shi, W. (eds.) HASP 2014, Hardware and Architectural Support for Security and Privacy, Minneapolis, MN, USA, June 15, 2014, pp. 7:1–7:9. ACM (2014)
29. Durvaux, François, Standaert, François-Xavier.: From improved leakage detection to the detection of points of interests in leakage traces. In: Fischlin, Marc, Coron, Jean-Sébastien. (eds.) EUROCRYPT 2016. LNCS, vol. 9665, pp. 240–262. Springer, Heidelberg (2016). https://doi.org/10.1007/978-3-662-49890-3_10
30. Marshall, B., Page, D., Webb, J.: MIRACLE: micro-architectural leakage evaluation. A study of micro-architectural power leakage across many devices. IACR Trans. Cryptogr. Hardw. Embed. Syst. 2022(1), 175–220 (2022)

Integrating Causality in Messaging Channels

Shan Chen[1]([✉]) and Marc Fischlin[2][ID]

[1] Southern University of Science and Technology, Shenzhen, China
chens3@sustech.edu.cn
[2] Cryptoplexity, Technische Universität Darmstadt, Darmstadt, Germany
marc.fischlin@tu-darmstadt.de
https://www.cryptoplexity.de

Abstract. Causal reasoning plays an important role in the comprehension of communication, but it has been elusive so far how causality should be properly preserved by instant messaging services. To the best of our knowledge, causality preservation is not even treated as a desired security property by most (if not all) existing secure messaging protocols like Signal. This is probably due to the intuition that causality seems already preserved when all received messages are intact and displayed according to their sending order. Our starting point is to notice that this intuition is wrong.

Until now, for messaging channels (where conversations take place), both the proper causality model and the provably secure constructions have been left open. Our work fills this gap, with the goal to facilitate the formal understanding of causality preservation in messaging.

First, we focus on the common two-user secure messaging channels and model the desired causality preservation property. We take the popular Signal protocol as an example and analyze the causality security of its cryptographic core (the double-ratchet mechanism). We show its inadequacy with a simple causality attack, then fix it such that the resulting Signal channel is causality-preserving, even in a strong sense that guarantees post-compromise security. Our fix is actually *generic*: it can be applied to any bidirectional channel to gain strong causality security.

Then, we model causality security for the so-called message franking channels. Such a channel additionally enables end users to report individual abusive messages to a server (e.g., the service provider), where this server relays the end-to-end-encrypted communication between users. Causality security in this setting further allows the server to retrieve the necessary causal dependencies of each reported message, essentially extending isolated reported messages to message flows. This has great security merit for dispute resolution, because a benign message may be deemed abusive when isolated from the context. As an example, we apply our model to analyze Facebook's message franking scheme. We show that a malicious user can easily trick Facebook (i.e., the server) to accuse an

---

Shan Chen is affiliated with both the Research Institute of Trustworthy Autonomous Systems and the Department of Computer Science and Engineering of SUSTech.

M. Joye and G. Leander (Eds.): EUROCRYPT 2024, LNCS 14653, pp. 251–282, 2024.
https://doi.org/10.1007/978-3-031-58734-4_9

innocent user. Then we fix this issue by amending the underlying message franking channel to preserve the desired causality.

Keywords: Causality · Secure messaging · Signal · Message franking

1   Introduction

Causality deals with the relationship of cause and effect. In computer systems causality preservation should ensure that events are processed in the right order. This is a long-standing topic in the area of distributed computing, e.g., Lamport's seminal work on logical clocks [23] and follow-up works on determining consistent global snapshots [8] and state recovery [34]. The ideas in these works, e.g., the ability to reconstruct the global state from local information, are still valid today.

Causality preservation has meanwhile also entered the area of cryptography. In particular, it was recently identified as a desired security property for secure instant messaging protocols, as discussed *informally* in [32,36]. However, there the goal of causality preservation is quite *weak*: "implementations can avoid displaying a message before messages that causally precede it" [36]. This may seem correct at first glance as it borrows the same intuition from distributed computing for ordering events, but a closer look shows that such a guarantee is actually not sufficient for secure messaging (SM). The reason is that message dependencies are much more subtle than event dependencies: the user's comprehension of a received message may be influenced by *any* messages displayed before it, even if some of them are causally *independent*. We illustrate this with a classic example below.

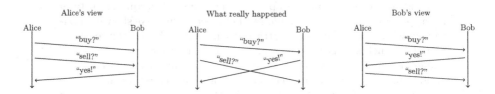

Fig. 1. Classic causality confusion example

As shown in Fig. 1, Alice asks Bob for investment advice using an instant messaging application. At first, Alice asks if she should buy a stock and Bob confirms, but Bob's response got delayed (e.g., due to network issues or attacks). From Alice's view, Bob remains silent, so Alice thinks he is currently offline. After a while, Alice tries to reach Bob again but this time she asks if she should sell the stock. Then, Alice receives Bob's response and mistakenly sells her stock.

It is worth noting that in the above example all messages are delivered and displayed in the correct order, so the causality confusion is *not* caused by out-of-order message display. The reason is that the message order cannot represent the exact causal relations of the real communication. In particular, the "yes!" response from Bob does not tell Alice which of her messages he replied to. One may then be tempted to address this issue with a "reply-to" feature provided by some instant messaging applications, however, Bob did not know that he had to "reply-to" the "buy?" message because his view was not ambiguous at all (i.e., only the "buy?" message was received before his response). Even if users are required to "reply-to" all messages, which significantly hampers usability, this feature usually cannot handle a response that depends on *multiple* messages.

Therefore, to resolve or mitigate causality confusion, it is better (or at least as a useful complement) to enable SM applications to extract the necessary causal information from their "channel-layer" protocols (through which users transmit application messages). This idea is formulated as a causality-preserving property in our model, which roughly captures an SM channel user's ability to locally reconstruct the global causal relations of the communication. Note that such security is against active man-in-the middle attacks, so it cannot be guaranteed by *unauthenticated* transport-layer protocols like TCP. Besides, our causality-preserving feature does not affect the *immediate decryption* property [1] usually required by SM channels. That is, when appended with the associated causal information, each received message can still be immediately decrypted upon receipt; meanwhile not only its sending order but also the exact message dependencies are reconstructed by the receiver.

Furthermore, compared to SM applications, it is probably more urgent and necessary to integrate causality in the so-called *message franking* schemes. Such a scheme additionally enables users to report abusive messages to the middle server who relays their end-to-end-encrypted communication. Clearly, the causal dependencies (i.e., the context) of an individually reported message is crucial for the server to determine if it is abusive.

For instance, a response to the question "what was the worst insult you have ever heard?" should be treated as benign, but it looks abusive when isolated from the context. A direct mitigation is to utilize timestamps that the server (e.g., Facebook) adds to each relayed message: the accused person can report the above question and argue that the seemingly abusive message is just a response to that question, as justified by their associated timestamps. However, this approach is not perfect, because timestamps reflect only the order of messages received by the server rather than the exact causal relations of the end-to-end conversation. For example, in Fig. 1 the server may still mistakenly view concurrent messages "sell?" "yes!" as sequential ones (i.e., as in either Alice's view or Bob's view). As another example, when Bob sends "my friend was insulted like this" followed by a message with abusive words, Alice can accuse Bob by reporting only the second message. Then, since in message franking only the message receiver (Alice) is allowed to report, the timestamp of the reported message does not help the server determine if Bob has ever sent a message right before the reported message.

In order to resolve causality issues in abuse reporting, one can enable the server to extract the entire (or necessary) context associated with the reported message. This is formulated as report causality preservation in our model.

1.1 Causality in Cryptographic Channels

Following previous work [1, 20], we treat (two-party) SM channels as *bidirectional* channels. In this work, we focus on their causality-preserving property.

In the cryptographic literature, channels were often defined as a *unidirectional* primitive where one party only sends messages and the other party only receives. For this simplified setting, the desired channel security is usually modeled with respect to a cryptographic primitive called stateful authenticated encryption. This primitive was proposed by Bellare *et al.* [5] and later adopted or refined by follow-up works [6, 21, 22, 27], mainly used to analyze the Transport Layer Security (TLS) record protocol. Recently, Marson and Poettering [26] initialized the formalization of bidirectional channels and their security, and showed how to securely combine two unidirectional channels to construct a bidirectional channel. Their results have later been extended to analyze multi-party broadcast channels [14], SM channels [20], and message-franking channels [19]. What all these approaches have in common is that they considered only channels on top of reliable networks (e.g., their constructions cease further functionality when a single message got lost). This however does not match the typical design of SM channels that could operate on *unreliable* networks, for which permanent message loss is possible. To tolerate message loss and meanwhile enable immediate decryption, Alwen *et al.* [1] extended the model for SM channels and applied it to analyze Signal's channel protocol, but they did not consider causality issues.

There were two formal analyses aiming to model causality for multi-party cryptographic channels [14, 25], but neither is satisfactory even for two parties. In particular, [25] defines causality as implied by ciphertext integrity, which should not be the case for a well-defined causality notion, e.g., Signal is proved to achieve ciphertext integrity [1] but causality confusions can still occur (e.g., the example in Fig. 1). The other work [14] focuses on a different object called broadcast channel, but their security notion captures only the aforementioned *weak* causality preservation goal (i.e., to avoid displaying a message before messages that causally precede it). Besides, *neither* work handles message loss or immediate decryption. Therefore, both the proper model of causality preservation for SM channels and the provably secure constructions remain open.

The other setting we consider for causality preservation is secure abuse reporting (also known as message franking). Here secure messaging is extended to enable users to report abusive messages to a server (e.g., the service provider), who relays their encrypted communication. Message franking was named and first introduced by Facebook's end-to-end-encrypted message system [15]. Its rough idea is to add message commitments to the underlying SM channel and let the server tag the encrypted messages transmitted through it. Formal analysis of message franking was initiated by Grubbs *et al.* [18] and continued by follow-up works on attachment franking [12] and asymmetric message franking [35], all of which treat message franking as an unidirectional primitive. Recently, bidirectional message franking channels were modeled in [19]. However, prior works on message franking essentially treat reported messages *individually* so do not consider their causality.

1.2 Our Contributions

The main contribution of our work is a formal study of the *proper* causality preservation model for messaging channels. We focus on two settings: two-party secure messaging and message franking. In each setting, we define a security model for it and propose provably secure constructions by adding causality to a popular real-world protocol. We hope that our formal results can help to clarify the subtleties of causality issues and facilitate the integration of causality in messaging channels. More details are summarized as follows.

Modeling Causality Preservation for Bidirectional Channels. Intuitively, causality is preserved by a bidirectional channel if the communicating parties are able to locally reconstruct the global view of their conversation. Such a global view is formalized in Sect. 2 as a so-called *causality graph*, a bipartite graph where each vertex represents a sending or receiving action and each edge represents a message transmission. It can be viewed as a simplified two-party version of the multi-party communication graph defined in [25]. With such a causality graph, we model causality preservation for bidirectional channels in Sect. 4. To match the practical design of SM channels, our model incorporates two important aspects that were *not* considered by previous causality works:

- Our model is compatible with *unreliable* networks, i.e., tolerating message loss and out-of-order delivery;
- Our causality security in its strong version captures *post-compromise security*, i.e., causality can be recovered even after a state compromise if the adversary stays *passive* during recovery [10]; this property is critical for SM channels since here a session may last for a very long time (e.g., months).

Relations to Integrity Notions. So far, all previous works on causality preservation essentially defined it as implied by ciphertext integrity. However, as mentioned before, this should not be the case if causality preservation is properly defined. In Sect. 4.5, we show that our causality preservation notion is completely separate from ciphertext integrity, as expected. Note that causality preservation, however, implies plaintext integrity, as otherwise the attacker can manipulate the message dependencies by simply modifying the messages (and causality becomes meaningless if the associated messages can be changed).

Causality Preservation of TLS 1.3. Before applying our model to analyze Signal, we first investigate a simpler bidirectional channel — the TLS 1.3 record protocol [30]. Since mitigating causality confusion for TLS may not seem very important, we do not claim this as our main contribution and leave it in the full version [9]. Nevertheless, adding causality to the TLS channel turns out to be very simple and practical, making it appealing to identify suitable use cases (a toy example is described in the full version [9]).

Formally, we first show that the TLS 1.3 channel cannot preserve causality even in our basic model (i.e., with no post-compromise security and assuming reliable in-order message delivery). Our causality attack essentially reflects the causality confusion illustrated in Fig. 1. To address that, we propose efficient fixes that add necessary causal information to each transmitted message, such that the resulting *causal* TLS 1.3 channels provably achieve causality preservation. Thanks to reliable in-order message delivery, one only has to add the number of *consecutively* received ciphertexts, denoted by δ, along with each sent message. This elegant idea has already appeared in [25, Remark 5, p.79] for constructing causal channels in their model, but not yet applied to any real-world protocols. For TLS 1.3, we show that δ can be securely added as part of the message, of the associated data, or even of the local nonce; the former two are very practical.

Causality Preservation of Signal. In Sect. 5, we analyze Signal's channel protocol (the double-ratchet mechanism [28]) with our strong causality preservation model that captures unreliable network and post-compromise security. First, we show that the Signal channel also suffers from a similar causality attack as in the TLS case, which actually implies its insecurity even in our weak model. To fix it, we also add necessary causal information to each transmitted message. However, since Signal may operate on unreliable networks, transmitting only δ is not enough to derive all causal dependencies of the communication. We resolve this by using a first-in-first-out queue Q to record the entire causal information before each sent message. As transmitting all previous causal information may incur too much overhead (i.e., linear in the number of exchanged messages), we further show how Q can be shortened such that in common scenarios the overhead is small enough for practical use. The resulting causal Signal channel is proved to preserve strong post-compromise causality. It turns out that our proposed fix is *generic*, i.e., it can be applied to any bidirectional channel to provide strong causality security. Finally, we show a concrete way for SM applications to integrate causality in their application-layer user interfaces.

Modeling Causality Preservation for Message Franking Channels. In Sect. 6, we present our causality preservation model for message franking channels. It captures two types of attackers. The first type considers a malicious server (which relays the end-to-end-encrypted communication) against honest users. Our security notion for this type is called *channel causality preservation*, which captures the security of the underlying SM channel and is defined in the same way as for bidirectional channels described above. The second type considers a malicious user that tries to fool the reporting system by tampering with causality. Causality preservation against such attacks is modeled as *report causality preservation*, which guarantees that successfully received messages must be reportable and successfully reported messages must be honest and carry the correct causal information. Note that, unlike the first type, here the second-type attacker knows the secret state used to encrypt and decrypt messages.

Causality Preservation of Facebook's Message Franking. Finally, in Sect. 7 we apply our model to analyze Facebook's message franking scheme. First, we show that it does not preserve channel causality, as the same causality attack against Signal works here. Then, we show that the scheme does not preserve report causality either, even if it uses our causal Signal channel. This is because no causal information associated with the reported message is carried in the report. We fix this in our provably secure generic construction by adding and committing the missing causal information (kept in a queue similar to the Signal case). Our construction allows the defendant to prove with causality that the reported abusive message has been taken out of context.

1.3 Further Related Work

Alwen *et al.* [1] formalized the property of *immediate decryption*. This property says that the receiver of a message can decrypt a ciphertext obtained from the sender instantaneously upon arrival, even in settings with out-of-order delivery. Moreover, the recipient can also identify the ordinal number in the sequence of received messages. The notion has later been refined in [11,29]. Immediate decryption thus focuses on a functional property, with some weak aspects of reliable ordering of received messages at a party's site. The bilateral (or potentially multilateral) view of causality, capturing dependencies between sent and received messages in communication, is thus orthogonal.

Continuing the line of research about immediate decryption, Barooti *et al.* [2] defined the notion of *recovering with immediate decryption* (RID), as an extension of the notions in [7,13]. The receiver version of the RID notion, denoted as r-RID, demands that the receiver can detect if a previously received ciphertext has been maliciously injected by the adversary. The sender version, s-RID, requires that the sender can detect that the receiver has obtained such a malicious ciphertext. The noteworthy extension in [2] is that the authors consider communication channels with out-of-order delivery. While RID is primarily an integrity notion, the solutions in [2] themselves share the idea of including history information in the ciphertexts with our constructions—which ultimately can be traced back to [25]. Namely, in [2] the receiver transmits the list of received ciphertexts (for r-RID) or a hash thereof (for s-RID). Our security goal, however, and the details of our constructions are different: we do not consider active attack detection while they do not handle causality.

Formal security treatments of out-of-order delivery in cryptographic channels can be found in [6,22,31]. Recently, Fischlin *et al.* [16] defined a more fine-grained *robustness* property for channels over unreliable networks. Robustness complements the classical integrity notion and states that maliciously injected ciphertexts on the network cannot disturb the receiver's expected behavior. In contrast, causality addresses dependencies on the message level, thus aiming at a different scope. One could, nonetheless, integrate a robustness notion as in [16] on top, on the channel level. Indeed, the Signal protocol already has robustness built in, which follows as in [16] for QUIC, because the receiver's state remains unchanged for an illegitimate ciphertext.

2   Causality Graphs

In order to formally define the causality preservation security, we introduce the notion of a *causality graph* associated with an interactive communication (often called a session) between two parties, say Alice (A) and Bob (B). We follow the idea of multi-party communication graphs described in [25], but focus on the two-party case and extract the most relevant aspects from their notions.[1]

Intuitively, a causality graph unambiguously identifies all causal information, i.e., dependencies of sending and receiving actions, in the associated communication session. Note that here only *successful* receiving actions are considered in the graph, i.e., each receiving action corresponds to an accepted message. The graph is *not* static: it grows with ongoing communications within the session and always reflects all dependencies of already performed actions. Formally, we have the following definition for the two-party case.

Definition 1. *The causality graph $G = (V_A, V_B, E, <)$ associated with a two-party communication session is a bipartite graph with two strict (or irreflexive) total orders respectively on the disjoint vertex sets V_A, V_B, and a strict partial order on all vertices, where the notation $<$ is overloaded to denote all orders.*

Each vertex represents either a sending action (called a sending vertex) or a receiving action (called a receiving vertex) performed by some party and V_A, V_B respectively denote the vertex sets of party A, B. The edge set E consists of only directed edges from sending to receiving vertices, each edge representing the transmission of a message. The orders on V_A and on V_B are naturally defined according to the increasing occurrence times of the represented actions. The order on $V_A \cup V_B$ is the transitive closure of the orders on V_A, V_B and the order implied by the directed edges (i.e., $(x, y) \in E \Rightarrow x < y$).[2]

G is correct *if and only if 1) the above defined order on $V_A \cup V_B$ is a strict partial order and 2) each receiving vertex is connected to* exactly one *sending vertex and each sending vertex is connected to* at most one *receiving vertex.*

With the strict partial order on $V_A \cup V_B$, the above causality graph unambiguously identifies all dependencies of the already performed sending and receiving actions. We say two edges $(x_1, y_1), (x_2, y_2) \in E$ are *concurrent* if 1) they are in opposite directions (i.e., x_1, x_2 cannot both belong to V_A or to V_B) and 2) $y_1 \not< x_2$ and $y_2 \not< x_1$; the latter means x_1, y_1, x_2, y_2 cannot be totally ordered. Intuitively, two concurrent edges do not depend on each other. We also say a (sending) vertex is *isolated* if it is not connected to any edge, which could happen when the message has not been delivered or got lost during transmission.

A pictorial description of an example causality graph is given in Fig. 2 (left). In the dashed box, we see two pairs of concurrent edges: $(a_1, b_3), (b_1, a_2)$ as well as $(a_1, b_3), (b_2, a_3)$. An example of a non-concurrent edge pair is (a_5, b_5) from Alice to Bob together with (b_6, a_7) from Bob to Alice in the lower part, where

---

[1] We note that [25] defined a notion called *causal graph*. This looks similar but is actually for reliable networks, while our causality graph captures unreliable networks.

[2] This is actually the strict partial order derived from Lamport's logical clock [23].

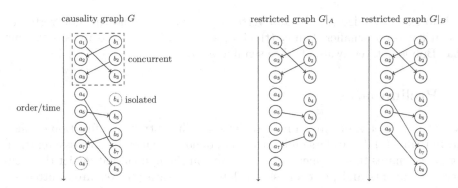

Fig. 2. An example causality graph G and the restricted graphs $G|_A, G|_B$ of Alice (left party) and Bob (right party).

the latter edge depends on the former one. The figure also shows two (dotted) isolated sending vertices a_8 and b_4.

Graph Addition. In order to model dynamic updates of the causality graph, we define a binary addition operation $+$ that inputs a graph and an action and outputs an updated graph. Let (S, P) denote a sending action of party $P \in \{A, B\}$. We write $G \leftarrow G + (\text{S}, P)$ to express that G is updated by capturing (S, P), i.e., adding a new sending vertex v to the vertex set V_P (then v will be the *largest* vertex in V_P with respect to $<$). Let (R, P, i) denote a receiving action of party P, with the associated sending action represented by the i-th sending vertex $\bar{v}_i$ in $V_{\bar{P}}$, where $\bar{P} = \{A, B\} \setminus P$; here $\bar{v}_i$ exists because this sending action occurred before (R, P, i). Similarly, we write $G \leftarrow G + (\text{R}, P, i)$ to express that G is updated by capturing (R, P, i): first add a new receiving vertex v to V_P and then add a directed edge $(\bar{v}_i, v)$.

Restricted Graph. Intuitively, the restricted graph $G|_P$ of party P captures the causality graph G restricted to P's view. Let v be the largest vertex in V_P. Formally, $G|_P$ is a subgraph of G that consists of v, all vertices in $V_A \cup V_B$ that are smaller than v, and all edges between those vertices; this is also known as the *v-prefix* of G as defined in [26]. $G|_P$ can be efficiently derived from G.

Note that $G|_P$ excludes any edge (and its receiving vertex) that is concurrent to, or larger than, the last edge from $\bar{P}$ to P. Consider the example causality graph G shown in Fig. 2. The restricted graph $G|_A$ of Alice excludes edges $(a_4, b_7), (a_6, b_8)$ (and vertices b_7, b_8) because they are concurrent to (b_6, a_7) (which is the last edge from Bob to Alice). This reflects the fact that Alice does not know whether the messages sent at a_4, a_6 have been delivered to Bob because she has not received any response regarding those messages yet. Alice at a_7 received a message sent from Bob at b_6; however, this receiving action only confirms the delivery of Alice's messages sent at a_1, a_5 but not those sent at a_4, a_6, since the latter are received after b_6. Similarly, the restricted graph $G|_B$

of Bob excludes edge (b_6, a_7) and vertex a_7. It also does not include vertex a_8 because it is not smaller than b_8 (the largest vertex in V_B); this reflects the fact that Bob is not yet aware of Alice sending at a_8.

3   Preliminaries

Notations. Let $\perp$ denote an invalid element. The output of a function or algorithm is all $\perp$(s) if any of its input is $\perp$. Let . denote the member access operation, e.g., $a.x$ denotes the x element of a. However, in the figures that depict the security experiments and protocols shown later, the state prefixes are omitted for simplicity, e.g., if a state st contains an element x then we simply write x instead of $st.x$.

In the full version [9], we recall the definitions of authenticated encryption with associated data (AEAD), message authentication codes (MACs), and commitment schemes with verification, as well as their corresponding advantage measures that this work focuses on: $\mathbf{Adv}_{\mathsf{AEAD}}^{\mathsf{auth}}$, $\mathbf{Adv}_{\mathsf{MAC}}^{\mathsf{euf\text{-}cma}}$, and $\mathbf{Adv}_{\mathsf{CS}}^{\mathsf{v\text{-}bind}}$.

4   Bidirectional Channels and Causality Preservation

4.1   Bidirectional Channels

A bidirectional channel allows two parties (or users), Alice (A) and Bob (B), to securely communicate with each other, where each party $P \in \{A, B\}$ can send messages to the other party $\bar{P} = \{A, B\} \setminus P$, and receive messages sent by $\bar{P}$. For security reasons, the sending party transforms messages to ciphertexts before transmitting them and the ciphertexts are later transformed back to messages by the receiving party. Both parties can keep states across their sending and receiving actions. Formally, we have the following definition based on the bidirectional channel notion proposed by [26].

Definition 2. *A bidirectional (cryptographic) channel is a three-tuple* $\mathsf{Ch} = (\mathsf{Init}, \mathsf{Snd}, \mathsf{Rcv})$ *associated with a key space* $\mathcal{K}_{\mathsf{Ch}}$, *a state space* $\mathcal{ST}$, *a message space* $\mathcal{M}$, *and an index space* $\mathcal{I}$:

$\mathsf{Init}(P, k) \rightarrow st_P$: *takes* $P \in \{A, B\}$, $k \in \mathcal{K}_{\mathsf{Ch}}$, *and outputs the initial state of* P;
$\mathsf{Snd}(P, st, m) \xrightarrow{\$} (st', c)$: *takes* $P \in \{A, B\}$, $st \in \mathcal{ST}$, $m \in \mathcal{M}$, *and outputs an updated state* $st' \in \mathcal{ST}$ *and a ciphertext* $c \in \{0, 1\}^*$;
$\mathsf{Rcv}(P, st, c) \rightarrow (st', m, i)$: *takes* $P \in \{A, B\}$, $st \in \mathcal{ST}$, $c \in \{0, 1\}^*$, *and outputs an updated state* $st' \in \mathcal{ST}$ *and a message* $m \in \mathcal{M} \cup \{\perp\}$ *with index* $i \in \mathcal{I}$.

Correctness requires that each party outputs the messages sent by the other party together with the correct index that indicates their sending order.

We say a party *accepts* a message m (and the ciphertext c) if Rcv processing c is successful, i.e., it outputs $m \neq \perp$. If the channel runs over an unreliable network, we follow [1] to require that (i) state st remains *unchanged* if Rcv

outputs $m = \perp$; (ii) Rcv never accepts two messages with the *same* index; and (iii) index i can be efficiently extracted from the ciphertext c (denoted by $c.i$).

Note that the message index i can be either a simple ordinal number in $\mathbb{N}$ that matches a send counter, or of any form as long as the indices are strictly ordered. For instance, in the SM syntax of [1], an index is a two-tuple that consists of an epoch number and a send counter within that epoch. However, due to the bijective mapping between indices and ordinals, our definitions for simplicity do not differentiate them explicitly.

Definitional Differences From [26]. First, our channel algorithms have the acting party's identity as an explicit input to capture the *different* behaviors of the communicating parties when running the same algorithm with the same inputs, e.g., TLS client and server use different components of the same session key (part of the input state) for encryption (in Snd) and decryption (in Rcv). Furthermore, for conciseness our Snd and Rcv algorithms do not take as input unencrypted application-level associated data, i.e., channel parties require the entire input message to be encrypted, which is often the case for real-world bidirectional channels (e.g., TLS 1.3, Signal, etc.). As we will show, there may be some associated data formed by the bidirectional channels and authenticated by their underlying authenticated encryption schemes, but such associated data is not specified by the channel users. However, it is easy to extend our definition to capture the application-level associated data if desired. Finally, our Rcv algorithm additionally outputs an index i to determine the sending order of received messages, which is necessary to model out-of-order delivery or message loss, but often omitted if the channel is over a reliable in-order network.

4.2 Local Graph and Its Update Function

Our security definitions utilize the notion of a *local graph* G_P to represent the causal information derived by a party P. The local graph can be constructed from the party's local protocol execution. Causality preservation of a channel should imply that each party's local graph always matches its restricted graph, i.e., $G_P = G|_P$. Intuitively, this means that local protocol execution is consistent with the party's expected view on causality: What the parties knows about the causality structure is accurate (up to what can be guaranteed).

A local graph update function localG is a function invoked after each successful Rcv execution. Function localG inputs a local graph and the Rcv execution's transcript T_{Rcv} and outputs an updated local graph. Note that the transcript consists of all the input, output, random coins, internal states, etc., used in the considered Rcv execution. The intuition behind localG is to update the local graph with the causal information extracted from the successful receiving action. Such a function is necessary because extracting causal information from received ciphertexts is the only way for a party P to correctly order the other party $\bar{P}$'s sending and receiving actions in its local graph G_P, as P does not have access to $\bar{P}$'s view. Furthermore, we define localG to concern only receiving actions because successful sending actions can be trivially added to the local graph in an unambiguous way, which is denoted by $G_P \leftarrow G_P + \mathsf{S}$.

4.3 Causality Preservation

Now, we formally define the security notion of *causality preservation (CP)*. The idea is that the adversary wins if it makes some party's local graph G_P deviate from the restricted graph $G|_P$, i.e., if the party's internal view on causality differs from the actual (local) view. We note that the adversary also wins (event Bad below) if it makes the receiver accept a malicious message, either one that has not been sent (if Ch is designed for unreliable networks) or one that has not been sent or is delivered in wrong order (if Ch is designed for reliable in-order networks). The former event occurs if the receiver outputs a message m with index i which has not been put on the wire, and the latter event further checks if the index i is as expected. Note that in the first case we cannot stipulate more since transmissions may get lost or be delivered later. Augmenting the security game by the Bad events ensures that the content of the message remains intact, thus guaranteeing that responses correspond to the right information.

Security Experiment. In Fig. 3, we depict the security experiment (or game) for causality preservation $\mathbf{Exp}^{cp}_{Ch,localG,\mathcal{A}}(1^\lambda)$ that is executed between a challenger and an adversary $\mathcal{A}$. The experiment is associated with a bidirectional channel $Ch = (Init, Snd, Rcv)$ and a local graph update function $localG$.

$\mathbf{Exp}^{cp}_{Ch,localG,\mathcal{A}}(1^\lambda):$	$\mathrm{Send}(P,m):$	$\mathrm{Recv}(P,c):$
1: $k \xleftarrow{\$} \mathcal{K}_{Ch}$	1: $(st_P,c) \xleftarrow{\$} Snd(P,st_P,m)$	1: $(st_P,m,i) \leftarrow Rcv(P,st_P,c)$ // T_{Rcv}: transcript
2: $st_A \leftarrow Init(A,k)$	2: if $c = \bot$ then return $\bot$	2: if $m = \bot$ then return $\bot,\bot$
3: $st_B \leftarrow Init(B,k)$	3: $G \leftarrow G + (S,P), G_P \leftarrow G_P + S$	3: if Bad then
4: $s_A, s_B, r_A, r_B \leftarrow 0$	4: add (P,s_P,m,c) to $\mathcal{R}$, $s_P \leftarrow s_P + 1$	4: $\quad$ terminate with 1 ($\mathcal{A}$ wins)
5: $G, G_A, G_B \leftarrow \varepsilon$	5: return c	5: $G \leftarrow G + (R,P,i)$
6: $\mathcal{R} \leftarrow \varnothing$		6: $G_P \leftarrow localG(G_P, T_{Rcv})$
7: $\mathcal{A}^{Send,Recv}$	unreliable networks:	7: if $G_P \neq G|_P$ then
8: terminate with 0	$\quad$ Bad $= [(\bar{P},i,m,\cdot) \notin \mathcal{R}]$	8: $\quad$ terminate with 1 ($\mathcal{A}$ wins)
	reliable in-order networks:	9: delete $(\bar{P},i,\cdot,\cdot)$ from $\mathcal{R}$, $r_P \leftarrow r_P + 1$
	$\quad$ Bad $= [(\bar{P},i,m,\cdot) \notin \mathcal{R}$ or $i \neq r_P]$	10: return m,i

Fig. 3. Security experiment for causality preservation

In the beginning, the challenger samples a random channel key k and calls Init with it to derive the initial states. All the states used in the game are also properly initialized, where in particular s_A, s_B, r_A, r_B are used to count sending and receiving actions. Then, $\mathcal{A}$ is given access to two oracles Send and Recv:

Send takes a party identity and a message, calls Snd on the input message, updates the graphs, records the message, and outputs the derived ciphertext. Note that for reliable in-order networks when a receiving action fails the state st_P may be set to $\bot$ by Rcv, and if so $Snd(P,st_P,\cdot)$ will always output $(\bot,\bot)$.

Recv takes a party identity and a ciphertext and calls Rcv on the input ciphertext. If the accepted message triggers the Bad event discussed above, $\mathcal{A}$ wins. Otherwise, the party's local graph G_P and the (global) causality graph G

are updated. Then, $\mathcal{A}$ wins if the local graph does not match the restricted graph. Finally, the oracle removes the accepted message from the record and outputs the message with its index.

Advantage Measure. The advantage is defined as $\mathbf{Adv}^{cp}_{Ch,localG}(\mathcal{A}) = \Pr[\mathbf{Exp}^{cp}_{Ch,localG,\mathcal{A}}(1^\lambda) \Rightarrow 1]$ for any arbitrary localG. We say a bidirectional channel Ch preserves causality (or is CP-secure) if one can *construct* an efficiently computable function localG* such that, for any efficient adversary $\mathcal{A}$, the advantage $\mathbf{Adv}^{cp}_{Ch,localG^\star}(\mathcal{A})$ is negligible.

The above security definition may look a bit elusive due to its reliance on the *constructibility* of localG* (which may not be unique), but the intuition is not complicated. Note that constructibility is a stronger requirement than existence because an existing function may be very hard to find (e.g., a function to output hash collisions). By definition, each party in a CP-secure channel can use localG* to extract all correct causal information associated with an ongoing session in the presence of an active attacker, which is impossible for an insecure channel due to the non-constructibility (or even non-existence) of localG*.

Note that a CP-secure channel only guarantees that each party is *in principle* able to derive *all* causal information captured by its restricted graph, which corresponds to the constructibility of some localG*. However, this does not imply that all correct causal information is indeed derived and utilized by the channel parties, e.g., they may use arbitrary functions to extract the necessary portion of causal information. This actually gives the practical channel constructions more flexibility for utilizing causality, i.e., it may be sufficient for a party to extract only *partial* causal information (rather than the entire local graph) to perform its causality-related functionality (see the TLS analysis in the full version [9] for example). In the future sections, we will illustrate in our analysis how exactly causality can be utilized to improve security for our proposed constructions.

4.4 Causality Preservation with Post-compromise Security

The above basic causality preservation notion is sufficient to analyze secure connection protocols like TLS 1.3 (see the full version [9]), for which state corruption leads to no security.[3] However, post-compromise security is an important concern for secure messaging (SM) protocols like Signal, since their sessions typically last for a long time (e.g., months). In order to capture this type of bidirectional channels, we define the notion of *strong causality preservation (SCP)* that recovers security after state compromise (and defaults to the basic weaker notion for uncompromised executions). Here for simplicity only unreliable networks are considered, as popular practical SM protocols like Signal usually do not assume reliable in-order message delivery.

---

[3] For secure connection protocols, our work focuses on their security within a basic connection, where no post-compromise security is guaranteed, but such protocols (e.g., TLS 1.3) could achieve post-compromise security across resumed sessions [33].

Epochs. In order to formalize post-compromise security, we follow the prior work to associate each party with a sequence of incrementing epochs $t = 0, 1, 2, \ldots$ that represents consecutive time periods. Each transmitted message and ciphertext are also associated with the same epoch as that of the party when it sent them. We assume that the epoch number t is part of the party's state st_P (denoted by $st_P.t$) and can be efficiently extracted from the ciphertext c (denoted by $c.t$). Then, for any ciphertext c *accepted* by a party P, we assume that $c.t \leq st_P.t + 1$. We will see that Signal satisfies the above assumptions. Finally, we let $(G_P)_{\geq t}$ and $(G|_P)_{\geq t}$ respectively denote subgraphs of G_P and $G|_P$ that consist of only vertices (and edges between them) created at epochs larger than or equal to t.

$\mathbf{Exp}^{\text{scp}}_{\text{Ch},\Delta,\text{localG},\mathcal{A}}(1^\lambda)$:

1: $k \xleftarrow{\$} \mathcal{K}_{\text{Ch}}$
2: $st_A \leftarrow \text{Init}(A, k)$
3: $st_B \leftarrow \text{Init}(B, k)$
4: $G, G_A, G_B \leftarrow \varepsilon$
5: $t_c \leftarrow -\infty$
6: $\mathcal{R}, \mathcal{R}_c \leftarrow \varnothing$
7: $\mathcal{A}^{\text{Send},\text{Recv},\text{Corr}}$
8: terminate with 0

$\text{Corr}(P)$:

1: add $\mathcal{R}.\text{get}(\bar{P})$ to $\mathcal{R}_c$
2: $t_c \leftarrow \max(st_A.t, st_B.t)$
3: return st_P

$\text{Send}(P, m)$:

1: $(st_P, c) \xleftarrow{\$} \text{Snd}(P, st_P, m)$
2: if $c = \bot$ then return $\bot$
3: $G \leftarrow G + (\text{S}, P), G_P \leftarrow G_P + \text{S}$
4: add $(P, c.i, m, c)$ to $\mathcal{R}$
5: if $c.t < t_c + \Delta$ then
6: | add $(P, c.i, m, c)$ to $\mathcal{R}_c$
7: return c

$\text{Invalid} = [\min(st_A.t, st_B.t) < t_c + \Delta$
          and $(\bar{P}, \cdot, \cdot, c) \notin \mathcal{R}]$

$\text{Bad} = [\min(st_A.t, st_B.t) \geq t_c + \Delta$
          and $(\bar{P}, i, m, \cdot) \notin \mathcal{R}$
          and $(\bar{P}, i, \cdot, \cdot) \notin \mathcal{R}_c]$

$\text{Recv}(P, c)$:

1: if Invalid then
2: | return $\bot, \bot$
3: $(st_P, m, i) \leftarrow \text{Rcv}(P, st_P, c)$ // T_{Rcv}: transcript
4: if $m = \bot$ then return $\bot, \bot$
5: if Bad then
6: | terminate with 1 ($\mathcal{A}$ wins)
7: if $(\bar{P}, i, m, \cdot) \in \mathcal{R}$ then
8: | $G \leftarrow G + (\text{R}, P, i)$
9: $G_P \leftarrow \text{localG}(G_P, T_{\text{Rcv}})$
10: if $(G_P)_{\geq t_c + \Delta} \neq (G|_P)_{\geq t_c + \Delta}$ then
11: | terminate with 1 ($\mathcal{A}$ wins)
12: delete $(\bar{P}, i, \cdot, \cdot)$ from $\mathcal{R}, \mathcal{R}_c$
13: return m, i

Fig. 4. Security experiment for strong causality preservation

Security Experiment. In Fig. 4 we depict the security experiment (or game) for strong causality preservation $\mathbf{Exp}^{\text{scp}}_{\text{Ch},\Delta,\text{localG},\mathcal{A}}(1^\lambda)$ that is executed between a challenger and an adversary $\mathcal{A}$. The experiment is additionally associated with a parameter $\Delta \geq 0$ that indicates how fast (in terms of epochs) parties recover from state compromise. Intuitively, strong causality preservation guarantees that even if at some epoch a party is corrupted, after Δ epochs the channel protocol resurrects causality again.

The experiment is more complicated than the CP experiment due to state compromise. In the beginning, the challenger initializes two additional states, t_c that stores the most recent (i.e., largest) compromised epoch and $\mathcal{R}_c$ that records the compromised messages (with the corresponding ciphertexts). Then, $\mathcal{A}$ is given oracle access to Send, Recv, Corr, where Corr is for state corruption.

Corr takes a party identity and outputs the party's current state; it also records all the outstanding messages sent by the other party as compromised (i.e., adding them to $\mathcal{R}_c$) and updates t_c.

Send works as before except that: if the party is still recovering from state compromise, i.e., $c.t < t_c + \Delta$, then the sent message and ciphertext are recorded as compromised.

Recv becomes more complicated to handle corruption, but it downgrades to the Recv oracle in the CP experiment when no corruption occurs (then $t_c = -\infty$ and $\mathcal{R}_c = \varnothing$). In the beginning, the Invalid condition is checked, which ensures that the adversary performs *passively* during channel recovery (i.e., no malicious ciphertext can be processed when either party's current epoch is less than $t_c + \Delta$). Then, if the ciphertext is successfully transformed to a message (i.e., the message is accepted), the Bad event is checked. Bad occurs if after recovery a party accepts a malicious message that was neither sent by the other party nor associated with a compromised epoch, and hence in this case $\mathcal{A}$ wins. Otherwise, the local graph G_P and (global) causality graph G are updated, where the latter is updated only when the accepted message is not modified since message dependencies captured by G are meaningless without the correct messages. Then, $\mathcal{A}$ wins if the after-recovery subgraph of either party's local graph $(G_P)_{\geq t_c + \Delta}$ does not match that of the party's restricted graph $(G|_P)_{\geq t_c + \Delta}$. Finally, the oracle removes the accepted message from the records and outputs the message with its index.

We remark that our model does *not* capture forward secrecy for causality. The key observation is that, even after state recovery, the part of a causality graph that corresponds to a previous uncompromised epoch may still be affected by a compromised message that carries malicious causal information. However, causality for already received messages is still guaranteed upon corruption.

Advantage Measure. The advantage is defined as $\mathbf{Adv}^{\mathsf{scp}}_{\mathsf{Ch},\Delta,\mathsf{localG}}(\mathcal{A}) = \Pr[\mathbf{Exp}^{\mathsf{scp}}_{\mathsf{Ch},\mathsf{localG},\Delta,\mathcal{A}}(1^\lambda) \Rightarrow 1]$ for any arbitrary localG. We say a bidirectional channel Ch preserves Δ-strong causality (or is Δ-SCP-secure) if one can *construct* an efficiently computable function localG* such that, for any efficient adversary $\mathcal{A}$, the advantage $\mathbf{Adv}^{\mathsf{scp}}_{\mathsf{Ch},\Delta,\mathsf{localG}^\star}(\mathcal{A})$ is negligible. Similarly, a Δ-SCP-secure channel also guarantees that each party is *in principle* able to derive *all* causal information captured by its restricted graph in epochs after recovery, but parties may choose to extract only *partial* causal information.

SCP $\Rightarrow$ CP and CP $\not\Rightarrow$ SCP. For SCP $\Rightarrow$ CP, we note that SCP downgrades to CP if the adversary makes no corruption query, in which case $t_c = -\infty$ and $\mathcal{R}_c = \varnothing$. The other direction is not true, e.g., causal TLS 1.3 channels (details in the full version [9]) offer no post-compromise security.

4.5   Relations to Integrity Notions

Our (S)CP notions are clearly orthogonal to confidentiality (i.e., causal relations can be simply observed by a network attacker), but one may think of them as complements to integrity. We show that this is not quite the case.

First, in Fig. 5 we formalize the security experiments of plaintext integrity (INT-PTXT) and ciphertext integrity (INT-CTXT) for bidirectional channels.[4]

---

[4] [26] initialized the formal security definitions for bidirectional channels, but their notions do not capture unreliable networks.

$\mathbf{Exp}^{\text{int-ptxt/int-ctxt}}_{\text{Ch},\mathcal{A}}(1^\lambda):$

1: $k \xleftarrow{\$} \mathcal{K}_{\text{Ch}}$
2: $st_A \leftarrow \text{Init}(A, k)$
3: $st_B \leftarrow \text{Init}(B, k)$
4: $s_A, s_B, r_A, r_B \leftarrow 0, \mathcal{R} \leftarrow \varnothing$
5: $\mathcal{A}^{\text{Send,Recv}}$
6: terminate with 0

$\text{Send}(P, m):$

1: $(st_P, c) \xleftarrow{\$} \text{Snd}(P, st_P, m)$
2: if $c = \bot$ then return $\bot$
3: $s_P \leftarrow s_P + 1$
4: add (P, s_P, m, c) to $\mathcal{R}$
5: return c

$\text{Recv}(P, c):$

1: $(st_P, m, i) \leftarrow \text{Rcv}(P, st_P, c)$
2: if $m = \bot$ then return $\bot, \bot$
3: if $\text{Bad}_{\text{ptxt}}/\text{Bad}_{\text{ctxt}}$ then
4: $\quad$ terminate with 1 ($\mathcal{A}$ wins)
5: $r_P \leftarrow r_P + 1$, delete $(\bar{P}, i, \cdot, \cdot)$ from $\mathcal{R}$
6: return m, i

Fig. 5. Security experiments for plaintext and ciphertext integrity, where $\text{Bad}_{\text{ptxt}} = \text{Bad}$ as defined in Fig. 3, $\text{Bad}_{\text{ctxt}} = [(\bar{P}, i, \cdot, c) \notin \mathcal{R}]$ for unreliable networks and $\text{Bad}_{\text{ctxt}} = [(\bar{P}, i, \cdot, c) \notin \mathcal{R} \text{ or } i \neq r_P]$ for reliable in-order networks.

Their advantage measures are defined naturally and denoted by $\mathbf{Adv}^{\text{int-ptxt}}_{\text{Ch}}(\mathcal{A})$ and $\mathbf{Adv}^{\text{int-ctxt}}_{\text{Ch}}(\mathcal{A})$ respectively.

$\mathbf{Exp}^{\text{s-int-ptxt/ctxt}}_{\text{Ch},\Delta,\mathcal{A}}(1^\lambda):$

1: $k \xleftarrow{\$} \mathcal{K}_{\text{Ch}}$
2: $st_A \leftarrow \text{Init}(A, k)$
3: $st_B \leftarrow \text{Init}(B, k)$
4: $t_c \leftarrow -\infty$
5: $\mathcal{R}, \mathcal{R}_c \leftarrow \varnothing$
6: $\mathcal{A}^{\text{Send,Recv,Corr}}$
7: terminate with 0

$\text{Send}(P, m):$

1: $(st_P, c) \xleftarrow{\$} \text{Snd}(P, st_P, m)$
2: if $c = \bot$ then return $\bot$
3: add $(P, c.i, m, c)$ to $\mathcal{R}$
4: if $c.t < t_c + \Delta$ then
5: $\quad$ add $(P, c.i, m, c)$ to $\mathcal{R}_c$
6: return c

$\text{Recv}(P, c):$

1: if Invalid then return $\bot, \bot$
2: $(st_P, m, i) \leftarrow \text{Rcv}(P, st_P, c)$
3: if $m = \bot$ then return $\bot, \bot$
4: if $\text{Bad}_{\text{s-ptxt}}/\text{Bad}_{\text{s-ctxt}}$ then
5: $\quad$ terminate with 1 ($\mathcal{A}$ wins)
6: delete $(\bar{P}, i, \cdot, \cdot)$ from $\mathcal{R}, \mathcal{R}_c$
7: return m, i

Fig. 6. Security experiments for strong plaintext integrity and strong ciphertext integrity, where Corr, Invalid and $\text{Bad}_{\text{s-ptxt}} = \text{Bad}$ are defined in Fig. 4 and $\text{Bad}_{\text{s-ctxt}} = [\min(st_A.t, st_B.t) \geq t_c + \Delta \text{ and } (\bar{P}, i, \cdot, c) \notin \mathcal{R} \text{ and } (\bar{P}, i, \cdot, \cdot) \notin \mathcal{R}_c]$.

Then, in Fig. 6 we define the security experiments for strong plaintext integrity (S-INT-PTXT) and strong ciphertext integrity (S-INT-CTXT) that offer post-compromise security for bidirectional channels. Similarly, we denote their advantage measures by $\mathbf{Adv}^{\text{s-int-ptxt}}_{\text{Ch},\Delta}(\mathcal{A})$ and $\mathbf{Adv}^{\text{s-int-ctxt}}_{\text{Ch},\Delta}(\mathcal{A})$ respectively.

To clarify the relationship of the above two notions, we define a notion called *robust correctness* (ROB-CORR) to capture correctness in a robust sense: after state recovery, decrypting ciphertexts created in a compromised epoch and decryption failure do not affect the correctness requirement, i.e., an honest ciphertext is always decrypted to the original message and index.[5] Its security experiment is the same as Fig. 6, except that the Bad event is replaced by $\text{Bad}_{\text{rob-corr}} = [\min(st_A.t, st_B.t) \geq t_c + \Delta \text{ and } (\bar{P}, i, \cdot, c) \in \mathcal{R} \text{ and } (\bar{P}, i, m, \cdot) \notin \mathcal{R} \text{ and } (\bar{P}, i, \cdot, \cdot) \notin \mathcal{R}_c]$. The advantage measure is denoted by $\mathbf{Adv}^{\text{rob-corr}}_{\text{Ch},\Delta}(\mathcal{A})$.

In the full version [9], we investigate the relations among the above integrity notions and our (S)CP notions; the results are summarized in Fig. 7.

---

[5] This notion is loosely connected to the idea behind the robust notion for unreliable channels recently put forward in [16], namely that malicious ciphertexts do not disturb the expected behavior. However, in our case the notion is closer to a correctness property after recovery. A similar correctness security notion was also defined in [1].

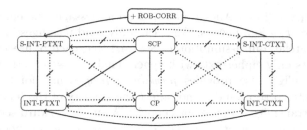

Fig. 7. Notion relations. Solid arrows mean an implication, dotted (crossed out) arrows mean a separation.

5 Causality Preservation of Signal

In this section, we analyze causality preservation of the Signal protocol [24, 28]. We focus on its double-ratchet component [28] without considering the X3DH key agreement [24] used to derive the initial shared key. First, we show that Signal as a bidirectional channel does not even achieve the basic CP security. Then, we propose simple fixes to construct SCP-secure causal Signal channels and describe a potential user interface for the SM applications to display the causal dependencies to end users.

5.1 The Signal Channel and Its Insecurity

The Signal Channel. According to our defined syntax (see Definition 2), we can view Signal as a bidirectional channel, denoted by $\mathsf{Ch}_{\mathsf{Signal}}$. Here we briefly summarize its main cryptographic design, and refer to the full version [9] for a more detailed description of the Signal channel based on its core building blocks.

Signal performs a so-called *continuous key agreement (CKA)* protocol to generate a series of shared secrets, such that after state compromise the channel parties are able to recover security with a *fresh* shared secret. Parties in the Signal channel send and receive messages in *alternate* epochs, with odd epochs for Alice to send and Bob to receive, and even epochs for Bob to send and Alice to receive. Therefore, concurrent messages sent by different parties are associated with *distinct* epochs. Recall that in Sect. 4.4 we assume each party P keeps the epoch number t in its local state st_P and the associated epoch number can be efficiently extracted from the ciphertext; this is the case for Signal.[6]

The epoch numbers of both parties are initialized as 0. For each party P, its epoch number $st_P.t$ is incremented from t to $t + 1$ in two cases: (1) after P receives from the other party a message with epoch number $t + 1$ (e.g., when $st_B.t = 0$ and Bob receives a message associated with epoch $t = 1$, Bob updates $st_B.t = 1$); or (2) before P sends a message while t is not the epoch for P to send

---

[6] Actually, Signal exploits the uniqueness of the latest CKA message (authenticated but not encrypted, as shown in the full version [9]) to index epochs. For simplicity, we follow [1] to assume an explicit epoch number is used.

(e.g., when $st_A.t = 2$ and Alice wants to send a message, the epoch number is incremented to $st_A.t = 3$ because Alice can only send messages in odd epochs). This design matches our assumption in Sect. 4.4 that each bidirectional channel party P accepts only ciphertexts with epoch number $\leq st_P.t + 1$.

The above CKA also provides *forward secrecy*, which for Signal roughly means that state corruption does not affect the security of the (encrypted) messages already transmitted in previous epochs. Actually, forward secrecy guaranteed by Signal is more fine-grained, i.e., even within the *same* epoch the already sent messages remain safe. To achieve such security, each party in Signal further updates its sending (or receiving) key after each sending (or receiving) action, such that past keys cannot be derived from new keys.

The message index of $\mathsf{Ch}_{\mathsf{Signal}}$ is hence a two-tuple (t, s), where t is the epoch number and s is the sent message counter within epoch t.

Causality Insecurity of $\mathsf{Ch}_{\mathsf{Signal}}$. We can follow the idea reflected in Fig. 1 to construct an efficient adversary $\mathcal{A}$ against causality preservation of $\mathsf{Ch}_{\mathsf{Signal}}$. First, $\mathcal{A}$ samples a random bit $b \xleftarrow{\$} \{0,1\}$. Then, consider the following queries for any three messages $m_1, m_2, m_3 \in \mathcal{M}$: ① $c_1 \xleftarrow{\$} \mathsf{Send}(A, m_1)$, ② $(m_1, (1, 0)) \leftarrow \mathsf{Recv}(B, c_1)$, ③ $c_2 \xleftarrow{\$} \mathsf{Send}(A, m_2)$, ④ $(m_2, (1, 1)) \leftarrow \mathsf{Recv}(B, c_2)$, ⑤ $c_3 \xleftarrow{\$} \mathsf{Send}(B, m_3)$, ⑥ $(m_3, (2, 0)) \leftarrow \mathsf{Recv}(A, c_3)$. If $b = 0$, $\mathcal{A}$ runs ①②③④⑤⑥; otherwise $b = 1$, $\mathcal{A}$ runs in a different order: ①②③⑤④⑥. These two cases are depicted in Fig. 8.

Fig. 8. Causality attack against Signal. Each ciphertext contains the epoch t for sending actions and the obtained epoch value $\bar{t}$ for receiving actions. The send counters are irrelevant for the attack and are omitted. The adversary chooses one of the execution flows randomly. Then, Alice's views (in the dashed boxes) in both cases are identical, whereas Alice's restricted graphs are different: the right hand side does not contain Bob's last vertex.

Clearly, the above two cases result in two different causality graphs (and different restricted graphs for Alice): in the left world ($b = 0$) Bob sent m_3 after receiving m_2 but in the right world ($b = 1$) that is not the case. Note that in both worlds Bob has received m_1 before sending m_3, so m_3 must belong to epoch $t = 2$.[7] Since c_3 carries no information about whether m_2 has been received, both worlds look identical to Alice. (This can be verified by checking the detailed

---

[7] Note that if Bob sends a message m before receiving any messages from Alice, then this message m belongs to epoch $t = 0$.

description of $\mathsf{Ch_{Signal}}$ in the full version [9].) Therefore, $G_A \neq G|_A$ happens with probability at least $1/2$, i.e., $\mathbf{Adv}^{\mathsf{cp}}_{\mathsf{Ch_{Signal}},\mathsf{localG}}(\mathcal{A}) \geq 1/2$ for any possible update function localG. By definition, $\mathsf{Ch_{Signal}}$ does not preserve causality.

5.2 Integrating Causality in Signal

Since Signal allows for out-of-order message delivery and message loss, transmitting only the δ value (i.e., the number of consecutively accepted messages before the sent message, more details discussed in the full version [9]) as for TLS is not enough to reconstruct the full causal relations. In order for the parties to build the correct restricted graph, along with each sent message the entire causal information before this message (that has not been known by the receiving party) has to be transmitted. We store this information in a queue Q (with the usual methods enq, deq, and front to enqueue and dequeue elements, and to read the front element without dequeuing it). Then, we propose a so-called *message-borne* causal Signal channel, indicating where Q is borne. Analogously, one can also construct an *associated-data-borne* causal Signal channel, by authenticating Q as part of the associated data rather than encrypting it.[8]

A Generic Causal Channel Compiler. In Fig. 9, we show a *generic* compiler that transforms an arbitrary bidirectional channel $\mathsf{Ch} = (\mathsf{Init}, \mathsf{Snd}, \mathsf{Rcv})$ into a message-borne causal channel Ch^m. In particular, when Ch is instantiated with $\mathsf{Ch_{Signal}}$, we get the message-borne causal Signal channel $\mathsf{Ch}^m_{\mathsf{cSignal}}$.

As shown in Fig. 9, Ch^m keeps indices i_S, i_R and queue Q as three additional states and encrypts the latter two states with the sent message. Formally, Q is a (first-in-first-out) queue that records a sequence of actions before the sent message in their correct time order: each action is recorded as the *index* of the associated sent or received message. We require that one can distinguish a sending index from a receiving index. Clearly, the receiving party is able to construct the correct restricted graph if *all* actions before the sent message are recorded in Q. However, this may incur too much overhead, e.g., a Signal communication session may last for months and hence involve many actions.

To mitigate overhead, we use indices i_S, i_R to update Q such that it records only the actions performed by party P but whose delivery has not yet been confirmed, i.e., P has not accepted any ciphertext sent from $\bar{P}$ that confirms the delivery of those actions. Let i_S denote, in P's view, the largest index of messages accepted by $\bar{P}$, then Q only needs to record P's actions after its i_S-th sending action, because earlier actions have been recorded and transmitted along with the sent messages accepted by $\bar{P}$. For instance, consider the message sent by Bob at b_6 in Fig. 2. This message has index 4 and queue Q consists of the (sending) message indices associated with b_3, b_4, b_5, i.e., $Q = (\bar{1}, 3, \bar{3})$ (where $\bar{i}$ indicates a receiving index), because the received message at b_5 already confirmed the

---

[8] As far as we know, the associated data is rarely used by instant messaging services for handling application-level data, so the message-borne version seems easier to understand and implement. It also matches our bidirectional channel syntax well.

$Ch^m.Init(P, k)$:
1: $st_{Ch} \leftarrow Ch.Init(P, k)$
2: $i_S, i_R \leftarrow -1, Q \leftarrow \varnothing$
3: return (st_{Ch}, i_S, i_R, Q)

$update(Q, \bar{i}, i_S, i_R, \bar{i}_R)$:
1: $Q.enq(\bar{i})$
2: if $i_R < \bar{i}$ then $i_R \leftarrow \bar{i}$
3: if $i_S < \bar{i}_R$ then
4:     while $Q.front() \neq \bar{i}_R$ do
5:         $Q.deq()$
6:         if $|Q| = 0$ then abort
7:     $Q.deq(), i_S \leftarrow \bar{i}_R$

$Ch^m.Snd(P, st, m)$:
1: $(st_{Ch}, c) \overset{\$}{\leftarrow} Ch.Snd(P, st_{Ch}, (m, (i_R, Q)))$
2: if $st_{Ch} = \perp$ then return $\perp, \perp$
3: $Q.enq(c.i)$
4: return st, c

$Ch^m.Rcv(P, st, c)$:
1: $(st_{Ch}, (m, (\bar{i}_R, \bar{Q})), \bar{i}) \leftarrow Ch.Rcv(P, st_{Ch}, c)$
2: if $m = \perp$ then return $st, \perp, \perp$
3: $update(Q, \bar{i}, i_S, i_R, \bar{i}_R)$
4: return $st, m, \bar{i}$

Fig. 9. The message-borne causal channel Ch^m (with dashed boxes highlighting the added causality-related operations). It deploys a queue Q and two indices i_S, i_R whose current values are always kept in the augmented state $st = (st_{Ch}, i_S, i_R, Q)$. Barred values represent the data output by the receiver of the underlying channel (as opposed to internal states). The value $\bar{Q}$ is not returned by Rcv, but it is part of the Rcv transcript T_{Rcv} so can be used by localG to update the local graph. When $Ch = Ch_{Signal}$, message indices are of the form (t, s) and ordered lexicographically (with -1 denoting a minimum).

delivery of messages sent at b_1 and b_2. In order to easily update i_S, we transmit an additional state i_R of P that records the largest index of accepted messages sent by $\bar{P}$, then i_S can be updated by comparing to $\bar{i}_R$ (i.e., the largest index of $\bar{P}$'s accepted messages sent by P) decrypted from ciphertexts sent by $\bar{P}$. This generalizes the idea of δ value, where it suffices to count the processed message in between; here we record all message indices since the last confirmation.

The actual procedures involving i_S, i_R, Q are described in the boxed content of Fig. 9. In Init, (i_S, i_R) are both initialized to -1, the minimum message index; Q is initialized to the empty queue. In Snd, (i_R, Q) are encrypted with the sent message, and after the encryption the message index (extracted from the ciphertext c) is recorded by Q. In Rcv, $(\bar{i}_R, \bar{Q})$ are decrypted along with the message from the received ciphertext, and if the decryption succeeds (Q, i_S, i_R) are updated by running update. This update function first records the index $\bar{i}$ of the accepted message, then updates i_R when it is smaller than $\bar{i}$; next, if $i_S < \bar{i}_R$ (i.e., some of P's early actions currently recorded by Q have been known by $\bar{P}$), then it deletes those early actions and updates i_S.

Note that Ch^m remains correct since the causality-related operations (dash-boxed in Fig. 9) do not affect the input of Snd nor the output of Rcv.

SCP Security of Ch^m. Consider a function localG$_m^*$ that updates G_P as follows. First, it extracts the decrypted queue $\bar{Q}$ and the output index $\bar{i}$ from the input transcript T_{Rcv}. Then, it processes $\bar{Q}$ from its front (oldest) element to its back (latest) element one by one. Recall that each element e_i in $\bar{Q}$ is a message index that represents an action. Consider the i-th element e_i in $\bar{Q}$. If e_i represents a sending action, the function checks if the e_i-th sending vertex in $V_{\bar{P}}$ has been added, and if not adds it and connects it to the corresponding receiving vertex (if any) in V_P. If e_i represents a receiving action, the function checks if the e_i-th sending vertex in V_P already connects to some receiving vertex in $V_{\bar{P}}$, and if not adds a new receiving (largest) vertex $\bar{v}$ to $V_{\bar{P}}$ and a directed edge from the e_i-th sending vertex of V_P to $\bar{v}$. After processing the entire queue $\bar{Q}$, it adds the $\bar{i}$-th sending vertex $\bar{v}'$ to $V_{\bar{P}}$ (if not yet added) and a new receiving (largest) vertex v' to V_P, then adds the edge $(\bar{v}', v')$. We illustrate the above procedures with a simple example in Fig. 10.

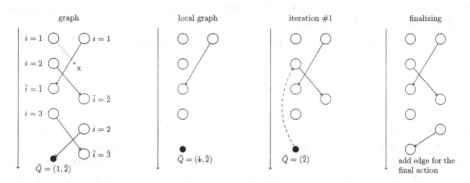

Fig. 10. Building local graph in Ch^m. The first figure shows the actual communication graph (with its first message being dropped on the network) where the left party eventually receives a ciphertext with queue $\bar{Q} = (1, \bar{2})$. Starting from its local graph (2nd figure) it iterates over the queue $\bar{Q}$, skipping the first sending vertex 1 (as it has been received) and adding the receiving vertex $\bar{2}$ as the largest vertex in the other party's vertex set and the edge (3rd figure). It finalizes the update by adding the vertices and edge of the final action (4th figure).

With $\mathsf{localG}_m^\star$, it is not hard to see that: (1) $G_P = G|_P$ always holds for a correct Ch^m execution and (2) $(G_P)_{\geq t_c + \Delta} = (G|_P)_{\geq t_c + \Delta}$ always holds for a correct Ch^m execution after recovery; we call this the correctness of $\mathsf{localG}_m^\star$. In the following theorem (with proof in the full version [9]), we show that the SCP security of the generic causal channel Ch^m can be reduced to the S-INT-CTXT and ROB-CORR security of its underlying bidirectional channel Ch.

Theorem 1. *For any $\Delta > 0$ and efficient adversary $\mathcal{A}$, there exist efficient adversaries $\mathcal{B}, \mathcal{C}$ such that*

$$\mathbf{Adv}^{\mathsf{scp}}_{\mathsf{Ch}^m, \Delta, \mathsf{localG}_m^\star}(\mathcal{A}) \leq \mathbf{Adv}^{\mathsf{s\text{-}int\text{-}ctxt}}_{\mathsf{Ch}, \Delta}(\mathcal{B}) + \mathbf{Adv}^{\mathsf{rob\text{-}corr}}_{\mathsf{Ch}, \Delta}(\mathcal{C}).$$

When Ch is instantiated with $\mathsf{Ch}_{\mathsf{Signal}}$, in the full version [9] we show that $\mathsf{Ch}^m_{\mathsf{cSignal}}$ provably achieves SCP security with $\Delta = 3$.

Integrating Causality in Application User Interfaces. Recall that SCP security ensures that the channel parties are in principal able to derive the correct causal information, but how to utilize it is up to the SM applications.

Here for completeness, we show a concrete method for application user interfaces to visualize causality offered by our causal channel.

Consider a message m accepted by a user, say, Alice. A causal channel can provide a causality feature that allows Alice to view which of her sent messages m depends on. To do this, the channel extracts the decrypted $\bar{Q}$ from the Rcv execution that outputs m, collects the recorded indices of messages sent by Alice, and returns those message indices along with m to the application. Then, the feature can be realized by highlighting the messages returned from the channel when Alice does a "press and hold" on the accepted message m. A toy example is described in the full version [9].

Such a causality-preserving feature helps users reduce or avoid misunderstanding caused by insufficient or incorrect causal dependencies displayed on a regular user interface (that does not preserve causality). There could be other more elegant ways to visualize causality, but finding the best visualization method and performing usability testing are beyond the scope of our work.

On the Size of Q. Recall that Q records all performed actions (as message indices) whose delivery has not yet been confirmed. From Fig. 9, we see that index queue Q dominates all overhead (computation, storage and communication). More precisely, all overhead is linear to the queue size $|Q|$. Clearly, $|Q|$ depends on the communication patterns of the conversations, for which we show two examples in the full version [9]. In practice, a straightforward way to limit such overhead is to set a *threshold* for the maximum number of elements in Q, similar to how Signal limits the maximum number of cached encrypted messages. Here, however, the causality security is slightly weakened to protect only the actions recorded in Q, for which a formal confirmation is left for future work.

6   Message Franking Channels and Causality Preservation

6.1   Message Franking Channels

In a message franking channel, besides exchanging messages the users are also allowed to report abusive messages to a third party (e.g., the messaging service provider). This additional functionality is called *message franking (MF)* by Facebook Messenger [15]. Such a setup concerns three parties: two users Alice (A), Bob (B), and a third party that we call a server (S). S routes (encrypted) messages exchanged between users (and hence S is referred to as a *router* in [19]). The role of the server is to authenticate the franking tag $c.c_f$ included in any ciphertext c routed through the server, such that the receiver (reporter) has a proof for the server to check that the other user has indeed sent that ciphertext.

A *message franking channel (MFC)* has been formalized by [19]. Similar to the discussion in Sect. 4.1, we extend their definition to capture the acting party's identity and the received index of the sending action (wrapped into the message auxiliary information), meanwhile ignoring the application-level associated data, sometimes referred to as a header. Besides, to match our bidirectional channel syntax and for better understanding, our definition is not nonce-based.

Definition 3. *A message franking channel is a five-tuple* MFCh $=$ (Init, Snd, Rcv, Tag, Rprt) *associated with a channel key space* $\mathcal{K}_{Ch}$, *a server key space* $\mathcal{K}_S$, *a state space* $\mathcal{ST}$, *a message space* $\mathcal{M}$, *an auxiliary information space* $\mathcal{U}$, *an index space* $\mathcal{I}$, *an opening key space* $\mathcal{K}_f$, *a franking tag space* $\mathcal{C}_f$, *and a tag space* $\mathcal{T}$:

Init$(P,k) \rightarrow st_P$: *takes* $P \in \{A,B,S\}$ *and a key* k, *where* $k \in \mathcal{K}_{Ch}$ *for* $P \in \{A,B\}$ *and* $k \in \mathcal{K}_S$ *for* $P = S$, *and outputs the initial state of* P;

Snd$(P, st, m) \xrightarrow{\$} (st', c)$ *takes* $P \in \{A,B\}$, $st \in \mathcal{ST}$, $m \in \mathcal{M}$, *and outputs an updated state* $st' \in \mathcal{ST}$ *and a ciphertext* $c \in \{0,1\}^*$, *where the ciphertext contains a franking tag* $c.c_f \in \mathcal{C}_f$ *and a message index* $c.i \in \mathcal{I}$;

Rcv$(P, st, c) \rightarrow (st', m, u, k_f)$ *takes* $P \in \{A,B\}$, $st \in \mathcal{ST}$, $c \in \{0,1\}^*$, *and outputs an updated state* $st' \in \mathcal{ST}$, *a message* $m \in \mathcal{M} \cup \{\perp\}$ *with auxiliary information* $u \in \mathcal{U}$ *that contains message index* $u.i \in \mathcal{I}$, *and an opening key* $k_f \in \mathcal{K}_f$;

Tag$(st_S, P, c_f) \rightarrow (st'_S, \tau)$: *takes* $st_S \in \mathcal{ST}$, *(sender identity)* $P \in \{A,B\}$, $c_f \in \mathcal{C}_f$, *and outputs an updated state* $st'_S \in \mathcal{ST}$ *and a server tag* $\tau \in \mathcal{T}$;

Rprt$(st_S, P, m, u, k_f, c_f, \tau) \rightarrow (st'_S, b)$ *takes* $st_S \in \mathcal{ST}$, *(reporter identity)* $P \in \{A,B\}$, $m \in \mathcal{M}$, $u \in \mathcal{U}$, $k_f \in \mathcal{K}_f$, $c_f \in \mathcal{C}_f$, $\tau \in \mathcal{T}$, *and outputs an updated state* $st'_S \in \mathcal{ST}$ *and a verification bit* $b \in \{0,1\}$.

Let Ch $=$ (Init', Snd, Rcv') *be the underlying bidirectional channel of* MFCh, *where* Init' *is* Init *with input* $P \in \{A,B\}$ *and* Rcv' *is* Rcv *with output* $(st', m, u.i)$. *Correctness requires that 1)* Ch *is correct and 2) all received messages can be successfully reported (i.e., $b = 1$).*

A message franking channel MFCh extends its underlying bidirectional channel in several ways: (i) Init further initializes the secret state of the server; (ii) Snd and Rcv respectively further output a franking tag and an opening key used by the server to verify authenticity of user messages; (iii) Rcv outputs auxiliary information (in addition to the message index) to capture potential causality information of the received message; and (iv) Tag and Rprt are used by the server to tag encrypted messages and verify reported messages.

6.2 Causality Preservation of Message Franking Channels

As briefly explained in the introduction, there are two types of causality preservation one would expect from a message franking channel. One is security for *honest users* against *a malicious server* that acts as a network attacker, resembling our causality preservation for bidirectional channels. The other one is security for *an honest server* against *one malicious user* who knows the channel key and tries to fool the reporting system by tampering with causality.

Trust Model. Before defining security, we first clarify the trust model for message franking channels. It is usually assumed that the server-user communications are *mutually authenticated*, which in practice can be realized by, e.g., server-authenticated TLS connections with user login. In particular, if the server is not authenticated, a user can send abusive messages that cannot be reported; if the user is not authenticated, a user can forge and successfully report abusive messages never sent by the other user. Note that such mutual authentication guarantees message integrity against network attackers, i.e., only a malicious server is able to play man-in-the-middle attacks.

Channel Causality Preservation. First, as with bidirectional channels, we define security notions to model causality preservation for honest users, which we call *channel causality preservation (CCP)* notions. The goal of the adversary is the same as the bidirectional channel case, i.e., to make some user's local view on causality deviate from the actual case or to make some user accept a malicious message. Under our trust model, the adversary is a malicious server that mirrors a network attacker in the bidirectional channel setting.

The security experiments for both the basic and strong causality preservation of a message franking channel MFCh are defined in the same way as depicted in Fig. 3 and Fig. 4, except that the bidirectional channel algorithms Init, Snd, Rcv are replaced by those of MFCh and the message index is extracted from the accepted auxiliary information. The corresponding advantage measures $\mathbf{Adv}^{cp}_{MFCh,localG}(\mathcal{A})$ and $\mathbf{Adv}^{scp}_{MFCh,\Delta,localG}(\mathcal{A})$ are also defined in the same way. Note that the server-related algorithms Tag, Rprt do not show up in the above security definitions because the adversary plays the role of a malicious server and knows the server secrets. One can also define the integrity notions for message franking channels as with Fig. 5 and Fig. 6 and derive similar relationship between CCP notions and integrity notions as with Fig. 7.

Report Causality Preservation. Then, we model the causality security that is directly related to the "message franking" functionality, which we call *report causality preservation (RCP)*. To define such security, it is convenient to view the adversary as either a malicious sender or a malicious receiver (reporter), like [18,19] defining *sender-binding* and *receiver-binding* notions for message franking schemes. Sender binding guarantees that no malicious user can make the other user accept a message that cannot be reported (and hence the correct causal information cannot be reported); receiver binding guarantees that no malicious user can successfully report a message that is never sent by the other user. Similarly, we split our RCP notion into two parts: RCP-S and RCP-R.

Our RCP-S notion (see Fig. 11 for its security experiment $\mathbf{Exp}^{rcp\text{-}s}_{MFCh,\mathcal{A}}(1^\lambda)$) is *equivalent* to the sender binding notion defined in [19], except that we add a Send oracle to allow an honest party to send messages and our MFC syntax uses probabilistic AEAD and ignores headers. This notion is a "bidirectional channel" extension of the "unidirectional" sender-binding property defined in [18], and the adversarial goal in our model is again to make an honest user accept an unreportable message. Note that in $\mathbf{Exp}^{rcp\text{-}s}_{MFCh,\mathcal{A}}(1^\lambda)$, the Recv oracle is required to process only ciphertexts with valid tags output by Tag, because the trust model assumes that users can only receive messages through the server (otherwise RCP-S is easy to break). Also note that although a malicious sender can manipulate the global causality graph, once the local graph is settled on the honest receiver side, this graph is deemed correct and cannot be modified; therefore, causality-related functionality is irrelevant to the definition of RCP-S. More detailed description of RCP-S is omitted here due to its high similarity to [19]. The RCP-S adversarial advantage of a message franking channel MFCh is defined as $\mathbf{Adv}_{\mathsf{MFCh}}^{\mathsf{rcp\text{-}s}}(\mathcal{A}) = \Pr[\mathbf{Exp}_{\mathsf{MFCh},\mathcal{A}}^{\mathsf{rcp\text{-}s}}(1^\lambda) \Rightarrow 1]$. We say MFCh is RCP-S-secure if its RCP-S advantage is negligible for any efficient adversary $\mathcal{A}$.

Our RCP-R notion (formally defined later) also follows the receiver-binding definitions [18,19], but it is extended to further allow the adversary to win if it successfully reports a message that carries *wrong or insufficient* causal information. As explained in the introduction, such information is very important for message franking because a benign message may look abusive when taken out of context. By design, RCP-R obviously implies receiver binding, which is defined as RCP-R excluding causality-related parts. Such a receiver binding notion (omitted here for conciseness) is essentially equivalent to receiver binding defined in [19]. However, the other direction is not true, i.e., receiver binding does not imply RCP-R. For instance, as shown in Sect. 7.1, Facebook's message franking channel MFCh$_{\mathsf{FB}}$ does not achieve RCP-R security, but with a theorem very similar to Theorem 3 (shown in Sect. 7.2) one can prove that MFCh$_{\mathsf{FB}}$ satisfies receiver binding.

We say a message franking channel *preserves report causality* (or is RCP-secure) if it is both RCP-S-secure and RCP-R-secure. In the following, we show the formal definition of our RCP-R security.

Message-Dependency Graph and its Extractor. First, we clarify what causal information is considered sufficient for a message m sent by an honest party P and reported by a malicious user $\bar{P}$. Ideally, the entire causal information until the sending action of the reported message could be carried by the m's auxiliary information, but this leads to expensive communication overhead. Instead, it suffices to carry only the causal information not yet confirmed by $\bar{P}$ in P's view, because the confirmed causal information has already been carried by the auxiliary information of messages accepted by P and hence can be reported. The above not-yet-confirmed causal information is exactly what queue Q records in the causal channel Ch^m (see Fig. 9) appended with the index i of the reported message m. We call the causality graph that represents the above causal information associated with each message the *message-dependency graph*. Let $G|_P^i$ denote the message-dependency graph of the i-th message sent by party P, which is a subgraph of $G|_P$. For instance, consider the message sent by Bob at b_6 in Fig. 2. This message has index 4 and $G|_B^4$ consists of (a_1, b_3), b_4, (a_5, b_5), and b_6, because the received message at b_5 already confirmed the delivery of messages sent at b_1 and b_2. Note that $G|_P^i$ is necessary for the server to construct the restricted causality graph $G|_P$ of the accused honest party P.

A message-dependency graph extractor Extr is a function that takes a message's auxiliary information and outputs a message-dependency graph.

$\mathbf{Exp}_{\mathsf{MFCh},\mathcal{A}}^{\mathsf{rcp\text{-}s}}(1^\lambda):$

1: $k_S \xleftarrow{\$} \mathcal{K}_S$
2: $k_{\mathsf{Ch}} \xleftarrow{\$} \mathcal{A}(1^\lambda)$
3: $st_S \leftarrow \mathsf{Init}(S, k_S)$
4: $st_A \leftarrow \mathsf{Init}(A, k_{\mathsf{Ch}})$
5: $st_B \leftarrow \mathsf{Init}(B, k_{\mathsf{Ch}})$
6: $\mathcal{R}_t, \mathcal{R}_r \leftarrow \varnothing$
7: $\mathcal{A}^{\mathsf{Send,Recv,Tag,Report}}(k_{\mathsf{Ch}})$
8: terminate with 0

$\mathsf{Send}(P, m):$

1: $(st_P, c) \xleftarrow{\$} \mathsf{Snd}(P, st_P, m)$
2: if $c = \bot$ then return $\bot$
3: return c

$\mathsf{Recv}(P, c, \tau):$ (require $(\bar{P}, c.c_f, \tau) \in \mathcal{R}_t$)

1: $(st_P, m, u, k_f) \leftarrow \mathsf{Rcv}(P, st_P, c)$
2: if $m \neq \bot$ then
3: | add $(P, m, u, k_f, c.c_f, \tau)$ to $\mathcal{R}_r$
4: return m, u, k_f

$\mathsf{Tag}(P, c_f):$

1: $(st_S, \tau) \leftarrow \mathsf{Tag}(st_S, P, c_f)$
2: add (P, c_f, τ) to $\mathcal{R}_t$
3: return τ

$\mathsf{Report}(P, m, u, k_f, c_f, \tau):$

1: $(st_S, b) \leftarrow \mathsf{Rprt}(st_S, P, m, u, k_f, c_f, \tau)$
2: if $b = 0$ and $(P, m, u, k_f, c_f, \tau) \in \mathcal{R}_r$ then
3: | terminate with 1 ($\mathcal{A}$ wins)
4: return b

$\mathbf{Exp}_{\mathsf{MFCh},\mathsf{Extr},\mathcal{A}}^{\mathsf{rcp\text{-}r}}(1^\lambda):$

1: $k_S \xleftarrow{\$} \mathcal{K}_S$
2: $k_{\mathsf{Ch}} \xleftarrow{\$} \mathcal{A}(1^\lambda)$
3: $st_S \leftarrow \mathsf{Init}(S, k_S)$
4: $st_A \leftarrow \mathsf{Init}(A, k_{\mathsf{Ch}})$
5: $st_B \leftarrow \mathsf{Init}(B, k_{\mathsf{Ch}})$
6: $\mathcal{R}, \mathcal{R}_f \leftarrow \varnothing, G \leftarrow \varepsilon$
7: $\mathcal{A}^{\mathsf{SendTag,Recv,Report}}(k_{\mathsf{Ch}})$
8: terminate with 0

$\mathsf{SendTag}(P, m):$

1: $(st_P, c) \xleftarrow{\$} \mathsf{Snd}(P, st_P, m)$
2: if $c = \bot$ then return $\bot$
3: $G \leftarrow G + (\mathsf{S}, P)$
4: $(st_S, \tau) \leftarrow \mathsf{Tag}(st_S, P, c.c_f)$
5: add (P, c, τ) to $\mathcal{R}$
6: add $(P, c.i, m, c.c_f)$ to $\mathcal{R}_f$
7: return c, τ

$\mathsf{Recv}(P, c, \tau):$ (require $(\bar{P}, c, \tau) \in \mathcal{R}$)

1: $(st_P, m, u, k_f) \leftarrow \mathsf{Rcv}(P, st_P, c)$
2: if $m \neq \bot$ then $G \leftarrow G + (\mathsf{R}, P, u.i)$
3: return m, u, k_f

$\mathsf{Report}(P, m, u, k_f, c_f, \tau):$

1: $(st_S, b) \leftarrow \mathsf{Rprt}(st_S, P, m, u, k_f, c_f, \tau)$
2: if $b = 1$ and $[(\bar{P}, u.i, m, c_f) \notin \mathcal{R}_f$ or $\mathsf{Extr}(u) \neq G|_{\bar{P}}^{u.i}]$
3: then terminate with 1 ($\mathcal{A}$ wins)
3: return b

Fig. 11. Security experiments for report causality preservation

Security Experiment for RCP-R.

On the bottom of Fig. 11, we depict the RCP-R security experiment $\mathbf{Exp}_{\mathsf{MFCh},\mathsf{Extr},\mathcal{A}}^{\mathsf{rcp\text{-}r}}(1^\lambda)$, which is associated with a message franking channel $\mathsf{MFCh} = (\mathsf{Init}, \mathsf{Snd}, \mathsf{Rcv}, \mathsf{Tag}, \mathsf{Rprt})$ and a message-dependency graph extractor Extr.

In the beginning, the challenger samples a random server key k_S and the adversary outputs an arbitrary channel key k_{Ch}, then the Init algorithm is executed to derive the initial states. All the states used in the game are also properly initialized. Then, $\mathcal{A}$ inputs the channel key k_{Ch} and is given access to three oracles SendTag, Recv and Report:

SendTag takes a user identity and a message, calls Snd on the input message, updates the graph, calls Tag on the franking tag (included in the derived ciphertext), records useful information in $\mathcal{R}$ and $\mathcal{R}_f$, and returns the derived ciphertext and server tag. This oracle models a user sending messages honestly through the server. Recall that malicious senders are already captured by RCP-S, whose goal is to make the other user accept unreportable messages.

Recv takes a user identity, a ciphertext and a server tag, calls Rcv on the input ciphertext, updates the graph, and outputs the derived message with auxiliary information and the derived opening key. Note that this oracle does not give the adversary much additional ability, because as a malicious receiver it already knows the secret user state to decrypt any ciphertext. The purpose of this oracle is to allow an honest party receive messages (through the server) and to update the global causality graph G (used to detect maliciously reported causal information). Therefore, we can require the oracle to only process ciphertexts and server tags output by SendTag queries.

Report takes a reporter (receiver) identity, a message with auxiliary information, an opening key, a franking tag, and a server tag, calls Rprt on the oracle input, and returns the derived verification bit b. The adversary wins if it reports successfully ($b = 1$) with either a message never output by an honest sender (($\bar{P}, u.i, m, c_f$) $\notin \mathcal{R}_f$) or incorrect causal information (Extr(u) $\neq G|_{\bar{P}}^{u.i}$).

Advantage Measure of RCP-R. The RCP-R advantage is defined as $\mathbf{Adv}_{\mathsf{MFCh,Extr}}^{\mathsf{rcp-r}}(\mathcal{A}) = \Pr[\mathbf{Exp}_{\mathsf{MFCh,Extr},\mathcal{A}}^{\mathsf{rcp-r}}(1^\lambda) \Rightarrow 1]$ for any arbitrary extractor Extr. We say a message franking channel MFCh is RCP-R-secure if one can *construct* an efficiently computable function Extr* such that, for any efficient adversary $\mathcal{A}$, the advantage $\mathbf{Adv}_{\mathsf{MFCh,Extr}^\star}^{\mathsf{rcp-r}}(\mathcal{A})$ is negligible. That is, a RCP-R-secure message franking channel guarantees that the server can use Extr* to derive all causal information captured by the associated message-dependency graph of each successfully reported message.

Remark on RCP-R Security. Note that RCP-R security both guarantees the authenticity of the reported message and extends it to the message flow. The reported flow itself, however, does not include the content of previous messages but only contains information about the related causal relations (to reduce the overhead). In case of a dispute, the accused party can then report the content of the previous messages for the server to reconstruct the communication. We discuss this process in more detail for the concrete case of Facebook Messenger at the end of Sect. 7.2.

7   Causality Preservation of Facebook's Message Franking

In this section, we first describe Facebook Messenger's message franking scheme [15] and show its insecurity for preserving report causality, then amend it to provably achieve the desired security.

7.1   Facebook's Message Franking Channel and Its Insecurity

Facebook's Message Franking Channel. Following our message franking channel syntax (see Definition 6.1), we present Facebook's MFC as a message franking channel MFCh$_{\mathrm{FB}}$ in Fig. 12, in a *generic* style for the benefit of modular design. That is, we abstract MFCh$_{\mathrm{FB}}$ as constructed with a bidirectional channel Ch = (Init, Snd, Rcv), a commitment scheme with verification CS = (Com, VerC), and a MAC MAC = ($\mathcal{K}$, Mac, Ver), where Facebook Messenger uses Signal as the underlying bidirectional channel protocol (i.e., Ch = Ch$_{\mathrm{Signal}}$) and instantiates both CS and MAC with HMAC-SHA-256 HMAC [4]. Correctness of MFCh$_{\mathrm{FB}}$ follows from that of its building blocks Ch, MAC, and CS.

Causality Insecurity of MFCh$_{\mathrm{FB}}$. First, as shown in Sect. 5.1, we know MFCh$_{\mathrm{FB}}$ does not preserve channel causality when Ch is instantiated with

$\mathsf{Init}(P, k)$:
- if $P = S$ then
  - return k
- $st_{\mathsf{Ch}} \leftarrow \mathsf{Ch.Init}(P, k)$
- $\boxed{s \leftarrow 1,\ i_S, i_R \leftarrow -1}$
- $\boxed{Q \leftarrow \varnothing}$
- return $(st_{\mathsf{Ch}}, \boxed{s, i_S, i_R, Q})$

$\mathsf{Snd}(P, st, m)$:
- if $P = S$ or $st = \perp$ then return $st, \perp$
- $(k_f, c_f) \leftarrow \mathsf{Com}((m, \boxed{s, Q}))$
- $(st, c_e) \xleftarrow{\$} \mathsf{Ch.Snd}(P, st_{\mathsf{Ch}}, (m, \boxed{i_R, Q}, k_f))$
- $\boxed{Q.\mathsf{enq}(s),\ s \leftarrow s + 1}$
- return $st, (c_e, c_f)$

$\mathsf{Tag}(st, P, c_f)$:
- if $P = S$ or $st = \perp$ then return $st, \perp$
- $\tau \leftarrow \mathsf{Mac}(st, c_f \| P \| \bar{P})$
- return st, τ

$\mathsf{Rcv}(P, st, c)$:
- if $P = S$ or $st = \perp$ then return $st, \perp, \perp, \perp$
- $(st, (m, \boxed{\bar{i}_R, \bar{Q}}, k_f), \bar{i}) \leftarrow \mathsf{Ch.Rcv}(P, st_{\mathsf{Ch}}, c.c_e)$
- if $m = \perp$ or $\mathsf{VerC}((m, \boxed{\bar{i}, \bar{Q}}), k_f, c.c_f) = 0$ then
  - return $st, \perp, \perp, \perp$
- $\boxed{\mathsf{update}(Q, \bar{i}, i_S, i_R, \bar{i}_R)}$
- return $st, m, (\bar{i}, \boxed{\bar{Q}}), k_f$

$\mathsf{Rprt}(st, P, m, u, k_f, c_f, \tau)$:
- if $P = S$ or $st = \perp$ then return $st, 0$
- return $st, \mathsf{Ver}(st, c_f \| \bar{P} \| P, \tau) \wedge \mathsf{VerC}((m, u), k_f, c_f)$

Fig. 12. Facebook's message franking channel $\mathsf{MFCh}_{\mathrm{FB}}$ (without boxed content) and the causal message franking channel $\mathsf{MFCh}_{\mathrm{cFB}}$ (with boxed content). The update function is the same as defined in Fig. 9.

$\mathsf{Ch}_{\mathrm{Signal}}$. Then, in the following we show that $\mathsf{MFCh}_{\mathrm{FB}}$ does not achieve RCP security (more specifically, RCP-R security) either, even if Ch is instantiated with our proposed causal Signal channel $\mathsf{Ch}^{m}_{\mathrm{cSignal}}$. The key observation is that the server receives only the reported message and its index, but not any other causal information. For instance, for the two execution flows considered in our Signal causality attack depicted in Fig. 8, when the message m_3 associated with c_3 is reported, the server cannot distinguish the two flows (that lead to different message-dependency graphs). That is, any extractor Extr will output an incorrect message-dependency graph associated with m_3 with probability at least $1/2$, i.e., $\mathbf{Adv}^{\mathsf{rcp\text{-}r}}_{\mathsf{MFCh}_{\mathrm{FB}},\mathsf{Extr}}(\mathcal{A}) \geq 1/2$ for any possible extractor Extr. By definition, $\mathsf{MFCh}_{\mathrm{FB}}$ does not achieve RCP-R security.

7.2 Integrating Causality in Facebook's Message Franking

The Causal Message Franking Channel. As shown in Fig. 12 with boxed content, our causal message franking channel $\mathsf{MFCh}_{\mathrm{cFB}}$ amends Facebook's message franking channel by adding a queue Q (defined in Sect. 5.2) to the auxiliary information of each sent message. This is quite similar to the Signal case, so the performance overhead introduced by $\mathsf{MFCh}_{\mathrm{cFB}}$ is also linear in $|Q|$ as discussed in Sect. 5.2. It is also easy to check that $\mathsf{MFCh}_{\mathrm{cFB}}$ remains correct.

CCP Security of $\mathsf{MFCh}_{\mathrm{cFB}}$**.** Consider a local graph update function $\mathsf{localG}^{\star}$ that extracts $\bar{Q}$ and $\bar{i}$ from the input transcript T_{Rcv} and proceeds as $\mathsf{localG}^{\star}_{m}$ for Ch^{m}. With a proof (omitted here) very similar to that of Theorem 1, we have the following theorem showing that the SCP security of our proposed causal message franking channel $\mathsf{MFCh}_{\mathrm{cFB}}$ can be reduced to the S-INT-CTXT and ROB-CORR security of the underlying bidirectional channel Ch.[9] In particular, the latter holds for $\Delta = 3$ when Ch is instantiated with $\mathsf{Ch}_{\mathrm{Signal}}$ (e.g., for Facebook Messenger), as discussed in the full version [9].

[9] A similar theorem (omitted here) holds for the case of basic causality preservation.

Theorem 2. *For any $\Delta > 0$ and any efficient adversary $\mathcal{A}$, there exist efficient adversaries $\mathcal{B}, \mathcal{C}$ such that*

$$\mathbf{Adv}^{\text{scp}}_{\text{MFCh}_{\text{cFB}}, \Delta, \text{localG}^*}(\mathcal{A}) \leq \mathbf{Adv}^{\text{s-int-ctxt}}_{\text{Ch}, \Delta}(\mathcal{B}) + \mathbf{Adv}^{\text{rob-corr}}_{\text{Ch}, \Delta}(\mathcal{C}).$$

RCP Security of MFCh_{cFB}. First, for almost the same reason why Facebook's message franking scheme satisfies perfect sender binding in [18], we can conclude that MFCh_{cFB} achieves perfect RCP-S security (i.e., $\mathbf{Adv}^{\text{rcp-s}}_{\text{MFCh}_{\text{cFB}}}(\mathcal{A}) = 0$). This is because Recv in the RCP-S security game (see top of Fig. 11) processes only ciphertexts with a *valid* server tag (i.e., sent through the server) and Rcv runs the *same* VerC check as in Rprt before accepting a message. Actually, with the same argument one can show that the original Facebook's MFC MFCh_{FB} is also RCP-S secure. Then, for RCP-R security, consider a message-dependency graph extractor Extr* that takes $(\bar{l}, \bar{Q})$ from the input auxiliary information u and then proceeds as localC^*_m for Ch^m, but now updating an empty local graph. The following theorem (proved in the full version [9]) shows that MFCh_{cFB} preserves report causality if its underlying MAC and CS schemes are secure. The latter holds when both instantiated with HMAC [3,18].

Theorem 3. *For any efficient adversary $\mathcal{A}$, there exist efficient adversaries $\mathcal{B}, \mathcal{C}$ such that*

$$\mathbf{Adv}^{\text{rcp-r}}_{\text{MFCh}_{\text{cFB}}, \text{Extr}^*}(\mathcal{A}) \leq \mathbf{Adv}^{\text{euf-cma}}_{\text{MAC}}(\mathcal{B}) + \mathbf{Adv}^{\text{v-bind}}_{\text{CS}}(\mathcal{C}).$$

Improving Dispute Handling with Causality. Here we show how causality can be utilized by a message franking server to handle disputes in a more reliable way. In particular, the MFCh_{cFB} server can construct Extr* to extract the message-dependency graph when dealing with abuse reports. Since now the server knows how the reported message depends on previous messages (without knowing the content), the server can ask the users to report those messages for further consideration if the accused user wants to defend himself. This process can continue until the fact is clear, which is always viable because in the worst case the entire communication with the correct causal information is revealed.

For instance, consider the attack discussed in the introduction: Alice asks Bob "what was the worst insult you have ever heard?" and reports the received response. The server now gets the exact message dependencies of the reported message (which may be visualized as a causality graph or something similar) and knows that Bob indeed received some message from Alice before sending the reported message, so it can ask Bob if he wants to report that message to defend himself. In this way, the above causality attack can be prevented.

8   Conclusion

We have seen that causality in two-user messaging channels can be preserved if one transmits sufficient information on the channel to be able to reconstruct the restricted graph. This coincides with the original idea in distributed computing to recover global states from local snapshots. It is an interesting open problem to investigate how causality can be integrated in secure *group messaging*. Another interesting problem to explore is to determine a lower bound on the time and space overhead for channels to guarantee causality security.

We remark that, from a channel perspective, we assume the *atomic* sending of messages, while for example TLS 1.3 is rather a stream-based interface [17]. Although it may seem first that our notion of causality is related only to an application-level viewpoint with atomic message processing, it is nonetheless tied to the receiving action Rcv of the channel protocol.

Finally, while not the focus of this work, it is certainly worthwhile to investigate how causality can be better visualized for users; one should also scrutinize how users respond to such designs.

Acknowledgments. We thank the anonymous reviewers for valuable comments. Shan Chen is funded by the research start-up grant by the Southern University of Science and Technology. Marc Fischlin is funded by the Deutsche Forschungsgemeinschaft (DFG, German Research Foundation) - SFB 1119 - 236615297.

References

1. Alwen, J., Coretti, S., Dodis, Y.: The double ratchet: Security notions, proofs, and modularization for the Signal protocol. In: Ishai, Y., Rijmen, V. (eds.) EURO-CRYPT 2019. Part I, volume 11476 of LNCS, pp. 129–158. Springer, Heidelberg (2019). https://doi.org/10.1007/978-3-030-17653-2_5
2. Barooti, K., Collins, D., Colombo, S., Huguenin-Dumittan, L., Vaudenay, S.: On active attack detection in messaging with immediate decryption. In: Handschuh, H., Lysyanskaya, A. (eds.) CRYPTO 2023, Part IV, volume 14084 of Lecture Notes in Computer Science, pp. 362–395. Springer, Cham (2023). https://doi.org/10.1007/978-3-031-38551-3_12
3. Bellare, M.: New proofs for NMAC and HMAC: security without collision-resistance. In: Dwork, C. (ed.) CRYPTO 2006. LNCS, vol. 4117, pp. 602–619. Springer, Heidelberg (2006). https://doi.org/10.1007/11818175_36
4. Bellare, M., Canetti, R., Krawczyk, H.: Keying hash functions for message authentication. In: Koblitz, N. (ed.) CRYPTO 1996. LNCS, vol. 1109, pp. 1–15. Springer, Heidelberg (1996). https://doi.org/10.1007/3-540-68697-5_1
5. Bellare, M., Kohno, T., Namprempre, C.: Authenticated encryption in SSH: provably fixing the SSH binary packet protocol. In: Atluri, V. (ed.) ACM CCS 2002, pp. 1–11. ACM Press (2002)
6. Boyd, C., Hale, B., Mjølsnes, S.F., Stebila, D.: From stateless to stateful: generic authentication and authenticated encryption constructions with application to TLS. In: Sako, K. (ed.) CT-RSA 2016. LNCS, vol. 9610, pp. 55–71. Springer, Cham (2016). https://doi.org/10.1007/978-3-319-29485-8_4
7. Caforio, A., Durak, F.B., Vaudenay, S.: Beyond security and efficiency: on-demand ratcheting with security awareness. In: Garay, J.A. (ed.) PKC 2021. LNCS, vol. 12711, pp. 649–677. Springer, Cham (2021). https://doi.org/10.1007/978-3-030-75248-4_23

8. Chandy, K.M., Lamport, L.: Distributed snapshots: determining global states of distributed systems. ACM Trans. Comput. Syst. **3**(1), 63–75 (1985)
9. Chen, S., Fischlin, M.: Integrating causality in messaging channels. Cryptology ePrint Archive, Paper 2024/362 (2024). https://eprint.iacr.org/2024/362
10. Cohn-Gordon, K., Cremers, C.J.F., Garratt, L.: On post-compromise security. In: Hicks, M., Köpf, B. (eds.) CSF 2016 Computer Security Foundations Symposium, pp. 164–178. IEEE Computer Society Press (2016)
11. Cremers, C., Zhao, M.: Provably post-quantum secure messaging with strong compromise resilience and immediate decryption. Cryptology ePrint Archive, Report 2022/1481 (2022). https://eprint.iacr.org/2022/1481
12. Dodis, Y., Grubbs, P., Ristenpart, T., Woodage, J.: Fast message franking: from invisible salamanders to encryptment. In: Shacham, H., Boldyreva, A. (eds.) CRYPTO 2018. LNCS, vol. 10991, pp. 155–186. Springer, Cham (2018). https://doi.org/10.1007/978-3-319-96884-1_6
13. Durak, F.B., Vaudenay, S.: Bidirectional asynchronous ratcheted key agreement with linear complexity. In: Attrapadung, N., Yagi, T. (eds.) IWSEC 2019. LNCS, vol. 11689, pp. 343–362. Springer, Cham (2019). https://doi.org/10.1007/978-3-030-26834-3_20
14. Eugster, P., Marson, G.A., Poettering, B.: A cryptographic look at multi-party channels. In: CSF 2018, pp. 31–45. IEEE (2018)
15. Facebook: Messenger secret conversations – technical whitepaper (2017)
16. Fischlin, M., Günther, F., Janson, C.: Robust channels: handling unreliable networks in the record layers of QUIC and DTLS 1.3. J. Cryptol. **37**(2), 9 (2024)
17. Fischlin, M., Günther, F., Marson, G.A., Paterson, K.G.: Data is a stream: security of stream-based channels. In: Gennaro, R., Robshaw, M. (eds.) CRYPTO 2015. LNCS, vol. 9216, pp. 545–564. Springer, Heidelberg (2015). https://doi.org/10.1007/978-3-662-48000-7_27
18. Grubbs, P., Lu, J., Ristenpart, T.: Message franking via committing authenticated encryption. In: Katz, J., Shacham, H. (eds.) CRYPTO 2017. LNCS, vol. 10403, pp. 66–97. Springer, Cham (2017). https://doi.org/10.1007/978-3-319-63697-9_3
19. Huguenin-Dumittan, L., Leontiadis, I.: A message franking channel. In: Yu, Yu., Yung, M. (eds.) Inscrypt 2021. LNCS, vol. 13007, pp. 111–128. Springer, Cham (2021). https://doi.org/10.1007/978-3-030-88323-2_6
20. Jaeger, J., Stepanovs, I.: Optimal channel security against fine-grained state compromise: the safety of messaging. In: Shacham, H., Boldyreva, A. (eds.) CRYPTO 2018. LNCS, vol. 10991, pp. 33–62. Springer, Cham (2018). https://doi.org/10.1007/978-3-319-96884-1_2
21. Jager, T., Kohlar, F., Schäge, S., Schwenk, J.: On the security of TLS-DHE in the standard model. In: Safavi-Naini, R., Canetti, R. (eds.) CRYPTO 2012. LNCS, vol. 7417, pp. 273–293. Springer, Heidelberg (2012). https://doi.org/10.1007/978-3-642-32009-5_17
22. Kohno, T., Palacio, A., Black, J.: Building secure cryptographic transforms, or how to encrypt and MAC. Cryptology ePrint Archive, Paper 2003/177 (2003). https://eprint.iacr.org/2003/177
23. Lamport, L.: Time, clocks, and the ordering of events in a distributed system. Communications (1978)
24. Marlinspike, M., Perrin, T.: The X3DH key agreement protocol (2016). https://www.signal.org/docs/specifications/x3dh/x3dh.pdf
25. Marson, G.A.: Real-World Aspects of Secure Channels: Fragmentation, Causality, and Forward Security. PhD thesis, Technische Universität (2017)

26. Marson, G.A., Poettering, B.: Security notions for bidirectional channels. IACR Trans. Symm. Cryptol. **2017**(1), 405–426 (2017)
27. Paterson, K.G., Ristenpart, T., Shrimpton, T.: Tag size *Does* matter: attacks and proofs for the TLS record protocol. In: Lee, D.H., Wang, X. (eds.) ASIACRYPT 2011. LNCS, vol. 7073, pp. 372–389. Springer, Heidelberg (2011). https://doi.org/10.1007/978-3-642-25385-0_20
28. Perrin, T., Marlinspike, M.: The double ratchet algorithm (2016). https://signal.org/docs/specifications/doubleratchet/doubleratchet.pdf
29. Pijnenburg, J., Poettering, B.: On secure ratcheting with immediate decryption. In: Agrawal, S., Lin, D. (eds.) ASIACRYPT 2022. Part III, volume 13793 of LNCS, pp. 89–118. Springer, Heidelberg (2022). https://doi.org/10.1007/978-3-031-22969-5_4
30. Rescorla, E.: The Transport Layer Security (TLS) Protocol Version 1.3. RFC 8446 (2018)
31. Rogaway, P., Zhang, Y.: Simplifying game-based definitions. In: Shacham, H., Boldyreva, A. (eds.) CRYPTO 2018. LNCS, vol. 10992, pp. 3–32. Springer, Cham (2018). https://doi.org/10.1007/978-3-319-96881-0_1
32. Rösler, P., Mainka, C., Schwenk, J.: More is less: on the end-to-end security of group chats in Signal, WhatsApp, and Threema. In: EuroS&P, pp. 415–429. IEEE (2018)
33. Scarlata, M.: Post-compromise security and TLS 1.3 session resumption (2020)
34. Strom, R.E., Yemini, S.: Optimistic recovery in distributed systems. ACM Trans. Comput. Syst. **3**(3), 204–226 (1985)
35. Tyagi, N., Grubbs, P., Len, J., Miers, I., Ristenpart, T.: Asymmetric message franking: content moderation for metadata-private end-to-end encryption. In: Boldyreva, A., Micciancio, D. (eds.) CRYPTO 2019. LNCS, vol. 11694, pp. 222–250. Springer, Cham (2019). https://doi.org/10.1007/978-3-030-26954-8_8
36. Unger, N., et al.: SoK: secure messaging. In: 2015 IEEE Symposium on Security and Privacy, pp. 232–249. IEEE Computer Society Press (2015)

Symmetric Signcryption and E2EE Group Messaging in Keybase

Joseph Jaeger[1]([✉])[iD], Akshaya Kumar[1][iD], and Igors Stepanovs[2][iD]

[1] School of Cybersecurity and Privacy, Georgia Institute of Technology,
Atlanta, GA, USA
{josephjaeger,akshayakumar}@gatech.edu
[2] Riga, Latvia
igors.stepanovs@gmail.com
https://cc.gatech.edu/~josephjaeger/, https://cc.gatech.edu/~akumar805/,
https://igors.org/

Abstract. We introduce a new cryptographic primitive called symmetric signcryption, which differs from traditional signcryption because the sender and recipient share a secret key. We prove that a natural composition of symmetric encryption and signatures achieves strong notions of security against attackers that can learn and control many keys. We then identify that the core encryption algorithm of the Keybase encrypted messaging protocol can be modeled as a symmetric signcryption scheme. We prove the security of this algorithm, though our proof requires assuming non-standard, brittle security properties of the underlying primitives.

1 Introduction

Keybase is a suite of encryption tools. It encompasses a public-key directory, an instant messenger, and a cloud storage service. Keybase was launched in 2014. In February 2020, it reported having accumulated more than 1.1M user accounts [27]. In May 2020, Keybase was acquired by Zoom. At the time, Zoom issued a public statement [36] saying that the Keybase's team was meant to play a critical part in building scalable end-to-end encryption for Zoom. The acquisition appears to have put an end to an active development of new Keybase features, but as of February 2024 it keeps receiving regular maintenance updates.

Instant Messaging in Keybase. Keybase implements its own end-to-end encrypted instant messaging protocol. This protocol is designed to support large groups. One-on-one chats are treated as group chats and hence use the same protocol. The protocol also allows to send large files as encrypted attachments in chat. It is impossible to opt out of end-to-end encryption in Keybase. In this work we analyze the security of this protocol.

The Keybase client is open source [24], but the server is not. Our security analysis primarily relies on the source code. Keybase also provides the "Keybase Book" website [22] with excellent documentation that explains its cryptographic design. The only prior security analysis of Keybase was done by NCC Group in

M. Joye and G. Leander (Eds.): EUROCRYPT 2024, LNCS 14653, pp. 283–312, 2024.
https://doi.org/10.1007/978-3-031-58734-4_10

2019 [31], which broadly looked at the security of the entire Keybase ecosystem. In comparison, we provide an in-depth analysis of a single component in Keybase.

Encrypted Group Chats. In this work we consider a setting in which an arbitrary number of users can form a group. All group members share a key for a symmetric encryption scheme. Each instant message within the group is encrypted with this key. Let us use g to denote the identity of a group and K_g to denote the key shared between the members of this group. In Keybase, every member of group g uses the same long-term key K_g to encrypt their outgoing chat messages. Each message is encrypted only once, simultaneously for all recipients. The resulting ciphertext is then broadcast to all members of the group.

The *Sender Keys* protocol [7,28] can be seen as building on this basic design idea. In *Sender Keys*, every member of the group owns a distinct symmetric encryption key; they share it with other group members. Each outgoing message is encrypted with the sender's own key, and the resulting ciphertext is broadcast to the group. Furthermore, each key is used to encrypt only a single message, and immediately afterwards a new key is derived to be used for the next encryption. So every group member tracks every other member's current encryption key, decrypting each incoming ciphertext with the corresponding sender's key and subsequently replacing it with an appropriately derived new key. Variants of the *Sender Keys* protocol are used in the *Signal* [28], *WhatsApp* [34], and *Matrix* [1,2] messengers. In addition, the *Messaging Layer Security* (MLS) [8] protocol contains a component called *FS-GAEAD* [3] or *TreeDEM* [33] that similarly uses a sender's key to encrypt and broadcast a message (but its overall design significantly differs from design of the *Sender Keys* protocol).

An encrypted group chat protocol should provide at least confidentiality and integrity of communication, with respect to an attacker that is not a member of the group. In part, this could be achieved by building the protocol from a symmetric encryption scheme that satisfies some notion of authenticated-encryption security. But care is needed to also prevent undesired message replays, reordering, or drops. These requirements are specific to a stateful protocol and do not necessarily follow from properties provided by the underlying stateless scheme.

Sender Authentication in Group Chats. Consider a group chat protocol that is built from a single symmetric encryption scheme and where every symmetric key is known to all group members. In such a protocol, group members are able to impersonate each other. This is true regardless of whether each group uses a single shared encryption key or has each member own a distinct encryption key. To prevent group members from impersonating each other, it is natural to use a digital signature scheme. Let us use u to denote the identity of a user and sk_u to denote this user's signing key for a digital signature scheme.

What is a sound way to compose a symmetric encryption scheme with a digital signature scheme? Let us consider two sequential compositions of a signing algorithm Sign with an encryption algorithm Encrypt. We call the resulting schemes Sign-then-Encrypt and Encrypt-then-Sign, and we show them in Fig. 1. The Sign-then-Encrypt scheme first signs a message m to obtain its digital signature s and then encrypts (s, m) to obtain and return a symmetric ciphertext

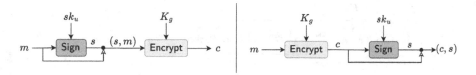

Fig. 1. Warmup schemes obtained by composing digital signatures with symmetric encryption. **Left pane:** Sign-then-Encrypt. **Right pane:** Encrypt-then-Sign.

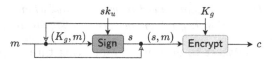

Fig. 2. A high-level representation of the SealPacket scheme in Keybase.

c. The Encrypt-then-Sign scheme first encrypts m as c and then computes a signature s over c; it returns the pair (c, s).

These compositions closely mirror those that are commonly used to build signcryption [5], which is a standard cryptographic primitive that combines digital signatures with public-key encryption [35], except we replace public-key encryption with symmetric encryption. It is well known that the corresponding compositions for signcryption are not secure in the multi-user setting, unless some effort is taken to bind together the message with the sender and recipient identities [5]. The standard advice is to always sign the recipient's identity and always encrypt the sender's identity. Our basic schemes in Fig. 1 would intuitively suffer from similar issues and benefit from similar countermeasures. However, the exact details would depend on what kind of security one expects from these schemes, so we defer this discussion.

The *Sender Keys* protocol [7] prescribes to sign a symmetric ciphertext; and this is indeed done by the *Signal, WhatsApp*, and *Matrix* messengers. The MLS protocol [8] protocol prescribes to encrypt a digital signature with a symmetric encryption scheme. So either protocol can be seen as using some variant of Encrypt-then-Sign or Sign-then-Encrypt as a subroutine. We will now discuss that Keybase can be seen as extending both of these basic schemes.

SealPacket: Sign-then-Encrypt in Keybase. Keybase uses a variant of the basic Sign-then-Encrypt scheme. It signs the symmetric encryption key along with the plaintext, meaning it signs (K_g, m) instead of just m. The resulting scheme is called SealPacket and is shown in Fig. 2. In the source code, the decision to sign K_g is explained as follows [26]:

> *simply using encryption and signing together isn't good enough ... the inner layer needs to assert something about the outer layer ... a better approach is to mix the outer key into the inner crypto, so that it's impossible to forget to check it ... That means the inner signing layer needs to assert*

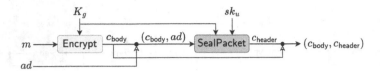

Fig. 3. A high-level representation of the BoxMessage scheme in Keybase.

the encryption key ... We don't need to worry about whether the signature might leak the encryption key either, because the signature gets encrypted.

Keybase uses SealPacket to encrypt the following three types of plaintexts: (1) a metadata header that is automatically created and sent along with every chat message, (2) a file that is sent as an attachment in chat, and (3) an arbitrary string chosen by a chat bot (for secure server-side storage of bot data).

BoxMessage: Encrypt-then-Sign in Keybase. The BoxMessage scheme in Keybase is a variant of the basic Encrypt-then-Sign scheme. This scheme, unlike SealPacket, is used only for one purpose: to encrypt the body of a chat message. So we denote by c_{body} the symmetric ciphertext that is created in the inner (encryption) layer of BoxMessage. The BoxMessage scheme extends the basic Encrypt-then-Sign scheme in two ways and is shown in Fig. 3. First, it takes an associated-data field ad and signs (c_{body}, ad) instead of just c_{body}. Second, rather than use a signature scheme, BoxMessage uses SealPacket to sign (c_{body}, ad).

Keybase uses the auxiliary-data field ad to authenticate a metadata header for the chat message. This header contains the group's identity and sender's identity among multiple other values. The data in ad is sent in plain over the network (along with c_{body}), meaning that SealPacket is not meant to provide confidentiality of ad. Indeed, the Keybase documentation explains that SealPacket is used to provide the confidentiality of the *signature* over (c_{body}, ad) [23]:

fields in the header aren't secret from the server, and it actually needs to know several of them ... The reason for sign-then-encrypting/signencrypting the header is instead to keep the signature itself private. Even though the server knows who's talking to whom, because it's delivering all the messages, it's better that it can't prove what it knows.

Interestingly, BoxMessage reuses the group's symmetric encryption key K_g between its calls to Encrypt and SealPacket. As mentioned above, SealPacket will itself first sign K_g and then run another instance of Encrypt with K_g as the key. In total, the same value of K_g is therefore used in 3 distinct contexts.

Symmetric Signcryption. We define *symmetric signcryption* as a new cryptographic primitive that combines symmetric encryption with digital signatures. We capture the setting where every user owns a signing key pair and in each group all users share a single symmetric encryption key. The encryption key is long-term, meaning it can be used an arbitrary number of times, simultaneously by all members of the group. This will allow us to formalize and analyze the SealPacket and BoxMessage schemes.

We note that the use of sender-specific encryption keys in the *Sender Keys* [7] and MLS [8] protocols can also be captured by symmetric signcryption. Indeed, in either protocol all symmetric encryption keys can seen as being independently sampled, and each individual key is used only once. This can be thought of as a collection of "one-time-use" symmetric signcryption schemes.

We adapt the standard syntax of (asymmetric) signcryption to suit our setting, defining algorithms SigEnc and VerDec. They both take explicit sender and group identities, nonces, and associated data.

Security of Symmetric Signcryption. We define two security notions for symmetric signcryption. The *out-group authenticated encryption* (OAE) security requires confidentiality and integrity of communication against an adversary that does not know the symmetric key of the group it attacks. This is required to hold even against an adversary that can assign to every user an arbitrary (possibly malformed) digital signature key pair. The *in-group unforgeability* (IUF) security requires unforgeability of messages sent by users whose signing keys are not known to the adversary. This is required to hold even against an adversary that can assign to every group an arbitrary (possibly malformed) symmetric key.

We show how to extend the basic Sign-then-Encrypt scheme, by carefully incorporating user and group identifiers, to achieve both of our security notions. We assume strong unforgeability of the underlying digital signature scheme and authenticated-encryption security of the underlying encryption scheme.

Implementation of SealPacket and BoxMessage. In the source code of the Keybase client, SealPacket is implemented in [26] and BoxMessage is implemented in [25]. These schemes are instantiated with the nonce-based authenticated encryption scheme XSalsa20-Poly1305 [15,16] and the digital signature scheme Ed25519 [17,18]. They also use SHA-512 and SHA-256 which does not significantly affect the design of either scheme so we omit discussing it here, but in the main body of the paper, we attempt to formalize both schemes precisely.

Keybase implements four versions of the BoxMessage scheme: V1, V2, V3, and V4. V1 is deprecated; the Keybase client allows to receive but not send messages that use V1. V2 is the default version that we formalize and analyze in this work. V3 is the same as V2, except it supports exploding messages; the body of an exploding message is encrypted using an ephemeral key instead of K_g. V4 is the same as V3, except it makes all group members use a dummy (zero) signing key and instead authenticate messages using pairwise MACs.

Provable Security Analysis. We model BoxMessage and SealPacket as symmetric signcryption schemes and provide formal reductions for their IUF and OAE security. Our analysis is done in a concrete security framework [11], and in a multi-key setting; we state precise bounds on the advantage of an attacker. The analysis of BoxMessage largely encompasses that of SealPacket, because BoxMessage uses SealPacket in a modular way. So we focus on the analysis of BoxMessage here. The main challenges arise from using K_g in 3 distinct contexts.

First, we aim to show it is hard to switch the context of the XSalsa20-Poly1305 ciphertexts c_{body} and c_{header}. Both are encrypted using the same key K_g, so there is a risk that an attacker could forge a valid encryption of some body-plaintext m from a known encryption of some header-plaintext (s, c_{body}, ad), or vice versa. To rule out such attacks, we rely on an observation that every application-layer message m that is queried to be encrypted by BoxMessage is encoded in a specific way, whereas every header-plaintext (s, c_{body}, ad) is expected to start with a valid Ed25519 signature. Based on the specification of Ed25519 we show (in the ROM and GGM) that it is hard to cast the encoding used in m as a valid Ed25519 signature (with respect to any verification key of adversary's choice).

Second, we need to show that XSalsa20-Poly1305 provides authenticated encryption even for certain messages derived from its secret key. This arises because in SealPacket the XSalsa20-Poly1305 key K_g is first signed with Ed25519 and then the resulting signature is encrypted using XSalsa20-Poly1305 under the same key. Here again we rely on the specification of Ed25519. An Ed25519 signature depends on two SHA-512 hash values of the message that is being signed, but it does not depend on the signed message beyond that. We use this (in the ROM) to eliminate the need to consider key-dependent messages and hence only require XSalsa20-Poly1305 to provide the standard notion of authenticated encryption.

We do not know any way to avoid the above analysis. The necessity to use non-standard security notions appears to be inherently implied by the design decisions made in Keybase. This could have been avoided (e.g. with out Sign-then-Encrypt scheme). Overall, our reductions (in the ROM and GGM) rely on the AEAD security of XSalsa20-Poly1305, collision resistance of SHA-256 and SHA-512, and strong unforgeability of Ed25519. We note that Keybase uses the version of Ed25519 that was recently shown to be SUF-CMA secure [10,20].

Limitations of Our Work. Our analysis of Keybase is intentionally narrow in scope. We perform an in-depth, algorithmic analysis of specific chat components that can be modeled as symmetric signcryption. Other analysis is outside the scope of our work, such as whether these algorithms are secure against timing attacks and whether they provide protection against message replays, reordering, or drops when used within the broader stateful chat protocol. More broadly, our analysis does not explicitly cover many other applications of cryptography in Keybase, including other versions of BoxMessage, encryption of attachments or bot data, the initial key exchange used to agree on group keys, the public-key directory used to share user keys, and the cloud storage service. These applications are important for the overall security of Keybase, and have the potential to interplay with each other in subtle ways. For example, user signing keys are used for multiple tasks in Keybase. We believe appropriate context separation is used for these purposes (e.g. all messages signed in SealPacket start with "Keybase-Chat-2"). If not, subtle cross-application attacks may be possible.

Related Work. The Hybrid Public-Key Encryption (HPKE) standard is specified in RFC 9180 [9]. Alwen, Janneck, Kiltz, and Lipp [4] analyze the "pre-shared key" modes from RFC 9180. They cast the HPKE$_{AuthPSK}$ mode as an asymmetric signcryption scheme that is augmented with a pre-shared symmetric key, and they define the corresponding security notions. They analyze the security that is achieved by $\mathsf{HPKE_{AuthPSK}}$ depending on which combinations of keys are secure. Our definitions are similar in the sense that both works define a signcryption-type primitive that in addition uses a symmetric key. However, the algorithms in [4] use one more set of keys, and the definitions in [4] are stated in the two-user setting. In essence, our primitives are similar in form, but are tailored to be used as tools in different settings.

2 Preliminaries

We use standard pseudocode notation and assume familiarity with hash functions, random oracles, nonce-based encryption, and digital signatures. Collision resistance is defined by $\mathsf{Adv}_{\mathsf{H}}^{\mathsf{CR}}(\mathcal{A}_{\mathsf{CR}}) = \Pr[\mathsf{H}(x) = \mathsf{H}(y) \wedge x \neq y : (x,y) \leftarrow \mathcal{A}_{\mathsf{CR}}]$.

2.1 Standard Security Notions in a Multi-key Setting

Key Management Oracles. Throughout this work we consider multi-key security notions. Adversaries in security games will be provided with three types of key management oracles. These oracles will allow (1) sampling new honest (i.e. challenge) keys, (2) exposing existing honest keys, and (3) adding corrupt keys of the adversary's choice. When an honest key is exposed it becomes corrupt, but it was initially sampled from a correct key distribution. In contrast, when an adversary adds its own corrupt key, such a key could be maliciously crafted in an arbitrary way. In basic security notions an adversary cannot benefit from crafting corrupt keys, because no challenge queries are permitted with respect to such keys. This changes for more complex systems built from more than one keyed primitive when some security is required to hold even if some underlying secrets are exposed. The ability to use malicious keys was modeled in prior work on (asymmetric) signcryption [14], and will be needed in this work.

Our security model for symmetric signcryption in Sect. 3 will define two sets of key management oracles. The set of *user oracles* $U = \{\textsc{NewHonUser}, \textsc{ExposeUser}, \textsc{NewCorrUser}\}$ will manage the keys for a digital signature scheme, whereas the set of *group oracles* $G = \{\textsc{NewHonGroup}, \textsc{ExposeGroup}, \textsc{NewCorrGroup}\}$ will manage the keys for a nonce-based encryption scheme. We adopt the same terminology and notation across all of the multi-key security notions; each notion for an *asymmetric* primitive will define a set of user oracles U, and each notion for a *symmetric* primitive will define a set of group oracles G. For consistency, we include oracles for adding corrupt keys even when an adversary cannot benefit from using them. When simulating user oracles in a security reduction, we write $\textsc{SimU}$ to denote the set $\{\textsc{SimNewHonUser}, \textsc{SimExposeUser}, \textsc{SimNewCorrUser}\}$ and do similarly for group oracles.

Nonce-Based Authenticated Encryption. Consider game G^{AEAD} of Fig. 4 for nonce-based encryption scheme NE and adversary $\mathcal{A}_{\mathsf{AEAD}}$. The advantage of

$\mathcal{A}_{\mathsf{AEAD}}$ in breaking the AEAD security of NE is defined as $\mathsf{Adv}_{\mathsf{NE}}^{\mathsf{AEAD}}(\mathcal{A}_{\mathsf{AEAD}}) = 2 \cdot \Pr[\mathcal{G}_{\mathsf{NE}}^{\mathsf{AEAD}}(\mathcal{A}_{\mathsf{AEAD}})] - 1$. The game samples a challenge bit b, and $\mathcal{A}_{\mathsf{AEAD}}$ is required to guess it. Adversary $\mathcal{A}_{\mathsf{AEAD}}$ is given the group oracles G, encryption oracle ENC, and decryption oracle DEC. Among the group oracles, NEWHONGROUP creates new groups with honestly generated NE keys, EXPOSEGROUP reveals the keys of existing groups, and NEWCORRGROUP instantiates new corrupt groups with NE keys of $\mathcal{A}_{\mathsf{AEAD}}$'s choice. We require NE to be nonce-misuse resistant [30], meaning that no challenge message m is allowed to be queried across two distinct calls to ENC with respect to the same set of g, n, ad. A corrupt group key can only be used to call ENC with $m_0 = m_1$, and a group key cannot be exposed after it has been used in ENC with $m_0 \neq m_1$. The decryption oracle DEC takes g, n, c, ad as input and decrypts this to the corresponding plaintext m. Following the all-in-one style of [30,32], it returns $\bot$ if $b = 0$, and it returns m otherwise. This oracle never decrypts a ciphertext with an exposed group's key, and it never decrypts ciphertexts previously produced by ENC (with the same g, c, ad).

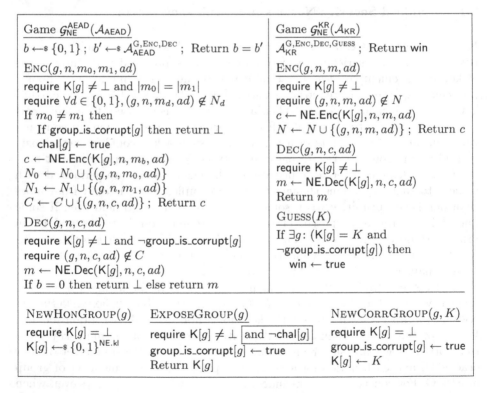

Fig. 4. Left pane: Game defining authenticated-encryption security of a nonce-based encryption scheme NE. **Right pane:** Game defining key-recovery security of NE. **Bottom pane:** Group oracles G = {NEWHONGROUP, EXPOSEGROUP, NEWCORRGROUP} that are provided to an adversary in either game, except that the boxed code only appears in the AEAD security game.

Key-Recovery Security of NE. Consider game G^{KR} of Fig. 4 for nonce-based encryption scheme NE and adversary $\mathcal{A}_{\text{KR}}$. The advantage of $\mathcal{A}_{\text{KR}}$ in breaking the KR security of NE is defined as $\text{Adv}_{\text{NE}}^{\text{KR}}(\mathcal{A}_{\text{KR}}) = \Pr[G_{\text{NE}}^{\text{KR}}(\mathcal{A}_{\text{KR}})]$.

Game $G_{\text{DS}}^{\text{SUFCMA}}(\mathcal{A}_{\text{SUFCMA}})$		$\text{SIGN}(u, m)$
$(u, m, s) \leftarrow_\$ \mathcal{A}_{\text{SUFCMA}}^{U, \text{SIGN}}$; If $\text{vk}[u] = \bot$ then return false		require $\text{sk}[u] \neq \bot$
$\text{win}_1 \leftarrow \neg\text{user\_is\_corrupt}[u]$; $\text{win}_2 \leftarrow ((u, m, s) \notin S)$		$s \leftarrow_\$ \text{DS.Sig}(\text{sk}[u], m)$
$\text{win}_3 \leftarrow \text{DS.Ver}(\text{vk}[u], m, s)$		$S \leftarrow S \cup \{(u, m, s)\}$
Return win_1 and win_2 and win_3		Return s
$\text{NEWHONUSER}(u)$	$\text{EXPOSEUSER}(u)$	$\text{NEWCORRUSER}(u, sk, vk)$
require $\text{sk}[u] = \text{vk}[u] = \bot$	require $\text{sk}[u] \neq \bot$	require $\text{sk}[u] = \text{vk}[u] = \bot$
$(\text{sk}[u], \text{vk}[u]) \leftarrow_\$ \text{DS.Kg}$	$\text{user\_is\_corrupt}[u] \leftarrow \text{true}$	$\text{user\_is\_corrupt}[u] \leftarrow \text{true}$
Return $\text{vk}[u]$	Return $\text{sk}[u]$	$\text{sk}[u] \leftarrow sk$; $\text{vk}[u] \leftarrow vk$

Fig. 5. Game defining strong unforgeability of a digital signature scheme DS, where $U = \{\text{NEWHONUSER}, \text{EXPOSEUSER}, \text{NEWCORRUSER}\}$.

Strong Unforgeability of Digital Signatures. Consider game G^{SUFCMA} of Fig. 5 for signature scheme DS and adversary $\mathcal{A}_{\text{SUFCMA}}$. The advantage of $\mathcal{A}_{\text{SUFCMA}}$ in breaking the SUFCMA security of DS is defined as $\text{Adv}_{\text{DS}}^{\text{SUFCMA}}(\mathcal{A}_{\text{SUFCMA}}) = \Pr[G_{\text{DS}}^{\text{SUFCMA}}(\mathcal{A}_{\text{SUFCMA}})]$.

3 Symmetric Signcryption

In this section we define syntax and security for multi-user symmetric signcryption. In symmetric signcryption, a user encrypts messages using their signing key and a symmetric key shared by a group of users. We want that nobody outside a group can learn what messages are being encrypted, and nobody at all can forge a message as having come from someone other than themselves.

Syntax. A symmetric signcryption scheme SS specifies algorithms SS.UserKg, SS.SigEnc, SS.VerDec, where SS.VerDec is deterministic. These algorithm use syntax $(sk, vk) \leftarrow_\$ \text{SS.UserKg}$, $c \leftarrow_\$ \text{SS.SigEnc}(g, K_g, u, sk_u, n, m, ad)$, and $m \leftarrow \text{SS.VerDec}(g, K_g, u, vk_u, n, c, ad)$. Associated to SS is a group-key length $\text{SS.gkl} \in \mathbb{N}$, a nonce space SS.NS, a plaintext space $\text{SS.MS} \subseteq \{0, 1\}^*$, and an associated-data space SS.AD. The user's key generation algorithm SS.UserKg returns a key pair (sk, vk) where sk is a signing key and vk is the corresponding verification key. The signcryption algorithm SS.SigEnc takes a group's identifier $g \in \{0, 1\}^*$ and its symmetric key $K_g \in \{0, 1\}^{\text{SS.gkl}}$, a sender's identifier $u \in \{0, 1\}^*$ and its signing key sk_u, a nonce $n \in \text{SS.NS}$, a plaintext $m \in \text{SS.MS}$, and associated data $ad \in \text{SS.AD}$; it returns a signcryption ciphertext c. The deterministic unsigncryption algorithm SS.VerDec takes $g, K_g, u, vk_u, n, c, ad$, where vk_u is the verification key of the sender u; it returns a plaintext $m \in \{0,1\}^* \cup \{\bot\}$, where $\bot$ indicates a failure to recover a plaintext. We say that SS is *deterministic* SS.SigEnc is deterministic. Correctness is defined in the natural way.

3.1   In-Group Unforgeability

The strongest variant of in-group unforgeability requires that an attacker cannot modify anything about ciphertexts. We also capture weaker variants. For example, the SealPacket encryption algorithm in Keybase (as defined in Sect. 4) uses a signing key to bind its ciphertexts to a group's symmetric key but not to a group's identifier. So we parameterize our security definition in order to capture the type of authenticity that is as restrictive as possible except for allowing (what can be described as) cross-group forgeries.

IUF Game. Consider game $\mathscr{G}^{\mathsf{IUF}}$ of Fig. 6, defined for symmetric signcryption scheme SS, ciphertext-triviality predicate $\mathsf{pred}_{\mathsf{trivial}}^{\mathsf{auth}}$, and adversary $\mathcal{A}_{\mathsf{IUF}}$. The advantage of $\mathcal{A}_{\mathsf{IUF}}$ in breaking the IUF security of SS is defined as $\mathsf{Adv}_{\mathsf{SS},\mathsf{pred}_{\mathsf{trivial}}^{\mathsf{auth}}}^{\mathsf{IUF}}(\mathcal{A}_{\mathsf{IUF}}) = \Pr[\mathscr{G}_{\mathsf{SS},\mathsf{pred}_{\mathsf{trivial}}^{\mathsf{auth}}}^{\mathsf{IUF}}(\mathcal{A}_{\mathsf{IUF}})]$. Adversary $\mathcal{A}_{\mathsf{IUF}}$ is given access to user oracles U, group oracles G, encryption oracle SIGENC, and decryption oracle VERDEC. Its goal is to set the win flag by forging a ciphertext for an honest user.

Among user oracles, NEWHONUSER creates honest users with honestly generated signing keys, NEWCORRUSER creates corrupt users with malicious signing keys, and EXPOSEUSER exposes signing keys of existing users. Among group oracles, NEWHONGROUP creates honest groups with honestly sampled symmetric keys, NEWCORRGROUP creates corrupt groups with malicious symmetric keys, and EXPOSEGROUP exposes symmetric keys of existing groups. Oracles NEWHONGROUP and NEWCORRGROUP take as input a set users identifying the new group's users; the encryption and decryption oracles then disallow queries that match a group to a non-member user. The user and group oracles use tables user_is_corrupt and group_is_corrupt in order to keep track of the users and groups whose keys are not secure, respectively. The IUF game never checks group_is_corrupt, deliberately giving the adversary full control over group keys.

The encryption oracle SIGENC takes (g, u, n, m, ad) and returns a ciphertext c that is produced by running SS.SigEnc$(g, \mathsf{K}[g], u, \mathsf{sk}[u], n, m, ad)$. Here note that the group and user keys $\mathsf{K}[g]$ and $\mathsf{sk}[u]$ are the only two inputs to SS.SigEnc that are not directly chosen by the adversary at the moment of querying the SIGENC oracle. At the end of each SIGENC query, the set C is updated to add the tuple $((g, u, n, m, ad), c)$ that can be interpreted as containing the input-output transcript of this query.

The decryption oracle VERDEC takes (g, u, n, c, ad) and returns the message m that is recovered by running SS.VerDec$(g, \mathsf{K}[g], u, \mathsf{vk}[u], n, c, ad)$. Keys $\mathsf{K}[g], \mathsf{sk}[g]$ are the only inputs to SS.VerDec not directly chosen by the adversary. If $m \neq \bot$, then the oracle determines if the current oracle query is a valid forgery and sets the win flag if so. In particular, VERDEC builds the tuple $z = ((g, u, n, m, ad), c)$ with all input and output values of the current decryption query. It checks z against the set C that contains the input-output behavior

---

Game $\mathcal{G}_{\mathsf{SS},\mathsf{pred}^{\mathsf{auth}}_{\mathsf{trivial}}}^{\mathsf{IUF}}(\mathcal{A}_{\mathsf{IUF}})$	Game $\mathcal{G}_{\mathsf{SS},\mathsf{pred}^{\mathsf{sec}}_{\mathsf{trivial}},\mathsf{func}^{\mathsf{sec}}_{\mathsf{out}}}^{\mathsf{OAE}}(\mathcal{A}_{\mathsf{OAE}})$
$\mathcal{A}_{\mathsf{IUF}}^{\mathsf{U},\mathsf{G},\textsc{SigEnc},\textsc{VerDec}}$	$b \leftarrow\!\!\$\ \{0,1\}\ ;\ b' \leftarrow\!\!\$\ \mathcal{A}_{\mathsf{OAE}}^{\mathsf{U},\mathsf{G},\textsc{SigEnc},\textsc{VerDec}}$
Return win	Return $b = b'$

$\underline{\textsc{SigEnc}(g,u,n,m,ad)}$	$\underline{\textsc{SigEnc}(g,u,n,m_0,m_1,ad)}$
require $\mathsf{K}[g] \neq \bot$	require $\mathsf{K}[g] \neq \bot$ and $\lvert m_0 \rvert = \lvert m_1 \rvert$
require $\mathsf{sk}[u] \neq \bot$ and $u \in \mathsf{members}[g]$	require $\mathsf{sk}[u] \neq \bot$ and $u \in \mathsf{members}[g]$
$c \leftarrow\!\!\$\ \mathsf{SS.SigEnc}(g,\mathsf{K}[g],u,\mathsf{sk}[u],n,m,ad)$	require $\forall d \in \{0,1\}, (g,u,n,m_d,ad) \notin N_d$
$C \leftarrow C \cup \{((g,u,n,m,ad),c)\}$	If $m_0 \neq m_1$ then
Return c	$\quad$ If $\mathsf{group\_is\_corrupt}[g]$ then return $\bot$

$\underline{\textsc{VerDec}(g,u,n,c,ad)}$	$\quad \mathsf{chal}[g] \leftarrow \mathsf{true}$
require $\mathsf{K}[g] \neq \bot$	$c \leftarrow\!\!\$\ \mathsf{SS.SigEnc}(g,\mathsf{K}[g],u,\mathsf{sk}[u],n,m_b,ad)$
require $\mathsf{vk}[u] \neq \bot$ and $u \in \mathsf{members}[g]$	$N_0 \leftarrow N_0 \cup \{(g,u,n,m_0,ad)\}$
$m \leftarrow \mathsf{SS.VerDec}(g,\mathsf{K}[g],u,\mathsf{vk}[u],n,c,ad)$	$N_1 \leftarrow N_1 \cup \{(g,u,n,m_1,ad)\}$
If $m = \bot$ then return $\bot$	$U \leftarrow U \cup \{((g,u,n,m_b,ad),c)\}$
$z \leftarrow ((g,u,n,m,ad),c)$	$Q \leftarrow Q \cup \{((g,u,n,m_0,m_1,ad),c)\}$
If $\mathsf{pred}^{\mathsf{auth}}_{\mathsf{trivial}}(z,C)$ then return m	Return c
If $\neg\mathsf{user\_is\_corrupt}[u]$ then win $\leftarrow \mathsf{true}$
Return m	$\underline{\textsc{VerDec}(g,u,n,c,ad)}$

	require $\mathsf{K}[g] \neq \bot$ and $\neg\mathsf{group\_is\_corrupt}[g]$
	require $\mathsf{vk}[u] \neq \bot$ and $u \in \mathsf{members}[g]$
	$m \leftarrow \mathsf{SS.VerDec}(g,\mathsf{K}[g],u,\mathsf{vk}[u],n,c,ad)$
	If $m = \bot$ then return $\bot$
	$z \leftarrow ((g,u,n,m,ad),c)$
	If $\mathsf{pred}^{\mathsf{sec}}_{\mathsf{trivial}}(z,C)$ then return $\mathsf{func}^{\mathsf{sec}}_{\mathsf{out}}(z,Q)$
	If $b = 0$ then return $\bot$ else return m

$\underline{\textsc{NewHonUser}(u)}$	$\underline{\textsc{NewHonGroup}(g,\mathsf{users})}$
require $\mathsf{sk}[u] = \mathsf{vk}[u] = \bot$	require $\mathsf{K}[g] = \bot$
$(\mathsf{sk}[u],\mathsf{vk}[u]) \leftarrow\!\!\$\ \mathsf{SS.UserKg}$	$\mathsf{K}[g] \leftarrow\!\!\$\ \{0,1\}^{\mathsf{SS.gkl}}$
Return $\mathsf{vk}[u]$	$\mathsf{members}[g] \leftarrow \mathsf{users}$
$\underline{\textsc{ExposeUser}(u)}$	$\underline{\textsc{ExposeGroup}(g)}$
require $\mathsf{sk}[u] \neq \bot$	require $\mathsf{K}[g] \neq \bot$ $\boxed{\text{and } \neg\mathsf{chal}[g]}$
$\mathsf{user\_is\_corrupt}[u] \leftarrow \mathsf{true}$	$\mathsf{group\_is\_corrupt}[g] \leftarrow \mathsf{true}$
Return $\mathsf{sk}[u]$	Return $\mathsf{K}[g]$
$\underline{\textsc{NewCorrUser}(u,sk,vk)}$	$\underline{\textsc{NewCorrGroup}(g,K,\mathsf{users})}$
require $\mathsf{sk}[u] = \mathsf{vk}[u] = \bot$	require $\mathsf{K}[g] = \bot$
$\mathsf{user\_is\_corrupt}[u] \leftarrow \mathsf{true}$	$\mathsf{group\_is\_corrupt}[g] \leftarrow \mathsf{true}$
$\mathsf{sk}[u] \leftarrow sk\ ;\ \mathsf{vk}[u] \leftarrow vk$	$\mathsf{K}[g] \leftarrow K\ ;\ \mathsf{members}[g] \leftarrow \mathsf{users}$

Fig. 6. Left pane: Game defining in-group unforgeability IUF of a symmetric signcryption scheme SS with respect to a ciphertext-triviality predicate $\mathsf{pred}^{\mathsf{auth}}_{\mathsf{trivial}}$. **Right pane:** Game defining out-group authenticated-encryption security OAE of SS with respect to a ciphertext-triviality predicate $\mathsf{pred}^{\mathsf{sec}}_{\mathsf{trivial}}$ and an output-guarding function $\mathsf{func}^{\mathsf{sec}}_{\mathsf{out}}$. **Bottom pane:** User oracles $\mathsf{U} = \{\textsc{NewHonUser}, \textsc{ExposeUser}, \textsc{NewCorrUser}\}$ and group oracles $\mathsf{G} = \{\textsc{NewHonGroup}, \textsc{ExposeGroup}, \textsc{NewCorrGroup}\}$ that are provided to an adversary in either game, except that the $\boxed{\text{boxed}}$ code only appears in the OAE security game.

$\mathsf{pred}_{\mathsf{trivial}}^{\mathsf{suf}}(z, C)$

Return $z \in C$

$\mathsf{pred}_{\mathsf{trivial}}^{\mathsf{euf}}(z, C)$

$((g, u, n, m, ad), c) \leftarrow z$

Return $\exists c' : ((g, u, n, m, ad), c') \in C$

$\mathsf{pred}_{\mathsf{trivial}}^{\mathsf{suf\text{-}except\text{-}group}}(z, C)$

$((g, u, n, m, ad), c) \leftarrow z$

Return $\exists g' : ((g', u, n, m, ad), c) \in C$

$\mathsf{pred}_{\mathsf{trivial}}^{\mathsf{suf\text{-}except\text{-}user}}(z, C)$

$((g, u, n, m, ad), c) \leftarrow z$

Return $\exists u' : ((g, u', n, m, ad), c) \in C$

Fig. 7. Sample ciphertext-triviality predicates which capture rules for deciding if a successfully decrypted VERDEC query was trivially obtainable or forgeable.

of all the prior encryption queries. If z is determined to be trivially obtainable from the information in C, then VERDEC exits early (with m as its output value); otherwise it sets the win flag. This check is performed by the *ciphertext-triviality predicate* $\mathsf{pred}_{\mathsf{trivial}}^{\mathsf{auth}}$. We will describe the syntax and the sample variants of $\mathsf{pred}_{\mathsf{trivial}}^{\mathsf{auth}}$ below.

Ciphertext-Triviality Predicates. The IUF security game is parameterized by ciphertext-triviality predicate $\mathsf{pred}_{\mathsf{trivial}}^{\mathsf{auth}}$ (we will also parameterize the OAE game with $\mathsf{pred}_{\mathsf{trivial}}^{\mathsf{auth}}$). Predicate $\mathsf{pred}_{\mathsf{trivial}}^{\mathsf{auth}}$ takes a tuple $z = ((g, u, n, m, ad), c)$ and a set C as input, where C contains tuples of the same format. Here z describes the input-output values of the current query to VERDEC oracle and each element of C contains an input-output transcript of a prior SIGENC oracle query. Predicate $\mathsf{pred}_{\mathsf{trivial}}^{\mathsf{auth}}$ returns true if z is considered to be trivially forgeable based on the information in C and false otherwise.

In Fig. 7 we define several ciphertext-triviality predicates. Predicate $\mathsf{pred}_{\mathsf{trivial}}^{\mathsf{suf}}$ checks if $z \in C$, capturing the strongest possible level of authenticity. This requires that only prior outputs of SIGENC can be successfully queried to the VERDEC oracle; any other successful decryption query causes the adversary to win the IUF game. This predicate can be thought of as making the IUF game capture the "strong" unforgeability of ciphertexts in our group setting. One could capture existential unforgeability by considering the predicate $\mathsf{pred}_{\mathsf{trivial}}^{\mathsf{euf}}$ that does not allow the adversary to win by merely producing new ciphertexts that decrypt to some tuple (g, u, n, m, ad) previously queried to SIGENC. Predicates $\mathsf{pred}_{\mathsf{trivial}}^{\mathsf{suf\text{-}except\text{-}group}}$ and $\mathsf{pred}_{\mathsf{trivial}}^{\mathsf{suf\text{-}except\text{-}user}}$ capture the authenticity of schemes where a ciphertext encrypting (g, u, n, m, ad) is not bound to the group's identifier or to the user's identifier, respectively. We use $\mathsf{pred}_{\mathsf{trivial}}^{\mathsf{suf}}$, $\mathsf{pred}_{\mathsf{trivial}}^{\mathsf{suf\text{-}except\text{-}group}}$ and $\mathsf{pred}_{\mathsf{trivial}}^{\mathsf{suf\text{-}except\text{-}user}}$ in our security analysis of Keybase. In this work, we do not use $\mathsf{pred}_{\mathsf{trivial}}^{\mathsf{suf\text{-}except\text{-}user}}$ with the IUF game – we need it for OAE.

3.2 Out-Group Authenticated Encryption

The strongest version of the out-group AE security requires that an attacker outside a chat group can neither learn any information about the exchanged messages, nor modify the exchanged ciphertexts in any way. We also capture weaker variants of this security notion. For example, the SealPacket encryption algorithm (as defined in Sect. 4) does not use a group's symmetric key to explicitly bind its ciphertexts to a user's signing key or a user's identifier when used in isolation. So we capture a variant of out-group AE security that is as restrictive as possible except for allowing an attacker to violate the sender's authenticity within any particular group.

OAE Game. Consider game G^{OAE} of Fig. 6 for symmetric signcryption scheme SS, ciphertext-triviality predicate $\mathsf{pred}^{\mathsf{auth}}_{\mathsf{trivial}}$, output-guarding function $\mathsf{func}^{\mathsf{sec}}_{\mathsf{out}}$, and adversary $\mathcal{A}_{\mathsf{OAE}}$. The advantage in breaking the OAE security of SS is defined as $\mathsf{Adv}^{\mathsf{OAE}}_{\mathsf{SS},\mathsf{pred}^{\mathsf{auth}}_{\mathsf{trivial}},\mathsf{func}^{\mathsf{sec}}_{\mathsf{out}}}(\mathcal{A}_{\mathsf{OAE}}) = \Pr[G^{\mathsf{OAE}}_{\mathsf{SS},\mathsf{pred}^{\mathsf{auth}}_{\mathsf{trivial}},\mathsf{func}^{\mathsf{sec}}_{\mathsf{out}}}(\mathcal{A}_{\mathsf{OAE}})]$. Adversary $\mathcal{A}_{\mathsf{OAE}}$ is given access to user and group oracles U and G and to the encryption and decryption oracles SIGENC and VERDEC. The goal of the adversary is to guess the challenge bit b. Our security game is defined in the all-in-one style of [20,00], where an adversary can learn the challenge bit by forging a ciphertext to its decryption oracle.

The user and group oracles in the OAE game are defined as in the IUF game, except it does not allow calling the EXPOSEGROUP oracle to expose the key of a group that was previously used for a left-or-right challenge-encryption query (as explained below). The OAE game never checks the contents of user_is_corrupt, deliberately giving the adversary full control over user keys.

The encryption oracle SIGENC takes (g, u, n, m_0, m_1, ad) and returns a ciphertext c by running $\mathsf{SS.SigEnc}(g, \mathsf{K}[g], u, \mathsf{sk}[u], n, m_b, ad)$. The group and user keys $\mathsf{K}[g]$ and $\mathsf{sk}[u]$ are the only inputs to SS.SigEnc not directly chosen by the adversary querying the SIGENC oracle (and the encrypted message m_b depends on the challenge bit). The SIGENC query requires that $|m_0| = |m_1|$ and will only use insecure group keys for non-challenge encryptions (i.e. for $m_0 = m_1$). This SIGENC oracle captures nonce-misuse resistance [30], using the sets N_d to prevent trivial wins. At the end of SIGENC queries, the set C is updated to add the tuple $((g, u, n, m_b, ad), c)$, and the set Q is updated to add the tuple $((g, u, n, m_0, m_1, ad), c)$. Here the Q set can contain the input-output "transcript" of SIGENC queries from the adversary's point of view, whereas the set C is more informative because it contains the message that was actually encrypted. We will explain the purpose of these sets below.

The decryption oracle VERDEC takes (g, u, n, c, ad) and returns the message m output by $\mathsf{SS.VerDec}(g, \mathsf{K}[g], u, \mathsf{vk}[u], n, c, ad)$. Keys $\mathsf{K}[g], \mathsf{sk}[g]$ are the only inputs to SS.VerDec not directly chosen by the adversary querying the VERDEC oracle. The VERDEC oracle disallows queries with corrupt group keys; if an adversary knows a group's key then it can decrypt ciphertexts for the group on its own. If SS.VerDec recovers a non-$\bot$ message m and the end of the VERDEC oracle is reached, then the challenge bit is meant to be revealed through returning m if $b = 1$ and $\bot$ otherwise. However, this intuition is not precise; it depends on how VERDEC responds to queries that are identified as being trivially forgeable. Similarly to how trivial forgeries were handled in the IUF game, here VERDEC builds $z = ((g, u, n, m, ad), c)$ and uses a ciphertext-triviality predicate $\mathsf{pred}^{\mathsf{sec}}_{\mathsf{trivial}}$ to check z against the set C from SIGENC. If z is considered *not* trivially obtainable from the information in C, then VERDEC proceeds to its last instruction that returns $\perp$ or m depending on the challenge bit. Otherwise, VERDEC should return an output that does not depend on the challenge bit to prevent trivial wins. Such an output is produced by the *output-guarding function* $\mathsf{func}_{\mathsf{out}}^{\mathsf{sec}}$, i.e. VERDEC returns the output of $\mathsf{func}_{\mathsf{out}}^{\mathsf{sec}}(z, Q)$. We now describe the syntax and variants of $\mathsf{func}_{\mathsf{out}}^{\mathsf{sec}}$.

Output-Guarding Functions. The OAE game can be parameterized by different choices of an output-guarding function $\mathsf{func}_{\mathsf{out}}^{\mathsf{sec}}$. We define $\mathsf{func}_{\mathsf{out}}^{\mathsf{sec}}$ to take a tuple $z = ((g, u, n, m, ad), c)$ and a set Q as input, where Q contains tuples with the format $((g, u, n, m_0, m_1, ad), c)$. Here z describes the input-output values of a single query to the VERDEC oracle, and each element of C specifies the input-output of a prior SIGENC oracle query. At a high level, z contains the message m that was recovered during an ongoing VERDEC call, and m is the only value in z, Q not necessarily known by the adversary. One might want to define VERDEC to return m whenever the input is identified as a trivial forgery, but m could potentially trivially reveal the challenge bit. So one could roughly think of $\mathsf{func}_{\mathsf{out}}^{\mathsf{sec}}$ as the function that should enable VERDEC to return m when possible. However, it should determine – from z and Q – if m would trivially help the adversary win and then "guard" VERDEC against returning this m.

$\mathsf{func}_{\mathsf{out}}^{\perp}(z, Q)$	$\mathsf{func}_{\mathsf{out}}^{\text{silence-with-}m_1}[\mathsf{pred}_{\mathsf{trivial}}](z, Q)$
Return $\perp$	For each $((g, u, n, m_0, m_1, ad), c) \in Q$ do
	$\quad$ If $m_0 \neq m_1$ then
	$\quad\quad$ If $\mathsf{pred}_{\mathsf{trivial}}(z, \{((g, u, n, m_0, ad), c)\})$ then return m_1
	$\quad\quad$ If $\mathsf{pred}_{\mathsf{trivial}}(z, \{((g, u, n, m_1, ad), c)\})$ then return m_1
	$((g, u, n, m, ad), c) \leftarrow z$; Return m

Fig. 8. Sample output-guarding functions $\mathsf{func}_{\mathsf{out}}^{\perp}$ and $\mathsf{func}_{\mathsf{out}}^{\text{silence-with-}m_1}$. Function $\mathsf{func}_{\mathsf{out}}^{\text{silence-with-}m_1}$ is parameterized by a ciphertext-triviality predicate $\mathsf{pred}_{\mathsf{trivial}}$.

In Fig. 8 we define two output-guarding functions. The function $\mathsf{func}_{\mathsf{out}}^{\perp}$ always returns $\perp$. This provides no useful information to the adversary and so captures a comparatively weaker security notion. The function $\mathsf{func}_{\mathsf{out}}^{\text{silence-with-}m_1}[\mathsf{pred}_{\mathsf{trivial}}]$ is parameterized by an arbitrary ciphertext-triviality predicate $\mathsf{pred}_{\mathsf{trivial}}$ and captures the following logic. For every element in Q that describes a challenge encryption (i.e. $m_0 \neq m_1$) performed by SIGENC, this function checks whether z is trivially forgeable based on the information that the adversary could have learned from the corresponding response. This is checked if z would be trivially forgeable for *both* choices of $b \in \{0, 1\}$ or only for *only one* choice of b. The output-guarding function returns m_1 when this condition passes. If no element of Q triggered the above, then the output-guarding function returns the m contained in z, i.e. the actual message recovered in VERDEC.

The Use of $\mathsf{func}_{\mathsf{out}}^{\text{silence-with-}m_1}$ in Our Work. We target $\mathsf{func}_{\mathsf{out}}^{\text{silence-with-}m_1}[\mathsf{pred}_{\mathsf{trivial}}]$ as the output-guarding function that provides the strongest possible security guarantees for the schemes that we analyze in this work. For every $\mathsf{pred}_{\mathsf{trivial}}$ we use,

---

BoxMessage.SigEnc$(g, K_g, u, sk_u, n, m_{body}, ad)$ // where $n = (n_{body}, n_{header})$
$c_{body} \leftarrow$ XSalsa20-Poly1305.Enc$(K_g, n_{body}, m_{body})$
$h_{body} \leftarrow$ SHA-256$(n_{body} \parallel c_{body})$
$m_{header} \leftarrow \langle ad, u, g, h_{body} \rangle$
$c_{header} \leftarrow$ SealPacket.SigEnc$(g, K_g, u, sk_u, n_{header}, m_{header}, \varepsilon)$
Return (c_{body}, c_{header})

SealPacket.SigEnc$(g, K_g, u, sk_u, n, m, ad)$ // where $ad = \varepsilon$
$h \leftarrow$ SHA-512(m) ; $m_s \leftarrow$ "Keybase-Chat-2" $\parallel \langle K_g, n, h \rangle$
$s \leftarrow$ Ed25519.Sig(sk_u, m_s) ; $m_e \leftarrow s \parallel m$
$c \leftarrow$ XSalsa20-Poly1305.Enc(K_g, n, m_e)
Return c

Fig. 9. The BoxMessage and SealPacket algorithms used in Keybase for encrypting chat messages from a user to a group. Here g is the group's identifier, K_g is the symmetric key shared by all group members, u is the sender's identifier, and sk_u is the sender's signing key.

$\mathsf{pred}_{trivial}(z, \{((g, u, n, m^*, ad), c)\})$ can only be true when z contains m^*. So for elements of Q with $m_0 \neq m_1$ only one of the two if conditions can pass, meaning it is necessary to silence the output. Otherwise the adversary can trivially win the game by building z, Q and evaluating $\mathsf{pred}_{trivial}$ to distinguish between $b = 0$ or $b = 1$. (This attack assumes the adversary can always compute $\mathsf{pred}_{trivial}(z, C)$ for SS, in spite of not knowing the challenge bit b that is needed to explicitly build C. This is true in all of our proofs.)

3.3 Symmetric Signcryption from Encryption and Signatures

In the full version, we introduce a provably secure version of Sign-then-Encrypt (StE). Its signcryption algorithm signs $s \leftarrow\!\!{}_\$ $ DS.Sig$(sk_u, \langle g, n, m, ad \rangle)$ then outputs ciphertext $c \leftarrow$ NE.Enc$(K_g, n, s \parallel m, \langle u, ad \rangle)$. We prove bounds of the form $\mathsf{Adv}^{IUF}_{StE, \mathsf{pred}^{suf}_{trivial}}(\mathcal{A}_{IUF}) \leq \mathsf{Adv}^{SUFCMA}_{DS}(\mathcal{A}_{SUFCMA})$ and $\mathsf{Adv}^{OAE}_{StE, \mathsf{pred}^{suf}_{trivial}, \mathsf{func}^{\perp}_{out}}(\mathcal{A}_{OAE}) \leq \mathsf{Adv}^{AEAD}_{NE}(\mathcal{A}_{AEAD})$.

4 Keybase Chat Encryption as Symmetric Signcryption

We analyze the security of the cryptographic algorithm BoxMessage that Keybase uses to encrypt and authenticate chat messages from a sender to a group. BoxMessage combines multiple cryptographic primitives to offer end-to-end encrypted messaging. In particular it uses XSalsa20-Poly1305, SHA-256, SHA-512, and Ed25519 as building blocks. Within BoxMessage, the SealPacket subroutine encrypts and authenticates message headers. We show the pseudocode for these algorithms in Fig. 9. We omit the decryption algorithms

BoxMessage.VerDec and SealPacket.VerDec from Fig. 9 as Keybase's implementation of these algorithms follows naturally from the corresponding SigEnc algorithms. We define the VerDec algorithms explicitly in our formalazation of BoxMessage and SealPacket.

To formalize the security of BoxMessage, it is crucial to first identify the formal primitive underlying this algorithm and the security goals it aims to achieve. None of the existing primitives in literature seem to aptly model this object, but it is naturally captured by the symmetric signcryption primitive that we defined in Sect. 3. Similarly, SealPacket can also be modeled as a symmetric signcryption scheme from which BoxMessage is built. In this section, we present modular constructions that cast BoxMessage and SealPacket as symmetric signcryption schemes. We first provide a general overview of the two algorithms.

The BoxMessage Chat-Encryption Algorithm. The BoxMessage.SigEnc algorithm accepts the following inputs – group's identifier g, symmetric group key K_g, sender identifier u, sender signing key sk_u, nonce $n = (n_{body}, n_{header})$, message m_{body}, and associated data ad. It performs the following steps. First it calls XSalsa20-Poly1305.Enc to encrypt m_{body} using key K_g and nonce n_{body}, and obtains the ciphertext c_{body}. It builds header plaintext m_{header} as $\langle ad, u, g, h_{body} \rangle$ (a unique encoding of ad, u, g, and hash $h_{body} = \text{SHA-256}(n_{body} \| c_{body})$). It then invokes SealPacket.SigEnc to encrypt m_{header} using sk_u, K_g, and n_{header}, and obtains the ciphertext c_{header}. Finally, it returns (c_{body}, c_{header}). To decrypt ciphertext (c_{body}, c_{header}), the algorithm BoxMessage.VerDec (not shown) ensures that c_{header} decrypts into the header plaintext m_{header} that is equal to the unique string $\langle ad, u, g, h_{body} \rangle$ composed from the inputs of BoxMessage.VerDec. In Keybase, the sender identifier u is their username and the group identifier g is constructed canonically from the usernames of the group members.

The SealPacket Header-Encryption Algorithm. The SealPacket algorithm accepts the same inputs as BoxMessage, except it does not take associated data ad as input. We capture this by setting SealPacket.AD $= \{\varepsilon\}$, meaning $ad = \varepsilon$ is always true When SealPacket.SigEnc is called from BoxMessage.SigEnc, it encrypts chat headers. To encrypt m with nonce n, it starts by hashing m to obtain $h = \text{SHA-512}(m)$. Then it builds an input m_s to the Ed25519 signature scheme by concatenating the prefix string "Keybase-Chat-2" with the unique encoding $\langle K_g, n, h \rangle$ of K_g, n, and h. It invokes Ed25519.Sig to produce a signature s over m_s using the signing key sk_u. Finally it calls XSalsa20-Poly1305.Enc to encrypt $m_e = s \| m$ using the key K_g and nonce n, and obtains the ciphertext c which is returned To decryption ciphertext c, the SealPacket.VerDec algorithm (not shown) first recovers m_e from c and then parses m_e to obtain $s \| m$. Note that m_e can be unambiguously parsed into $s \| m$ because Ed25519 produces fixed-length signatures. Then SealPacket.VerDec reconstructs m_s and ensures that s verifies as a valid signature for m_s under the sender's public key vk_u. We study the security of SealPacket in the context of the BoxMessage algorithm, but this is not the only context in which Keybase uses SealPacket. It is also used independently for the encryption of long strings and attachments. In the full version we detail other uses of SealPacket in Keybase.

Analysis Challenges. The descriptions of BoxMessage and SealPacket that we have given so far already present the following challenges in their analysis.

Key Reuse in BoxMessage. The same symmetric key K_g is used in BoxMessage and SealPacket. This violates the principle of key separation, which says that one should always use distinct keys for distinct algorithms and modes of operation. Without context separation, this potentially allows an attacker to forward ciphertexts produced by one algorithm to another. There is no explicit context separation, so our analysis will "extract" separation by making assumptions of Ed25519 and using low-level details of how messages are encoded.

Cyclic Key Dependency in SealPacket. The message m_s signed in SealPacket is derived from the symmetric group key K_g which is also used to encrypt the signature. This produces what is known as an "encryption cycle", a generalization of encrypting one's own key [10]. Standard AEAD security does not guarantee security when messages being encrypted depend on the key used for encryption. We use an extension of AEAD security allowing key-dependent messages and prove (in the random oracle model) that XSalsa20-Poly1305 achieves it for the particular key-dependent messages required.

Lack of Group/User Binding in SealPacket. By looking at the SealPacket algorithm in Fig. 9 we can see that the inputs u and g are never used by the algorithm. This means that a SealPacket ciphertext does not, in general, bind to the group's or user's identifiers. This could potentially allow a malicious user to impersonate another group member. When SealPacket is used within BoxMessage, it is always invoked on a message that contains the group's and the user's identifier, so the lack of group/user binding in SealPacket is not consequential there.

Nonce Repetition in Keybase. XSalsa20-Poly1305 is not secure when nonces repeat so our security analysis disallows nonce repetition between BoxMessage and/or SealPacket. The Keybase implementation uses uniformly random nonces, making collisions highly unlikely. Moreover, our results show that BoxMessage is robust to accidental non-uniformity in randomness as long nonces do not repeat. The XSalsa20-Poly1305 authenticated encryption scheme combines the XSalsa20 stream cipher and the Poly1305 *one-time* message authentication code. The stream is derived from the key and nonce and is used for keying Poly1305, so if nonces repeat then privacy and integrity may both be broken.

Message Encryption Scheme BM. Our modular symmetric signcryption construction BM models the BoxMessage chat-encryption algorithm as follows.

Construction 1. *Let* $\mathcal{M} \subseteq \{0,1\}^*$. *Let* NE *be a nonce-based encryption scheme. Let* H *be a hash function. Let* SP *be a deterministic symmetric signcryption scheme. Then* BM = BOX-MESSAGE-SS$[\mathcal{M}, \text{NE}, \text{H}, \text{SP}]$ *is the deterministic symmetric signcryption scheme as defined in Fig. 10, with message space* BM.MS = $\mathcal{M}$ *and associated-data space* BM.AD = $\{0,1\}^*$. *We require the following. The group key taken by* BM *is used as the key for both* NE *and* SP*, so* BM.gkl = NE.kl = SP.gkl. *The nonce taken by* BM *is a pair containing a separate nonce for each of* NE *and* SP*, so* BM.NS = $\{0,1\}^{\text{NE.nl}} \times$ SP.NS.

BM.UserKg

$(sk, vk) \leftarrow^\$ \text{SP.UserKg}$; Return (sk, vk)

BM.SigEnc$(g, K_g, u, sk_u, n, m_{\text{body}}, ad)$ // $K_g \in \{0,1\}^{256}$

$(n_{\text{body}}, n_{\text{header}}) \leftarrow n$ // $n_{\text{body}}, n_{\text{header}} \in \{0,1\}^{192}$
// Encrypt the message body
$c_{\text{body}} \leftarrow \text{NE.Enc}(K_g, n_{\text{body}}, m_{\text{body}})$ // NE = XSalsa20-Poly1305
// Create and encrypt the message header
$h_{\text{body}} \leftarrow \text{H}(n_{\text{body}} \| c_{\text{body}})$; $m_{\text{header}} \leftarrow \langle ad, u, g, h_{\text{body}} \rangle$ // H = SHA-256
$c_{\text{header}} \leftarrow \text{SP.SigEnc}(g, K_g, u, sk_u, n_{\text{header}}, m_{\text{header}}, \varepsilon)$ // SP = SEAL-PACKET-SS
Return $(c_{\text{body}}, c_{\text{header}})$

BM.VerDec$(g, K_g, u, vk_u, n, c, ad)$

$(n_{\text{body}}, n_{\text{header}}) \leftarrow n$; $(c_{\text{body}}, c_{\text{header}}) \leftarrow c$
// Recover and verify the message header
$m_{\text{header}} \leftarrow \text{SP.VerDec}(g, K_g, u, vk_u, n_{\text{header}}, c_{\text{header}}, \varepsilon)$
$h_{\text{body}} \leftarrow \text{H}(n_{\text{body}} \| c_{\text{body}})$
If $m_{\text{header}} \neq \langle ad, u, g, h_{\text{body}} \rangle$ then return $\bot$
// Recover and return the message body
$m_{\text{body}} \leftarrow \text{NE.Dec}(K_g, n_{\text{body}}, c_{\text{body}})$; Return m_{body}

Fig. 10. Symmetric signcryption scheme BM = BOX-MESSAGE-SS[$\mathcal{M}$, NE, H, SP]. The right-aligned comments provide a guideline for modeling Keybase.

SP.UserKg

$(sk, vk) \leftarrow^\$ \text{DS.Kg}$; Return (sk, vk)

SP.SigEnc$(g, K_g, u, sk_u, n, m, ad)$ // $K_g \in \{0,1\}^{256}, n \in \{0,1\}^{192}, ad = \varepsilon$

$h \leftarrow \text{H}(m)$ // H = SHA-512
$m_s \leftarrow \text{"Keybase-Chat-2"} \| \langle K_g, n, h \rangle$
$s \leftarrow \text{DS.Sig}(sk_u, m_s)$; $m_e \leftarrow s \| m$ // DS = Ed25519
$c \leftarrow \text{NE.Enc}(K_g, n, m_e)$; Return c // NE = XSalsa20-Poly1305

SP.VerDec$(g, K_g, u, vk_u, n, c, ad)$ // $ad = \varepsilon$

$m_e \leftarrow \text{NE.Dec}(K_g, n, c)$
If $m_e = \bot$ then return $\bot$
$s \| m \leftarrow m_e$ // s.t. $|s| = \text{DS.sl}, |m| \geq 0$
$h \leftarrow \text{H}(m)$
$m_s \leftarrow \text{"Keybase-Chat-2"} \| \langle K_g, n, h \rangle$
If $\neg\text{DS.Ver}(vk_u, m_s, s)$ then return $\bot$ else return m

Fig. 11. Symmetric signcryption scheme SP = SEAL-PACKET-SS[H, DS, NE]. The right-aligned comments provide a guideline for modeling Keybase.

Header Encryption Scheme SP. Our modular symmetric signcryption construction SP models the header-encryption algorithm SealPacket as follows.

Construction 2. *Let* H *be a hash function. Let* DS *be a deterministic digital signature scheme. Let* NE *be a nonce-based encryption scheme. Then* SP = SEAL-PACKET-SS[H, DS, NE] *is the symmetric signcryption scheme as defined in Fig. 11, with group-key length* SP.gkl = NE.kl, *nonce space* SP.NS = $\{0,1\}^{\text{NE.nl}}$, *message space* SP.MS = $\{0,1\}^*$, *and associated-data space* SP.AD = $\{\varepsilon\}$.

5 Security Analysis of Keybase Chat Encryption

In this section we analyze the security of the symmetric signcryption schemes BM and SP defined in Sect. 4. In Sect. 5.1, we show the in-group unforgeability of BM and SP. In Sects. 5.2 and 5.3, we show the out-group AE security of BM and SP. This requires us to introduce two weaker variants of the OAE security notion, one each for BM and SP, by relaxing the level of nonce-misuse requirements of the OAE game defined in Fig. 6. The SP analysis requires two new security notions, $\mathcal{M}$ *opacity* for digital signature schemes and *authenticated encryption for key-dependent messages* for nonce-based encryption schemes.

5.1 In-Group Unforgeability of BoxMessage and SealPacket

In-Group Unforgeability of BoxMessage. In-group unforgeability of BM = BOX-MESSAGE-SS[$\mathcal{M}$, NE, H, SP] reduces to the security of SP and H. A BM ciphertext is a pair $(c_{\text{body}}, c_{\text{header}})$ comprising an NE ciphertext c_{body} and an SP ciphertext c_{header}, which encrypts $\langle ad, u, g, h_{\text{body}} \rangle$. The adversary's objective is to forge a BM ciphertext by either forging c_{body} or c_{header}. The adversary can use a corrupt group key K_g, so c_{body} ciphertexts are easily forged. However, this does not suffice to produce a BM forgery because c_{header} encrypts the hash of c_{body}. Therefore, it would need to forge a corresponding c_{header} ciphertext. The IUF security of SP prevents the adversary from forging c_{header} ciphertexts. As a result, the adversary can only reuse honestly generated c_{header} from its prior queries to SigEnc in its forgery attempts. Since an honest c_{header} effectively commits to ad, u, g, h_{body}, and n_{header}, using an old c_{header} to construct a new BM ciphertext requires finding a new NE nonce-ciphertext pair that hashes to the same h_{body} under H. Collision resistance of H prevents this. The formal proof of Theorem 1 is in the full version.

Theorem 1. *Let* BM = BOX-MESSAGE-SS[$\mathcal{M}$, NE, H, SP] *be the symmetric signcryption scheme built from some* $\mathcal{M}$, NE, H, SP *as specified in Construction 1. Let* $\text{pred}_{\text{trivial}}^{\text{suf}}$ *and* $\text{pred}_{\text{trivial}}^{\text{suf-except-group}}$ *be the ciphertext-triviality predicates as defined in Fig. 7. Let* $\mathcal{A}_{\text{IUF-of-BM}}$ *be any adversary against the* IUF *security of* BM *with respect to* $\text{pred}_{\text{trivial}}^{\text{suf}}$. *Then we can build adversaries* $\mathcal{A}_{\text{IUF-of-SP}}$ *and* $\mathcal{A}_{\text{CR}}$ *such that*

$$\text{Adv}_{\text{BM},\text{pred}_{\text{trivial}}^{\text{suf}}}^{\text{IUF}}(\mathcal{A}_{\text{IUF-of-BM}}) \leq \text{Adv}_{\text{SP},\text{pred}_{\text{trivial}}^{\text{suf-except-group}}}^{\text{IUF}}(\mathcal{A}_{\text{IUF-of-SP}}) + \text{Adv}_{\text{H}}^{\text{CR}}(\mathcal{A}_{\text{CR}}).$$

In-Group Unforgeability of SealPacket. In-group unforgeability of the symmetric signcryption scheme SP = SEAL-PACKET-SS[H, DS, NE] reduces to the

Fig. 12. A summary of the reductions that we provide for the wOAE security of SP and the bwOAE security of BM.

security of DS and H. We parameterize the IUF security of SP to aim for a relaxed version of strong unforgeability because SP ciphertexts do not directly depend on the group's identifier g (even though it depends on the group key K_g).

An SP ciphertext encrypts $s \parallel m$ under K_g. The adversary can use a corrupt K_g, but forging an SP ciphertext still requires the signature s. So the adversary must either forge a new signature or reuse an honest signature from a prior SigEnc query. The SUFCMA security of DS prevents the former. An honest signature s is computed over "Keybase-Chat-2" $\parallel \langle K_g, n, h \rangle$ where h is the hash of the message m. Hence reusing an honest signature could use a new SP ciphertext that encrypts $s \parallel m$ with K_g, n, but the tidiness of NE prevents this. So reusing an honest signature requires finding a new message that hashes to the same h under H. Collision resistance of H prevents this. The formal proof of Theorem 2 is in the full version.

Theorem 2. *Let* SP $=$ SEAL-PACKET-SS[H, DS, NE] *be the symmetric sign-cryption scheme built from some* H, DS, *and* NE *as specified in Construction 2. Let* $\mathrm{pred}_{\mathrm{trivial}}^{\mathrm{suf\text{-}except\text{-}group}}$ *be the ciphertext-triviality predicate as defined in Fig. 7. Let* $\mathcal{A}_{\mathrm{IUF\text{-}of\text{-}SP}}$ *be any adversary against the* IUF *security of* SP *with respect to* $\mathrm{pred}_{\mathrm{trivial}}^{\mathrm{suf\text{-}except\text{-}group}}$. *Then we can build adversaries* $\mathcal{A}_{\mathrm{SUFCMA}}$ *and* $\mathcal{A}_{\mathrm{CR}}$ *such that*

$$\mathrm{Adv}_{\mathrm{SP},\mathrm{pred}_{\mathrm{trivial}}^{\mathrm{suf\text{-}except\text{-}group}}}^{\mathrm{IUF}}(\mathcal{A}_{\mathrm{IUF\text{-}of\text{-}SP}}) \leq \mathrm{Adv}_{\mathrm{DS}}^{\mathrm{SUFCMA}}(\mathcal{A}_{\mathrm{SUFCMA}}) + \mathrm{Adv}_{\mathrm{H}}^{\mathrm{CR}}(\mathcal{A}_{\mathrm{CR}}).$$

5.2   Out-Group AE Security of BoxMessage

Out-group AE security of BM $=$ BOX-MESSAGE-SS[$\mathcal{M}$, NE, H, SP] reduces to the security of its underlying primitives as summarized by the rightmost arrows of Fig. 12. At a high level, we show that BM achieves a variant of OAE security (bwOAE) if SP achieves another variant of OAE security (wOAE) and H is collision-resistant. Because NE $=$ XSalsa20-Poly1305 in Keybase (which is not nonce-misuse resistant), both variants disallow nonce repetition.

Intuition. An BM ciphertext is a pair $(c_{\mathrm{body}}, c_{\mathrm{header}})$ consisting of an NE ciphertext c_{body} and an SP ciphertext c_{header}. One way the adversary could learn the challenge bit is by querying its VerDec oracle on a forged BM ciphertext that decrypts successfully. In order to accomplish that, the adversary must either forge the underlying SP ciphertext c_{header} or reuse an honestly generated c_{header}.

The former is prevented by the out-group AE security of SP. The latter is prevented by the collision resistance of H because of the following. An honestly generated c_{header} effectively commits to ad, u, g, h_{body}, and n_{header}. In order to reuse c_{header}, an adversary must find a new NE nonce-ciphertext pair that hashes to h_{body}, hence producing a collision. It follows that the VERDEC oracle is essentially useless to the adversary; it can only serve to decrypt non-challenge ciphertexts that were previously returned by SIGENC. So it remains to show that the adversary cannot learn the challenge bit solely based on the BM ciphertexts that it receives from SIGENC. For any ciphertext (c_{body}, c_{header}) returned by SIGENC, the SP ciphertext c_{header} encrypts a hash of c_{body} but otherwise does not depend on the challenge bit. So the adversary gains no advantage from observing c_{header}. Finally, the AEAD security of NE guarantees that c_{body} does not reveal the challenge bit.

Because the header encryption scheme SP and the body encryption scheme NE use the same symmetric key K_g, we require integrity of SP ciphertexts produced using K_g hold even when the adversary can obtain other NE encryptions under the same key. Similarly, the NE ciphertexts generated using the symmetric key K_g should be indistinguishable even when the adversary can obtain SP encryptions and decryptions under the same key. We introduce a variant of the OAE game in Definition 3 to capture these joint requirements.

Restrictions on Nonce Misuse in BM and SP. We now define new variants of out-group AE security for our analysis of Keybase. The BM and SP schemes in Keybase are not nonce-misuse resistant so we modify the OAE game to disallow nonce repetition. We start with wOAE security for SP.

Definition 1. *Let* SS *be a symmetric signcryption scheme. Consider the* OAE *security game for* SS *of Fig. 6 (w.r.t. any* $pred_{trivial}^{sec}$, $func_{out}^{sec}$). *We define a new variant of this game as follows. The instruction preventing nonce misuse*

require $\forall d \in \{0,1\}, (g, u, n, m_d, ad) \notin N_d$ *is replaced with*   require $(g, n) \notin N$.

In addition, the instructions updating the nonce set

$$N_0 \leftarrow N_0 \cup \{(g, u, n, m_0, ad)\}$$
$$N_1 \leftarrow N_1 \cup \{(g, u, n, m_1, ad)\}$$ *are replaced with* $N \leftarrow N \cup \{(g, n)\}$.

We denote the resulting game (and security notion) by wOAE. *It is a weak variant of* OAE *that does not require nonce-misuse resistance. We define an adversary's advantage in breaking the* wOAE *security of* SS *in the natural way.*

Now we define bwOAE security for BM. The nonce of BM is a pair of two separate nonces $n = (n_{body}, n_{header})$. The bwOAE security game independently applies the group-nonce uniqueness condition introduced in Definition 1 to each of (g, n_{body}) and (g, n_{header}), *and* it also requires that $n_{body} \neq n_{header}$. This is a necessary because BM calls NE.Enc on (g, n_{body}), and SP calls NE.Enc on (g, n_{header}). In Keybase both NE schemes are XSalsa20-Poly1305 using the same key.

Definition 2. *Let* $\mathcal{X}, \mathcal{Y}$ *be any sets. Let* SS *be a symmetric signcryption scheme with the nonce space* SS.NS $= \mathcal{X} \times \mathcal{Y}$. *Consider the* OAE *security game for* SS *of Fig. 6 (w.r.t. any* $pred_{trivial}^{sec}$, $func_{out}^{sec}$). *We define a new variant of this game as follows. The instruction preventing nonce misuse*

require $\forall d, (g, u, n, m_d, ad) \notin N_d$ *is replaced with*
$$\begin{array}{l}(n_{\text{body}}, n_{\text{header}}) \leftarrow n \\ \text{If } n_{\text{body}} = n_{\text{header}} \text{ then return } \bot \\ \text{If } (g, n_{\text{body}}) \in N \text{ then return } \bot \\ \text{If } (g, n_{\text{header}}) \in N \text{ then return } \bot.\end{array}$$

In addition, the instructions updating the nonce set

$$\begin{array}{l}N_0 \leftarrow N_0 \cup \{(g, u, n, m_0, ad)\} \\ N_1 \leftarrow N_1 \cup \{(g, u, n, m_1, ad)\}\end{array} \quad \textit{are replaced with} \quad \begin{array}{l}N \leftarrow N \cup \{(g, n_{\text{header}})\} \\ N \leftarrow N \cup \{(g, n_{\text{body}})\}.\end{array}$$

We denote the resulting game (and security notion) by bwOAE. *Beyond being defined for* SS *with a bipartite nonce space, this variant of* OAE *is weak in that it does not require nonce-misuse resistance. We define an adversary's advantage in breaking the* bwOAE *security of* SS *in the natural way.*

The Joint Security Required of SP and NE. Here we define the security notion required from SP when it is used in the presence of arbitrary NE encryptions under the same symmetric group keys that are used by SP. We call this notion wOAE[ENC[$\mathcal{M}$, NE]]. It is a parameterized version of the wOAE game defined in Definition 1. We use it for our analysis of the bwOAE security of BM.

At the start of this section we discussed that the security reduction for BM intuitively requires that it is hard to forge an SP ciphertext (without knowing the corresponding group key K_g) in the presence of NE encryptions. Our definition of wOAE[ENC[$\mathcal{M}$, NE]] captures this by providing the adversary access to an NE encryption oracle ENC in addition to the SIGENC and VERDEC oracles in the out-group AE security game of SP. We stress that proving the security of BM does not, in principle, require us to provide the SIGENC oracle to the adversary. We choose to require this stronger level of security from SP because of the following reasons. On the one hand, in Sect. 4 we explained why it is beneficial to prove that SP satisfies a strong security notion, going beyond what is required by BM. On the other hand, this stronger security notion that we require from SP will not come at the cost of introducing additional assumptions or achieving looser concrete-security bounds in our analysis of BM.

Definition 3. *Let* SS *be a symmetric signcryption scheme. Let* $\mathcal{M} \subseteq \{0,1\}^*$. *Let* NE *be a nonce-based encryption scheme. Consider the* wOAE *security game for* SS *as defined in Definition 1 (w.r.t. any* $\text{pred}_{\text{trivial}}^{\text{sec}}$, $\text{func}_{\text{out}}^{\text{sec}}$). *We define a variant of this game by adding an oracle that is defined as follows.*

ENC[$\mathcal{M}$, NE]$(g, n_{\text{body}}, m_{\text{body},0}, m_{\text{body},1})$

require $\mathsf{K}[g] \neq \bot$ and $|m_{\text{body},0}| = |m_{\text{body},1}|$
require $(g, n_{\text{body}}) \notin N$ and $m_{\text{body},0}, m_{\text{body},1} \in \mathcal{M}$
If $m_{\text{body},0} \neq m_{\text{body},1}$ then
    If group_is_corrupt[g] then return $\bot$
    chal[g] $\leftarrow$ true
$c_{\text{body}} \leftarrow$ NE.Enc($\mathsf{K}[g], n_{\text{body}}, m_{\text{body},b}$)
$N \leftarrow N \cup \{(g, n_{\text{body}})\}$; *Return* c_{body}

It shares set N, *bit* b, *and the tables* K, group_is_corrupt, chal *with the rest of the security game. We denote the resulting game (and security notion) by* wOAE[ENC[$\mathcal{M}$, NE]]. *It simultaneously requires out-group AE security of* SS *(without nonce repetition) and an IND-style security of* NE. *We define an adversary's advantage in breaking this security notion in the natural way.*

Note that we require the messages that the adversary queries to the ENC oracle to be in $\mathcal{M}$. Intuitively, in our security analysis of BM, an adversary will only be able to obtain NE encryptions of messages in the message space of BM. So in the security reduction for BM we will use $\mathcal{M} = $ BM.MS.

Out-Group AE Security of BoxMessage. We prove bwOAE security of BM. The formal proof of Theorem 3 is in the full version.

Theorem 3. *Let* BM $=$ BOX-MESSAGE-SS[$\mathcal{M}$, NE, H, SP] *be the symmetric signcryption scheme built from some* $\mathcal{M}$, NE, H, SP *as specified in Construction 1. Let* $\text{pred}_{\text{trivial}}^{\text{suf}}$ *and* $\text{pred}_{\text{trivial}}^{\text{suf-except-user}}$ *be the ciphertext-triviality predicates as defined in Fig. 7. Let* $\text{func}_{\text{out}}^{\perp}$ *be the output-guarding functions as defined in Fig. 8. Let* wOAE[ENC[$\mathcal{M}$, NE]] *be the security notion as defined in Definition 3. Let* $\mathcal{A}_{\text{bwOAE-of-BM}}$ *be any adversary against the* bwOAE *security of* BM *with respect to* $\text{pred}_{\text{trivial}}^{\text{suf}}$ *and* $\text{func}_{\text{out}}^{\text{sec}}$. *Then we build adversaries* $\mathcal{A}_{\text{wOAE-of-SP}}$ *and* $\mathcal{A}_{\text{CR}}$ *such that*

$$\text{Adv}_{\text{BM},\text{pred}_{\text{trivial}}^{\text{suf}},\text{func}_{\text{out}}^{\perp}}^{\text{bwOAE}}(\mathcal{A}_{\text{bwOAE-of-BM}}) \leq \text{Adv}_{\text{SP},\text{pred}_{\text{trivial}}^{\text{suf-except-user}},\text{func}_{\text{out}}^{\perp}}^{\text{wOAE}[\text{ENC}[\mathcal{M},\text{NE}]]}(\mathcal{A}_{\text{wOAE-of-SP}})$$
$$+ \text{Adv}_{\text{H}}^{\text{CR}}(\mathcal{A}_{\text{CR}}).$$

Note that we prove the security of BM with respect to $\text{pred}_{\text{trivial}}^{\text{suf}}$ and $\text{func}_{\text{out}}^{\perp}$. As discussed in Sect. 3, $\text{pred}_{\text{trivial}}^{\text{suf}}$ essentially requires BM to have ciphertext integrity. Our result relies on the security of SP with respect to $\text{pred}_{\text{trivial}}^{\text{suf-except-user}}$ and $\text{func}_{\text{out}}^{\perp}$. Recall that $\text{pred}_{\text{trivial}}^{\text{suf-except-user}}$ basically requires SP to have ciphertext integrity, except it allows for an honest ciphertext to be successfully decrypted even with respect to a wrong user identifier; the latter is not considered a "valid" forgery. This does not translate to an attack against BM because it only uses SP to encrypt header messages $m_{\text{header}} = \langle ad, u, g, h_{\text{body}} \rangle$ that contain u, and the BM.VerDec algorithm verifies that the group identifier it received as input matches the one that was parsed from m_{header}.

5.3   Out-Group AE Security of SealPacket

Out-group AE security of SP $=$ SEAL-PACKET-SS[H, DS, NE] reduces to the security NE and DS (see Fig. 12). In particular, wOAE[ENC[$\mathcal{M}$, NE]] security holds if NE provides authenticated encryption for key-dependent messages and DS produces $\mathcal{M}$-sparse signatures. We introduce these security notions below.

Intuition. Recall that in the wOAE[ENC[$\mathcal{M}$, NE]] game, the adversary is provided with (un)signcryption oracles SIGENC and VERDEC for SP, and an encryption oracle ENC for NE. Each of these returns output based on a challenge bit that is shared between them. The adversary can use three approaches to learn the challenge bit. It can (a) attempt SP forgeries by calling its SP decryption oracle VERDEC; (b) make left-or-right queries to its NE encryption oracle ENC; (c) make left-or-right queries to its SP encryption oracle SIGENC.

The adversary is allowed to expose users' signing keys so it could attempt to forge an SP ciphertext using an exposed DS signing key and its ENC oracle. The adversary would then query the resulting ciphertext to its VERDEC oracle in an attempt to trivially win the game. We show that the adversary is unable to accomplish this. The ENC oracle is defined to only produce encryptions of the messages from the set $\mathcal{M}$. In the implementation of Keybase, the messages from $\mathcal{M}$ have a specific encoding; we will rely on this property in our proof. In contrast, any ciphertext successfully decrypted by VERDEC must encrypt a message of the form $m_e = s \,\|\, m$ where s is a valid DS signature. So the adversary needs to find a signature s that is consistent with the message encoding that is permitted by ENC. The $\mathcal{M}$-sparseness of DS signatures, which we formalize below, prevents this. It follows that the VERDEC oracle does not help the adversary to win the game by querying ciphertexts that were previously returned by ENC.[1]

Now we can reimagine the ENC and SIGENC oracles as producing NE encryptions of key-dependent messages. The SIGENC oracle requires messages to be derived as a specific function of the symmetric group key K_g. The ENC oracle can be thought of as allowing to messages that are derived from "constant" functions, meaning the chosen messages do not depend on K_g. We can also view the VERDEC oracle as an NE decryption oracle that prevents the adversary from trivially winning the game by merely querying the ciphertexts it previously obtained from either ENC or SIGENC. We define the AE security of NE for key-dependent messages and show that the adversary can only win the wOAE[ENC[$\mathcal{M}$, NE]] game against SP if it can win the KDMAE game against NE.

Reliance on the Message Encoding in Keybase. We mentioned in the intuition that we rely on the encoding of messages in $\mathcal{M}$ in our proof. We emphasize that avoiding this dependency is non-trivial. The cyclic key dependency within SP and the key reuse between BM and SP pose significant challenges when considering the possibility of an alternate proof.

$\mathcal{M}$-sparse Signatures. Consider game $\mathcal{G}^{\mathsf{SPARSE}}$ of Fig. 13, defined for a digital signature scheme DS, a set $\mathcal{M} \subseteq \{0,1\}^*$, and an adversary $\mathcal{A}_{\mathsf{SPARSE}}$. The advantage of $\mathcal{A}_{\mathsf{SPARSE}}$ in breaking the $\mathcal{M}$-SPARSE security of DS is defined as $\mathrm{Adv}^{\mathsf{SPARSE}}_{\mathsf{DS},\mathcal{M}}(\mathcal{A}_{\mathsf{SPARSE}}) = \Pr[\mathcal{G}^{\mathsf{SPARSE}}_{\mathsf{DS},\mathcal{M}}(\mathcal{A}_{\mathsf{SPARSE}})]$. Intuitively, this game captures the inability of an adversary to produce a signature that conforms to the message space $\mathcal{M}$ even though the adversary chooses the public key used to verify the signature. More formally, the adversary wins if it is able to return (vk, m, s, γ) such that s verifies as a signature over the message m under the verification key vk and $s \,\|\, \gamma \in \mathcal{M}$. We stress that the adversary is allowed to choose an arbitrary – possibly malformed – verification key. The adversary is not required to know the corresponding signing key, and such a key may in fact not exist.

---

[1] The wOAE[ENC[$\mathcal{M}$, NE]] game itself also prevents the adversary from trivially winning by querying VERDEC on a ciphertext that was previously returned by SIGENC.

We verify our intuition about the $\mathcal{M}$-sparsity of the Ed25519 signature scheme underlying SP in the full version. Ed25519 is a deterministic signature scheme introduced by Bernstein, Duif, Lange, Schwabe, and Yang in [17]. It is obtained by applying the commitment-variant of the Fiat-Shamir transform to an identification scheme. Therefore a signature produced by Ed25519 consists of the commitment and response of the identification scheme. The adversary can only win the SPARSE game of Ed25519 if it is able to produce an accepting conversation transcript for the identification scheme such that the corresponding commitment conforms to $\mathcal{M}$. Commitments in the identification scheme underlying Ed25519 are elements of a prime-order group. We prove that finding such a commitment is only possible if the adversary is able to find a group element and its discrete logarithm such that the group element is in $\mathcal{M}$ which we show is hard in the generic group model.

The Message Space $\mathcal{M}$. Keybase uses the MessagePack serialization format [21] to encode plaintext messages. Plaintext messages are represented using a custom data structure in Keybase. So the serialized MessagePack encoding of a plaintext is a byte sequence that not only stores the plaintext itself but also some metadata

$$
\begin{array}{|l|}
\hline
\mathcal{G}_{\text{DS},\mathcal{M}}^{\text{SPARSE}}(\mathcal{A}_{\text{SPARSE}}) \\
\hline
(vk, m, s, \gamma) \leftarrow\!\!\$ \; \mathcal{A}_{\text{SPARSE}} \\
\text{win}_0 \leftarrow \text{DS.Ver}(vk, m, s) \\
\text{win}_1 \leftarrow (s \,\|\, \gamma \in \mathcal{M}) \\
\text{Return win}_0 \text{ and win}_1 \\
\hline
\end{array}
$$

Fig. 13. Game defining $\mathcal{M}$-sparsity of a digital signature scheme DS for a set $\mathcal{M}$.

about the data structure that represents it. For messages encrypted by BM, the metadata about the data structure happens be located in the first 17 bytes of the encoding. This means that the encoding of every plaintext encrypted by BM contains a fixed 17-byte prefix. Let this 17-byte prefix be pre. Then we define the message space of BM by BM.MS $= \{\text{pre} \,\|\, \nu \mid \nu \in \{0,1\}^*\}$.

Message-Deriving Functions. Let ϕ be any function that takes a symmetric key K as input and uses it to derive and return some message m. We call ϕ a *message-deriving* function and will consider some classes (i.e. sets) Φ of message-deriving functions. We require that the length of an output returned by ϕ must not depend on its input; we denote the output length of ϕ by $\|\phi\|$.

AE Security of NE for Key-Dependent Messages. Consider game $\mathcal{G}^{\text{KDMAE}}$ of Fig. 14, defined for a nonce-based encryption scheme NE, a class of message-deriving functions Φ, and an adversary $\mathcal{A}_{\text{KDMAE}}$. The advantage of $\mathcal{A}_{\text{KDMAE}}$ in breaking the Φ-KDMAE security of NE is defined as $\text{Adv}_{\text{NE},\Phi}^{\text{KDMAE}}(\mathcal{A}) = 2 \cdot \Pr[\mathcal{G}_{\text{NE},\Phi}^{\text{KDMAE}}(\mathcal{A})] - 1$. This game can be thought of as a modification of the AEAD security game for NE (Fig. 4) which does not require nonce-misuse resistance. The core difference is that the ENC oracle now takes message-deriving functions $\phi_0, \phi_1 \in \Phi$ as input. The challenge message is derived as $m_b \leftarrow \phi_b(K[g])$ for $b \in \{0,1\}$, where $K[g]$ is the symmetric group key associated to g. Trivial attacks are prevented by requiring that ϕ_0, ϕ_1 have the same output length and that $\phi_0 = \phi_1$ whenever ENC is called for a corrupt group. Our definition is based on prior work [6,12,13,19]. There are strong impossibility results [12] regarding

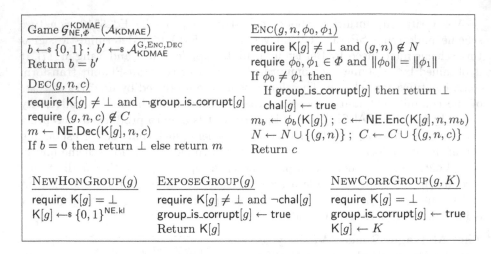

Fig. 14. Game defining authenticated-encryption security of NE for Φ-key-dependent messages, where Φ is a class of message-deriving functions and G = {NEWHONGROUP, EXPOSEGROUP, NEWCORRGROUP}.

the existence of schemes that are secure with respect to very large classes of message-deriving functions Φ. We sidestep these results by considering a very narrow and simple class Φ_{SP} that we define below.

The Class of Message-Deriving Functions Φ_{Sp} Earlier we discussed that in the wOAE[ENC[$\mathcal{M}$, NE]] security game for SP, the SIGENC and ENC oracles can be thought of as returning an NE ciphertext that encrypts an output of some message-deriving function. We now define the class Φ_{SP} containing all message-deriving functions that are used by either SIGENC or ENC.

Construction 3. *Let* NE *be a nonce-based encryption scheme. Let* H *be a hash function. Let* DS *be a digital signature scheme. Let* SIGENC-DER *and* ENC-DER *be the parameterized message-deriving functions that are defined as follows, each taking an* NE *key* $K \in \{0,1\}^{NE.kl}$ *as input.*

SIGENC-DER[NE, H, DS, m, n, sk](K)	ENC-DER[m](K)
$h \leftarrow H(m)$; $m_s \leftarrow$ "Keybase-Chat-2" $\Vert \langle K, n, h \rangle$	*Return* m
$s \leftarrow$ DS.Sig(sk, m_s) ; $m_e \leftarrow s \Vert m$; *Return* m_e	

Then Φ_{SP} = MSG-DER-FUNC[NE, H, DS] *is the class of all message-deriving functions of these forms.*

Note that SIGENC-DER only uses K as a part of the message m_s signed by DS.Sig. Keybase instantiates DS with Ed25519 which computes two SHA-512 hashes of m_s (mixed with other inputs). The resulting signature does not depend on m_s in any other way. Using this observation and an indifferentiability result of Bellare, Davis, and Di [10] (for SHA-512 with output reduced modulo a prime) we capture SIGENC-DER as a special class of message-deriving functions for which we can prove security in the random oracle model.

KDMAE Security for Messages Derived from a Hashed Key. Let H be a hash function. Let Φ be a class of message-deriving functions such that each $\phi \in \Phi$ on input K is only allowed to derive messages from the hash value $H(K)$, and never directly from K. We will roughly show that every AEAD-secure nonce-based encryption scheme NE is also Φ-KDMAE-secure, provided that H is modeled as a random oracle. We formalize this class of functions as follows.

Definition 4. *We say Φ derives messages from a hashed key if there exists a set Γ and a function H (modeled as a random oracle) such that $\Phi = \{\phi_\gamma \mid \phi_\gamma(\cdot) = \gamma(H(\cdot)), \gamma \in \Gamma\}$.*

In the full version we show how to capture Φ_{SP} as satisfying this definition. Thereby, the following result will give us Φ_{SP}-KDMAE security.

Proposition 1. *Let NE be a nonce-based encryption scheme. Let Φ be a class of message-deriving functions that derives messages from a hash key. Let $\mathcal{A}_{\mathsf{KDMAE}}$ be an adversary against the Φ-KDMAE security of NE making $q_{\mathrm{NEWHONGROUP}}$ queries to its $\mathrm{NEWHONGROUP}$ oracle. Then we can build adversaries $\mathcal{A}_{\mathsf{KR}}$ and $\mathcal{A}_{\mathsf{AEAD}}$ such that (in the random oracle model)*

$$\mathsf{Adv}_{\mathsf{NE},\Phi}^{\mathsf{KDMAE}}(\mathcal{A}_{\mathsf{KDMAE}}) \leq 2 \cdot \mathsf{Adv}_{\mathsf{NE}}^{\mathsf{KR}}(\mathcal{A}_{\mathsf{KR}}) + \mathsf{Adv}_{\mathsf{NE}}^{\mathsf{AEAD}}(\mathcal{A}_{\mathsf{AEAD}}) + \frac{q_{\mathrm{NEWHONGROUP}}^2}{2^{\mathsf{NE.kl}}}.$$

The constructed adversaries will not repeat (g, n) across ENC queries, so non-nonce-misuse resistant NE suffices. To prove this, we first assert that a Φ-KDMAE adversary $\mathcal{A}_{\mathsf{KDMAE}}$ can never directly query the random oracle on any of the (non-exposed) honest keys; otherwise, we could use $\mathcal{A}_{\mathsf{KDMAE}}$ in order to break the key-recovery security of AEAD. But then $\mathcal{A}_{\mathsf{KDMAE}}$ cannot distinguish between messages derived from $H(K[g])$ or from some $H^*(g)$. Here H is the actual random oracle and H^* is a simulated random oracle whose output depends on a group's identifier g instead of this group's key $K[g]$. We switch from using $H(K[g])$ to $H^*(g)$, thus breaking the dependency of each challenge message on the corresponding NE key. The AEAD security of NE then guarantees that $\mathcal{A}_{\mathsf{KDMAE}}$ cannot guess the challenge bit. The formal proof of Proposition 1 is in the full version.

Out-Group AE Security of SealPacket. We prove wOAE security of SP. The formal proof of Theorem 4 is in the full version.

Theorem 4. *Let $\mathcal{M} \subseteq \{0,1\}^*$. Let SP = SEAL-PACKET-SS[H, DS, NE] be the symmetric signcryption scheme built from some H, DS, NE as specified in Construction 2. Let $\mathsf{pred}_{\mathsf{trivial}}^{\mathsf{suf\text{-}except\text{-}user}}$ be the ciphertext-triviality predicate as defined in Fig. 7. Let $\mathsf{func}_{\mathsf{out}}^{\perp}$ be the output-guarding function as defined in Fig. 8. Let wOAE[ENC[$\mathcal{M}$, NE]] be the security notion as defined in Definition 3. Let $\Phi_{\mathsf{SP}} =$ MSG-DER-FUNC[NE, H, DS] be the class of message-deriving functions defined in Construction 3. Let $\mathcal{A}_{\mathsf{wOAE\text{-}of\text{-}SP}}$ be an adversary against the wOAE[ENC[$\mathcal{M}$, NE]] security of SP with respect to $\mathsf{pred}_{\mathsf{trivial}}^{\mathsf{suf\text{-}except\text{-}user}}$ and $\mathsf{func}_{\mathsf{out}}^{\perp}$. Then we can build adversaries $\mathcal{A}_{\mathsf{KDMAE}}$ and $\mathcal{A}_{\mathsf{SPARSE}}$ such that*

$$\mathsf{Adv}_{\mathsf{SP},\mathsf{pred}_{\mathsf{trivial}}^{\mathsf{suf\text{-}except\text{-}user}},\mathsf{func}_{\mathsf{out}}^{\perp}}^{\mathsf{wOAE[ENC[\mathcal{M},NE]]}}(\mathcal{A}_{\mathsf{wOAE\text{-}of\text{-}SP}}) \leq \mathsf{Adv}_{\mathsf{NE},\Phi_{\mathsf{SP}}}^{\mathsf{KDMAE}}(\mathcal{A}_{\mathsf{NE}}) + 2 \cdot \mathsf{Adv}_{\mathsf{DS},\mathcal{M}}^{\mathsf{SPARSE}}(\mathcal{A}_{\mathsf{SPARSE}}).$$

The OAE security results in Theorems 3 and 4 used the weaker output guarding function $\text{func}_{\text{out}}^{\perp}$. In the full version of this paper, we show that for $\text{SS} \in \{\text{BM}, \text{SP}\}$, the OAE security of SS with respect to $\text{func}_{\text{out}}^{\perp}$ implies its OAE security with respect to the stronger output guarding function $\text{func}_{\text{out}}^{\text{sec}}$.

6 Conclusions

Combining Theorem 1 with Theorem 2 and Theorem 3 with Theorem 4 establishes the in-group unforgeability and out-group authenticated encryption security of Keybase's BoxMessage algorithm. These results rely on some standard security assumptions (unforgeability of Ed25519 and collision resistance of SHA-256) as well as some non-standard assumptions (key-dependent message security of XSalsa20-Poly1305 and sparsity of Ed25519). These non-standard assumptions arose, respectively, from the key cycle in SealPacket and the key reuse without explicit context separation BoxMessage. While we were able to justify these assumptions, we consider them brittle as they are not well studied, their justifications required ideal models, and (in the case of sparsity) they required properties of the specific messaging encoding format used by Keybase.

The comparative simplicity of our Sign-then-Encrypt construction speaks to the value of formalizing the syntax and security of symmetric signcryption. Explicit goals allow designing schemes in parallel with writing proofs to identify precisely what is needed.

References

1. Albrecht, M., Dowling, B., Jones, D.: Device-oriented group messaging: a formal cryptographic analysis of matrix'core. In: IEEE S&P 2024 (2023)
2. Albrecht, M.R., Celi, S., Dowling, B., Jones, D.: Practically-exploitable cryptographic vulnerabilities in matrix. In: 2023 IEEE Symposium on Security and Privacy (SP), pp. 1419–1436. IEEE Computer Society (2022)
3. Alwen, J., Coretti, S., Dodis, Y., Tselekounis, Y.: Modular design of secure group messaging protocols and the security of MLS. In: Vigna, G., Shi, E. (eds.) ACM CCS 2021, pp. 1463–1483. ACM Press, November 2021. https://doi.org/10.1145/3460120.3484820
4. Alwen, J., Janneck, J., Kiltz, E., Lipp, B.: The pre-shared key modes of HPKE. In: Guo, J., Steinfeld, R. (eds.) Advances in Cryptology - ASIACRYPT 2023. Springer, Heidelberg (2023). https://doi.org/10.1007/978-981-99-8736-8_11
5. An, J.H., Dodis, Y., Rabin, T.: On the security of joint signature and encryption. In: Knudsen, L.R. (ed.) EUROCRYPT 2002. LNCS, vol. 2332, pp. 83–107. Springer, Heidelberg (2002). https://doi.org/10.1007/3-540-46035-7_6
6. Backes, M., Pfitzmann, B., Scedrov, A.: Key-dependent message security under active attacks - BRSIM/UC-soundness of symbolic encryption with key cycles. In: Sabelfeld, A. (ed.) CSF 2007 Computer Security Foundations Symposium, pp. 112–124. IEEE Computer Society Press (2007). https://doi.org/10.1109/CSF.2007.23
7. Balbás, D., Collins, D., Gajland, P.: WhatsUpp with sender keys? Analysis, improvements and security proofs. In: Guo, J., Steinfeld, R. (eds.) Advances in Cryptology - ASIACRYPT 2023, pp. 307–341. Springer, Heidelberg (2023). https://doi.org/10.1007/978-981-99-8733-7_10

8. Barnes, R., Beurdouche, B., Robert, R., Millican, J., Omara, E., Cohn-Gordon, K.: The Messaging Layer Security (MLS) Protocol. RFC 9420, July 2023. https://doi.org/10.17487/RFC9420
9. Barnes, R., Bhargavan, K., Lipp, B., Wood, C.A.: Hybrid Public Key Encryption. RFC 9180, February 2022. https://doi.org/10.17487/RFC9180
10. Bellare, M., Davis, H., Di, Z.: Hardening signature schemes via derive-then-derandomize: stronger security proofs for EdDSA. In: Boldyreva, A., Kolesnikov, V. (eds.) PKC 2023, Part I. LNCS, vol. 13940, pp. 223–250. Springer, Heidelberg (2023). https://doi.org/10.1007/978-3-031-31368-4_9
11. Bellare, M., Desai, A., Jokipii, E., Rogaway, P.: A concrete security treatment of symmetric encryption. In: 38th FOCS, pp. 394–403. IEEE Computer Society Press, October 1997. https://doi.org/10.1109/SFCS.1997.646128
12. Bellare, M., Keelveedhi, S.: Authenticated and misuse-resistant encryption of key-dependent data. In: Rogaway, P. (ed.) CRYPTO 2011. LNCS, vol. 6841, pp. 610–629. Springer, Heidelberg (2011). https://doi.org/10.1007/978-3-642-22792-9_35
13. Bellare, M., Meiklejohn, S., Thomson, S.: Key-versatile signatures and applications: RKA, KDM and joint Enc/Sig. In: Nguyen, P.Q., Oswald, E. (eds.) EUROCRYPT 2014. LNCS, vol. 8441, pp. 496–513. Springer, Heidelberg (2014). https://doi.org/10.1007/978-3-642-55220-5_28
14. Bellare, M., Stepanovs, I.: Security under message-derived keys: Signcryption in iMessage. In: Canteaut, A., Ishai, Y. (eds.) EUROCRYPT 2020, Part III. LNCS, vol. 12107, pp. 507–537. Springer, Heidelberg (2020). https://doi.org/10.1007/978-3-030-45727-3_17
15. Bernstein, D.J.: The Poly1305-AES message-authentication code. In: Gilbert, H., Handschuh, H. (eds.) FSE 2005. LNCS, vol. 3557, pp. 32–49. Springer, Heidelberg (2005). https://doi.org/10.1007/11502760_3
16. Bernstein, D.J.: The Salsa20 family of stream ciphers. In: Robshaw, M., Billet, O. (eds.) New Stream Cipher Designs. LNCS, vol. 4986, pp. 84–97. Springer, Heidelberg (2008). https://doi.org/10.1007/978-3-540-68351-3_8
17. Bernstein, D.J., Duif, N., Lange, T., Schwabe, P., Yang, B.Y.: High-speed high-security signatures. In: Preneel, B., Takagi, T. (eds.) CHES 2011. LNCS, vol. 6917, pp. 124–142. Springer, Heidelberg (2011). https://doi.org/10.1007/978-3-642-23951-9_9
18. Bernstein, D.J., Duif, N., Lange, T., Schwabe, P., Yang, B.Y.: High-speed high-security signatures. J. Cryptogr. Eng. 2(2), 77–89 (2012). https://doi.org/10.1007/s13389-012-0027-1
19. Black, J., Rogaway, P., Shrimpton, T.: Encryption-scheme security in the presence of key-dependent messages. In: Nyberg, K., Heys, H.M. (eds.) SAC 2002. LNCS, vol. 2595, pp. 62–75. Springer, Heidelberg (2003). https://doi.org/10.1007/3-540-36492-7_6
20. Brendel, J., Cremers, C., Jackson, D., Zhao, M.: The provable security of Ed25519: theory and practice. In: 2021 IEEE Symposium on Security and Privacy, pp. 1659–1676. IEEE Computer Society Press, May 2021. https://doi.org/10.1109/SP40001.2021.00042
21. Furuhashi, S.: Messagepack. https://msgpack.org/
22. Keybase: Keybase Book. https://book.keybase.io/
23. Keybase: Keybase Book—Chat—Crypto. https://github.com/keybase/book-content/blob/master/D-docs/04-chat/01-crypto.md?plain=1#L89-L93
24. Keybase: Keybase client. https://github.com/keybase/client
25. Keybase: Keybase client—boxer.go—BoxMessage. https://github.com/keybase/client/blob/v6.2.2/go/chat/boxer.go/#L1564-L1566

26. Keybase: Keybase client—codec.go—Design Notes. https://github.com/keybase/client/blob/v6.2.2/go/chat/signencrypt/codec.go/#L95-L110
27. Keybase: Keybase stats. https://web.archive.org/web/20200207065125/https://keybase.io/. Accessed 28 Feb 2024
28. Marlinspike, M.: Private group messaging, May 2014. https://signal.org/blog/private-groups/
29. Rogaway, P.: Nonce-based symmetric encryption. In: Roy, B.K., Meier, W. (eds.) FSE 2004. LNCS, vol. 3017, pp. 348–359. Springer, Heidelberg (2004). https://doi.org/10.1007/978-3-540-25937-4_22
30. Rogaway, P., Shrimpton, T.: A provable-security treatment of the key-wrap problem. In: Vaudenay, S. (ed.) EUROCRYPT 2006. LNCS, vol. 4004, pp. 373–390. Springer, Heidelberg (2006). https://doi.org/10.1007/11761679_23
31. Ryan, K., Pornin, T., Fitzgerald, S.: Keybase protocol security review, February 2019. https://keybase.io/docs-assets/blog/NCC_Group_Keybase_KB2018_Public_Report_2019-02-27_v1.3.pdf
32. Shrimpton, T.: A characterization of authenticated-encryption as a form of chosen-ciphertext security. Cryptology ePrint Archive, Report 2004/272 (2004). https://eprint.iacr.org/2004/272
33. Wallez, T., Protzenko, J., Beurdouche, B., Bhargavan, K.: TreeSync: authenticated group management for messaging layer security. In: 32nd USENIX Security Symposium, pp. 1217–1233. USENIX Association, Anaheim, CA, August 2023
34. WhatsApp: Whatsapp encryption overview: Technical white paper, September 2023. https://www.whatsapp.com/security/WhatsApp-Security-Whitepaper.pdf
35. Zheng, Y.: Digital signcryption or how to achieve cost(signature & encryption) ≪ cost(signature) + cost(encryption). In: Kaliski Jr., B.S. (ed.) CRYPTO 1997. LNCS, vol. 1294, pp. 165–179. Springer, Heidelberg (1997). https://doi.org/10.1007/BFb0052234
36. Zoom: Zoom acquires keybase and announces goal of developing the most broadly used enterprise end-to-end encryption offering, May 2020. https://blog.zoom.us/zoom-acquires-keybase-and-announces-goal-of-developing-the-most-broadly-used-enterprise-end-to-end-encryption-offering/

Theoretical Foundations (I/II)

Trapdoor Memory-Hard Functions

Benedikt Auerbach[ID], Christoph U. Günther[✉][ID], and Krzysztof Pietrzak

Institute of Science and Technology Austria, Klosterneuburg, Austria
{benedikt.auerbach,cguenthe,pietrzak}@ista.ac.at

Abstract. Memory-hard functions (MHF) are functions whose evaluation provably requires a lot of memory. While MHFs are an unkeyed primitive, it is natural to consider the notion of *trapdoor* MHFs (TMHFs). A TMHF is like an MHF, but when sampling the public parameters one also samples a trapdoor which allows evaluating the function much *cheaper*.

Biryukov and Perrin (Asiacrypt'17) were the first to consider TMHFs and put forth a candidate TMHF construction called DIODON that is based on the SCRYPT MHF (Percival, BSDCan'09). To allow for a trapdoor, SCRYPT's initial hash chain is replaced by a sequence of squares in a group of unknown order where the order of the group is the trapdoor. For a length n sequence of squares and a group of order N, DIODON's cumulative memory complexity (CMC) is $O(n^2 \log N)$ without the trapdoor and $O(n \log(n) \log(N)^2)$ with knowledge of it.

While SCRYPT is proven to be optimally memory-hard in the random oracle model (Alwen et al., Eurocrypt'17), DIODON's memory-hardness has not been proven so far. In this work, we fill this gap by rigorously analyzing a specific instantiation of DIODON. We show that its CMC is lower bounded by $\Omega(\frac{n^2}{\log n} \log N)$ which almost matches the upper bound. Our proof is based Alwen et al.'s lower bound on SCRYPT's CMC but requires non-trivial modifications due to the algebraic structure of DIODON. Most importantly, our analysis involves a more elaborate compression argument and a solvability criterion for certain systems of Diophantine equations.

1 Introduction

Moderately-hard functions have many applications, the most prominent one being password hashing. Early constructions of such functions aimed to be moderately hard in terms of computation. For example, PBKDF2 [25] is essentially a regular hash function repeated sufficiently many times.

Unfortunately, computationally expensive functions are not *egalitarian*. Attackers can use specialized hardware (like FPGAs or ASICs) to evaluate some specific computationally expensive function several orders of magnitude more efficiently (in terms of energy and hardware cost) than general-purpose hardware. This creates an asymmetry between the cost for honest users and attackers. Specifically with password hashing in mind, Percival [30] introduced the notion of *memory-hard functions* (MHFs).

© International Association for Cryptologic Research 2024
M. Joye and G. Leander (Eds.): EUROCRYPT 2024, LNCS 14653, pp. 315–344, 2024.
https://doi.org/10.1007/978-3-031-58734-4_11

1.1 Memory-Hard Functions

Informally, a function is memory-hard if its evaluation cost on general-purpose hardware is dominated by the memory (rather than CPU) cost. Since memory costs are roughly the same for specialized- and general-purpose hardware, MHFs are more egalitarian than computationally-hard functions. The first MHF construction was SCRYPT [30] followed by many others (e.g., [2,11,14,15,17]). These constructions primarily differ in their notion of memory-hardness and side-channel resistance.

Memory-Hardness. A popular way to measure the memory-hardness of a function is the *cumulative memory complexity* (CMC) [7]. It basically sums the memory cost over all steps[1] of an evaluation. A secure MHF not only ensures that the CMC of the honest evaluation algorithm is high, but also that any other, adversarial evaluation algorithm has a CMC not much lower than the honest evaluation algorithm. While the honest evaluation algorithm uses little to no parallelism, the adversarial algorithm is allowed arbitrarily many parallel queries to the random oracle.

Unfortunately, the definition of CMC does not exclude time-memory trade-offs. In particular, an MHF may be evaluated in more steps where each step requires less memory [31]. A stronger notion is sustained space complexity [4] which only counts steps where the memory usage is sufficiently high.

Finally, let us mention the related notion of bandwidth-hardness [16,32] capturing the number of cache-misses rather than the memory usage. This captures the energy cost of evaluating a function more accurately, whereas CMC is a better measure for the hardware cost.

Side-Channel Resistance. MHFs come in two flavors, *data-dependent* and *data-independent MHFs* (dMHF and iMHF, respectively), which classify the side-channel resistance of MHFs. The memory-access patterns during the evaluation of an iMHF do not depend on the input but are fixed. In contrast, dMHFs allow the memory-access patterns to depend on the input. While dMHFs are easier to construct and can provably achieve higher evaluation cost [3], their security can be compromised by side-channel attacks which leak memory access patterns. A notion aiming to combine the advantages of iMHFs and dMHFs using computational assumptions was proposed in [9].

1.2 Trapdoor MHFs

An MHF is an unkeyed primitive, but like for other unkeyed primitives, say, one-way permutations or collision-resistant hash functions, it is natural to consider a keyed version. Biryukov and Perrin [13] introduced *asymmetrically memory-hard functions* which are essentially MHFs admitting a trapdoor. So similarly

---

[1]   MHFs are typically constructed from hash functions. In security proofs, these are modelled as random oracles. So a "step" may be thought of as a query (or many independent queries in parallel) to the random oracle.

to an MHF, evaluating the function is guaranteed to cost a lot of memory in general. However, in contrast to an MHF, when sampling the parameters one also generates a secret trapdoor. Knowledge of this trapdoor allows evaluating the function much cheaper using less memory. Therefore, we call such functions *trapdoor MHFs* (TMHFs) and note that the PURED framework [12]—an effort to classify all types of resource-hard functions—also uses the word "trapdoor" to describe such functions.

In this work, we focus on a data-dependent TMHF that provably achieves high CMC. To precisely quantify the gap between the honest evaluation algorithms (with and without knowledge of the trapdoor) we use the notation (c_{hon}, c_{td})-TMHF. This means that the honest evaluation algorithms without and with knowledge of the trapdoor have a CMC of c_{hon} and c_{td}, respectively.

Applications. One potential application of TMHFs are proofs of CMC that benefit from efficient private verification. For example, consider an e-mail server that wants to combat junk mail [21] by requiring e-mail senders to solve a TMHF. Thanks to the trapdoor, the server can verify the sender's response with fewer resources than the sender. So the server can choose larger parameters that would otherwise be too costly, especially if the gap between c_{hon} and c_{td} is large.[2]

Another application is password hashing, albeit a less convincing one. In principle, the trapdoor allows a server to verify logins more cheaply compared to using an MHF. However, the trapdoor needs to be stored securely (e.g., in an HSM) and then it is conceivable to simply encrypt the passwords instead of hashing them. One downside of encryption is that a compromise of the key (e.g., the HSM is broken) reveals all passwords, a catastrophical failure. Since TMHFs would still require some bruteforcing in this case, they might still be preferable.

Related Primitives. Memory-hard puzzles [8] are closely related, yet different. Solving a puzzle is memory-hard, but it is easy to sample a puzzle that will evaluate to a specific solution. While the first property is comparable to evaluating a TMHF without knowledge of the trapdoor, the second property can roughly be seen as the opposite of the trapdoor evaluation.

1.3 The DIODON TMHF

DIODON [13] is the first construction aiming to be TMHF. It is based on SCRYPT [30], a well-known data-dependent MHF that has provably high memory-hardness [5,6]. DIODON as stated in [13] offers multiple parameters to fine-tune the security and performance of the function. In this paper, we stick to the natural choice of parameters that most closely resembles SCRYPT[3] and

---

[2] In a similar vein, some proof of work blockchains use MHFs, but the parameters cannot be too large as otherwise the verification of blocks becomes too expensive. Sadly, TMHF are not suited for blockchains since it is unclear who would possess the trapdoor.

[3] Using notation from [13], $M := n$, $L := n$, and $\eta := 1$.

also work in a slightly different algebraic setting. To avoid confusion, we call this specific instantiation TDSCRYPT.

TDSCRYPT essentially replaces the sequential hashing done in SCRYPT's initial phase with sequential squaring in a group of unknown order. More precisely, TDSCRYPT is defined with respect to a group of unknown order where the trapdoor is the group order N. Given a parameter n which basically specifies the memory requirement of the evaluation and input group element $W =: W_0$, first define $W_i := W_{i-1}^2$ for $0 < i < n$. Then set $S_0 := h(W_n, 0 \cdots 0)$, and, for $0 < i \le n$, define $S_i := h(W_j, S_{i-1})$ where $j := S_{i-1} \bmod n$ and h is a hash function. Finally, S_n is the output of TDSCRYPT on input W.

Evaluation Algorithms. The honest evaluation algorithm without knowledge of the trapdoor repeatedly squares W, and stores all intermediate values (i.e., all W_i) in memory. Then it computes all S_i in sequence, looking up W_j on demand. Adding up the memory consumed over all steps, we get a CMC of $\Theta(n^2 \log N)$ because the algorithm stores n group elements of size roughly $\log N$ bits while computing the values from S_0 to S_n within n steps.[4]

In comparison, the trapdoor evaluation algorithm first computes $W_n = W^{2^n}$ directly by first reducing $2^n \bmod N$. Then, it computes the S_i sequentially while computing the W_j on demand similarly to W_n. This has a cost of roughly $\Theta(n \log(N)^2 \log(n))$ and we defer the details to Sect. 3.2. In summary, TDSCRYPT is approximately an $(n^2 \log(N), n \log(n) \log(N)^2)$-TMHF.

1.4 Contributions and Technical Overview

Our main contribution is a rigorous proof of the following lower bound. It bounds the CMC required by any TDSCRYPT evaluation algorithm without knowledge of the trapdoor.

Theorem 1 (Informal). *In the random oracle and generic group model, assuming that factoring is hard, any algorithm $\mathcal{A}$ evaluating TDSCRYPT has a cumulative memory complexity lower bounded by $\Omega(\frac{n^2}{\log n} \log N)$.*

Recall that the honest evaluation algorithm (without trapdoor) has a cumulative-memory complexity of $\Theta(n^2 \log N)$, so our lower bound is a factor $1/\log(n)$ loose. We do not know of any evaluation algorithm achieving $O(\frac{n^2}{\log n} \log N)$ and believe that the loss in tightness is an artifact of our proof.

Proof Strategy. We follow the proof of Alwen et al. [6] who proved that SCRYPT has a CMC of $\Omega(n^2 \omega_h)$—which is tight—in the *random oracle model* (ROM).[5] Naturally, we also work in the ROM, but also need to consider Shoup's

---

[4] We assume that a hash- and group operations take the same amount of time.

[5] Note that ω_h is the output length of the random oracle which corresponds to $\log N$ in our bounds.

generic-group model (GGM) [36]. Their proof first considers a *single-challenge time-memory trade-off* which is then generalized to get a *multi-challenge memory complexity lower bound*. We will elaborate how these two concepts are related to CMC in the following paragraphs.

We remark that our single-challenge time-memory trade-off proof is more involved and differs considerably from Alwen et al. [6] where this part of the proof was fairly simple. The generalization to the multi-challenge memory complexity lower bound—by far the most complicated part in [6]—is fortunately essentially identical. Thus, most of our proof focuses on the single-challenge case and we only sketch the multi-challenge argument while referring to [6] for details.

Single-Challenge Time-Memory Trade-Off. Consider the following *single-challenge game*. Like when evaluating TDSCRYPT the adversary $\mathcal{A}$ receives an input group element W but does not know the group order N. It is then given the *challenge* $j \xleftarrow{\$} \{0, \ldots, n-1\}$ and needs to output $W_j = W^{2^j}$ as quickly as possible. Before being challenged, $\mathcal{A}$ is allowed to perform precomputation and to store the resulting advice string. Clearly, if the advice string is large enough, $\mathcal{A}$ can store $W_0, \ldots, W_{n-1}$ and answer every challenge instantly. Inspired by this, we are interested in a time-memory trade-off: *How fast (on average) can $\mathcal{A}$ answer a challenge in relation to the size of the advice string?*

To this end, we first show that if $\mathcal{A}$ answers a large fraction of the challenges quickly, it must have a lot of group elements stored, else it could factor. Our approach draws inspiration from proofs showing that repeated squaring (i.e., on input W computing W^{2^j}) [33] is sequential in generic models if factoring is hard [27,34,35]. On a high level, they first lower bound the number of queries required by algorithms oblivious to the group order. Using this lower bound, they show that if an adversarial algorithm is faster, its query behavior reveals a non-trivial factor of N. While the lower bound for sequential squaring trivially equals the prescribed number of iterations, figuring out a tight enough bound for the single-challenge game with respect to TDSCRYPT is substantially more complex. Without delving into the details, we prove a bound by analyzing the solvability of certain systems of Diophantine equations.[6] We use powerful mathematical tools such as a lemma due to van der Waerden [28] and a generalization of the famous distinct subset sums problem due to Erdős [23, C8].

Second, again assuming hardness of factoring, we show that storing k group elements roughly requires a memory of $k \log(N)$ as otherwise we could encode a random injection (the GGM's labeling function) more efficiently than information-theoretically possible. Our proof is inspired by Corrigan-Gibbs and Kogan [18] who analyze how helpful preprocessing is for computing discrete logarithms by using an incompressibility argument [20]. In contrast to their work, our argument is more involved. On the one hand, the single-challenge game is more complex than the discrete logarithm problem. On the other, the group order is unknown which complicates bookkeeping in the encoding routine.

---

[6] This means that the systems have integer coefficients. Intuitively, if an algorithm is oblivious to the group order, its query behavior might as well be analyzed over $\mathbb{Z}$ instead of $\mathbb{Z}_N$.

Combining the two results above, we get that if an adversary answers challenges quickly on average, then the advice string must be large—assuming factoring is hard.

Multi-challenge Time-Memory Trade-Off. When an algorithm evaluates TDSCRYPT and outputs S_n, it almost surely must have computed $S_1, \ldots, S_n$ in sequence because h is a modeled as a random oracle. Computing S_i given S_{i-1} requires W_j by definition where is $j := S_{i-1} \bmod n$ (almost) uniformly random because, again, h is a random oracle. It follows that evaluating TDSCRYPT requires playing n single-challenge games in sequence. So, a lower bound on the memory complexity of solving multiple challenges implies a lower bound on the CMC of TDSCRYPT.

1.5 Open Problems

First, TDSCRYPT has a CMC of $O(n^2 \log N)$ whereas the lower bound is only $\Omega(\frac{n^2}{\log n} \log N)$. Ideally, this bound should be tight. Looking ahead, one possible way of achieving this is strengthening Lemma 2, a solvability criterion for certain systems of Diophantine equations. Essentially, one would need to show $\mathrm{rank}(A) \geq \ell/(ct)$ for some constant c.

Second, TDSCRYPT's drop in CMC when using the trapdoor is only due to the much lower memory requirement of the trapdoor evaluation. The computation actually increases from n to $n \log(N)$, as in the 2nd phase of the evaluation (where we compute the S_i's) the normal evaluation just makes n group operations (modular multiplications), while the trapdoor evaluation needs to do n exponentiations. An open problem is constructing a TMHF where the trapdoor evaluation not only improves CMC, but strictly improves on memory usage and computation individually (or at least improves on one of them without decreasing the other).

Finally, coming up with a TMHF that fulfills different notions of memory hardness would be interesting. For example, a data-independent TMHF or a TMHF that ensures high sustained space complexity.

2 Preliminaries

2.1 Notation

$\mathbb{N}, \mathbb{Z}, \mathbb{Z}_N, \mathbb{Q}$, and $\mathbb{R}$ are the sets of natural numbers including 0, integers, integers modulo N, rational, and real numbers, respectively. For these sets, the superscript $^+$ denotes the strictly positive subset (e.g., $\mathbb{N}^+ = \{1, 2, \ldots\}$). $[a, b]$ denotes the set $\{a, \ldots, b\}$, $[a, b) = \{a, \ldots, b - 1\}$, and $[n]$ is a shorthand for $[1, n]$. Furthermore, $\mathrm{Inj}(A, B)$ is the set of all injections from set A to set B and $x \xleftarrow{\$} X$ samples an element from the set X uniformly at random. Vectors are written in boldface (e.g., $\boldsymbol{x}$) and matrices in upper case. $|x|$ denotes the absolute value or the length of x depending on whether x is a number or a list, vector, etc., and $\|x\|$ is the number of bits required to encode x. Algorithms are usually typeset sans-serif (e.g., Alg), $x := y$ or $x := \mathsf{Alg}(\dots)$ denote assignment or the output of a deterministic algorithm, and $a \leftarrow \mathsf{Alg}(\dots)$ the output of a probabilistic one.

λ always denotes the security parameter and $\mathrm{negl}(\lambda)$ (resp. $\mathrm{poly}(\lambda)$) are the set of all functions that are negligible (resp. polynomial) in λ. Furthermore, we use standard Big O notation such as O, Ω, Θ, and ω. When working with groups, group elements are written upper case, and their exponents with respect to the group generator lower case. Lastly, log denotes the binary logarithm.

2.2   Algebraic Setting

To allow for a trapdoor, we require some algebraic structure: the group of quadratic residues with respect to RSA moduli. As a consequence, the memory-hardness of TDSCRYPT is based on factoring assumptions. In the following, we define modulus generation, related factoring assumptions, and the group of quadratic residues.

Definition 1 (Safe-prime Generator). *Let* GenSP *be an algorithm that samples two distinct safe primes of the same bit length uniformly at random. More precisely, define* $(p', q') \leftarrow \mathsf{GenSP}(\lambda)$ *and let* $p := (p' - 1)/2$ *and* $q := (q' - 1)/2$. *It holds that* p', p, q' *and* q *are prime,* $p \neq q$, *and* $\|p\| = \|q\| = k(\lambda)$ *with* $k(\lambda) \in \mathrm{poly}(\lambda)$.

In terms of notation, let $N := pq$ and $N' := p'q'$ in the rest of the paper.[7]. Next, we give two hardness assumptions stating that factoring N' as well as N is hard.

Definition 2 (Factoring N'). *The game* $\mathsf{Fac}'_{\mathsf{GenSP}, \mathcal{A}}(\lambda)$ *is defined with respect to* GenSP *and a probabilistic polynomial-time (PPT) adversary* $\mathcal{A}$. *On input of a security parameter* λ *it runs* $(p', q') \leftarrow \mathsf{GenSP}(\lambda)$, *sets* $N' := p'q'$, *and invokes the adversary, yielding* $(p^*, q^*) \leftarrow \mathcal{A}(N')$. *The game returns 1 if* $\{p^*, q^*\} = \{p', q'\}$ *and 0 otherwise.*

We say that factoring N' *is hard if, for every PPT algorithm* $\mathcal{A}$, *the advantage is negligible, i.e.,* $\mathrm{Adv}^{\mathsf{Fac}'}_{\mathsf{GenSP}, \mathcal{A}}(\lambda) := \Pr[1 \leftarrow \mathsf{Fac}'_{\mathsf{GenSP}, \mathcal{A}}(\lambda)] \in \mathrm{negl}(\lambda)$ *where the probability is taken over the randomness of* GenSP *and* $\mathcal{A}$.

Definition 3 (Factoring N). *The game* $\mathsf{Fac}_{\mathsf{GenSP}, \mathcal{A}}(\lambda)$ *is defined similarly to* $\mathsf{Fac}'_{\mathsf{GenSP}, \mathcal{A}}(\lambda)$ *but with* N' *replaced by* N. *So the game invokes* $(p^*, q^*) \leftarrow \mathcal{A}(N)$ *and returns 1 if and only if* $\{p^*, q^*\} = \{p, q\}$. *We say that* factoring N *is hard if, for every PPT algorithm* $\mathcal{A}$, $\mathrm{Adv}^{\mathsf{Fac}}_{\mathsf{GenSP}, \mathcal{A}}(\lambda) := \Pr[1 \leftarrow \mathsf{Fac}_{\mathsf{GenSP}, \mathcal{A}}(\lambda)] \in \mathrm{negl}(\lambda)$ *where the probability is taken over the randomness of* GenSP *and* $\mathcal{A}$.

Let us briefly analyze both assumptions. It is conjectured that the density of safe primes p' in the interval $[2^{k-1}, 2^k]$ is of order $1/k^2$ (e.g., [22]). Note that the

---

[7] Note that usually N and N' are defined the other way around. However, most parts of the paper are only concerned with N, so we chose this notation to avoid clutter.

map $p' \mapsto (p'-1)/2$ is injective, so this statement implies the same regarding the density of $(p'-1)/2 = p$ in $[2^{k-2}, 2^{k-1}]$. Thus, assuming the conjecture holds, the standard factoring assumption (i.e., factoring the product of two uniformly sampled arbitrary k-bit primes is hard) implies that factoring N' as well as N is hard. For simplicity, we say that *factoring is hard* with respect to GenSP if factoring N as well as factoring N' are hard with respect to GenSP.

Equipped with these definitions, we finally define the group of quadratic residues modulo N'.

Definition 4 (Group of Quadratic Residues). *For $(p', q') \leftarrow$ GenSP(λ), let $p := (p'-1)/2$, $q := (q'-1)/2$, $N' := p'q'$, and $N := pq$. The group of quadratic residues modulo N' is a subgroup of $\mathbb{Z}_{N'}^*$ defined as $\mathbb{QR}_{N'} := \{X^2 \mid X \in \mathbb{Z}_{N'}^*\}$.*

Since p' and q' are safe primes (and thereby Blum integers), $\mathbb{QR}_{N'}$ is a cyclic group of order $|\mathbb{QR}_{N'}| = N$ and a uniformly sampled element $X \leftarrow \mathbb{QR}_{N'}$ is a generator with overwhelming probability $\varphi(N)/N = 1 - \frac{q+p-1}{N} \in (1 - \text{negl}(\lambda))$ where φ denotes Euler's totient function.

2.3   Generic Group Model

In the proof of our main result we model the cyclic group $\mathbb{QR}_{N'} = \langle g \rangle$ of order $N := pq$ as a generic group in the style of Shoup's generic group model (GGM) [36]. In the GGM algorithms do not get direct access to the group (that we may identify with the group $(\mathbb{Z}_N, +)$ by using the isomorphism $\mathbb{Z}_N \to \mathbb{QR}_{N'}$; $z \mapsto g^z$). Instead, access to group elements is provided via abstract labels $\sigma \in \mathcal{L}$ where $\mathcal{L} := \{0,1\}^{\omega_{\mathcal{L}}}$ (with $\omega_{\mathcal{L}} \geq \lceil \log(N) \rceil$) and group operations are performed using an oracle $\mathcal{G}$ that allows for multiplication, division, and inversion.

More precisely, let $\text{Inj}(\mathbb{Z}_N, \mathcal{L})$ be the set of all injections from $\mathbb{Z}_N$ to $\mathcal{L}$ and let $\Sigma \xleftarrow{\$} \text{Inj}(\mathbb{Z}_N, \mathcal{L})$ be one such injection chosen uniformly at random. Σ is called the *labeling function*, and it defines the oracle $\mathcal{G} \colon \{+, -, \text{inv}\} \times \mathcal{L} \times \mathcal{L} \to \mathcal{L} \cup \{\bot\}$. $\mathcal{G}$ answers a query $(\circ, \sigma_1, \sigma_2)$ as follows. If σ_1 and σ_2 are not in the image of Σ, it returns $\bot$. Otherwise, if $\circ \in \{+, -\}$, it returns $\Sigma(\Sigma^{-1}(\sigma_1) \circ \Sigma^{-1}(\sigma_2) \mod N)$, and if $\circ = \text{inv}$, it returns $\Sigma(-\Sigma^{-1}(\sigma_1) \mod N)$.

Abusing notation, we will almost always write Σ instead of $\mathcal{G}$ when talking about a concrete instantiation of the generic group oracle.

2.4   Machine Model and Complexity Measure

Parallel Oracle Model. To define a memory complexity measure, we first require a machine model. Prior work uses the *parallel random oracle model* [6,7] which allows algorithms to perform an unlimited number of random oracle queries in parallel. Similarly, we define the *parallel oracle model* which additionally allows for generic group queries. That is, a *polynomial-time* (PT) algorithm $\mathcal{A}$ has access to two oracles: $\mathcal{G}$, a group-operation oracle, and h, a random oracle. We will sometimes explicitly state the oracles in superscript, i.e., $\mathcal{A}^{\mathcal{G}, \text{h}}$, and omit them when they are clear from context.

The random oracle $\mathsf{h} \colon \{0,1\}^* \to \{0,1\}^{\omega_\mathsf{h}}$ maps inputs to bit strings of length ω_h and we require that $\omega_\mathsf{h} \in \Theta(\log N)$. To ensure that the set of random oracles is finite, we assume some sufficiently large, finite bound $*$ on the inputs.

Algorithm $\mathcal{A}$'s execution proceeds in *rounds* starting with round 1. Within each round, $\mathcal{A}$ performs local computation and submits oracle queries at the end of it. Then, at the beginning of the next round, $\mathcal{A}$ receives the response to its queries. Formally, *states* capture $\mathcal{A}$'s progress throughout the rounds and its queries to both oracles. At the end of round i, $\mathcal{A}$ produces an *output state* $\overline{\mathsf{st}}_i := (\tau_i, \mathbf{qrs}_i^{\mathcal{G}}, \mathbf{qrs}_i^\mathsf{h})$ where τ is a bit string, and $\mathbf{qrs}^{\mathcal{G}}$ and $\mathbf{qrs}^\mathsf{h}$ are vectors containing queries to $\mathcal{G}$ and h, respectively. Consequently, in round $i + 1$, it receives the *input state* $\mathsf{st}_i := (\tau_i, \mathbf{res}_i^{\mathcal{G}}, \mathbf{res}_i^\mathsf{h})$ where $\mathbf{res}_i^{\mathcal{G}}$ and $\mathbf{res}_i^\mathsf{h}$ are vectors containing the results of the queries $\mathbf{qrs}_i^{\mathcal{G}}$ and $\mathbf{qrs}_i^\mathsf{h}$.

We will only consider *deterministic* algorithms in the interest of keeping proofs readable and concise. This is essentially without loss of generality in our setting since we only care about algorithms that correctly evaluate TDSCRYPT with sufficiently high, i.e., noticeable, success probability. Such algorithms can be derandomized by trying out a few choices of the randomness, checking each randomness on a polynomial number of random inputs, and then fix the randomness on which the algorithm performed best. This will with overwhelming probability result in a deterministic algorithm whose success probability is close to the randomized one.

Complexity Measure. To evaluate the memory complexity of an algorithm, we use a notion called *cumulative memory complexity* (CMC) [7]. Essentially, CMC is the sum of an algorithm's memory consumption at every point in time, i.e., the area under the memory usage curve.

More formally, consider an algorithm $\mathcal{A}$ running in the parallel oracle model on some input x. Its execution results in a sequence of input states $\mathsf{st}_i = (\tau_i, \mathbf{res}_i^{\mathcal{G}}, \mathbf{res}_i^\mathsf{h})$. Then, its CMC is given by $\mathsf{cc}_\mathsf{mem}(\mathcal{A}^{\mathcal{G},\mathsf{h}}(x)) := \sum_i \|\mathsf{st}_i\|$ where the bit length of the input state st_i is defined as $\|\mathsf{st}_i\| := \|\tau_i\| + |\mathbf{res}_i^{\mathcal{G}}|\omega_\mathcal{L} + |\mathbf{res}_i^\mathsf{h}|\omega_\mathsf{h}$. Without loss of generality, an algorithm submits at least one query per round, so $\|\mathsf{st}_i\| \geq \min\{\omega_\mathcal{L}, \omega_\mathsf{h}\} \in \Theta(\log N)$ by definition.

Preprocessing Algorithms. Instead of working with a single deterministic PT algorithm $\mathcal{A}$, we often view it as a pair of deterministic PT algorithms $\mathcal{A} = (\mathcal{A}_0, \mathcal{A}_1)$. Intuitively, $\mathcal{A}_0$ performs preprocessing and outputs some advice which $\mathcal{A}_1$ receives as input. It follows that we do not charge $\mathcal{A}_0$ for any memory usage and that we do not count its number of rounds (but emphasize that, unlike in other works, $\mathcal{A}_0$'s computation is not completely unbounded as we cannot allow it to factor N with noticeable probability).

In the terms of the parallel oracle model, given public parameters pp and online input x, to evaluate $\mathcal{A}^{\mathcal{G},\mathsf{h}}(\mathsf{pp}, x)$, first execute $\mathcal{A}_0^{\mathcal{G},\mathsf{h}}(\mathsf{pp})$ resulting in an input state st_0. Then, starting in round 1, run $\mathcal{A}_1^{\mathcal{G},\mathsf{h}}(\mathsf{st}_0, x)$ with the online input x yielding the output of $\mathcal{A}$. The CMC of $\mathcal{A}$ is defined as $\mathsf{cc}_\mathsf{mem}(\mathcal{A}^{\mathcal{G},\mathsf{h}}(\mathsf{pp}, x)) := \mathsf{cc}_\mathsf{mem}(\mathcal{A}_1^{\mathcal{G},\mathsf{h}}(\mathsf{st}_0, x))$.

3   A Trapdoor Memory-Hard Function from Factoring

3.1   Trapdoor Memory-Hard Functions

A *trapdoor memory-hard function* (TMHF) is defined by a triple of polynomial-time algorithms (Setup, Eval, TDEval) as follows (with the security parameter λ left implicit).

- Setup() $\rightarrow$ (pp, td). The probabilistic setup algorithm samples public parameters pp and corresponding trapdoor td. The public parameters implicitly determine the domain Dom(pp) and range Ran(pp) of the TMHF.
- Eval(pp, w) =: y. The deterministic evaluation algorithm takes public parameters pp and $w \in$ Dom(pp) as inputs and returns a $y \in$ Ran(pp).
- TDEval(pp, td, w) =: y. The deterministic trapdoor evaluation algorithm takes public parameters pp, trapdoor td, and $w \in$ Dom(pp) as inputs and returns $y \in$ Ran(pp).

We require correctness, i.e., for all (pp, td) $\leftarrow$ Setup() and all $w \in$ Dom(pp), it holds that Eval(pp, w) = TDEval(pp, td, w). To quantify the quality of a TMHF we have to analyze the cumulative memory required to evaluate it with and without access to the trapdoor. Accordingly, if the required CMC is given by functions c_{hon} and c_{td}, i.e.,

$$c_{\text{hon}}(\text{pp}) = \text{cc}_{\text{mem}}(\text{Eval}(\text{pp}, w)) \text{ and } c_{\text{td}}(\text{pp}) = \text{cc}_{\text{mem}}(\text{TDEval}(\text{pp}, \text{td}, w))$$

the TMHF is referred to as a $(c_{\text{hon}}, c_{\text{td}})$-TMHF.

Naturally, trapdoor evaluations must have a lower CMC than the standard evaluation algorithm. That is, for all (pp, td) $\leftarrow$ Setup, there exists some $0 < \Delta(\text{pp}) < 1$ (ideally $\Delta(\text{pp}) \in o(1)$), such that, for all inputs $w \in$ Dom(pp), we have $c_{\text{td}}(\text{pp}) < \Delta(\text{pp}) \cdot c_{\text{hon}}(\text{pp})$. Moreover, we want our function to be a good MHF when ignoring the trapdoor. This means the CMC of Eval(pp, w) should be high by construction, but no adversarial evaluation algorithm should exist that can evaluate the function with much lower CMC. This must hold even when the other adversarial algorithm is allowed to make many parallel queries to the oracles and when it is given some advice that was computed (by any polynomial time preprocessing) dependent on pp (but of course not the input w or the trapdoor).

3.2   Description of TdScrypt

We will analyze TdScrypt which can be viewed as a concrete instantiation of Diodon [13]. Specifically, using notation from [13], we set $M := n$, $L := n$, and $\eta = 1$. Furthermore, TdScrypt is defined over the group of quadratic residues $\mathbb{QR}_{N'}$ instead of $\mathbb{Z}_{N'}$ due to technicalities.

Construction. TdScrypt is defined with respect to integer $n \in \mathbb{N}$ corresponding to the number of iterated steps (i.e., repeated squarings). It relies on computations in the group $\mathbb{QR}_{N'}$ of quadratic residues modulo N' as defined

Setup()	Eval(pp, W)	TDEval(pp, td, W)
00 $(p', q') \leftarrow$ GenSP()	07 $W_0 := W$	16 $W_0 := W$
01 $N' := p'q'$	08 For $i := 1, \ldots, n-1$:	17 $m := 2^n \bmod N$
02 $N := (p'-1)(q'-1)/4$	09 $\quad W_i := W_{i-1}^2$	18 $W_n := W_0^m$
03 pick h	10 $\quad$ Store W_i	19 $S_0 := \mathsf{h}(W_n, 0^{\omega_\mathsf{h}})$
04 pp $:= (N', \mathsf{h}, n)$	11 $S_0 := \mathsf{h}(W_n, 0^{\omega_\mathsf{h}})$	20 For $i := 1, \ldots, n$:
05 td $:= N$	12 For $i := 1, \ldots, n$:	21 $\quad j_i := S_{i-1} \bmod n$
06 Return (pp, td)	13 $\quad j_i := S_{i-1} \bmod n$	22 $\quad m_i := 2^{j_i} \bmod N$
	14 $\quad S_i := \mathsf{h}(W_{j_i}, S_{i-1})$	23 $\quad W_{j_i} := W_0^{m_i}$
	15 Return S_n	24 $\quad S_i := \mathsf{h}(W_{j_i}, S_{i-1})$
		25 Return S_n

Fig. 1. Trapdoor memory-hard function $\textsc{TdScrypt}_n^\mathsf{h}$ defined with respect to number of steps $n \in \mathbb{N}$. The TMHF uses a hash function $\mathsf{h} \colon \{0,1\}^* \to \{0,1\}^{\omega_\mathsf{h}}$, domain $\mathrm{Dom}(\mathsf{pp}) = \mathbb{QR}_{N'}$ and range $\{0,1\}^{\omega_\mathsf{h}}$. The exponentiations W_i^2, W_0^m, and $W_0^{m_i}$ are in $\mathbb{QR}_{N'}$.

in Definition 4. Accordingly, its public parameters pp consist of an RSA modulus $N' := p'q'$, where p' and q' are safe primes generated using safe prime generator GenSP (see Definition 1), a hash function $\mathsf{h} \colon \{0,1\}^* \to \{0,1\}^{\omega_\mathsf{h}}$, and n. The corresponding trapdoor is $\mathsf{td} := N = (p'-1)(q'-1)/4 = |\mathbb{QR}_{N'}|$. $\textsc{TdScrypt}$'s formal description is in Fig. 1.

In the following, we will assume that the time of evaluating h approximately matches the time of evaluating a group operation, i.e., computing a multiplication in modulo N'. This could for example be implemented by setting $\mathsf{h}(s) := \mathsf{h}''(\mathsf{h}'(s) \cdot \mathsf{h}'(s) \bmod N')$, where $\mathsf{h}' \colon \{0,1\}^* \to \mathbb{QR}_{N'}$ and $\mathsf{h}'' \colon \mathbb{QR}_{N'} \to \{0,1\}^{\omega_\mathsf{h}}$ are cryptographic hash functions.

To evaluate the TMHF on input $W \in \mathrm{Dom}(\mathsf{pp}) := \mathbb{QR}_{N'}$ algorithm Eval sets $W_0 := W$ and computes and stores the group elements $W_i := W_{i-1}^2 = W^{2^i}$ for $i \in [n-1]$. Then it sets $S_0 := \mathsf{h}(W_n, 0^{\omega_\mathsf{h}})$, and, for $i := [n]$, computes $S_i := \mathsf{h}(W_{j_i}, S_{i-1})$ where the index $j_i := S_{i-1} \bmod n$. The output of Eval is $S_n \in \mathrm{Ran}(\mathsf{pp}) := \{0,1\}^{\omega_\mathsf{h}}$.

TDEval computes the values S_i without storing the group elements W_{j_i}, but instead recomputes them efficiently using its knowledge of $N = |\mathbb{QR}_{N'}|$. It sets $W_0 := W$, computes $W_n := W_0^m$, and $S_0 := \mathsf{h}(W_n, 0^{\omega_\mathsf{h}})$, where $m := 2^n \bmod N$. Then for $i \in [n]$ it computes, in order, $j_i := S_{i-1} \bmod n$, $m_i := 2^{j_i} \bmod N$, $W_i = W_0^{m_i}$, and $S_i := \mathsf{h}(W_{j_i}, S_{i-1})$. Its output is S_n.

Cumulative Memory Complexity. Recall that the CMC is the memory usage summed over all steps. In the following analysis of $\textsc{TdScrypt}$ we will give a brief estimate of Eval and TDEval's CMC where we define a "step" to constitute the time taken by one group operation. For details on this choice and an in-depth CMC analysis we refer to the full version [10].

For Eval, note that its CMC is dominated by the second loop (Lines 12–14). During the loop, Eval keeps n group elements $W_0, \ldots, W_n$ in memory, amounting to $\Theta(n \log(N'))$ bits. The loop requires $\Theta(n)$ group operations in total as every evaluation of h takes the time of one group operation by definition. We thus obtain

$$cc_{mem}(Eval(pp, x)) \in \Theta(n \log(N') \cdot n) = \Theta(n^2 \log(N')).$$

TDEval's CMC is also dominated by the loop (Lines 20–24). In contrast to Eval, the memory usage during the loop is low because it does not store n group elements. However, every loop iteration requires more steps since TDEval reduces n-bit integers of the form 2^j with $j \in [0, n)$ modulo N (Line 22) and performs exponentiations in $\mathbb{QR}_{N'}$ (Line 23). In general, the former operations requires $\Theta(n \log(N'))$ group operations which can be reduced to $\log(n)$ group operations by using a lookup table of size $\Theta(\log(n) \log(N'))$. The exponentation requires $\Theta(\log N')$ group operations using square-and-multiply. So during the loop, TDEval stores the lookup table using $\Theta(\log(n) \log(N'))$ bits, and every iteration takes $\Theta(\log(n) + \log(N'))$ group operations, resulting in

$$cc_{mem}(TDEval(pp, td, x)) \in \Theta(\log(n) \log(N') \cdot n (\log(N') + \log(n)))$$
$$= \Theta(n \log(N')^2 \log(n)).$$

Summing up, TDSCRYPT is a $(n^2 \log(N'), n \log(n) \log(N')^2)$-TMHF.

4   Overview of the Lower Bound Proof

In the previous section, we established that Eval has a CMC of $\Theta(n^2 \log N)$ and TDEval one of $\Theta(n \log n \log N)$. These analyses only hold for the specific algorithms stated in Fig. 1. However, an adversary (without knowledge of the trapdoor) need not follow Eval. The rest of this paper is devoted to showing that no evaluation algorithm is meaningfully faster than Eval.

Theorem 1 (Restated). *Let $n \in \mathrm{poly}(\lambda)$ with $n \geq 8$ and let $\mathcal{A}$ be a deterministic parallel oracle machine that evaluates TDSCRYPT correctly with probability $\chi(\lambda)$ over the choice of the parameters and input W. Then, assuming that factoring is hard, in the GGM and ROM with probability at least $\chi(\lambda) - \epsilon(\lambda)$,*

$$cc_{mem}(\mathcal{A}^{PP}(W)) \in \Omega\left(\frac{n^2}{\log n} \log N\right)$$

where pp are the public parameters, $\epsilon(\lambda) \in \mathrm{negl}(\lambda)$, and the probability is taken over the choice of parameters.

So we show a lower bound on the CMC of evaluating TDSCRYPT that almost matches Eval and is only a factor of $1/\log n$ loose. Note that $\log n \in O(\log \lambda)$ by definition of n, so the loss in tightness is small asymptotically.

To prove our lower bound, we assume that factoring is hard and work in generic models. This is in line with lower bounds on the memory complexity of (non-trapdoor) memory-hard functions which are situated in the ROM. The rest of the paper is divided into two sections similar to Alwen et al. [6]

Single-Challenge Time-Memory Trade-Off (Sect. 5). Before considering the whole TDSCRYPT execution, we focus on the hardness of computing $W_j := W^{2^j}$ for $j \xleftarrow{\$} [n]$ given M bits of precomputed advice. This is closely related to the second phase of TDSCRYPT which, for all $i \in [n]$, requires computing $S_i := h(W^{2^{j_i}}, S_{i-1})$ given challenge $j_i := S_{i-1} \bmod n$. Note that j_i is chosen (almost) uniformly from $[0, n)$ when modeling h as a random oracle. Here, the precomputed advice can be thought of as the state of the algorithm before learning challenge j_i. Our goal is to show that if the advice is short, computing W_j takes a long time on average. Stated differently, if $\mathcal{A}$ computes W_j quickly on average, the advice must be large.

Multi-challenge Memory Complexity Lower-Bound (Sect. 6). We abstract the whole evaluation of TDSCRYPT as a multi-challenge game to get the lower bound on $cc_{mem}(\mathcal{A})$. To this end, the single-challenge trade-off is applied to every challenge, i.e., to the moment in time before it is known *and every point in time before the preceding challenge has been issued*. This idea closely follows the corresponding proof in Alwen et al. [6], and we refer interested readers to the paper for details.

5 Single-Challenge Time-Memory Trade-Off

We consider a pair of deterministic parallel oracle machines $\mathcal{A} = (\mathcal{A}_0, \mathcal{A}_1)$ where $\mathcal{A}_0$ receives the input W and performs preprocessing, resulting in an advice string. In the context of TDSCRYPT, this is best thought of as the computation performed by the (adversarial) evaluation algorithm up to learning challenge j. $\mathcal{A}_1$, on input of challenge $j \xleftarrow{\$} [0, n)$, uses the advice string to query W^{2^j} to h in as few rounds as possible. For now, we explicitly pass the challenge j as an input. Our goal is to relate the advice string size to the number of rounds required by $\mathcal{A}_1$ on average across all possible choices of j.

To formalize the preceding description, we first specify the set of parameters which determine an execution of TDSCRYPT and then the game sketched above.

Definition 5 (Parameters). *For security parameter $\lambda \in \mathbb{N}$, let $\mathsf{params}(\lambda)$ be the set of all possible parameters. It contains all quadruples (N, Σ, h, w) where $(p', q') \leftarrow \mathsf{GenSP}(\lambda)$ with $p := (p' - 1)/2$ and $q := (q' - 1)/2$ defines the group order $N := pq$, the labeling function Σ is an injection $\mathrm{Inj}(\mathbb{Z}_N, \mathcal{L})$, h is a random oracle, and the input w is non-zero, i.e., $w \in \mathbb{Z}_N \setminus \{0\}$. Here, w is the discrete logarithm of W, i.e., $\Sigma^{-1}(W) = w$ in the GGM. Furthermore, recall that we require $\omega_{\mathcal{L}}$, the length of labels in $\mathcal{L}$, and ω_h, the output length of h, to be larger than $\log N$ and of order $\log N$ respectively.*

To avoid clutter, we sometimes leave λ implicit and write params instead.

Definition 6 (Single-challenge Game). *Let $(N, \Sigma, h, w) \in \mathsf{params}$ and $\mathcal{A} = (\mathcal{A}_0, \mathcal{A}_1)$ be deterministic parallel oracle machines. To the challenge $j \in [0, n)$*

and state $\mathsf{st}_0 := \mathcal{A}_0^{\Sigma,\mathsf{h}}(\Sigma(1), \Sigma(w))$ *we associate*

$$\mathsf{TimeSC}_{\mathcal{A}_1}^{\Sigma,\mathsf{h}}(\mathsf{st}_0, j) = \begin{cases} \min\{i \colon \Sigma(w^{2^j}) \in \mathbf{qrs}_i^{\mathsf{h}}\}, & \textit{if the minimum exists} \\ \infty, & \textit{otherwise.} \end{cases}$$

So TimeSC is the earliest round $i \in \mathbb{N}^+$ in which $\mathcal{A}_1^{\mathcal{G},\mathsf{h}}(\mathsf{st}_0, j)$ queries $\Sigma(w^{2^j})$ to h or ∞ if it never does.

Next, we answer the following question: *How small can* TimeSC *be relative to the size of* st_0? That is, we are interested in a time-memory trade-off when playing TimeSC.

A preliminary observation is that if $\|\mathsf{st}_0\| \geq n\omega_{\mathcal{L}}$, then there exists a simple strategy $\mathcal{SS}$ achieving $\mathsf{TimeSC}_{\mathcal{SS}} = 1$. Indeed, $\mathcal{SS}$ simply stores the answers to every possible challenge in st_0. Generalizing to any $\|\mathsf{st}_0\| = M$, we get the following strategy $\mathcal{SS}$: $\mathcal{SS}_0$ encodes $\rho := \lfloor M/\omega_{\mathcal{L}} \rfloor$ group elements in st_0 where the elements are of the form W^{2^i} with the i equidistantly spaced across $0, \ldots, n-1$. $\mathcal{SS}_1$, on input j, picks the maximum $i \leq j$ such that W^{2^i} is stored in st_0 and, if necessary, repeatedly squares it until reaching W^{2^j}. So $\mathsf{TimeSC}_{\mathcal{SS}} > n/(2\rho)$ for at least half of the challenges.

We want to show that if factoring is hard, no algorithm $\mathcal{A}$ can meaningfully beat $\mathcal{SS}$ for most choices of parameters. That is, there exists a partition of params into sets good and bad such that bad contains a negligible fraction of params and $\mathcal{A}$ can only beat the strategy when the chosen parameters are in bad. Note that we cannot give guarantees for all possible parameter choices since, e.g., sometimes N might be easy to factor. This leads us to Lemma 1 that characterizes the set bad.

Lemma 1 (Single-challenge Trade-Off). *For every pair of deterministic parallel oracle machines* $\mathcal{A} = (\mathcal{A}_0, \mathcal{A}_1)$, *all* $c \in \mathbb{N}$ *with security parameter* λ *large enough, and all* $n, M, Q \in \mathrm{poly}(\lambda)$ *with* $n \geq 8$ *and subsets* bad $\subseteq$ params(λ), *if, for every* $(N, \Sigma, \mathsf{h}, w) \in$ bad, $\mathcal{A}_1$ *makes at most* Q *queries,* $\mathsf{st}_0 := \mathcal{A}_0^{\Sigma,\mathsf{h}}(\Sigma(1), \Sigma(w))$ *is of size* $|\mathsf{st}_0| \leq M$ *and*

$$\Pr_{j \overset{\$}{\leftarrow} [0,n)} \left[\mathsf{TimeSC}_{\mathcal{A}_1}^{\Sigma,\mathsf{h}}(\mathsf{st}_0, j) \leq \frac{n}{6\rho \log(n/2)} \right] \geq 1/2$$

where $\rho = (M + \log n + \log Q + c \log \lambda + 1)/(\log(N) - 3(\log Q - \log n) - 3)$, *then* $|\mathrm{bad}| < \lambda^{-c} |\,\mathrm{params}(\lambda)|$.

In other words, bad is the set of parameters where, for every choice of parameters contained therein, $\mathcal{A}_1$ answers more quickly than expected. It is also possible to define the single-challenge trade-off the other way around. So there exists a large set good, and the trade-off holds for any parameters in good. Corollary 1 captures this view and also simplifies Lemma 1 by not stating all constants explicitly.

Corollary 1. *For every pair of deterministic parallel oracle machines* $\mathcal{A} = (\mathcal{A}_0, \mathcal{A}_1)$, *there exists a negligible function* $\epsilon(\lambda) \in \mathrm{negl}(\lambda)$ *such that, for all* $n, M, Q \in \mathrm{poly}(\lambda)$ *with* $n \geq 8$, *there exists a subset* good $\subseteq$ params(λ) *such that,*

for every $(N, \Sigma, \mathsf{h}, w) \in$ good, $\mathcal{A}_1$ *makes at most* Q *queries,* $\mathsf{st}_0 := \mathcal{A}_0^{\Sigma,\mathsf{h}}(\Sigma(w))$
is of size $|\mathsf{st}_0| \le M$,

$$\Pr_{j \overset{\$}{\leftarrow} [0,n)} \left[\mathsf{TimeSC}_{\mathcal{A}_1}^{\Sigma,\mathsf{h}}(\mathsf{st}_0, j) > \frac{n}{6\rho \log(n/2)} \right] \ge 1/2$$

where $\rho \in \Theta((M + \log n + \log Q + \log \lambda)/(\log(N) - (\log Q - \log n)))$ *and* $|\mathsf{good}| \ge (1 - \epsilon(\lambda))|\mathsf{params}(\lambda)|$.

Let us now compare Corollary 1's guarantees to the simple strategy $\mathcal{SS}$. ρ is asymptotically close to $\lfloor M/\log N \rfloor \le \lfloor M/\log \omega_{\mathcal{L}} \rfloor$ as in $\mathcal{SS}$. However, $n/(6\rho \log(n/2))$ is roughly a $1/\log(n)$ factor looser than $n/(2\rho)$. This seemingly is an artifact of our proof (looking ahead, Lemma 2), and we leave possible improvements to future work. The remainder of the section is devoted to the proof and structured as follows: First, we explain how to reason about $\mathcal{A}_1$'s query behavior algebraically and state some algebraic tools related to that. Second, we give the high-level structure of the proof and highlight three central claims. Finally, we prove each claim to complete the proof.

5.1   Reasoning About $\mathcal{A}_1$'s Queries Algebraically

Algebraic Representation of Labels. Algorithm $\mathcal{A}_1$ receives st_0 (the output of preprocessing algorithm $\mathcal{A}_0(\Sigma(1), \Sigma(w))$) and challenge j as input. It then uses the GGM oracle to generate the label $\Sigma(w2^j)$. As is typical in the GGM (e.g., [18,36]), the reduction in our proof exploits $\mathcal{A}_1$'s query behavior. To this end, the reduction associates an algebraic representation to every label that $\mathcal{A}_1$ queries to or receives from the oracle. More precisely, the algebraic representations are linear terms over $\mathbb{Z}_N$ in several indeterminates $x_1, \ldots, x_m$. The reduction stores the mapping of algebraic representations to labels in an (initially empty) table T to ensure consistency between queries.

Whenever $\mathcal{A}_1$ makes a query $\mathcal{G}(+, \sigma_1, \sigma_2)$, the reduction does the following:[8] First, it checks whether T already contains the label σ_1. If not, it represents σ_1 by a new indeterminate x_i and stores this mapping in T. Then, σ_2 is processed analogously before the reduction computes the label $\sigma_3 = \mathcal{G}(+, \sigma_1, \sigma_2)$. If T does not contain a representation for σ_3, its representation is set to the sum of the ones of σ_1 and σ_2. Queries for the operations $\circ \in \{-, \mathsf{inv}\}$ are handled in the analogous way.

We stress that $\mathcal{A}_1$ only receives the (bit string) st_0 and the challenge j as input but not any labels. As a consequence, T is initially empty. Thus, all algebraic representations will not contain any constant terms. This is in contrast to similar approaches (e.g., [36]) where constant terms arise as a consequence of the adversary explicitly receiving the group generator as input at the beginning of the game. Intuitively, in our scenario $\mathcal{A}_0$ must store some labels (e.g., $\Sigma(w)$) in st_0 in order for the hint to be useful.

---

[8] The following explanation is high-level and thus omits technicalities such as collision handling.

System of Equations. In the above explanation, the reduction executed $\mathcal{A}_1$ with some arbitrary challenge $j \in [n]$. In the actual proof, the reduction cares about specific challenges, in particular, the subset $J \subseteq [0, n)$ of challenges that are answered within in at most t rounds (t will be set later). For every $j \in J$, the reduction starts $\mathcal{A}_1(\mathsf{st}_0, j)$. Then, it executes all instances of $\mathcal{A}_1$ in parallel in lockstep while only keeping track of a *single* table T. In more detail: First, the reduction initializes the empty table T. Second, for every $j \in J$, it runs the $\mathcal{A}_1(\mathsf{st}_0, j)$ until the first batch of parallel queries to the GGM oracle is made. Iterating over all $j \in J$, the reduction responds to the queries and adds labels to T as described above. Then, it resumes the execution of all $\mathcal{A}_1$ instances until they query the GGM a second time. The reduction repeats this procedure for t rounds.

This parallel and lockstep execution gives rise to a system of linear equations corresponding to the challenges $j \in J$ as follows. By definition of J, all challenges j lead to $\mathcal{A}_1(\mathsf{st}_0, j)$ querying the label $\Sigma(w2^j)$ within t rounds. In turn, the table must contain this label with a corresponding representation of the form $a_{j,1}x_1 + \cdots + a_{j,m}x_m$ (here in, say, m indeterminates). By correctness, it must satisfy

$$a_{j,1}x_1 + \cdots + a_{j,m}x_m = w2^j \bmod N. \tag{1}$$

Collecting these equations for all $j \in J$, we obtain a system of equations over $\mathbb{Z}_N$ of the form $A\boldsymbol{x} = \boldsymbol{b}$, where $A = (a_{ji})_{j \in J, i \in [m]}$ and $\boldsymbol{b} = \left(2^j w \bmod N \mid j \in J\right)^{\top}$. Since Eq. (1) holds for every equation, the system must have a solution $\boldsymbol{x} \in \mathbb{Z}_m$. Intuitively, the solution $\boldsymbol{x}$ corresponds to the discrete logarithm of group elements queried by $\mathcal{A}_1$ out of the blue (represented by indeterminates) of which there are m in total. In practice, $\mathcal{A}_1$ must have (mostly) stored these group elements in st_0 as a randomly guessed group element will most likely not be useful in computing a challenge.

Groups of Unknown Order. The above characterization of A requires knowledge of the group order N. However, assuming that factoring is hard, the reduction and, more importantly, $\mathcal{A}_1$ do not know N. Therefore, we will argue that it is almost always valid to consider the system $A\boldsymbol{x} = \boldsymbol{b}$ as being defined over $\mathbb{Z}$ instead of $\mathbb{Z}_N$. That is, $A \in \mathbb{Z}^{\ell \times m}$, $\boldsymbol{x} \in \mathbb{Z}^m$, and $\boldsymbol{b} \in \mathbb{Z}^\ell$ with $\boldsymbol{b} = \left(2^j w \mid j \in J\right)^{\top}$ Since $\mathcal{A}_1$ is executed for t rounds, for every entry $a_{ji} \in A$, we have $|a_{ji}| \leq 2^t$ as a consequence.[9] Furthermore, $A\boldsymbol{x} = \boldsymbol{b}$ constitutes a system of Diophantine equations since A, $\boldsymbol{x}$, and $\boldsymbol{b}$ only have integer components.[10] Since we are working with integers, this system might not have a solution $\boldsymbol{x}$. However, looking ahead, it almost always will, assuming that factoring is hard.

Solving a system of equations $A\boldsymbol{x} = \boldsymbol{b}$ over $\mathbb{Z}$ works similarly to solving one over a field. Recall that in a field one commonly uses Gaussian elimination to transform A into a row- or column-reduced echelon form (i.e., a triangular matrix with pivot entries equal to 1) because then the solution can easily be

---

[9] In fact, for every row $\boldsymbol{a}_j$, one can even show that $\|\boldsymbol{a}_j\|_1 \leq 2^t$ (cf. the full version [10]).

[10] A precise definition of A, $\boldsymbol{x}$, and $\boldsymbol{b}$ appears in the full version [10].

found algorithmically. The integer analogue to the column reduced echelon form is the well-known column-style *Hermite normal form (HNF)* which we define as in [29].

Definition 7 (Hermite Normal Form). *A matrix $H \in \mathbb{Z}^{\ell \times m}$ is in Hermite normal form if (i) there exists a sequence of integers $1 \le i_1 < \cdots < i_r \le \ell$ such that $h_{ij} = 0$ for all $i < i_j$ where r is the number of non-zero columns; and (ii) $0 \le h_{i_j k} < h_{i_j j}$ for all $0 \le k < j \le m$.*

So by Item (i), H is a lower-triangular matrix and all its zero columns are to the right. Furthermore, taking Item (ii) into account, for every matrix A, there exists a unique HNF H such that $H = AU$ where $U \in \mathbb{Z}^{m \times m}$ is unimodular (i.e., invertible over $\mathbb{Z}$). Moreover, H has $r := \text{rank}(A)$ non-zero columns [24]. In the rest of the paper, we denote the HNF of A by $\text{HNF}(A) = (H, U)$.

Note that the definition of $\text{rank}(\cdot)$ might differ to one's own intuitive definition. This is due to $\mathbb{Z}^{\ell \times m}$ being a module and not a vector space. In contrast to linear algebra, different definitions of rank are not equivalent, so we define $\text{rank}(\cdot)$ below.

Definition 8 (Rank). $\text{rank}(A)$ *is the size of largest subset of A's columns that are linearly independent. A set of columns $\{c_1, \ldots, c_k\}$ is linearly dependent if there exist $\alpha_1, \ldots, \alpha_k \in \mathbb{Z}$ with at least one $\alpha_i \ne 0$ such that $\sum_{i=1}^{k} \alpha_i c_i = \mathbf{0}$.*

5.2   Proof Skeleton

We first give a high-level overview of the proof. Assume that Lemma 1 does not hold. So we have a large set of parameters bad where the trade-off does not hold for at least half of the challenges. That is, we have an upper bound on how many rounds the adversary needs to answer them. Thus, we can derive a system of equations $A\boldsymbol{x} = \boldsymbol{b}$ over $\mathbb{Z}$ where the $a_{ij} \in A$ are bounded in magnitude due to the trade-off not holding. Then, we prove the following claims about this system:

– Assuming factoring is hard, $A\boldsymbol{x} = \boldsymbol{b}$ behaves identically over $\mathbb{Z}$ and $\mathbb{Z}_N$ almost always. For example, $A\boldsymbol{x} = \boldsymbol{b}$ having a solution over $\mathbb{Z}_N$ does not necessarily imply the same holds over $\mathbb{Z}$, yet the implication will almost always hold under the factoring assumption.
– Assuming that $A\boldsymbol{x} = \boldsymbol{b}$ over $\mathbb{Z}$ has a solution, $\text{rank}(A) \ge \rho$ for every choice of parameters in bad.
– $\text{rank}(A) < \rho$ for some choice of parameters in bad. Otherwise, a random labeling function Σ could be compressed more efficiently than information-theoretically possible.

Notice that the last two claims contradict each other, so Lemma 1 must hold. We now give the detailed version of the above sketch.

Proof of Lemma 1. We distinguish two cases depending on ρ, the first one being trivial.

Case $\rho > n/(6\log(n/2))$: Then $n/(6\rho\log(n/2)) < 1$ and so the trade-off holds for any $j \in [0, n)$ since TimeSC ≥ 1 by Definition 6.

Case $\rho \leq n/(6\log(n/2))$: Towards contradiction, assume that Lemma 1 does not hold. That is, there exists a pair of deterministic parallel oracle machines $\mathcal{A} = (\mathcal{A}_0, \mathcal{A}_1)$, $c \in \mathbb{N}$ with security parameter λ large enough and, for infinitely many security parameters λ, there exist $n, M, Q \in \text{poly}(\lambda)$ with $n \geq 8$ and a subset bad $\subseteq$ params(λ), such that, for every $(N, \Sigma, \mathsf{h}, w) \in$ bad, $\mathcal{A}_1$ makes at most Q queries, $\mathsf{st}_0 := \mathcal{A}_0^{\Sigma,\mathsf{h}}(\Sigma(1), \Sigma(w))$ is of size $|\mathsf{st}_0| \leq M$ and

$$\Pr_{j \xleftarrow{\$} [0,n)}\left[\mathsf{TimeSC}_{\mathcal{A}_1}^{\Sigma,\mathsf{h}}(\mathsf{st}_0, j) \leq \frac{n}{6\rho\log(n/2)}\right] \geq 1/2$$

where $\rho = (M + \log n + \log Q + c\log\lambda + 1)/(\log(N) - 3(\log Q - \log n) - 3)$ and $|\mathsf{bad}| \geq \lambda^{-c}|\,\mathsf{params}(\lambda)|$.

So for parameters in bad, it holds that $\mathcal{A}_1$ will answer at least $n/2$ challenges correctly by the end of round $\frac{n}{6\rho\log(n/2)}$. By the definition of rounds (cf. Sect. 2.4), to compute these answers, it can make and receive the results of $t := \frac{n}{6\rho\log(n/2)} - 1$ rounds of queries.

As in Sect. 5.1, consider the system of Diophantine equations $A\boldsymbol{x} = \boldsymbol{b}$ where $A \in \mathbb{Z}^{(n/2)\times m}$ for some $m \in \mathbb{N}^+$ arising from $\mathcal{A}_1$'s query behavior. In the case that $\mathcal{A}_1$ answers more than $n/2$ challenges, we avoid ambiguities by selecting $n/2$ challenges in some deterministic order (e.g., low challenge numbers first). Note that every matrix element $|a_{ij}| \leq 2^t$ and that the vector $\boldsymbol{b}$ does not contain 0, its elements are pairwise distinct, and of the form $b_i = 2^j w$ for $j \in [0, n)$.

First, assuming factoring is hard, $A\boldsymbol{x} = \boldsymbol{b}$ behaves similarly to $A\boldsymbol{x} = \boldsymbol{b} \bmod N$ almost always. It is proven in Sect. 5.3.

Claim 1. If Lemma 1 does not hold, there exists a negligible function $\epsilon(\lambda) \in$ negl(λ) such that (i) $A\boldsymbol{x} = \boldsymbol{b}$ has a solution; (ii) $\mathsf{HNF}(A)$ and $\mathsf{HNF}(A) \bmod N$ have the same shape (i.e., $\mathsf{HNF}(A) \bmod N$ has no additional zero entries); and (iii) the diagonal entries of $\mathsf{HNF}(A) \bmod N$ are invertible over $\mathbb{Z}_N$ except for probability $\epsilon(\lambda)$ where the probability is taken over the choice of $(N, \Sigma, \mathsf{h}, w) \in$ params(λ).

Second, since $\mathcal{A}$ answers a lot of challenges quickly, its rank must be large as proven in Sect. 5.4.

Claim 2. If Lemma 1 does not hold and $\rho \leq n/(6\log n)$, for all $(N, \Sigma, \mathsf{h}, w) \in$ bad, rank$(A) \geq \rho$.

Last, rank(A) cannot be too large by an incompressibility argument presented in Sect. 5.5.

Claim 3. If Lemma 1 does not hold, there exists a $(N, \Sigma, \mathsf{h}, w) \in$ bad, such that rank$(A) < \rho$.

The latter two claims contradict each other, completing the proof.

5.3   Analyzing the Behavior of $Ax = b$

The proof of Claim 1 follows from the assumed hardness of factoring. In particular, Item (i) and Item (ii) reduce to factoring N', and Item (iii) to factoring N.

Proof of Claim 1. Let E_i denote the event that item i does not hold. We will show that all events happen with negligible probability.

- There exists a negligible function $\epsilon(\lambda) \in \text{negl}(\lambda)$ such that $\Pr_{\text{params}}[E_{\text{(iii)}}] \leq \epsilon(\lambda)$. To see this, consider the algorithm $\mathcal{B}$ playing the game $\text{Fac}_{\text{GenSP},\mathcal{B}}(\lambda)$ (cf. Definition 3). It uses $\mathcal{A}$ (guaranteed by the assumption that Lemma 1 does not hold) as a subroutine.
  On input N, $\mathcal{B}$ picks $w \leftarrow \mathbb{Z}_N \setminus \{0\}$, and lazily samples h and Σ to respond to $\mathcal{A}$'s queries. Note that $\mathcal{B}$ can simulate Σ and h perfectly because it knows N. Assuming that N, w and what has been sampled of Σ and h so far is consistent with bad, $\mathcal{B}$ is able to derive the system $Ax - b$. Then, it computes $\text{HNF}(A) \bmod N$ and checks whether any diagonal element a cannot be inverted. If so, $\mathcal{B}$ outputs (p^*, q^*) where $p^* = \gcd(a, N)$ and $q^* = N/p^*$.
  $\mathcal{B}$ is a PPT algorithm and $(N, \Sigma, \text{h}, w) \in$ bad with probability at least λ^{-c}. Hence, $\Pr[E_{\text{(iii)}}] \leq \lambda^c \text{Adv}^{\text{Fac}}_{\text{GenSP},\mathcal{B}}(\lambda)$ which is negligible as factoring N is assumed to be hard.
- There exists a negligible function $\epsilon(\lambda) \in \text{negl}(\lambda)$ such that $\Pr_{\text{params}}[E_{\text{(i)}}] + \Pr_{\text{params}}[E_{\text{(ii)}}] \leq \epsilon(\lambda)$.
  The reduction is similar to the previous item except for two differences. First, $\mathcal{B}$ only knows N' but not N, so it cannot simulate Σ perfectly. However, this is not an issue as $\mathcal{B}$ can approximate lazy sampling Σ by using $N'/4$ instead of N. Since $N'/4 = N + O(\sqrt{N})$, answering a polynomial number of Σ queries using lazy sampling with $N'/4$ is statistically close to lazy sampling with N. Second, $\mathcal{B}$ factors N' instead of N. If $Ax = b$ has a solution over $\mathbb{Z}$ but not $\mathbb{Z}_N$ or if a matrix entry is non-zero over $\mathbb{Z}$ but zero over $\mathbb{Z}_N$, $\mathcal{B}$ learns a multiple of the group order N. Such a multiple can be used to factor N' with probability at least $1/2$ [26, Thm. 8.50].

Combining the two items above completes the proof. $\qquad\qquad\qquad\square$

5.4   Combinatorial Proof of the rank(A) Lower Bound

The key result of this section is the following number-theoretical lemma. Given a system of Diophantine equations $Ax = b$, it bounds rank(A) from below as a function of A's number of rows and the magnitude of its entries.

Lemma 2 *Let* $\ell \in \mathbb{N}$ *with* $\ell \geq 4$, $t \in \mathbb{N}$, *and* $m, w \in \mathbb{N}^+$. *For any matrix* $A = (a_{i,j})_{i \in [\ell], j \in [m]} \in \mathbb{Z}^{\ell \times m}$ *with* $|a_{i,j}| \leq 2^t$ *for all* i, j *and vector* $b = (2^{j_1}w, \ldots, 2^{j_\ell}w)^\top$ *with pairwise distinct* $j_1, \ldots, j_\ell \in \mathbb{N}$, *if the system* $Ax = b$ *has a solution* $x \in \mathbb{Z}^m$, *then* $\text{rank}(A) \geq \frac{\ell}{3\max\{t, \log \ell\}}$.

In the context of the single-challenge trade-off, the lemma states the following: If $\mathcal{A}_1$ solves a lot of challenges, either it must take a long time or rank(A) is high. This makes sense since the rank approximately corresponds to the number of group elements stored in st_0 which is at most $M/\log N \approx \rho$. Note that Claim 2 formalizes precisely this intuition, so it follows from Lemma 2 almost directly.

Proof of Claim 2. By the assumption that Lemma 1 does not hold, $\mathcal{A}_1$ answers at least $\ell := n/2 \geq 4$ challenges within $t := n/(6\rho \log(n/2)) - 1$ rounds of queries. By Claim 1 Item (i), we may assume that bad only contains parameters where the system $Ax = b$ has a solution. So we apply Lemma 2 to get rank(A) $\geq \frac{n}{6 \max\{t, \log(n/2)\}}$ and we consider two cases depending on max: First, if rank(A) $\geq n/(6t)$, it follows that rank(A) $\geq n/(6(t+1))$ and substituting for t, we arrive at rank(A) $\geq \rho \log(n/2) \geq \rho$ as desired since $\log(n/2) \geq 2$. Second, if rank(A) $\geq n/(6\log(n/2))$, by the assumption that $n/(6\log(n/2)) \geq \rho$, we also get rank(A) $\geq \rho$ completing the proof. □

We now turn to the proof of Lemma 2. The first ingredient is an elegant number-theoretic lemma due to van der Waerden (restated and proven in [28]) which precisely describes when a system of Diophantine equations has a solution.

Lemma 3 (van der Waerden). *Consider the Diophantine system of linear equations $Ax = b$ with $A \in \mathbb{Z}^{\ell \times m}$ and $b \in \mathbb{Z}^\ell$. The system has a solution $x \in \mathbb{Z}^m$ if and only if, for every rational vector $v \in \mathbb{Q}^\ell$ such that $vA \in \mathbb{Z}^m$, it also holds that $vb \in \mathbb{Z}$.*

We will show that if rank(A) is too small, such a vector v always exists. To this end, we introduce the second ingredient which is a combinatorial claim. It is a vector version of the famous distinct subset sums problem and associated conjecture[11] due to Erdős [23, C8].

Claim 4. For $t, m, \ell \in \mathbb{N}$ with $\ell \geq 4$, let $R \subset \mathbb{Z}^m$ with $|R| = \ell$ and every $r \in R$ satisfying $\|r\|_\infty \leq 2^t$.[12] If $m < \ell/(3\max\{t, \log \ell\})$, two subsets $R_1, R_2 \subseteq R$ exist such that at least one subset is non-empty ($R_1 \cup R_2 \neq \emptyset$), they are disjoint ($R_1 \cap R_2 = \emptyset$), and their sums are equal ($\sum_{r_1 \in R_1} r_1 = \sum_{r_2 \in R_2} r_2$).

Note that the above claim is slightly more general than the vector version considered by Costa et al. [19, Prop. 2.1], but their proof is easily adapted to our setting.

Proof. First, for any subset's sum, notice that the largest absolute value of any resulting vector coordinate is bounded by $2^t \ell$, which follows directly from the triangle inequality and the fact that subsets contain at most ℓ elements.

---

[11] Consider a subset $S \subseteq \{1, \ldots, 2^t\}$ of size $|S| = m$. *What is the maximum size m so that all subsets of S have distinct sums?* The best-known lower bound is $t + 2 \leq m$ and upper bounds are roughly $m < t + \log t$ (ignoring constants). Erdős conjectured that $m = t + O(1)$ and offered $500 for proof or refutation [23, C8].

[12] $\|r\|_\infty$ is the infinity norm of the vector $r = (r_1, \ldots, r_m)$ and defined as $\max_i |r_i|$.

Second, there exist 2^ℓ distinct (not necessarily disjoint) subsets. Assuming that all subsets' sums are distinct, by the pigeonhole principle, it must hold that

$$|\{-2^t\ell, -2^t\ell + 1, \ldots, 2^t\ell - 1, 2^t\ell\}|^m \geq 2^\ell$$
$$(2^{t+2}\ell)^m \geq 2^\ell$$
$$m(t + 2 + \log \ell) \geq \ell$$
$$m \geq \ell/(3\max\{t, \log \ell\})$$

where the second line follows by overapproximating the size of the set, the third by applying log to both sides, and the fourth by $2 \leq \log \ell \leq \max\{t, \log \ell\}$ since $\ell \geq 4$ by assumption. As a consequence, if $m < \ell/(3\max\{t, \log \ell\})$, then there exist two distinct, but not necessarily disjoint subsets R_1' and R_2' with equal subset-sum.

To get disjoint sets R_1 and R_2, we remove all common elements by defining $R_i := R_i' \setminus (R_1' \cap R_2')$ for $i \in \{1, 2\}$. Notice that at least one set is non-empty since R_1' and R_2' are distinct. This completes the proof. □

Equipped with these tools, the proof of Lemma 2 is straightforward.

Proof of Lemma 2. Towards contradiction, assume that there exist A as well as b satisfying the constraints in the lemma's statement and that the system $Ax = b$ has a solution, but $\mathrm{rank}(A) < \frac{\ell}{3\max\{t, \log \ell\}}$. We will show that this implies the existence of a vector $v \in \{-1, 0, 1\}^\ell$ with $v \neq 0$ and $vA = 0$.

For finding such a v, we may assume that $\mathrm{rank}(A) = m$ (i.e., A is full-rank). This almost directly follows from linear independence (cf. full version [10]).

Now we use Claim 4 to construct v. Whenever A contains two identical rows, it is straightforward to define an appropriate v. Thus, we may assume that the rows of A are distinct and form a set $R \subset \mathbb{Z}^m$ of size $|R| = \ell$. Combining this with the assumption $m = \mathrm{rank}(A) < \ell/(3\max\{t, \log \ell\})$, Claim 4 applies, so there exist two disjoint subsets R_1 and R_2 with equal sum with one of them being non-empty. Hence, we initialize $v := 0$, and set $v_i := 1$ if $r_i \in R_1$ and $v_j := -1$ if $r_j \in R_2$. This is unambiguous as the subsets are disjoint. Further, notice that $v \neq 0$ since one subset is non-empty, and, since the subsets' sums are equal, $vA = 0$ as required.

Last, we apply Lemma 3 to $Ax = b$ and v. By definition, $b \in \mathbb{Z}^\ell$ contains no element $b_i = 0$, all b_i are pairwise distinct and exponentially far apart. Thus, $vb = \beta \in \mathbb{Z}$ with $\beta \neq 0$ since $v \in \{-1, 0, 1\}$. Setting $v' := \frac{1}{|\beta|+1}v$, we arrive at the conclusion that the system $Ax = b$ does not have a solution by van der Waerden (Lemma 3). This is a contradiction, completing the proof. □

5.5 Incompressibility Argument

Recall that Claim 3 claims the existence of parameters in bad such that $\mathrm{rank}(A) < \rho$. To this end, we will show that $\mathrm{rank}_{\min} < \rho$ where $\mathrm{rank}_{\min}$ is the minimum rank over all possible parameters in bad, that is,

$$\mathrm{rank}_{\min} := \min_{\mathrm{bad}}(\mathrm{rank}(A)). \tag{2}$$

Our proof use an incompressibility argument (e.g., [1,6,18,20,37]) to bound $\mathsf{rank}_{\min}$ in terms of $|\mathsf{st}_0| = M$ and since ρ depends on M, we get the desired bound. Formally, we follow the framework of De, Trevisan, and Tulsiani [20] stated below.

Lemma 4 (De, Trevisan, and Tulsiani [20]). *Let* $\mathsf{Enc} \colon \mathcal{S} \times \{0,1\}^\mu \to \{0,1\}^r$ *and* $\mathsf{Dec} \colon \{0,1\}^\mu \times \{0,1\}^r \to \mathcal{S}$ *be randomized encoding and decoding procedures such that, for every* $s \in \mathcal{S}$, $\Pr_{r \leftarrow \{0,1\}^r}[\mathsf{Dec}(\mathsf{Enc}(s;r);r) = s] \geq \delta$. *Then* $\mu \geq \log|\mathcal{S}| - \log 1/\delta$.

Intuitively, the analysis of preprocessing algorithms $\mathcal{A} = (\mathcal{A}_0, \mathcal{A}_1)$ using the framework proceeds as follows. $\mathcal{S}$ is usually a set of functions, injections, etc. where $\mathcal{A}$ has oracle access to one $s \in \mathcal{S}$. Enc, knowing $s \in \mathcal{S}$, runs $\mathcal{A}_0^s$ to get st_0 and then $\mathcal{A}_1(\mathsf{st}_0)^s$ such that $\mathcal{A}_1$'s query behavior implicitly allows one to reconstruct parts of s. It outputs an encoding comprised of st_0 and an additional hint. Dec receives this encoding and runs $\mathcal{A}_1(\mathsf{st}_0)^{\mathsf{hint}}$ where the hint is used to simulate the oracle. Given $\mathcal{A}_1$'s query behavior, Dec recovers s at the cost of $\|\mathsf{st}_0\| + \|\mathsf{hint}\|$ bits where the hint is carefully designed to be smaller than $\log|\mathcal{S}|$ bits. Since encoding s using less than $\log|\mathcal{S}|$ bits would constitute information-theoretically impossible compression, st_0 must be large enough to contain the remaining information.

  In our case, we work with $\mathcal{S} := \mathsf{bad}$, but effectively we only efficiently encode the labeling function $\varSigma \in \mathsf{Inj}(\mathbb{Z}_N, \mathcal{L})$ while using a naive encoding for N, h, and w. Our argument then follows the strategy outlined in the previous paragraph. As in Sect. 5.1, $\mathcal{A}_1$ induces the system of Diophantine equations $A\boldsymbol{x} = \boldsymbol{b}$ where A and $\boldsymbol{b}$ are known. Every element of $\boldsymbol{x} \bmod N$ corresponds to the discrete logarithm of some label in $\mathcal{L}$ and Dec can solve the system to extract $\boldsymbol{x}$, effectively learning some discrete logarithms, and, in turn, the labels for the corresponding group elements without them being encoded in the hint. Given usual linear algebra intuition, the solvability of this system and the uniqueness of its solution are related to the rank of A. Here, this is $\mathsf{rank}_{\min}$ which allows us to connect $\|\mathsf{st}_0\| = M$ to $\mathsf{rank}_{\min}$.

  Equipped with this high-level explanation, we now state Claim 5. It posits the existence of $(\mathsf{Enc}, \mathsf{Dec})$ that efficiently encode the labeling function $\varSigma \in \mathsf{Inj}(\mathbb{Z}_N, \mathcal{L})$ where the encoding size depends on M and $\mathsf{rank}_{\min}$.

Claim 5. If Lemma 1 does not hold, for $(N, \varSigma, \mathsf{h}, w) \in \mathsf{bad}$, there exist $(\mathsf{Enc}, \mathsf{Dec})$ which, given auxiliary inputs N, h, and w, encodes the labeling function $\varSigma$ using

$$\log \binom{|\mathcal{L}|}{N} + \log(N!) + M + \log n + \log Q - \mathsf{rank}_{\min} \cdot (\log N - 3(\log n + \log Q) - 3)$$

bits with probability 1.

Before constructing such $(\mathsf{Enc}, \mathsf{Dec})$, we show how their existence implies Claim 3.

Proof of Claim 3. In general, optimally encoding an element of params requires $\log|\mathsf{params}| = \mu' + \log\binom{|\mathcal{L}|}{N} + \log(N!)$ bits where μ' is the length of an optimal encoding of N, h, and w. Since bad contains at least a $1/\lambda^c$ fraction of params, it follows from elementary logarithmic identities that an optimal encoding of a tuple in bad requires

$$\mu' + \log \binom{|\mathcal{L}|}{N} + \log(N!) + \log(\lambda^{-c}) = \mu' + \log \binom{|\mathcal{L}|}{N} + \log(N!) - c\log \lambda$$

bits. Now, by Claim 5 and applying Lemma 4 while canceling common terms (implicitly accounting for μ'), it must hold that

$$-c\log \lambda \leq M + \log n + \log Q - \mathsf{rank}_{\min} \cdot (\log N - 3(\log n + \log Q) - 3)$$

which implies

$$\mathsf{rank}_{\min} \leq \frac{M + \log n + \log Q + c\log \lambda}{\log N - 3(\log Q - \log n) - 3}.$$

By the definition of ρ in Lemma 1, it follows that $\mathsf{rank}_{\min} < \rho$, so there exists a $(N, \Sigma, \mathsf{h}, w) \in$ bad such that $\mathrm{rank}(A) < \rho$ as desired.   □

The only thing left to show is that $(\mathsf{Enc}, \mathsf{Dec})$ for Σ as in Claim 5 exist. This requires careful handling of various technicalities, so we will only sketch the proof here and defer the complete proof to the appendix of the full version [10].

Proof of Claim 5 (Sketch). The high-level idea is that Enc and Dec both run $\mathcal{A}_1$ as a subroutine. $\mathcal{A}_1$ induces a system of equations $A\boldsymbol{x} = \boldsymbol{b}$ with $\mathrm{rank}(A) \geq \mathsf{rank}_{\min}$. This allows Enc to encode the discrete logarithm of $\mathsf{rank}_{\min}$ many group element labels using a short hint instead of the naive encoding that costs roughly $\log N$ bits.

Given input Σ and auxiliary inputs N, h and w, Enc computes st_0 by running $\mathcal{A}_0^{\Sigma,\mathsf{h}}(\Sigma(1), \Sigma(w))$ and then executes $\mathcal{A}_1^{\Sigma,\mathsf{h}}(\mathsf{st}_0)$ on every challenge $j \in [0, n)$ for at most $t := \frac{n}{6\rho \log(n/2)} - 1$ rounds in parallel in lockstep. During this, Enc successively constructs an encoding of Σ. This encoding contains the information necessary for Dec to also run $\mathcal{A}_1$ without knowing the oracle Σ.

In particular, Enc (and also Dec) track the algebraic representation of queries as in Sect. 5.1. The algebraic representation of a label might include some indeterminates which correspond to labels that $\mathcal{A}_1$ input to Σ out of the blue (i.e., either it guessed the label or it extracted it from st_0).

On the one hand, Enc needs to ensure that Dec can answer oracle queries to the labeling function Σ correctly. To this end, it first encodes the image of Σ using $\log \binom{|\mathcal{L}|}{N}$ bits, and, for some queries, it adds a hint of circa $\log N$ bits which specify the label to be returned. Note that this hint is only required for *some* queries since the output of a query is sometimes uniquely determined by the algebraic representations of the preceding queries (e.g., when $\mathcal{A}_1$ repeats a query). Since Dec tracks those representations, it can answer such queries without additional help from Enc.

On the other hand, Enc also needs to tell Dec when the label $\Sigma(w^{2^j})$ is queried to h. This requires a hint of $\log n + \log Q$ bits; $\log n$ bits to identify the instance of $\mathcal{A}_1$ and $\log Q$ to specify the query within that instance. Given rank_{min} many hints, Dec derives a system of equations $A\boldsymbol{x} = \boldsymbol{b}$. The vector $\boldsymbol{b} \in \mathbb{Z}^{\mathsf{rank}_{min}}$ contains the $2^i w$ specified by the hints and the rows of A the corresponding algebraic representations. So $\boldsymbol{x} \in \mathbb{Z}^m$, when taken modulo N, corresponds to the discrete logarithms of some indeterminates within these algebraic representations.

Computing $\mathsf{HNF}(A) = (H, U)$ yields a lower triangular matrix H such that $A\boldsymbol{x} = \boldsymbol{b}$ has a solution if and only if $H\boldsymbol{y} = \boldsymbol{b}$ has a solution where $\boldsymbol{x} = U\boldsymbol{y}$. Recall that H has rank_{min} many non-zero columns and, due to the triangular shape of H, every non-zero column constrains one entry of $\boldsymbol{x}$.

Next, reduce every matrix and vector modulo N. Notice that Claim 1 Items (ii) and (iii) guarantee that $H \bmod N$ still has the same shape and that the pivot elements are invertible. This implies that every non-zero column of $H \bmod N$ uniquely constrains one entry in $\boldsymbol{y} \bmod N$ and thus effectively one indeterminate. So given $\mathcal{A}_1$'s query behavior, Dec derives the discrete logarithm of rank_{min} many indeterminates with a hint of only $\mathsf{rank}_{min}(\log n + \log Q)$ bits.

Last, we analyze the encoding size relative to the naive encoding of $\log \binom{|\mathcal{L}|}{N} + \log(N!)$ bits. Answering queries in general requires no more bits than the naive encoding: $\log \binom{|\mathcal{L}|}{N}$ bits for the image and roughly $\log N$ bits for every query. For every indeterminate recovered from the system of equations, the hint is only $\log n + \log Q$ bits which is smaller than $\log(N/2)$ for λ large enough. Thus, the total encoding size is

$$\underbrace{\log \binom{|\mathcal{L}|}{N} + \log(N!) + \underbrace{M}_{|\mathsf{st}_0|}}_{\text{Cost of DLogs in general}} - \underbrace{\mathsf{rank}_{min} \cdot (\log N - 1 - \log n - \log Q)}_{\text{Savings due to DLogs from } A\boldsymbol{x}=\boldsymbol{b}}.$$

$\square$

Note that the savings in the claim's actual statement are lower since Enc has to handle colliding Σ queries which introduce additional overhead.

6   Multi-challenge Memory Complexity

We now consider the whole evaluation of TDSCRYPT, and we want to prove that it requires $\Omega(\frac{n^2}{\log n} \log N)$ memory almost always—no matter the evaluation strategy. This is formalized in the theorem below which is in the spirit of Alwen et al. [6, Thm. 1].

Theorem 1. Let $n \in \mathrm{poly}(\lambda)$ with $n \geq 8$ and let $\mathcal{A}$ be a deterministic parallel oracle machine that evaluates TDSCRYPT correctly with probability $\chi(\lambda)$ over the choice of the parameters and input W. Then, assuming that factoring is hard, in the GGM and ROM with probability at least $\chi(\lambda) - \epsilon(\lambda)$,

$$\mathsf{cc}_{mem}(\mathcal{A}^{\Sigma, \mathsf{h}}(\Sigma(1), \Sigma(w))) \in \Omega\left(\frac{n^2}{\log n} \log N\right)$$

where $\epsilon(\lambda) \in \mathrm{negl}(\lambda)$, and the probability is taken over $(N, \Sigma, \mathsf{h}, w) \xleftarrow{\$} \mathrm{params}(\lambda)$.

As stated before, our proof follows Alwen et al.'s [6] line of reasoning closely, that is, considering the single-challenge game and then generalizing it to the multi-challenge setting which roughly equals any actual evaluation. While our single-challenge trade-off proof differed considerably, the multi-challenge proof is almost identical. On a high level, the single-challenge trade-offs can simply be swapped out, and this only affects constants. Alwen et al. [6] took great care to state these explicitly. In contrast, we stick to asymptotics since our primary focus is showing that a TMHF exists.

TDSCRYPT **Definition** Recall the definition of TDSCRYPT. Given input $\Sigma(w)$, compute the powers $\Sigma(2^i w)$, $0 \leq i < n$. Then, define $S_0 = \mathsf{h}(\Sigma(2^n w), 0^\ell)$ and, for $1 < i \leq n$, $S_i = \mathsf{h}(\Sigma(2^{j_i} w), S_{i-1})$ where $j_i = S_{i-1} \bmod n$ is the *ith challenge*. For $k \in [n]$, we define s_k to be the round in which the kth challenge is issued, i.e., when the value S_{k-1} is the result of a query.

High-Level Proof Strategy. On a high-level, the proof strategy is as follows. We modify Corollary 1 to work with a single adversary $\mathcal{A}$ that can be thought of as a (potentially dishonest) evaluation strategy for TDSCRYPT. For some $k \in [n]$, we split the execution of $\mathcal{A}$ into two parts, up to round s_k when the kth challenge $j_k = S_{k-1} \bmod n$ is issued and afterward. These parts map to $\mathcal{A}_0$ and $\mathcal{A}_1$ as in Corollary 1 where the explicit input j to $\mathcal{A}_1$ is replaced by slightly altering (i.e., programming) the random oracle such that $S_{k-1} \bmod n = j$ (but $\lfloor S_{k-1}/n \rfloor$ is unchanged) and the advice st_0 is now the input state st_{s_k}. So we get a time-memory trade-off in the style of Corollary 1 that intuitively states: For at least half of the n possible values j_k may take, either $\mathcal{A}$ needs a lot of rounds to answer the challenge, or all the input state st_r with $r \leq s_k$ have a size $\|\mathsf{st}_r\|$ that is increasing with r and reasonably large when r is closer to s_k. Then, we can argue that this trade-off must hold for roughly half of all n challenges by Hoeffding's inequality, and we can thus add the input state sizes $\|\mathsf{st}_r\|$ for all n challenges to get the desired memory complexity.

Proof Sketch. As a first step, we characterize parameter combinations that are not amenable to our proof strategy.

Definition 9 (Collisions). *For given N, Σ, and w, the set* $\mathsf{colliding}_k$ *contains all random oracles h that cause a collision amongst the preceding $\{S_0, \dots, S_{k-1}\}$ during the honest* $\mathsf{Eval}(\mathsf{pp}, \Sigma(w))$.

Definition 10 (Rounding Impossible). *For given N, Σ, and w, the set* $\mathsf{rounding}_k(n)$ *contains all random oracles h that are not amenable to programming some challenge $j \in [0, n)$. That is, there exists $0 \leq i \leq k$ such that $S_i > \lfloor 2^\ell/n \rfloor n - 1$.*

Intuitively, the above two definitions characterize random oracles where we cannot program $j_k = S_{k-1} \bmod n$ uniformly. Either the value is not independent of previously issued challenges due to collisions, or S_{k-1} might overflow for some choices of j_k. The next definition then tells us that any fixed adversary $\mathcal{A}$ almost always learns the values $(S_i)_{0 \leq i \leq n}$ in sequential order.

Definition 11 (Wrong Evaluation Order). *For given N, Σ, w, and $\mathcal{A}$, the set wrongOrder$_k$ contains all random oracles h where during the execution of $\mathcal{A}^{\Sigma,h}(\Sigma(w))$ a query to h of the form $(\cdot, S_j)$ occurs before one of the form $(\cdot, S_i)$ for $0 \leq i < j < k$.*

With the above definitions in place, we can now define the time-memory trade-off. Essentially, this is a modified version of the single-challenge game (cf. Definition 6) merged with the time-memory trade-off Lemma 1 (resp. Corollary 1).

Definition 12 (Hard Challenge). *Let $\lambda, n \in \mathbb{N}$ with $n \geq 8$, $k, j \in [0, n)$, $(N, \Sigma, h, w) \in \mathsf{params}(\lambda)$ with $h \notin \mathsf{colliding}_{k-1} \cup \mathsf{rounding}_{k-1}(n)$, and $\mathcal{A}$ a deterministic oracle machine making at most $Q \in \mathsf{poly}(\lambda)$ queries. Consider the execution $\mathcal{A}^{\Sigma,h}(\Sigma(1), \Sigma(w))$ up to round $s_k \in \mathbb{N}^+$, which is the earliest round where the query $(W^{2^{j_{k-1}}}, S_{k-2}) \in \mathbf{qrs}^h$ with $j_{k-1} = S_{k-2} \bmod n$ occurs (in the case $k = 1$, the query is $(W^{2^n}, 0^\ell)$). For any round r with $0 \leq r \leq s_k$, let $M_r = \|\mathsf{st}_r\|$, and associate a fixed value ρ_r to it similarly to Lemma 1.[13] It follows that*

$$\rho_r \in \Theta(M_r + \log n + \log Q + \log \lambda) / (\log(N) - \log Q - \log n).$$

Define $h' = h$ except for S_{k-1} which will be changed to S'_{k-1} with $\lfloor S'_{k-1}/n \rfloor = \lfloor S_{k-1}/n \rfloor$ but $S'_{k-1} \bmod n = j$, and consider the execution $\mathcal{A}^{\Sigma,h'}(\Sigma(1), \Sigma(x))$. Let $t_{k,j,r} \in \mathbb{N}^+$ be minimal such that the query $(W^{2^j}, S_{k-1}) \in \mathbf{qrs}^{h'}$ occurs after s_k in round $r + t_{k,j,r} > s_k$ where $t_{k,j,r} = \infty$ if it never does. Then, let

$$r_k = \underset{0 \leq r \leq s_k}{\arg\max} \left\{ \frac{n}{6\rho_r \log(n/2)} - (s_k - r) \right\},$$

and define

$$\mathsf{Hard}_{\mathcal{A}(w)}^{\Sigma,h,n}(k,j) = 1 \text{ if and only if } t_{k,j,r_k} > \frac{n}{6\rho_{r_k} \log(n/2)}.$$

We will re-use the notation introduced in these definitions and use it to state the modified single-challenge trade-off. Essentially, it says that most parameters do not fall into colliding, rounding or wrongOrder, and that the time-memory trade-off holds for them.

Lemma 5. *For every deterministic parallel oracle machine $\mathcal{A}$, there exist negligible functions $\epsilon(\lambda) \in \mathsf{negl}(\lambda)$ such that, for all $n \in \mathsf{poly}(\lambda)$ with $n \geq 8$, there exists a subset $\mathsf{good} \subseteq \mathsf{params}(\lambda)$ such that, for every $(N, \Sigma, h, w) \in \mathsf{good}$ and $k \in \mathbb{N}$ with $1 \leq k \leq n$, $|\mathsf{good}| \geq (1 - \epsilon(\lambda))|\mathsf{params}(\lambda)|$ and the following holds:*

---

[13] To be precise, $\rho = (M + \log n + 2\log Q + c\log \lambda + 1)/(\log(N) - 3(\log Q - \log n) - 3)$ where c is as in Lemma 1.

- $h \notin \mathsf{colliding}_{k-1}$;
- $h \notin \mathsf{rounding}_{k-1}(n)$;
- $h \notin \mathsf{wrongOrder}_{k-1}$; and
- $\Pr_{j \xleftarrow{\$} [0,n)} \left[\mathsf{Hard}_{\mathcal{A}(w)}^{\Sigma,h,n}(k,j) \right] \geq 1/2$.

Proof (Sketch). As in the proof of Lemma 1, towards contradiction, we assume that for some n and k, bad is large, i.e., $|\mathsf{bad}| \geq \lambda^{-c}|\,\mathsf{params}(\lambda)|$, and we consider four cases. We will show that every case leads to a contradiction.

- $h \in \mathsf{colliding}_{k-1}$: View N, Σ and w as fixed and count how many choices of h cause a collision. There are at most $k^2 \leq n^2$ possible colliding pairs S_i and S_j and, for every pair, a collision happens for at most a $2^{-\log N}$ fraction of random oracles as h's output length is at least $\log N$. So, at most an $n^2/2^{\log N}$ fraction of random oracles might cause a collision which is negligible and therefore contradicts the assumption that bad covers a polynomial fraction of params (cf. [6, Clm. 15]).
- $h \in \mathsf{rounding}_{k-1}$ and $h \in \mathsf{wrongOrder}_{k-1}$: Both analyses are analogous the previous case with the fraction of random oracles being in the order of $1/N$ as well (cf. [6, Clms. 16 & 18]).
- $\Pr_{j \xleftarrow{\$} [n]} \left[\mathsf{Hard}_{\mathcal{A}(w)}^{\Sigma,h,n}(k,j) \right] < 1/2$: This case follows the proof of Lemma 1 with some modifications. Instead of considering explicit preprocessing- and online algorithms $(\mathcal{A}_0, \mathcal{A}_1)$, we split the execution of $\mathcal{A}$ into two parts—up to round r (preprocessing) and everything afterward (online). In this setting, we cannot pass the challenge j to the online algorithm explicitly anymore. Instead, we will program the random oracle h to include the challenge implicitly, i.e., setting $S_{k-1} \bmod n = j$. Programming is always possible as long as $h \notin \mathsf{colliding}_{k-1} \cup \mathsf{rounding}_{k-1}(n)$, and we may assume that this is the case by the preceding case analyses. For Dec to know when to program h, $\log Q$ additional bits of hint are required to recognize the query $(W^{2^{j_k-1}}, S_{k-2})$ (cf. Definition 12). Apart from these modifications, the proof is identical to the one of Lemma 1.

This discussion completes the proof sketch.   □

We now use Lemma 5's trade-off to lower bound the sum $\sum_{r=1}^{s_n+1} \rho_r$ where we note that ρ_r is a quantity related to the size of the input state $\|\mathsf{st}_r\|$. Note that the sum covers all rounds up to round $s_n + 1$, i.e., the round in which $\mathcal{A}$ first computes S_n, the output of TDSCRYPT. This strategy is taken from [6, Sec. 5] so we refer interested readers there for more details.

Claim 6 (Lower Bound on $\sum \rho_r$). If $(N, \Sigma, h, w) \in \mathsf{good}$ and $\mathcal{A}^{\Sigma,h}(\Sigma(1), \Sigma(w))$ queries S_n, then $\sum_{r=1}^{s_n+1} \rho_r \in \Omega(n^2/\log n)$.

Proof (Sketch). First, note that if the parameters are in good, whenever $\mathcal{A}$ queries S_n, it must have received all $\{S_i\}_{0 \leq i \leq n}$ during its execution, and it must receive them in order. Second, if $\mathsf{Hard}_{\mathcal{A}(w)}^{\Sigma,h,n}(k,j) = 1$, then, for any $0 \leq r \leq s_k$,

$$t_{k,j,r} > \frac{n}{6\rho_r \log(n/2)} \tag{3}$$

by the choice of r_k (cf. [6, Clms. 5 & 10]). Third, by a generalization of Hoeffding's inequality (cf. [6, Clm. 7]), we argue that for any fixing of challenges, at least $n(1/2 - \epsilon)$ challenges are Hard where $\epsilon > 0$ (cf. [6, Clm. 19]).

Given the above, we apply [6, Clm. 8] to $\rho_r > \frac{n}{6t_{k,j,r}\log(n/2)}$, which is Eq. (3) rearranged. This gets us $\sum_{r=1}^{s_n+1} \rho_r \in \Omega(n^2/\log n)$ as desired (cf. [6, Clm. 11]).$\square$

Finally, we prove Theorem 1 by converting the quantity $\sum \rho_r$ to memory complexity.

Proof of Theorem 1 (Sketch). By Lemma 5, an overwhelming fraction of parameters is in good, and $\mathcal{A}$ queries S_n with probability $\chi(\lambda)$. Applying Claim 6, we get a lower bound of $\sum_{r=1}^{s_n+1} \rho_r \in \Omega(n^2/\log n)$. Since $M_r \in \Omega(\rho_r \log N)$ for all $r \in \mathbb{N}$ by definition, it follows that $\sum_{r=1}^{s_n+1} M_r \in \Omega(\frac{n^2}{\log n}\log N)$. Note that this sum is equivalent to the cc_{mem} of $\mathcal{A}$ which completes the proof sketch. $\square$

Acknowledgement. We thank the Eurocrypt reviewers for their thorough review and for pointing out related works. This research was funded in whole or in part by the Austrian Science Fund (FWF) 10.55776/F85.

References

1. Abusalah, H., Alwen, J., Cohen, B., Khilko, D., Pietrzak, K., Reyzin, L.: Beyond Hellman's time-memory trade-offs with applications to proofs of space. In: Takagi, T., Peyrin, T. (eds.) ASIACRYPT 2017. LNCS, vol. 10625, pp. 357–379. Springer, Cham (2017). https://doi.org/10.1007/978-3-319-70697-9_13

2. Alwen, J., Blocki, J., Harsha, B.: Practical graphs for optimal side-channel resistant memory-hard functions. In: Thuraisingham, B.M., Evans, D., Malkin, T., Xu, D. (eds.) ACM CCS 2017, pp. 1001–1017. ACM Press (2017). https://doi.org/10.1145/3133956.3134031

3. Alwen, J., Blocki, J., Pietrzak, K.: Depth-robust graphs and their cumulative memory complexity. In: Coron, J.-S., Nielsen, J.B. (eds.) EUROCRYPT 2017. LNCS, vol. 10212, pp. 3–32. Springer, Cham (2017). https://doi.org/10.1007/978-3-319-56617-7_1

4. Alwen, J., Blocki, J., Pietrzak, K.: Sustained space complexity. In: Nielsen, J.B., Rijmen, V. (eds.) EUROCRYPT 2018. LNCS, vol. 10821, pp. 99–130. Springer, Cham (2018). https://doi.org/10.1007/978-3-319-78375-8_4

5. Alwen, J., Chen, B., Kamath, C., Kolmogorov, V., Pietrzak, K., Tessaro, S.: On the complexity of scrypt and proofs of space in the parallel random oracle model. In: Fischlin, M., Coron, J.-S. (eds.) EUROCRYPT 2016. LNCS, vol. 9666, pp. 358–387. Springer, Heidelberg (2016). https://doi.org/10.1007/978-3-662-49896-5_13

6. Alwen, J., Chen, B., Pietrzak, K., Reyzin, L., Tessaro, S.: Scrypt is maximally memory-hard. In: Coron, J.-S., Nielsen, J.B. (eds.) EUROCRYPT 2017. LNCS, vol. 10212, pp. 33–62. Springer, Cham (2017). https://doi.org/10.1007/978-3-319-56617-7_2

7. Alwen, J., Serbinenko, V.: High parallel complexity graphs and memory-hard functions. In: Servedio, R.A., Rubinfeld, R. (eds.) 47th ACM STOC, pp. 595–603. ACM Press (2015). https://doi.org/10.1145/2746539.2746622

8. Ameri, M.H., Block, A.R., Blocki, J.: Memory-hard puzzles in the standard model with applications to memory-hard functions and resource-bounded locally decodable codes. In: Galdi, C., Jarecki, S. (eds.) Security and Cryptography for Networks, pp. 45–68. Springer, Cham (2022). https://doi.org/10.1007/978-3-031-14791-3_3
9. Ameri, M.H., Blocki, J., Zhou, S.: Computationally data-independent memory hard functions. In: Vidick, T. (ed.) ITCS 2020. vol. 151, pp. 36:1–36:28. LIPIcs (2020). https://doi.org/10.4230/LIPIcs.ITCS.2020.36
10. Auerbach, B., Günther, C.U., Pietrzak, K.: Trapdoor memory-hard functions. Cryptology ePrint Archive, Paper 2024/312 (2024). https://eprint.iacr.org/2024/312
11. Biryukov, A., Dinu, D., Khovratovich, D.: Argon2: new generation of memory-hard functions for password hashing and other applications. In: 2016 IEEE European Symposium on Security and Privacy (EuroS&P), pp. 292–302 (2016). https://doi.org/10.1109/EuroSP.2016.31
12. Biryukov, A., Lombard-Platet, M.: Pured: a unified framework for resource-hard functions. Cryptology ePrint Archive, Paper 2023/1809 (2023). https://eprint.iacr.org/2023/1809
13. Biryukov, A., Perrin, L.: Symmetrically and asymmetrically hard cryptography. In: Takagi, T., Peyrin, T. (eds.) ASIACRYPT 2017. LNCS, vol. 10626, pp. 417–445. Springer, Cham (2017). https://doi.org/10.1007/978-3-319-70700-6_15
14. Blocki, J., Harsha, B., Kang, S., Lee, S., Xing, L., Zhou, S.: Data-independent memory hard functions: new attacks and stronger constructions. In: Boldyreva, A., Micciancio, D. (eds.) CRYPTO 2019. LNCS, vol. 11693, pp. 573–607. Springer, Cham (2019). https://doi.org/10.1007/978-3-030-26951-7_20
15. Blocki, J., Holman, B.: Sustained space and cumulative complexity trade-offs for data-dependent memory-hard functions. In: Dodis, Y., Shrimpton, T. (eds.) CRYPTO 2022, Part III. LNCS, vol. 13509, pp. 222–251. Springer, Heidelberg (2022). https://doi.org/10.1007/978-3-031-15982-4_8
16. Blocki, J., Ren, L., Zhou, S.: Bandwidth-hard functions: reductions and lower bounds. In: Lie, D., Mannan, M., Backes, M., Wang, X. (eds.) ACM CCS 2018, pp. 1820–1836. ACM Press (2018). https://doi.org/10.1145/3243734.3243773
17. Boneh, D., Corrigan-Gibbs, H., Schechter, S.: Balloon hashing: a memory-hard function providing provable protection against sequential attacks. In: Cheon, J.H., Takagi, T. (eds.) ASIACRYPT 2016. LNCS, vol. 10031, pp. 220–248. Springer, Heidelberg (2016). https://doi.org/10.1007/978-3-662-53887-6_8
18. Corrigan-Gibbs, H., Kogan, D.: The discrete-logarithm problem with preprocessing. In: Nielsen, J.B., Rijmen, V. (eds.) EUROCRYPT 2018. LNCS, vol. 10821, pp. 415–447. Springer, Cham (2018). https://doi.org/10.1007/978-3-319-78375-8_14
19. Costa, S., Dalai, M., Della Fiore, S.: Variations on the Erdős distinct-sums problem. Discrete Appl. Math. **325**, 172–185 (2021). https://doi.org/10.1016/j.dam.2022.10.015, https://www.sciencedirect.com/science/article/pii/S0166218X22004103
20. De, A., Trevisan, L., Tulsiani, M.: Time space tradeoffs for attacks against one-way functions and PRGs. In: Rabin, T. (ed.) CRYPTO 2010. LNCS, vol. 6223, pp. 649–665. Springer, Heidelberg (2010). https://doi.org/10.1007/978-3-642-14623-7_35
21. Dwork, C., Naor, M.: Pricing via processing or combatting junk mail. In: Brickell, E.F. (ed.) CRYPTO 1992. LNCS, vol. 740, pp. 139–147. Springer, Heidelberg (1993). https://doi.org/10.1007/3-540-48071-4_10
22. von zur Gathen, J., Shparlinski, I.E.: Generating safe primes. J. Math. Cryptol. **7**(4), 333–365 (2013). https://doi.org/10.1515/jmc-2013-5011

23. Guy, R.K.: Unsolved Problems in Number Theory. Problem Books in Mathematics. Springer, New York, NY, 2 edn. (1994). https://doi.org/10.1007/978-1-4899-3585-4

24. Hermite, C.: Sur l'introduction des variables continues dans la théorie des nombres, Cambridge Library Collection - Mathematics, vol. 1, pp. 164–192. Cambridge University Press (2009). https://doi.org/10.1017/CBO9780511702754.015

25. Kaliski, B.: Pkcs# 5: Password-based cryptography specification version 2.0. Request for Comments 2898, Internet Engineering Task Force (September 2000). https://www.rfc-editor.org/rfc/rfc2898.html

26. Katz, J., Lindell, Y.: Introduction to Modern Cryptography, 2nd edn. Chapman & Hall/CRC (2014)

27. Katz, J., Loss, J., Xu, J.: On the security of time-lock puzzles and timed commitments. In: Pass, R., Pietrzak, K. (eds.) TCC 2020. LNCS, vol. 12552, pp. 390–413. Springer, Cham (2020). https://doi.org/10.1007/978-3-030-64381-2_14

28. Lazebnik, F.: On systems of linear diophantine equations. Math. Mag. **69**(4), 261–266 (1996). https://doi.org/10.2307/2690528, http://www.jstor.org/stable/2690528

29. Micciancio, D., Warinschi, B.: A linear space algorithm for computing the hermite normal form. In: Proceedings of the 2001 International Symposium on Symbolic and Algebraic Computation, pp. 231–236. ISSAC 2001. Association for Computing Machinery, New York (2001). https://doi.org/10.1145/384101.384133

30. Percival, C.: Stronger key derivation via sequential memory-hard functions. In: BSDCan 2009 (2009)

31. Ren, L., Devadas, S.: Proof of space from stacked expanders. In: Hirt, M., Smith, A. (eds.) TCC 2016. LNCS, vol. 9985, pp. 262–285. Springer, Heidelberg (2016). https://doi.org/10.1007/978-3-662-53641-4_11

32. Ren, L., Devadas, S.: Bandwidth hard functions for ASIC resistance. In: Kalai, Y., Reyzin, L. (eds.) TCC 2017. LNCS, vol. 10677, pp. 466–492. Springer, Cham (2017). https://doi.org/10.1007/978-3-319-70500-2_16

33. Rivest, R.L., Shamir, A., Wagner, D.A.: Time-lock puzzles and timed-release crypto. Tech. rep, USA (1996)

34. Rotem, L.: Revisiting the uber assumption in the algebraic group model: Fine-grained bounds in hidden-order groups and improved reductions in bilinear groups. In: Dachman-Soled, D. (ed.) 3rd Conference on Information-Theoretic Cryptography (ITC 2022). Leibniz International Proceedings in Informatics (LIPIcs), vol. 230, pp. 13:1–13:13. Schloss Dagstuhl – Leibniz-Zentrum für Informatik, Dagstuhl, Germany (2022). https://doi.org/10.4230/LIPIcs.ITC.2022.13, https://drops.dagstuhl.de/opus/volltexte/2022/16491

35. Rotem, L., Segev, G.: Generically speeding-up repeated squaring is equivalent to factoring: sharp thresholds for all generic-ring delay functions. In: Micciancio, D., Ristenpart, T. (eds.) CRYPTO 2020. LNCS, vol. 12172, pp. 481–509. Springer, Cham (2020). https://doi.org/10.1007/978-3-030-56877-1_17

36. Shoup, V.: Lower bounds for discrete logarithms and related problems. In: Fumy, W. (ed.) EUROCRYPT 1997. LNCS, vol. 1233, pp. 256–266. Springer, Heidelberg (1997). https://doi.org/10.1007/3-540-69053-0_18

37. Yao, A.C.C.: Coherent functions and program checkers (extended abstract). In: 22nd ACM STOC, pp. 84–94. ACM Press (1990). https://doi.org/10.1145/100216.100226

Probabilistically Checkable Arguments
for All NP

Shany Ben-David[✉]

Department of Computer Science, Bar-Ilan University, Petah Tikva, Israel
shany.ben-david@biu.ac.il

Abstract. A probabilistically checkable argument (PCA) is a computational relaxation of PCPs, where soundness is guaranteed to hold only for false proofs generated by a computationally bounded adversary. The advantage of PCAs is that they are able to overcome the limitations of PCPs. A *succinct* PCA has a proof length that is polynomial in the witness length (and is independent of the non-deterministic verification time), which is impossible for PCPs, under standard complexity assumptions. Bronfman and Rothblum (ITCS 2022) constructed succinct PCAs for NC that are publicly-verifiable and have constant query complexity under the sub-exponential hardness of LWE.

We construct a publicly-verifiable succinct PCA with constant query complexity for all NP in the adaptive security setting. Our PCA scheme offers several improvements compared to the Bronfman and Rothblum construction: (1) it applies to all problems in NP, (2) it achieves adaptive security, and (3) it can be realized under any of the following assumptions: the *polynomial* hardness of LWE; $O(1)$-LIN; or sub-exponential DDH.

Moreover, our PCA scheme has a *succinct prover*, which means that for any NP relation that can be verified in time T and space S, the proof can be generated in time $O_{\lambda,m}(T \cdot \text{polylog}(T))$ and space $O_{\lambda,m}(S \cdot \text{polylog}(T))$. Here, $O_{\lambda,m}$ accounts for polynomial factors in the security parameter and in the size of the witness. En route, we construct a new *complexity-preserving* RAM Delegation scheme that is used in our PCA construction and may be of independent interest.

Keywords: succinct probabilistically checkable argument · PCA

1 Introduction

Probabilistically Checkable Proofs (PCPs) play a significant role in complexity theory and cryptography, leading to groundbreaking results in various fields. This is evidenced by the remarkable PCP theorem which is one of the most important results in theoretical computer science. The PCP theorem states that the satisfiability of a formula of size n can be proved in poly(n) time and can be verified by querying only a constant number of bits from the proof.

Sponsored in part by the Israel Science Foundation (Grant No. 2302/22), and by the BIU Center for Research in Applied Cryptography and Cyber Security in conjunction with the Israel National Cyber Bureau in the Prime Minister's Office.

M. Joye and G. Leander (Eds.): EUROCRYPT 2024, LNCS 14653, pp. 345–374, 2024.
https://doi.org/10.1007/978-3-031-58734-4_12

While PCPs are a very powerful tool, they have several limitations. For example, Fortnow and Santhanam [10] showed that PCPs cannot be *succinct* unless the polynomial hierarchy collapses. A PCP proof is succinct if, for a formula of size n with witness length m, the proof length is $\text{poly}(m)$, rather than $\text{poly}(n, m)$. Beyond showing a limit to the efficiency of PCPs, this fact has broader implications. Harnik and Naor [11] raised the *instance compression* (IC) question, in which we ask if it is possible to take any instance in any NP relation and compress it to a short instance while preserving the information of whether the instance is in the language or not. The main focus of this question is instances of size n with a witness of size m, where the instance is much larger than the witness, i.e., $m \ll n$. A line of work [4,9–11] shows different use cases for instance compression, including constructing a variety of fundamental cryptographic primitives. Unfortunately, Fortnow and Santhanam showed that instance compression also implies succinct PCPs, which means that instance compression does not exist (unless the polynomial hierarchy collapses).

Probabilistically Checkable Arguments (PCA). The notion of PCA was introduced as a *computational* analog of PCPs [5,15,19]. That is, soundness is required to hold only against *computationally bounded* adversaries. This allows PCAs to bypass information-theoretic barriers that limit PCP constructions.

In more detail, PCAs rely on a (honestly generated) common reference string (CRS) which is given to both the prover and the verifier. The key parameters of interest in a PCA scheme include the size of the proof, the verifier's query complexity and randomness complexity, and the prover's running time. Unlike typical cryptographic primitives, PCAs aim for *constant* soundness error against polynomially bounded adversaries. This is inherent since PCAs additionally aim for *constant* query complexity (independent of the security parameter). Note that the soundness error is defined over the randomness of generating the CRS, the adversary, and the verifier.

Succinct PCAs. A PCA for an NP relation $\mathcal{R}$ with verification time $t = t(n, m)$ is said to be *succinct* if the PCA proof is of length $\text{poly}(\lambda, m, \log t)$, where n is the instance size, m is the witness size, and λ is the security parameter. Importantly, poly refers to a fixed universal polynomial (that does not depend on the relation $\mathcal{R}$).

Previous Work on PCAs. Kalai and Raz [15] constructed a *privately-verifiable* PCA. In the privately-verifiable setting, the verifier must hold a trapdoor to the common reference string in order to verify the proof. Their PCA construction relies on exponential hardness assumptions for PIR schemes, providing *non-adaptive* soundness, ensuring security for instances that are chosen independently of the common reference string. Their construction gives $\text{poly}(d, m)$ proof size and polylog(n) query complexity for languages that can be verified with circuits of size n and depth d, using witness of size m.

Later on, Bronfman and Rothblum [5] were the first to construct a *publicly-verifiable succinct* PCA with constant query complexity, also with *non-adaptive* soundness. Their results were a big step forward. However, they have two significant drawbacks. First, their PCA construction applies only to relations in NC rather than to the entire NP class. Second, their PCA construction is under the sub-exponential hardness assumption of the learning with error (LWE) problem.

Our PCA. We construct a publicly-verifiable succinct PCA with constant query complexity in the *adaptive* security setting for *all* NP. Compared to the Bronfman and Rothblum construction, our PCA scheme exhibits improvements in several aspects: (1) it applies to all problems in NP, (2) it achieves adaptive security, (3) it can be realized under any of the following assumptions: the polynomial hardness of LWE; $O(1)$-LIN; or sub-exponential Decisional Diffie-Hellman (DDH), and (4) an efficient prover, which we denote as a *succinct prover*.

PCA with a Succinct Prover. We say that a PCA scheme has a *succinct prover* if, for any NP relation $\mathcal{R}$ that can be verified in time $t = \mathrm{poly}(n, m)$ and space $s = \mathrm{poly}(n, m)$, the PCA prover (given the instance and the witness) generates the proof in time $t \cdot \mathrm{poly}(\lambda, m, \log t)$ and space $s \cdot \mathrm{poly}(\lambda, m, \log t)$. Here, poly refers to a fixed universal polynomial (that does not depend on the relation $\mathcal{R}$).[1]

Theorem 1 (Informal). *Every* NP *relation has a publicly-verifiable succinct* PCA *with constant query complexity under any one of the following assumptions: (1)* polynomial *hardness of* LWE*; (2)* $O(1)$-LIN*; or (3) sub-exponential Decisional Diffie-Hellman (*DDH*).*

Moreover, the PCA *protocol is adaptively sound and has a succinct prover.*

In fact, our PCA construction (along with the argument presented in Theorem 2) relies on two general components, non-interactive batch argument for NP and a rate-1 OT.[2] Both components can be constructed under any of the assumptions mentioned in the theorem, which enables us to obtain our results.

Computational Instance Compression (CIC). An instance compression (IC) is a very strong and useful tool. Unfortunately, it cannot be constructed under standard assumptions. Bronfman and Rothblum [5] solved this problem by introducing *computational instance compression* or CIC, which is the cryptographic

---

[1] Recall that a succinct PCA has proof size $\mathrm{poly}(\lambda, m, \log t)$. In our construction, the prover's time and space has a multiplicative factor in that proof size. It remains open to achieve an additive factor, i.e., $O(t) + \mathrm{poly}(\lambda, m, \log t)$ running time and $O(s) + \mathrm{poly}(\lambda, m, \log t)$ space.

[2] Both components are formally defined in [13].

equivalent for instance compression (IC). For a false statement, the new instance computed by the scheme might be in the language, but it is computationally infeasible to find a witness for the new instance. Bronfman and Rothblum show that PCA implies CIC. Their CIC is for the class NC and can be realized under the sub-exponential hardness assumption of the learning with error (LWE) problem. We combine their CIC construction with Theorem 1 and immediately get CIC for *all* NP, under the same hardness assumptions as for our PCA.

Theorem 2 (Informal). *Every* NP *relation has a* CIC *scheme under any one of the following assumptions: (1)* polynomial *hardness of* LWE; *(2)* $O(1)$-LIN; *or (3)* sub-exponential Decisional Diffie-Hellman *(*DDH*).*

Our main building block in our PCA construction (which in turn, leads to our results in Theorem 1 and Theorem 2) is a RAM Delegation scheme. However, existing RAM Delegation schemes in the literature do not meet our specific requirements. This leads us to construct a new RAM Delegation scheme.[3]

RAM Delegation. Efficient verification of computation is a fundamental notion in computer science both in theory and, recently, has been deployed in practice in cloud services and block-chains. This usage makes verification of computation schemes highly motivated in theory and practice.

In this paper, the computation we wish to delegate is described as a RAM machine. In a RAM Delegation scheme, a verifier wishes to evaluate the output of a RAM machine M on an input x without investing the computational resources required for the computation. Instead, the verifier delegates the computation to an untrusted prover, which generates the output of the computation $y = M(x)$ together with a proof Π that supports the correctness of the computation (given a suitable common reference string crs). We would like to minimize the computation time for both the prover and the verifier. The prover should run in time proportional to the original computation (polynomial or even linear in the actual computation). Ideally, the verifier running time should be sub-linear (or even poly-logarithmic) in the input size. In order to facilitate sub-linear computation time, the verifier is given a digest $d = \mathsf{Digest}(\mathsf{crs}, x)$ of its input rather than the input itself.

Previous Work on RAM Delegation. Our focus is on publicly-verifiable RAM Delegation schemes that are constructed based on falsifiable and standard assumptions. There has been significant research trying to construct such delegation schemes: [14,18] constructions achieve $\text{poly}(\lambda, t^\epsilon)$ verification time for any constant $\epsilon > 0$ under either the standard decisional assumptions on groups with bilinear maps or the $O(1)$-LIN assumption in prime-order groups. In contrast, [8] achieves $\text{poly}(\lambda, \log t)$ verification time from LWE.

---

[3] The discussion regarding the RAM Delegation scheme necessary for our PCA construction can be found in Sect. 2.2.

Kalai, Lombardi, Vaikuntanathan, and Wichs [13] construct the first RAM Delegation scheme under any of the following assumptions: (1) LWE; (2) $O(1)$-LIN; or (3) sub-exponential Decisional Diffie-Hellman (DDH). Their scheme has verification time $\mathrm{poly}(\lambda, \log t)$. They prove their results using a novel transformation from any non-trivial batch argument to a highly efficient, strongly sound RAM Delegation scheme. Roughly, they begin with a non-trivial batch argument (BARG) and boost it into a highly efficient one. Then they transform the efficient BARG into an efficient RAM Delegation scheme. The [13] construction has another interesting property, which is *strong soundness*. Note that their construction focuses on *read-only* RAM machines (where the machine's memory cannot be modified).

Our RAM Delegation Scheme. We construct publicly-verifiable RAM Delegation scheme for *read-write* RAM machines and $\mathrm{poly}(\lambda, \log t)$ verification time. Our RAM Delegation is also *complexity-preserving*, a property left unexplored in previous work. That is, for any RAM machine that runs in time T and space S, the honest RAM Delegation prover generates the proof in time that has quasi-linear dependence in T and space that has linear dependence in S and poly-logarithmic dependence in T. Our construction uses falsifiable assumptions (as mentioned in Theorem 1), while providing the *strong soundness* guarantee (as defined in [13]).[4]

Theorem 3 (Informal). *Under any of the assumptions mentioned in Theorem 1, there exists a publicly-verifiable* RAM Delegation *scheme with* strong soundness *for any* read-write RAM *machine. Moreover, the verifier running time is* $\mathrm{poly}(\lambda, \log t)$, *while the prover runs in time* $\tilde{O}_\lambda(t+n)$ *and uses* $\tilde{O}_\lambda(w \cdot \mathrm{polylog}(t) + n)$ *space.*

Here, $t = t(n)$ *is the running time of the* RAM *machine, and* $w = w(n)$ *is the number of distinct memory locations written by the machine.*

Here, the $\tilde{O}_\lambda$ notation accounts for polynomial factors in the security parameter and in the size of the local state of the machine. Note that similar to Theorem 1, our RAM Delegation construction actually relies on two general components, a non-interactive batch argument for NP and a rate-1 OT. Both of which can be realized under any of the assumptions mentioned in Theorem 1. For the formal theorem statement, please refer to the full version.

Observe that w may be much smaller than both the running time and the total read-write memory of the RAM machine. On close inspection of the construction of [13], their prover runs in time at least $\tilde{O}_\lambda(t^2 + n)$ and space $\tilde{O}_\lambda(t + n)$. In comparison, the prover of Theorem 3, when applied to read-only RAM machines, has running time $\tilde{O}_\lambda(t + n)$ and uses $\tilde{O}_\lambda(\mathrm{polylog}(t) + n)$ space.

---

[4] Both the standard soundness and strong soundness notions are sufficient for obtaining our results. However, the strong soundness guarantee may be useful for other applications.

Future Work on Efficient RAM Delegation Prover. Our current research on RAM delegation schemes has yielded an efficient prover, where the running time has a quasi-linear dependency on the running time of the original RAM computation, and the space has a quasi-linear linear dependency on the space of the original RAM computation. Achieving linear dependency on the original computation complexity remains an open question.

Future Work on PCAs. In [5], Bronfman and Rothblum introduced the implications of PCAs on the hardness of approximation. They demonstrated that if P $\neq$ NP and there exists a publicly verifiable constant-query PCA for SAT, then there exists $\epsilon > 0$ for which there is no polynomial-time algorithm solving approximate MaxSATϵ[5]. The hardness of MaxSATϵ is expected, as it follows from the PCP theorem. The interesting aspect is that we can get this result using the notion of PCAs. We believe that our new results on *succinct* PCAs for NP can be useful in achieving new hardness of approximation results.

One potential direction suggested by Bronfman and Rothblum is the hardness of approximation in Fine-Grained complexity. Previously, PCPs were used to demonstrate the hardness of approximation in the Fine-Grained complexity of problems in P [1,6], where a significant barrier to achieving the result was the size of the PCP proofs. We believe that the use of *succinct* PCAs (instead of PCPs) may have new implications in this field.

2   Our Techniques

In this section, we begin by introducing our techniques for constructing a PCA scheme. Initially, the prover in the PCA construction is not succinct. Once we achieve our PCA results, we'll describe how to refine our implementation to ensure a succinct prover.

To elaborate further, the primary tool for our PCA construction is RAM Delegation scheme. We start by presenting a generic PCA construction from RAM Delegation scheme (Sect. 2.1). This construction leads us to obtain a PCA protocol for all NP that is (1) succinct and (2) has constant query complexity. The construction relies on the assumption that there exists a succinct RAM Delegation scheme for all deterministic *read-write* RAM machines, where here, succinct means that the proof size and verification time are poly-logarithmic in the original computation. It is important to note that, at this stage, the resulting PCA protocol does not have a succinct prover.

In Sect. 2.2, we describe how to construct the required succinct RAM Delegation scheme for any deterministic *read-write* RAM machines. The RAM Delegation scheme is also publicly verifiable and adaptively sound, which implies

---

[5] In the MaxSAT problem, the goal is to find an assignment that maximizes the number of satisfied clauses in a formula. In the approximate MaxSAT$_\epsilon$ problem, the goal is to find an assignment that is ϵ close to maximizing the number of satisfied clauses in a formula.

the same properties for our PCA scheme. The RAM Delegation scheme, and accordingly, the PCA scheme can be realized under any of the following assumptions: (1) *polynomial* hardness of LWE, (2) $O(1)$-LIN, or (3) sub-exponential Decisional Diffie-Hellman (DDH).

Subsequently, in Sect. 2.3, we delve into the implementation details of the same RAM Delegation protocol introduced in Sect. 2.2, with a specific emphasis on achieving a complexity-preserving prover. Integrating this RAM Delegation protocol into our PCA construction naturally leads us to obtain a PCA with a succinct prover.

2.1 Adaptive PCA for All NP

The primary objective of this subsection is to provide an overview of our PCA construction. Here, our focus is on constructing a PCA protocol for all NP that is (1) succinct and (2) has constant query complexity. Recall that a succinct PCA has a proof size that is polynomial in the witness size, and constant query complexity indicates that the verifier makes a constant number of queries to the proof. Note that here, the resulting PCA prover is not succinct.

While achieving either succinctness or constant query complexity separately might be relatively straightforward, the challenge arises when we aim to achieve both properties simultaneously. In what follows, we begin with an overview of this challenge. Then, we describe the Bronfman and Rothblum [5] construction, which successfully addresses this challenge and results in a PCA protocol for any problem in NC. Finally, we describe our PCA construction that achieves both properties simultaneously and provides a PCA protocol for any relation in NP.

An Attempt to Balance Succinctness and Constant Query Complexity. Succinctness alone can be achieved by simply sending the entire witness to the verifier. The difficulty arises when we aim to combine this with constant query complexity. A standard approach would be to encode the witness using an error-correcting code and add a probabilistically checkable proof of proximity (PCPP) certifying that the NP verifier would have accepted had it read the entire witness. In such construction, for any instance $x \in \{0,1\}^n$ and witness $w \in \{0,1\}^m$, the proof is: $\pi = (\mathsf{Enc}(w), \Pi_{\mathsf{PCPP}})$.

This PCA construction has constant query complexity, but the proof size is $\mathrm{poly}(n,m)$, while our goal is to have the proof size sub-linear in n. This large proof size follows from the fact that known PCPPs have a proof length that depends polynomially on the running time of the computation that the PCPP certifies (as described in [3]). In our case, the computation being certified is the NP verifier, whose running time is at least linear in n.

This issue can be resolved by replacing the NP verifier with an alternative verifier that has a significantly smaller running time. In our case, as well as in the previous construction by Bronfman and Rothblum, the new verifier will run in time $\mathrm{poly}(\log n, m)$.

The Bronfman and Rothblum PCA. Bronfman and Rothblum [5] constructed the first publicly verifiable succinct PCA. Their construction uses the idea described above of replacing the NP verifier with a more efficient one. In order to replace the NP verifier, [5] used SNARGs for P (PSNARGs). PSNARG schemes are powerful tools that allow us to verify a long deterministic computation in time that is sub-linear in the computation. Essentially, they apply a PSNARG to the NP verifier's computation, thus reducing the verification time. The resulting PCPP proof is $\pi = (\text{Enc}(w \parallel \Pi_{\text{PSNARG}}), \Pi_{\text{PCPP}})$.

Unfortunately, this is not enough. The PSNARG verifier needs to at least read its input, which in our case is of size $n + m$ (the NP verifier, when thought of as a P computation, takes as input $x' = (x, w)$). The PCPP proof size in this construction is again $\text{poly}(n, m)$. To solve this problem, [5] used a specific type of PSNARG called a *holographic* PSNARG. In a holographic PSNARG the verifier is given oracle access to an (honestly generated) encoding of the input (rather than input explicitly). This enables the verifier to run in sub-linear time in the input size.

This still does not suffice, since PCPPs are not designed for computations involving an oracle. To cope with this issue, they added a pre-processing phase that hashes the encoding of the input. For this final phase to work, they need a PSNARG with even more specific requirements. For example, the prover needs to know which are the input locations that the verifier is going to query. These requirements limit [5] to using a very specific PSNARG construction due to [12]. The use of this PSNARG limits their PCA to work only for NC computations, and under sub-exponential LWE.

We take a different approach to lowering the verifier running time. Rather than working with PSNARGs, we use a RAM Delegation scheme. This enables us to get around the limitations of Bronfman and Rothblum's PCA.

RAM Delegation. Before delving into the details of our PCA construction, we introduce the concept of a RAM Delegation scheme. It is worth noting that RAM Delegation schemes can have different definitions in the literature. For our construction, we adopt the notion introduced in [13] and extend it to apply to *read-write* RAM machines.

In more detail, we consider read-write RAM computations where the machine is given its input in *read-only* memory and has access to a large *read-write* memory initially filled with zeros. It can access both memory modules at an arbitrary location with unit cost. To allow for later flexibility, we think of the input to the RAM machine as a pair $x = (x^{\text{imp}}, x^{\text{exp}})$, where we call x^{imp} the implicit input (which we think of as large), and x^{exp} the explicit input (which we think of as small).

In a RAM Delegation scheme, the prover wants to convince the verifier that $M(x) = y$ for some RAM machine M, input x, and output y. In the completeness experiment, the prover is given as input a common reference string crs and an input $x = (x^{\text{imp}}, x^{\text{exp}})$. The prover generates a proof Π and sends it to the verifier. The verifier is given as input the crs, a digest of the implicit input $d \leftarrow$

Digest(crs, x^{imp}), the explicit input x^{exp}, and an output y. The verifier outputs accept or reject. The soundness guarantee implies that it is computationally hard to generate $(M, x = (x^{\text{imp}}, x^{\text{exp}}), \pi, y)$ such that $M(x) \neq y$, and yet the verifier accepts the proof with respect to d ← Digest(crs, x^{imp}).

For the efficiency parameters, we want the proof size and the verification time to be sub-linear in the size of the (large) implicit input x^{imp} and sub-linear in the running time t of the original RAM computation. To capture this notation, we define a RAM Delegation scheme as *succinct* if both the proof size and verification time are at most poly($\lambda, |x^{\text{exp}}|, \log |x^{\text{imp}}|, \log t$).

PCA from RAM Delegation. We turn back to constructing PCAs. Recall that our starting point is a proof of the following structure: $\pi = (\text{Enc}(w), \Pi_{\text{PCPP}})$, where Enc(w) is an encoding of the witness, and Π_{PCPP} is a PCPP proof certifying that the NP verifier would have accepted had it read the entire witness w. Our goal is to replace the NP verifier with a more efficient computation. For this purpose, we will use a *succinct* RAM Delegation scheme, in which the verifier runs in poly-logarithmic time in the input size (given a digest of the input).

Fix a relation $\mathcal{R}$ in NP, and a RAM machine M that verifies the relation. Given an instance x and a witness w, consider a RAM Delegation scheme certifying that $M(x^{\text{imp}}, x^{\text{exp}}) = 1$, where $x^{\text{imp}} = x$ is the NP instance, and $x^{\text{exp}} = w$ is the NP witness. Observe that the running time of the succinct RAM Delegation verifier is poly($\lambda, m, \log n$) given the digest of x, where m refers to the witness size and n refers to the instance size.

We can now describe our PCA construction:

- Prover:
  1. Compute the following
     1.1 Π_{RAM}, the RAM Delegation proof certifying $M(x, w) = 1$.
     1.2 d, the digest of the input x.
     1.3 Π_{PCPP}, the PCPP proof certifying that after decoding Enc(w $\|$ Π_{RAM}) the RAM Delegation verifier accepts given (d, w, Π_{RAM}).
  2. Output $\Pi = (\text{Enc}(w \mid \Pi_{\text{RAM}}), \Pi_{\text{PCPP}})$.
- Verifier:
  1. Compute d, the digest of the input x.
  2. Check that the PCPP verifier accepts.

This construction achieves constant query complexity directly by the PCPP scheme. To establish succinctness, we need to bound the size of the proof, where $\Pi = (\text{Enc}(w \| \Pi_{\text{RAM}}), \Pi_{\text{PCPP}})$. By the running time vt = poly($\lambda, m, \log n$) of the RAM Delegation verifier, we get that $|\Pi_{\text{RAM}}| \leq$ poly($\lambda, m, \log n$). Recall that a PCPP proof is of size polynomial in the original computation. In our case, this is the computation of the RAM Delegation verifier. Therefore, $|\Pi| \leq$ poly(vt) + poly($\lambda, m, \log n$) $\leq$ poly($\lambda, m, \log n$). Overall, we get that the construction achieves both succinctness and constant query complexity.

Regarding the publicly verifiable and adaptively sound properties of the PCA scheme, these properties naturally follow when the RAM Delegation scheme is publicly verifiable and adaptively sound.

We now turn to construct our RAM Delegation scheme.

2.2 RAM Delegation

In this subsection, we outline the construction of the succinct RAM Delegation scheme essential for our PCA construction discussed in Sect. 2.1. By incorporating the resulting RAM Delegation scheme into our PCA construction, we achieve publicly verifiable succinct PCA with constant query complexity in the adaptive security setting under various standard assumptions. However, it is important to note that this PCA *prover* is not yet succinct. We will address the succinctness of the prover in Sect. 2.3 by constructing complexity-preserving RAM Delegation . The RAM Delegation notion we use in our PCA construction is the notion presented in [13]. This notion differentiates itself from standard RAM Delegation by splitting the input into explicit and implicit components, where the explicit input is considered small and the implicit input is considered large. The verifier receives the explicit input in the clear and obtains only the digest of the implicit input. This distinction is reflected in the soundness definition, which we inherently use for proving security for our PCA construction. However, the RAM Delegation construction presented in [13] is not sufficient for our PCA construction as it specifically applies to read-only RAM machines.

There are two immediate potential approaches for achieving construction for read-write RAM machines under the required notion. We could modify existing constructions that apply to read-write RAM machines [8,14,18] to support explicit and implicit input. This can be achieved relatively easily. However, as we will see in Sect. 2.3, updating the RAM Delegation construction from [13] to apply to any read-write RAM machines allows us to leverage the specific structure of the prover in that construction to achieve a complexity-preserving prover. Ultimately, this leads to the desired succinct prover for our PCA scheme.

Moreover, extending the construction in [14] maintains a stronger soundness security notion than achieved in previous RAM Delegation constructions.[6] Additionally, it provides a RAM Delegation scheme for any read-write RAM machine assuming two generic components. That is, a batch argument scheme and rate-1 OT (as formally defined in [13]). These components can, in turn, be constructed from either one of the following assumptions: (1) polynomial hardness of LWE; (2) $O(1)$-LIN; or (3) sub-exponential Decisional Diffie-Hellman (DDH), and achieve our PCA construction under those assumptions.

In what follows we describe the techniques we used for constructing our RAM Delegation scheme. The main tool that we use is a somewhere extractable batch argument (BARG) scheme.

---

[6] Our construction maintains the same *strong soundness* guarantee as defined in [13]. The weaker notion is sufficient for our construction. See Definition 6 for the formal definition of both security notions.

Somewhere Extractable Batch Arguments (seBARGs). In a batch argument scheme (BARG), the goal is to efficiently verify a batch of k NP statements. The prover is given a batch of k NP statements $x_1, \ldots, x_k$ along with their corresponding witnesses $w_1, \ldots, w_k$, and sends a short proof to the verifier. We want the proof size and verification time to be significantly smaller than the total size of the witnesses. Specifically, the main interest is to have a sub-linear (or ideally, poly-logarithmic) dependence in the number of statements.

Our construction actually uses a stronger primitive called somewhere extractable batch argument (seBARG). A BARG is said to be somewhere extractable if, for some (hidden) pre-choice of i, given a trapdoor to the crs and an accepting proof, it is possible to extract a witness w_i for the i-th NP statement.

We upgrade any BARG to be seBARG using *somewhere extractable hash with local opening* (SEH). An SEH family is a family of hash functions with local openings where, given a hashed value and a suitable trapdoor for the i-th bit (generated during the SEH setup), one can efficiently extract the i-th bit of the hashed input. Upgrading BARG to be seBARG using SEH can be done by first committing to all the witnesses using the SEH, and then modifying the NP statements to include consistency with the hashed value. In our construction, we replace BARG with seBARG without loss of generality since we also use SEH explicitly (as previously done implicitly in [8,16], and explicitly in [13]).

Our RAM Delegation Scheme. Our RAM Delegation construction extends the Kalai, Lombardi, Vaikuntanathan, and Wichs [13] construction which, in turn, is inspired by the transformations of [8,16]. To prove that $M(x) = y$ using a BARG scheme, [13] employs a step-by-step approach, dividing the computation into smaller steps. The *read-only* RAM machine M starts with an initial state st_0. At each step $i \in [t]$, it reads one bit from the input x at some location j_i and transitions from state st_i to state st_{i+1}. The BARG proof should certify that each computation step is performed correctly.

In more detail, for computing the proof, the prover in [13] first computes the digest of the input $d \leftarrow \mathsf{Digest}(x)$ (using a hash family with local openings) and a somewhere extractable hash $\mathsf{com_{st}} \leftarrow \mathsf{SEH.Hash}(st_1, \ldots, st_t)$. Then, the prover constructs a seBARG proof for the following batch NP statement: For each $i \in [t]$, (1) the values (st_{i-1}, st_i) are consistent with $\mathsf{com_{st}}$, (2) the bit $x[j_i]$ is consistent with d, (3) the machine transformation $st_{i-1} \rightarrow st_i$ consist with the bit $x[j_i]$, (4) if $i = t$ then check that st_t is an accepting state. The witness w_i includes the values $(st_{i-1}, st_i, x[j_i])$ along with local opening certifying the consistency of the values with their digest.

Moving forward to constructing *read-write* RAM Delegation, in addition to the input and the intermediate states, to describe one computation step of a *read-write* RAM machine, we need more information. The *read-write* machine M starts with an initial state st_0 and an all-zero memory D_0. Then, at each step, the machine reads one bit from the input, reads one bit from the memory, and writes one bit to the memory. The state of the machine is then transformed from $(\mathsf{st}_{i-1}, D_{i-1})$ to (st_i, D_i).

One possible strategy is to reconsider the definition of the machine's state to include both the local state and the memory: $\mathsf{st}'_i = (\mathsf{st}_1, D_i)$. Then we can use the same algorithm in [13]. The witness, w_i, is now the values $(\mathsf{st}'_{i-1}, \mathsf{st}'_i, x[j_i])$ along with local opening certifying the consistency of the values with their digest. However, incorporating the memory into the state definition introduces a challenge in terms of proof size. The size of the state includes the description of the entire memory, which can be arbitrarily large (even exceeding the computation time t). Consequently, the size of one witness, and accordingly the resulting seBARG proof, may become too large (larger than the computation itself).

We combine techniques from [8,14] to overcome this obstacle and gain succinctness again. Instead of directly computing $\mathsf{com}_{\mathsf{st}} \leftarrow \mathsf{SEH.Hash}(\mathsf{st}'_1, \ldots, \mathsf{st}'_t)$, we introduce an intermediate step. First, we compute the Merkle roots $\mathsf{rt}_0, \ldots, \mathsf{rt}_t$ of the memory states $D_0, \ldots, D_t$. These Merkle roots serve as compact representations of the entire memory throughout the computation. Next, we compute $\mathsf{com} \leftarrow \mathsf{SEH.Hash}((\mathsf{st}_1, \mathsf{rt}_1), \ldots, (\mathsf{st}_t, \mathsf{rt}_t))$. Our batch NP statement is now: For each $i \in [t]$, (1) the values $((\mathsf{st}_{i-1}, \mathsf{rt}_{i-1}), (\mathsf{st}_i, \mathsf{rt}_i))$ are consistent with com, (2) the bit $x[j_i]$ is consistent with d, (3) the bit $D_{i-1}[k]$ is consistent with rt_{i-1}, (4) assuming the bit $x[j_i], D_{i-1}[k]$ has been read, the machine transformation is $(\mathsf{st}_{i-1}, \mathsf{rt}_{i-1}) \rightarrow (\mathsf{st}_i, \mathsf{rt}_i)$, and (5) if $i = t$ then check that st_t is an accepting state. The witness w_i includes the values $((\mathsf{st}_{i-1}, \mathsf{rt}_{i-1}), (\mathsf{st}_i, \mathsf{rt}_i), x[j_i])$ along with local opening certifying the consistency of the values with their digest, and the proof that the transformation $\mathsf{rt}_{i-1} \rightarrow \mathsf{rt}_i$ is correct.

Our RAM Delegation construction is then:

- Prover:
  1. Compute the following:
     1.1 d, the digest of the input.
     1.2 $(\mathsf{st}_0, D_0), \ldots, (\mathsf{st}_t, D_t)$, the states of the machine through the computation.
     1.3 $\mathsf{rt}_0, \ldots, \mathsf{rt}_t$, the Merkle roots of the values $D_0, \ldots, D_t$.
     1.4 com, the SEH of $((\mathsf{st}_1, \mathsf{rt}_1), \ldots, (\mathsf{st}_t, \mathsf{rt}_t))$, along with correlated openings to each one of the values.
     1.5 $\mathsf{w}_1, \ldots, \mathsf{w}_t$, the witnesses for the NP statements.
     1.6 Π, the seBARG proof for the NP statements (using $\mathsf{w}_1, \ldots, \mathsf{w}_t$).
  2. Output (Π, com).
- Verifier:
  1. Given the digest d, check that the BARG proof accepts (relative to the hashed value com).

Our analysis is based on the analysis in [13]. However, in our case, we need to pay special attention to the proof of each computation step, verifying efficiently that the transformation $((\mathsf{st}_{i-1}, \mathsf{rt}_{i-1}) \rightarrow (\mathsf{st}_i, \mathsf{rt}_i))$ is done correctly.[7]

---

[7] The formal and full analysis appears in the full version of this work.

Note that the space complexity of the prover is at least $\tilde{O}_\lambda(t + S + n)$ since the prover simulates the RAM machine that uses space of size S, and it holds a list of t elements in the memory. Moreover, the running time of the prover is at least $\tilde{O}_\lambda(t^2 + t \cdot S + n)$ since it computes the hash of the memory at each step (which takes time $t \cdot S$), and in step 1.4 it computes the t openings to com (which takes t time for each opening). In the following subsection, we improve the time and space complexity of the prover.

2.3   Complexity-Preserving RAM Delegation

Up to this point, we constructed a publicly verifiable succinct PCA with constant query complexity for all NP in the adaptive security setting. However, the PCA prover is not yet succinct. The running time of our PCA prover (described in Sect. 2.2) is dominated by the running time of the RAM Delegation prover. Ultimately, improving the running time of the RAM Delegation prover to be complexity-preserving results in a PCA scheme with a succinct prover.[8]

This subsection presents an efficient implementation of the RAM Delegation prover introduced in Sect. 2.2, that achieves complexity-preserving RAM Delegation scheme.

The implementation of the prover presented in Sect. 2.2 demonstrates a time complexity of $\tilde{O}_\lambda(t^2 + t \cdot S + n)$, and space complexity of at least $\tilde{O}_\lambda(t + S + n)$, where S denotes the size of the *large* read-write memory used by the machine. Here, $\tilde{O}_\lambda$ notation accounts for polynomial factors in the security parameter and in the size of the machine's local state. For simplicity, in what follows, we will focus on a specific inefficient part of the prover's computation and see how to improve both the running time and space complexity. By applying the same approach to other parts of the computation, we can achieve time complexity $\tilde{O}_\lambda(t + n)$ and a space complexity $\tilde{O}_\lambda(w \cdot \mathrm{polylog}(t) + n)$, where w is the number of *distinct* memory locations written by the RAM machine.

For this high-level overview, we are specifically targeting a simplified version of the prover, with a focus on enhancing selected steps. These steps include the computation of:

1. $(\mathsf{st}_1, \ldots, \mathsf{st}_t)$ - the machine's states list through the process.
2. $(\mathsf{com}, \rho_1, \ldots, \rho_t)$ - a commitment to the machine's states list and the corresponding openings.
3. $(\mathsf{w}_1, \ldots, \mathsf{w}_t)$ - the witnesses to the NP statement.
4. (Π) - the BARG proof for the NP statements generating given $(\mathsf{w}_1, \ldots, \mathsf{w}_t)$.

Note that the underlying structure of the commitment scheme in our construction is essentially a Merkle tree. Hence, in the subsequent discussion, we will refer to the commitment mentioned in step 2 as a Merkle root, and the openings as the authentication paths within this tree.

We divided the description of our improved implementation into three phases. The starting point is the naive implementation as described above that achieves

---

[8] See Sect. 4 for the running time analysis.

$\tilde{O}_\lambda(t^2 + t \cdot S + n)$ running time and $\tilde{O}_\lambda(t + S + n)$ space. Then, in each phase, we incrementally improve these parameters as follows:

- In phase one, we achieve $\tilde{O}_\lambda(t^2 + t \cdot w + n)$ running time and $\tilde{O}_\lambda(t + w + n)$ space.
- In phase two, we achieve $\tilde{O}_\lambda(t \cdot w + n)$ running time and $\tilde{O}_\lambda(w \cdot \mathrm{polylog}(t) + n)$ space.
- In phase three, we achieve $\tilde{O}_\lambda(t + n)$ running time and $\tilde{O}_\lambda(w \cdot \mathrm{polylog}(t) + n)$ space.

Phase one: Our first step towards complexity-preserving is to reduce the large read-write space factor and achieve $\tilde{O}_\lambda(t^2 + t \cdot w + n)$ running time and $\tilde{O}_\lambda(t + w + n)$ space.

For generating the RAM proof, the prover is required to at least simulate the RAM computation. It is important to note that even though the machine might have access to a large read-write memory, it might only write to a small number of locations. In other words, the memory might be sparse. In our construction, we take advantage of this property by emulating the machine's read-write memory using a *sparse hash tree* scheme.

Sparse Hash Tree. A *sparse hash tree* scheme is a data structure that represents a Merkle tree, particularly suited for sparse Merkle trees, meaning that most of the leaf nodes are empty. The sparsity of the tree enables efficient simulation of the tree, with time complexity proportional to the tree's depth and the number of non-empty elements, rather than being proportional to the entire tree's size. Specifically, we construct a sparse hash tree where each operation takes time and space that is linear in the number of non-zero elements.

The RAM machine starts with all zero memory and writes to at most w distinct locations in the memory, which allows us to emulate the read-write memory of size S with $\tilde{O}_\lambda(w)$ space. This naturally results in a time complexity of $\tilde{O}_\lambda(t^2 + t \cdot w + n)$ and a space complexity of $\tilde{O}_\lambda(t + w + n)$.

Phase two: In what follows, we reduce the running time to $\tilde{O}_\lambda(t \cdot w + n)$ and space to $\tilde{O}_\lambda(w \cdot \mathrm{polylog}(t) + n)$. For that purpose, the focus of this phase is to maintain a running time that is quasi-linear in t, and simultaneously, avoid storing t elements in the memory.

Initially, our RAM Delegation prover stores the entire computation history $(\mathsf{st}_1, \ldots, \mathsf{st}_t)$ in memory, leading to a memory overhead of $\tilde{O}_\lambda(t)$. Instead, we construct a stream of the following data: $(\mathsf{st}_1, \ldots, \mathsf{st}_t)$. However, simply creating a stream of states is not sufficient, as we need to access this information multiple times for various computations.[9] Same challenges also apply for the list of openings $(\rho_1, \ldots, \rho_t)$ and for the list of witnesses $(\mathsf{w}_1, \ldots, \mathsf{w}_t)$. To address this issue, we introduce the new notion of *rewindable stream*.

---

[9] Note that naively traversing the entire stream from the beginning for each access to st_i would result in an overhead of at least $\tilde{O}_\lambda(t^2)$ running time.

Rewindable Stream. A *stream* is a sequence of elements that are accessed incrementally over time. In our context, we introduce the concept of a *rewindable stream*, which refers to the ability to return to a specific point in the stream and continue generating the stream from that point onward. In more detail, a rewindable stream allows a client to efficiently create a backup of the stream's state at any time and later restore the stream's state to that specific time point.

In what follows, we describe how to (1) construct rewindable stream of states $(\mathsf{st}_1, \ldots, \mathsf{st}_t)$, (2) compute the commitment com to the state's list based on the stream of states, (3) compute a rewindable stream of openings $(\rho_1, \ldots, \rho_t)$ using the stream of states, and (4) generate the BARG proof in step 4 based on a stream of witnesses (which is essentially the stream of openings).

Rewindable Stream of States. The computation of a RAM machine progresses in a step-by-step manner. Given a configuration of the machine, which includes its state and the contents of its read-write memory, the next configuration can be computed efficiently. Leveraging this structure, we can design a rewindable stream where the states of the stream correspond to an intermediate configuration of the RAM machine. For the backup operation, we simply copy the entire intermediate configuration of the RAM machine. This process can be implemented using $\tilde{O}_\lambda(w)$ time and space, as we use a sparse hash tree to emulate the machine's memory.

In what follows we explain how to compute the commitment com to the state's list based on the stream of states. Recall that we refer to the commitment in step 2 as a Merkle root, and the openings are the authentication paths in the Merkle tree. This brings us to the broader challenge of efficiently computing a Merkle root when provided with rewindable stream access to the data.

Computing the Commitment com. Our task is to efficiently compute Merkle root given a rewindable stream access to the data. It is well-known that computing a Merkle root can be done in quasi-linear time while storing only a logarithmic number of elements in memory (as proved in [17]). A careful look at the algorithm will show that this can be done using a single pass over the data, allowing us to use the stream of states to implement step 2 while storing only $\log t$ elements in the memory, and in time $\tilde{O}_\lambda(t \cdot \log t)$.

We have explained how to efficiently compute the commitment com, and reduce the space complexity required for this operation. Now, we will describe how to efficiently construct a rewindable stream of openings. Both steps together ensure the time and space efficiency of step 2.

Rewindable Stream of Openings. Recall that each opening to com is essentially an authentication path in a Merkle tree. An authentication path can be computed in a quasi-linear time while storing only a logarithmic number of elements in memory (as proved in [17]). We can use the algorithm to generate a stream of t

authentication paths while storing only $\log t$ elements in the memory. However, each authentication path is computed in time $\tilde{O}_\lambda(t \cdot \log t \cdot w)$, which concludes with an overall running time of $\tilde{O}_\lambda(t^2 \cdot \log t \cdot w)$ for computing all the authentication paths.

Our next challenge is to reduce the running time of the stream. Instead of generating each authentication path auth_{i+1} from scratch, our algorithm leverages the information in the previous authentication path auth_i. An authentication path represents the path from a leaf to the root and consists of the sibling's values encountered along the way. By exploiting the concept of the *lowest common ancestor*, we observe that the leaves $(i, i+1)$ share the same path from the lowest common ancestor to the root and, therefore, also share the same siblings from the lowest common ancestor to the root. Consequently, for the lowest common ancestor of height h, these two authentication paths have $(\log t - h)$ identical values. With this insight, we can split the computation of Next into two steps. The first step will take the relevant data from the previous authentication path auth_i, and the second step will compute the authentication path within the subtree of height h. By utilizing the *rewind* property of the stream, which allows us to start from a specific point in the stream, the second step will take $\tilde{O}_\lambda(2^h \cdot h \cdot w)$ time rather than $\tilde{O}_\lambda(t \cdot \log^2 t \cdot w)$.

This approach achieves a running time of $\tilde{O}_\lambda(t \cdot \log^2 t \cdot w)$ for one pass over the entire stream. In other words, in the amortized case, the running time is $\tilde{O}_\lambda(\log^2 t \cdot w)$.[10]

To efficiently compute the list of witnesses (step 3), we construct a rewindable stream of witnesses that contain the machine's states and the corresponding openings to com by simply wrapping the rewindable streams we constructed. The following step computes the BARG proof efficiently using only rewindable stream access to the witnesses, thereby avoiding the need for explicit access to the witness list.

Computing the BARG Proof. For this step, we need to construct an efficient BARG with stream rewind access to the witnesses. For t instances, the BARG prover will run in time $\tilde{O}(t \cdot |\mathsf{w}| + t) \cdot \mathrm{poly}(\lambda)$, and use space of size $\tilde{O}(|\mathsf{w}| \cdot \mathrm{polylog}(t) + t) \cdot \mathrm{poly}(\lambda)$. Moreover, the prover will access each element in the stream at most $\mathrm{polylog}(t)$ times. Note that the bounded access to the stream will allow us to start with a stream that is efficient only in the amortized case, and yet conclude with $\tilde{O}(t \cdot |\mathsf{w}| + t) \cdot \mathrm{poly}(\lambda)$ time complexity.

We use the BARG scheme constructed in [13], but we suggest an alternative implementation for the prover. The implementation will use the same techniques as described above for the RAM Delegation efficient prover (for the formal construction and analysis, please refer to the full version).

---

[10] More detailed analysis of the algorithm's efficiency appears in the full version of this work.

Overall, we reduced the t^2 overhead in the running time and t space overhead. This leads us to $\tilde{O}_\lambda(t \cdot w + t + n)$ running time and $\tilde{O}_\lambda(w \cdot \text{polylog}(t) + n)$ space complexity.

Phase three : As a final step toward complexity-preserving, in this phase, we achieve $\tilde{O}_\lambda(t + n)$ running time and $\tilde{O}_\lambda(w \cdot \text{polylog}(t) + n)$ space.

To achieve this, we implement the rewindable stream of states in a way that each operation in the stream, including backup, restore, and advancing to the next element, only takes $\tilde{O}_\lambda(\text{polylog}(t))$ time, rather than $\tilde{O}_\lambda(w \cdot \text{polylog}(t))$. By following a similar analysis as in Phase 2, but with the improved stream running time, we attain the necessary complexity parameters for the prover.

The challenge arises in the stream backup operation that requires copying the entire memory of the RAM machine. Here, instead of copying the entire memory, we use a data structure that represents the RAM memory and allows for efficient backup operation.

Memory Scheme. A _memory scheme_ is a data structure that represents a memory of a deterministic program, allowing for reading, writing, backing up, and restoration of the memory.

We construct a memory scheme, where each operation, including backups, takes time that is poly-logarithmic in the size of the original memory. This construction allows us to implement the rewindable stream of states efficiently, and consecutively, to achieve our desirable complexity parameters.

3   Preliminaries

Notations. We denote the set of all positive integers up to n as $[n] := \{1, ..., n\}$. For any two string $x, y \in \Sigma^*$ over alphabet Σ, we denote $(a \mathbin{\|} b)$ to be the concatenation of the two strings. The relative distance between strings $x, y \in \Sigma^\ell$ over alphabet Σ is $\Delta(x, y) := \frac{|\{i \mid x_i \neq y_i\}|}{\ell}$. The relative distance between $x \in \Sigma^\ell$ and a non-empty set $S \subseteq \Sigma^\ell$ is $\Delta(x, S) := \min_{y \in S}(\Delta(x, y))$.

3.1   Probabilistically Checkable Proofs

A probabilistically checkable proof (PCP) is a special format for writing a proof that can be verified by reading only a few bits. The following definition is taken from [5].

Definition 1 (PCP). _A probabilistically checkable proof (PCP) for language_ $L \in$ NTIME(t) _consists of a_ poly(t) _prover_ PCP.P, _that gets as input the instance_ x _as well as a witness_ w, _and a_ poly$(|\mathrm{x}|, \log t)$ _time oracle machine_ PCP.V, _that recieves_ x _as input as well as an oracle to a proof string_ π.

Completness. _For every_ $(\mathrm{x}, \mathrm{w}) \in \mathcal{R}$ _it holds that:_

$$\Pr\left[\, \mathsf{PCP.V}^\pi(\mathrm{x}) = 1 \;\mid\; \pi \leftarrow \mathsf{PCP.P}(\mathrm{x}, \mathrm{w}) \,\right] = 1.$$

Soundness. *For every* $\mathrm{x} \notin L$, *and for every oracle* $\tilde{\pi}$ *it holds that*

$$\Pr\left[\mathsf{PCP.V}^{\tilde{\pi}}(\mathrm{x}) = 1\right] < \frac{1}{2}$$

The length of π *as a function of* $|\mathrm{x}|$ *and* $|\mathrm{w}|$ *is called the proof length. In order to verify its oracle, the verifier* $\mathsf{PCP.V}$ *tosses* $\mathsf{r} = \mathsf{r}(|\mathrm{x}|)$ *random coins, and makes* $\mathsf{q} = \mathsf{q}(|\mathrm{x}|)$ *queries to* π. *The functions* r *and* q *are called the randomness complexity and query complexity, respectively.*

Theorem 4 ([2]). *Every* $L \in \mathrm{NP}$ *has a* PCP *with constant query complexity and logarithmic randomness complexity.*

Succinct PCP*s.* A PCP for $L \in \mathrm{NP}$ is said to be succinct [10,15] if there exists a polynomial p (which may depend on L), such that for every $(\mathrm{x}, \mathrm{w}) \in \mathcal{R}$ it holds that $|\pi| = \mathsf{p}(|\mathrm{w}|, \log(|\mathrm{x}|))$, for $\pi = \mathsf{PCP.P}(\mathrm{x}, \mathrm{w})$.

3.2   Probabilistically Checkable Proofs of Proximity

In what follows, we define probabilistically checkable proofs of proximity (PCPP). The definition is taken from [5].

PCPPs, much like PCPs, allows the verifier to read only a small number of bits from the proof. However, the key distinction between PCPs and PCPPs is that a PCPP verifier also reads only a small number of bits from its *input*, and is therefore, only required to reject inputs that are far from its language. In what follows, we define PCPP for pair languages.

Pair Languages. A language L is said to be a pair language if $L \subseteq \{0,1\}^* \times \{0,1\}^*$. Given instance x, the projection of L on x is the set $L(\mathrm{x}) = \{y \mid (\mathrm{x}, y) \in L\}$.

Definition 2 (PCPP). *A probabilistically checkable proof of proximity (PCPP) for a pair language* $L \in \mathrm{DTIME}(t)$ *consists of a* $\mathrm{poly}(t)$ *prover* $\mathsf{PCPP.P}$, *that gets as input the pair* (x, y) *and a* $\mathrm{poly}(|\mathrm{x}|, \log t)$ *time oracle machine* $\mathsf{PCPP.V}$, *that recieves* x *as an explicit input, oracle access to implicit input* y, *and oracle access to a proof string* π. *The verifier also recieves (explicitly) a proximity parameter* $\delta > 0$. *For proximity parameter* $\delta \in [0,1]$ *and input* (x, y) *the following holds:*

Completness. *For every* $(\mathrm{x}, y) \in L$ *it holds that*

$$\Pr\left[\mathsf{PCPP.V}^{y,\pi}(\mathrm{x}, |y|, |\pi|, \delta) = 1 \mid \pi \leftarrow \mathsf{PCPP.P}(\mathrm{x}, y)\right] = 1.$$

Soundness. *For every* $\Delta(y, L(\mathrm{x})) \geq \delta$, *and for every oracle* $\tilde{\pi}$ *it holds that*

$$\Pr\left[\mathsf{PCPP.V}^{y,\tilde{\pi}}(\mathrm{x}, |y|, |\pi|, \delta) = 1\right] < \frac{1}{2}$$

The length of π as a function of $|\mathrm{x}|$ and $|y|$ is called the proof length. In order to verify its oracles, the verifier PCPP.V *tosses* $\mathrm{r} = \mathrm{r}(|\mathrm{x}|, |y|, \delta)$ *random coins, and makes* $\mathrm{q} = \mathrm{q}(|\mathrm{x}|, |y|, \delta)$ *queries to* y *and* π. *The functions* r *and* q *are called the randomness complexity and query complexity, respectively.*

Theorem 5 ([3]). *Let L be a pair language, with instances (x, y), computable in time $t = t(|\mathrm{x}|, |y|)$, and let $\delta \in [0,1]$. There exists a* PCPP *for L with respect to proximity parameter δ, with query complexity $O(1/\delta)$, randomness complexity $O(\log \frac{t}{\delta})$, and proof length* $\mathrm{poly}(t)$. *The verifier runs in time* $\mathrm{polylog}(t, \frac{1}{\delta})$ *and the prover runs in time* $\mathrm{poly}(t)$.

3.3 Probabilistically Checkable Arguments

In what follows, we define probabilistically checkable argument (PCA). The definition is taken from [5].

Much like a PCPs, PCAs are a special format in which the verifier only has to read a few bits from the proof. Unlike PCPs, in which any proof for a false statement is rejected with high probability, for PCAs, accepting proofs may exist, but we require that it is computationally hard to find them.

Definition 3 (Publicly-Verifiable PCA.). *A publicly-verifiable probabilistically checkable argument (PCA) for an* NP *relation $\mathcal{R}$ is a triplet of* $\mathrm{poly}(n, m, \lambda)$-*time algorithms* (PCA.G, PCA.P, PCA.V), *with deterministic* PCA.P *and probabilistic* PCA.G *and* PCA.V, *such that for every instance length n and witness length m the following holds:*

Completness. *For every* $\mathrm{x} \in \{0,1\}^n$ *and* $\mathrm{w} \in \{0,1\}^m$, *such that $(\mathrm{x}, \mathrm{w}) \in \mathcal{R}$, every $\lambda \in \mathbb{N}$, and every* $\mathrm{crs} \leftarrow$ PCA.G$(1^n, 1^m, 1^\lambda)$ *it holds that:*

$$\Pr\left[\mathrm{PCA.V}^\pi(\mathrm{crs}, \mathrm{x}) = 1 \mid \pi \leftarrow \mathrm{PCA.P}(\mathrm{crs}, \mathrm{x}, \mathrm{w}) \right] = 1.$$

Computational Adaptive Soundness. *For every $\lambda \in \mathbb{N}$, and poly-size adversary $\tilde{\mathrm{P}}$, with all but* $\mathrm{negl}(\lambda)$ *probability over the choice of* $\mathrm{crs} \leftarrow$ PCA.G$(1^n, 1^m, 1^\lambda)$ *it holds that:*

$$\Pr\left[\begin{matrix} \mathrm{PCA.V}^{\tilde{\pi}}(\mathrm{crs}, \mathrm{x}) = 1 \\ \mathcal{R}(\mathrm{x}) = \emptyset \end{matrix} \,\middle|\, (\mathrm{x}, \tilde{\pi}) \leftarrow \tilde{\mathrm{P}}(\mathrm{crs}) \right] < \frac{1}{2}.$$

The length of π, as a function of n, m, and λ is called the proof length. In order to verify its oracle, the verifier PCA.V *tosses* $\mathrm{r} = \mathrm{r}(n, m, \lambda)$ *random coins, and makes* $\mathrm{q} = \mathrm{q}(n, m, \lambda)$ *queries to π. The functions r and q are called the randomness complexity and query complexity, respectively.*

Note that in Definition 3 we distinguish between the randomness used for generating the crs and the randomness of the verifier. This separation allows us to define the crs as "good" with overwhelming probability while the verifier only guarantees constant soundness (since the verifier only makes a small number of queries).

Succinct PCA*s.* A PCA for an NP relation $\mathcal{R}$, which is decidable in some time $t = t(n,m) \geq n$, is said to be succinct if the PCA proof is of length $\text{poly}(m, \lambda, \log t)$, where poly refers to a fixed universal polynomial (that does not depend on the relation $\mathcal{R}$).

PCA with a Succinct Prover. We say that a PCA scheme has a *succinct prover* if for any NP relation $\mathcal{R}$ that can be verified in time $t = \text{poly}(n,m)$ and space $s = \text{poly}(n,m)$, the PCA prover (given the instance and the witness) generates the proof in time $t \cdot \text{poly}(\lambda, m, \log t)$ and space $s \cdot \text{poly}(\lambda, m, \log t)$. Here, poly refers to a fixed universal polynomial (that does not depend on the relation $\mathcal{R}$).

3.4 Batch Arguments

In what follows, we define batch argument (BARG) scheme for BatchCSAT. The definition is taken from [13].

Let CSAT be the following language:

$$\text{CSAT} = \{(C, \mathbf{x}) \mid \exists \mathbf{w} \in \{0,1\}^m \text{ s.t. } C(\mathbf{x}, \mathbf{w}) = 1\}$$

where $C : \{0,1\}^n \times \{0,1\}^m \to \{0,1\}$ is a Boolean circuit and $\mathbf{x} \in \{0,1\}^n$ is an instance.

Let BatchCSAT be the following language:

$$\text{BatchCSAT} = \{C \mid \exists \mathbf{w}_1, \dots, \mathbf{w}_k \in \{0,1\}^m \text{ s.t. } \forall i \in [k], \ C(i, \mathbf{w}_i) = 1\}$$

Definition 4 (BARG for BatchCSAT). *A non-interactive batch argument for the index language* BARG $=$ (BARG.G, BARG.P, BARG.V) *has the following syntax:*

BARG.G$(1^\lambda, k, s, i^*) \to (\text{crs}, \text{td})$. *This is a randomized algorithm that takes as input a security parameter 1^λ, a number of instances k, a circuit size 1^s, and an index $i^* \in [k]$. It outputs a common reference string* crs, *and a trapdoor* td.

BARG.P$(\text{crs}, C, \mathbf{w}_1, \dots, \mathbf{w}_k) \to \pi$. *This is a deterministic poly-time algorithm that takes as input a common reference string* crs, *a circuit $C : \{0,1\}^n \times \{0,1\}^m \to \{0,1\}$ and a witnesses $\mathbf{w}_1, \dots, \mathbf{w}_k \in \{0,1\}^m$. It outputs a proof π.*

BARG.V$(\text{crs}, C, \pi) \to \{0,1\}$. *This is a deterministic poly-time algorithm that takes as input a circuit $C : \{0,1\}^n \times \{0,1\}^m \to \{0,1\}$, and a proof π. It outputs an acceptance bit.*

An $\mathcal{L}(\cdot, \cdot)$-succinct BARG *protocol for the relation $\mathcal{R}$ satisfies the following requirements:*

$\mathcal{L}$-**Succinct.** *The running time of* BARG.G *is at most $\mathcal{L}(k, \lambda) \cdot \text{poly}(s)$, and the length of the* crs *and the proof π is at most $\mathcal{L}(k, \lambda) \cdot \text{poly}(s)$.*

$\mathcal{L}$-**Verifier Efficiency.** *The running time of* BARG.V *is at most $\mathcal{L}(k, \lambda) \cdot \text{poly}(s)$.*

Prover Efficiency. *The running time of* BARG.P *is polynomial in its input.*

Completeness. *For every* $k = k(\lambda), m = m(\lambda), s = s(\lambda)$ *of size at most* 2^λ, *witnesses* $w_1, \ldots, w_k \in \{0,1\}^m$, *and circuit* $C \in \{0,1\}^s$ *such that* $\forall i \in [k]$ $C(i, w_i) = 1$, *and for every index* $i^* \in [k]$, *there exists a negligible function* μ *such that for any* $\lambda \in \mathbb{N}$:

$$\Pr\left[\text{BARG.V}(\text{crs}, C, \pi) = 1 \,\middle|\, \begin{array}{l} (\text{crs}, \text{td}) \leftarrow \text{BARG.G}(1^\lambda, s, k, m, i^*) \\ \pi \leftarrow \text{BARG.P}(\text{crs}, C, (w_1, \ldots, w_k)) \end{array} \right] = 1 - \mu(\lambda).$$

Indistiguishability. *For every poly-size adversary A, and any polynomials* $k = k(\lambda), m = m(\lambda), s = s(\lambda)$, *there exists a function* μ *such that for every* $\lambda \in \mathbb{N}$ *and two indexes* $i_1, i_2 \in [k]$:

$$\left| \begin{array}{l} \Pr\left[A(\text{crs}) = 1 \mid (\text{crs}, \cdot) \leftarrow \text{BARG.G}(1^\lambda, s, k, m, i_1) \right] \\ - \Pr\left[A(\text{crs}) = 1 \mid (\text{crs}, \cdot) \leftarrow \text{BARG.G}(1^\lambda, s, k, m, i_2) \right] \end{array} \right| \leq \mu(\lambda).$$

Semi-adaptive Soundness. *For every poly-size adversary A, and any polynomials* $k = k(\lambda), m = m(\lambda), s = s(\lambda)$, *there exists a function* μ *such that for every* $\lambda \in \mathbb{N}$ *and index* $i^* \in [k]$:

$$\Pr\left[\begin{array}{l} \text{BARG.V}(\text{crs}, C, \pi) = 1 \\ (C, i^*) \notin \text{CSAT} \end{array} \,\middle|\, \begin{array}{l} (\text{crs}, \text{td}) \leftarrow \text{BARG.G}(1^\lambda, s, k, m, i^*) \\ (C, \pi) \leftarrow A(\text{crs}) \end{array} \right] \leq \mu(\lambda).$$

Definition 5 (seBARG for BatchCSAT). *A somewhere extractable non-interactive batch argument for the index language* seBARG = (BARG.G, BARG.P, BARG.V, BARG.E) *is a BARG with the following augmented syntax:*

BARG.E(td, C, π) → w^*. *This is a deterministic poly-time algorithm that takes as input a trapdoor key* td, *a circuit* $C : \{0,1\}^n \times \{0,1\}^m \rightarrow \{0,1\}$, *and a proof* π. *It outputs a witness* $w \in \{0,1\}^m$.

An $\mathcal{L}(\cdot, \cdot)$-*succinct* seBARG *protocol for the relation* $\mathcal{R}$ *satisfies the following additional requirements to that of an* $\mathcal{L}(\cdot, \cdot)$-*succinct* BARG

Somewhere Argument of Knowledge. *For every poly-size adversary A, and any polynomials* $k = k(\lambda), m = m(\lambda), s = s(\lambda)$, *there exists a function* μ *such that for every* $\lambda \in \mathbb{N}$ *and index* $i^* \in [k]$:

$$\Pr\left[\begin{array}{l} \text{BARG.V}(\text{crs}, C, \pi) = 1 \\ C(i^*, w^*) \neq 1 \end{array} \,\middle|\, \begin{array}{l} (\text{crs}, \text{td}) \leftarrow \text{BARG.G}(1^\lambda, s, k, m, i^*) \\ (C, \pi) \leftarrow A(\text{crs}) \\ w^* \leftarrow \text{BARG.E}(\text{td}, \pi) \end{array} \right] \leq \mu(\lambda).$$

The following theorem follows by implying the [13] BARG transformation on the BARG constructions from [7,8,18].

Theorem 6 ([7,8,13,18]). *There exist poly*$(\lambda, \log k)$-*succinct index BARGs for* BatchCSAT *with somewhere argument of knowledge under any of the following assumptions:*

1. *The* $O(1)$-LIN *assumption on a pair of cryptographic groups with efficient bilinear map.*
2. *The hardness of Learning with errors* (LWE) *problem against polynomial time adversaries.*
3. *The sub-exponential Decisional Diffie-Hellman* (DDH) *assumptions.*

3.5   RAM Delegation

In what follows we define RAM Delegation scheme for *read-write* RAM machines. The definition is taken from [13].

A *read-write* RAM machine is modeled as a deterministic machine with random access to a *read-write* memory of large size. In its standard definition, the machine has a local state of length logarithmic in the memory size. At each time step, the machine reads or writes to a single memory cell and updates its local state. Often it is assumed that the machine has no input outside of its memory.

We say that without loss of generality, the RAM machine has random access to a *read-only* memory of size n and a large *read-write* memory initially filled with zeros. We refer to the specific memory locations where the machine performs write operations as the *write-memory* of the machine. We denote $t(n)$ as the number of steps executed by the machine, and $w(n)$ as the size of the write-memory. The input to the RAM machine is represented as a pair $x = (x^{\mathsf{imp}}, x^{\mathsf{exp}})$, where x^{imp} is large and stored in the random access memory, and x^{exp} is a compact explicit input. Having defined this model, we can now proceed to formalize the concept of RAM Delegation.

Definition 6. *An* $\mathcal{L}$-*succinct* RAM Delegation $=$ (RAM.G, RAM.D, RAM.P, RAM.V) *for a* RAM *computation* M *with local state of size* $\mathsf{L_{st}} \geq |x^{\mathsf{exp}}| + \log |x^{\mathsf{imp}}|$, *satisfies the following properties:*

$\mathcal{L}$-**Succinct.** *The running time of* RAM.G *is at most* $\mathcal{L}(\lambda, t) \cdot \mathrm{poly}(\mathsf{L_{st}})$, *and the length of a proof* π *is at most* $\mathcal{L}(\lambda, t) \cdot \mathrm{poly}(\mathsf{L_{st}})$.

$\mathcal{L}$-**Verifier Efficiency.** *The running time of* RAM.V *is at most* $\mathcal{L}(\lambda, t) \cdot \mathrm{poly}(\mathsf{L_{st}})$.

Prover Efficiency. *The running time of* RAM.P *is polynomial in its input and the read-write memory of the machine.*

Digest Efficiency. *The running time of* RAM.D *is linear in its input,* $|x| \cdot \mathrm{poly}(\lambda)$.

Completeness. *For any* $\lambda, n \in \mathbb{N}$ *such that* $n \leq w(n) \leq t(n) \leq 2^\lambda$, *and for any* $x = (x^{\mathsf{imp}}, x^{\mathsf{exp}}) \in \{0,1\}^n$ *such that* $M(x)$ *halts within* t *time steps, we have that*

$$\Pr\left[\begin{array}{l} \mathsf{RAM.V}(\mathsf{crs}, \mathsf{d}^{\mathsf{imp}}, x^{\mathsf{exp}}, b, \pi) = 1 \\ M(x) = 1 \end{array} \middle| \begin{array}{l} \mathsf{crs} \leftarrow \mathsf{RAM.G}(1^\lambda, t) \\ \mathsf{d}^{\mathsf{imp}} = \mathsf{RAM.D}(\mathsf{crs}, x^{\mathsf{imp}}) \\ (b, \pi) \leftarrow \mathsf{RAM.P}(\mathsf{crs}, x^{\mathsf{imp}}, x^{\mathsf{exp}}) \end{array} \right] = 1 - \mathsf{negl}(\lambda).$$

Collision Resistance of RAM *Digest*. *For any poly-size adversary* A, *and polynomial* $t = t(\lambda)$, *there exists a negligible function* $\mathsf{negl}(\cdot)$ *such that for every* $\lambda \in \mathbb{N}$,

$$\Pr\left[\begin{array}{l} \mathsf{RAM.D}(\mathsf{crs}, x) = \mathsf{RAM.D}(\mathsf{crs}, x') \\ x \neq x' \end{array} \middle| \begin{array}{l} \mathsf{crs} \leftarrow \mathsf{RAM.G}(1^\lambda, t) \\ (x, x') \leftarrow A(\mathsf{crs}) \end{array} \right] \leq \mathsf{negl}(\lambda).$$

Weak Soundness. *For any poly-size adversary* A, *and polynomial* $t = t(\lambda)$, *there exists a negligible function* $\mathsf{negl}(\cdot)$ *such that for every* $\lambda \in \mathbb{N}$,

$$\Pr\left[\begin{array}{l} \mathsf{RAM.V}(\mathsf{crs}, \mathsf{d}^{\mathsf{imp}}, x^{\mathsf{exp}}, 0, \pi_0) = 1 \\ \mathsf{RAM.V}(\mathsf{crs}, \mathsf{d}^{\mathsf{imp}}, x^{\mathsf{exp}}, 1, \pi_1) = 1 \end{array} \middle| \begin{array}{l} \mathsf{crs} \leftarrow \mathsf{RAM.G}(1^\lambda, t) \\ (x = (x^{\mathsf{imp}}, x^{\mathsf{exp}}), \pi_0, \pi_1) \leftarrow A(\mathsf{crs}) \\ \mathsf{d}^{\mathsf{imp}} \leftarrow \mathsf{RAM.D}(\mathsf{crs}, x^{\mathsf{imp}}) \end{array} \right] \leq \mathsf{negl}(\lambda).$$

We say that the RAM Delegation *scheme has a* strong soundness *if it also satisfies the following strong soundness definition:*

Strong Soundness. For any poly-size adversary A, and polynomial $t = t(\lambda)$, there exists a negligible function negl$(\cdot)$ *such that for every $\lambda \in \mathbb{N}$,*

$$\Pr \left[\begin{array}{l} \mathsf{RAM.V}(\mathsf{crs}, \mathsf{d}^{\mathsf{imp}}, x^{\mathsf{exp}}, 0, \pi_0) = 1 \\ \mathsf{RAM.V}(\mathsf{crs}, \mathsf{d}^{\mathsf{imp}}, x^{\mathsf{exp}}, 1, \pi_1) = 1 \end{array} \middle| \begin{array}{l} \mathsf{crs} \leftarrow \mathsf{RAM.G}(1^\lambda, t) \\ (\mathsf{d}^{\mathsf{imp}}, x^{\mathsf{exp}}, \pi_0, \pi_1) \leftarrow A(\mathsf{crs}) \end{array} \right] \leq \mathsf{negl}(\lambda).$$

4 PCA from RAM Delegation

In this section we construct a publicly-verifiable and adaptively sound succinct PCA with constant query complexity for any relation in NP. The construction is introduced in Sect. 4.1. We then proceed to prove the completeness, efficiency, and soundness of the scheme in Sect. 4.2. By combining these results, we establish the following theorem.

Theorem 7. *Assume there exists a* poly$(\log t, \lambda)$*-succinct* RAM Delegation *with weak soundness for any read-write* RAM *machine, then for any relation $\mathcal{R}$ in* NP *there exists a publicly-verifiable and adaptively sound succinct* PCA *with constant query complexity.*
    Furthermore,

- *The verifier runs in time $n \cdot$ poly(λ) + polylog$(\lambda, m, \log n)$.*
- *The verifier has randomness size $O(\log m + \log\log n + \log \lambda)$.*
- *The prover runs in time $T + n \cdot$ poly(λ) + poly$(\lambda, m, \log n)$, and uses space $S + n \cdot$ poly(λ) + poly$(\lambda, m, \log n)$, where T, S are the running time and space complexity of the* RAM Delegation *prover.*

Where n is the instance size, and m is the witness size.

By combining Theorem 7 with Theorem 9 we get the following corollary.

Corollary 1. *For any relation $\mathcal{R}$ in* NP *there exists a publicly-verifiable and adaptively sound succinct* PCA *with constant query complexity under any of the following assumptions:*

1. *The $O(1)$-*LIN *assumption on a pair of cryptographic groups with efficient bilinear map.*
2. *The hardness of Learning with errors (*LWE*) problem against polynomial time adversaries.*
3. *The sub-exponential Decisional Diffie-Hellman (*DDH*) assumptions.*

    Furthermore,

- *The verifier runs in time $n \cdot$ poly(λ) + polylog$(\lambda, m, \log n)$.*
- *The verifier has randomness size $O(\log m + \log\log n + \log \lambda)$.*
- *The prover runs in time $T \cdot$ poly$(\lambda, m, \log T)$, and uses space $S \cdot$ poly$(\lambda, m, \log T)$, where T, S are the time and space required for verifying the language.*

4.1 Construction

In this section, we present the construction of a publicly-verifiable and adaptively sound succinct PCA with constant query complexity for any relation in NP. We begin by introducing relevant notations that will be used throughout the construction.

Notations. Fix a relation $\mathcal{R}$ in NP. Let M' be a deterministic Turing machine that can verify whether an instance of size n and a witness of size m belong to $\mathcal{R}$ in time $t = \text{poly}(n)$. We denote M as a RAM machine that, given an implicit input $x^{\text{imp}} = \text{x}$ and an explicit input w, emulates $M'(\text{x}, \text{w})$. The machine will output 1 if and only if $M'(\text{x}, \text{w})$ accepts. The running time of M is t. The read-write memory of the machine is of size $S = t + n + m$. The local state of the machine includes the description of the state of the Turing machine and the last location read from memory, which requires at most $\text{polylog}(t, n, m)$. We define the size of the local state of the machine to be $\mathsf{L_{st}} = |x^{\text{exp}}| + \log |x^{\text{imp}}| + \text{polylog}(t, n, m) = m + \text{polylog}(t, n, m)$.

Let $(\mathsf{RAM.G}, \mathsf{RAM.D}, \mathsf{RAM.P}, \mathsf{RAM.V})$ be a RAM Delegation scheme for the machine M, and let Enc be an efficiently encodable and decodable error correcting code ensemble with relative distance $\delta > 0$. Denote by Enc^{-1} the (poly-time) decoding algorithm for Enc. We require the decoding algorithm to work only for valid codewords. The language L' is defined as follows:

$$L' = \left\{ \left(\mathsf{crs}, \mathsf{d}^{\text{imp}}\right), \mathsf{Enc}(\text{w}\|\pi) \mid \mathsf{RAM.V}(\mathsf{crs}, \mathsf{d}^{\text{imp}}, \text{w}, 1, \pi) \right\}$$

In other words, the language L' is the set of pairs of the following structure:

1. The first component consists of inputs known to $\mathsf{RAM.V}$ explicitly, namely, the common reference string crs and a digest of the implicit input.
2. The second component consists of inputs given to $\mathsf{RAM.V}$ by the prover, namely, the witness w, and the RAM Delegation proof π. All of these are encoded by the error correcting code Enc.

We define $\mathsf{PCPP} = (\mathsf{PCPP.P}, \mathsf{PCPP.V})$ scheme to be a PCPP scheme for the language L'.

Construction 8. The construction of the PCA scheme is as follows:

- $\mathsf{PCA.G}(1^n, 1^m, 1^\lambda)$.
  1. Output $\mathsf{crs} \leftarrow \mathsf{RAM.G}(1^\lambda, t(n, m))$.
- $\mathsf{PCA.P}(\mathsf{crs}, \text{x}, \text{w})$.
  1. Set $\pi_1 = \mathsf{RAM.P}(\mathsf{crs}, \text{x}, \text{w})$.
  2. Set $\mathsf{d}^{\text{imp}} = \mathsf{RAM.D}(\mathsf{crs}, \text{x})$.
  3. Set $\pi_2 = \mathsf{PCPP.P}((\mathsf{crs}, \mathsf{d}^{\text{imp}}), \mathsf{Enc}(\text{w}\|\pi_1))$.
  4. Output a proof $\pi = (\mathsf{Enc}(\text{w}\|\pi_1)\|\pi_2)$.
- $\mathsf{PCA.V}^\pi(\mathsf{crs}, \text{x})$.
  1. Set $\mathsf{d}^{\text{imp}} = \mathsf{RAM.D}(\mathsf{crs}, \text{x})$.
  2. Parse π as $\mathsf{Enc}(\text{w}\|\pi_1)\|\pi_2$.
  3. Output $\mathsf{PCPP.V}^{\mathsf{Enc}(\text{w}\|\pi_1), \pi_2}((\mathsf{crs}, \mathsf{d}^{\text{imp}}), \frac{\delta}{2})$.

4.2   Analysis

In what follows, we will provide proofs for completeness, efficiency, and soundness for the PCA construction in section Sect. 4.1.

Completeness. Follows directly from the completeness properties of the underlying encoding, RAM Delegation and PCPP schemes.

Efficiency. We start by defining the efficiency properties of the underlying RAM Delegation scheme. Let $\mathsf{L_{st}}$ be the size of the local state of M, let vt be the running time of RAM.V, let $\mathsf{L_{crs}}$ be the size of crs, and let L_{π_1} be the size of the proof π_1. By the $\mathrm{poly}(\lambda, \log t)$-verifier efficiency and the $\mathrm{poly}(\lambda, \log t)$-succinctness of the underlying RAM Delegation scheme, we get that for $\mathsf{L_{st}} \geq |x^{\mathsf{exp}}| + \log |x^{\mathsf{imp}}|$ the following holds (Definition 6),

$$\mathsf{vt}, \mathsf{L_{crs}}, \mathsf{L}_{\pi_1} \leq \mathrm{poly}(\lambda, \log t) \cdot \mathrm{poly}(\mathsf{L_{st}}).$$

Given that $\mathsf{L_{st}} = m + \mathrm{polylog}(t, n, m)$, we get that $\mathsf{L_{st}} \geq |x^{\mathsf{exp}}| + \log |x^{\mathsf{imp}}|$. Therefore, by the above equation,

$$\mathsf{vt}, \mathsf{L_{crs}}, \mathsf{L}_{\pi_1} \leq \mathrm{poly}(\lambda, \log t) \cdot \mathrm{poly}(\log t, \log n, m)$$
$$\leq \mathrm{poly}(\lambda, \log n, m). \tag{1}$$

Furthermore, we define the running time required for verifying the language L' to be the t'. By the efficiency of the underlying RAM Delegation scheme and the efficiency of the underlying encoding scheme, we get that,

$$t' = \mathsf{vt} + \mathrm{poly}(m, \mathsf{L}_{\pi_1}).$$

By combining the above equation with Eq. 1 we get that:

$$t' \leq \mathrm{poly}(\lambda, \log n, m). \tag{2}$$

Now, we can proceed to prove the succinctness of our scheme.

- Proof Size: By the efficiency of the underlying encoding scheme, and by the size of π_1 described in Eq. 1, we get that,

$$|\mathsf{Enc}(\mathsf{w}||\pi_1)| \leq \mathrm{poly}(\lambda, \log n, m). \tag{3}$$

By the running time of RAM.V described in Eq. 1, combining with Theorem 5, we get that,

$$|\pi_2| \leq \mathrm{poly}(\lambda, \log n, m). \tag{4}$$

Overall, by combining Eqs. 3, 4 we get that,

$$|\pi| = |(\mathsf{Enc}(\mathsf{w}||\pi_1)||\pi_2)| \leq \mathrm{poly}(\lambda, \log n, m),$$

as required.

– Prover Complexity: We start by analyzing the running time of all the steps except for the RAM Delegation prover execution. The PCA prover first computes π_1, the RAM Delegation proof. Then, the PCA prover computes the digest of x using RAM.D. By the efficiency of the underlying RAM Delegation, this step takes time:

$$|\mathbf{x}| \cdot \text{poly}(\lambda) = n \cdot \text{poly}(\lambda). \tag{5}$$

Finally, the prover computes π_2 by encoding $(\mathbf{w} \,\|\, \pi_1)$, followed by the computation of a PCPP proof for the language L'. Since the running time of verifying L' is t', this step takes $\text{poly}(t')$ (Theorem 5). By Eq. 2, we get that this step takes time:

$$\text{poly}(\lambda, \log n, m). \tag{6}$$

By Eq. 1 we get that,

$$\text{poly}(\mathsf{vt}, m, \mathsf{L}_{\pi_1}) \leq \text{poly}(\lambda, \log n, m). \tag{7}$$

By Eq. 5 to Eq. 7, we get that all the steps of the PCA prover, except for the execution of the RAM Delegation prover, takes time:

$$n \cdot \text{poly}(\lambda) + \text{poly}(\lambda, \log n, m). \tag{8}$$

Overall, for a RAM Delegation prover with running time bounded by T, we get that the running time of the PCA prover is bounded by:

$$T + n \cdot \text{poly}(\lambda) + \text{poly}(\lambda, \log n, m).$$

Regarding the space complexity of the PCA prover, it is determined by the space used by the RAM Delegation prover and the runtime of the remaining steps. Therefore, referring to Eq. 8, for a RAM Delegation prover with space complexity bounded by S, the space complexity of the PCA prover is bounded by:

$$S + n \cdot \text{poly}(\lambda) + \text{poly}(\lambda, \log n, m)$$

as required.

– Verifier Running Time: The PCA verifier starts by computing the digest of x using RAM.D. By the efficiency of the underlying RAM Delegation scheme, this step takes time

$$|\mathbf{x}| \cdot \text{poly}(\lambda) = n \cdot \text{poly}(\lambda). \tag{9}$$

Then, the PCA verifier validates the PCPP proof. By Theorem 5, verifying the PCPP proof takes time:

$$\text{polylog}(\mathsf{vt}, m, \mathsf{L}_{\pi_1}). \tag{10}$$

By Eq. 1 we get that,

$$\text{polylog}(\mathsf{vt}, m, \mathsf{L}_{\pi_1}) \leq \text{polylog}(\lambda, m, \log n). \tag{11}$$

Overall, by combining Eq. 9 to Eq. 11 we get that the verifier runs in time $n \cdot \text{poly}(\lambda) + \text{polylog}(\lambda, m, \log n)$, as required.

- <u>Verifier's Randomness Size:</u> The PCA verifier only uses randomness required for the PCPP verifier. Therefore, by Theorem 5, the randomness complexity is $O(\log t')$. By Eq. 2 we get that the randomness complexity is

$$O(\log(\mathrm{poly}(\lambda, \log n, m))) \leq O(\log(\lambda) + \log\log(n) + \log(m)),$$

as requires.
- <u>Query Complexity:</u> The PCA verifier only queries its oracle when running the PCPP verifier. Therefore, for a fixed proximity parameter, by Theorem 5, the query complexity is $O(1)$, as required.

Soundness. Fix some $n, m \in \mathbb{N}$, security parameter $\lambda \in \mathbb{N}$, and deterministic malicious prover $\tilde{\mathsf{P}}$ of size $s(\lambda) = \mathrm{poly}(\lambda)$.

Fix a crs generated by $\mathsf{PCA.G}(1^n, 1^m, 1^\lambda)$, a malicious prover message $(\mathrm{x}, \tilde{\pi}) = \tilde{\mathsf{P}}(\mathsf{crs})$ such that $\mathcal{R}(\mathrm{x}) = \emptyset$, and a digest of the input $\mathsf{d}^{\mathsf{imp}} = \mathsf{RAM.D}(\mathsf{crs}, \mathrm{x})$. Parse the proof as $\tilde{\pi} = \tilde{\tau}_1 \| \tilde{\tau}_2$. Consider the case where:

$$\Delta(\tilde{\tau}_1, \mathsf{Image}(\mathsf{Enc})) \geq \frac{\delta}{2}.$$

In this case, since $L'(\mathsf{crs}, \mathsf{d}^{\mathsf{imp}}) \subseteq \mathsf{Image}(\mathsf{Enc})$, it holds that:

$$\Delta(\tilde{\tau}_1, L'(\mathsf{crs}, \mathsf{d}^{\mathsf{imp}})) \geq \frac{\delta}{2}.$$

By the soundness property of the PCPP, we get that:

$$\Pr\left[\mathsf{PCPP.V}^{\tilde{\tau}_1, \tilde{\tau}_2}((\mathsf{crs}, \mathsf{d}^{\mathsf{imp}}), \tfrac{\delta}{2}) = 1 \;\middle|\; \begin{array}{l} (\mathrm{x}, \tilde{\pi}) \leftarrow \tilde{\mathsf{P}}(\mathsf{crs}) \\ \mathsf{d}^{\mathsf{imp}} \leftarrow \mathsf{RAM.D}(\mathsf{crs}, \mathrm{x}) \\ \tilde{\pi} := \tilde{\tau}_1 \| \tilde{\tau}_2 \\ \Delta(\tilde{\tau}_1, L'(\mathsf{crs}, \mathsf{d}^{\mathsf{imp}})) \geq \frac{\delta}{2} \end{array} \right] < \frac{1}{2}.$$

By the above equation, for the case where $\Delta(\tilde{\tau}_1, \mathsf{Image}(\mathsf{Enc})) \geq \frac{\delta}{2}$, the following holds:

$$\Pr\left[\mathsf{PCA.V}^{\tilde{\pi}}(\mathsf{crs}, \mathrm{x}) = 1 \wedge \mathcal{R}(\mathrm{x}) \;\middle|\; (\mathrm{x}, \tilde{\pi}) \leftarrow \tilde{\mathsf{P}}(\mathsf{crs}) \right] < \frac{1}{2},$$

as required.

Therefore, moving forward, we will only consider the case where:

$$\Delta(\tilde{\tau}_1, \mathsf{Image}(\mathsf{Enc})) < \frac{\delta}{2}.$$

In this case, the prefix $\tilde{\tau}_1$ can be decoded efficiently into $\tilde{\mathrm{w}} \| \tilde{\pi}_1 = \mathsf{Enc}^{-1}(\tilde{\tau}_1)$.

Given a crs we define the event BAD_b to be the following event:

$$\mathsf{BAD}_b := \left[\begin{array}{c|c} \mathsf{RAM.V}(\mathsf{crs}, \mathsf{d}^{\mathsf{imp}}, \tilde{w}, 1, \tilde{\pi}_1) = b & (\mathsf{x}, \tilde{\pi}) \leftarrow \tilde{\mathsf{P}}(\mathsf{crs}) \\ \mathcal{R}(\mathsf{x}) = \emptyset & \begin{array}{l} \mathsf{d}^{\mathsf{imp}} \leftarrow \mathsf{RAM.D}(\mathsf{crs}, \mathsf{x}) \\ \tilde{\pi} := \tilde{\pi}_1 || \tilde{\tau}_2 \\ \tilde{w} || \tilde{\pi}_1 \leftarrow \mathsf{Enc}^{-1}(\tilde{\tau}_1) \end{array} \end{array} \right].$$

In other words, the occurrence of event BAD_1 implies that the proof $\tilde{\pi}$ consists of a false witness $\tilde{w}$ and an accepting RAM Delegation proof $\tilde{\pi}_1$. We'll argue that (1) the probability of sampling a PCA common reference string such that the event BAD_1 occurs is negligible, and (2) the probability of sampling a PCA common reference string such that the event BAD_0 occurs and that the PCA verifier accepts is at most $\frac{1}{2}$. Combining both claims will give us the required soundness guarantee for our PCA.

By the soundness property of the underlying RAM Delegation scheme, we get that:

$$\Pr\left[\mathsf{BAD}_1 \mid \mathsf{crs} \leftarrow \mathsf{PCA.G}(1^n, 1^m, 1^\lambda)\right] \le \mathsf{negl}(\lambda).$$

Otherwise, we could use $(\mathsf{x}, \tilde{\pi}) \leftarrow \tilde{\mathsf{P}}(\mathsf{crs})$ to construct an adversary for the RAM Delegation scheme that breaks the weak soundness with the same probability that the event BAD_1 occurs. The adversary for the RAM Delegation scheme will extract the witness $\tilde{w}$ and the proof $\tilde{\pi}_1$ from $\tilde{\pi}$. Then, the adversary will generate an honest proof π_0 for the statement that $M(\mathsf{x}, \mathsf{w}) = 0$ (which can be done by the completeness of the RAM Delegation scheme). The adversary will output $(x = (\mathsf{x}, \mathsf{w}), \pi_0, \pi_1 = \tilde{\pi}_1)$.

Next, we want to bound the following probability of BAD_0. By the definition of BAD_0, this means that $\mathsf{RAM.V}$ rejects its input. Therefore, the claim proven by $\tilde{\tau}_2$ is false. In this case, by the soundness of the PCPP verifier for L' it holds that the probability of $\mathsf{PCPP.V}$ accepting input $((\mathsf{crs}, \mathsf{d}^{\mathsf{imp}}), \mathsf{Enc}(\tilde{w} || \tilde{\pi}_1))$ with proof $\tilde{\tau}_2$ is at most $\frac{1}{2}$. Therefore, we get that:

$$\Pr\left[\begin{array}{c} \mathsf{PCA.V}^{\tilde{\pi}}(\mathsf{crs}, \mathsf{x}) = 1 \ \wedge \ \mathcal{R}(\mathsf{x}) \\ \mathsf{BAD}_0 \end{array} \middle| \mathsf{crs} \leftarrow \mathsf{PCA.G}(1^n, 1^m, 1^\lambda) \right] < \frac{1}{2}.$$

Overall, with all but $\mathsf{negl}(\lambda)$ probability over the choice of crs, the probability of $\mathsf{PCPP.V}$ accepting x with proof $\tilde{\pi}$ is at most $\frac{1}{2}$.

5   Complexity-Preserving RAM Delegation Scheme

In this section we construct a $\mathsf{poly}(\lambda, \log t)$-succinct RAM Delegation scheme for any read-write RAM machine.

Theorem 9. *There exist* $\mathsf{poly}(\lambda, \log t)$-*succinct* RAM Delegation *scheme for any read-write* RAM *machine under any of the following assumptions:*

1. *The $O(1)$-LIN assumption on a pair of cryptographic groups with efficient bilinear map.*
2. *The hardness of Learning with errors (LWE) problem against polynomial time adversaries.*
3. *The sub-exponential Decisional Diffie-Hellman (DDH) assumptions.*

   Moreover, the RAM prover has the following properties:

   - *The prover runs in time $(t \cdot \mathrm{poly}(\mathsf{L_{st}}, \log t) + |x^{\mathsf{imp}}|) \cdot \mathrm{poly}(\lambda)$.*
   - *The prover uses sapce $(w \cdot \mathrm{poly}(\mathsf{L_{st}}, \log t) + |x^{\mathsf{imp}}|) \cdot \mathrm{poly}(\lambda)$.*

where $(x^{\mathsf{imp}}, x^{\mathsf{exp}})$ is the input to M, t is the running time of $M(x^{\mathsf{imp}}, x^{\mathsf{exp}})$, and w is the space used by $M(x^{\mathsf{imp}}, x^{\mathsf{exp}})$.

The proof of this theorem appears in the full version of this work.

Acknowledgments. We thank Eylon Yogev and Gal Arnon for invaluable and useful discussions.

References

1. Abboud, A., Rubinstein, A., Williams, R.R.: Distributed PCP theorems for hardness of approximation in P. In: Umans, C. (ed.) 58th IEEE Annual Symposium on Foundations of Computer Science, FOCS 2017, Berkeley, 15–17 October 2017, pp. 25–36. IEEE Computer Society (2017)
2. Arora, S., Lund, C., Motwani, R., Sudan, M., Szegedy, M.: Proof verification and the hardness of approximation problems. J. ACM **45**(3), 501–555 (1998)
3. Ben-Sasson, E., Goldreich, O., Harsha, P., Sudan, M., Vadhan, S.P.: Short PCPS verifiable in polylogarithmic time. In: 20th Annual IEEE Conference on Computational Complexity (CCC 2005), 11–15 June 2005, San Jose, pp. 120–134. IEEE Computer Society (2005)
4. Bodlaender, H.L., Downey, R.G., Fellows, M.R., Hermelin, D.: On problems without polynomial kernels. J. Comput. Syst. Sci. **75**(8), 423–434 (2009). https://doi.org/10.1016/j.jcss.2009.04.001
5. Bronfman, L., Rothblum, R.D.: PCPs and instance compression from a cryptographic lens. In: Braverman, M. (ed.) 13th Innovations in Theoretical Computer Science Conference, ITCS 2022, 31 January–3 February 2022, Berkeley. LIPIcs, vol. 215, pp. 30:1–30:19. Schloss Dagstuhl - Leibniz-Zentrum für Informatik (2022)
6. Chen, L., Goldwasser, S., Lyu, K., Rothblum, G.N., Rubinstein, A.: Fine-grained complexity meets IP = PSPACE. In: Chan, T.M. (ed.) Proceedings of the Thirtieth Annual ACM-SIAM Symposium on Discrete Algorithms, SODA 2019, San Diego, 6–9 January 2019, pp. 1–20. SIAM (2019)
7. Choudhuri, A.R., Garg, S., Jain, A., Jin, Z., Zhang, J.: Correlation intractability and snargs from sub-exponential DDH. In: Handschuh, H., Lysyanskaya, A. (eds.) Advances in Cryptology, CRYPTO 2023. LNCS, vol. 14084, pp. 635–668. Springer, Cham (2023). https://doi.org/10.1007/978-3-031-38551-3_20
8. Choudhuri, A.R., Jain, A., Jin, Z.: Snargs for $\mathcal{P}$ from LWE. In: 62nd IEEE Annual Symposium on Foundations of Computer Science, FOCS 2021, Denver, 7–10 February 2022, pp. 68–79. IEEE (2021)

9. Drucker, A.: New limits to classical and quantum instance compression. SIAM J. Comput. **44**(5), 1443–1479 (2015)
10. Fortnow, L., Santhanam, R.: Infeasibility of instance compression and succinct PCPs for NP. In: Dwork, C. (ed.) Proceedings of the 40th Annual ACM Symposium on Theory of Computing, Victoria, 17–20 May 2008, pp. 133–142. ACM (2008)
11. Harnik, D., Naor, M.: On the compressibility of np instances and cryptographic applications. SIAM J. Comput. **39**(5), 1667–1713 (2010)
12. Jawale, R., Kalai, Y.T., Khurana, D., Zhang, R.Y.: Snargs for bounded depth computations and PPAD hardness from sub-exponential LWE. In: Khuller, S., Williams, V.V. (eds.) STOC 2021, pp. 708–721. ACM (2021)
13. Kalai, Y.T., Lombardi, A., Vaikuntanathan, V., Wichs, D.: Boosting batch arguments and RAM delegation. IACR Cryptol. ePrint Arch. p. 1320 (2022)
14. Kalai, Y.T., Paneth, O., Yang, L.: How to delegate computations publicly. In: Charikar, M., Cohen, E. (eds.) Proceedings of the 51st Annual ACM SIGACT Symposium on Theory of Computing, STOC 2019, Phoenix, 23–26 June 2019, pp. 1115–1124. ACM (2019)
15. Kalai, Y.T., Raz, R.: Probabilistically checkable arguments. In: Halevi, S. (ed.) Advances in Cryptology. CRYPTO 2009. LNCS, vol. 5677, pp. 143–159. Springer, Heidelberg (2009). https://doi.org/10.1007/978-3-642-03356-8_9
16. Kalai, Y.T., Vaikuntanathan, V., Zhang, R.Y.: Somewhere statistical soundness, post-quantum security, and SNARGs. In: Nissim, K., Waters, B. (eds.) Theory of Cryptography, TCC 2021. LNCS, vol. 13042, pp. 330–368. Springer, Cham (2021). https://doi.org/10.1007/978-3-030-90459-3_12
17. Szydlo, M.: Merkle tree traversal in log space and time. In: Cachin, C., Camenisch, J. (eds.) Advances in Cryptology. EUROCRYPT 2004. LNCS, vol. 3027, pp. 541–554. Springer, Heidelberg (2004). https://doi.org/10.1007/978-3-540-24676-3_32
18. Waters, B., Wu, D.J.: Batch arguments for NP and more from standard bilinear group assumptions. IACR Cryptol. ePrint Arch. p. 336 (2022)
19. Zimand, M.: Probabilistically checkable proofs the easy way. In: Baeza-Yates, R.A., Montanari, U., Santoro, N. (eds.) Foundations of Information Technology in the Era of Networking and Mobile Computing, IFIP 17th World Computer Congress - TC1 Stream/2nd IFIP International Conference on Theoretical Computer Science (TCS 2002), 25–30 August 2002, Montreal. IFIP Conference Proceedings, vol. 223, pp. 337–351. Kluwer (2002)

The Complexity of Algebraic Algorithms for LWE

Matthias Johann Steiner[✉][iD]

Alpen-Adria-Universität Klagenfurt, Klagenfurt am Wörthersee, Austria
matthias.steiner@aau.at

Abstract. Arora & Ge introduced a noise-free polynomial system to compute the secret of a Learning With Errors (LWE) instance via linearization. Albrecht et al. later utilized the Arora-Ge polynomial model to study the complexity of Gröbner basis computations on LWE polynomial systems under the assumption of semi-regularity. In this paper we revisit the Arora-Ge polynomial and prove that it satisfies a genericity condition recently introduced by Caminata & Gorla, called being in generic coordinates. For polynomial systems in generic coordinates one can always estimate the complexity of DRL Gröbner basis computations in terms of the Castelnuovo-Mumford regularity and henceforth also via the Macaulay bound.

Moreover, we generalize the Gröbner basis algorithm of Semaev & Tenti to arbitrary polynomial systems with a finite degree of regularity. In particular, existence of this algorithm yields another approach to estimate the complexity of DRL Gröbner basis computations in terms of the degree of regularity. In practice, the degree of regularity of LWE polynomial systems is not known, though one can always estimate the lowest achievable degree of regularity. Consequently, from a designer's worst case perspective this approach yields sub-exponential complexity estimates for general, binary secret and binary error LWE.

In recent works by Dachman-Soled et al. the hardness of LWE in the presence of side information was analyzed. Utilizing their framework we discuss how hints can be incorporated into LWE polynomial systems and how they affect the complexity of Gröbner basis computations.

Keywords: LWE · LWE with hints · Gröbner bases

1 Introduction

With the emerging threat of Shor's quantum polynomial time algorithms for factoring and discrete logarithms [33] on the horizon, cryptographers in the past 20 years have been in desperate search for new cryptographic problems that cannot be solved in polynomial time on classical as well as quantum computers. So far, lattice-based cryptography built on *Learning With Errors* (LWE) and the *Short Integer Solution* (SIS) [1] has emerged as most promising candidate for cryptography in the presence of quantum computers.

© International Association for Cryptologic Research 2024
M. Joye and G. Leander (Eds.): EUROCRYPT 2024, LNCS 14653, pp. 375–403, 2024.
https://doi.org/10.1007/978-3-031-58734-4_13

In this paper we revisit polynomial models to solve the Search-LWE problem via Gröbner basis computations. Solving LWE via a polynomial system was first done by Arora & Ge [6], though they solved the system via linearization not via Gröbner bases. Albrecht et al. [2,3] studied the complexity of Gröbner basis computations for the Arora-Ge polynomial model under the assumption that the polynomial system is *semi-regular* [24,28]. Moreover, for binary error LWE Sun et al. [37] refined the complexity estimates for linearization under the semi-regularity assumption. For a general review of the computational hardness of LWE we refer to [4].

We stress that the complexity estimates of [2,3,37] are still hypothetical since both works do not provide a proof that a LWE polynomial system is semi-regular except for very special cases, see e.g. [3, Theorem 11]. Moreover, the complexity bounds rely on asymptotic studies of the Hilbert series of a semi-regular polynomial system. Needless to say that a priori is not guaranteed that these complexity estimates apply for practical LWE instantiations.

In this paper we consider two new approaches to estimate the complexity of Gröbner basis computations. Caminata & Gorla [12] revealed that the solving degree of polynomial system in *generic coordinates* is always upper bounded by the Castelnuovo-Mumford regularity and henceforth also by the Macaulay bound, see [12, Theorem 10]. For our first approach we prove that any fully determined LWE polynomial system is in generic coordinates. In particular this implies that for any LWE polynomial system there exists a Gröbner basis algorithm in exponential time as well as memory complexity. Semaev & Tenti [32] revealed that the complexity of Gröbner basis algorithms can also be estimated via the *degree of regularity* of a polynomial system. Though, their bound is only applicable over finite fields and the polynomial system must contain the field equations, see [32, Theorem 2.1] and [38, Theorem 3.65]. We generalize their result to any polynomial system that admits a finite degree of regularity regardless of the underlying field. For a fixed degree of regularity we will determine the minimal number of LWE samples necessary so that the polynomial system could achieve the degree of regularity. Hence, for a designer this implies that there *could* exist Gröbner basis algorithms in sub-exponential time as well as memory to solve Search-LWE.

In two recent works Dachman-Soled et al. [18,19] introduced a framework to study the complexity of attacks on Search-LWE in the presence of side information. In Sect. 6 we shortly review their framework and describe how hints can be incorporated into LWE polynomial systems. Moreover, in Example 28 we showcase the complexity impact of hints on Gröbner basis computations.

Finally, Semaev & Tenti [32] also investigated the probability that a uniformly and independently distributed polynomial system $\mathcal{F} \subset \mathbb{F}_q[x_1, \ldots, x_n]/$ $(x_1^q - x_1, \ldots, x_n^q - x_n)$ achieves a certain degree of regularity. Their proof depends only on combinatorial properties, hence we expect that a similar result can be proven for uniformly and independently distributed polynomial system $\mathcal{F} \subset \mathbb{F}_q[x_1, \ldots, x_n]/(f(x_1), \ldots, f(x_n))$, where f is univariate and $\deg(f) \geq 2$ is arbitrary. In Appendix A of the full version [35] we study the related problem whether a LWE polynomial is close to the uniform distribution or not. We find a negative answer for this question, in particular we show that the statistical distance between the highest degree component of a LWE polynomial and the uniform distribution is always $\geq \frac{1}{2}$ and has limit 1 if the degree of the LWE polynomial goes to infinity. Hence, even if Semaev & Tenti's analysis generalizes it is not applicable to LWE polynomial systems.

2 Preliminaries

By k we will always denote a field, by $\bar{k}$ we denote its algebraic closure, and by $\mathbb{F}_q$ we denote the finite field with q elements. Let $I \subset k[x_1, \ldots, x_n]$ be an ideal, then we denote the zero locus of I over $\bar{k}$ as

$$\mathcal{Z}(I) = \left\{ \mathbf{x} \in \bar{k}^n \mid f(\mathbf{x}) = 0, \ \forall f \in I \right\} \subset \mathbb{A}_{\bar{k}}^n. \tag{1}$$

If in addition I is homogeneous, then we denote the projective zero locus over $\bar{k}$ by $\mathcal{Z}_+(I) \subset \mathbb{P}_{\bar{k}}^{n-1}$.

Let $f \in K[x_1, \ldots, x_n]$ be a polynomial, and let x_0 be an additional variable, we call

$$f^{\mathrm{hom}}(x_0, \ldots, x_n) = x_0^{\deg(f)} \cdot f\left(\frac{x_1}{x_0}, \ldots, \frac{x_n}{x_0}\right) \in K[x_0, \ldots, x_n] \tag{2}$$

the homogenization of f with respect to x_0, and analog for the homogenization of ideals $I^{\mathrm{hom}} = \{f^{\mathrm{hom}} \mid f \in I\}$ and finite systems of polynomials $\mathcal{F}^{\mathrm{hom}} = \{f_1^{\mathrm{hom}}, \ldots, f_m^{\mathrm{hom}}\}$. Further, we will always assume that we can extend a term order on $k[x_1, \ldots, x_n]$ to a term order on $k[x_0, \ldots, x_n]$ according to [12, Definition 8].

For a term order $>$ and an ideal $I \subset k[x_1, \ldots, x_n]$ we denote with

$$\mathrm{in}_>(I) = \{\mathrm{LT}_>(f) \mid f \in I\} \tag{3}$$

the initial ideal of I, i.e. the ideal of leading terms of I, with respect to $>$.

Every polynomial $f \in [x_1, \ldots, x_n]$ can be written as $f = f_d + f_{d-1} + \ldots + f_0$, where f_i is homogeneous of degree i. We denote the highest degree component f_d of f with f^{top}, and analog we denote $\mathcal{F}^{\mathrm{top}} = \{f_1^{\mathrm{top}}, \ldots, f_m^{\mathrm{top}}\}$.

For a homogeneous ideal $I \subset P$ and an integer $d \geq 0$ we denote

$$I_d = \{f \in I \mid \deg(f) = d, \ f \text{ homogeneous}\}, \tag{4}$$

and analog for the polynomial ring P.

Let $I, J \subset k[x_1, \ldots, x_n]$ be ideals, then we denote with

$$I : J = \{f \in k[x_1, \ldots, x_n] \mid \forall g \in J : f \cdot g \in I\} \tag{5}$$

the usual ideal quotient, and with $I : J^\infty = \bigcup_{i \geq 1} I : J^i$ the saturation of I with respect to J.

Let $I, \mathfrak{m} \in k[x_0, \ldots, x_n]$ be homogeneous ideals where $\mathfrak{m} = (x_0, \ldots, x_n)$, then we call $I^{\mathrm{sat}} = I : \mathfrak{m}^\infty$ the saturation of I.

We will often encounter the lexicographic and the degree reverse lexicographic term order which we will abbreviate as LEX and DRL respectively.

For $\mathbf{x}, \mathbf{y} \in k^n$ we denote the standard inner product as

$$\langle \mathbf{x}, \mathbf{y} \rangle = \mathbf{x}^\mathsf{T} \mathbf{y} = \sum_{i=1}^{n} x_i \cdot y_i. \tag{6}$$

By log we denote the natural logarithm and by $\log_2$ the logarithm in base 2.

2.1   Learning with Errors

Learning With Errors (LWE) was introduced by Ajtai in his seminal work [1]. In its base form it can be formulated as a simple computational linear algebra problem.

Definition 1 (Learning with errors, [1]). *Let q be a prime, let $n \geq 1$ be an integer, and let χ be a probability distribution on $\mathbb{Z}$. For a secret vector $\mathbf{s} \in \mathbb{F}_q^n$ the LWE distribution $A_{\mathbf{s},\chi}$ over $\mathbb{F}_q^n \times \mathbb{F}_q$ is sampled by choosing $\mathbf{a} \in \mathbb{F}_q^n$ uniformly at random, choosing $e \leftarrow \chi$, and outputting $(\mathbf{a}, \langle \mathbf{s}, \mathbf{a} \rangle + e \in \mathbb{F}_q)$.*

In Search-LWE we are given m LWE samples $(\mathbf{a}_i, b_i)$ sampled according to some probability distribution. Our task is then to recover the secret vector $\mathbf{s} \in \mathbb{F}_q^n$ that has been used to generate the samples.

As probability distribution one typically chooses a discrete Gaussian distribution with mean 0 and standard deviation σ. For ease of computation in this paper, we ignore the discretization and assume $\chi = \mathcal{N}(0, \sigma)$ if not specified otherwise, hence we do not discuss discretization techniques further. Assume that $X \sim \mathcal{N}(0, \sigma)$, we will utilize the following well-known property of the Gaussian distribution several times in this paper

$$\mathbb{P}\left[|X| > t \cdot \sigma\right] \leq \frac{2}{t \cdot \sqrt{2 \cdot \pi}} \cdot \exp\left(-\frac{t^2}{2}\right). \tag{7}$$

It is well-known that solving Search-LWE for a discrete Gaussian error distribution and $\sigma \in \mathcal{O}(\sqrt{n})$ is at least as hard as solving several computational lattice problems, see e.g. [10,27,29,30].

Moreover, on top of LWE many cryptographic functions can be built, e.g. Regev's public key cryptosystem [30] as well as a key exchange mechanism [9].

2.2   Gröbner Bases

For an ideal $I \subset k[x_1, \ldots, x_n]$ and a term order $>$ on the polynomial ring, a $>$-Gröbner basis $\mathcal{G} = \{g_1, \ldots, g_m\}$ is a finite set of generators such that

$$\mathrm{in}_{>}(I) = \left(\mathrm{LT}_{>}(g_1), \ldots, \mathrm{LT}_{>}(g_m) \right). \tag{8}$$

Gröbner bases were introduced by Bruno Buchberger in his PhD thesis [11]. With Gröbner bases one can solve many computational problems on ideals like the ideal membership problem or the computation of the zero locus [17]. For a general introduction to the theory of Gröbner bases we refer to [17].

Today, two classes of Gröbner basis algorithms are known: *Buchberger's algorithm* and *linear algebra-based algorithms*. In this paper we only study the latter family.

Let $\mathcal{F} = \{f_1, \ldots, f_m\} \subset P = k[x_1, \ldots, x_n]$ be a homogeneous polynomial system, and let $>$ be a term order on P. The *homogeneous Macaulay matrix* in degree d, denoted as M_d, has columns indexed by monomials in P_d sorted from left to right with respect to $>$. The rows of M_d are indexed by polynomials $s \cdot f_i$, where $s \in P$ is a monomial such that $\deg(s \cdot f_i) = d$. The entry of row $s \cdot f_i$ at column t is the coefficient of $s \cdot f_i$ at the monomial t. For an inhomogeneous polynomial system M_d is replaced by $M_{\leq d}$ and the degree equalities by inequalities. By performing Gaussian elimination on $M_0, \ldots, M_d$ respectively $M_{\leq d}$ for d big enough one will produce a $>$-Gröbner basis of $\mathcal{F}$. This idea can be traced back to Lazard [26]. Since d determines the complexity of this algorithm in space and time, the least suitable d is of special interest [20].

Definition 2 (Solving degree, [12, Definition 6]). *Let $\mathcal{F} = \{f_1, \ldots, f_m\} \subset k[x_1, \ldots, x_n]$ and let $>$ be a term order. The solving degree of $\mathcal{F}$ is the least degree d such that Gaussian elimination on the Macaulay matrix $M_{\leq d}$ produces a Gröbner basis of $\mathcal{F}$ with respect to $>$. We denote it by $\mathrm{sd}_>(\mathcal{F})$.*

If $\mathcal{F}$ is homogeneous, we consider the homogeneous Macaulay matrix M_d and let the solving degree of $\mathcal{F}$ be the least degree d such that Gaussian elimination on $M_0, \ldots, M_d$ produces a Gröbner basis of $\mathcal{F}$ with respect to $>$.

Today, the most efficient variants of linear algebra-based Gröbner basis algorithms are Faugére's F4 [22] and Matrix-F5 [23] algorithms. These algorithms utilize efficient selection criteria to avoid redundant rows in the Macaulay matrices. Moreover, they construct the matrices for increasing values of d. Therefore, they also need stopping criteria, though one could artificially stop the computation once the solving degree is reached since then a Gröbner basis must already be contained in the system produced by Gaussian elimination. Hence, we do not discuss termination criteria further.

Let $\mathcal{F} \subset k[x_1, \ldots, x_n]$ be a polynomial system, and let $\mathcal{F}^{\mathrm{hom}}$ be its homogenization. We always have that, see [12, Theorem 7],

$$\mathrm{sd}_{DRL}(\mathcal{F}) \leq \mathrm{sd}_{DRL}(\mathcal{F}^{\mathrm{hom}}). \tag{9}$$

Complexity Estimate via the Solving Degree. For a matrix $\mathbf{A} \in k^{n \times m}$ of rank r the reduced row echelon form can be computed in $\mathcal{O}(n \cdot m \cdot r^{\omega-2})$ [36, §2.2], where $2 \leq \omega < 2.37286$ is a linear algebra constant [5].

Let $\mathcal{F} \subset P = k[x_1, \ldots, x_n]$ be a system of m homogeneous polynomials, it is well-known that the number of monomials in P_d is given by $\binom{n+d-1}{d}$. Moreover, at most $\binom{n+d-\deg(f_i)-1}{d-\deg(f_i)} \leq \binom{n+d-1}{d}$ many columns can stem from the polynomial f_i. Therefore, the cost of Gaussian elimination on $M_0, \ldots, M_d$ is bounded by

$$\mathcal{O}\left(m \cdot d \cdot \binom{n+d-1}{d}^{\omega}\right). \tag{10}$$

Thus, by estimating the solving degree $\mathrm{sd}_{DRL}(\mathcal{F})$ we yield a complexity upper bound for linear algebra-based Gröbner basis computations.

2.3   Generic Coordinates and the Solving Degree

For completeness, we shortly recall the definition of the Castelnuovo-Mumford regularity [21, Sect. 4], a well-established invariant from commutative algebra and algebraic geometry. Let $P = k[x_0, \ldots, x_n]$ be the polynomial ring and let

$$\mathbf{F} : \cdots \to F_i \to F_{i-1} \to \cdots \tag{11}$$

be a graded complex of free P-modules, where $F_i = \sum_j P(-a_{i,j})$.

Definition 3. *The Castelnuovo-Mumford regularity of* $\mathbf{F}$ *is defined as*

$$\mathrm{reg}\,(\mathbf{F}) = \sup_i a_{i,j} - i.$$

By Hilbert's Syzygy theorem [21, Theorem 1.1] any finitely graded P-module has a finite free graded resolution. I.e., for every homogeneous ideal $I \subset P$ the regularity of I is computable.

Next we introduce the notion of generic coordinates which first appeared in the seminal work of Bayer & Stillman [8]. Let $I \subset P$ be an ideal, and let $r \in P$. We use the shorthand notation "$r \nmid 0 \mod I$" for expressing that r is not a zero-divisor on P/I.

Definition 4. ([12,13, **Definition 5**]). *Let* k *be an infinite field. Let* $I \subset k[x_0, \ldots, x_n]$ *be a homogeneous ideal with* $|\mathcal{Z}_+(I)| < \infty$. *We say that* I *is in generic coordinates if either* $|\mathcal{Z}_+(I)| = 0$ *or* $x_0 \nmid 0 \mod I^{\mathrm{sat}}$.

Let k *be any field, and let* $k \subset K$ *be an infinite field extension.* I *is in generic coordinates over* K *if* $I \otimes_k K[x_0, \ldots, x_n] \subset K[x_0, \ldots, x_n]$ *is in generic coordinates.*

Provided a polynomial system is in generic coordinates, then the solving degree is always upper bounded by the Castelnuovo-Mumford regularity.

Theorem 5. ([12, **Theorem 9, 10**]). *Let* K *be an algebraically closed field, and let* $\mathcal{F} = \{f_1, \ldots, f_m\} \subset K[x_1, \ldots, x_n]$ *be an inhomogeneous polynomial system such that* $(\mathcal{F}^{\mathrm{hom}})$ *is in generic coordinates. Then*

$$\mathrm{sd}_{DRL}\,(\mathcal{F}) \leq \mathrm{reg}\,\left(\mathcal{F}^{\mathrm{hom}}\right).$$

By a classical result one can always bound the regularity of an ideal with the Macaulay bound (see [15, Theorem 1.12.4]).

Corollary 6. (Macaulay bound, [26, Theorem 2], [12, Corollary 2]). *Consider a system of equations* $\mathcal{F} = \{f_1, \ldots, f_m\} \subset k[x_1, \ldots, x_n]$ *with* $d_i = \deg\,(f_i)$ *and* $d_1 \geq \ldots \geq d_m$. *Set* $l = \min\{n+1, m\}$. *Assume that* $|\mathcal{Z}_+\,(\mathcal{F}^{\mathrm{hom}})| < \infty$ *and that* (F^{hom}) *is in generic coordinates over* $\bar{k}$. *Then*

$$\mathrm{sd}_{DRL}\,(\mathcal{F}) \leq \mathrm{reg}\,\left(\mathcal{F}^{\mathrm{hom}}\right) \leq d_1 + \ldots + d_l - l + 1.$$

In particular, if $m > n$ and $d = d_1$, then

$$\mathrm{sd}_{DRL}(\mathcal{F}) \leq (n+1) \cdot (d-1) + 1.$$

In the proof of [12, Theorem 11] Caminata & Gorla implicitly revealed an efficient criterion to prove that a polynomial system is in generic coordinates. This observation was later formalized by Steiner in terms of the highest degree components of a polynomial system [34].

Theorem 7 ([34, **Theorem 3.2**]). *Let k be an algebraically closed field, and let $\mathcal{F} = \{f_1, \ldots, f_m\} \subset k[x_1, \ldots, x_n]$ be an inhomogeneous polynomial system such that*

(i) $(\mathcal{F}) \neq (1)$, and
(ii) $\dim(\mathcal{F}) = 0$.

Then the following are equivalent.

(1) $(\mathcal{F}^{\mathrm{hom}})$ is in generic coordinates and $\left| \mathcal{Z}_+ \left(\mathcal{F}^{\mathrm{hom}} \right) \right| \neq 0$.
(2) $\sqrt{\mathcal{F}^{\mathrm{top}}} = (x_1, \ldots, x_n)$.
(3) $(\mathcal{F}^{\mathrm{top}})$ is zero-dimensional in $k[x_1, \ldots, x_n]$.
(4) For every $1 \leq i \leq n$ there exists an integer $d_i \geq 1$ such that $x_i^{d_i} \in \mathrm{in}_{DRL}\left(\mathcal{F}^{\mathrm{hom}} \right)$.

In particular, (4) implies that every inhomogeneous polynomial system that contains a zero-dimensional DRL Gröbner basis is already in generic coordinates.

2.4 A Refined Solving Degree

In the Gröbner basis complexity literature there is another quantity that is also known as solving degree that refines Definition 2, cf. [14, §1]. Again let $\mathcal{F} = \{f_1, \ldots, f_m\} \subset P = k[x_1, \ldots, x_n]$ be a finite set of polynomials, and let $>$ be a term order on P. We start with $M_{\leq d}$ the Macaulay matrix for $\mathcal{F}$ up to degree d and compute a basis $\mathcal{B}$ of the row space of $M_{\leq d}$ via Gaussian elimination. Now we construct the Macaulay matrix $M_{\leq d}$ for the polynomial system $\mathcal{B}$ and again compute the basis $\mathcal{B}'$ of the row space via Gaussian elimination. We repeat this procedure until $\mathcal{B} = \mathcal{B}'$, at this point multiplying the polynomials in $\mathcal{B}'$ with all monomials up to degree $\leq d$ does not add any new elements to the basis after Gaussian elimination. We denote the final Macaulay matrix for $\mathcal{F}$ with $\hat{M}_d$, and we also denote $\hat{M}_d$'s row space via $\mathrm{rowsp}\left(\hat{M}_d \right)$. It is clear that

$$\mathrm{rowsp}\left(\hat{M}_d \right) \subset (\mathcal{F})_{\leq d} = \{f \in (\mathcal{F}) \mid \deg(f) \leq d\}, \tag{12}$$

and for d big enough $\mathrm{rowsp}\left(\hat{M}_d \right)$ will contain a $>$-Gröbner basis for $\mathcal{F}$. This motivates the following definition.

Definition 8 (Refined solving degree, see [14, Definition 1.1]). *Let* $\mathcal{F} = \{f_1, \ldots, f_m\} \subset k[x_1, \ldots, x_n]$ *and let* $>$ *be a term order. The refined solving degree of* $\mathcal{F}$ *is the least degree* d *such that* $\text{rowsp}\left(\hat{M}_d\right)$ *contains a Gröbner basis of* $\mathcal{F}$ *with respect to* $>$. *We denote it by* $\overline{\text{sd}}_>(\mathcal{F})$.

It is clear from the definitions that

$$\overline{\text{sd}}_> (\mathcal{F}) \leq \text{sd}_> (\mathcal{F}), \tag{13}$$

but the inequality might be strict.

Complexity Estimate via the Refined Solving Degree. Let $\mathcal{F} \subset P = k[x_1, \ldots, x_n]$ be a system of m homogeneous polynomials, let $\overline{\text{sd}}_>(\mathcal{F}) \leq d$ for some term order $>$ on P, and let D denote the number of monomials in P of degree $\leq d$. Then the dimensions of the Macaulay matrix $M_{\leq d}$ for $\mathcal{F}$ are bounded by $D \cdot m \times D$. Without loss of generality we can assume that $\mathcal{F}$ does not contain redundant elements, then the row space basis of $M_{\leq d}$ has either at least $m + 1$ elements or it contains a Gröbner basis with $\leq m$ many elements. In the first case, we have to build a new Macaulay matrix whose size is bounded by $D \cdot (m+1) \times D$. Iterating this argument we can build at most $(D - m)$ many Macaulay matrices, and we have to perform Gaussian elimination at most $D - m$ times. With $D \leq d \cdot \binom{n+d-1}{d}$ and our estimation from Eq. (10) we obtain the following worst case complexity estimate

$$\mathcal{O}\left(\sum_{i=0}^{D-m-1} (m+i) \cdot d \cdot \binom{n+d-1}{d}^\omega \right) \tag{14}$$

$$\in \mathcal{O}\left(\left(m \cdot D + \frac{(D-m-1) \cdot (D-m-2)}{2} \right) \cdot d \cdot \binom{n+d-1}{d}^\omega \right) \tag{15}$$

$$\in \mathcal{O}\left(m \cdot D^2 \cdot d \cdot \binom{n+d-1}{d}^\omega \right) \tag{16}$$

$$\in \mathcal{O}\left(m \cdot d^3 \cdot \binom{n+d-1}{d}^{\omega+2} \right). \tag{17}$$

2.5   Approximation of Binomial Coefficients

We recall the following well-known approximation of binomial coefficients.

Lemma 9. *([16, Lemma 17.5.1]). For* $0 < p < 1$, $q = 1 - p$ *such that* $n \cdot p$ *is an integer*

$$\frac{1}{\sqrt{8 \cdot n \cdot p \cdot q}} \leq \binom{n}{n \cdot p} \cdot 2^{-n \cdot H_2(p)} \leq \frac{1}{\sqrt{\pi \cdot n \cdot p \cdot q}}.$$

With $p = \frac{k}{n}$ the inequality then becomes

$$\sqrt{\frac{n}{8 \cdot k \cdot (n-k)}} \leq \binom{n}{k} \cdot 2^{-n \cdot H_2\left(\frac{k}{n}\right)} \leq \sqrt{\frac{n}{\pi \cdot k \cdot (n-k)}}. \tag{18}$$

In case the solving degree is an integer polynomial in the number of variables, then we have the following generic estimation for the binomial coefficient.

Proposition 10. *Let $n \geq 2$ be an integer, let $\alpha \geq 1$, and let $p \in \mathbb{Z}[x]$.*

(1) If $p(n) \geq n - 1$ for all $n \geq 2$, then

$$\left(\frac{n + p(n) - 1}{p(n) \cdot (n - 1)} \right)^{\alpha} \leq \frac{2^{\alpha}}{n - 1}.$$

(2) If $p(n) \geq 0$ for all $n \geq 2$, then

$$H_2 \left(\frac{p(n)}{n + p(n) - 1} \right) \leq \left(4 \cdot \frac{(n - 1) \cdot p(n)}{(n + p(n) - 1)^2} \right)^{\frac{1}{\log(4)}} \leq \left(4 \cdot \frac{p(n)}{n - 1} \right)^{\frac{1}{\log(4)}}.$$

In particular if $\alpha \geq 2$ and $p(n) \geq n - 1$ for all $n \geq 2$, then

$$\binom{n + p(n) - 1}{p(n)}^{\alpha} \in \mathcal{O} \left(\frac{1}{n - 1} \cdot 2^{\alpha \cdot \left(\frac{4 \cdot (n-1) \cdot p(n)}{\left(n+p(n)-1 \right)^{2 - \log(4)}} \right)^{\frac{1}{\log(4)}}} \right).$$

Proof. For (1), since $\alpha \geq 1$ and $n \geq 2$ we have that

$$\left(\frac{n + p(n) - 1}{p(n) \cdot (n - 1)} \right)^{\alpha} = \left(\frac{1}{p(n)} + \frac{1}{n - 1} \right)^{\alpha} \leq \left(\frac{2}{n - 1} \right)^{\alpha} \leq \frac{2^{\alpha}}{n - 1},$$

which proves the claim.

For (2), let $0 < p < 1$ we recall the following inequality for the binary entropy [39, Theorem 1.2]

$$H_2(p) \leq \left(4 \cdot p \cdot (1 - p) \right)^{\frac{1}{\log(4)}}.$$

Then

$$H_2 \left(\frac{p(n)}{n + p(n) - 1} \right) \leq \left(4 \cdot \frac{(n - 1) \cdot p(n)}{(n + p(n) - 1)^2} \right)^{\frac{1}{\log(4)}}.$$

Since $\log(4) \approx 1.3863$ we have that $n - 1 \leq n + p(n) - 1 \Rightarrow (n - 1)^{\frac{1}{\log(4)}} \leq (n + p(n) - 1)^{\frac{1}{\log(4)}}$, so the second inequality follows.

The last claim follows from Eq. (18) combined with the two inequalities. □

3 Refined Solving Degree and Degree of Regularity

Another measure to estimate the complexity of linear algebra-based Gröbner basis algorithms is the so-called degree of regularity.

Definition 11 (Degree of regularity, [7, Definition 4]). *Let k be a field, and let $\mathcal{F} \subset P = k[x_1, \ldots, x_n]$. Assume that $(\mathcal{F}^{\mathrm{top}})_d = P_d$ for some integer $d \geq 0$. The degree of regularity is defined as*

$$d_{\mathrm{reg}}(\mathcal{F}) = \min\left\{d \geq 0 \mid (\mathcal{F}^{\mathrm{top}})_d = P_d\right\}.$$

Note that by Theorem 7 and the projective weak Nullstellensatz [17, Chapter 8 §3 Theorem 8] $\mathcal{F}$ is in generic coordinates if and only if $d_{\mathrm{reg}}(\mathcal{F}) < \infty$.

Let $\mathcal{F} = \{f_1, \ldots, f_m, x_1^q - x_1, \ldots, x_n^q - x_n\} \subset \mathbb{F}_q[x_1, \ldots, x_n]$ be a polynomial system such that $d_{\mathrm{reg}}(\mathcal{F}) \geq \max\{q, \deg(f_1), \ldots, \deg(f_m)\}$, Semaev & Tenti [32, Theorem 2.1] showed that all S-polynomials appearing in Buchberger's algorithm have degree $\leq 2 \cdot d_{\mathrm{reg}}(\mathcal{F}) - 2$. Due to the requirement $d_{\mathrm{reg}}(\mathcal{F}) \geq q$ we do not expect that Semaev & Tenti's bound outperforms the Macaulay bound in practice. On the other hand, the inclusion of the field equations was only made to restrict to the $\mathbb{F}_q$-valued solutions of a polynomial system, the proof of [32, Theorem 2.1] only requires that $d_{\mathrm{reg}}(\mathcal{F}) < \infty$. Moreover, we will see that LWE polynomial systems contain a univariate polynomial $f_i \mid x_i^q - x_i$ for all variables x_i. Hence, LWE polynomial systems can restrict to the $\mathbb{F}_q$-valued solutions with polynomials of much smaller degrees than q. Therefore, we will now generalize [32, Theorem 2.1] to the general case $d_{\mathrm{reg}}(\mathcal{F}) < \infty$.

Let $\mathcal{F} = \{f_1, \ldots, f_m\} \subset k[x_1, \ldots, x_n]$ be such that $d_{\mathrm{reg}}(\mathcal{F}) < \infty$. Moreover, let $>$ be a degree compatible[1] term order on $k[x_1, \ldots, x_n]$. In principle, we simply repeat the refined analysis presented in [38, §3.4]:

(1) Compute the Macaulay matrices $M_{\leq d_{\mathrm{reg}}(\mathcal{F})}$ of the sequence $f_1, \ldots, f_m$ with respect to $>$, and put the matrix into row echelon form.
(2) Choose a finite set of generators $(\mathcal{B}) = I$ such that every element of $\mathcal{B}$ has degree $\leq d_{\mathrm{reg}}(\mathcal{F})$, and every monomial in $k[x_1, \ldots, x_n]$ of degree $\geq d_{\mathrm{reg}}(\mathcal{F})$ is divisible by at least one monomial in $\left(\mathrm{LM}_>(\mathcal{B})\right)$.[2] Then we perform Buchberger's algorithm on $\mathcal{B}$ to obtain a Gröbner basis $\mathcal{G}$.
(3) Compute a reduced Gröbner basis of $(\mathcal{F})$ via $\mathcal{G}$.

Let us now collect some properties of the basis $\mathcal{B}$.

Proposition 12. *Let k be a field, let $>$ be a degree compatible term order on $P = k[x_1, \ldots, x_n]$, and let $\mathcal{F} = \{f_1, \ldots, f_m\} \subset P$ be such that $d_{\mathrm{reg}}(\mathcal{F}) < \infty$. There exists a finite generating set $\mathcal{B}$ for $(\mathcal{F})$ such that*

(1) $\max_{f \in \mathcal{B}} \deg(f) \leq d_{\mathrm{reg}}(\mathcal{F})$.
(2) Every monomial $m \in k[x_1, \ldots, x_n]$ with $\deg(m) \geq d_{\mathrm{reg}}(\mathcal{F})$ is divisible by some $\mathrm{LM}_>(f)$, where $f \in \mathcal{B}$.
(3) For $f \in \mathcal{B}$ with $\deg(f) = d_{\mathrm{reg}}(\mathcal{F})$ one has $\deg\left(f - \mathrm{LT}_>(f)\right) < d_{\mathrm{reg}}(\mathcal{F})$.

---

[1] A term order $>$ on P is called degree compatible if for $f, g \in P$ with $\deg(f) > \deg(f)$ one also has that $f > g$.
[2] For ease of writing we introduce the shorthand notation: $\mathcal{B} = \{h_1, \ldots, h_r\}$, then $\left(\mathrm{LM}_>(\mathcal{B})\right) = \left(\mathrm{LM}_>(h_1), \ldots, \mathrm{LM}_>(h_r)\right)$.

Proof. We abbreviate $d_{\mathrm{reg}}(\mathcal{F}) = d_{\mathrm{reg}}$. First we construct the Macaulay matrix $M_{\leq d_{\mathrm{reg}}}$ of $\mathcal{F}$ with respect to $>$ and denote with $\mathcal{B}$ basis of the row space of $M_{\leq d_{\mathrm{reg}}}$. By assumption, we have that $d_{\mathrm{reg}} = d_{\mathrm{reg}}(\mathcal{B})$.

For $f \in \mathcal{F}$, if $\deg(f) \leq d_{\mathrm{reg}}$, then by construction $f \in (\mathcal{B})_{\leq d_{\mathrm{reg}}}$. If $\deg(f) > d_{\mathrm{reg}}$, then we compute the remainder r_f of f modulo $\mathcal{B}$ with respect to $>$ and add it to $\mathcal{B}$. By elementary properties of multivariate polynomial division, see [17, Sect. 2 §3 Theorem 3], and the degree of regularity we then have that $\deg(r_f) < d_{\mathrm{reg}}$.

Obviously, we have that $(\mathcal{B}) = (\mathcal{F})$ and (1) follows by construction, (2) follows from $d_{\mathrm{reg}} = d_{\mathrm{reg}}(\mathcal{B})$, and lastly basis elements that satisfy (3) can always be constructed with another round of Gaussian elimination on the elements of $\mathcal{B}$ of degree d_{reg}. □

Now we can prove the generalization of Semaev & Tenti's bound.

Theorem 13. *Let k be a field, let $>$ be a degree compatible term order on $\Gamma = k[x_1, \ldots, x_n]$, and let $\mathcal{F} = \{f_1, \ldots, f_m\} \subset P$ such that $d_{\mathrm{reg}}(\mathcal{F}) < \infty$. If $d_{\mathrm{reg}}(\mathcal{F}) \geq \max\{\deg(f_1), \ldots, \deg(f_m)\}$, then*

$$\overline{\mathrm{sd}}_{>}(\mathcal{F}) \leq 2 \cdot d_{\mathrm{reg}}(\mathcal{F}) - 1.$$

Proof. We abbreviate $d_{\mathrm{reg}}(\mathcal{F}) = d_{\mathrm{reg}}$. Let $\mathcal{B} = \{g_1, \ldots, g_t\}$ be the ideal basis from Proposition 12 for $(\mathcal{F})$. By assumption, we have that $\mathcal{F} \subset (\mathcal{B})_{\leq d_{\mathrm{reg}}}$, and by construction $\mathcal{B} \subset \mathrm{rowsp}(M_{d_{\mathrm{reg}}}(\mathcal{F}))$. Starting from $\mathcal{B}$ we compute a $>$-Gröbner basis via Buchberger's algorithm, see [17, Sect. 2 §7]. Let $g_i, g_j \in \mathcal{B}$, we consider their $>$-S-polynomial

$$S_{>}(g_i, g_j) = \frac{x^{\gamma}}{\mathrm{LM}_{>}(g_i)} \cdot g_i - \frac{x^{\gamma}}{\mathrm{LM}_{>}(g_j)} \cdot g_j,$$

where $x^{\gamma} = \mathrm{lcm}(\mathrm{LM}_{>}(g_i), \mathrm{LM}_{>}(g_j))$. Note that by [17, Sect. 2 §9 Proposition 4] we only have to consider the pairs with $\gcd(\mathrm{LM}_{>}(g_i), \mathrm{LM}_{>}(g_j)) \neq 1$. Since $\mathrm{LM}_{>}(g_i)$ and $\mathrm{LM}_{>}(g_j)$ must coincide in at least one variable and their degree is $\leq d_{\mathrm{reg}}$ we can conclude that

$$\deg\left(\frac{x^{\gamma}}{\mathrm{LM}_{>}(g_i)} \cdot g_i\right), \deg\left(\frac{x^{\gamma}}{\mathrm{LM}_{>}(g_j)} \cdot g_j\right) \leq 2 \cdot d_{\mathrm{reg}} - 1.$$

After performing division by remainder of the S-polynomial with respect to $\mathcal{B}$ we then also have that the remainder has degree $< d_{\mathrm{reg}}$ since $(\mathrm{LM}_{>}(\mathcal{B}))_d = (k[x_1, \ldots, x_n])_d$ for all $d \geq d_{\mathrm{reg}}$. Therefore, we can construct all S-polynomials within Buchberger's algorithm with non-trivial remainder via polynomials whose degree is $\leq 2 \cdot d_{\mathrm{reg}} - 1$. Since Buchberger's algorithm always produces a $>$-Gröbner basis we can conclude that $\overline{\mathrm{sd}}_{>}(\mathcal{F}) \leq 2 \cdot d_{\mathrm{reg}} - 1$. □

Corollary 14. *In the scenario of Theorem 13, the largest degree of S-polynomials appearing in Buchberger's algorithm is less than or equal to $2 \cdot d_{\mathrm{reg}}(\mathcal{F}) - 2$.*

Proof. Let us take another look at the S-polynomial

$$S_>(g_i, g_j) = \frac{x^\gamma}{\mathrm{LM}_>(g_i)} \cdot g_i - \frac{x^\gamma}{\mathrm{LM}_>(g_j)} \cdot g_j$$

$$= \frac{x^\gamma}{\mathrm{LM}_>(g_i)} \cdot \tilde{g}_i - \frac{x^\gamma}{\mathrm{LM}_>(g_j)} \cdot \tilde{g}_j,$$

where $x^\gamma = \mathrm{lcm}\left(\mathrm{LM}_>(g_i), \mathrm{LM}_>(g_j)\right)$ and $\tilde{g}_l = g_l - \mathrm{LM}_>(g_l)$ for $l = i, j$. Since the leading monomials are not coprime we have that

$$\deg\left(\frac{x^\gamma}{\mathrm{LM}_>(g_i)}\right), \deg\left(\frac{x^\gamma}{\mathrm{LM}_>(g_j)}\right) \leq d_{\mathrm{reg}} - 1.$$

Moreover, by Proposition 12 we have that $\deg(\tilde{g}_i), \deg(\tilde{g}_j) < d_{\mathrm{reg}}$. $\square$

4 Affine-Derived Polynomial Systems

LWE polynomial systems follow a very special structure. To construct one polynomial one starts with a univariate polynomial f and then substitutes a multivariate affine equation $\langle \mathbf{a}, \mathbf{x} \rangle + b$ into f. Many properties of LWE polynomial systems solely stem from this substitution, this motivates the following definition.

Definition 15 (Affine-derived polynomial systems). *Let k be a field, let $n, m \geq 1$ be integers, let $g_1, \ldots, g_m \in k[x]$ be non-constant polynomials, let $\mathbf{a}_1, \ldots, \mathbf{a}_m \in k^n$, and let $b_1, \ldots, b_m \in k$. In the polynomial ring $k[x_1, \ldots, x_n]$, we call*

$$g_1(\mathbf{a}_1^\mathsf{T} \mathbf{x} + b_1) = 0,$$

$$\ldots$$

$$g_m(\mathbf{a}_m^\mathsf{T} \mathbf{x} + b_m) = 0,$$

where $\mathbf{x} = (x_1, \ldots, x_n)^\mathsf{T}$, the affine-derived polynomial system of $g_1, \ldots, g_m$ by $(\mathbf{a}_1, b_1), \ldots, (\mathbf{a}_m, b_m)$. We also abbreviate affine-derived polynomial systems as tuple $\left((g_1, \mathbf{a}_1, b_1), \ldots, (g_m, \mathbf{a}_m, b_m)\right)$.

Next let us collect some properties of zero-dimensional affine-derived polynomial systems.

Theorem 16. *Let k be a field and let $\bar{k}$ be its algebraic closure, let $n \geq 1$ be an integer, and let $\mathcal{F} = \left((g_1, \mathbf{a}_1, b_1), \ldots, (g_n, \mathbf{a}_n, b_n)\right) \subset k[x_1, \ldots, x_n]$ be an affine-derived polynomial system. Assume that the matrix*

$$\mathbf{A} = (\mathbf{a}_1 \ldots \mathbf{a}_n)^\mathsf{T} \in k^{n \times n}$$

has rank n. Then

(1) LEX and DRL Gröbner bases of $\mathcal{F}$ can be computed via an affine transformation.

(2) $\mathcal{F}$ is a 0-dimensional polynomial system.

(3) $\dim_k \left(k[x_1,\ldots,x_n]/(\mathcal{F}) \right) = \prod_{i=1}^{n} \deg{(g)}_i$.

(4) Let $\mathcal{G} \subset \bar{k}[x_1,\ldots,x_n]$ be such that $\mathcal{F} \subset \mathcal{G}$ and $(\mathcal{G}) \neq (1)$. Then $(\mathcal{G}^{\mathrm{hom}})$ is in generic coordinates.

If in addition k is a finite field with q elements, and $g_i \mid x^q - x$ for all $1 \leq i \leq n$. Then

(5) Any ideal $I \subset k[x_1,\ldots,x_n]$ such that $\mathcal{F} \subset I$ is radical.

Proof. For (1), we define new variables via

$$\begin{pmatrix} y_1 \\ \vdots \\ y_n \end{pmatrix} = (\mathbf{a}_1 \ldots \mathbf{a}_n)^\mathsf{T} \begin{pmatrix} x_1 \\ \vdots \\ x_n \end{pmatrix} + \begin{pmatrix} b_1 \\ \vdots \\ b_n \end{pmatrix},$$

and since the matrix $\mathbf{A}$ has full rank this construction is invertible. Then the polynomial system is of the form $g_1(y_1) = \ldots = g_n(y_n) = 0$, so under any LEX and DRL term order the leading monomials of the polynomials are pairwise coprime, so by [17, Sect. 2 §9 Theorem 3, Proposition 4] we have found a Gröbner basis.

For (2), follows from [17, Sect. 5 §3 Theorem 6].

For (3), the quotient space dimension can be computed by counting the number of monomials not contained in $\left(y_1^{\deg(g_1)}, \ldots, y_n^{\deg(g_n)} \right)$.

For (4), follows from Theorem 7.

For (5), let $F = (x_1^q - x_1, \ldots, x_n^q - x_n) \subset k[x_1,\ldots,x_n]$ be the ideal of field equations. It is well-known that for any ideal $I \subset k[x_1,\ldots,x_n]$ the ideal $I + F$ is radical, see for example [25, Lemma 3.1.1]. Since $g_i \mid x^q - x$ we have for all $1 \leq i \leq n$ that

$$(\mathbf{a}_i^\mathsf{T}\mathbf{x} + c_i)^q - (\mathbf{a}_i^\mathsf{T}\mathbf{x} + c_i) = (\mathbf{a}_i^\mathsf{T}\mathbf{x})^q - (\mathbf{a}_i^\mathsf{T}\mathbf{x})$$

$$= \sum_{j=1}^{n} a_{i,j} \cdot (x_j^q - x_j) = \mathbf{a}_i^\mathsf{T} \begin{pmatrix} x_1^q - x_1 \\ \vdots \\ x_n^q - x_n \end{pmatrix} \in (\mathcal{F}).$$

So by invertibility $\mathbf{A}$ we have that $x_i^q - x_i \in (\mathcal{F})$ for all $1 \leq i \leq n$ which proves the claim. $\square$

Remark 17. Note that being in generic coordinates also follows from [12, Remark 13].

Corollary 18. *Let k be an algebraically closed field, let $m > n \geq 1$, let $\mathcal{F} = \left((g_1, \mathbf{a}_1, b_1), \ldots, (g_m, \mathbf{a}_m, b_m) \right) \subset k[x_1,\ldots,x_n]$ be an affine-derived polynomial system such that $\deg{(g_1)} \geq \ldots \geq \deg{(g_m)}$. Assume that the matrix*

$$\mathbf{A} = (\mathbf{a}_1 \ldots \mathbf{a}_m)^\mathsf{T} \in k^{m \times n}$$

has rank n. Then

$$\text{sd}_{DRL}(\mathcal{F}) \leq \sum_{i=1}^{n+1} (\deg(g_i) - 1) + 1.$$

In particular if $d \geq \deg(g_1)$, then

$$\text{sd}_{DRL}(\mathcal{F}) \leq (n+1) \cdot (d-1) + 1$$

Proof. Follows from Theorem 16 and the Macaulay bound Corollary 6.   □

4.1   LWE Polynomial Systems

Arora & Ge proposed a noise-free polynomial system to solve the Search-LWE problem [6]. If the error is distributed via a Gaussian distribution $\mathcal{N}(0, \sigma)$, then one assumes that the error always falls in the range $[-t \cdot \sigma, t \cdot \sigma]$ for some $t \in \mathbb{Z}$ such that $d = 2 \cdot t + 1 < q$. As we saw in Eq. (7), the probability of falling outside this interval decreases exponentially in t. Therefore, up to some probability, in $\mathbb{F}_q$ the error is then always a root of the polynomial

$$f(x) = x \cdot \prod_{i=1}^{t} (x+i) \cdot (x-i) \in \mathbb{F}_q[x]. \tag{19}$$

Since by construction $2 \cdot t + 1 < q$ there cannot exist $1 \leq i < j \leq t$ such that $i \equiv -j \mod q$. So f is a square-free polynomial and therefore divides the field equation $x^q - x$. For LWE samples $(\mathbf{a}_i, c_i) = (\mathbf{a}_i, \mathbf{a}_i^\mathsf{T}\mathbf{s} + e_i) \in \mathbb{Z}_q^n \times \mathbb{Z}_q$ one then has that in $\mathbb{F}_q[x_1, \ldots, x_n]$

$$f(c_i - \mathbf{a}_i^\mathsf{T}\mathbf{x}) = 0 \tag{20}$$

with probability $\geq 1 - \frac{2}{t \cdot \sqrt{2 \cdot \pi}} \cdot \exp\left(-\frac{t^2}{2}\right)$. Given m LWE samples one then constructs m polynomials of the form of Eq. (20), we call this polynomial system the LWE polynomial system $\mathcal{F}_{\text{LWE}}$. Obviously, the LWE polynomial system is an affine-derived polynomial system. The failure probability, i.e. the probability that at least one error term does not lie in the interval $[-t \cdot \sigma, t \cdot \sigma]$, can be estimated via the union bound

$$p_{fail} = m \cdot \mathbb{P}\left[|X| > t \cdot \sigma\right] \leq m \cdot \frac{2}{t \cdot \sqrt{2 \cdot \pi}} \cdot \exp\left(-\frac{t^2}{2}\right). \tag{21}$$

Moreover, by Theorem 16 for the polynomial system to be fully determined we have to require that $m \geq n$ and that n sample vectors are linearly independent.

To devise the complexity of Gröbner basis computations we in principle follow the strategy of [3, §5]. We assume that $\sigma = n^\epsilon$, where $0 \leq \epsilon \leq 1$, and let θ be such that $0 \leq \theta \leq \epsilon \leq 1$. We consider sample numbers of the following form

$$m_{\text{GB}} = e^{\gamma_\theta}, \tag{22}$$

where $\gamma_\theta = 2^{2 \cdot (\epsilon - \theta)}$.

Lemma 19 ([3, **Lemma 5**]). *Let q, n, σ be parameters of an LWE instance. Let $(\mathbf{a}_1, b_1), \ldots, (\mathbf{a}_m, b_m)$ be elements of $\mathbb{Z}_q^n \times \mathbb{Z}$ sampled according to LWE. If $t = \sqrt{2 \cdot \log(m)}$, then the LWE polynomial system vanishes with probability at least*

$$p_g = 1 - \sqrt{\frac{1}{\pi \cdot \log(m)}}.$$

By [3, Remark 1] $m \in \mathcal{O}(n)$ implies that $p_g \in 1 - o(1)$.

Therefore, we can deduce the degree D_{GB} required for $m_{\mathrm{GB}} = e^{\gamma_\theta}$ equations in the LWE polynomial system. By the previous lemma, we have to fix $t_{\mathrm{GB}} = \sqrt{2 \cdot \log(m_{\mathrm{GB}})} = \sqrt{2 \cdot \gamma_\theta}$, so

$$D_{\mathrm{GB}} = 2 \cdot \sqrt{2 \cdot \log(m_{\mathrm{GB}})} \cdot \sigma + 1$$
$$\in \mathcal{O}\left(\sqrt{\log(m_{\mathrm{GB}}) \cdot \sigma}\right) = \mathcal{O}\left(\sqrt{\gamma_\theta} \cdot \sigma\right) = \mathcal{O}\left(n^{\frac{1}{2} \cdot \iota - \theta}\right) = \mathcal{O}\left(\gamma_\theta \cdot n^\theta\right). \tag{20}$$

Theorem 20. *Let $q, n \geq 2, \sigma = \sqrt{\frac{n}{2 \cdot \pi}}$ be parameters of an LWE instance. Let $m_{GB} = e^{\frac{\pi \cdot n}{4}}$, and let $(\mathbf{a}_i, b_i)_{1 \leq i \leq m_{GB}}$ be elements of $\mathbb{F}_q^n \times \mathbb{F}_q$ sampled according to LWE. If the matrix $\mathbf{A} = (\mathbf{a}_1 \ldots \mathbf{a}_m)^{\mathsf{T}}$ has rank n, then a linear algebra-based Gröbner basis algorithm that computes a DRL Gröbner basis has time complexity*

$$\mathcal{O}\left(n \cdot 2^{\omega \cdot 2^{\frac{1}{\log(2)}}} \cdot n^{2 - \frac{1}{\log(4)} + \frac{\pi \cdot \log_2(e)}{4}} \cdot n\right)$$

and memory complexity

$$\mathcal{O}\left(n \cdot 2^{2^{1 + \frac{1}{\log(2)}}} \cdot n^{2 - \frac{1}{\log(4)} + \frac{\pi \cdot \log_2(e)}{4}} \cdot n\right).$$

The algorithm has success probability $\geq 1 - \frac{2}{\pi \cdot \sqrt{n}}$.

Proof. As in Lemma 19 let $t = \sqrt{2 \cdot \log(m_{\mathrm{GB}})}$. By our assumptions and Equation (23) we have that

$$D_{\mathrm{GB}} = 2 \cdot \sqrt{2 \cdot \log(m_{\mathrm{GB}})} \cdot \sigma + 1 = 2 \cdot \sqrt{2 \cdot \frac{\pi \cdot n}{4}} \cdot \sqrt{\frac{n}{2 \cdot \pi}} + 1 = n + 1.$$

Since the matrix $\mathbf{A}$ has full rank we can apply Corollary 18 to estimate the solving degree of the LWE polynomial system

$$\mathrm{sd}_{DRL}(\mathcal{F}_{\mathrm{LWE}}) \leq (n+1) \cdot (D_{\mathrm{GB}} - 1) + 1 = n^2 + n + 1.$$

Now we apply Proposition 10 with $p(n) = n^2 + n + 1$, then we perform the additional estimations

$$n^3 - 1 < n^3,$$
$$\left(n^2\right)^{2 - \log(4)} \leq \left(n^2 + 2 \cdot n\right)^{2 - \log(4)},$$

for all $n \geq 1$. Also note that $2 - \log(4) \approx 0.6137$, so we can divide by the expressions in the last inequality without affecting the sign. Therefore,

$$(n + p(n) - 1) \cdot H_2\left(\frac{p(n)}{n + p(n) - 1}\right) \leq 2^{\frac{1}{\log(2)}} \cdot n^{2 - \frac{1}{\log(4)}}.$$

The final claim then follows by converting m_{GB} into base 2.   □

Numerically we have that $2 - \frac{1}{\log(4)} \approx 1.2787$.

4.2   LWE with Small Errors

Suppose that the LWE error distribution χ can only take values in $\mathcal{E} \subset \mathbb{F}_q$ with $|\mathcal{E}| = D \ll \sqrt{n}$. Then the error polynomial is

$$f(x) = \prod_{e \in \mathcal{E}} (x - e) \tag{24}$$

of degree D. Moreover, for any LWE sample $(\mathbf{a}, b)$ we have $f(b - \mathbf{a}^\mathsf{T}\mathbf{x}) = 0$ with probability 1. Analog to Theorem 20 we can estimate the complexity of a DRL Gröbner basis computation.

Theorem 21. *Let q be a prime, and let $m > n \geq 2$ be integers. Let $(\mathbf{a}_i, b_i)_{1 \leq i \leq m}$ be elements of $\mathbb{F}_q^n \times \mathbb{F}_q$ sampled according to a LWE distribution $A_{\mathbf{s},\chi}$ such that the error distribution that χ can take at most D values. If the matrix $\mathbf{A} = (\mathbf{a}_1 \dots \mathbf{a}_m)^\mathsf{T}$ has rank n, then a linear algebra-based Gröbner basis algorithm that computes a DRL Gröbner basis has time complexity*

$$\mathcal{O}\left(m \cdot (D - 1) \cdot n \cdot 2^{\omega \cdot \left(8 \cdot D^{\log(4)} - 1\right)^{\frac{1}{\log(4)}} \cdot n}\right)$$

and memory complexity

$$\mathcal{O}\left(m \cdot (D - 1) \cdot n \cdot 2^{2 \cdot \left(8 \cdot D^{\log(4)} - 1\right)^{\frac{1}{\log(4)}} \cdot n}\right).$$

Proof. The LWE polynomial has degree D, therefore by Corollary 18

$$\mathrm{sd}_{DRL}(\mathcal{F}_{\mathrm{LWE}}) \leq (n + 1) \cdot (D - 1) + 1.$$

We apply Proposition 10 with $p(n) = (n+1) \cdot (D-1) + 1$ and do the estimations

$$\frac{(n + 1) \cdot (D - 1) + 1}{n - 1} = \frac{(n - 1) \cdot (D - 1) + 2 \cdot D - 1}{n - 1} \in \mathcal{O}(1),$$

for all $n \geq 2$,

$$((n + 1) \cdot (D - 1) + 1) \cdot (n - 1) = (n^2 - 1) \cdot (D - 1) + n - 1 \leq 2 \cdot n^2 \cdot D,$$
$$(n \cdot D)^{2 - \log(4)} \leq (n \cdot D + D - 1)^{2 - \log(4)},$$

for all $n \geq 1$.   □

4.3   LWE with Small Secrets

Suppose that the entries of the secret $\mathbf{s}$ of a LWE distribution $A_{\mathbf{s},\chi}$ can only take values in $\mathcal{S} \subset \mathbb{F}_q$ with $|\mathcal{S}| = D$. Then for $1 \leq i \leq n$ we can add the equations

$$f_i(x_i) = \prod_{s \in \mathcal{S}} (x_i - s) \tag{25}$$

to the LWE polynomial system. Trivially, $f_1, \ldots, f_n$ is a DRL Gröbner basis, so the monomials $g \notin \mathrm{in}_{DRL}(f_1, \ldots, f_n)$ have degree $\leq n \cdot (D - 1)$. Moreover, any univariate polynomial is trivially affine-derived.

Theorem 22. *Let q be a prime, and let $m > n \geq 2$ be integers. Let $(\mathbf{a}_i, b_i)_{1 \leq i \leq m}$ be elements of $\mathbb{Z}_q^n \times \mathbb{Z}_q$ sampled according to a LWE distribution $A_{\mathbf{s},\chi}$ such that the components of the secret can only take values in a set of size D. If the error polynomial f has $\deg(f) > D$, then a linear algebra-based Gröbner basis algorithm that computes a DRL Gröbner basis has time complexity*

$$\mathcal{O}\left(m \cdot (D-1) \cdot n^2 \cdot 2^{\omega \cdot 2^{\frac{1}{\log(2)}} \cdot (D-1)^{1 - \frac{1}{\log(4)}} \cdot n^{2 - \frac{1}{\log(4)}}} \right)$$

and memory complexity

$$\mathcal{O}\left(m \cdot (D-1)^2 \cdot n^3 \cdot 2^{2^{1 + \frac{1}{\log(2)}} \cdot (D-1)^{1 - \frac{1}{\log(4)}} \cdot n^{2 - \frac{1}{\log(4)}}} \right).$$

Proof. Let $\mathcal{F}_{\mathrm{LWE}}$ be the affine-derived LWE polynomial system, and let $\mathcal{F}_\mathcal{S}$ be the polynomials that have all possible values of the secret components as zeros, see Eq. (25). As preprocessing we compute the remainder of all polynomials in $\mathcal{F}_{\mathrm{LWE}}$ with respect to $\mathcal{F}_\mathcal{S}$ and DRL, then the remainder polynomials can at most have degree $n \cdot (D-1)$, see [17, Sect. 2 §6 Proposition 1]. Now we join the remainders and $\mathcal{F}_\mathcal{S}$ in a single system $\mathcal{F}$ and start the Gröbner basis computation. By Theorem 7 this polynomial system is in generic coordinates, therefore

$$\mathrm{sd}_{DRL}(\mathcal{F}) \leq (n+1) \cdot (n \cdot (D-1) - 1) + 1.$$

Now we apply Proposition 10 with $p(n) = (n+1) \cdot n \cdot (D-1) + 1$ and perform the additional estimations

$$\frac{(n+1) \cdot (n \cdot (D-1) - 1) + 1}{n-1} \leq \frac{(D-1) \cdot (n+1)^2}{n-1} \in \mathcal{O}((D-1) \cdot n)$$

for all $n \geq 2$, and

$$((n+1) \cdot n \cdot (D-1) + 1) \cdot (n-1) \leq n^3 \cdot (D-1),$$
$$n^2 \cdot (D-1) \leq n + (n+1) \cdot n \cdot (D-1),$$

for all $n \geq 1$. Then

$$\frac{n^3 \cdot (D-1)}{\left(n^2 \cdot (D-1) \right)^{2 - \log(4)}} = n^{2 \cdot \log(4) - 1} \cdot (D-1)^{\log(4) - 1}$$

which proves the claim. $\square$

LWE with Small Secrets and Small Errors. Lastly, let us shortly analyze the case of small secret small error LWE. Suppose that the errors are drawn from a set of size $D_{\mathcal{E}}$ and that the secrets are drawn from a set of size $D_{\mathcal{S}}$. As for Theorem 22 we can compute the DRL remainder of the LWE polynomials with respect to the n univariate polynomials limiting the possible solutions for the secret.

– If $D_{\mathcal{E}} \gg D_{\mathcal{S}}$, then we can estimate the degrees of the remainders as $\leq n \cdot (D_{\mathcal{S}} - 1)$, then we obtain the Macaulay bound

$$\mathrm{sd}_{DRL}(\mathcal{F}) \leq (n+1) \cdot n \cdot (D_{\mathcal{S}} - 1) + 1. \tag{26}$$

– If $n \cdot (D_{\mathcal{S}} - 1) \gg D_{\mathcal{E}} \geq D_{\mathcal{S}}$, then we can always estimate the degrees of the remainders as $\leq D_{\mathcal{E}}$, then

$$\mathrm{sd}_{DRL}(\mathcal{F}) \leq (n+1) \cdot (D_{\mathcal{E}} - 1) + 1. \tag{27}$$

– If $n \cdot (D_{\mathcal{S}} - 1) \gg D_{\mathcal{S}} > D_{\mathcal{E}}$, then we perform a variable transformation so that the LWE polynomials $\mathcal{F}_{\mathrm{LWE}}$ include n univariate polynomials, i.e. we exchange the roles of $\mathcal{F}_{\mathcal{S}}$ and $\mathcal{F}_{\mathrm{LWE}}$. The degrees of the remainders of $\mathcal{F}_{\mathcal{S}}$ are then bounded by $\leq D_{\mathcal{S}}$, and we obtain

$$\mathrm{sd}_{DRL}(\mathcal{F}) \leq n \cdot (D_{\mathcal{S}} - 1) + D_{\mathcal{E}}. \tag{28}$$

So the first case reduces to Theorem 22 and the second and the third one to Theorem 21, though the third case has a different constant term in the solving degree bound than small error LWE.

5 Sub-exponential Complexity Estimates via the Refined Solving Degree

In this section we use Theorem 13 to show that in an ideal scenario general LWE, binary secret LWE and binary error LWE admit sub-exponential Gröbner basis algorithms.

5.1 LWE with Exponential Many Samples

For general LWE the lowest achievable degree of regularity is the degree D of the error polynomial. In that degree there exist $\binom{n+D-1}{D}$ many monomials, hence to achieve degree of regularity m the number of samples m has to be at least the aforementioned binomial coefficient.

Theorem 23. *Let q, n, σ be parameters of an LWE instance, and let $D = 2 \cdot t \cdot \sigma + 1$ be the degree of the LWE polynomial. Let $m \in \mathcal{O}\left(\binom{n+D-1}{D}\right)$ be such that $d_{\mathrm{reg}}\left(\mathcal{F}_{LWE}^{\mathrm{top}}\right) = D$. Then a linear algebra-based Gröbner basis algorithm that computes a DRL Gröbner basis has time complexity*

$$\mathcal{O}\left(D^3 \cdot 2^{(\omega+3) \cdot 2^{\frac{1}{\log(2)}} \cdot (2 \cdot D - 1)^{\frac{1}{\log(4)}} \cdot (n-1)^{1 - \frac{1}{\log(4)}}}\right)$$

and memory complexity

$$\mathcal{O}\left(D^3 \cdot 2^{5 \cdot 2^{\frac{1}{\log(2)}}} \cdot (2 \cdot D - 1)^{\frac{1}{\log(4)}} \cdot (n-1)^{1 - \frac{1}{\log(4)}}\right).$$

For $t \to \infty$ the success probability of the algorithm approaches 1.

Proof. We can use Theorem 13 and Eq. (17) to estimate the complexity of a linear algebra based Gröbner basis algorithm. Then

$$\mathcal{O}\left(m \cdot (2 \cdot D - 1)^3 \cdot \binom{n + 2 \cdot D - 2}{2 \cdot D - 1}^{w+2}\right) \in \mathcal{O}\left(D^3 \cdot \binom{n + 2 \cdot D - 2}{2 \cdot D - 1}^{w+3}\right).$$

To estimate the binomial coefficient we use Eq. (18) and [39, Theorem 1.2]. Similar to Proposition 10, the term in the square root is estimated by $\mathcal{O}(1)$. For the entropy term we have that

$$(n + 2 \cdot D - 2) \cdot H_2\left(\frac{2 \cdot D - 1}{n + 2 \cdot D - 2}\right) \leq \left(4 \cdot \frac{(2 \cdot D - 1) \cdot (n-1)}{(n + 2 \cdot D - 2)^{2 - \log(4)}}\right)^{\frac{1}{\log(4)}}.$$

Without loss of generality $D \geq 1$, so $n - 1 \leq n + 2 \cdot D - 2$ which implies the complexity claim.

For the success probability, recall that by Equation (21)

$$\begin{aligned}
p_{fail} &\in \mathcal{O}\left(m \cdot \frac{2}{t \cdot \sqrt{2 \cdot \pi}} \cdot \exp\left(-\frac{t^2}{2}\right)\right) \\
&\in \mathcal{O}\left(\binom{n + D - 1}{D} \cdot \frac{2}{t \cdot \sqrt{2 \cdot \pi}} \cdot \exp\left(-\frac{t^2}{2}\right)\right) \\
&\in \mathcal{O}\left(\sqrt{\frac{n + D - 1}{D \cdot (n-1)}} \cdot 2^{2 \cdot \sqrt{D \cdot n}} \cdot \frac{2}{t \cdot \sqrt{2 \cdot \pi}} \cdot \exp\left(-\frac{t^2}{2}\right)\right) \\
&\in \mathcal{O}\left(\exp\left(2 \cdot \log(2) \cdot \sqrt{2} \cdot t \cdot \sigma \cdot n - \frac{t^2}{2}\right)\right),
\end{aligned}$$

which proves the claim. $\square$

In particular, for $\sigma = \sqrt{n}$ and $t = \frac{k}{\sqrt{\sigma}}$, where $k \in \mathbb{Z}$ we obtain the complexity estimate

$$\mathcal{O}\left((k \cdot \sqrt{n})^3 \cdot 2^{(w+3) \cdot 2^{\frac{1}{\log(2)}}} \cdot (4 \cdot k + 1)^{\frac{1}{\log(4)}} \cdot n^{1 - \frac{1}{2 \cdot \log(4)}}\right). \tag{29}$$

Since $1 - \frac{1}{2 \cdot \log(4)} \approx 0.6393$ this complexity estimate is sub-exponential.

5.2   Sub-exponential Complexity for Binary Secret LWE

Recall that binary secret LWE is the simplest case of small secret LWE, see Sect. 4.3. Let $F = (x_1^2 - x_1, \ldots, x_n^2 - x_n)$, and let $\mathcal{F}_{\text{LWE}} = \{f_1, \ldots, f_m\}$ be a binary secret LWE polynomial system where the (univariate) LWE error polynomial is of degree D. Without loss of generality we can first reduce the polynomials in $\mathcal{F}_{\mathrm{LWE}}$ modulo F with respect to the DRL term order. Let $f \in \mathcal{F}_{\mathrm{LWE}}$, after the preprocessing step only monomials of the form

$$m = x_1^{\alpha_1} \cdots x_n^{\alpha_n}, \tag{30}$$

where $\alpha_i \in \{0, 1\}$ for all i, are present in f and by elementary properties of multivariate polynomial division, see [17, Sect. 2 §3], also $\deg(f) \leq D$ after the reduction.

Suppose that all $f \in \mathcal{F}_{\mathrm{LWE}}$ are of degree D after the reduction, we want to find the minimal achievable degree of regularity $d_{\mathrm{reg}}((\mathcal{F}_{\mathrm{LWE}}) + F)$. Let $g \in P = \mathbb{F}_q[x_1, \ldots, x_n]$ be a monomial such that $x_i^2 \mid g$ for some i. Such a monomial can always be generated by some element in F^{top}, therefore we only have to consider monomials as in Eq. (30). Necessarily, these monomials must be generated by the elements in $\mathcal{F}_{\mathrm{LWE}}^{\mathrm{top}}$. Moreover, by elementary combinatorics there exist $\binom{n}{d}$ many monomials of the form of Eq. (30) in degree d.

To compute $d_{\mathrm{reg}}((\mathcal{F}_{\mathrm{LWE}}) + F)$ one iterates through:

(1) Let $d = 0$, and $\mathcal{G} = (\mathcal{F}_{\mathrm{LWE}}^{\mathrm{top}})$.
(2) Perform Gaussian elimination on $\mathcal{G}$ to obtain a minimal generating set. If $|\mathcal{G}| = \binom{n}{D+d}$ return $D + d$, else set $d = d + 1$.
(3) Compute $\mathcal{G} = \sum_{i=1}^{n} x_i \cdot (\mathcal{G}) \mod (x_1^2, \ldots, x_n^2)$, and return to step (2).

In order to achieve $d_{\mathrm{reg}}((\mathcal{F}_{\mathrm{LWE}}) + F) \leq D + d$, for some $d \geq 0$, we must require that

$$m \cdot \binom{n}{d} \overset{!}{\geq} \binom{n}{D+d} \tag{31}$$

$$\Leftrightarrow m \overset{!}{\geq} \frac{\binom{n}{D+d}}{\binom{n}{d}} = \prod_{i=1}^{D} \frac{n-d-i+1}{d+i}. \tag{32}$$

I.e., $m \in \mathcal{O}(n^D)$ many samples can be sufficient to achieve $d_{\mathrm{reg}}((\mathcal{F}_{\mathrm{LWE}}) + F) \leq D + 1$.

Provided that $m \in \mathcal{O}(n^D)$ and $d_{\mathrm{reg}}(\mathcal{F}_{\mathrm{LWE}}) \leq D + 1$, then we obtain analog to Theorem 23 the following complexity estimate

$$\mathcal{O}\left(n^D \cdot D^3 \cdot 2^{(\omega+2) \cdot 2^{\frac{1}{\log(2)}}} \cdot (2 \cdot D + 1)^{\frac{1}{\log(4)}} \cdot (n-1)^{1 - \frac{1}{\log(4)}}\right). \tag{33}$$

If $D = 2 \cdot t \cdot \sigma + 1$ and $\sigma = \sqrt{n}$, then we can further estimate $2 \cdot D + 1 \in \mathcal{O}(\sqrt{n})$. In particular, the exponent of n then becomes

$$\frac{1}{2 \cdot \log(4)} + 1 - \frac{1}{\log(4)} = 1 - \frac{1}{2 \cdot \log(4)} \approx 0.6393, \tag{34}$$

so the complexity estimate is indeed sub-exponential.

5.3   Polynomial Complexity for Binary Error LWE

Recall that binary error LWE is the simplest case of small error LWE, see Sect. 4.2. Every polynomial has degree 2. Analog to Theorem 21, we first pick n linearly independent samples $(\mathbf{a}_i, b_i)$ and perform a coordinate transformation. So without loss of generality we assume that $\mathbf{a}_i$ is the ith standard basis vector of $\mathbb{F}_q^n$. After the transformation these n LWE equations become $x_i^2 - x_i = 0$. We allocate them in the ideal $F = (x_1^2 - x_1, \ldots, x_n^2 - x_n)$, the remaining $m - n$ LWE polynomials we collect in $\mathcal{F}_{\text{LWE}}$. Therefore, we can interpret binary error LWE as special case of binary secret LWE, see Sect. 5.2. Suppose that we want to achieve $d_{\text{reg}}((\mathcal{F}_{\text{LWE}}) + F) \leq 2 + d$ for some $d \geq 0$, then by Equation (32)

$$m - n \overset{!}{\geq} \frac{(n - d - 1) \cdot (n - d)}{(d + 1) \cdot (d + 2)} \tag{35}$$

many LWE samples are necessary. In particular, for $d = 0$ this reduces to Arora & Ge's analysis [6]. Analog to Theorem 23 and Eq. (33), for $m \in \mathcal{O}(n^2)$ we then obtain the complexity estimate

$$\mathcal{O}\left(n^2 \cdot d^3 \cdot \binom{n + 2 \cdot d + 2}{2 \cdot d + 3}^{\omega + 2}\right) \in \mathcal{O}\left(d^3 \cdot n^{(\omega+2) \cdot (2 \cdot d + 3) + 2}\right). \tag{36}$$

It is easy to see from Eq. (35) that the higher the value of d the fewer samples are necessary to achieve a certain degree of regularity. Let us see an example.

Example 24. Let q be a prime, and let $n = 256$, and

(1) Let $m = 2 \cdot n$. The minimum $d \in \mathbb{Z}_{\geq 0}$ such that Equation (35) is satisfied is $d = 14$. Analog to Equation (36) with $m = 2 \cdot n$ we yield the complexity of a DRL Gröbner basis computation

$$\mathcal{O}\left(2 \cdot n \cdot d^3 \cdot \binom{n + 30}{31}^{\omega + 2}\right) \in \mathcal{O}\left(n^{31 \cdot \omega + 64}\right).$$

If we use $\omega \leq 3$, then direct evaluation of the left complexity yields 434 bits.

(2) Let $m = n^{\frac{3}{2}}$. The minimum $d \in \mathbb{Z}_{\geq 0}$ such that Equation (35) is satisfied is $d = 3$. Then we yield the complexity of a DRL Gröbner basis computation

$$\mathcal{O}\left(n^{\frac{3}{2}} \cdot d^3 \cdot \binom{n + 8}{9}^{\omega + 2}\right) \in \mathcal{O}\left(n^{9 \cdot \omega + 19.5}\right).$$

If we use $\omega \leq 3$, then direct evaluation of the left complexity yields 178 bits.

5.4   A Conjecture on the Castelnuovo-Mumford Regularity

Experimentally we observed the following property for all LWE polynomial systems studied in this paper.

Conjecture 25. *Let $\mathbb{F}_q$ be a finite field, and let $\mathcal{F}_{LWE} \subset \mathbb{F}_q[x_1, \ldots, x_n]$ be a LWE polynomial system.*

(1) For small secret LWE where the error is drawn from the interval $[-N, N]$

$$\mathrm{reg}\left(\mathcal{F}_{LWE}^{\mathrm{hom}}\right) \leq d_{\mathrm{reg}}\left(\mathcal{F}_{LWE}\right) + N - 1.$$

(2) For binary secret or binary error LWE

$$\mathrm{reg}\left(\mathcal{F}_{LWE}^{\mathrm{hom}}\right) \leq d_{\mathrm{reg}}\left(\mathcal{F}_{LWE}\right) + 1.$$

In case the conjecture holds, then the complexity estimates discussed in this section improve significantly since we can utilize the complexity estimate for Gaussian elimination on a *single* Macaulay matrix (Eq. (10)).

– The binary error LWE estimate from Eq. (33) improves to

$$\mathcal{O}\left(n^D \cdot D \cdot 2^{\omega \cdot 2^{\frac{1}{\log(2)}} \cdot (D+2)^{\frac{1}{\log(4)}} \cdot (n-1)^{1 - \frac{1}{\log(4)}}}\right). \tag{37}$$

– The binary secret LWE estimate from Eq. (36) improves to

$$\mathcal{O}\left(d \cdot n^{\omega \cdot (d+3)+2}\right). \tag{38}$$

E.g., under the conjecture the numeric complexities of Example 24 improve to 279 bits and 96 bits respectively.

We also note that for the conservative cryptanalyst there is a non-hypothetical alternative to Conjecture 25. By [14, Theorem 5.3] for a polynomial system $\mathcal{F}^{\mathrm{hom}} \subset P[x_0]$ in generic coordinates one always has that

$$d_{\mathrm{reg}}\left(\mathcal{F}\right) \leq \mathrm{reg}\left(\mathcal{F}^{\mathrm{hom}}\right). \tag{39}$$

Thus, one can estimate the lowest achievable complexity estimate for Gaussian elimination on the Macaulay matrix to produce a Gröbner basis of $\mathcal{F}_{\mathrm{LWE}}$ as follows:

(1) Compute/Estimate the lowest achievable degree of regularity $\hat{d}$ for $\mathcal{F}_{\mathrm{LWE}}$.
(2) Use Eq. (10) with $d = \hat{d}$ and $\omega = 2$ to estimate the lowest achievable complexity upper bound of a Gröbner basis computation for $\mathcal{F}_{\mathrm{LWE}}$.

We also recommend utilizing Eq. (10) itself for numerical computations rather than our complexity estimations. Our estimations are not tight but merely showcase the complexity class, i.e. exponential, sub-exponential & polynomial, for various LWE Gröbner basis computations.

5.5 Complexity Estimation of Kyber768

Finally, let us showcase our complexity estimation methods for a concrete crypto-graphic example: Kyber768 [31], a selected algorithm in the NIST post-quantum competition. Kyber768 is based on the Module-LWE problem, it has parameters $q = 3329$, $n = 3 \cdot 256$, $m = n$, $D = 2$ and errors as well as secrets are drawn from the interval $[-D, D]$. I.e., it is an instance of small error and small secret LWE. Thus, it induces a polynomial system of 1536 equations in 768 variables, where 768 polynomials stem from LWE samples. The lowest achievable degree of regularity for Kyber768 is estimated via

$$m \cdot \binom{n+d-1}{d} \overset{!}{\geq} \binom{n + (2 \cdot D + 1) + d - 1}{(2 \cdot D + 1) + d}. \tag{40}$$

In Table 2 we list our complexity estimates together with estimates for various lattice-based attacks. The complexities for lattice-based attacks have been computed via the lattice estimator tool[3] by Albrecht et al. [4].

Table 1. Bit complexity estimation for various attack strategies on Kyber768. Complexity of lattice-based attacks are computed via the lattice estimator [4]. For attacks where the lattice estimator provides estimations for multiple steps in an attack the most difficult step is shown in the table. For Gröbner basis attacks, the proven complexity estimate is computed via Eq. (10) and the Macaulay bound (Corollary 6). The optimistic complexity estimate is computed via Eq. (17), Theorem 13 and the lowest achievable degree of regularity. The lowest achievable complexity estimate is computed via Eq. (10) with sd$_{DRL}$ $(\mathcal{F}_{\text{Kyber768}}) \leq d_{\text{reg}}(\mathcal{F}_{\text{Kyber768}}) + (2 \cdot D + 1) - 1$ (Conjecture 25). Gröbner basis complexity estimates are computed with $\omega = 2$.

Method	BKW	USVP	BDD	BDD Hybrid	BDD MiTM Hybrid	Dual	Dual Hybrid	Proven complexity estimate		Optimistic complexity estimate		Lowest achievable complexity estimate	
Samples	2^{226}	768	768	768	768	768	768	768	768^4	768	768^4	768	768^4
Complexity (bits)	239	205	201	201	357	214	206	5554	5581	4717	419	1588	203
Solving degree	n.a.							3077		n.a.		n.a.	
Lowest achievable degree of regularity	n.a.							n.a.		232	7	232	7

6 Integrating Hints into LWE Polynomial Models

In two recent works Dachman-Soled et al. [18,19] introduced a framework for cryptanalysis of LWE in the presence of side information. E.g., in presence of

---

[3] https://github.com/malb/lattice-estimator.

a side-channel the information can come from the power consumption, electro-magnetic radiation, sound emission, etc. of a device. Once side information has been obtained it has to be modeled as mathematical hints. Dachman-Soled et al. categorize hints for LWE into four classes [18, §1]:

- Perfect hints: $\langle \mathbf{s}, \mathbf{v} \rangle = l \in \mathbb{F}_q$.[4]
- Modular hints: $\langle \mathbf{s}, \mathbf{v} \rangle \equiv l \mod k$.
- Approximate hints: $\langle \mathbf{s}, \mathbf{v} \rangle + e_\sigma = l \in \mathbb{F}_q$.
- Short vector hints: $\mathbf{v} \in \Lambda$, where Λ is the lattice associated to a LWE instance.

Dachman-Soled et al. [18,19] then discuss how these hints can be incorporated into Distorted Bounded Distance Decoding (DBDD) problems and lattice reduction algorithms to attack LWE. For readers interested how such hints can be obtained in practice we refer to [18, §4, 6]. Except for short vector hints that do not involve the LWE secret, we can incorporate these hints into LWE polynomial models.

Integrating a perfect hint is straight-forward since including an affine equation to the polynomial systems simply eliminates one variable.

If we are given a modular hint, then in principle one can compute a subset $\Omega \in \mathbb{F}_q$ such that $\langle \mathbf{s}, \mathbf{v} \rangle - l \in \Omega$ (in $\mathbb{F}_q$). Hence, we can set up a new polynomial with roots in Ω, substitute $\langle \mathbf{s}, \mathbf{v} \rangle - l$ into the polynomial and add it to the LWE polynomial system. Although this sounds simple, in practice the computation of Ω can be a challenge. In particular, if $\mathbf{s}$ and $\mathbf{v}$ can take all values in $\mathbb{F}_q^n$, then we expect the set Ω to be too big to improve Gröbner basis computations. On the other hand, if $\mathbf{s}, \mathbf{v} \in \{0, 1\}^n$ and we have the modular equation $\langle \mathbf{s}, \mathbf{v} \rangle \equiv 1 \mod 2$, then only the odd numbers in the interval $[0, n]$ can be in Ω, so the univariate polynomial with roots in Ω is of degree $\leq \lceil \frac{n}{2} \rceil$.

More interesting are approximate hints. Such hints are obtained from noisy side-channel information. In case the probability distribution of e_σ has smaller width than the one of the LWE error, then we can reduce the degree of a polynomial in the LWE polynomial system. Another class of hints that we interpret as approximate hints are Hamming weight hints. Suppose that the LWE secret entry s_1 is drawn from $D \subset \mathbb{F}_q$ and that we know the Hamming weight $H(s_1) = k$. Then we can add a univariate polynomial in x_1 to the LWE polynomial system whose roots are exactly the elements of D of Hamming weight k. I.e., Hamming weight hints restrict the number of possible solutions. We illustrate this with an example.

Example 26. Let q be a 16 bit prime number, and let $(\mathbf{a}_i, b_i)_{1 \leq i \leq m} \subset \mathbb{F}_q^n \times \mathbb{F}_q$ be a LWE sample generated with secret $\mathbf{s} \subset [-5, 5]^n$. As discussed in Sect. 4.3, for every variable x_i we can add a polynomial of degree 11 to the polynomial system to restrict the solutions to the interval. Suppose that s_i is represented

---

[4]   Dachman-Soled et al. [18] considered perfect hints over $\mathbb{Z}^n$, our notion of perfect hint corresponds to their modular hint, where the modulus is the characteristic of $\mathbb{F}_q$. They made this distinction, because affine equations over $\mathbb{Z}^n$ and $\mathbb{F}_q^n$ require different integration into lattice algorithms, see [18, §4.1, 4.2]. Though, for integration into polynomial systems perfect hints are always projected to $\mathbb{F}_q$.

by a signed 16 bit integer and that we learned its Hamming weight $H(s_i) = 2$, then $s_i \in \{3, 5\}$ and we can replace the degree 11 polynomial by a polynomial of degree 2.

Note that such Hamming weight biases can also persist if one opts for a more efficient memory representation of the secret entries.

Example 27. Let q be a 16 bit prime number, and let $(\mathbf{a}_i, b_i)_{1 \leq i \leq m} \subset \mathbb{F}_q^n \times \mathbb{F}_q$ be a LWE sample generated with secret $\mathbf{s} \subset [-2, 2]^n$. As discussed in Sect. 4.3, for every variable x_i we can add a polynomial of degree 5 to the polynomial system to restrict the solutions to the interval. Assume that the entries of $\mathbf{s}$ are stored as signed integers in the interval $\left[-\frac{q}{2}, \frac{q}{2}\right]$, then

– if $H(s_i) = 0$, then $s_1 = 0$,
– if $H(s_i) = 1$, then $s_1 \in \{1, 2\}$, and
– if $H(s_i) = 2$, then $s_1 \in \{-1, -2\}$.

So if one can learn the Hamming weight of s_i, then one either obtains a perfect hint or one can replace the degree 5 polynomial by a degree 2 polynomial.

Moreover, modular and approximate hints can be combined in a hybrid manner.

Example 28. Let q be a 16 bit prime number, and let $(\mathbf{a}_i, b_i)_{1 \leq i \leq m} \subset \mathbb{F}_q^n \times \mathbb{F}_q$ be a LWE sample generated with secret $\mathbf{s} \subset [-5, 5]^n$. Assume that the entries of $\mathbf{s}$ are stored as signed integers in the interval $\left[-\frac{q}{2}, \frac{q}{2}\right]$. If $H(s_i) = 2$ and $s_i \equiv 1$ mod 3, then $s_i \in \{-2, 4\}$. So we can replace the degree 11 polynomial by a polynomial of degree 2.

In practice this can have devastating consequences. If we can reduce a small secret LWE instance to binary secret LWE or even worse to binary secret binary error LWE, then we expect to achieve a lower degree of regularity with less number of samples necessary compared to the plain polynomial system. We numerically showcase this in the following example.

Example 29. Let q be a 16 bit prime number, assume that we are given small secret small error LWE over $\mathbb{F}_q^{256}$ whose secrets and error are drawn from $[-2, 2]$. Let $m = 256^{\frac{3}{2}}$ samples be given, and assume that we have enough Hamming weight hints for the secret and the error terms to transform the LWE polynomial system to either

(i) binary secret LWE, or
(ii) binary secret binary error LWE.

In Table 2 we record the least integer d such that $d_{\text{reg}} (\mathcal{F}_{\text{LWE}}) \leq D + d$ together with the optimistic complexity estimate from Eq. (17) and the lowest achievable complexity estimate implied by Eq. (39) for various numbers of perfect hints.

Table 2. Complexity estimates for small secret small error LWE, binary secret LWE and binary secret binary error LWE over $\mathbb{F}_q^{256}$ with error polynomial degree $D = 5$ and $m = 256^{\frac{3}{2}}$. The column d lists the least integer such that $d_{\mathrm{reg}}(\mathcal{F}_{\mathrm{LWE}}) \leq D + d$ for a given number of perfect hints. The optimistic complexity estimate is computed via Equation (17) and the lowest achievable complexity estimate is computed via Equation (10) with $\mathrm{sd}_{DRL}(\mathcal{F}_{\mathrm{LWE}}) = d_{\mathrm{reg}}(\mathcal{F}_{\mathrm{LWE}}) + D - 1$ where $D = 5, 2$ (Conjecture 25).

	Small Secret Small Error LWE $D = 5$			Binary Secret LWE $D = 5$			Binary Secret Binary Error LWE $D = 2$		
Perfect hints	d	Optimistic complexity estimate (bits)	Lowest achievable complexity estimate (bits)	d	Optimistic complexity estimate (bits)	Lowest achievable complexity estimate (bits)	d	Optimistic complexity estimate (bits)	Lowest achievable complexity estimate (bits)
$\omega = 2$									
0	57	1391	481	38	1118	370	3	237	92
50	45	1122	393	30	906	303	2	188	78
150	22	596	221	15	499	174	1	127	59
190	13	387	152	8	320	117	0	80	45
$\omega = 3$									
0	57	1731	712	38	1389	547	3	291	131
50	45	1394	580	30	1125	336	2	229	110
210	8	339	165	5	290	127	0	88	56

7 Discussion

In this paper we proved that any fully-determined LWE polynomial system is in generic coordinates. Therefore, bounds for the complexity of DRL Gröbner basis computations can be found via the Castelnuovo-Mumford regularity. In particular, this permits provable complexity estimates without relying on strong but unproven theoretical assumptions like semi-regularity [24,28].

We also demonstrated how the degree of regularity of a LWE polynomial system can be used to derive complexity estimates. Though, in practice one has to keep in mind that a degree of regularity computation usually requires a non-trivial Gröbner basis computation for the highest degree components. Hence, we interpret complexity bounds based on the lowest achievable degree of regularity as worst-case bounds from a designer's perspective that *could* be achievable by an adversary.

Based on the lowest achievable degree of regularity, we discussed that a conservative cryptanalyst should assume that Gaussian elimination on a single Macaulay matrix in the degree of regularity is sufficient to solve Search-LWE.

Moreover, we discussed how side information can be incorporated into LWE polynomial systems, and we showcased how it can affect the complexity of Gröbner basis computations.

Overall, we have presented a new framework to aid algebraic cryptanalysis for LWE-based cryptosystems under minimal theoretical assumptions on the polynomial system.

Acknowledgments. The author would like to thank the anonymous reviewers at Eurocrypt 2024 for their valuable comments and helpful suggestions which improved both the quality and presentation of the paper. The author would like to thank Prof. Elisabeth Oswald at Alpen-Adria-Universität Klagenfurt for her suggestion to study LWE polynomial system as well as the hints framework of Dachman-Soled et al. Matthias Steiner has been supported by the European Research Council (ERC) under the European Union's Horizon 2020 research and innovation program (grant agreement No. 725042).

References

1. Ajtai, M.: Generating hard instances of lattice problems (extended abstract). In: 28th Annual ACM Symposium on Theory of Computing, Philadephia, PA, USA, 22–24 May pp. 99–108. ACM Press, (1996). https://doi.org/10.1145/237814. 237838

2. Albrecht, M.R., Cid, C., Faugère, J.C., Fitzpatrick, R., Perret, L.: Algebraic algorithms for LWE problems. ACM Commun. Comput. Algebra **49**(2), 62 (2015). https://doi.org/10.1145/2815111.2815158

3. Albrecht, M.R., Cid, C., Faugère, J.C., Perret, L.: Algebraic algorithms for LWE. Cryptology ePrint Archive, Report 2014/1018 (2014). https://eprint.iacr. org/2014/1018

4. Albrecht, M.R., Player, R., Scott, S.: On the concrete hardness of Learning with errors. J. Math. Cryptol. **9**(3), 169–203 (2015). https://doi.org/10.1515/jmc-2015-0016

5. Alman, J., Williams, V.V.: A refined laser method and faster matrix multiplication. In: Marx, D. (ed.) 32nd Annual ACM-SIAM Symposium on Discrete Algorithms, pp. 522–539. ACM-SIAM, Virtual Conference, 10–13 Jan (2021). https://doi.org/ 10.1137/1.9781611976465.32

6. Arora, S., Ge, R.: New algorithms for learning in presence of errors. In: Aceto, L., Henzinger, M., Sgall, J. (eds.) ICALP 2011. LNCS, vol. 6755, pp. 403–415. Springer, Heidelberg (2011). https://doi.org/10.1007/978-3-642-22006-7_34

7. Bardet, M., Faugère, J.C., Salvy, B.: On the complexity of Gröbner basis computation of semi-regular overdetermined algebraic equations. In: Proceedings of the International Conference on Polynomial System Solving, pp. 71–74 (2004)

8. Bayer, D., Stillman, M.: A criterion for detecting m-regularity. Invent. Math. **87**(1), 1–11 (1987). https://doi.org/10.1007/BF01389151

9. Bos, J.W., Costello, C., Ducas, L., Mironov, I., Naehrig, M., Nikolaenko, V., Raghunathan, A., Stebila, D.: Frodo: Take off the ring! Practical, quantum-secure key exchange from LWE. In: Weippl, E.R., Katzenbeisser, S., Kruegel, C., Myers, A.C., Halevi, S. (eds.) ACM CCS 2016: 23rd Conference on Computer and Communications Security, 24–28 Oct, Vienna, Austria, pp. 1006–1018. ACM Press (2016). https://doi.org/10.1145/2976749.2978425

10. Brakerski, Z., Langlois, A., Peikert, C., Regev, O., Stehlé, D.: Classical hardness of learning with errors. In: Boneh, D., Roughgarden, T., Feigenbaum, J. (eds.) 45th Annual ACM Symposium on Theory of Computing, Palo Alto, CA, USA, 1–4 Jun, pp. 575–584. ACM Press (2013).https://doi.org/10.1145/2488608.2488680

11. Buchberger, B.: Ein Algorithmus zum Auffinden der Basiselemente des Restklassenringes nach einem nulldimensionalen Polynomideal. Ph.D. thesis, Universität Innsbruck (1965)

12. Caminata, A., Gorla, E.: Solving multivariate polynomial systems and an invariant from commutative algebra. In: Bajard, J.C., Topuzoğlu, A. (eds.) WAIFI 2020. LNCS, vol. 12542, pp. 3–36. Springer, Cham (2021). https://doi.org/10.1007/978-3-030-68869-1_1

13. Caminata, A., Gorla, E.: Solving multivariate polynomial systems and an invariant from commutative algebra. arXiv: 1706.06319 (2022), Version: 7

14. Caminata, A., Gorla, E.: Solving degree, last fall degree, and related invariants. J. Symb. Comput. **114**, 322–335 (2023). https://doi.org/10.1016/j.jsc.2022.05.001

15. Chardin, M.: Some results and questions on Castelnuovo-Mumford regularity. In: Peeva, I. (ed.) Syzygies and Hilbert Functions. Lecture Notes in Pure and Applied Mathematics, vol. 254, pp. 1–40. Chapman and Hall/CRC (2007)

16. Cover, T.M., Joy, T.A.: Elements of Information Theory, 2 edn. John Wiley & Sons, Ltd., Hoboken, New Jersey (2006). https://doi.org/10.1002/0471200611

17. Cox, D.A., Little, J., O'Shea, D.: Ideals, Varieties, and Algorithms. UTM, Springer, Cham (2015). https://doi.org/10.1007/978-3-319-16721-3

18. Dachman-Soled, D., Ducas, L., Gong, H., Rossi, M.: LWE with side information: attacks and concrete security estimation. In: Micciancio, D., Ristenpart, T. (eds.) CRYPTO 2020. LNCS, vol. 12171, pp. 329–358. Springer, Cham (2020). https://doi.org/10.1007/978-3-030-56880-1_12

19. Dachman-Soled, D., Gong, H., Hanson, T., Kippen, H.: Revisiting security estimation for LWE with hints from a geometric perspective. In: Handschuh, H., Lysyanskaya, A. (eds.) CRYPTO 2023, Part V. LNCS, vol. 14085, pp. 748–781. Springer, Heidelber (2023). https://doi.org/10.1007/978-3-031-38554-4_24

20. Ding, J., Schmidt, D.: Solving degree and degree of regularity for polynomial systems over a finite fields. In: Fischlin, M., Katzenbeisser, S. (eds.) Number Theory and Cryptography. LNCS, vol. 8260, pp. 34–49. Springer, Heidelberg (2013). https://doi.org/10.1007/978-3-642-42001-6_4

21. Eisenbud, D.: The Geometry of Syzygies: A Second Course Commutative Algebra and Algebraic Geometry, 1 edn. Springer New York (2005). https://doi.org/10.1007/b137572

22. Faugère, J.C.: A new efficient algorithm for computing Gröbner bases (F4). J. Pure Appl. Algebra **139**(1), 61–88 (1999). https://doi.org/10.1016/S0022-4049(99)00005-5

23. Faugère, J.C.: A new efficient algorithm for computing Gröbner bases without reduction to zero (F5). In: Proceedings of the 2002 International Symposium on Symbolic and Algebraic Computation, ISSAC 2002, pp. 75–83. Association for Computing Machinery (2002). https://doi.org/10.1145/780506.780516

24. Fröberg, R.: An inequality for Hilbert series of graded algebras. Math. Scand. **56**, 117–144 (1985). https://doi.org/10.7146/math.scand.a-12092

25. Gao, S.: Counting Zeros over Finite Fields Using Gröbner Bases. Master's thesis, Carnegie Mellon University (2009). https://www.cs.cmu.edu/~sicung/papers/MS_thesis.pdf

26. Lazard, D.: Gröbner bases, Gaussian elimination and resolution of systems of algebraic equations. In: van Hulzen, J.A. (ed.) EUROCAL 1983. LNCS, vol. 162, pp. 146–156. Springer, Heidelberg (1983). https://doi.org/10.1007/3-540-12868-9_99

27. Micciancio, D.: On the hardness of learning with errors with binary secrets. Theory Comput. **14**(13), 1–17 (2018). https://doi.org/10.4086/toc.2018.v014a013

28. Pardue, K.: Generic sequences of polynomials. J. Algebra **324**(4), 579–590 (2010). https://doi.org/10.1016/j.jalgebra.2010.04.018

29. Peikert, C.: Public-key cryptosystems from the worst-case shortest vector problem: extended abstract. In: Mitzenmacher, M. (ed.) 41st Annual ACM Symposium on Theory of Computing, Bethesda, MD, USA, 31 May–2 Jun, pp. 333–342. ACM Press (2009). https://doi.org/10.1145/1536414.1536461

30. Regev, O.: On lattices, learning with errors, random linear codes, and cryptography. In: Gabow, H.N., Fagin, R. (eds.) 37th Annual ACM Symposium on Theory of Computing, Baltimore, MA, USA, 22–24 May, pp. 84–93. ACM Press (2005). https://doi.org/10.1145/1060590.1060603

31. Schwabe, P., et al.: CRYSTALS-KYBER. Tech. rep., National Institute of Standards and Technology (2022). https://csrc.nist.gov/Projects/post-quantum-cryptography/selected-algorithms-2022

32. Semaev, I., Tenti, A.: Probabilistic analysis on Macaulay matrices over finite fields and complexity of constructing Gröbner bases. J. Algebra **565**, 651–674 (2021). https://doi.org/10.1016/j.jalgebra.2020.08.035

33. Shor, P.W.: Algorithms for quantum computation: Discrete logarithms and factoring. In: 35th Annual Symposium on Foundations of Computer Science, Santa Fe, NM, USA, 20–22 Nov, pp. 124–134. IEEE Computer Society Press (1994). https://doi.org/10.1109/SFCS.1994.365700

34. Steiner, M.J.: Solving degree bounds for iterated polynomial systems. IACR Trans. Symm. Cryptol. **2024**(1), 357–411 (2024). https://doi.org/10.46586/tosc.v2024.i1.357-411

35. Steiner, M.J.: The complexity of algebraic algorithms for LWE. Cryptology ePrint Archive, Paper 2024/313 (2024). https://eprint.iacr.org/2024/313

36. Storjohann, A.: Algorithms for matrix canonical forms. Doctoral thesis, ETH Zurich, Zürich (2000). https://doi.org/10.3929/ethz-a-004141007, diss., Technische Wissenschaften ETH Zürich, Nr. 13922, 2001

37. Sun, C., Tibouchi, M., Abe, M.: Revisiting the hardness of binary Error LWE. In: Liu, J.K., Cui, H. (eds.) ACISP 2020. LNCS, vol. 12248, pp. 425–444. Springer, Cham (2020). https://doi.org/10.1007/978-3-030-55304-3_22

38. Tenti, A.: Sufficiently overdetermined random polynomial systems behave like semiregular ones. Ph.D. thesis, University of Bergen (2019). https://hdl.handle.net/1956/21158

39. Topsøe, F.: Bounds for entropy and divergence for distributions over a two-element set. J. Ineq. Pure Appl. Math. **2**(2), Paper No. 25, 13 p.–Paper No. 25, 13 p. (2001). http://eudml.org/doc/122035

Pauli Manipulation Detection Codes and Applications to Quantum Communication over Adversarial Channels

Thiago Bergamaschi[✉]

Department of EECS, UC Berkeley, Berkeley, USA
thiagob@berkeley.edu

Abstract. We introduce and explicitly construct a quantum error-detection code we coin a "Pauli Manipulation Detection" code (or PMD), which detects every Pauli error with high probability. We apply them to construct the first near-optimal codes for two tasks in quantum communication over adversarial channels.

Our main application is an approximate quantum code over qubits which can efficiently correct from a number of (worst-case) erasure errors approaching the quantum Singleton bound. Our construction is based on the composition of a PMD code with a stabilizer code which is list-decodable from erasures, a variant of the stabilizer list-decodable codes studied by Leung and Smith [49], and Bergamaschi et al. [17].

Our second application is a quantum authentication code for "qubit-wise" channels, which does not require a secret key. Remarkably, this gives an example of a task in quantum communication which is provably impossible classically. Our construction is based on a combination of PMD codes, stabilizer codes, and classical non-malleable codes (Dziembowski et al. [33]), and achieves "minimal redundancy" (rate $1 - o(1)$).

Keywords: Quantum Error Correction · Secret Sharing · Non-Malleability

1 Introduction

Algebraic Manipulation Detection (AMD) codes, introduced by Cramer, Dodis, Fehr, Padró and Wichs [26], are a fundamental primitive at the intersection of coding theory and cryptography. They are a form of keyless message authentication code, which offers error-detection guarantees against additive errors by assuming that the tampering adversary cannot "see" the codeword. In other words, AMDs detect arbitrary bit-flip errors with high probability, so long as the error is independent of the internal randomness in the code. Although their error-detection guarantees may seem a bit restrictive at first, AMD codes have found numerous applications as building blocks to stronger cryptographic primitives,

© International Association for Cryptologic Research 2024
M. Joye and G. Leander (Eds.): EUROCRYPT 2024, LNCS 14653, pp. 404–433, 2024.
https://doi.org/10.1007/978-3-031-58734-4_14

including secret sharing schemes [24], non-malleable codes [33], fuzzy extractors [26], and more.[1]

In this paper we consider a quantum analog of AMD codes. In particular, we introduce and explicitly construct quantum error-detection codes - subspaces of complex vector spaces - that can detect arbitrary Pauli errors (of arbitrarily large weight). This error model includes both bit-flip and phase-flip errors, generalizing in a sense their classical counterparts. Inspired by their name, we refer to our codes as "Pauli Manipulation Detection" codes (or PMDs):[2]

Definition 1. *We refer to a subspace Π of an n-qubit Hilbert space as an ε-PMD if, for every n-qubit Pauli error $E \neq \mathbb{I}$,*

$$\|\Pi E \Pi\|_{\infty} \leq \varepsilon. \tag{1}$$

In the (informal) definition above, Π plays both the role of code-space, and the projection onto it. This definition implies that every Pauli error on the code is detected *almost-deterministically*: if a code-state $|\psi\rangle \in \Pi$ is corrupted by a Pauli error $E \neq \mathbb{I}$, the projective measurement onto the PMD code-space $(\Pi, \mathbb{I} - \Pi)$ does not detect the Pauli tampering with probability at most

$$\langle \psi | E^{\dagger} \Pi E | \psi \rangle \leq \|\Pi E^{\dagger} \Pi E \Pi\|_{\infty} = \|\Pi E \Pi\|_{\infty}^{2} \leq \varepsilon^{2}. \tag{2}$$

Crucially, the gentle-measurement lemma then implies that PMD codes are able to detect whether they were corrupted by a Pauli, without disturbing the corrupted code-state. That is, conditioned on measuring $\mathbb{I} - \Pi$,

$$(\mathbb{I} - \Pi)E|\psi\rangle \approx E|\psi\rangle. \tag{3}$$

We leverage this key idea to construct the first efficient quantum codes approaching the information-theoretically optimal rate (or "minimal redundancy") for two tasks in quantum coding theory and cryptography.

Applications. Our main application is an approximate quantum code over qubits for the adversarial erasures channel, which is able to efficiently correct from a near-optimal number of erasure errors. Due to a well-known connection between quantum error correction and secret sharing [23,29,36,56], this result can also be understood as a near-optimal *ramp* quantum secret sharing scheme with qubit shares.

Our second application is a quantum *tamper-detection* code for "qubit-wise" channels. In turn, this result can be thought of as a quantum authentication code for a restricted, un-entangled, adversarial model, which does not require a secret key. Curiously, these codes provide a form of error-detection which is provably impossible with classical messages.

---

[1] We refer the reader to [27] for a review of AMD codes, and Sect. 1.2 for more related work.

[2] $\|\cdot\|_{\infty}$ is the operator norm, or Schatten infinity norm.

1.1 Our Results

Constructions of PMD Codes. Our first result is an explicit construction of PMD codes, which achieves rate near 1 and inverse-exponential error.

Theorem 1. *For all sufficiently large integers n and $\lambda | n$, there exists an ε-PMD encoding $n - \lambda$ qubits into n qubits with error $\varepsilon \leq n^{1/2} \cdot 2^{1-\lambda/4}$. Moreover, it can be constructed and encoded efficiently.*

Our construction is based on the stabilizer "Purity Testing" codes (PTCs) introduced by Barnum, Crepeau, Gottesman, Smith and Tapp [11] in the context of quantum message authentication. Informally, a PTC is a pseudorandom set of stabilizer codes[3] $\{Q_k\}_{k \in K}$ which detects every Pauli error with high probability (over random choice of the key k). We show that the natural approach of encoding a message state $|\psi\rangle$ into a superposition of PTC encodings,

$$\mathsf{Enc_{PMD}} \, |\psi\rangle = |K|^{-1/2} \sum_{k \in K} |k\rangle \otimes \mathsf{Enc}_{Q_k} |\psi\rangle, \qquad (4)$$

almost defines a PMD.[4] Unfortunately, in general this construction is not a PMD. Nevertheless, we show that the family of PTC's designed in [11] satisfy a certain form of "key manipulation security", which guarantees this construction is secure (and maybe of independent interest).

Approximate Quantum Erasure Codes on the Quantum Singleton Bound. Our first application of PMD codes is to approximate quantum error correction.

An erasure error (or detectable leakage) on a quantum error correcting code corresponds to an error on a known location of the code. Erasure correction has recently found renewed interest in the quantum computing community, due to connections with quantum secret sharing [23], fault tolerance [59], the information-disturbance tradeoff [47], and even information retrieval in black holes [60].

The quantum Singleton or "no-cloning" bound imposes an information-theoretic limit on the maximum number of erasures a quantum code can (even approximately) correct from. It states that no quantum code of rate r can correct from more than a $\frac{1}{2}(1 - r) + o(1)$ fraction of erasures, for any assymptotically small recovery error [37,46,54]. Moreover, to approach this bound over small alphabet sizes, one fundamentally needs *approximate* quantum error correction: A famous result by Rains [53] showed that no exact quantum code on qubits can correct from more than even a $1/3$ fraction of erasures.

---

[3] Stabilizer codes [35] are a quantum analog of linear codes, defined by the joint $+1$ eigenspace of a set of commuting Pauli operators (the generators). A Pauli error is said to be detectable if it anti-commutes with one of the generators.

[4] $\mathsf{Enc_{PMD}}$ and the Enc_{Q_k} are unitaries, acting on a message register and ancilla qubits initialized to $|0\rangle$ (omitted for clarity).

Our main result in this work is a randomized construction of an efficient and near-optimal approximate quantum code over qubits for the adversarial (worst-case) erasures channel.

Theorem 2 (Main Result). *For every rate* $0 < r < 1$ *and sufficiently large* $n \in \mathbb{N}$, *there exists a Monte Carlo construction of an* n *qubit quantum code of rate* r *which corrects from a fraction* $\delta \geq \frac{1}{2}(1-r) - O(\log^{-1} n)$ *of erasures, up to an inverse-exponentially small recovery error* $\varepsilon = 2^{-\tilde{\Omega}(n)}$. *The construction succeeds with probability* $1 - 2^{-\tilde{\Omega}(n)}$.

Moreover, one can encode, decode, and sample a classical description of our codes efficiently in $\text{poly}(n)$ time. We describe the relation between Theorem 2 and quantum secret sharing in Sect. 1.2.

A challenging consequence of the relaxation to approximate erasure correction is that non-adaptive (or oblivious) adversaries are fundamentally very different than adaptive adversaries [50], which can use the erased qubits to learn partial information about the message (and modify their corruption). While against the former one can often borrow ideas from the well-studied random erasure error model [38,41], in the adaptive setting we require very different techniques.

Our code construction is based on a recent approach to design quantum codes against adversarial errors, list-decodable stabilizer codes [17,49]. However, known approaches to use list decoding for approximate quantum error correction either assume shared randomness between sender and receiver, or require a large qudit alphabet size. Thereby, they are unable to approach the quantum Singleton bound over qubits, at least in a "one-shot" setting.

Our new insights lie in combining our PMD codes, with a new type of stabilizer code which is list-decodable *from erasures*, an analog to the classical notion introduced by Guruswami [39]. In this application, our main technical contribution is a reduction from approximate quantum erasure correction to PMDs and erasure list-decoding, and is inspired by a classical result by Cramer et al. [24] (Eurocrypt 2015) on the construction of classical secret sharing schemes from AMDs and list-decodable codes.

Quantum Tamper-Detection Codes for Qubit-Wise Channels. Our second application of PMD codes is to designing quantum tamper-detection codes.

Tamper-detection [20,44] is an adversarial coding-theoretic guarantee which is closely related to error-detection and authentication, but *without* a secret key. Informally, both quantum tamper-detection codes (TDCs) and quantum authentication schemes (QASs) [11,40] are protocols in which a sender (Alice) conveys a (quantum) message ψ to a receiver (Bob) over some insecure quantum channel Λ, with the guarantee that Bob either receives a state close to ψ, or aborts $\perp$.[5]

---

[5] See Definition 3 for a formal definition.

Their distinction lies in the adversarial model: whereas QASs are secure against arbitrary channels Λ, TDCs only hope to address certain restricted tampering models. Naturally, the stronger adversarial model also comes with a drawback. Barnum et al. [11] showed that, in general, sending an authenticated k qubit message requires a secret key of at least $2k \cdot (1 - o(1))$ bits shared between Alice and Bob. The motivating question we ask here is:

Are there simpler adversarial models for which quantum tamper-detection is possible without a secret key?

The model we study in this paper is that of "qubit-wise" channels, where $\Lambda = \otimes_{i \in [n]} \Lambda_i$. Informally, this corresponds to Alice sending each qubit of her n qubit code-state to n distinct, non-communicating and un-entangled parties. These parties may strategize ahead of time and decide on a nefarious combination of distinct channels $\Lambda_i \neq \Lambda_j$, but they must act on the code-state independently of each other.[6]

It should be clear that this task remains impossible classically. Indeed, in the absence of shared randomness between sender and receiver, the n parties can always collude ahead of time, and substitute the entire message with a valid encoding of any other pre-agreed message $\hat{m}$. Bob will be none the wiser, and will decode to $\hat{m}$ without noticing that Alice's message has been completely replaced. Nonetheless, we show that in the quantum setting the scenario is drastically different:

Theorem 3. *For every sufficiently large $n \in \mathbb{N}$, there exists a Monte Carlo construction of a quantum tamper code for qubit-wise channels, of blocklength n qubits, rate $1 - O(\log^{-1} n)$, and error $\varepsilon \leq 2^{-\tilde{\Omega}(n)}$. The construction succeeds with probability $1 - 2^{-\tilde{\Omega}(n)}$.*

Although classical tamper detection is impossible in the "bit-wise" setting, the closely related goal known as *non-malleability* is possible. Classical non-malleable codes [33] are a relaxation of authentication and error correcting codes, where Bob is tasked with decoding Alice's message m to either the original message m, rejection $\perp$, or a completely unrelated value $\tilde{m}$. In contrast to authentication and error correction, non-malleable codes are much more versatile and can be constructed in a number of limited-adversarial settings, even without a secret key.

Our code construction combines non-malleable codes with PMD codes and stabilizer codes, and is inspired by the design of a classical bit-wise non-malleable code by Cheraghchi and Guruswami [22]. However, we emphasize that our result is fundamentally stronger than any form of classical or quantum non-malleability (for qubit-wise channels, see Sect. 2.3). In this application, our main technical contribution draws ideas from the quantum circuit lower bounds for quantum

---

[6] Quantum channels are completely positive and trace preserving maps on linear operators. We remark that by an averaging argument, the adversaries are allowed shared randomness, just not shared entanglement.

error correcting codes by Anshu and Nirhke [7], to show how to use entanglement to evade the previously mentioned "substitution" attack, and detect adversarial tampering without a secret key.

1.2 Additional Related Work

Tamper-Detection Codes and Secret Sharing. Our work is inspired by constructions of classical secret sharing schemes from ideas in tamper-resilient cryptography [24–26,28,50]. A key ingredient in that line of work is the concept of an algebraic manipulation detection (AMD) code [26]. Simply put, an "algebraic manipulation" is a form of adversarial data tampering, without prior knowledge of the data values. For instance, if our data is a value x in a group $\mathcal{G}$, then an "algebraic manipulation" corresponds to adding some value $\delta \in \mathcal{G}$ (without knowing x), resulting in $x + \delta$. An AMD code corresponds to an encoding of data into $\mathcal{G}$, in a way that any algebraic manipulation $\delta \neq 0$ is detected with high probability. [44] generalized AMD codes to other tampering families, including low-degree polynomial and low-depth circuit tampering.

[20] were the first to explore tamper-detection codes in the quantum setting. Their work focused on the concept of a "Unitary Tamper Detection Code", a quantum code which can faithfully detect errors chosen from a restricted family of unitary operators. Among other results, they constructed explicit quantum codes for classical messages which could detect arbitrary Pauli errors, which they referred to as "Quantum AMDs". Our PMDs arose as a natural generalization to quantum messages, albeit our techniques depart significantly. Moreover, [20] don't attempt to address tampering *channels* (just unitaries), whose lack of reversibility imply a unique set of challenges.

Approximate Quantum Error Correction. [48] were the first to showcase the benefits of approximate error correction to quantum communication. They constructed a 4 qubit code which could correct a single amplitude dampening error, violating the "Hamming bound" for quantum codes based on the Pauli basis. Several results then studied conditions in which approximate quantum error correction is even possible [12,14,15,30,41,47,51,52,55].

In this context, most related to our work are the results of [17,29,49], who studied the adversarial error channel. While it is well known consequence of the Knill-Laflamme conditions [46] that no exact quantum code can correct from more than $n/4$ adversarial errors, [29] constructed approximate quantum codes which could correct $(n-1)/2$ adversarial errors, all the way up to the no-cloning bound! Their codes relied on an insightful combination of quantum error correction, quantum authentication, and classical secret sharing, but came at a cost of an exponentially large alphabet size and assymptotically decaying rate.

[17,49] address these issues using the list-decoding of stabilizer codes. [49] presented a quantum code over qubits which beat the quantum Gilbert-Varshamov (GV) bound, albeit relied on an inefficient decoding algorithm, and a secret key shared between sender and receiver. [17] showed how to efficiently approach the

quantum Singleton bound over (large, but) constant-sized alphabets, by combining purity testing codes and classical secret sharing with efficient constructions of list-decodable stabilizer codes. While in this work we share many of the same tools as [17], what distinguishes our approaches is that (1) our goal is to design codes over qubits, and (2) we correct from a number of (erasure) errors much larger than the underlying code distance. Thereby, we cannot rely on techniques such as "code-blocking" to hide shared randomness back into the code[7], nor can we leverage "privacy" by relying on exact local-indistinguishability.

Quantum Secret Sharing. [23,29,36,56] showed that exact and approximate quantum error correction and quantum secret sharing are deeply connected. In a quantum (n,t)-threshold secret sharing scheme, a secret quantum state is encoded into n shares such that any t can be used to reconstruct the secret, but any $\leq t-1$ contain no information about the secret. By definition, this is already a quantum error correcting code, and [23] noted that the converse is also true. Via the information-disturbance paradigm, even approximately correcting from quantum erasures implies the approximate privacy of the erased subset [47].

A natural extension to threshold secret sharing is the concept of a (n,t,p) *ramp* secret sharing scheme, where the "reconstruction" and "privacy" thresholds are distinct. Any t suffice to reconstruct the secret, but no p of them reveal any information. Our result in Theorem 2 can be understood as a near-optimal quantum ramp secret sharing scheme encoding secrets of $r \cdot n$ qubits into n binary shares, where $t = (\frac{1+r}{2} + \gamma) \cdot n, p = (\frac{1-r}{2} - \gamma) \cdot n$, with recovery and privacy error $2^{-\Omega(\gamma \cdot n)}$.

Non-malleable Codes. The first construction of an efficient non-malleable code by [33] was for "bit-wise" tampering functions, which is the conceptual classical analog to the qubit-wise channels we study. Their construction was based on combinations of AMD codes and error-correcting codes (with extra secret-sharing properties). Subsequent works then built on their results by developing explicit and "minimal redundancy" (rate $1 - o(1)$) constructions [4,5,22]. Qualitatively, our construction of tamper detection codes is inspired by [22], who combined a "concatenated" non-malleable code with a pseudorandom permutation. The secret key for the permutation was then itself hidden back into the code, using a smaller, sub-optimal non-malleable code.

Outside of the bit-wise setting, other notable examples of non-malleable codes include the well studied "split-state" model [1–3,32,45], as well as AC^0 [8] and poly-sized [9] circuits.

In subsequent work, [18] introduced the notion of a quantum non-malleable code. Informally, in their definition, the receiver Bob is tasked with either outputting the original quantum message ψ (preserving any side-entanglement), or a fixed state σ (decoupled from any side-entanglement). They constructed said codes in the split-state model, even against entangled adversaries, by relying on techniques closely related to those of Sect. 2.3 in combination with *quantum-secure* versions of non-malleable codes [19].

---

[7] As similarly done by [29,41] to approach the no-cloning bound.

We remark that while our (un-entangled) qubit-wise adversarial model is strictly weaker than their (entangled) split-state model, we emphasize that our tamper detection security guarantee is fundamentally stronger than non-malleability - and indeed, tamper detection is impossible against adversaries with unbounded entanglement. We further discuss the differences between these models in Sect. 2.3.

2 Technical Overview

In this section, we present a brief overview of the main ideas in this work. We assume familiarity with basic definitions of Pauli operators and stabilizer codes. A review of these concepts is presented in Appendix A of the full version.

In Sect. 2.1, we show how the intuition that PMDs detect Pauli errors without perturbing the corrupted code-states can be bootstrapped into correcting from "sparse" Pauli channels. Then, in Sect. 2.2, we overview how list-decoding from erasures can be used to reduce approximate quantum erasure correction to correcting from sparse Pauli channels.

In Sect. 2.3, we overview our construction of tamper detection codes for qubit-wise channels from classical non-malleable codes, PMD codes, and stabilizer codes. Finally, in Sect. 2.4, we overview our explicit constructions of PMD codes from the PTC codes of [11].

2.1 The Sparse Pauli Channel Lemma

The motivating idea behind our use of PMDs in approximate quantum error correction is to ask when a Pauli error E can also be identified (and corrected), if it can be detected. To make this concrete, consider the following distinguishing task:

Task 1 (Sparse Pauli Channel Correction). *Let $|\psi\rangle \in \Pi$ be a PMD code-state and E_1, E_2 be two Pauli operators. Then, given the quantum state $E_i |\psi\rangle$ for unknown i and the classical description of E_1, E_2, can we recover $|\psi\rangle$?*

Naturally, there is a simple algorithm to recover a state close to $|\psi\rangle$. First apply $E_1^\dagger$ and measure $(\Pi, \mathbb{I} - \Pi)$. If the outcome is $\mathbb{I} - \Pi$, then, by the gentle-measurement lemma, we are left with a state $\approx E_1^\dagger E_2 |\psi\rangle$. One can then revert E_1, attempt the next correction $E_2^\dagger$, and measure Π again.

We refer to this task as "Sparse Pauli Channel Correction" because it encapsulates the case where a receiver, Bob, is handed a probabilistic mixture of $\psi \in \Pi$ corrupted by a random Pauli error chosen from a small, known set of errors. In Lemma 1 we formalize this approach, and show how to bootstrap the gentle-measurement lemma into recovering ψ even when the error comes from a short list of L possible candidate errors:

Lemma 1 (Informal). *Let $\mathcal{E} = \{E_1, \cdots, E_L\}$ be a list of L distinct n qubit Pauli operators. Then, given a classical description of $\mathcal{E}$, there exists a unitary $\mathsf{Dec}_\mathcal{E}$ on $n + L$ qubits which approximately recovers states in Π from errors in $\mathcal{E}$:*

$$\forall |\psi\rangle \in \Pi \text{ and } E \in \mathcal{E} : \|\mathsf{Dec}_\mathcal{E}(E|\psi\rangle \otimes |0^L\rangle) - |\psi\rangle \otimes |\mathsf{Aux}_E\rangle\|_2 \leq 2 \cdot L \cdot \varepsilon, \quad (5)$$

for some L qubit state $|\mathsf{Aux}_E\rangle$ which only depends on E and $\mathcal{E}$.

If $L = o(1/\varepsilon)$, then PMDs can correct from Sparse Pauli Channels with asymptotically decaying error. In fact, in Sect. 5 we present a quantum algorithm which can coherently correct from superpositions of errors in the span of $\mathcal{E}$, and thus generalizes the proposition above on mixtures of Pauli errors. As we later discuss, this coherent correction step is what later allows us to recover from *adaptive* erasure errors.

2.2   From List Decoding to Approximately Correcting Quantum Erasures

Our quantum erasure code construction combines PMD codes with stabilizer codes which are *list-decodable from erasures*, a variant of the list-decodable stabilizer codes studied by [17,49]. In particular, we consider their code composition:

$$\mathsf{Enc}(|m\rangle) \equiv \mathsf{Enc}\,|m\rangle \otimes |0^{a_{\mathsf{PMD}}}\rangle \otimes |0^{a_Q}\rangle = \mathsf{Enc}_Q\big(\mathsf{Enc}_{\mathsf{PMD}} \otimes \mathbb{I}^{a_Q}\big)\,|m\rangle \otimes |0^{a_{\mathsf{PMD}}}\rangle \otimes |0^{a_Q}\rangle$$

where the unitaries $\mathsf{Enc}_Q, \mathsf{Enc}_{\mathsf{PMD}}$ encode into the erasure list-decodable code and the PMD code respectively, and a_{PMD}, a_Q correspond to ancilla qubits. Figure 1 represents this encoding setup, and the erasure process.

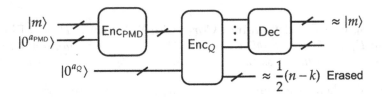

Fig. 1. The composition of a PMD and QLDE codes, and an erasure error.

One of our main technical contributions is designing an efficient decoding channel Dec for our code construction, that is, a reduction from approximate erasure correction to list-decoding from erasures and Pauli Manipulation Detection. In the rest of this subsection, we overview how an outer list-decoding step can be used to reduce the erasure channel to a sparse Pauli channel, which we can then handle with the inner PMD code and Lemma 1.

In classical coding theory, list-decoding [34,58] arose as a natural relaxation to "unique" decoding, where the decoder is tasked with recovering a list of candidate messages from a corrupted codeword, when recovering a unique one may no longer be possible. Formally, a code $C \subset \Sigma^n$ is said to be (τ, L) list-decodable if there are at most L codewords of C in any hamming ball of radius $\tau \cdot n$ in Σ^n. If C is linear, with parity check matrix H, then this definition implies that at most L additive errors $e_1, \cdots, e_L$ of bounded weight $\leq \tau \cdot n$ can have the same parity check syndrome $s = He_i$.

Analogously to linear codes, in a stabilizer code which is (τ, L) list-decodable, there are at most L logically-distinct Pauli errors of weight $\leq \tau \cdot n$ consistent with any syndrome measurement [17,49]. Operationally, what this implies is that measuring the syndrome of a bounded weight adversarial error channel, collapses the channel into a mixture over Pauli errors in a discrete list $\mathcal{E} = \{E_1, \cdots, E_L\}$, i.e., a sparse Pauli channel!

The notion of list-decoding *from erasures* was introduced by [39], and conceptually corresponds to the natural extension to list-decoding when the error locations are known. Based on their work, we define:

Definition 2. *A stabilizer code on n qubits is (τ, L) list-decodable from erasures (QLDE) if for all syndrome vectors s and subsets $T \subset [n]$, $|T| \leq \tau \cdot n$, there are at most L logically-distinct Pauli operators supported on T and of syndrome s.*

Indeed we show that a syndrome measurement on a QLDE code analogously "collapses" the quantum erasure channel into a mixture of Pauli errors in a list $\mathcal{E}$. More importantly, (given the syndrome) we reason that one can always compute such a list of Pauli errors $\mathcal{E} = \{E_1, \cdots, E_L\}$ efficiently in terms of n and L, since list-decoding stabilizer codes *from erasures* actually corresponds to solving a linear system.[8]

Together with our Sparse Pauli Channel Lemma 1, we conclude that the code composition $\mathsf{Enc} = \mathsf{Enc}_Q \circ \mathsf{Enc}_{\mathsf{PMD}}$ efficiently corrects erasures:

Lemma 2. *The code composition of an ε-PMD with a (τ, L) erasure list-decodable code corrects from a τ fraction of adversarially chosen erasures with up to a $O(\varepsilon^{1/2} \cdot L^{3/4})$ recovery error in poly(n, L) time.*

To instantiate Lemma 2, in Appendix C of the full version we show how to build (τ, L)-QLDE codes from the CSS construction [21,57] of classical linear codes which are list-decodable from erasures, and present a simple randomized code construction. Our randomized construction is based on random CSS codes, and we show that they are list-decodable from a number of erasures approaching the quantum Singleton bound via the classical results of [31,39]:

Theorem 4. *For all $0 < r, \gamma < 1$ and sufficiently large positive integer n, a random rate r CSS code on n qubits is $(\frac{1}{2}(1 - r - \gamma), 2^{O(1/\gamma)})$-QLDE with probability $\geq 1 - n^{O(1)} \cdot 2^{-\Omega((1-r) \cdot n)}$.*

---

[8] In contrast to normal list-decoding of linear codes, erasure list-decoding linear codes simply corresponds to solving a linear system, and thereby is efficient in terms of n and L. See [39], or Appendix C of the full version for a review.

Unfortunately, we don't know yet of deterministically constructable stabilizer codes with these list-decoding guarantees (see Sect. 3). However, our randomized constructions are efficiently sampleable, encodable and erasure list-decodable, and their construction succeeds (i.e. has the desired list decoding property) with exponentially high probability.

2.3   Quantum Tamper Detection for Qubit-Wise Channels

The definition of quantum tamper detection we consider[9] is a special case of that of [20], and can be understood as a keyless version of the definition of quantum authentication by [40]. We consider a public and keyless pair of channels (Enc, Dec), where Enc encodes k qubits into an n qubit mixed state, and Dec decodes n qubits into $k+1$ qubits, consisting of a message register M and a flag F indicating acceptance $|\text{Acc}\rangle$ or rejection $|\text{Rej}\rangle$.

Definition 3 quantifies standard correctness and robust error-detection guarantees, when a quantum state on the register M (possibly entangled with a side register R) is encoded into the code.

Definition 3. *A pair of quantum channels* (Enc, Dec) *is an ε-secure quantum tamper detection code for qubit-wise channels if they satisfy*

1. **Correctness.** *In the absence of tampering, for all messages* ψ_{MR}:

$$(\text{Dec} \circ \text{Enc} \otimes \mathbb{I}_R)(\psi_{MR}) = \text{Acc} \otimes \psi_{MR} \qquad (6)$$

2. **Tamper Detection.** *For every set of n single qubit channels* $(\Lambda_1, \cdots, \Lambda_n)$, *there exists a constant $p_\Lambda \in [0,1]$ such that,* $\forall \psi_{MR}$:

$$\left(\text{Dec} \circ \left(\otimes_i^n \Lambda_i \right) \circ \text{Enc} \otimes \mathbb{I}_R \right)(\psi_{MR}) \approx_\varepsilon p_\Lambda \cdot \text{Acc} \otimes \psi + (1 - p_\Lambda) \cdot \bot \otimes \psi_R. \quad (7)$$

Where the error is measured in trace distance, and $\bot$ on M and F indicates the message is rejected.

This definition allows the adversaries to share randomness, but explicitly does not allow them to communicate, share entanglement, nor be entangled with the message. Therefore, it is not composable in the standard (authentication) sense. Nevertheless, it still provides meaningful guarantees in a "one-shot" setting. For instance, it can be used to establish entanglement, a secret key, or teleport over a state between Alice and Bob.[10]

---

[9] In the first posting of this work, we stated an alternative definition referred to as "keyless authentication" based on [40]. For this submission, we changed the definition to the more standard simulation paradigm below, but none of the proofs were modified.

[10] Here, we comment on the distinction between this model and the recent quantum non-malleable codes of [18]. In a tamper-detection code, if Bob accepts with non-negligible probability $\omega(\varepsilon)$, then he is guaranteed to have preserved entanglement with Alice. In a quantum non-malleable code, the adversaries may have decoupled Alice and Bob, and Bob will be none-the-wiser.

In the rest of this subsection we overview Theorem 3. We begin by presenting a simplification of our main result, a tamper detection code of rate approaching $1/3$, which showcases the main techniques. For completeness, we present a self-contained proof of this simpler construction in Appendix E of the full version. Afterwards, we present a high-level description of how we leverage code concatenation and pseudorandomness to achieve our rate $1 - o(1)$ construction.

The Rate 1/3 Construction. The key tool we use is a classical non-malleable code against bit-wise tampering functions [4,5,22,33]. Informally, a classical non-malleable code ($\mathsf{Enc_{NM}}$, $\mathsf{Dec_{NM}}$) is a relaxation of error-correction and error-detection codes, where the decoder is tasked with either outputting (1) the original message, (2) rejecting $\perp$, **or** (3) outputting a message which is completely uncorrelated from the original message. The role of the non-malleable code in our construction is to establish a "non-malleable secret key" between Alice and Bob. That is, a $\approx 2/3$ fraction of the qubit-wise channels will be used to send over an encoding $\mathsf{Enc_{NM}}(s)$ of a uniformly random bitstring s, which will later be used to encrypt Alice's message state.

Alice encodes her message $|\psi\rangle$ first into the composition $\tilde{Q}$ of a PMD code, and a stabilizer code Q of block-length N_Q and near-linear distance d. Then, she one-time-pads her state with a random N_Q qubit Pauli P^s, indexed by a $2 \cdot N_Q$ bit long secret key s, which is then encoded into NM (see Fig. 2).

$$\mathsf{Enc}(\psi) = \mathbb{E}_s \mathsf{Enc_{NM}}(s) \otimes P^s \cdot \mathsf{Enc}_{\tilde{Q}}(\psi) \cdot (P^s)^{\dagger}, \qquad (8)$$

$$\text{where } \mathsf{Enc}_{\tilde{Q}} = \mathsf{Enc}_Q \circ \mathsf{Enc_{PMD}}. \qquad (9)$$

If the PMD code, the stabilizer code Q, and the classical non-malleable code NM all have rate $\approx 1 - o(1)$, then the resulting construction has rate $\approx \frac{1}{3}(1 - o(1))$.

Our decoding algorithm is relatively simple to describe. After receiving Alice's message, Bob first decodes the non-malleable code using $\mathsf{Dec_{NM}}$. Assuming he doesn't immediately reject, Bob obtains some string $\tilde{s}$, and uses it to revert the Pauli one-time-pad applied on the quantum half of the encoding. After doing so, Bob measures the syndrome of Q, and if successful, projects onto the PMD code-space. Assuming all of these steps accept, at the end of the protocol Bob outputs the "message" register of the PMD.

Informally, the classical non-malleability guarantees that the distribution over Bob's recovered key $\tilde{s}$ is close to a convex combination over the original key s, and an uncorrelated key drawn from some arbitrary distribution $\mathcal{D}^A$. In our analysis, we can essentially consider these two cases separately:

In the first case, if Bob recovers the original key s, then on average over random s he receives the outcome of a Pauli channel:

$$\mathbb{E}_s(P^s)^{\dagger} \circ \Lambda \circ P^s \circ \mathsf{Enc}_{\tilde{Q}}(\psi) = \sum_{E \in \text{Pauli}} |c_E|^2 \cdot E \cdot \mathsf{Enc}_{\tilde{Q}}(\psi) \cdot E^{\dagger} \qquad (10)$$

Indeed, the operation on the left-hand-side above is the well known Pauli Twirl operation [6]. Since the effective channel is a Pauli channel, we can rely on the

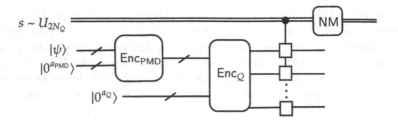

Fig. 2. Enc for the rate $1/3-o(1)$ construction. The unlabeled controlled gate represents the Pauli One-Time-Pad.

properties of the PMD code to detect any adversarial tampering (cf Appendix E of the full version).

Conversely, if Bob does not recover the original key s, then since Pauli's are 1-Designs, on average over a random Pauli he receives a uniformly random (encrypted) message:

$$\mathbb{E}_s \Lambda \circ P^s \circ \mathsf{Enc}_{\tilde{Q}}(\psi_{MR}) = \Lambda \circ \left(\mathbb{E}_s P^s \cdot \mathsf{Enc}_{\tilde{Q}}(\psi_{MR}) \cdot (P^s)^\dagger \right) \quad (11)$$

$$= \psi_R \otimes \Lambda(\mathbb{I}/2^{N_Q}) = \psi_R \otimes_i^{N_Q} \Lambda_i(\mathbb{I}/2) \quad (12)$$

Moreover, from Bob's perspective, the state he receives $\otimes_i \Lambda_i(\mathbb{I}/2)$ is completely uncorrelated from Alice's message ψ! Conceptually, this guarantees that our code construction is already sort of a quantum "non-malleable code". However, we can in fact say something much stronger.

What makes this construction a tamper detection code, instead of just a non-malleable code, is the fact that if Bob does not receive the original key then his syndrome measurement will reject with high probability. This follows from the fact that his received state, on average over random s, is the (unentangled) *product state* $\otimes_i \Lambda_i(\mathbb{I}/2)$. However, product states should be very far from the highly entangled code-spaces of stabilizer codes. We leverage a lemma by Anshu and Nirkhe [7] to show that the probability Bob's syndrome measurement accepts (that is, outputs syndrome 0), if the key has been tampered with is $\leq 2^{-\Omega(d^2/N_Q)}$, exponentially decaying with the distance d of the stabilizer code (See Lemma 22 of the full version).

Here, it is instructive to pause briefly and discuss why this or related constructions wouldn't be able to achieve tamper-detection if the adversaries were entangled. The first obstacle is that the classical non-malleable codes we used are, apriori, not robust to adversaries which can leverage quantum correlations. Nevertheless (modulo rate considerations), this obstacle is quite surmountable by leveraging recent constructions of quantum-secure non-malleable codes and extractors [19]. The truly fundamental issue is to quantify how far the adversaries pre-shared state is from the code-space of the stabilizer code. Indeed, if they could pre-prepare an arbitrary entangled state, they could replace the code-state themselves, ensuring that tamper-detection is impossible.

Rate Amplification. Our approach to improve the rate is inspired by a construction of classical non-malleable codes by [22]. The bottleneck in the previous construction is the amount of classical randomness used, and thus our first step is to replace the uniformly random Pauli one-time-pad P^s by a t-wise independent Pauli Pad $P^{G(s)}$, generated using a short seed of length $\sigma = O(t \log k)$. Unfortunately, under a t-wise independent pad, the quantum half of Enc is no longer perfectly encrypted, and our proof techniques in the previous section (the Pauli Twirl and [7]'s result) break.

To address these issues, we use quantum code concatenation. Alice first encodes her message ψ into a high rate, near-linear distance stabilizer code, and then encodes the symbols of the outer code[11] into the composition $\tilde{Q}$ of a PMD code and another high rate stabilizer code of smaller block-length (See Fig. 3).

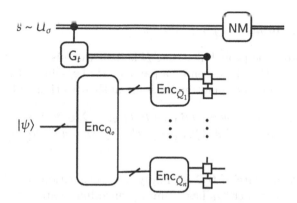

Fig. 3. The concatenated code with a pseudorandom Pauli Pad. Ancilla qubits removed for clarity.

Intuitively, if the block-length of the inner codes is $b < t$, then via the t-wise independence the marginal density matrix on each inner code is truly encrypted, and we can leverage the proof techniques of the uniformly random case. While this intuition does capture the case where Bob does not recover the key, the case where Bob recovers the original key is a little more subtle. Since $G(s)$ is only t-wise independent, we can no longer argue that the effective channel on the entire code is simply a Pauli channel.

The key insight to address the case where the key is recovered is to further divide into cases on whether each block is significantly tampered, or whether each tampering channel Λ_j is "sparse" in the Pauli basis. While we defer the details to Appendix E of the full version, the underlying intuition is that if many of the channels in any given inner block $\tilde{Q}_i$ are not "sparse" in the Pauli

---

[11] Technically, the symbols are first bundled up into blocks of size $k/\log^c k$, and then each block is encoded into $\tilde{Q}$.

basis, then the Pauli twirl argument should still imply that block i rejects with high probability. Conversely, if many of the channels in any given inner block are "sparse", then the PMD in that block should detect the presence of errors without distorting the state.

2.4   Explicit PMDs from Pairwise-Detectable Purity Testing

To conclude our technical overview, we discuss our construction of PMD codes from the stabilizer Purity Testing Codes (PTCs) by [11]. A PTC is a set of stabilizer codes which detects every Pauli error "on average":

Definition 4. *A set of stabilizer codes $\{Q_k\}_{k \in K}$ is called an ε-strong* PTC *if for all non-trivial Pauli operators $E \neq \mathbb{I}$, it holds that*

$$\mathbb{P}_{k \leftarrow K}\big[E \in N_k\big] \leq \varepsilon. \tag{13}$$

where N_k is the normalizer group (the undetectable errors) of Q_k.

In other words, the probability that E is detectable is $\geq 1 - \varepsilon$, for a random choice of code $k \leftarrow K$. [11] presented a particularly key-efficient family of PTCs, and used them to develop quantum message authentication codes:

Theorem 5 ([11]). *For every sufficiently large $n, \lambda \in \mathbb{N}, \lambda | n$, there exists a set of $[[n, n-\lambda]]_2$ stabilizer codes $\{Q_\alpha\}_{\alpha \in \mathbb{F}_{2^\lambda}}$ which form an ε-strong* PTC *with error $\varepsilon \leq n \cdot 2^{-\lambda}$.*

A natural "candidate" PMD is simply a superposition over keys and PTC encodings. That is, if each Q_k has a unitary encoding map Enc_k acting on some number $\mathsf{Anc}_{\mathsf{PTC}}$ of ancillas and the message state $|\phi\rangle$, then our PMDs encode $|\phi\rangle$ as a uniform superposition over keys (on a "key" register) and PTC encodings (on a "code" register):

$$\mathsf{Enc}\,|\phi\rangle = |K|^{-1/2} \sum_k |k\rangle \otimes \mathsf{Enc}_k\,|\phi\rangle \tag{14}$$

There is a natural associated projection $\Pi = \mathsf{Enc}(\mathbb{I} \otimes |0\rangle\langle 0|^{\mathsf{Anc}_{key}+\mathsf{Anc}_{\mathsf{PTC}}})\mathsf{Enc}^\dagger$ onto the codespace as well (see Sect. 4).

Intuitively, one expects that Pauli errors supported only on the "code" register should be handled by the PTC property. The challenge really lies in what happens when the key register itself is corrupted. To build a rough idea on our proof technique, consider the following "Key Manipulation" experiment:

Let us encode some state $|m\rangle$ into the ath stabilizer code Q_a, and then measure the syndrome of the bth code. When $a = b$, there is no tampering and the syndrome measurement naturally "accepts" (i.e. we measure syndrome 0). When $a \neq b$, the probability we mistakenly accept is

$$\langle m|\,\mathsf{Enc}_a^\dagger \Pi_b \mathsf{Enc}_a\,|m\rangle \leq \|\Pi_a \Pi_b \Pi_a\|_\infty, \tag{15}$$

where Π_k corresponds to the projection onto the kth stabilizer code-space Q_k. If Q_k has stabilizer group S_k, then the projector onto Q_k can be written as $\Pi_k = |S_k|^{-1} \sum_{\sigma \in S_k} \sigma$. We note that for any Pauli σ, $\Pi_k \sigma \Pi_k = 0$ unless $\sigma \in N_k$, thus

$$\|\Pi_a \Pi_b \Pi_a\|_\infty \le |S_b|^{-1} \sum_{\sigma \in S_b \cap N_a} \|\sigma\|_\infty \le |S_b|^{-1} \cdot |S_b \cap N_a|. \tag{16}$$

That is, a measure of how many stabilizers of S_b are "undetectable" to the code Q_a. We remark that on average over a, b, and, assuming all the stabilizer groups have size $|S_b| = 2^\lambda$, linearity of expectation and the ε-strong condition tells us that

$$\mathbb{E}_{a \leftarrow K} \|\Pi_a \Pi_b \Pi_a\|_\infty \le 2^{-\lambda} \left(1 + \sum_{E \in S_b \setminus \{\mathbb{I}\}} \mathbb{P}_{a \leftarrow K}[E \in N_a] \right) \le 2^{-\lambda} + \varepsilon \tag{17}$$

That is, these code-space projectors are almost orthogonal on average (for random a, b).

Unfortunately, this doesn't tell us much about correlated pairs of keys (a, b). For instance, what about the pairs $(a, b = a + s)$, where s is some fixed "bit-flip" error? In particular, let us assume the set of keys K form a group under addition, and consider pairs $(a, a + s)$ for uniformly random $a \leftarrow K$ and a fixed non-zero shift $s \in K$. We refer to the set of stabilizer codes $\{Q_a\}_{a \in K}$ as pairwise detectable, if over random $a \in K$ the probability some operator of S_a is undetectable to the code Q_{a+s} is small.

Definition 5. *A set of stabilizer codes $\{Q_k\}_{k \in K}$ is called δ pairwise-detectable if, for all $s \ne 0$,*

$$\mathbb{P}_{k \leftarrow K}[S_k \cap N_{k+s} \ne \{\mathbb{I}\}] \le \delta \tag{18}$$

In which case, $\mathbb{E}_{a \leftarrow K} \|\Pi_a \Pi_{a+s} \Pi_a\|_\infty \le 1/2^\lambda + \delta$ for all non-zero $s \in K$. In Sect. 4, we prove that pairwise-detectability is precisely what we need to construct PMD codes, resulting in the following lemma:

Lemma 3. *If a set of $[[n, n - \lambda]]_2$ stabilizer codes $\{Q_k\}_{k \in K}$ is a ε-strong PTC and is δ pairwise-detectable, then the code defined by* Enc, Π *above is a $(n + \log K, n - \lambda, \Delta)$-PMD with $\Delta \le \max(\varepsilon, \sqrt{2^{-\lambda} + \delta})$.*

It only remains to instantiate our lemma with a viable set of stabilizer codes. In the full version, we prove that the PTCs introduced by [11] provide a particularly key-efficient family of pairwise detectable stabilizer codes, which gives us our PMD construction of Theorem 1.

Lemma 4. *The family of $[[n, n - \lambda]]_2$ stabilizer codes considered by [11] is $\le n \cdot 2^{1-\lambda}$ pairwise-detectable.*

2.5 Organization

We organize the rest of this paper as follows.

- In Sect. 3 we discuss and raise interesting questions left by our work.
- In Sect. 4, we discuss properties of PMDs and present their construction from pairwise-detectable purity testing codes. In the full version, we show that the purity testing codes of [11] are pairwise-detectable.
- In Sect. 5, we show how to construct approximate quantum codes for erasures/quantum secret sharing schemes from PMDs and erasure list-decoding.

For conciseness, we defer to the full version our constructions of quantum codes which are list decodable from erasures, and out constructions of tamper detection codes for qubit-wise channels.

3 Discussion

We dedicate this section to a discussion on the interesting directions and open problems raised here.

The first question lies in developing new explicit constructions and lower bounds for PMD codes. While lower bounds and near-optimal constructions have been studied in a multitude of settings for AMD codes [10,26,28,42,43], our attempts at adapting their techniques to the quantum setting have been far from fruitful.

In recent work, [13] devised (classical) binary codes which are near-optimally erasure list-decodable. That is, they constructed codes which could correct from $(1 - \tau)$ fraction of erasures with list sizes $L = O(\log 1/\tau)$ and rate $\tau^{1+\gamma}$, for any value of $\tau > n^{-\Omega(1)}$. These codes have the remarkable property that they provably have smaller list sizes (for fixed τ) than the best possible linear code [39]. Since stabilizer codes are built on classical linear codes (and thus inherit their lower bounds), one could ask whether efficient non-stabilizer codes exist with even better list sizes than our random CSS construction. Unfortunately, even asking for deterministically constructible erasure list-decodable stabilizer codes seems to be a challenge.

An interesting case of our construction corresponds to the $k = 1$ case, that is, encoding a single logical qubit. In this limit, our codes encode the logical qubit into n physical qubits such that it is recoverable from a $\frac{1}{2} - O(\log^{-1} n)$ fraction of erasures. It is the list sizes in our construction that arise as the key bottleneck to further approaching the no-cloning bound of $1/2$. One could analogously ask, is there an efficient quantum code to approximately correct from a $\frac{1}{2} - n^{-\Omega(1)}$ fraction of erasures?

Finally, the main and arguably most interesting question is, what other adversarial quantum channels can be used to send authenticated quantum messages without a secret key? Perhaps a simpler question, what about "non-malleable" quantum messages? While we focus on qubit-wise channels as a proof-of-concept here, generalizing our approach to other settings such as LOCC (local operations and classical communication) channels, qubit-wise channels with entangled parties, or the split-state model [1], all require fundamentally new insights.[12]

4 Pauli Manipulation Detection

In this section, we discuss properties and our explicit construction of Pauli Manipulation Detection (PMD) codes (Theorem 1). Here, we present a slightly more formal definition:

Definition 6. *A q^k-dimensional subspace of $\mathbb{C}^{q^n}$ with code-space projector Π is said to be an $(n, k, \varepsilon)_q$-PMD if, for all non-trivial Pauli operators $E \in \mathcal{P}_q^n \setminus \{\mathbb{I}\}$[13],*

$$\|\Pi E \Pi\|_\infty \leq \varepsilon \tag{19}$$

Definition 6 implies that corrupting any code-state $|\psi_1\rangle$ with any non-identity Pauli E, leads to a state which is near-orthogonal to the code space.

$$|\langle \psi_1| E^\dagger |\psi_2\rangle| = |\langle \psi_1| E^\dagger \Pi |\psi_2\rangle \langle \psi_2 |\Pi E |\psi_1\rangle|^{1/2} \tag{20}$$

$$\leq \|\Pi E^\dagger \Pi E \Pi\|_\infty^{1/2} = \|\Pi E \Pi\|_\infty \leq \varepsilon \tag{21}$$

For all code-states $|\psi_2\rangle \in \Pi$. In a sense, this suggests that one can check if a given code-state was perturbed by a Pauli, without corrupting it. We make this connection precise in Lemma 5. Subsequently, we prove our main result on the construction of PMDs from "pairwise-detectable" sets of stabilizer codes.

Theorem 6 *(Theorem 1, Restatement). For every prime power q, sufficiently large $n \in \mathbb{N}$, and $\lambda | n$, there exists an explicit and efficient $(n, n - 2\lambda, \varepsilon)_q$-PMD with error $\varepsilon \leq 2 \cdot n^{1/2} \cdot q^{-\lambda/2}$.*

4.1 Robust Manipulation Detection

To begin, in Lemma 5 we formalize the property that PMDs detect errors without disturbing the corrupted code-state. Let Enc be the unitary which encodes into the PMD code, $\mathsf{Enc}\,|\psi\rangle\,|0^{\mathsf{Anc}}\rangle = |\bar{\psi}\rangle$, using $|\mathsf{Anc}| = n - k$ qudit ancillas. We show that there exists a n qudit $+1$ qubit unitary Auth which either exactly accepts, or approximately rejects code-states corrupted by Paulis. The extra qubit in register F acts as a "flag", indicating acceptance/rejection:

Lemma 5. *If Π is an (n, k, ε)-PMD, then there exists a unitary $\mathsf{Auth} : \mathbb{C}^{q^n} \otimes \mathbb{C}^2 \to \mathbb{C}^{q^n} \otimes \mathbb{C}^2$, satisfying*

1. **Correctness.** *Auth exactly recovers code-states, $\forall |\psi\rangle \in \mathbb{C}^{q^k}$:*

$$\mathsf{Auth}\big(\mathsf{Enc}\,|\psi\rangle\,|0^{\mathsf{Anc}}\rangle\,\big)\,|0\rangle_F = |\psi\rangle\,|0^{\mathsf{Anc}}\rangle\,|1\rangle_F$$

---

[12] See [16, 18] for recent progress in this direction.

[13] We refer to $\mathcal{P}_q$ as the q-ary Pauli group, a.k.a the Weyl-Heisenberg group. See Appendix A of the full version for basic definitions.

2. **Robust Error-Detection.** *For every Pauli $E \in \mathcal{P}_q^n \setminus \{\mathbb{I}\}$ and k qudit states ψ, let $|\phi_E\rangle = E \cdot \mathsf{Enc}\,|\psi\rangle \otimes |0^{\mathsf{Anc}}\rangle \otimes |0\rangle_F$ correspond to a corrupted code-state. Then,*

$$\| \mathsf{Auth}\,|\phi_E\rangle\,|0\rangle_F - |\phi_E\rangle\,|0\rangle_F \|_2 \leq \sqrt{2}\cdot\varepsilon \qquad (22)$$

At a high level, item (1) above stipulates that if there is no corruption, then we recover the original message state. Item 2 indicates that Auth detects the Pauli error $E \neq \mathbb{I}$ while approximately preserving the corrupted code-state $|\phi_E\rangle$.

Proof. To define the authentication unitary Auth, we first measure Π coherently, and write out the outcome on the binary side-register (the flag F). Conditioned on the measurement outcome, we revert the encoding $\mathsf{Enc}^\dagger$ on the code-register. Formally, $\mathsf{Auth} = C(\mathsf{Enc}^\dagger)U$, where U performs the measurement, and $C(\mathsf{Enc}^\dagger)$ performs the controlled gate

$$U = \Pi \otimes X_F + (1-\Pi)\otimes Z_F, \text{ and } C(\mathsf{Enc}^\dagger) = \mathsf{Enc}_Q^\dagger \otimes |1\rangle\langle 1|_F + \mathbb{I}_Q \otimes |0\rangle\langle 0|_F \quad (23)$$

Correctness is immediate. To prove the error-detection property, note that $|\phi_E\rangle\,|0\rangle_F = E \cdot \mathsf{Enc}(|\psi\rangle)\,|0\rangle_F$ and $\mathsf{Auth}\,|\phi_E\rangle\,|0\rangle_F$ are pure states, where the real part of their inner product satisfies

$$\mathcal{R}e\left[\langle\phi_E|\langle 0|_F \mathsf{Auth}\,|\phi_E\rangle\,|0\rangle_F \right] = \langle\psi|\,\mathsf{Enc}^\dagger E^\dagger(\mathbb{I}-\Pi)E\mathsf{Enc}\,|\psi\rangle \qquad (24)$$

$$\geq 1 - \|\Pi E\Pi E\Pi\|_\infty = 1 - \|\Pi E\Pi\|_\infty^2 \geq 1 - \varepsilon^2 \qquad (25)$$

The relation $\|x-y\|_2 = \sqrt{2(1-\mathcal{R}e[x\cdot y])}$ gives us the desired bound.

4.2 PMDs from Pairwise-Detectable Purity Testing

In this subsection we describe a construction of PMDs based on the PTC's of [11], and prove Theorem 6. Recall the definition of PTCs and our notion of pairwise detectability:

Definition 7 (Purity Testing). *A set of stabilizer codes $\{Q_k\}_{k\in K}$ is called an ε-strong PTC if for all non-trivial Pauli operators $E \in \mathcal{P}_q^n \setminus \{\mathbb{I}\}$,*

$$\mathbb{P}_{k\leftarrow K}\left[E \in N(Q_k)\right] \leq \varepsilon \qquad (26)$$

In other words, the probability that E is detectable is $\geq 1-\varepsilon$, for a random choice of code $k \leftarrow K$. [11] presented a particularly key-efficient family of PTC's, and used them to develop quantum message authentication codes:

Theorem 7 ([11]). *For every prime power q and sufficiently large $n, \lambda \in \mathbb{N}, \lambda | n$, there exists a set of $[[n, n-\lambda]]_q$ stabilizer codes $\{Q_\alpha\}_{\alpha\in\mathbb{F}_{q^\lambda}}$ which form an ε-strong PTC with error $\varepsilon \leq n\cdot q^{-\lambda}$.*

Definition 8 (Pairwise Detectability). *A set of stabilizer codes $\{Q_k\}_{k \in K}$ is called δ pairwise-detectable if, for all $s \neq 0$,*

$$\mathbb{P}_{k \leftarrow K}[S(Q_k) \cap N(Q_{k+s}) \neq \{\mathbb{I}\}] \leq \delta \tag{27}$$

In the full version, we show the family of PTC's in [11] is pairwise-detectable. For now, we simply import the result and use it to construct PMDs.

Lemma 6 (Lemma 4, restatement). *The family of $[[n, n - \lambda]]_q$ PTC's considered by [11] are δ pairwise-detectable with $\delta \leq 2 \cdot n \cdot q^{-\lambda}$.*

We define our PMDs as follows. If each Q_k has a unitary encoding map Enc_k acting on some number a of ancillas and the message state $|\phi\rangle$, then our PMDs encode $|\phi\rangle$ as superpositions of PTC encodings, where a "key register" S holds k, and a "code register" C holds $\mathsf{Enc}_k |\phi\rangle |0^{\mathsf{Anc}}\rangle$:

$$\mathsf{Enc} = \sum_k |k\rangle \langle k|_S H_S \otimes \mathsf{Enc}_k, \mathsf{Enc}(|\psi\rangle) = |K|^{-1/2} \sum_k |k\rangle \otimes \mathsf{Enc}_k(|\phi\rangle), \tag{28}$$

where H_S prepares the uniform superposition over keys, $H_S |0^{key}\rangle = |K|^{-1/2} \sum_k |k\rangle$. There is a natural projection Π onto the codespace,

$$\Pi = \mathsf{Enc}(\mathbb{I} \otimes 0^{\mathsf{Anc}+key})\mathsf{Enc}^\dagger = |K|^{-1} \sum_{k,k'} |k\rangle \langle k'| \otimes \mathsf{Enc}_k(\mathbb{I} \otimes 0^{\mathsf{Anc}})\mathsf{Enc}_{k'}^\dagger. \tag{29}$$

Recall that $\Pi_k = \mathsf{Enc}_k(\mathbb{I} \otimes 0^{\mathsf{Anc}})\mathsf{Enc}_k^\dagger$ is simply the projector onto Q_k. We readily inspect $\Pi^2 = \Pi$, and $\Pi\mathsf{Enc} |\phi\rangle = \mathsf{Enc} |\phi\rangle$ for all ϕ.

Lemma 7. *If a set of $[[n, n - \lambda]]_q$ stabilizer codes $\{Q_k\}_{k \in K}$ is a ε-strong PTC and is δ pairwise-detectable, then the code defined by Enc, Π is a $(n + \log_q K, n - \lambda, \Delta)_q$-PMD with $\Delta \leq \max(\varepsilon, \sqrt{q^{-\lambda} + \delta})$*

We obtain Theorem 6 by instantiating the lemma above with the PTCs in [11] and Lemma 6. We divide the proof of this lemma in two steps. First, in Lemma 8, we show that the probability any Pauli error E is undetected is roughly related to the key manipulation security experiment we devised in Sect. 2.4. Then, in Lemma 9, we show that pairwise-detectability implies that our candidate PMD doesn't fail the experiment except for assymptotically small probability.

Lemma 8. *Let $E = E_K \otimes E_C \neq \mathbb{I}_K \otimes \mathbb{I}_C$ be a Pauli error, where $E_K = X^a Z^b$ is supported on the key register K and E_C on the code C.*

$$\|\Pi E \Pi\|_\infty \leq |K|^{-1} \sum_k \|\Pi_k E_C \Pi_{k+a}\|_\infty \tag{30}$$

Moreover, if $E_C = \mathbb{I}$ and $E_K = Z^b$ is a phase, then $\|\Pi E \Pi\|_\infty = 0$.

Lemma 9. *If $a = 0$ and $E_C \neq \mathbb{I}$, $\|\Pi E \Pi\|_\infty \leq \varepsilon$. Moreover, if $a \neq 0$, then $\|\Pi E \Pi\|_\infty \leq \sqrt{q^{-\lambda} + \delta}$*

Combined, Lemma 8 and Lemma 9 show that $\|\Pi E \Pi\|_\infty \leq \varepsilon$ for all $E \neq \mathbb{I}$, and thus we have proved Lemma 7. It remains now to prove the claims:

Proof. [of Lemma 8] Let $E = E_S \otimes E_C \neq \mathbb{I}$ be any Pauli operator acting on the key S and code register C. We begin by writing out $\Pi E \Pi =$

$$|K|^{-2} \sum_{k_1,k_2,k_3,k_4 \in K} \langle k_2| E_S |k_3\rangle \cdot |k_1\rangle \langle k_4| \otimes \mathsf{Enc}_{k_1} \mathsf{Enc}_{k_2}^\dagger \Pi_{k_2} E_C \Pi_{k_3} \mathsf{Enc}_{k_3} \mathsf{Enc}_{k_4}^\dagger \tag{31}$$

We make the explicit assumption that the Pauli operators acting on the key register S obey the additive group structure of the set of PTC keys K. That is $X^a Z^b |k\rangle_S = \omega^{ib \cdot k} |k+a\rangle_S$, and $\sum_{z \in K} \omega^{ib \cdot z} = |K| \cdot \delta_{b,0}$.

First, if $E_C = \mathbb{I}$ and E_K is a phase error, then $\langle k_2| Z^e |k_3\rangle = \delta_{k_2,k_3} \cdot w^{ib \cdot k_3}$, and $b \neq 0$. Note that $E_C = \mathbb{I}$ implies $\mathsf{Enc}_{k_2}^\dagger \Pi_{k_2} E_C \Pi_{k_2} \mathsf{Enc}_{k_2} = (\mathbb{I} \otimes 0^{\mathsf{Anc}})$. Thus, summing over $k_2 \in K$,

$$\Pi E \Pi = |K|^{-2} \Big(\sum_{k_2} w^{ib \cdot k_2} \Big) \cdot \sum_{k_1,k_4 \in K} \cdot |k_1\rangle \langle k_4| \otimes \mathsf{Enc}_{k_1} (\mathbb{I} \otimes 0^{\mathsf{Anc}}) \mathsf{Enc}_{k_4}^\dagger = 0. \tag{32}$$

To conclude this claim, if $E_K = X^a Z^b$, we use the unitary invariance of $\|\cdot\|_\infty$, the factorization of the norm of tensor products, and the triangle inequality, to write $\|\Pi E \Pi\|_\infty \leq$

$$|K|^{-2} \Big\| \sum_{k_1,k_4 \in K} |k_1\rangle \langle k_4| \Big\|_\infty \Big\| \sum_{k_2 \in K} \omega^{i(k_2-a) \cdot b} \mathsf{Enc}_{k_2}^\dagger \Pi_{k_2} E_C \Pi_{k_2-a} \mathsf{Enc}_{k_2-a} \Big\|_\infty \tag{33}$$

$$\leq |K|^{-1} \sum_{k_2} \big\| \Pi_{k_2} E_C \Pi_{k_2-a} \big\|_\infty \tag{34}$$

Where we used $\| \sum_{x,y \in K} |x\rangle \langle y| \|_\infty = |K|$.

Proof. [of Lemma 9] If $a = 0$ but $E_C \neq \mathbb{I}$, then we have

$$\|\Pi E \Pi\|_\infty \leq |K|^{-1} \sum_k \|\Pi_k E_C \Pi_k\|_\infty = \mathbb{P}_{k \leftarrow K}[E \in Q_k^\dagger] \leq \varepsilon. \tag{35}$$

If $a \neq 0$,

$$\|\Pi_k E_C \Pi_{k+a}\|_\infty^2 = \|\Pi_k E_C \Pi_{k+a} E_C^\dagger \Pi_k\|_\infty \leq |S_{k+a}|^{-1} \sum_{\sigma \in S_{k+a} \cap Q_k^\perp} \|\sigma\|_\infty \tag{36}$$

$$\leq |S_{k+a}|^{-1} \cdot |S_{k+a} \cap Q_k^\perp| = q^{-\lambda} + \mathbb{I}[S_{k+a} \cap Q_k^\perp \neq \{\mathbb{I}\}]. \tag{37}$$

Since $\{Q_k\}$ is δ pairwise-detectable, in expectation over k this is simply $1/q^\lambda + \delta$. By Jensen's inequality,

$$\|\Pi E \Pi\|_\infty \leq \sqrt{q^{-\lambda} + \delta}. \tag{38}$$

5   Approximate Quantum Erasure Correction

In this section, we prove our main result on the application of PMD codes to approximate quantum erasure correction (Theorem 2).

We begin in Sect. 5.1, where we describe our code construction from PMDs and stabilizer codes which are list-decodable from erasures. In the remaining subsections (Sect. 5.2 and Sect. 5.3), we analyze and prove the theorem. We refer the reader to the full version for formal definitions of the adaptive & non-adaptive erasures model and approximate quantum error correction, and for formal definitions and constructions of quantum codes which are list-decodable from erasures.

5.1   The Code Construction

Encoding. We combine

- An $(m, k, \varepsilon)_q$ PMD code Π, with associated encoding and authentication unitaries $(\mathsf{Enc_{PMD}}, \mathsf{Auth_{PMD}})$ (See Definition 6 and Lemma 5). In particular, the PMD code of Theorem 1.

- An $[[n, m]]_q$ stabilizer code Q with encoding unitary Enc_Q, which is (δ, L)-QLDE. In particular, that of Theorem 4.

We encode any k qudit message state $|\psi\rangle$ first with the encoding unitary $\mathsf{Enc_{PMD}}$, and then with Enc_Q:

$$\mathsf{Enc}(|\psi\rangle) \equiv \mathsf{Enc}\,|\psi\rangle \otimes |0^{\mathsf{Anc}}\rangle = \mathsf{Enc}_Q\left(\mathsf{Enc_{PMD}} \otimes \mathbb{I}^{\mathsf{Anc}_Q}\right)|\psi\rangle \otimes |0^{\mathsf{Anc}}\rangle \qquad (39)$$

Note $|\mathsf{Anc}| = n - k$, and $\mathsf{Anc}_Q = n - m$. See Fig. 1 for an illustration.

Decoding. Our decoding algorithm Dec is composed of two phases, a list-decoding step in Algorithm 1 to obtain a discrete set of correction operators, followed by a coherent decoding phase in Algorithm 2 to correct these errors in superposition. While for simplicity we describe the algorithm in the context of non-adaptive adversaries, the algorithm for adaptive adversaries is exactly the same.

The first phase follows the ideas in [17] adapted to erasure list-decoding. Upon receiving a reduced density matrix ρ_T of a code-state $\mathsf{Enc}(\psi)$ for some $T \subset [n]$, we first measure the syndrome s of $\rho_T \otimes 0^{n-|T|}$ using a description of the stabilizers of Q. If $|T| \geq (1 - \delta) \cdot n$ and Q is (δ, L)-QLDE, then the syndrome measurement collapses the state into a superposition of at most L logically-distinct errors acting on the n-qudit code register, and we can efficiently obtain a list $E_1 \cdots E_L$ of candidate Pauli corrections.

Algorithm 1: Dec

Input: $T \subset [n]$, and a reduced density matrix of a code-state

$$\rho_T = \text{Tr}_{[n]\backslash T}[\text{Enc}(\psi \otimes 0^{\text{Anc}})]$$

Output: A k qudit state $\psi' \approx \psi$ close to the original message

1: Prepare the state $\rho_T \otimes 0^{n-|T|}$ on an n qudit register C, and measure the syndrome s of Q.

2: Apply erasure list-decodability to the syndrome s and T to obtain a list $E_1, \ldots, E_L$ of potential errors.

3: Coherently Correct using Algorithm 2, producing a state supported on the register C and L extra qubits.

4: Output the first k qudits of C.

In the second phase (Algorithm 2), we filter through each list element coherently, attempting each correction operator sequentially and relying on the PMD authentication unitary Auth to "catch" invalid corrections. Recall that Auth coherently measures the projection onto the PMD code-space, and reverts the encoding if successful (Lemma 5).

In slightly more detail, we begin by preparing L extra "flag" qubit registers $F_1 \cdots F_L$ initialized to $|0^L\rangle$, which will be used to coherently keep track of whether the state has been decoded already. First, we apply $\text{Enc}_Q^\dagger E_1^\dagger$ to the code register C to revert the state back into a corrupted codeword of a PMD, and we proceed by applying Auth on the PMD register and the first Flag qubit F_1. Conditioned on F_1 failing, we apply $\text{Enc}_Q^\dagger (E_{i+1}^\dagger E_i) \text{Enc}_Q$ to attempt the next correction. We repeat this process iteratively over $i \in [2, L]$, conditioning on the absense of previous success.

We show that Algorithm 2 succeeds in coherently producing the message ψ, by relying on the guarantee that the PMD approximately preserves the corrupted code-state when the authentication fails. In this manner, we are able to sequentially try elements of the list until one succeeds, without the error accumulating excessively.

Lemma 10. *Let* PMD *be a* $(m, k, \varepsilon)_q$*-PMD and* Q *be a* $[[n, m]]_q$ *stabilizer code which is* (δ, L)*-QLDE, both defined over the* q*-ary Pauli basis* $\mathcal{P}_q$. *Then* (Enc, Dec) *define a quantum code encoding* k *qudits into* n *qudits, which* $(\delta, 3 \cdot \varepsilon^{1/2} \cdot L^{3/4})$ *approximately corrects erasures.*

We can now instantiate the lemma above with our constructions of list decodable codes and PMD codes, to arrive at Theorem 2.

Corollary 1. *For all* $0 < r < 1$, *every sufficiently large* $n \in \mathbb{N}$, *and* $\gamma \geq (\log n)^{-1}$, *there exists a Monte Carlo construction of a family of* $((n, r \cdot n))_q$ *quantum codes which* $(\frac{1}{2}(1 - r - \gamma), 2^{-\Omega(\gamma \cdot n)})$ *approximately corrects erasures in time* $n^{O(1)}$. *The construction succeeds with probability* $1 - 2^{-\Omega(\gamma \cdot n)}$.

Algorithm 2: U: Coherently Correcting using PMDs and QLDs

Input: A list $\{E_i\}_{i\in[L]}$ of Pauli operators, and an n qudit register C with the state $|\phi\rangle$

Output: The pure state $U|\phi\rangle_C|0\rangle^L$ supported on n qudits and L qubits.

1: Prepare the state $|\phi\rangle_C \otimes |0^{\otimes L}\rangle_F$, by appending L extra "Flag" qubit registers $F_1 \cdots F_L$.

2: Apply $(\mathsf{Enc}_Q^\dagger E_1^\dagger)_C \otimes \mathbb{I}_F$ to revert the state to a corrupted PMD code-state, followed by $(\mathsf{Auth}_{\mathsf{PMD},F_1} \otimes \mathbb{I}_{\mathsf{Anc}_Q} \otimes \mathbb{I}_{F_{[n]\setminus\{1\}}})$ and authenticate it and write the output on F_1

3: Revert the candidate correction, controlled on the F_1

$$U_1 = \mathsf{Enc}_Q^\dagger(E_?^\dagger E_1)\mathsf{Enc}_Q \otimes |0\rangle\langle 0|_{F_1} + \mathbb{I}_C \otimes |1\rangle\langle 1|_{F_1} \quad (40)$$

4: For $i \in [2, L]$

5: Apply Auth to the PMD register and the ith flag, controlled on the $i-1$st flag,

$$A_i = \mathsf{Auth}_{C,F_i} \otimes |0\rangle\langle 0|_{F_{i-1}} + \mathbb{I}_C \otimes X_{F_i} \otimes |1\rangle\langle 1|_{F_{i-1}} \quad (41)$$

6: Attempt the next correction, controlled on the ith flag,

$$U_i = \mathsf{Enc}_Q^\dagger(E_{i+1}^\dagger E_i)\mathsf{Enc}_Q \otimes |0\rangle\langle 0|_{F_i} + \mathbb{I}_C \otimes |1\rangle\langle 1|_{F_i} \quad (42)$$

Proof. [of Corollary 1 and Theorem 2] If the PMD has rate r_{PMD} and Q has rate r_Q, then $R = r_{\mathsf{PMD}} \cdot r_Q$. We use the family of PMDs from Theorem 1, such that $\varepsilon_{\mathsf{PMD}} = n^{O(1)} \cdot 2^{-\Omega(\lambda)}$, where $\lambda = r_Q \cdot (1 - r_{\mathsf{PMD}}) \cdot n$.

We use the family of $(\frac{1}{2}(1 - r_Q - \gamma_Q), 2^{O(1/\gamma_Q)})$ erasure list decodable codes from Theorem 4. We pick a γ' s.t. (1) $r + \gamma \geq R + \gamma' = r_Q + \gamma_Q$, to match the desired erasure decoding radius, and thereby $\lambda = (\gamma' - \gamma_Q) \cdot n = \gamma_Q \cdot n$ if $\gamma_Q = \gamma'/2$. The theorem statement is vacuous unless $R < 1 - \gamma'$, and thereby $r_Q = R + \gamma'/2$ is well defined.

The corresponding $r_{\mathsf{PMD}} = 1 - \frac{\gamma_Q}{\gamma_Q + R}$, is only well defined in Theorem 1 if (2) the fraction is rational and $<1/3$. If the desired rate $r \geq \gamma/2$, then we pick $R = r$ and $\gamma_Q = \gamma/50$. If the desired rate $r \leq \gamma/2$, then we pick $R = \gamma/2$, and $\gamma_Q = \gamma/50$. In both situations, we satisfy conditions (1, 2), have rate $\geq r$, decoding radius $\geq \frac{1}{2}(1 - r - \gamma)$, error $2^{O(1/\gamma_Q)} \cdot 2^{-\Omega(\gamma_Q n)} = 2^{-\Omega(\gamma \cdot n)}$, and runtime $2^{O(1/\gamma_Q)} \cdot n^{O(1)} = n^{O(1)}$. The construction of Q succeeds with probability $\geq 1 - n^{O(1)} \cdot 2^{-\Omega(\gamma_Q \cdot n)} = 1 - 2^{-\Omega(\gamma \cdot n)}$.

5.2   Analysis

Recall that Algorithm 1 performs a syndrome measurement, collapsing the n qudit corrupted code-state $\mathcal{A} \circ \mathsf{Enc}(\psi)$ into a superposition of Pauli errors $|\phi\rangle = \sum_{i \in [L]} a_i \cdot E_i \mathsf{Enc}(|\psi\rangle)$ of the same syndrome. Since Q is (δ, L)-QLDE, there are at most L logically-distinct elements in the superposition. Thus, it suffices to show that the unitary U defined in Algorithm 2 approximately recovers from these superpositions, producing a state close to a product state with the original message $|\psi\rangle$.

We first claim that U approximately recovers from single Pauli errors in Lemma 11, corresponding essentially to our "Sparse Pauli Channel" Lemma 1 in the overview. This is the most technical part of the analysis, and we defer its proof to the bottom of this section. Then, in Lemma 12 we show how to boot-strap this claim into recovering from superpositions of at most L errors, which all but immediately gives us Lemma 10 as a corollary.

Lemma 11 (Single Pauli Errors). *Let* $|\phi_i\rangle = E_i \mathsf{Enc}(|\psi\rangle)$, *where* E_i *is logically equivalent to the* ith *list element in Algorithm 1. Then* U *approximately recovers the encoded message, i.e.,* $\forall \psi$:

$$\left\| \, |\psi\rangle \otimes |\mathsf{Aux}_i\rangle - U \cdot (|\phi_i\rangle \otimes |0^L\rangle) \right\|_2 \leq 2 \cdot L \cdot \varepsilon \qquad (43)$$

For some choice of $n - k$ *qudit and* L *qubit ancilla* $|\mathsf{Aux}_i\rangle$. *Moreover,* $\langle \mathsf{Aux}_i | \, |\mathsf{Aux}_j\rangle = \delta_{ij}$.

The intuition behind the proof of the single Pauli error case of Lemma 11 lies in considering an "ideal" PMD, with error $\varepsilon = 0$. In which case, all the authentication steps don't change the state, until a "correct" list element $E_j^\dagger$ is accepted by the PMD, returning the original message ψ.

To lift our Sparse Pauli Channel correction to correcting from *superpositions* of errors, we fundamentally leverage the fact that corrupted code-states of PMD codes are near-orthogonal. We show that this limits the quantum interference between distinct Pauli errors, and enables us to correct from sparse superpositions with only a slight degrade in accuracy:

Lemma 12 (Sparse Superpositions of Pauli Errors). *If* $|\phi\rangle = \sum_{i \in [L]} a_i |\phi_i\rangle$ *where* $\langle \phi | \, |\phi\rangle = 1$ *and* $|\phi_i\rangle = E_i \mathsf{Enc}(|\psi\rangle)$, *then* U *approximately recovers the encoded message* ψ, *i.e.*

$$\left\| \psi \otimes \mathsf{Aux} - U \circ (\phi \otimes 0^L) \right\|_1 \leq 3 \cdot \varepsilon^{1/2} \cdot L^{3/4} \qquad (44)$$

For some choice of $n - k$ *qudit and* L *qubit state* $|\mathsf{Aux}\rangle$.

This concludes the proof that Dec recovers the message $|\psi\rangle$ from adversarial erasure channels, thus $(\mathsf{Enc}, \mathsf{Dec})$ forms an erasure AQECC as in Lemma 10.

5.3   The Proofs

We dedicate the rest of this section to proofs of the lemmas above.

Proof. [of Lemma 11] Since Q is (δ, L)-QLDE, the ith list element E corrects $|\phi_i\rangle$, i.e., $E_i^\dagger |\phi_i\rangle = \mathsf{Enc}(\psi)$. If the previous authentication steps didn't corrupt the state, then the authentication should correctly accept on the ith iteration of Algorithm 2:

$$\mathsf{Auth}\left(\mathsf{Enc}_Q^\dagger E_i^\dagger E_i \mathsf{Enc}(|\psi\rangle)\right)|0\rangle_{F_i} = \mathsf{Auth}\left(\mathsf{Enc}_{\mathsf{PMD}}(|\psi\rangle)\right)|0\rangle_{F_i} \qquad (45)$$

$$= |\psi\rangle \otimes |0^{\mathsf{Anc}}\rangle \otimes |1\rangle_{F_i} \qquad (46)$$

During the previous iterations $t \in (1 \cdots i-1)$, we sequentially apply the operators $E_{i+1}^\dagger E_i$ to change between code-states of Q. We emphasize that $E_{i+1}^\dagger E_i$ is a logical operator of Q, and thus $E_{ij} = \mathsf{Enc}_Q^\dagger E_j^\dagger E_i \mathsf{Enc}_Q$ is a n-qudit Pauli operator, with non-trivial support only on the m-qudit message register corresponding to the PMD.

Consider the pure state $|D_t\rangle$ defined after the t-th iteration of Algorithm 2, and assume $1 \le t < i$. Let the ideal pure state $|v_t\rangle$ be

$$|v_t\rangle = \left(\mathsf{Enc}_Q^\dagger E_t^\dagger E_i \mathsf{Enc}(|\psi\rangle)\right)|00\cdots 0\rangle_F \qquad (47)$$

We prove by induction that $\| |D_t\rangle - |v_t\rangle \|_2 \le 2 \cdot t \cdot \varepsilon$ for $1 \le t < i$. We note that $t = 1$ corresponds to Lemma 5. For $t > 1$, we observe the recurrences

$$|D_t\rangle = U_t A_t |D_{t-1}\rangle, \text{ and } |v_t\rangle = U_t |v_{t-1}\rangle \qquad (48)$$

Consider the decomposition $|D_t\rangle = U_t A_t |v_{t-1}\rangle + U_t A_t(|D_{t-1}\rangle - |v_{t-1}\rangle)$. Note that by Lemma 5,

$$\| |v_t\rangle - U_t A_t |v_{t-1}\rangle \|_2 = \| |v_{t-1}\rangle - A_t |v_{t-1}\rangle \|_2 \le 2 \cdot \varepsilon \qquad (49)$$

and that by the inductive hypothesis, we have $\| |D_{t-1}\rangle - |v_{t-1}\rangle \|_2 \le 2 \cdot (t-1) \cdot \varepsilon$. Thus,

$$\| |D_t\rangle - |v_t\rangle \|_2 \le \| |D_{t-1}\rangle - |v_{t-1}\rangle \|_2 + \|U_t A_t |v_{t-1}\rangle - |v_t\rangle \|_2 \le 2 \cdot t \cdot \varepsilon \qquad (50)$$

After succeeding at the ith attempt, the remaining gates $\prod_{k=i+1}^L (A_k U_k)$ in Algorithm 2 only increment the counter F and don't act on the code C. Thus, the output state is $\le 2 \cdot L \cdot \varepsilon$ close to the pure state

$$\prod_{k=i+1}^L (A_k U_k) A_i |v_i\rangle = |\psi\rangle \otimes |0^{\mathsf{Anc}}\rangle \otimes |0_1 0_2 \cdots 0_{i-1} 1_i 1_{i+1} \cdots 1_L\rangle_F \qquad (51)$$

Orthogonality follows from the fact that no two logically distinct operators $i \ne j$ are accepted by the PMD at the same iteration.

It remains now to show the proof of Lemma 12 from Lemma 11.

Proof. [of Lemma 12] We first show that the corrupted code-states are approximately orthogonal, $|\langle \phi_i | \phi_j \rangle| \leq \varepsilon$, which via the normalization constraint $|\langle \phi | \phi \rangle| = 1$, tells us $\sum_i |a_i|^2 \approx 1$. Then we show Algorithm 2 produces a state close to $\psi \otimes \mathsf{Aux}$, where Aux is the superposition of aux states, $|\mathsf{Aux}\rangle \propto \sum_{i \in [L]} a_i |\mathsf{Aux}_i\rangle$.

Recall from Lemma 11 that $\mathsf{Enc}_Q E_i^\dagger E_j \mathsf{Enc}_Q = E_{ij}$ is some Pauli operator acting on the PMD register. Thus, using Definition 6,

$$|\langle \phi_i | \phi_j \rangle| = |\langle 0^{\mathsf{Anc}} | \langle \psi | \mathsf{Enc}^\dagger E_i^\dagger E_j \mathsf{Enc} |\psi\rangle |0^{\mathsf{Anc}}\rangle| \leq \|\Pi E \Pi\|_\infty \leq \varepsilon \qquad (52)$$

Let $|aux\rangle = N^{-1/2} \sum_{i \in [L]} a_i |aux\rangle_i$, where the orthogonality of the $|aux\rangle_i$ tells us $N = \sum_i |a_i|^2$. Using the normalization constraint on $|\phi\rangle$, we obtain a bound on N:

$$1 = \langle \phi | \phi \rangle = \sum_i |a_i|^2 + \sum_{i \neq j} a_i^* a_j \langle \phi_i | \phi_j \rangle \geq \sum_i |a_i|^2 - \varepsilon \cdot \sum_{i \neq j} |a_i^* a_j| \geq (1 - \varepsilon \cdot L) \cdot \sum_i |a_i|^2,$$
$$(53)$$

via the Cauchy-Schwartz inequality. Thereby $N = \sum_i |a_i|^2 \leq 1/(1 - \varepsilon \cdot L)$.

Finally, we consider the desired inner product:

$$N^{1/2} \cdot |(\langle \psi | \otimes \langle \mathsf{Aux} |) U |\phi\rangle \otimes |0^L\rangle| = |\sum a_j^* \langle \psi | \otimes \langle \mathsf{Aux}_j | U |\phi\rangle \otimes |0^L\rangle| \qquad (54)$$

$$\geq \langle \phi \rangle - \sum |a_j| \cdot \left| \left(\langle \psi | \otimes \langle \mathsf{Aux}_j | U - \langle \phi_j | \otimes \langle 0^L | \right) |\phi\rangle \otimes |0^L\rangle \right| \geq \qquad (55)$$

$$\geq 1 - \sum_j |a_j| \cdot \| |\psi\rangle \otimes |\mathsf{Aux}_j\rangle - U \cdot (|\phi_j\rangle \otimes |0^L\rangle)\|_2 \geq 1 - -2 \cdot L^{3/2} \cdot \varepsilon \cdot (\sum_i |a_i|^2)^{1/2} \quad (56)$$

Where we used the triangle inequality, the Cauchy-Schwartz inequality twice, and then Lemma 11. Thus,

$$|(\langle \psi | \otimes \langle \mathsf{Aux} |) U |\phi\rangle \otimes |0^L\rangle| \geq (1 - L \cdot \varepsilon)^{1/2} - 2 \cdot L^{3/2} \cdot \varepsilon \geq 1 - 3 \cdot L^{3/2} \cdot \varepsilon \quad (57)$$

The relation between inner product and trace distance of pure states gives us the desired bound.

References

1. Aggarwal, D., Ball, M., Obremski, M.: Survey: non-malleable code in the split-state model. Cryptology ePrint Archive, Paper 2022/1326 (2022). https://eprint.iacr.org/2022/1326
2. Aggarwal, D., Dodis, Y., Lovett, S.: Non-malleable codes from additive combinatorics. Cryptology ePrint Archive, Paper 2013/201 (2013). https://eprint.iacr.org/2013/201
3. Aggarwal, D., Sekar, S., Kanukurthi, B., Obremski, M., Obbattu, S.L.B.: Rate one-third non-malleable codes. Cryptology ePrint Archive, Paper 2021/1042 (2021). https://eprint.iacr.org/2021/1042

4. Agrawal, S., Gupta, D., Maji, H.K., Pandey, O., Prabhakaran, M.: Explicit non-malleable codes resistant to permutations and perturbations. Cryptology ePrint Archive, Paper 2014/841 (2014). https://eprint.iacr.org/2014/841
5. Agrawal, S., Gupta, D., Maji, H.K., Pandey, O., Prabhakaran, M.: A rate-optimizing compiler for non-malleable codes against bit-wise tampering and permutations. Cryptology ePrint Archive, Paper 2014/842 (2014). https://eprint.iacr.org/2014/842
6. Aharonov, D., Ben-Or, M., Eban, E.: Interactive proofs for quantum computations. In: International Conference on Supercomputing (2008)
7. Anshu, A., Nirkhe, C.: Circuit lower bounds for low-energy states of quantum code Hamiltonians. In: Information Technology Convergence and Services (2020)
8. Ball, M., Dachman-Soled, D., Guo, S., Malkin, T., Tan, L.Y.: Non-malleable codes for small-depth circuits. Cryptology ePrint Archive, Paper 2018/207 (2018). https://eprint.iacr.org/2018/207
9. Ball, M., Dachman-Soled, D., Loss, J.: (nondeterministic) hardness vs. non-malleability. Cryptology ePrint Archive, Paper 2022/070 (2022). https://eprint.iacr.org/2022/070
10. Bao, J., Ji, L., Wei, R., Zhang, Y.: New existence and nonexistence results for strong external difference families. Discret. Math. **341**, 1798–1805 (2016)
11. Barnum, H., Crépeau, C., Gottesman, D., Smith, A., Tapp, A.: Authentication of quantum messages. In: The 43rd Annual IEEE Symposium on Foundations of Computer Science, 2002. Proceedings, pp. 449–458. IEEE (2002)
12. Barnum, H., Knill, E.: Reversing quantum dynamics with near-optimal quantum and classical fidelity. J. Math. Phys. **43**, 2097–2106 (2000)
13. Ben-Aroya, A., Doron, D., Ta-Shma, A.: Near-optimal erasure list-decodable codes. In: Proceedings of the 35th Computational Complexity Conference (2020)
14. Bény, C.: Conditions for the approximate correction of algebras. In: Childs, A., Mosca, M. (eds.) TQC 2009. LNCS, vol. 5906, pp. 66–75. Springer, Heidelberg (2009). https://doi.org/10.1007/978-3-642-10698-9_7
15. Bény, C., Oreshkov, O.: General conditions for approximate quantum error correction and near-optimal recovery channels. Phys. Rev. Lett. **104**(12), 120501 (2010)
16. Bergamaschi, T., Boddu, N.G.: On split-state quantum tamper detection and non-malleability (2023). https://api.semanticscholar.org/CorpusID:265456980
17. Bergamaschi, T., Golowich, L., Gunn, S.: Approaching the quantum singleton bound with approximate error correction. arXiv **abs/2212.09935** (2022)
18. Boddu, N.G., Goyal, V., Jain, R., Ribeiro, J.L.: Split-state non-malleable codes and secret sharing schemes for quantum messages. ArXiv **abs/2308.06466** (2023). https://api.semanticscholar.org/CorpusID:260886799
19. Boddu, N.G., Jain, R.: Non-malleable code in the split-state model. Entropy **24** (2022). https://api.semanticscholar.org/CorpusID:208058906
20. Boddu, N.G., Kapshikar, U.: Tamper detection against unitary operators. ArXiv **abs/2105.04487** (2021)
21. Calderbank, S.: Good quantum error-correcting codes exist. Phys. Rev. A Atom. Mol. Opt. Phys. **54**(2), 1098–1105 (1996)
22. Cheraghchi, M., Guruswami, V.: Non-malleable coding against bit-wise and split-state tampering. J. Cryptol. **30**, 191–241 (2013)
23. Cleve, R., Gottesman, D., Lo, H.K.: How to share a quantum secret. Phys. Rev. Lett. **83**, 648–651 (1999)
24. Cramer, R., Damgård, I., Döttling, N., Fehr, S., Spini, G.: Linear secret sharing schemes from error correcting codes and universal hash functions. IACR Cryptol. ePrint Arch. **2015**, 1089 (2015)

25. Cramer, R., Damgård, I., Fehr, S.: On the cost of reconstructing a secret, or vss with optimal reconstruction phase. In: Annual International Cryptology Conference (2001)
26. Cramer, R., Dodis, Y., Fehr, S., Padró, C., Wichs, D.: Detection of algebraic manipulation with applications to robust secret sharing and fuzzy extractors. In: International Conference on the Theory and Application of Cryptographic Techniques (2008)
27. Cramer, R., Fehr, S., Padró, C.: Algebraic manipulation detection codes. Sci. China Math. **56**, 1349–1358 (2013). https://api.semanticscholar.org/CorpusID:31391230
28. Cramer, R., Padró, C., Xing, C.: Optimal algebraic manipulation detection codes in the constant-error model. In: Theory of Cryptography Conference (2015)
29. Crépeau, C., Gottesman, D., Smith, A.D.: Approximate quantum error-correcting codes and secret sharing schemes. In: International Conference on the Theory and Application of Cryptographic Techniques (2005)
30. Devetak, I.: The private classical capacity and quantum capacity of a quantum channel. IEEE Trans. Inf. Theory **51**, 44–55 (2005)
31. Ding, Y., Jin, L., Xing, C.: Erasure list-decodable codes from random and algebraic geometry codes. IEEE Trans. Inf. Theory **60**, 3889–3894 (2014)
32. Dziembowski, S., Kazana, T., Obremski, M.: Non-malleable codes from two-source extractors. Cryptology ePrint Archive, Paper 2013/498 (2013). https://eprint.iacr.org/2013/498
33. Dziembowski, S., Pietrzak, K., Wichs, D.: Non-malleable codes (2018). https://api.semanticscholar.org/CorpusID:14293524
34. Elias, P.: List decoding for noisy channels. In: Technical Report 335. Research Laboratory of Electronics, MIT (1957)
35. Gottesman, D.: Stabilizer codes and quantum error correction. arXiv: Quantum Physics (1997)
36. Gottesman, D.: Theory of quantum secret sharing. Phys. Rev. A **61**, 042311 (1999)
37. Grassl, M., Huber, F., Winter, A.J.: Entropic proofs of singleton bounds for quantum error-correcting codes. IEEE Trans. Inf. Theory **68**, 3942–3950 (2020)
38. Gullans, M.J., Krastanov, S., Huse, D.A., Jiang, L., Flammia, S.T.: Quantum coding with low-depth random circuits. Phys. Rev. X **11**, 031066 (2020)
39. Guruswami, V.: List decoding from erasures: bounds and code constructions. IEEE Trans. Inf. Theory **49**, 2826–2833 (2001)
40. Hayden, P.M., Leung, D.W., Mayers, D.: The universal composable security of quantum message authentication with key recyling. arXiv: Quantum Physics (2016)
41. Hayden, P.M., Penington, G.: Approximate quantum error correction revisited: introducing the alpha-bit. Commun. Math. Phys. **374**, 369–432 (2017)
42. Huczynska, S., Paterson, M.B.: Existence and non-existence results for strong external difference families. Discret. Math. **341**, 87–95 (2016)
43. Huczynska, S., Paterson, M.B.: Weighted external difference families and R-optimal AMD codes. Discret. Math. **342**, 855–867 (2018)
44. Jafargholi, Z., Wichs, D.: Tamper detection and continuous non-malleable codes. In: Theory of Cryptography Conference (2015)
45. Kanukurthi, B., Obbattu, S.L.B., Sekar, S.: Four-state non-malleable codes with explicit constant rate. Cryptology ePrint Archive, Paper 2017/930 (2017). https://eprint.iacr.org/2017/930
46. Knill, E., Laflamme, R.: Theory of quantum error-correcting codes. Phys. Rev. A **55**, 900–911 (1996)

47. Kretschmann, D., Schlingemann, D., Werner, R.F.: The information-disturbance tradeoff and the continuity of Stinespring's representation. IEEE Trans. Inf. Theory **54**, 1708–1717 (2006)
48. Leung, D.W., Nielsen, M.A., Chuang, I.L., Yamamoto, Y.: Approximate quantum error correction can lead to better codes. Phys. Rev. A **56**, 2567–2573 (1997)
49. Leung, D.W., Smith, G.: Communicating over adversarial quantum channels using quantum list codes. IEEE Trans. Inf. Theory **54**, 883–887 (2006)
50. Lin, F., Cheraghchi, M., Guruswami, V., Safavi-Naini, R., Wang, H.: Secret sharing with binary shares. In: IACR Cryptol. ePrint Arch. (2018)
51. Mandayam, P., Ng, H.K.: Towards a unified framework for approximate quantum error correction. Phys. Rev. A **86**, 012335 (2012). https://doi.org/10.1103/PhysRevA.86.012335. https://link.aps.org/doi/10.1103/PhysRevA.86.012335
52. Ng, H.K., Mandayam, P.: Simple approach to approximate quantum error correction based on the transpose channel. Phys. Rev. A **81**, 062342 (2010). https://doi.org/10.1103/PhysRevA.81.062342. https://link.aps.org/doi/10.1103/PhysRevA.81.062342
53. Rains, E.M.: Quantum shadow enumerators. IEEE Trans. Inf. Theory **45**, 0001–2366 (1996)
54. Rains, E.M.: Nonbinary quantum codes. IEEE Trans. Inf. Theory **45**, 1827–1832 (1997)
55. Schumacher, B., Westmoreland, M.D.: Approximate quantum error correction. Quantum Inf. Process. **1**(1-2), 5–12 (2002). https://doi.org/10.1023/A%3A1019653202562
56. Smith, A.D.: Quantum secret sharing for general access structures. arXiv: Quantum Physics (2000)
57. Steane: Simple quantum error-correcting codes. Phys. Rev. A Atom. Mol. Opt. Phys. **54 6**, 4741–4751 (1996)
58. Wozencraft., J.M.: List Decoding. Quarterly Progress Report, Research Laboratory of Electronics, vol. 48, pp. 90–95. MIT (1958)
59. Wu, Y., Kolkowitz, S., Puri, S., Thompson, J.D.: Erasure conversion for fault-tolerant quantum computing in alkaline earth Rydberg atom arrays. Nat. Commun. **13**, 4657 (2022)
60. Yoshida, B., Kitaev, A.Y.: Efficient decoding for the Hayden-Preskill protocol. arXiv: High Energy Physics - Theory (2017)

Certified Everlasting Secure Collusion-Resistant Functional Encryption, and More

Taiga Hiroka[1], Fuyuki Kitagawa[2,3], Tomoyuki Morimae[1], Ryo Nishimaki[2,3(✉)], Tapas Pal[4], and Takashi Yamakawa[1,2,3]

[1] Yukawa Institute for Theoretical Physics, Kyoto University, Kyoto, Japan
[2] NTT Social Informatics Laboratories, Tokyo, Japan
ryo.nishimaki@ntt.com
[3] NTT Research Center for Theoretical Quantum Information, Atsugi, Japan
[4] Karlsruhe Institute of Technology, KASTEL Security Research Labs, Karlsruhe, Germany

Abstract. We study certified everlasting secure functional encryption (FE) and many other cryptographic primitives in this work. Certified everlasting security roughly means the following. A receiver possessing a quantum cryptographic object (such as ciphertext) can issue a certificate showing that the receiver has deleted the cryptographic object and information included in the object (such as plaintext) was lost. If the certificate is valid, the security is guaranteed even if the receiver becomes computationally unbounded after the deletion. Many cryptographic primitives are known to be impossible (or unlikely) to have information-theoretical security even in the quantum world. Hence, certified everlasting security is a nice compromise (intrinsic to quantum).

In this work, we define certified everlasting secure versions of FE, compute-and-compare obfuscation, predicate encryption (PE), secret-key encryption (SKE), public-key encryption (PKE), receiver non-committing encryption (RNCE), and garbled circuits. We also present the following constructions:
- Adaptively certified everlasting secure collusion-resistant public-key FE for all polynomial-size circuits from indistinguishability obfuscation and one-way functions.
- Adaptively certified everlasting secure bounded collusion-resistant public-key FE for NC^1 circuits from standard PKE.
- Certified everlasting secure compute-and-compare obfuscation from standard fully homomorphic encryption and standard compute-and-compare obfuscation.
- Adaptively (resp., selectively) certified everlasting secure PE from standard adaptively (resp., selectively) secure attribute-based encryption and certified everlasting secure compute-and-compare obfuscation.

Technical details are omitted due to page limitations in this version. Please, see the full version [HKM+23] *for the technical details.*
T. Pal—The research was conducted while the author was a postdoc at NTT Social Informatics Laboratories.

M. Joye and G. Leander (Eds.): EUROCRYPT 2024, LNCS 14653, pp. 434–456, 2024.
https://doi.org/10.1007/978-3-031-58734-4_15

- Certified everlasting secure SKE and PKE from standard SKE and PKE, respectively.
- Cetified everlasting secure RNCE from standard PKE.
- Cetified everlasting secure garbled circuits from standard SKE.

1 Introduction

1.1 Background

Computational security in cryptography relies on assumptions that some problems are hard to solve. However, such assumptions could be broken in the future when revolutionary novel algorithms are discovered, or computing devices are drastically improved. One solution to the problem of computational security is to construct information-theoretically-secure protocols. However, many cryptographic primitives are known to be impossible (or unlikely) to satisfy information-theoretical security even in the quantum world [LC97, May97, MW18].

Good compromises (intrinsic to quantum!) have been studied recently [Unr15, BI20, KT20, HMNY21, HMNY22b, Por23]. In particular, certified everlasting security, which was introduced in [HMNY22b] based on [Unr15, BI20], achieves the following security: After receiving quantum-encrypted data, a receiver can issue a certificate to prove that (s)he deleted its quantum-encrypted data. If the certificate is valid, its security is guaranteed even if the receiver becomes computationally unbounded later. A (private or public) verification key for certificates is also generated along with quantum-encrypted data. This security notion is weaker than information-theoretical security since a malicious receiver could refuse to issue a valid certificate. However, it is still a useful security notion because, for example, a sender can penalize receivers who do not issue valid certificates. In addition, certified everlasting security is an intrinsically quantum property because it implies information-theoretical security in the classical world.[1]

Certified everlasting security can bypass the impossibility of information-theoretical security. In fact, several cryptographic primitives have been shown to have certified everlasting security, such as commitments and zero-knowledge [HMNY22b]. An important open problem in this direction is

Which cryptographic primitives can have certified everlasting security?

Functional encryption (FE) is one of the most advanced cryptographic primitives and achieves considerable flexibility in controlling encrypted data [BSW11].

---

[1] This is because a malicious receiver can copy the encrypted data freely. Hence, the encrypted data must be secure against an unbounded malicious receiver at the point when the receiver obtains the encrypted data. The same discussion does not go through in the quantum world because even a malicious receiver cannot copy the quantum-encrypted data due to the quantum no-cloning theorem.

In FE, an owner of a master secret key MSK can generate a functional decryption key sk_f that hardwires a function f. When a ciphertext ct_m of a message m is decrypted by sk_f, we can obtain the value $f(m)$, and no information beyond $f(m)$ is leaked. Information-theoretically secure FE is impossible, and all known constructions are computationally secure [GVW12, GGH+16, AP20, AV19, JLS21, JLS22]. A motivating application of FE is analyzing sensitive data and computing new data from personal data without sacrificing data privacy. In this example, users must store their encrypted data on a remote server since users delegate the computation. At some point, users might request the server to "forget" their data (even if they are encrypted). European Union [GDP16] and California [CCP18] adopted data deletion clauses in legal regulations for such users. Encryption with certified deletion could be useful for implementing the right to be forgotten. However, suppose that FE does not have *certified everlasting security*. In that case, the rapid growth of computational power potentially breaks the privacy of sensitive personal data (such as DNA) in the future. This risk ("recalling" in the future) is great because descendants inherit DNA information. Certified everlasting security is desirable for such practical applications of FE.

Hence, we have the following open problem:

Is it possible to construct certified everlasting secure FE?

We note that certified everlasting secure FE is particularly useful compared to certified everlasting secure public key encryption (PKE) (or more generally "all-or-nothing encryption"[2] [GMM17]) because it ensures security even against an honest receiver who holds a decryption key. That is, we can ensure that a receiver who holds a decryption key sk_f for a function f cannot learn more than $f(m)$ even if the receiver can run an unbounded-time computation after issuing a valid certificate. In contrast, certified everlasting PKE does not ensure any security against an honest receiver since the receiver can simply keep a copy of a plaintext after honestly decrypting a ciphertext.

Another useful advanced cryptographic primitive is obfuscation for compute-and-compare programs [WZ17] (a.k.a. lockable obfuscation [GKW17]). A compute-and-compare obfuscation scheme can obfuscate a compute-and-compare circuit parameterized by a polynomial-time computable circuit P along with a lock value lock and a message m. The circuit takes an input x and outputs m if $P(x) = \mathsf{lock}$ and $\perp$ otherwise. Point functions, conjunction with wild cards, plaintext checkers, and affine testers are examples of such circuits [GKW17, WZ17]. Hence, certified everlasting secure compute-and-compare obfuscation achieves certified deletion for obfuscated programs in the restricted class of functionalities. In addition, compute-and-compare obfuscation has many cryptographic applications [GKW17, WZ17, CVW+18, FFMV23, AYY22, AKYY23]. We can generically convert all-or-nothing encryption into anonymous one via compute-and-compare obfuscation. In particular, we can

---

[2] Such as identity-based encryption (IBE), attribute-based encryption (ABE), fully homomorphic encryption (FHE), or witness encryption (WE).

obtain predicate encryption (PE) [KSW08,GVW15] from ABE and compute-and-compare obfuscation. PE is an attribute-hiding variant of ABE and an intermediate primitive between ABE and FE. If we can achieve certified everlasting secure compute-and-compare obfuscation, it is possible to achieve certified everlasting secure PE (and anonymous IBE and PKE).

Hence, we have the following second open problem:

Is it possible to construct certified everlasting secure compute-and-compare obfuscation?

1.2 Our Results

We solve the above questions in this work. Our contributions are as follows.

1. We formally define certified everlasting versions of many cryptographic primitives: FE, compute and compare obfuscation, PE, secret-key encryption (SKE), PKE, receiver non committing encryption (RNCE), and a garbling scheme.
2. We construct adaptively certified everlasting secure collusion-resistant public-key FE for P/poly from indistinguishability obfuscation (IO) and one-way functions (OWFs). We also construct adaptively certified everlasting secure bounded collusion-resistant public-key FE for NC^1 from standard PKE.
3. We construct certified everlasting secure compute-and-compare obfuscation from standard FHE and standard compute-and-compare obfuscation. Both building blocks can be instantiated with the learning with errors (LWE) assumption. We also construct adaptively (resp., selectively) certified everlasting secure PE from standard adaptively (resp., selectively) secure ABE and certified everlasting secure compute-and-compare obfuscation.
4. To achieve adaptively certified everlasting secure bounded collusion-resistant FE, we construct many certified everlasting secure cryptographic primitives:
   - Two constructions of certified everlasting secure SKE from standard SKE. An advantage of the first construction is that the certificate is classical, but a disadvantage is that the security proof relies on the quantum random oracle model (QROM) [BDF+11]. The security of the second construction holds without relying on the QROM, but the certificate is quantum.
   - Two constructions of certified everlasting secure PKE with the same properties of the SKE constructions above from standard PKE.
   - A construction of certified everlasting secure RNCE from certified everlasting PKE.
   - A construction of certified everlasting secure garbling scheme for P/poly from certified everlasting SKE.

All our constructions are privately verifiable, so we must keep verification keys (for deletion certificate) secret. It is open to achieving certified everlasting secure bounded collusion-resistant FE for P/poly from standard PKE.

We introduce fascinating techniques to achieve certified everlasting secure collusion-resistant FE and certified everlasting secure compute-and-compare obfuscation. We developed an authentication technique for BB84 state to satisfy both the functionality of FE and certified everlasting security. (See Sect. 2.1 for the detail.) This authentication technique for BB84 states is of independent interest and we believe that it has further applications.[3] We also developed a deferred evaluation technique using dummy lock values to satisfy both the functionality of compute-and-compare obfuscation and certified everlasting security. (See Sect. 2.3 for the detail.)

1.3   Concurrent and Independent Work

Certified Everlasting Secure SKE and PKE. Recently, Bartusek and Khurana concurrently and independently obtained similar results [BK23]. They introduce a generic compiler that can convert several cryptographic primitives to certified everlasting secure ones, such as PKE, ABE, FHE, WE, and timed-release encryption. Their constructions via the generic compiler have the advantage that the certificates are classical *and* no QROM is required. Our constructions of certified everlasting SKE and PKE cannot achieve both: if the certificates are classical, QROM is required, and if QROM is not used, the certificates have to be quantum. We note that their certified everlasting SKE and PKE can be used as building blocks of our RNCE, garbling, and bounded collusion-resistant FE constructions instead of our SKE and PKE schemes.

While their work focuses on all-or-nothing encryption, our work presents certified everlasting secure garbling and FE, which are not given in their work. It is unclear how to apply their generic compiler to garbling and FE.

One might think that certified everlasting garbling can be constructed from certified everlasting SKE, which is constructed from their generic compiler. However, it is non-trivial whether certified everlasting garbling can be immediately constructed from certified everlasting SKE because garbling needs double-encryption. (For details, see Sect. 2.2.)

Moreover, a direct application of their generic compiler to FE does not work because of the following reason. If we directly apply their generic compiler to FE, we have a ciphertext consisting of classical and quantum parts. The classical part is the original FE ciphertext whose plaintext is $m \oplus r$ with random r, and the quantum part is random BB84 states whose computational basis states encode r. The decryption key of the function f consists of functional decryption key sk_f and the basis of the BB84 states. However, in this construction, a receiver with the ciphertext and the decryption key cannot obtain $f(m)$, because what the receiver obtains is only $f(m \oplus r)$ and r, which cannot recover $f(m)$.

Bartusek-Khurana's Results and Our Collusion-Resistant FE, PE, and Compute-and-Compare Obfuscation. While our certified everlasting secure bounded

---

[3] Indeed, an application was found by Kitagawa, Nishimaki, and Yamakawa [KNY23]. See Sect. 1.4.

collusion-resistant FE (and its building block SKE, PKE, garbling, and RNCE) schemes are concurrent and independent work, our certified everlasting secure collusion-resistant FE, PE, and compute-and-compare obfuscation schemes use the certified everlasting lemma by Bartusek and Khurana[4] Those three schemes were added after the paper by Bartusek and Khurana was made public. *Their work does not consider FE, PE, and compute-and-compare obfuscation.*

If we directly apply their generic compiler to PE, we cannot hide the attribute part though we can hide the plaintext part. Even if we apply the same technique to the attribute part, say, we also set the attribute to $a \oplus r'$ with random r', and put random BB84 states whose computational basis states encode r' in a ciphertext, the idea does not work. A receiver cannot obtain the plaintext even if $P(a) = 1$ because the predicate computes $P(a \oplus r')$ instead of $P(a)$, and the correctness does not hold.

It is non-trivial whether we can obtain certified everlasting compute-and-compare obfuscation by their framework for encryption with certified deletion because we need to hide information about circuits while preserving the functionality. Savvy readers might think it may be possible by applying the framework to the compute-and-compare obfuscation from circular *insecure* FHE by Klucz-niak [Klu22]. However, we need compute-and-compare obfuscation to instantiate circular insecure FHE. This is a circular argument.

Certified Everlasting Secure FE. Bartusek, Garg, Goyal, Khurana, Malavolta, Raizes, and Roberts [BGG+23] concurrently and independently obtained adaptively certified everlasting secure collusion-resistant FE for P/poly from IO and OWFs. They use subspace coset states [CLLZ21], while we use BB84 states (with one-time signatures). Hence, the techniques are different. Their scheme is publicly verifiable thanks to the subspace coset state approach. Another technical difference is that they directly rely on adaptively secure multi-input FE (MIFE) [GGG+14, GJO16] while we do not. Hence, their scheme incurs an additional sub-exponential loss (from IO to adaptively secure MIFE [GJO16]). Our scheme uses selectively secure MIFE and does not incur sub-exponential loss. We note that selectively secure MIFE and IO are equivalent without any security loss [GGG+14]. They also present several certified everlasting secure primitives that are not considered in our work. However, the results on RNCE, garbled circuits, compute-and-compare obfuscation, and PE are unique to our work.

1.4   Subsequent Work

A subsequent work by Kitagawa, Nishimaki, and Yamakawa [KNY23] shows another application of our authentication technique for BB84 states which we

---

[4] This is because this paper is a major update version of the paper by Hiroka et al. [HMNY22a] with new additional results (i.e., collusion-resistant FE, PE, and compute-and-compare obfuscation). The content in the work by Hiroka et al. [HMNY22a] is a concurrent and independent work of the work by Bartusek and Khurana [BK23].

develop for the construction of certified everlasting secure collusion-resistant FE. Specifically, they use the technique to construct a generic compiler to add the publicly verifiable deletion property for various kinds of cryptographic primitives solely based on OWFs.

1.5 More on Related Works

Ciphertext Certified Deletion. Unruh [Unr15] introduced the concept of revocable quantum time-released encryption. In this primitive, a receiver possessing quantum encrypted data can obtain its plaintext after a predetermined time T. The sender can revoke the quantum encrypted data before time T. If the revocation succeeds, the receiver cannot obtain the plaintext information even if its computing power becomes unbounded.

Broadbent and Islam [BI20] constructed one-time SKE with certified deletion. It is standard one-time SKE except that once the receiver issues a valid classical certificate, the receiver cannot obtain the plaintext information even if the receiver later becomes a computationally *unbounded* adversary. (See also [KT20].)

Hiroka, Morimae, Nishimaki, and Yamakawa [HMNY21] constructed reusable SKE, PKE, and ABE with certified deletion. These reusable SKE, PKE, and ABE with certified deletion are standard reusable SKE, PKE, and ABE with additional properties, respectively. Once the receiver issues a valid classical certificate, the receiver cannot obtain the plaintext information even if it obtains some secret information (e.g., the master secret key of ABE). In these primitives, the security holds against computationally bounded adversaries, unlike in this work. Poremba [Por23] achieved FHE with certified deletion. In addition, certificates for deletion are publicly verifiable in his construction. The security holds against computationally bounded adversaries, unlike in this work. However, the security of the construction relies on a strong conjecture that a particular hash function is "strong Gaussian-collapsing".

Hiroka, Morimae, Nishimaki, and Yamakawa [HMNY22b] constructed commitments with statistical binding and certified everlasting hiding. From it, they also constructed a certified everlasting zero-knowledge proof system for QMA based on the zero-knowledge protocol of [BG20].

Key Certified Deletion. Kitagawa and Nishimaki [KN22] introduced the notion of FE with secure key leasing, where functional decryption keys are quantum states and we can generate certificates for deleting the keys. This can be seen as certified deletion of keys and the dual of certified deletion of ciphertexts. They achieved bounded collusion-resistant secret-key FE with secure key leasing for P/poly from standard SKE.

Secure Software Leasing. Ananth and La Place introduced the notion of secure software leasing and achieved it for a sub-class of evasive functions from public-key quantum money (need IO and OWFs) and the LWE assumption [AL21]. Secure software leasing encode classical program into quantum program and has an explicit returning process. After a lessor verifies that a returned quantum program is valid, a lessee cannot run the leased program anymore. Later, several secure software leasing schemes for a sub-class of evasive functions or cryptographic functionalities (or its variant) with various properties (such as classical communication, without assumptions) were presented [CMP20, BJL+21, KNY21, ALL+21]. None of them are certified everlasting secure.

Compute-and-Compare Obfuscation, PE, and FE. There are tremendous amount of previous works on standard FE and PE for general circuits and standard compute-and-compare obfuscation. We focus on strongly related works. No previous work consider certified everlasting secure FE, PE, and compute-and-compare obfuscation.

Gorbunov, Vaikuntanathan, and Wee [GVW12] constructed bounded collusion-resistant adaptively secure PKFE for P/poly from standard PKE (and either the DDH or LWE assumption). Later, Ananth and Vaikuntanathan improved ciphertext size and assumptions. They constructed adaptively secure bounded collusion-resistant PKFE for P/poly with optimal ciphertext size from standard PKE. Garg, Gentry, Halevi, Raykova, and Sahai [GGH+16] constructed selectively secure collusion-resistant PKFE for P/poly from IO and OWFs. Waters [Wat15] constructed adaptively secure PKFE collusion-resistant for P/poly from IO and OWFs. Ananth, Brakerski, Segev, and Vaikuntanathan [ABSV15] presented a transformation from selectively secure collusion-resistant FE for P/poly to adaptively secure collusion-resistant FE for P/poly. Jain, Lin, and Sahai constructed IO for P/poly from well-founded assumptions [JLS21, JLS22]. However, their constructions are not post-quantum secure.[5]

Gorbunov, Vaikuntanathan, and Wee [GVW15] constructed PE for P/poly from the LWE assumption. Goyal, Koppula, and Waters [GKW17] and Wichs and Zirdelis [WZ17] presented the notion of compute-and-compare obfuscation (or lockable obfuscation) and achieved it from the LWE assumption. These two works also presented a general transformation from ABE to PE using compute-and-compare obfuscation. Kluczniak [Klu22] constructed compute-and-compare obfuscation from circular *insecure* FHE. However, all known instantiations of circular insecure FHE rely on compute-and-compare obfuscation.

1.6   Organization

If we put any self-contained part of the technical sections, it breaks the page limitations. Hence, we omit all the technical details in this version. Please see the full version [HKM+23] for the technical details. In Sec. 2.1, we provide a technical overview for constructing certified everlasting secure collusion-resistant FE. In Sec. 2.2, we provide a technical overview for constructing certified everlasting secure bounded collusion-resistant FE. In Sec. 2.3, we provide a technical overview for constructing compute-and-compare obfuscation.

---

[5] There are a few candidate constructions of post-quantum secure IO [BGMZ18, CHVW19, AP20].

2   Technical Overview

2.1   Technical Overview: Collusion-Resistant FE

Certified everlasting lemma of Bartusek and Khurana. Our construction is based on a lemma which we call *certified everlasting lemma* proven by Bartusek and Khurana [BK23], which is described as follows.

Suppose that $\{\mathcal{Z}(m)\}_{m \in \{0,1\}^{\lambda+1}}$ is a family of distributions over classical strings such that $\mathcal{Z}(m)$ is computatioally indistinguishable from $\mathcal{Z}(0^{\lambda+1})$ for any $m \in \{0,1\}^{\lambda+1}$. Intuitively, $\mathcal{Z}(m)$ can be regarded as an "encryption" of m. For $b \in \{0,1\}$ and a QPT adversary, let $\widetilde{\mathcal{Z}}(b)$ be the following experiment:

- The experiment samples $z, \theta \leftarrow \{0,1\}^{\lambda}$.
- The adversary takes $|z\rangle_{\theta}$, and $\mathcal{Z}(\theta, b \oplus \bigoplus_{j:\theta_j=0} z_j)$ as input where z_j is the j-th bit of z and outputs a classical string $z' \in \{0,1\}^{\lambda}$ and a quantum state ρ.
- The experiment outputs ρ if $z'_j = z_j$ for all j such that $\theta_j = 1$ and otherwise outputs a special symbol $\bot$.

Then for any QPT adversary, the trace distance between $\widetilde{\mathcal{Z}}(0)$ and $\widetilde{\mathcal{Z}}(1)$ is $\mathsf{negl}(\lambda)$.[6]

The above lemma can be regarded as a generic compiler that adds certified everlasting security. For example, we can construct a certified everlasting PKE scheme from any plain PKE scheme as follows. For encrypting a message $b \in \{0,1\}$, a ciphertext is set to be $|z\rangle_{\theta}, \mathsf{Enc}(\theta, b \oplus \bigoplus_{j:\theta_j=0} z_j)$ where $z, \theta \leftarrow \{0,1\}^{\lambda}$ and Enc is the encryption algorithm of the underlying PKE scheme. Here, we omit an encryption key for simplicity and keep using a similar convention throughout this subsection. The deletion algorithm simply measures $|z\rangle_{\theta}$ in the Hadamard basis to output a certificate z' and the verification algorithm checks if $z'_j = z_j$ for all j such that $\theta_j = 1$. Then the above lemma implies that an adversary's internal state has no information about b conditioned on the acceptance, which means certified everlasting security.

Public-slot FE. Unfortunately, their compiler does not directly work for FE in general. The problem is that for a function f, there may not exist a function f' such that $f(m)$ can be recovered from $f'(m \oplus \bigoplus_{j:\theta_j=0} z_j, \theta)$ and z. To overcome this issue, we introduce an extension of FE which we call public-slot FE. In public-slot FE, a decryption key is associated with a *two-input* function where the first and second inputs are referred to as the secret and public inputs, respectively. Given a ciphertext of a message m and a decryption key for a function f, one can compute $f(m, \mathsf{pub})$ for all public inputs pub. Its security is defined similarly to that of plain FE except that the challenge message pair $(m^{(0)}, m^{(1)})$

---

[6] In fact, we need an "interactive version" of the lemma. We believe that such an interactive version is implicitly proven and used in [BK23]. See the full version for the formal statement of the lemma and a comparison with [BK23].

must satisfy $f(m^{(0)}, \mathsf{pub}) = f(m^{(1)}, \mathsf{pub})$ for all key queries f and public inputs pub.

We observe that many existing constructions of FE based on IO (e.g., [GGH+16]) can be naturally extended to public-slot FE. In particular, we show that a simple modification of the FE scheme of Ananth and Sahai [AS16] yields an adaptively secure public-slot FE based on IO.

First Attempt. Our first attempt to construct a collusion-resistant FE scheme with certified everlasting security is as follows. Let Enc be an encryption algorithm of a public-slot FE scheme. A ciphertext for a message $m = m_1 \ldots m_n \in \{0,1\}^n$ consists of $\{|z_i\rangle_{\theta_i}\}_{i \in [n]}$ and $\mathsf{Enc}(\theta_1, \ldots, \theta_n, \beta_1, \ldots, \beta_n)$ where $z_i, \theta_i \leftarrow \{0,1\}^\lambda$ for $i \in [n]$, and $\beta_i := m_i \oplus \bigoplus_{j:\theta_{i,j}=0} z_{i,j}$ where $z_{i,j}$ is the j-th bit of z_i. A decryption key for a function f is a decryption key of the underlying public-slot FE for a two-input function $g[f]$ defined as follows. The function $g[f]$ takes a secret input $(\theta_1, \ldots, \theta_n, \beta_1, \ldots, \beta_n)$ and a public input $(b_1, \ldots, b_n) \in \{0,1\}^{\lambda \times n}$, computes $m_i := \beta_i \oplus \bigoplus_{j:\theta_{i,j}=0} b_{i,j}$ for $i \in [n]$, and outputs $f(m_1, \ldots, m_n)$. To see decryption correctness, we first observe that if we first measure $\{|z_i\rangle_{\theta_i}\}_{i \in [n]}$ in the computational basis to get $(b_1, \ldots, b_n)$, then we have $b_{i,j} = z_{i,j}$ for all i, j such that $\theta_{i,j} = 0$. Thus, if we run the decryption algorithm of the public-slot FE scheme with the public input $(b_1, \ldots, b_n)$, then this yields the correct output $f(m_1, \ldots, m_n)$. We remark that the decryption can actually be done without measuring $\{|z_i\rangle_{\theta_i}\}_{i \in [n]}$ by running the above procedure coherently. The deletion and verification algorithms can be defined similarly to those for the certified everlasting PKE scheme as explained above: The deletion algorithm simply measures $\{|z_i\rangle_{\theta_i}\}_{i \in [n]}$ in the Hadamard basis to get $\{z_i'\}_{i \in [n]}$ and the verification algorithm checks if $z_{i,j}' = z_{i,j}$ for all i, j such that $\theta_{i,j} = 1$.

However, the above scheme is insecure. The problem is that public-slot FE does not force an adversary to use a legitimate public input. By running the decryption algorithm with different public inputs many times, an adversary can learn more than $f(m_1, ..., m_n)$, which would even break security as a plain FE scheme. For example, if the adversary uses a public input $(b_1, ..., b_i', ..., b_n)$ such that b_i' is the same as b_i except that $b_{i,j}' \neq b_{i,j}$ for some j such that $\theta_{i,j} = 0$, then it can obtain $f(m_1, ..., 1 - m_i, ..., m_n)$.

Certify the Public Input by One-time Signatures. Our idea to resolve the above issue is to certify $\{z_i\}_{i \in [n]}$ in the quantum part of the ciphertext by using one-time signatures. Specifically, the encryption algorithm first generates a pair of a verification key $\mathsf{vk}_{i,j}$ and a signing key $\mathsf{sk}_{i,j}$ of a deterministic one-time signature for $i \in [n]$ and $j \in [\lambda]$. A ciphertext for a message $m = m_1 \ldots m_n \in \{0,1\}^n$ consists of $\{|\psi_{i,j}\rangle\}_{i \in [n], j \in [\lambda]}$ and $\mathsf{Enc}(\{\mathsf{vk}_{i,j}\}_{i \in [n], j \in [\lambda]}, \theta_1, \ldots, \theta_n, \beta_1, \ldots, \beta_n)$ where $z_i, \theta_i \leftarrow \{0,1\}^n$ for $i \in [n]$, $\beta_i := m_i \oplus \bigoplus_{j:\theta_{i,j}=0} z_j$, and

$$|\psi_{i,j}\rangle := \begin{cases} |z_{i,j}\rangle |\sigma_{i,j,z_{i,j}}\rangle & \text{if } \theta_{i,j} = 0 \\ |0\rangle |\sigma_{i,j,0}\rangle + (-1)^{z_{i,j}} |1\rangle |\sigma_{i,j,1}\rangle & \text{if } \theta_{i,j} = 1 \end{cases} \quad (1)$$

where $\sigma_{i,j,b}$ is a signature generated by using the signing key $\mathsf{sk}_{i,j}$ on the message $b \in \{0,1\}$. Note that $|\psi_{i,j}\rangle$ is the state obtained by coherently running the signing algorithm with the signing key $\mathsf{sk}_{i,j}$ on j-th qubit of $|z_i\rangle_{\theta_i}$. We modify the function $g[f]$ associated with the decryption key of the public-slot FE to additionally check the validity of the signatures for $b_{i,j}$ for i, j such that $\theta_{i,j} = 0$. That is, $g[f]$ takes a secret input $(\{\mathsf{vk}_{i,j}\}_{i \in [n], j \in [\lambda]}, \theta_1, \ldots, \theta_n, \beta_1, \ldots, \beta_n)$ and a public input $(b_1, \ldots, b_n, \sigma_1, \ldots, \sigma_n)$, parses $\sigma_i = (\sigma_{i,1}, \ldots, \sigma_{i,\lambda})$ for each $i \in [n]$, and checks if $\sigma_{i,j}$ is a valid signature for $b_{i,j}$ (i.e., if $\sigma_{i,j} = \sigma_{i,j,b_{i,j}}$) for all i, j such that $\theta_{i,j} = 0$. If it is not the case, it just outputs $\perp$. Otherwise, it computes $m_i := \beta_i \oplus \bigoplus_{j:\theta_{i,j}=0} b_{i,j}$ for $i \in [n]$ and outputs $f(m_1, \ldots, m_n)$. Note that $|\psi_{i,j}\rangle$ contains the valid signature $\sigma_{i,j,z_{i,j}}$ on the message $z_{i,j}$ whenever $\theta_{i,j} = 0$. Thus, the decryption correctness is unaffected. In addition, if we measure $|\psi_{i,j}\rangle$ in the Hadamard basis for i, j such that $\theta_{i,j} = 1$, then the outcome $(c_{i,j}, d_{i,j})$ satisfies $z_{i,j} = c_{i,j} \oplus d_{i,j}(\sigma_{i,j,0} \oplus \sigma_{i,j,1})$. By modifying the verification algorithm to check the above equality, the verification correctness also holds. By the security of one-time signatures, an adversary cannot arbitrarily modify the public input when running the decryption algorithm of the underlying public-slot FE.

While this authentication technique seems to prevent obvious attacks, we still do not know how to prove certified everlasting security of this scheme. In particular, we want to rely on the certified everlasting lemma of [BK23]. However, the lemma only enables us to perform bit-wise game hops. For example, if $n = 3$ and the challenge messages are 000 and 111, we would need to consider hybrid experiments where the challenge message evolves as $000 \rightarrow 100 \rightarrow 110 \rightarrow 111$.[7] However, the restriction on the adversary only ensures $f(000) = f(111)$ for decryption key queries f and does not ensure, say, $f(000) = f(100)$. Without this condition, we cannot rely on the security of the underlying public-slot FE. Hence, it seems impossible to prove indistinguishability between neighboring intermediate hybrids.

Redundant Encoding. Our idea for resolving the above issue is to encode the message in a redundant way so that there is a space for a "spare message". Specifically, we first encode a message $m = m_1 \ldots m_n \in \{0,1\}^n$ into a $(2n + 1)$-bit string $m_1 \ldots m_n \| 0^{n+1}$. The rest of the scheme is identical to that in the previous paragraph, except that i's range is $[2n+1]$ instead of $[n]$ and $g[f]$ chooses which part to use for deriving the output depending on the value of the $(2n+1)$-th bit. Specifically, $g[f]$ takes a secret input $(\{\mathsf{vk}_{i,j}\}_{i \in [2n+1], j \in [\lambda]}, \theta_1, \ldots, \theta_{2n+1}, \beta_1, \ldots, \beta_{2n+1})$ and a public input $(b_1, \ldots, b_{2n+1}, \sigma_1, \ldots, \sigma_{2n+1})$ and first checks the validity of the signatures on positions corresponding to i, j such that $\theta_{i,j} = 0$ as before. Then it computes $m_i := \beta_i \oplus \bigoplus_{j:\theta_{i,j}=0} b_{i,j}$ for $i \in [2n + 1]$, and outputs

---

[7] Note that an FE scheme with 3-bit messages itself is trivial to construct from any PKE scheme. We are considering this toy example just to explain a technical difficulty.

$F(m_1, \ldots, m_{2n+1})$ where F is defined as

$$F(m_1, \ldots, m_{2n+1}) := \begin{cases} f(m_1, \ldots, m_n) & \text{if } m_{2n+1} = 0 \\ f(m_{n+1}, \ldots, m_{2n}) & \text{if } m_{2n+1} = 1 \end{cases}. \tag{2}$$

The decryption correctness is unaffected because we always have $m_{2n+1} = 0$ when decrypting an honestly generated message. The verification correctness is also unaffected since the way of encoding messages is irrelevant. We explain why this enables us to avoid the issue mentioned in the previous paragraph. Intuitively, the advantage of such a redundant encoding is that we can ensure that the encoded challenge message contains either of two challenge messages in all intermediate hybrids. Let $m^{(0)}$ and $m^{(1)}$ be a pair of challenge messages. Note that they correspond to $m^{(0)} \| 0^{n+1}$ and $m^{(1)} \| 0^{n+1}$ after encoding. Then we consider intermediate hybrids where the corresponding challenge messages after the encoding evolves as follows:

1. Starting from $m^{(0)} \| 0^{n+1}$, we change the $(n+1)$-th to $2n$-th bits one-by-one toward $m^{(0)} \| m^{(1)} \| 0$.
2. Flip the $(2n+1)$-th bit, which results in $m^{(0)} \| m^{(1)} \| 1$.
3. Change the first to n bits one-by-one toward $m^{(1)} \| m^{(1)} \| 1$.
4. Flip the $(2n+1)$-th bit, which results in $m^{(1)} \| m^{(1)} \| 0$.
5. Change the $(n+1)$-th to $2n$-th bits one-by-one toward $m^{(1)} \| 0^{2n+1}$.

Importantly, the value of F on the encoded challenge message is equal to $f(m^{(0)}) = f(m^{(1)})$ at any point of the hybrids. This enables us to rely on the security of the underlying public-slot FE along with certified everlasting lemma in every hybrid.

What One-Time Signatures to Use? Finally, we remark that we have to choose an instantiation of one-time signatures carefully. Roughly speaking, the reason why we are using one-time signatures is to prevent an adversary from using "unauthorized" $b_{i,j}$, i.e., those for which the valid signature $\sigma_{i,j,b_{i,j}}$ is not given to the adversary. However, by the correctness of one-time signatures, a valid signature must exist on every message. This means that a valid signature on an "unauthorized" $b_{i,j}$ must exist even if it is difficult for an adversary to find. This situation is not compatible with the security definition of public-slot FE. Recall that its security requires that the challenge message pair $(m^{(0)}, m^{(1)})$ must satisfy $f(m^{(0)}, \mathsf{pub}) = f(m^{(1)}, \mathsf{pub})$ for all key queries f and *all* public inputs pub. That is, the security is not applicable if there is at least one pub such that $f(m^{(0)}, \mathsf{pub}) \neq f(m^{(1)}, \mathsf{pub})$ even if such pub is difficult to find. To overcome this issue, we use Lamport signatures instantiated with a PRG. Let $\mathsf{PRG} : \{0,1\}^\lambda \to \{0,1\}^{2\lambda}$ be a PRG. When the message length is 1, a signing key is set to be $(u_0, u_1) \in \{0,1\}^{\lambda \times 2}$ and a verification key is set to be $(v_0 = \mathsf{PRG}(u_0), v_1 = \mathsf{PRG}(u_1)) \in \{0,1\}^{2\lambda \times 2}$. A signature for a bit b is defined to be u_b. This scheme has a special property in that we can program a verification key so that it does not have a valid signature for a particular message. For example, if we want to ensure that a message 0 does not have a valid signature, then we can set v_0 to be a uniformly random 2λ-bit string. Then, with probability $1 - 2^{-\lambda}$, there is no preimage of v_0, which means that there is no valid signature on the massage 0. By using this property, whenever $b_{i,j}$ is unauthorized, we can switch to a hybrid where there is no valid signature for $b_{i,j}$. This effectively resolves the above issue.

2.2   Technical Overview: Bounded Collusion-Resistant FE

In this subsection, we give a high-level overview of our certified everlasting secure bounded collusion-resistant FE schemes. It is known that the (bounded collusion-resistant) plain FE is constructed from (standard) PKE, RNCE, and garbling [GVW12]. A natural strategy is constructing PKE, RNCE, and garbling with certified everlasting security and using them as building blocks. We show that PKE with certified everlasting security can be constructed using the techniques of [Unr15, HMNY22b]. RNCE with certified everlasting security for *classical messages* can be constructed from certified everlasting PKE in the same way as standard RNCE [KNTY19]. However, such an RNCE scheme is insufficient for our purpose (constructing adaptively-secure FE) because it is not for *quantum messages*. We also need a new idea to construct garbling with certified everlasting security. The following explains these ideas and how to construct FE with certified everlasting security.

Certified Everlasting Garbling for P/poly *Circuits.* In classical cryptography, it is known that we can construct plain garbling from plain SKE using double-encryption [Yao86, LP09]. Double-encryption means we generate a nested ciphertext $ct_2 \leftarrow Enc(sk', ct_1)$, where $ct_1 \leftarrow Enc(sk, m)$, m is the message, Enc is the encryption algorithm of SKE, and sk, sk' are secret keys of SKE. This double-encryption is an essential technique for garbling. However, it is an obstacle to our purpose. First, we do not know SKE with certified everlasting security for *quantum* messages. Second, even if the first problem is solved, we have another problem: We can obtain a valid certificate showing that ct_1 has been deleted by running the deletion algorithm on ct_2. However, such a certificate does not necessarily mean the deletion of m. We bypass the problem using XOR secret sharing instead of double-encryption.[8] More precisely, we uniformly randomly sample p and compute $(vk', ct') \leftarrow Enc(sk', p)$ and $(vk, ct) \leftarrow Enc(sk, p \oplus m)$ to encrypt message m. Here, Enc is the encryption algorithm of certified everlasting SKE, and vk', vk are the verification keys that are used to verify the correctness of deletion certificates. The receiver with (ct', ct) can obtain m only if it has both sk' and sk, and nothing else otherwise, as in the case of double-encryption. Furthermore, once the receiver issues the deletion certificate of (ct', ct), it can no longer obtain the information of m even if it becomes computationally unbounded.

It is easy to see that we can implement the well-known gate garbling [Yao86, LP09] by using the double encryption in the parallel way above instead of the sequential double encryption. We can prove its computational security via a

---

[8]   A similar technique was used by Gentry, Halevi, and Vaikuntanathan [GHV10].

similar discussion as that in [LP09]. (Although [LP09] uses double-encryption, we can show the security for the XOR secret sharing case similarly.) Furthermore, we can prove its certified everlasting security by using the certified everlasting security of the SKE. Hence, we can obtain certified everlasting garbling.

FE with Non-adaptive Security. Our next task is achieving certified everlasting FE using certified everlasting garbling. It is known that plain FE with *non-adaptive security* can be constructed by running the encryption algorithm of (plain) PKE on labels of a plain garbling scheme [SS10].[9] In our certified everlasting garbling scheme (explained in the previous paragraph), the labels are classical bit strings and the deletion algorithm does not take the labels as input. Therefore, this classical construction for plain FE by Sahai and Seyalioglu [SS10] can be directly applied to the construction of our 1-bounded certified everlasting FE for P/poly circuits with *non-adaptive security*.

FE with Adaptive Security. Now, we want to convert non-adaptive security to adaptive one.[10] However, the conversion is non-trivial. Let us first review the conversion for plain FE. In classical cryptography, we can convert non-adaptively secure FE into adaptively secure FE by using RNCE. Roughly speaking, RNCE is the same as PKE except that we can generate a fake ciphertext $\tilde{ct} \leftarrow \mathsf{Fake}(\mathsf{pk})$ without plaintext and we can generate a fake secret key $\tilde{sk} \leftarrow \mathsf{Reveal}(\mathsf{pk}, m)$ that decrypts $\tilde{ct}$ to m. The security of RNCE guarantees that $(\mathsf{Enc}(\mathsf{pk}, m), \mathsf{sk})$ and $(\mathsf{Fake}(\mathsf{pk}), \mathsf{Reveal}(\mathsf{pk}, m))$ are computationally indistinguishable, where Enc is the real encryption algorithm, and sk is the real secret key. Adaptively secure FE can be constructed by running the real encryption algorithm Enc of the RNCE on the ciphertext $\mathsf{nad.ct}$ of the FE. We can prove its adaptive security as follows. The adversary of adaptive security can send key queries after the challenge encryption query. However, the sender can simulate the challenge encryption query without generating $\mathsf{nad.ct}$. This is because, from the security of RNCE, we can switch $(\mathsf{Enc}(\mathsf{pk}, \mathsf{nad.ct}), (\mathsf{sk}, \mathsf{nad.sk}_f))$ to the fake one $(\mathsf{Fake}(\mathsf{pk}), (\mathsf{Reveal}(\mathsf{pk}, \mathsf{nad.ct}), \mathsf{nad.sk}_f))$, where $\mathsf{nad.sk}_f$ is the functional secret key of the non-adaptively secure FE. Therefore, the sender needs not generate $\mathsf{nad.ct}$ before generating $\mathsf{nad.sk}_f$ for the simulation of the adversary's queries, which means that we can reduce the adaptive security to the non-adaptive security.

How can we adopt the above classical idea of the conversion to the certified everlasting case? From the discussion above, a straightforward way is to encrypt the ciphertext $\mathsf{nad.ct}$ of certified everlasting FE with non-adaptive security using certified everlasting RNCE as follows: $(\mathsf{vk}, \mathsf{ct}) \leftarrow \mathsf{Enc}(\mathsf{pk}, \mathsf{nad.ct})$, where vk is the verification key, pk is the public key, and Enc is the real encryption algorithm of the certified everlasting RNCE. However, this idea fails for the following two

---

[9] The non-adaptive security means that the adversary can call the key queries only before the challenge encryption query.

[10] The adaptive security means that the adversary can call key queries before and after the challenge encryption query.

reasons. First, nad.ct is a quantum state. Our certified everlasting RNCE scheme does not support quantum messages. Second, even if we can construct RNCE for quantum messages, we have another problem: A valid certificate of ct is issued by running the deletion algorithm on ct. However, such a certificate does not necessarily mean the deletion of the plaintext of nad.ct. The first problem is about security, and the second problem is about correctness.

Our idea to resolve the first problem is to use quantum teleportation. We construct RNCE for quantum messages from RNCE for classical messages by using quantum teleportation.[11] (We believe that the idea of using quantum teleportation in the following way will be useful in many other applications beyond RNCE.) As the ciphertext and the secret key of adaptively secure FE, we take

$$\frac{1}{2^{2N}} \sum_{a,b\in\{0,1\}^N} (Z^b X^a(\text{nad.ct})X^a Z^b)_{C_1} \otimes \text{Enc}(\text{pk},(a,b))_{C_2} \otimes (\text{nad.sk}_f,\text{sk})_S,$$

where nad.ct is an N-qubit state, the registers C_1 and C_2 are the ciphertext, and the register S is the secret key. Here, $X^a := \bigotimes_{j=1}^N X_j^{a_j}$, $Z^b := \bigotimes_{j=1}^N Z_j^{b_j}$, a_j is the jth bit of a, and b_j is the jth bit of b. Moreover, Enc is the real encryption algorithm of RNCE for classical messages, nad.sk$_f$ is the secret key of non-adaptively secure FE, and sk is the real secret key of RNCE for classical messages. We want to show the adaptive security of the construction by reducing it to the non-adaptive security of the building block FE. In the first step of hybrids, we switch the state to

$$\frac{1}{2^{2N}} \sum_{a,b} (Z^b X^a(\text{nad.ct})X^a Z^b)_{C_1} \otimes \text{Fake}(\text{pk})_{C_2} \otimes (\text{nad.sk}_f,\text{Reveal}(\text{pk},(a,b)))_S$$

by using the property of RNCE for classical messages. In the second step of hybrids, we switch the state to

$$\frac{1}{2^{2N}} \sum_{x,z\in\{0,1\}^N} \mathcal{T}_{A',A}^{x,z}[\text{nad.ct}_{A'} \otimes |\Phi_N\rangle\langle\Phi_N|_{A,C_1}] \otimes \text{Fake}(\text{pk})_{C_2} \otimes (\text{nad.sk}_f,\text{Reveal}(\text{pk},(x,z)))_S,$$

where $|\Phi_N\rangle$ is the N Bell pairs between the registers A and C_1. $\mathcal{T}_{A',A}^{x,z}[\text{nad.ct}_{A'} \otimes |\Phi_N\rangle\langle\Phi_N|_{A,C_1}]$ is the state on the register C_1 obtained in the following way: the state nad.ct$_{A'}$ on the register A' is coupled with the halves of N Bell pairs on the register A, and the teleportation measurement $\mathcal{T}_{A',A}^{x,z}$ with the result (x,z) is applied on the registers A and A'. Now, we can generate the states on the registers C_1 and C_2 without knowing nad.ct, which means that the sender can simulate the challenge encryption query without nad.ct. In other words, the sender does not need to generate nad.ct before generating nad.sk$_f$ for the simulation of adversary queries.

This idea solves the first problem. However, the second problem remains. The receiver with $(Z^b X^a(\text{nad.ct})X^a Z^b, \text{Enc}(\text{pk},(a,b)))$ can issue a deletion certificate

---

[11] A similar technique was used in the context of multi-party quantum computation [BCKM21].

of $Z^b X^a (\mathsf{nad.ct}) X^a Z^b$. The deletion certificate does not necessarily pass the verification algorithm for the deletion of nad.ct. This is an obstacle to achieving correctness. We solve this problem by introducing an efficient algorithm that we call the modification algorithm. Let nad.cert* be the deletion certificate of $Z^b X^a (\mathsf{nad.ct}) X^a Z^b$. The modification algorithm takes (a, b) and nad.cert* as input, and outputs nad.cert that is the deletion certificate of nad.ct. Therefore, by using the modification algorithm, we can convert the deletion certificate nad.cert* of $Z^b X^a (\mathsf{nad.ct}) X^a Z^b$ to the deletion certificate nad.cert of nad.ct. We observe that the modification algorithm exists for many natural constructions, including our construction.[12]

q-bounded FE for NC^1 *circuits.* Finally, we explain how to convert 1-bounded one to the q-bounded one.[13] Unfortunately, we do not know how to obtain q-bounded certified everlasting FE for P/poly circuits. What we can construct in this paper is that only for NC^1 circuits. (It is an open problem to obtain q-bounded certified everlasting FE for P/poly circuits.)

Let us explain how to convert 1-bounded certified everlasting FE for P/poly circuits to q-bounded certified everlasting FE for NC^1 circuits. In classical cryptography, it is known that [GVW12] multi-party computation (MPC) can convert plain 1-bounded FE for P/poly circuits to plain q-bounded FE for NC^1 circuits. The idea is, roughly speaking, the view of each party in the MPC protocol is encrypted using 1-bounded FE scheme. In this classical construction, no encryption is done on the ciphertexts of plain FE, and therefore this classical construction can be directly applied to our certified everlasting case. (It is an open problem to obtain q-bounded certified everlasting FE for P/poly circuits.)

2.3 Technical Overview: Compute-and-Compare Obfuscation

This section provides a high-level overview of our certified everlasting compute-and-compare obfuscation. Recall that a compute-and-compare obfuscation scheme obfuscates a circuit P along with a lock value lock and a message m and outputs an obfuscated circuit $\widetilde{P}$. In the evaluation phase, one can recover m from $\widetilde{P}$ using an input x to the circuit such that $P(x) = \mathsf{lock}$. A certified everlasting compute-and-compare obfuscation scheme additionally generates a verification key vk while obfuscating circuit P. A user can generate a deletion certificate cert from $\widetilde{P}$. If we have vk, we can verify whether the certificate is valid or not. The certified everlasting security ensures that no information about P, lock and m is available to the user after producing a valid certificate. This means that the user actually deleted the obfuscated circuit.

---

[12] If the deletion algorithm is the computational-basis measurements followed by Clifford gates, the modification algorithm is just modifying the Pauli one-time pad, $X^a Z^b$. In fact, all known constructions use only Hadamard basis measurements.

[13] q-bounded means that the adversary can call key queries q times with an a priori bounded polynomial q.

Compute-and-Compare Obfuscation without a Message. We first explain our idea to construct a certified everlasting compute-and-compare obfuscation without any message. That is, the evaluation returns 1 if $P(x) = $ lock holds. Let CC.Obf be the obfuscation algorithm of a standard compute-and-compare obfuscation scheme and Enc, Dec be the encryption, and decryption algorithms of FHE. The main idea is to compute an FHE ciphertext ct_P encrypting the circuit P and use CC.Obf to produce an obfuscated circuit $\widetilde{Dec}$ of the decryption circuit of FHE with lock value lock and message 1. The obfuscated circuit $\widetilde{P}$ consists of ct_P and $\widetilde{Dec}$. Given an input x, we first apply the evaluation procedure of FHE to get a ciphertext $ct_{P(x)} = Enc(P(x))$ (we omit the encryption key) and then run the evaluation algorithm of the compute-and-compare obfuscation with input $ct_{P(x)}$ to check whether $P(x) = $ lock. Note that we cannot use certified everlasting FHE [BK23] in a black-box manner since CC.Obf is a classical algorithm that cannot obfuscate a quantum circuit, in particular, the decryption algorithm of the FHE. Instead, we use BB84 states along with classical FHE as follows. The obfuscated circuit $\widetilde{P}$ consists of $\widetilde{Dec} := CC.Obf(Dec(sk, \cdot), lock, 1)$ and $\{|z_i\rangle_{\theta_i}, ct_i\}_{i \in [\ell_P]}$ where $ct_i := Enc(\theta_i \| \widetilde{b}_i)$, $z_i, \theta_i \leftarrow \{0,1\}^\lambda$ for $i \in [\ell_P]$, $\widetilde{b}_i := b_i \oplus \bigoplus_{j:\theta_{i,j}=0} z_{i,j}$ and b_i is the i-th bit of the binary string of length ℓ_P representing the circuit P. The verification key is $vk = (\{z_i, \theta_i\}_{i \in [\ell_P]})$. To evaluate the obfuscated circuit with an input x, we first coherently compute an evaluated FHE ciphertext $|ct_{U_x(P)}\rangle$ where U_x is a circuit that on input $(\{z_i, \theta_i, \widetilde{b}_i\}_{i \in [\ell_P]})$ first recovers b_i, the bits representing P, and then outputs $P(x)$. Then, we coherently evaluate the obfuscated circuit $\widetilde{Dec}$ with input $|ct_{U_x(P)}\rangle$ and check that the measured outcome is 1 to decide $P(x) = $ lock. The deletion and verification algorithm works similarly as in the certified everlasting PKE scheme described in Sec. 2.1. That is, we use the concrete certified everlasting secure FHE scheme by Bartusek and Khurana in a non-black-box way.

However, the above scheme cannot guarantee certified everlasting security. The reason is that the classical compute-and-compare obfuscation cannot hide the lock value from an unbounded adversary. More precisely, the unbounded adversary is given a target circuit and an auxiliary input and can easily distinguish between the obfuscated circuit $\widetilde{Dec} \leftarrow CC.Obf(1^\lambda, Dec, lock, 1)$ and the corresponding simulated circuit $\widetilde{Dec} \leftarrow CC.Sim(1^\lambda, pp_{Dec}, 1^1)$ if the auxiliary input and lock are correlated, where pp_{Dec} consists of parameters of Dec (input and output length and circuit size).

We solve this problem by masking the obfuscated circuit that encodes lock using the XOR function in combination with the BB84 states. In particular, we sample "dummy" lock value $R \leftarrow \{0,1\}^\lambda$ and set the obfuscated circuit $\mathcal{L}_C$ as $(\widetilde{Dec} := CC.Obf(Dec(sk, \cdot), R, 1), \{|z_i\rangle_{\theta_i}, ct_i\}_{i \in [\ell]})$ where $\ell = \ell_P + \ell_{\widetilde{I}}$ and $\{ct_i\}_{i \in [\ell]}$ encrypts the binary string representing the circuits $(P \| \widetilde{I})$ where $\widetilde{I} := CC.Obf(I, lock, R)$. We denote I by the identity circuit that is $I(x) = x$ for all x. The evaluation algorithm works as before except that the circuit U_x on input $(\{z_i, \theta_i, \widetilde{b}_i\}_{i \in [\ell]})$ first reconstructs $(P \| \widetilde{I})$ and then outputs the result obtained in the evaluation of $\widetilde{I}$ with input $P(x)$. Hence, checking $P(x) = $ lock is deferred until evaluating $\widetilde{I}$, which is hidden due to the certified everlasting security of FHE. The correctness follows from the fact that U_x returns R if $P(x) = \mathsf{lock}$ and evaluation of $\widetilde{\mathsf{Dec}}$ outputs 1 if $U_x(P\|\widetilde{I}) = R$.

The simulated circuit $\widetilde{\mathcal{P}}$ consists of $\widetilde{\mathsf{Dec}} = \mathsf{CC.Obf}(\mathsf{Dec}(\mathsf{sk},\cdot), R, 1)$ and $\{|z_i\rangle_{\theta_i}, \mathsf{ct}_i\}_{i\in[\ell]}$ where $\mathsf{ct}_i := \mathsf{Enc}(\theta_i\|\widetilde{b}_i)$ and $\widetilde{b}_i := 0 \oplus \bigoplus_{j:\theta_{i,j}=0} z_{i,j}$ for $i \in [\ell]$. Note that, $\widetilde{\mathcal{P}}$ does not contain any information about P and lock. We rely on the certified everlasting lemma of [BK23] to show that the real obfuscated circuit is indistinguishable from the simulated circuit for any unbounded adversary who produces a valid certificate of deletion. Although an unbounded adversary can recover sk from $\widetilde{\mathsf{Dec}}$, sk is useless for distinguishing after the deletion. Since the lemma only allows us to flip one bit at a time, we use a sequence of ℓ hybrid experiments. In the i-th hybrid, we change the bit b_i from 1 to 0. If we can show that $\mathsf{Enc}(\theta_i\|\widetilde{b}_i)$ is computationally indistinguishable from $\mathsf{Enc}(0\|\widetilde{b}_i)$ and then it is possible to apply the certified everlasting lemma to flip the bit b_i without noticing the unbounded adversary. To establish the computational indistinguishability, we first replace the circuit $\widetilde{I}$: $\mathsf{CC.Obf}(I, \mathsf{lock}, R)$ with the simulated one $\widetilde{I} \leftarrow \mathsf{CC.Sim}(1^\lambda, \mathsf{pp}_I, 1^{|R|})$ and then change the circuit $\widetilde{\mathsf{Dec}} \leftarrow \mathsf{CC.Obf}(\mathsf{Dec}, \mathsf{lock}, 1)$ to the corresponding simulated circuit $\widetilde{\mathsf{Dec}} \leftarrow \mathsf{CC.Sim}(1^\lambda, \mathsf{pp}_{\mathsf{Dec}}, 1^1)$ depending on the security of the underlying compute-and-compare obfuscation scheme. Since the FHE secret key sk is no longer required to simulate the adversary's view, we can change $\mathsf{Enc}(\theta_i\|\widetilde{b}_i)$ to $\mathsf{Enc}(0\|\widetilde{b}_i)$ using the IND-CPA security of FHE. Hence, b_i can be set to 0 by employing the certified everlasting lemma.

Compute-and-Compare Obfuscation with a Message. Next, we discuss extending the above construction into a certified everlasting compute-and-compare obfuscation scheme that obfuscates a circuit P along with lock and a message $m = m_1 \ldots m_n \in \{0,1\}^n$. Our idea is to encrypt the message using FHE in combination with the BB84 states and recover the message bits during evaluation depending on the outcome of the obfuscated circuit $\widetilde{\mathsf{Dec}}$. The obfuscated circuit $\widetilde{\mathcal{P}}$ now additionally includes $\{|z_{\ell+k}\rangle_{\theta_{\ell+k}}, \mathsf{ct}_{\ell+k}\}_{k\in[n]}$ where $z_{\ell+k}, \theta_{\ell+k} \leftarrow \{0,1\}^\lambda$, $\mathsf{ct}_{\ell+k} := \mathsf{Enc}(\theta_{\ell+k}\|\widetilde{b}_{\ell+k})$ and $\widetilde{b}_{\ell+k} := m_k \oplus \bigoplus_{j:\theta_{\ell+k,j}=0} z_{\ell+k,j}$ for $k \in [n]$. The evaluation procedure works as before except the U_x on input $((\{z_i, \theta_i, \widetilde{b}_i\}_{i\in[\ell]}), (z_{\ell+k}, \theta_{\ell+k}, \widetilde{b}_{\ell+k}))$ first reconstructs $(P\|\widetilde{I})$ from $\{z_i, \theta_i, \widetilde{b}_i\}_{i\in[\ell]}$ and m_k from $(z_{\ell+k}, \theta_{\ell+k}, \widetilde{b}_{\ell+k})$, and then outputs $m_k \cdot \widetilde{I}(P(x))$. We can similarly define the deletion and verification algorithms as before. The scheme correctly recovers m in a bit-by-bit manner. Let us consider $P(x) = \mathsf{lock}$ and $m_k = 1$. Then, by the definition of U_x and the correctness of compute-and-compare obfuscation, we have $m_k \cdot \widetilde{I}(P(x)) = R$. Consequently, $\widetilde{\mathsf{Dec}}$ evaluates to 1 for an input $\mathsf{ct}_{m_k \cdot \widetilde{I}(P(x))}$. If the result of the evaluation is not 1, then we set $m_k := 0$. We prove the certified everlasting security of the scheme using the same idea as discussed for the compute-and-compare obfuscation scheme without a message. The only difference is that we additionally delete the information of m using the IND-CPA security of FHE and certified everlasting lemma of [BK23] after we erase the information about P and lock.

452   T. Hiroka et al.

Certified Everlasting Predicate Encryption. Goyal, Koppula and Waters [GKW17] and Wichs and Zirdelis [WZ17] showed a generic construction of PE[14] from compute-and-compare obfuscation and ABE. The construction works as follows. The setup and key generation algorithms are the same as the underlying ABE. Let Enc and Dec be the encryption and decryption algorithms of ABE. To encrypt a message m with attribute x, the encryption algorithm samples a random lock $R \in \{0,1\}^\ell$ and computes $ct := \mathsf{Enc}(x, R)$ and $\widetilde{\mathsf{Dec}} := \mathsf{CC.Obf}(\mathsf{Dec}(\cdot, ct), R, m)$. The ciphertext is the obfuscated circuit $\widetilde{\mathsf{Dec}}$. Given a secret key sk_P for a policy P, a user simply evaluates $\widetilde{\mathsf{Dec}}$ with input sk_P to recover the message m. Note that, if $P(x) = 1$ then by the correctness of ABE, $\mathsf{Dec}(sk_P, ct) = R$ and hence $\widetilde{\mathsf{Dec}}(sk_P)$ returns m.

One might hope that replacing the compute-and-compare obfuscation and ABE with their certified everlasting counterparts in the classical construction yields a certified everlasting PE. This would not work since our certified everlasting compute-and-compare obfuscation cannot obfuscate a quantum decryption circuit $\mathcal{D}ec(\cdot, ct)$ of the certified everlasting ABE. However, we need to erase the information about R from the ABE ciphertext ct in order to apply the certified everlasting security of the compute-and-compare obfuscation. In other words, after a valid certificate of deletion is produced, an unbounded adversary should not be able to distinguish between $\mathsf{Enc}(x, R)$ and $\mathsf{Enc}(x, \mathbf{0})$. A classical ABE alone can not guarantee such indistinguishability. We solve this problem by using a classical ABE coupled with BB84 states and a certified everlasting compute-and-compare obfuscation in the above construction. In particular, we first sample $z_i, \theta_i \leftarrow \{0,1\}^\ell$, set $\widetilde{r}_i := r_i \oplus \bigoplus_{j:\theta_{i,j}=0} z_{i,j}$ and then compute $ct := \mathsf{Enc}(x, (\theta_1, \ldots, \theta_\ell, \widetilde{r}_i, \ldots, \widetilde{r}_\ell))$ where r_i denotes the i-th bit of R. The ciphertext consists of $\widetilde{\mathcal{D}ec} := CCObf(\mathsf{Dec}(\cdot, ct), R, m)$ and $\{|z_i\rangle_{\theta_i}\}_{i \in [\ell]}$. The verification key associated with the ciphertext includes $\{z_i, \theta_i\}_{i \in [\ell]}$ and a verification key vk_{Dec} corresponding to the circuit Dec. The deletion and verification algorithms can be defined in a natural way. That is, we use the concrete certified everlasting secure ABE scheme by Bartusek and Khurana in a non-black-box way.

Suppose an adversary queries secret keys sk_P such that $P(x) = 0$ and becomes unbounded after delivering a valid certificate of deletion of the ciphertext. Our idea is to use the security of ABE and the certified everlasting lemma of [BK23] to delete the information of R. Then, we utilize the certified everlasting security of compute-and-compare obfuscation for replacing $\widetilde{\mathcal{D}ec}$ with a simulated circuit that does not contain any information about m, x.

Acknowledgement. TM is supported by JST Moonshot JPMJMS2061-5-1-1, JST FOREST, MEXT QLEAP, the Grant-in-Aid for Scientific Research (B) No. JP19H04066, the Grant-in Aid for Transformative Research Areas (A) 21H05183, and the Grant-in-Aid for Scientific Research (A) No. 22H00522. TH is supported by JSPS research fellowship and by JSPS KAKENHI No. JP22J21864.

---

[14] It satisfies one-sided attribute-hiding security, meaning that the attribute and message are both hidden to a user who does not have a secret key for successful decryption.

References

ABSV15. Ananth, P., Brakerski, Z., Segev, G., Vaikuntanathan, V.: From selective to adaptive security in functional encryption. In: Gennaro, R., Robshaw, M. (eds.) CRYPTO 2015. LNCS, vol. 9216, pp. 657–677. Springer, Heidelberg (2015). https://doi.org/10.1007/978-3-662-48000-7_32

AKYY23. Agrawal, S., Kumari, S., Yadav, A., Yamada, S.: Broadcast, trace and revoke with optimal parameters from polynomial hardness. In: Hazay, C., Stam, M. (eds.) Advances in Cryptology - EUROCRYPT 2023. EUROCRYPT 2023, LNCS, Part III, vol. 14006, pp. 605–636. Springer, Cham (2023). https://doi.org/10.1007/978-3-031-30620-4_20

AL21. Ananth, P., La Placa, R.L.: Secure software leasing. In: Canteaut, A., Standaert, F.-X. (eds.) EUROCRYPT 2021, Part II. LNCS, vol. 12697, pp. 501–530. Springer, Cham (2021). https://doi.org/10.1007/978-3-030-77886-6_17

ALL+21. Aaronson, S., Liu, J., Liu, Q., Zhandry, M., Zhang, R.: New approaches for quantum copy-protection. In: Malkin, T., Peikert, C. (eds.) CRYPTO 2021, Part I. LNCS, vol. 12825, pp. 526–555. Springer, Cham (2021). https://doi.org/10.1007/978-3-030-84242-0_19

AP20. Agrawal, S., Pellet-Mary, A.: Indistinguishability obfuscation without maps: attacks and fixes for noisy linear FE. In: Canteaut, A., Ishai, Y. (eds.) EUROCRYPT 2020, Part I. LNCS, vol. 12105, pp. 110–140. Springer, Cham (2020). https://doi.org/10.1007/978-3-030-45721-1_5

AS16. Ananth, P., Sahai, A.: Functional encryption for turing machines. In: Kushilevitz, E., Malkin, T. (eds.) TCC 2016, Part I. LNCS, vol. 9562, pp. 125–153. Springer, Heidelberg (2016). https://doi.org/10.1007/978-3-662-49096-9_6

AV19. Ananth, P., Vaikuntanathan, V.: Optimal bounded-collusion secure functional encryption. In: Hofheinz, D., Rosen, A. (eds.) TCC 2019, Part I. LNCS, vol. 11891, pp. 174–198. Springer, Cham (2019). https://doi.org/10.1007/978-3-030-36030-6_8

AYY22. Agrawal, S., Yadav, A., Yamada, S.: Multi-input Attribute Based Encryption and Predicate Encryption. In: Dodis, Y., Shrimpton, T. (eds.) Advances in Cryptology - CRYPTO 2022. CRYPTO 2022, LNCS, vol. 13507, pp. 590–621. Springer, Cham (2022). https://doi.org/10.1007/978-3-031-15802-5_21

BCKM21. Bartusek, J., Coladangelo, A., Khurana, D., Ma, F.: On the round complexity of secure quantum computation. In: Malkin, T., Peikert, C. (eds.) CRYPTO 2021, Part I. LNCS, vol. 12825, pp. 406–435. Springer, Cham (2021). https://doi.org/10.1007/978-3-030-84242-0_15

BDF+11. Boneh, D., Dagdelen, Ö., Fischlin, M., Lehmann, A., Schaffner, C., Zhandry, M.: Random oracles in a quantum world. In: Lee, D.H., Wang, X. (eds.) ASIACRYPT 2011. LNCS, vol. 7073, pp. 41–69. Springer, Heidelberg (2011). https://doi.org/10.1007/978-3-642-25385-0_3

BG20. Broadbent, A., Grilo, A.B.: QMA-hardness of consistency of local density matrices with applications to quantum zero-knowledge. In: 61st FOCS, pp. 196–205. IEEE Computer Society Press, November 2020

BGG+23. Bartusek, J., et al.: Obfuscation and outsourced computation with certified deletion. Cryptology ePrint Archive, Report 2023/265 (2023). https://eprint.iacr.org/2023/265

BGMZ18. Bartusek, J., Guan, J., Ma, F., Zhandry, M.: Return of GGH15: provable security against Zeroizing attacks. In: Beimel, A., Dziembowski, S. (eds.) TCC 2018, Part II. LNCS, vol. 11240, pp. 544–574. Springer, Cham (2018). https://doi.org/10.1007/978-3-030-03810-6_20

BI20. Broadbent, A., Islam, R.: Quantum encryption with certified deletion. In: Pass, R., Pietrzak, K. (eds.) TCC 2020, Part III. LNCS, vol. 12552, pp. 92–122. Springer, Cham (2020). https://doi.org/10.1007/978-3-030-64381-2_4

BJL+21. Broadbent, A., Jeffery, S., Lord, S., Podder, S., Sundaram, A.: Secure software leasing without assumptions. In: Nissim, K., Waters, B. (eds.) TCC 2021, Part I. LNCS, vol. 13042, pp. 90–120. Springer, Cham (2021). https://doi.org/10.1007/978-3-030-90459-3_4

BK23. Bartusek, J., Khurana, D.: Cryptography with certified deletion. In: Handschuh, H., Lysyanskaya, A. (eds.) Advances in Cryptology - CRYPTO 2023. CRYPTO 2023, Part V, LNCS, vol. 14085, pp. 192–223. Springer, Cham (2023). https://doi.org/10.1007/978-3-031-38554-4_7

BSW11. Boneh, D., Sahai, A., Waters, B.: Functional encryption: definitions and challenges. In: Ishai, Y. (ed.) TCC 2011. LNCS, vol. 6597, pp. 253–273. Springer, Heidelberg (2011). https://doi.org/10.1007/978-3-642-19571-6_16

CCP18. California consumer privacy act (2018)

CHVW19. Chen, Y., Hhan, M., Vaikuntanathan, V., Wee, H.: Matrix PRFs: constructions, attacks, and applications to obfuscation. In: Hofheinz, D., Rosen, A. (eds.) TCC 2019, Part I. LNCS, vol. 11891, pp. 55–80. Springer, Cham (2019). https://doi.org/10.1007/978-3-030-36030-6_3

CLLZ21. Coladangelo, A., Liu, J., Liu, Q., Zhandry, M.: Hidden Cosets and applications to unclonable cryptography. In: Malkin, T., Peikert, C. (eds.) CRYPTO 2021, Part I. LNCS, vol. 12825, pp. 556–584. Springer, Cham (2021). https://doi.org/10.1007/978-3-030-84242-0_20

CMP20. Coladangelo, A., Majenz, C., Poremba, A.: Quantum copy-protection of compute-and-compare programs in the quantum random oracle model. Cryptology ePrint Archive, Report 2020/1194 (2020). https://eprint.iacr.org/2020/1194

CVW+18. Chen, Y., Vaikuntanathan, V., Waters, B., Wee, H., Wichs, D.: Traitor-tracing from LWE made simple and attribute-based. In: Beimel, A., Dziembowski, S. (eds.) TCC 2018. LNCS, vol. 11240, pp. 341–369. Springer, Cham (2018). https://doi.org/10.1007/978-3-030-03810-6_13

FFMV23. Francati, D., Friolo, D., Malavolta, G., Venturi, D.: Multi-key and multi-input predicate encryption from learning with errors. In: Hazay, C., Stam, M. (eds.) Advances in Cryptology - EUROCRYPT 2023. EUROCRYPT 2023, Part III, LNCS, vol. 14006, pp. 573–604. Springer, Cham (2023). https://doi.org/10.1007/978-3-031-30620-4_19

GDP16. Regulation (EU) 2016/679 of the European parliament and of the council of 27 April 2016 on the protection of natural persons with regard to the processing of personal data and on the free movement of such data, and repealing directive 95/46 (general data protection regulation). Official Journal of the European Union (OJ), pp. 1–88 (2016)

GGG+14. Goldwasser, S., et al.: Multi-input functional encryption. In: Nguyen, P.Q., Oswald, E. (eds.) EUROCRYPT 2014. LNCS, vol. 8441, pp. 578–602. Springer, Heidelberg (2014)

GGH+16. Garg, S., Gentry, C., Halevi, S., Raykova, M., Sahai, A., Waters, B.: Candidate indistinguishability obfuscation and functional encryption for all circuits. SIAM J. Comput. **45**(3), 882–929 (2016)

GHV10. Gentry, C., Halevi, S., Vaikuntanathan, V.: i-hop homomorphic encryption and rerandomizable yao circuits. In: Rabin, T. (ed.) CRYPTO 2010. LNCS, vol. 6223, pp. 155–172. Springer, Heidelberg (2010). https://doi.org/10.1007/978-3-642-14623-7_9

GJO16. Goyal, V., Jain, A., O'Neill, A.: Multi-input functional encryption with unbounded-message security. In: Cheon, J.H., Takagi, T. (eds.) ASIACRYPT 2016, Part II. LNCS, vol. 10032, pp. 531–556. Springer, Heidelberg (2016). https://doi.org/10.1007/978-3-662-53890-6_18

GKW17. Goyal, R., Koppula, V., Waters, B.: Lockable obfuscation. In: Umans, C. (ed.), 58th FOCS, pp. 612–621. IEEE Computer Society Press, October 2017

GMM17. Garg, S., Mahmoody, M., Mohammed, A.: Lower bounds on obfuscation from all-or-nothing encryption primitives. In: Katz, J., Shacham, H. (eds.) CRYPTO 2017, Part I. LNCS, vol. 10401, pp. 661–695. Springer, Cham (2017). https://doi.org/10.1007/978-3-319-63688-7_22

GVW12. Gorbunov, S., Vaikuntanathan, V., Wee, H.: Functional encryption with bounded collusions via multi-party computation. In: Safavi-Naini, R., Canetti, R. (eds.) CRYPTO 2012. LNCS, vol. 7417, pp. 162–179. Springer, Heidelberg (2012). https://doi.org/10.1007/978-3-642-32009-5_11

GVW15. Gorbunov, S., Vaikuntanathan, V., Wee, H.: Predicate encryption for circuits from LWE. In: Gennaro, R., Robshaw, M. (eds.) CRYPTO 2015. LNCS, vol. 9216, pp. 503–523. Springer, Heidelberg (2015). https://doi.org/10.1007/978-3-662-48000-7_25

HKM+23. Hiroka, T., Kitagawa, F., Morimae, T., Nishimaki, R., Pal, T., Yamakawa, T.:. Certified everlasting secure collusion-resistant functional encryption, and more. Cryptology ePrint Archive, Paper 2023/236 (2023). https://eprint.iacr.org/2023/236

HMNY21. Hiroka, T., Morimae, T., Nishimaki, R., Yamakawa, T.: Quantum encryption with certified deletion, revisited: public key, attribute-based, and classical communication. In: Tibouchi, M., Wang, H. (eds.) ASIACRYPT 2021. LNCS, vol. 13090, pp. 606–636. Springer, Cham (2021). https://doi.org/10.1007/978-3-030-92062-3_21

HMNY22a. Hiroka, T., Morimae, T., Nishimaki, R., Yamakawa, T.: Certified everlasting functional encryption. Cryptology ePrint Archive, Report 2022/969 (2022). https://eprint.iacr.org/2022/969

HMNY22b. Hiroka, T., Morimae, T., Nishimaki, R., Yamakawa, T.: Certified everlasting zero-knowledge proof for QMA. In: Dodis, Y., Shrimpton, T. (eds.) Advances in Cryptology - CRYPTO 2022. CRYPTO 2022. LNCS, Part I, vol. 13507, pp. 239–268. Springer, Cham (2022). https://doi.org/10.1007/978-3-031-15802-5_9

JLS21. Jain, A., Lin, H., Sahai, A.: Indistinguishability obfuscation from well-founded assumptions. In: Khuller, S., Williams, V.V., (eds.), 53rd ACM STOC, pp. 60–73. ACM Press, June 2021

JLS22. Jain, A., Lin, H., Sahai, A.: Indistinguishability obfuscation from LPN over $\mathbb{F}_p$, DLIN, and PRGs in NC^0. In: Dunkelman, O., Dziembowski, S. (eds.), EUROCRYPT 2022, Part I, vol. 13275 of LNCS, pp. 670–699. Springer, Heidelberg, May/June 2022

Klu22. Kluczniak, K.: Lockable obfuscation from circularly insecure fully homomorphic encryption. In: Hanaoka, G., Shikata, J., Watanabe, Y. (eds.), PKC 2022, Part II, vol. 13178 of LNCS, pp. 69–98. Springer, Cham (2022)

KN22. Kitagawa, F., Nishimaki, R.: Functional encryption with secure key leasing. In: Asiacrypt 2022 (2022)

KNTY19. Kitagawa, F., Nishimaki, R., Tanaka, K., Yamakawa, T.: Adaptively secure and succinct functional encryption: improving security and efficiency, simultaneously. In: Boldyreva, A., Micciancio, D. (eds.) CRYPTO 2019, Part III. LNCS, vol. 11694, pp. 521–551. Springer, Cham (2019). https://doi.org/10.1007/978-3-030-26954-8_17

KNY21. Kitagawa, F., Nishimaki, R., Yamakawa, T.: Secure software leasing from standard assumptions. In: Nissim, K., Waters, B. (eds.) TCC 2021. LNCS, vol. 13042, pp. 31–61. Springer, Cham (2021). https://doi.org/10.1007/978-3-030-90459-3_2

KNY23. Kitagawa, F., Nishimaki, R., Yamakawa, T.: Publicly verifiable deletion from minimal assumptions. In: Rothblum, G., Wee, H. (eds) Theory of Cryptography. TCC 2023. LNCS, vol. 14372, pp. 228–245. Springer, Cham (2023). https://doi.org/10.1007/978-3-031-48624-1_9

KSW08. Katz, J., Sahai, A., Waters, B.: Predicate encryption supporting disjunctions, polynomial equations, and inner products. In: Smart, N. (ed.) EUROCRYPT 2008. LNCS, vol. 4965, pp. 146–162. Springer, Heidelberg (2008). https://doi.org/10.1007/978-3-540-78967-3_9

KT20. Kundu, S., Tan, E.: Composably secure device-independent encryption with certified deletion. arXiv, 2011.12704 (2020)

LC97. Lo, H.-K., Chau, H.F.: Is quantum bit commitment really possible? Phys. Rev. Lett. **78**, 3410–3413 (1997)

LP09. Lindell, Y., Pinkas, B.: A proof of security of Yao's protocol for two-party computation. J. Cryptol. **22**(2), 161–188 (2009)

May97. Mayers, D.: Unconditionally secure quantum bit commitment is impossible. Phys. Rev. Lett. **78**, 3414–3417 (1997)

MW18. Menda, S., Watrous, J.: Oracle separations for quantum statistical zero-knowledge. arXiv:1801.08967 (2018)

Por23. Poremba, A.: Quantum proofs of deletion for learning with errors. In: Kalai, Y.T. (ed.), 14th Innovations in Theoretical Computer Science Conference, ITCS 2023, 10–13 January 2023, MIT, Cambridge, Massachusetts, USA, vol. 251 of LIPIcs, pp. 90:1–90:14. Schloss Dagstuhl - Leibniz-Zentrum für Informatik (2023)

SS10. Sahai, A., Seyalioglu, H.: Worry-free encryption: functional encryption with public keys. In: Al-Shaer, E., Keromytis, A.D., Shmatikov, V. (eds.) ACM CCS 2010, pp. 463–472. ACM Press, October 2010

Unr15. Dominique Unruh. Revocable quantum timed-release encryption. J. ACM **62**(6), 49:1–49:76 (2015)

Wat15. Waters, B.: A punctured programming approach to adaptively secure functional encryption. In: Gennaro, R., Robshaw, M. (eds.) CRYPTO 2015, Part II. LNCS, vol. 9216, pp. 678–697. Springer, Heidelberg (2015). https://doi.org/10.1007/978-3-662-48000-7_33

WZ17. Wichs, D., Zirdelis, G.: Obfuscating compute-and-compare programs under LWE. In: Umans, C. (ed.) 58th FOCS, pp. 600–611. IEEE Computer Society Press, October 2017

Yao86. Yao, A.C.C.: How to generate and exchange secrets (extended abstract). In: 27th FOCS, pp. 162–167. IEEE Computer Society Press, October 1986

Early Stopping for Any Number of Corruptions

Julian Loss[1(✉)] and Jesper Buus Nielsen[2]

[1] CISPA Helmholtz Center for Information Security, Saarbrücken, Germany
lossjulian@gmail.com
[2] Aarhus University, Aarhus, Denmark

Abstract. Minimizing the round complexity of byzantine broadcast is a fundamental question in distributed computing and cryptography. In this work, we present the first *early stopping* byzantine broadcast protocol that tolerates up to $t = n-1$ malicious corruptions and terminates in $\mathcal{O}(\min\{f^2, t+1\})$ rounds for any execution with $f \leq t$ actual corruptions. Our protocol is deterministic, adaptively secure, and works assuming a plain public key infrastructure. Prior early-stopping protocols all either require honest majority or tolerate only up to $t = (1 - \epsilon)n$ malicious corruptions while requiring either trusted setup or strong number theoretic hardness assumptions. As our key contribution, we show a novel tool called a *polariser* that allows us to transfer certificate-based strategies from the honest majority setting to settings with a dishonest majority.

1 Introduction

In the problem of byzantine broadcast [21], a sender P_s holds a value v that it wants to share among n parties $P_1, \ldots, P_n$ using a distributed protocol Π with the following properties: 1) *validity*: if the sender is honest (i.e., it follows the protocol description of Π correctly), all honest parties output v 2) *agreement*: all honest parties output the same value v' from Π. Broadcast is an integral building block in many cryptographic and distributed protocols, e.g., multi-party computation, verifiable secret sharing, and state-machine replication. One of the most important efficiency metrics for a broadcast protocol is its *round complexity*: how many rounds does the protocol run for until all parties have terminated?

A seminal result of Dolev and Strong [12] shows that any broadcast protocol tolerating $t < n$ malicious parties runs for at least $t + 1$ rounds in some runs. In the same work, they also give a protocol that shows the tightness of their bound. However, their bound is known to be loose for protocol executions where the number of corruptions f is less than t, i.e., $f < t$, and where eventual agreement is allowed. In [11] the authors define two notions of agreement,

This work is funded by the European Union, ERC-2023-STG, Project ID: 101116713. Views and opinions expressed are however those of the author(s) only and do not necessarily reflect those of the European Union. Neither the European Union nor the granting authority can be held responsible for them.
Funded by the Danish Independent Research Council under Grant-ID DFF-3103-00077B (CryptoDigi).

M. Joye and G. Leander (Eds.): EUROCRYPT 2024, LNCS 14653, pp. 457–488, 2024.
https://doi.org/10.1007/978-3-031-58734-4_16

simultaneous agreement (SA) and eventual agreement (EA). In SA the parties must give output in the same round. In EA they are allowed to give output in different rounds, but must of course still agree on the output itself. They show that for SA any protocol will have runs with $t + 1$ rounds even when $f = 0$. But for EA they only show a lower bound of $f + 2$ rounds.[1] They did not give a protocol matching this bound. Intrigued by this gap, a long line of work has studied so-called *early stopping* protocols which terminate in $O(g(f)) = o(t)$ rounds (for some function g) in any execution where the actual number of corrupted parties f is sufficiently small compared to t. Early stopping protocols are known for both the information theoretic setting with $t < n/3$ malicious corruptions [2,6,17,22] and the authenticated setting with $t < n/2$ corruptions [27]. To the best of our knowledge, however, little is known about early stopping protocols for the setting of $n/2 \le t < n$ malicious corruptions. On one hand, several randomized protocols achieve sublinear (in n) round complexity for broadcast in the dishonest majority setting [7,15,16,29,30]. However, these protocols require the maximum number t of corruptions to be at most a constant fraction of n in order to stop early (some require t to be much smaller).

All in all, for the full corruption threshold $t = n-1$, the tightest lower bound says that any protocol must run for at least $f+2$ rounds, whereas the best protocol uses n rounds in all runs, even for low f. Clearly, there is a fundamental gap in our understanding of early stopping protocols when $t = n - 1$. Motivated by this discussion, we pose the following question: *Are there early stopping broadcast protocols tolerating up to $t = n - 1$ corruptions?*

1.1   Our Contribution

In this work, we answer this question in the affirmative by providing the first early stopping protocol CDC for arbitrary majority corruption, i.e., $t = n - 1$. Concretely, its properties can be summarized as follows:

- CDC tolerates any number $t < n$ of malicious corruptions.
- For any execution with $f \le \sqrt{t}$ faults, CDC terminates in $O(f^2)$ rounds. It always terminates within $O(t)$ rounds. Prior work achieves either $t+1$ rounds deterministically or requires that the maximum number of faults satisfy $t = (1 - \epsilon) \cdot n$ for some $\epsilon > 0$ in order to achieve early stopping.
- Our protocol is secure with respect to a *strongly adaptive adversary*. This type of adversary can observe an honest party's messages, corrupt it, and replace its messages with its own before these messages are delivered. This sets our work apart from existing early stopping protocols for the dishonest majority regime with a strongly adaptive adversary. Namely, existing protocols require either 1) strong number theoretic hardness assumptions (i.e., time-locked puzzles) [28,29] or 2) tolerate only $t = n/2 + O(1)$ malicious corruptions [15,16] in order to stop early.

---

[1] The proof uses a hybrid argument appealing to agreement $e^{\text{poly}(t)}$ times, so holds only for protocols with agreement error $e^{-\text{poly}(t)}$. The argument appeals to validity only twice so the validity error may be any constant $< 1/2$.

- CDC is deterministic and works in the plain public key model. By comparison, existing early stopping protocols for majority corruption are all randomized and, in many cases, require strong setup assumptions.

In summary, CDC is the first early stopping protocol for $t = n - 1$ and makes a significant improvement over the state of the art for any execution with $f = o(\sqrt{n})$ corruptions. We give further comparison with existing literature in the related work section.

1.2 Technical Overview

We now give an overview of our techniques. We begin by giving a brief recap of the classical Dolev-Strong protocol [12] DSC. We then explain the difficulty of making this protocol early stopping and our key insights to overcome it.

Recap: the Dolev-Strong Protocol. DSC achieves a round complexity of $t + 1$ against a strongly adaptive malicious adversary corrupting up to $t < n$ parties. It works as follows for a sender P_s holding a message m:

- In round 1, P_s signs m and sends it to all parties.
- In any round $i \le t$, a party P_j does as follows. If it receives a message m together with a list of valid signatures from i distinct parties for the first time, it adds m to a set of accepted messages $\mathcal{A}$. Then, P_i adds its own signature to the list, and forwards it to all parties so that they add it to $\mathcal{A}$ at most one round later.
- In round $t + 1$, a party P_i executes the above rule to update $\mathcal{A}$, but does not forward a new list. Instead P_i, determines its output as follows. If $\mathcal{A} = \{\}$ or $|\mathcal{A}| > 1$, output a default output NoMsg. If $\mathcal{A} = \{m\}$, output m.

Clearly, if an honest P_i adds m to $\mathcal{A}$ at any point during the first t rounds of the protocol, all honest parties add it to $\mathcal{A}$ at most one round later. If P_i adds m to $\mathcal{A}$ in round $t + 1$, it sees m with $t + 1$ signatures and thus knows that at least one honest party P_j has previously signed m in a previous round. Since P_j was honest in that round, it would have added its own signature to the list of t signatures it needed to add m to $\mathcal{A}$ and passed on the resulting list of $t + 1$ signatures to all parties. Hence, all honest parties add m to $\mathcal{A}$ by round $t + 1$.

Why Making DSC Early Stopping is Hard. Stopping DSC early turns out to be very challenging. Surprisingly, however, this does not result from a fully malicious sender P_s that sends conflicting (signed) messages in DSC to break consistency, as this allows all honest parties to detect and prove that P_s is acting dishonestly. The central difficulty arises already from crash faults: P_s can simply not send any message to (some of) the parties. Note that if P_s sends no signature then DSC runs in silence for $t + 1$ rounds before outputting NoMsg. We would like to terminate this earlier. However, the sender might send a signature only to a single honest party in round 1. Or send it to no honest party but collude with some P_i forwarding the signature from P_s to a single honest party in round 2, *et cetera.* To detect this and stop early it would help if honest parties from round 1 could prove that they did not get a message from P_s. But how to prove this? This is a comparatively simple task in the honest majority setting where there are $n - t \geq t + 1$ honest parties. At a high-level, parties can simply collect a certificate of accusations against the sender for not sending them a message. If they can obtain $t + 1$ signed accusations, they can disqualify the sender and stop the protocol. On the other hand, if P_s cannot be disqualified, then at least one honest party must have received a message from P_s and can forward it to all other parties. Unfortunately, this strategy fails when $t \geq n/2$, as there are only $n - t < t + 1$ honest parties so a certificate might not be constructible. Thus, the obstacle we must overcome is to design an analogue of a certificate for the dishonest majority setting.

Polarisers to the Rescue. Our key tool for achieving this is a novel primitive called a *polariser*. Informally, a polariser partitions the parties into two 'polarized' sets Alive and Corrupt. Polarisers are updated continuously throughout the protocol and maintain the following properties. First, an honest party P_i accepts a polariser from another party (and subsequently updates its own polariser) only if it itself is in Alive. Moreover, for any party $P \in$ Corrupt, a polariser contains accusation against P from *all* parties in Alive. And it is ensured that honest parties never accuse honest parties. As it turns out, these properties make it possible for an honest party P_i to justify any decision in our protocol and convince other honest parties to take the same decision. A crucial observation is that it follows from the properties that all honest parties are in Alive and therefore P_i knows it can forward the polariser and have it accepted by other *honest* parties: they too are in Alive. Thus, polarisers act as our replacement for certificates. The idea behind creating a polariser is surprisingly simple. As an example, suppose the sender P_s does not send a party P_i a message in the first round. Now, P_i can publicly accuse P_s. To deal with having accusations levelled against honest senders, note that honest parties will move P_s to Corrupt only if it was accused by all parties in Alive. Since P_i never accuses an honest sender P_s and is itself in Alive, this precludes honest parties from moving an honest P_s to Corrupt. However, this creates a different problem: if P_j is also dishonest, but is itself in Alive, it can simply not accuse P_s. In this case, P_s cannot be moved from Alive to Corrupt, since not all parties in Alive have accused P_s. To deal with this type of behaviour from dishonest parties, we present a recursive solution for generating a polariser. In our running example from above, we require that either P_j sends whatever it got from P_s or it accuses P_s of cheating. If P_i receives neither of those two things from P_j, P_i knows that P_j is itself corrupt and accordingly accuses P_j. And, importantly, P_i expects every other party P_k to accuse P_j too, or send to P_i the reason that it did not accuse P_j, namely an accusation of P_j against P_s (which would resolve the issue). If P_k does not send an accusation or resolvement, then P_i will accuse P_k, *et cetera*. In each recursive step one more corrupt party is accused, and there are at most f corrupt parties, so the recursion stops in at most f steps. When it stops, then in the view of every honest party either P_s can be moved from Alive to Corrupt or a signature from P_s was received. Hence each honest party receives either a signed message from P_s or a polariser showing that P_s is corrupt.

Justifying Outputs and Graded Broadcast. Polarisers can be used to justify the output (or non-output) of any subprotocol to other parties. To do so, parties will either send their entire view of the protocol transcript so far in case a subprotocol produces output, or send a polariser to justify not having output. We show a protocol GSTM for *graded broadcast* that is inspired by the protocol of Koo et al. [16]. Roughly, GSTM outputs a message m together with a grade $g \in \{0, 1, 2\}$ and a proof π that justifies the combination of m and g. The grade g reflects a party's confidence in its output. Grade $g = 2$ indicates high confidence, meaning that m should be output, and all other parties have grade at least 1 for the same message m. Grade $g = 1$ indicates low confidence in m, meaning that some parties might not have received the message m. Finally, $g = 0$ indicates that the message was not received, the sender was corrupt, and some dummy NoMsg should be output. Validity ensures that all parties output $(m, 2)$ whenever the sender is honest. The crucial property of GSTM, however, is that if a dishonest party can produce a justified output then the grading rules from above apply too. So a corrupted party basically cannot justify an output unless that output could have been produced by an honest party.

Putting Things Together: Protocol DC. Using GSTM we are able to run a broadcast protocol DC that resembles the well-known phase-king approach [5] from the honest majority setting. In this style of protocol, one rotates through $f+1$ leaders until agreement on an output is detected. Essentially, each leader is instructed to broadcast via GSTM whatever it received from the previous instance. The crucial idea is that a malicious leader can never undo the progress that the protocol has made so far by making them choose a different output from one that they have already agreed on (or not choosing the output of an honest sender). This is because each time a new broadcast is initiated by a leader, its input must be justified by the entire view of the protocol so far. Therefore it must use an input which some honest party could have used, or choose to abort the protocol. More precisely, once an output m is received with a positive grade g in the jth leader iteration, parties set $m_j = m$ and broadcast this message once it is their turn to be the leader. (If the previous king aborted then they pick the most recent such value, if there is one, and otherwise they pick a fixed default output). The consistency properties of GSTM and the justification that comes along with any new output ensures that a dishonest leader can never introduce a new message once parties have already agreed on a message m. Once parties see an output m with grade 2, they can detect agreement, forward the justification for this output to all parties, and terminate. After $f + 1$ leader rotations, at least one of the leaders will be honest, giving grade 2, at which point the agreement detection is triggered and the protocol terminates.

CDC: *Ensuring $O(t)$ Round-Complexity.* In the worst case, each of the leader iterations in DC identifies only a single party (i.e., the leader) as malicious. Since each of these steps takes roughly f rounds, we end up with an overall complexity of $O(f^2)$ for DC. To avoid exceeding $O(t)$ for the round complexity, we can simply stop the protocol after running for $\ell = O(t)$ rounds. At this point, we can afford to run an additional instance of DSC to reach agreement. More precisely, any party that has not terminated by round $\ell - 1$ will thus use DSC to broadcast its view of the protocol so far to all parties after completing iteration ℓ. (Running for one more iteration ensures that all parties have time to be forwarded justifications from already terminated parties). Once DSC terminates after another $O(t)$ rounds, all parties can locally decide on a correct output which, by the justification properties of GSTM, will be consistent with parties who have already terminated. This solution, however, still has an undesirable property: honest parties can terminate $O(t)$ rounds apart, whenever one party terminates in iteration $\ell - 1$, but other parties keep on running. This would make the protocol very difficult to use as a subroutine in higher-level application. To have parties terminate one round apart, our actual protocol CDC replaces DSC with a new protocol WES (WES stands for *weak early stopping*) that terminates in $O(f)$ rounds if the sender is honest and $O(t)$ rounds in any other case—furthermore, parties terminate at most one round apart. This allows honest parties who terminate early in DC to always broadcast their justified outputs via WES. If any WES reports a justified output of DC that will be the final output, otherwise the final output will be NoMsg. Parties can terminate immediately upon receiving output from the first terminating instance of WES reporting a justified output of DC. If an honest party saw a justified output of DC it gets reported in $\mathcal{O}(f)$ rounds and the overall protocol terminates in $\mathcal{O}(f^2)$ rounds. If no honest party saw a justified output from DC in $O(t)$ rounds, there are (at least) $f = \sqrt{t}$ corruptions and then the protocol is allowed to run for $\mathcal{O}(t)$ rounds. We believe that WES may have other natural applications.

Achieving Polynomial Complexity. A final wrinkle is that sending along the protocol's entire transcript in every step would result in exponential communication complexity. However, this turns out to be unnecessary, as P_i can simulate another party P_j's behaviour from its past messages. This means that P_j need only send information associated with the most recent protocol step every time it is asked to justify one of its outputs. Thus, our combined protocol CDC ends up with a communication complexity of $O(n^4\lambda)$, where λ is the length of a signature.

1.3 Related Work

Below, we summarize some early stopping protocols from the literature.

Deterministic Protocols. To the best of our knowledge, the first early stopping protocol for byzantine agreement (which implies broadcast for $t < n/2$) with optimal resilience $t < n/3$ in the information theoretic setting was due to Berman et al. [6], who gave a protocol with (optimal) round complexity $\min\{f+2, t+1\}$ and exponential communication. Their work builds on earlier work of Berman and Garay [4] who achieved the same round complexity with polynomial complexity and $n > 4t$. Garay and Moses [17,18] later improved the communication and computation for the corruption-optimal protocol to polynomial. However, their protocol achieves a slightly worse round complexity for the early stopping case of $\min\{f + 5, t + 1\}$. Much later, Abraham and Dolev [2] gave the first protocol with optimal round complexity $\min\{f + 2, t + 1\}$ and polynomial communication/computation. In the authenticated setting with $t < n/2$ and plain PKI, Perry and Toueg [27] showed a protocol with polynomial communication and computation complexity and a round complexity of $\min\{2f + 4, 2t + 2\}$.

Randomized Protocols. In the following, we let δ denote the failure probability of a protocol. There are various randomized protocols for the honest majority setting with constant expected round complexity for both the $t < n/3$ (information theoretic) setting [14,24] and $t < n/2$ (authenticated) setting [1,19]. They can all be made to terminate early with worst-case failure probability δ by running them for $O(\log(1/\delta))$ iterations (each iteration has constant many rounds).

One can use similar ideas to turn expected constant round protocols in the dishonest majority setting with $t < n$ corruptions into protocols that always stop early and have failure probability δ. Here, randomized protocols were first explored by Garay et al., who showed an expected $O(2t - n)^2$-round protocol from plain PKI for any $t < n$ [16]. Their approach was later improved by Fitzi and Nielsen [15], who showed a protocol with $O(2t - n)$ complexity in the same setting. These protocols lead to early stopping protocols with round complexities $O(\log(1/\delta) + (2t - n)^2)$ and $O(\log(1/\delta) + 2t - n)$, respectively, and failure probability δ. However, since $O(2t - n) = O(n)$ (regardless of f) whenever $t = (1 - \epsilon) \cdot n$ where $\epsilon > 0$, these protocols are not early stopping.

Chan et al. [7] presented a randomized broadcast protocol with trusted setup and tolerating any $(1 - \epsilon)$-fraction of adaptive corruptions (for an arbitrary constant $\epsilon > 0$) by assuming no after-the-fact removal of messages. Their protocol achieves a round complexity of $O(\log(1/\delta)) \cdot (n/(n - t))$ for failure probability δ. Also assuming trusted setup and no after-the-fact removals, but tolerating up to $t = n - 1$ corruptions, Wan et al. [30] give a protocol achieving expected $O((n/(n - t))^2)$ round complexity and $O(\log(1/\delta)/\log(n/t)) \cdot (n/(n - t))$ complexity for failure probability δ. Protocols tolerating adaptive corruptions with after-the-fact message removals and $t < (1 - \epsilon)n$ corruptions were studied by Wan et al. [30] and more recently by Srinivasan et al. [28], who gave protocols from time-lock-assumptions achieving round complexities of $(n/(n - t))^2 \cdot \text{polylog}(\lambda)$ (for failure probability negligible in λ) and $O(\log(1/\delta)) \cdot (n/(n - t))$, respectively. Most recently, Alexandru et al. [3] showed how to remove the need for trusted setup in order to obtain $O(\log(1/\delta)) \cdot (n/(n - t))$ round complexity. Although these protocols all achieve early stopping (with failure probability δ) for $t = (1 - \epsilon) \cdot n$, they are also not early stopping when $t = n - O(1)$. Namely, in this case, their round complexity is at least $O(n/(n - t)) = O(n)$.

Lower Bounds, Communication Optimizations, and Weaker Models. As mentioned above [11] showed that the round complexity of an early stopping algorithm with eventual agreement in an execution with f faults is lower bounded by $\min\{f + 2, t + 1\}$. This was later extended by Keidar and Rajsbaum [20] to the setting of omission faults, which can fail to send or receive some of their messages. They demonstrate that early stopping broadcast/agreement algorithms require the same complexity as in the malicious setting if agreement is required to be *uniform*, i.e., omission faulty parties that output, must output consistently with the honest parties. Chandra et al. present reliable broadcast protocols achieving $f + 2$ rounds in the crash fault model and $2f + 3$ rounds in the omission fault model [8]. The latter result was later improved to $f + 2$ by Parvédy and Raynal [26] to $\min\{f + 2, t + 1\}$ round complexity and $O(n^2 \cdot f)$ communication complexity in the omission fault model.

From the perspective of communication complexity, a result by Dolev and Lenzen [9] shows that any (deterministic) early stopping algorithm with optimal round complexity requires sending $O(nt + t^2 f)$ messages. This tightens the famous Dolev-Reischuk bound for the early stopping case [10]. On the other hand, the recent result of Lenzen and Sheikholeslami [22] demonstrate that this bound can be circumvented by presenting an early stopping protocol with (suboptimal) $O(f)$ round complexity but significantly improved $O(nt)$ communication complexity.

2   Preliminaries

We work with directed trees Tree with a single root and edges pointing towards the leafs. For a tree Tree we use path $\in$ Tree to denote a path $(r, \ldots, l)$ from the root r to a leaf l. We let $\mathsf{depth}(\mathsf{Tree}) = \max_{\mathsf{path} \in \mathsf{Tree}}(|\mathsf{path}| - 1)$. The tree with only a root thus has $\mathsf{depth}(\mathsf{Tree}) = 0$ and if the tree is empty $\mathsf{depth}(\mathsf{Tree}) = -1$. For $\mathsf{path} = (r, \ldots, l)$ we let $\mathsf{leaf}(\mathsf{path}) = l$. We assume a synchronous model with n parties $\mathbb{P} = \{\mathsf{P}_1, \ldots, \mathsf{P}_n\}$. The computation proceeds in rounds where in each round each party can send a message to each other parties that is guaranteed to arrive by the end of that round. We assume a rushing adversary that can adaptively corrupt parties and replace or delete any of the messages they sent for a round and which have not yet been delivered. We use t to denote the maximum number of corrupted parties and $f \leq t$ to denote the actual number of corrupted parties. We allow t to take any value $0 \leq t \leq n$.

We assume a PKI. In an initial setup round each party P_i generates a keypair $(\mathsf{sk}_i, \mathsf{vk}_i)$ for a signature scheme and announces vk_i to a public bulletin board. As is standard for this line of work, we assume the Dolev-Yao model [13] and treat signatures as information theoretic objects with perfect unforgeability. Throughout, we denote the size of a signature in bits as λ.

Definition 1 (Broadcast).   *Let Π be a protocol executed by n parties $\mathsf{P}_1, \ldots, \mathsf{P}_n$, where a designated* sender P_s *holds input x and each party P_i terminates upon giving output y_i. We say that Π is a* broadcast protocol *if it has these properties:*

- *Validity: If P_s is honest, each honest party P_i outputs $y_i = x$.*
- *Agreement: For honest parties P_i and P_j, $y_j = y_i$.*

Sequential Composition of Protocols Without Simultaneous Termination. When describing our protocols we will assume that all parties get input in the same round. If a party has no input in a protocol we assume that they nonetheless get a tacit, dummy input, to ensure they know in which round to start running. We also assume that all sub-protocols give outputs in the same round. This ensures that if the parties call a sub-protocol and then proceed when it gives output, then they are still synchronized. Under these conditions we will design protocol where parties might terminate at most one round apart. This leads to problems with composition: when using a protocol as a subroutine, we assume parties give outputs in the same round. But in many of our protocols, parties terminate one round apart. This can, however, be handled using known techniques for sequential composition of protocols without simultaneous termination at a blowup in round complexity of just 2. Details can be found in [23] and Chap. 7 in [25]. Here, we sketch the main idea for completeness. Protocols which assume that the parties start in the same round will be compiled into protocols tolerating that they start one round apart. The compiler works as follows. If parties start a protocol Π one communication round apart, then after P_i sends its messages for protocol round r of Π, it will wait for two underlying communication rounds to ensure it received messages from honest parties sending their messages one underlying communication round later than P_i. Then, P_i computes its messages for the next protocol round and sends them out, waits for two communication rounds *et cetera*. This leaves the problem that the parties might terminate two communication rounds apart. This would be a problem for sequential composition as we want them to start the next protocol only one communication round apart. This can be mitigated when Π has justified outputs. When the first party gets an output it sends it to the other parties. The output will arrive within 1 *communication* round. When a party sees a valid incoming protocol output, they adopt this as their own output and forward it to all parties. Now all parties terminate at most one communication round apart. We will call this the *staggering compiler*.

3   Polarisers and Transferable Justifiers

We first put in place a tool which will allow us to write later protocols more concisely. The tool is called a *polariser* as it polarises the n parties into two disjoint sets S and T of which we know all honest parties are fully inside one of the sets. An external party might not know whether S or T contain the honest parties, but an honest party will of course know which set it is in.

Polarisers are used for proving that a corrupted party P_i did *not* send a message. To motivate their design we first discuss this issue. Consider a party P_i which is to send a message m of a particular form to P_k, say it should be signed. We would like to know when this was *not* done and have a *transferable* proof of this. If we have a bound $t < n/2$ on how many corruptions there can be then this is easy. You can ask P_i to send m via all other parties P_j and have all P_j forward m to P_k or a signature $\sigma_j = \mathsf{Sig}_{\mathsf{sk}_j}((\mathrm{ACC}, \mathsf{P}_i, \mathsf{P}_j))$ which is a signed accusation of P_i that P_j did not send a message. Now P_k either gets m or a certificate of $t + 1$ accusations which can act as a transferable proof that P_j did not send a message. In contrast, in the dishonest majority setting, simple majority voting about whether the message was sent will not solve the problem.

The solution is polarisers. The core of a polariser will be a tuple (Alive, Corrupt, Accuse), where $\mathbb{P} = $ Alive $\cup$ Corrupt and for all parties in Alive, we have a signed accusation for each party in Corrupt. Assuming that all honest parties send all intended messages and honest parties only accuse parties which fail to send a message, this leaves only two cases when seeing (Alive, Corrupt, Accuse). Either all the honest parties are in Alive or all the honest parties are in Corrupt (if there is an honest party in both Alive and Corrupt then an honest party accused an honest party). But it might of course be that all the parties in Alive are corrupted and falsely accusing the parties in Corrupt. This is hard to catch in the dishonest majority case where it can happen that |Alive| > |Corrupt| and all parties in Alive are corrupt. This prevents external agreement on who is corrupt.

The trick is to give up on externally valid certificates and go for a weaker type of certificate which maintains transferability only within the context of the current protocol. An honest party P_i can check whether $P_i \in$ Alive or $P_i \in$ Corrupt. If $P_i \in$ Corrupt, then reject the polariser. Note that in this case *all* honest parties are in Corrupt and will therefore also reject the polariser if it is sent to them. If $P_i \in$ Alive, then accept the polariser. Note that in this case *all* honest parties are in Alive and will therefore also accept the polariser.

Definition 2 (Polariser). *Let* Pol $= $ (Alive, Corrupt, Accuse) *be a tuple where we refer to set* Alive *as the* alive parties, *to set* Corrupt *as the* corrupt parties, *and to set* Accuse *as the* accusations. *We define the following* structural *properties:*

- *__Justifiability.__ For every* $P_j \in$ Corrupt *and for every party* $P_i \in$ Alive, *there exists* $A_{i,j} \in$ Accuse, *where* $A_{i,j}$ *denotes a value* $(\text{ACC}, P_i, P_j, \sigma_i)$, *where* $\text{Ver}_{\text{vk}_i}((\text{ACC}, P_i, P_j), \sigma_i) = \top$.
- *__Completeness.__* Alive $\cap$ Corrupt $= \emptyset$ *and* Alive $\cup$ Corrupt $= \mathbb{P}$.

We define the following contextual *property:*

- *__Accusation Soundness.__ If* P_i *and* P_j *are honest then the adversary cannot construct a valid* $A_{i,j}$ *in PPT, in particular there is no such* $A_{i,j}$ *in* Accuse.

We call a polariser Pol *a* P_i-polariser if $P_i \in$ Pol.Corrupt. *We use* $\overset{i}{\not\rightarrow}$ *to denote the set of* P_i-polarisers. *As with the Landau notation for asymptotic complexity we misuse notation and use* Pol $= \overset{i}{\not\rightarrow}$ *to denote that* Pol $\in \overset{i}{\not\rightarrow}$. *We also sometimes let* $\overset{i}{\not\rightarrow}$ *denote a generic element from* $\overset{i}{\not\rightarrow}$.

In all our protocols constructing polarisers we only sign messages of the form $(\text{ACC}, P_i, P_j, \sigma_i)$ if P_j is corrupt. Therefore:

Lemma 1 (Polarisation Lemma). *Let* Honest *be the set of honest parties and let* Pol *be a polariser. Then* Honest $\subset$ Pol.Alive *or* Honest $\subset$ Pol.Corrupt.

Proof. By Completeness, Honest $\subset$ Pol.Alive $\cup$ Pol.Corrupt, and it cannot be the case that $\mathsf{P}_i \in$ Pol.Alive and $\mathsf{P}_j \in$ Pol.Corrupt are honest, because then by Justifiability $\mathsf{A}_{i,j} \in$ Accuse, contradicting Accusation Soundness.   □

3.1   Transferable Justifiers

Our second general tool is the concept of a transferable justifier for a protocol output. Recall that the purpose of polarisers is to get a transferable proof that some party did not send a message. From these, we build increasingly complex messages and eventually a justified output. It is helpful to have some general machinery for talking about transferable justifiers.

Definition 3 (Justifier). *We call a PPT predicate* $J : \mathbb{P} \times \{0,1\}^* \times \{0,1\}^* \rightarrow \{\top, \bot\}$ *a justifier predicate. If for a party* P_i, *a message* m *and a proof* π *we have that* $J(\mathsf{P}_i, m, \pi) = \top$ *then we say that* P_i *accepts the message* m *with justifier* π. *We require that justifiers are transferable, i.e., if* P_i *and* P_j *are honest then* $J(\mathsf{P}_i, m, \pi) = \top$ *implies that* $J(\mathsf{P}_j, m, \pi) = \top$. *We use* $J(m, \pi) = \top$ *to denote that* $J(\mathsf{P}_i, m, \pi) = \top$ *for all honest* P_i. *By transferability this is the implied if it holds for a single honest* P_i.

As an example consider a protocol where P_j was to send a message and let $\mathrm{NoMsg}^{(j)}$ be a special symbol denoting that P_j sent no message. Then a justifier predicare for this could be $J(\mathsf{P}_i, \mathrm{NoMsg}^{(j)}, \mathsf{Pol}) \equiv \mathsf{P}_i \in \mathsf{Pol.Honest} \wedge \mathsf{Pol} = \overset{j}{\not\rightarrow}$, i.e., P_i accepts that P_j sent nothing if Pol proves that P_j is corrupt and that P_i is honest. This is a transferable justification qua Lemma 1.

Definition 4 (Justified Inputs/Outputs). *We say that a protocol* Π *has justified inputs if it takes an input justifier* J_{In} *as parameter and works for any justifier predicate* J_{In}. *We write* $\Pi_{J_{\mathsf{In}}}$ *to specify the value of* J_{In} *being used in a given run. When a protocol* $\Pi_{J_{\mathsf{In}}}$ *with justified inputs is being called by an honest party* P_i *with input* x_i *then* x_i *must be of the form* $x_i = (m_i, \pi_i)$ *such that* $J_{\mathsf{In}}(\mathsf{P}_i, m_i, \pi_i) = \top$. *We say that a protocol* Π *has an output justifier if the protocol, as part of its code, specifies a justifier predicate* J_{Out}. *We denote the output justifier of* Π *by* $\Pi.J_{\mathsf{Out}}$. *We say that a protocol* P_i *has justified outputs if it has an output justifier and the outputs* y_i *of honest* P_i *are of the form* $y_i = (m_i, \pi_i)$ *and it always holds that* $\Pi.J_{\mathsf{Out}}(\mathsf{P}_i, m_i, \pi_i) = \top$ *after a run of the protocol with a PPT adversary.*

An important tool in our protocols is that justified outputs can be passed on to other parties. Therefore, not even adversarial parties should be able to claim wrong outputs. The following notion is later used to phrase this.

Definition 5 (Adversarial Justified Output (AJO)). *Let* Π *be a protocol with an output justifier and let* $\mathcal{A}$ *be a PPT adversary. Consider the following experiment: Execute* Π *with* $\mathcal{A}$ *in the role of the adversary. When all honest parties* P_i *have produced an output* $y_i = (m_i, \pi_i)$, *give all* y_i *to* $\mathcal{A}$. *We say that*

$\mathcal{A}$ *generates* ℓ adversarial justified outputs (AJOs) $(m^1, \ldots, m^\ell)$ *if it outputs* $(\mathsf{P}^1, m^1, \pi^1), \ldots, (\mathsf{P}^\ell, m^\ell, \pi^\ell)$ *such that for all* $j = 1, \ldots, \ell$ *such that* P^j *is honest and* $\Pi.J_{\mathsf{Out}}(\mathsf{P}^j, m^j, \pi^j) = \top$. *Otherwise, we say that no outputs were generated.*

Note that the triple $(\mathsf{P}^j, m^j, \pi^j)$ with $\Pi.J_{\mathsf{Out}}(\mathsf{P}^j, m^j, \pi^j) = \top$ does not mean that P^j *produced* the output (m^j, π^j). It merely means that P^j would *accept* the output (m^j, π^j) given its current state and the predicate $\Pi.J_{\mathsf{Out}}$. Note also that if a property holds for all AJOs it also holds for honest outputs as the adversary are given the honest outputs and can reuse them as a triple in $(\mathsf{P}^1, m^1, \pi^1), \ldots, (\mathsf{P}^\ell, m^\ell, \pi^\ell)$.

4   Send Transferable Messages

We now present a protocol which forces a potentially corrupt sender to send a message, solving the *missing message problem* discussed earlier. Throughput, we let NoMsg be a designated symbol where NoMsg $\notin \{0, 1\}^*$. We use it to signal that a sender was corrupt and did not send a normal message. Ultimately, NoMsg could be mapped to a normal message, like the empty string, but it helps the exposition to assume NoMsg $\notin \{0, 1\}^*$. We also use another such symbol $\perp$ and assume that $\perp \notin \{0, 1\}^*$ and $\perp \neq$ NoMsg.

Definition 6 (Send Transferable Message Protocol). *Let* $\Pi_{J_{\mathsf{Msg}}}$ *be a protocol run among* n *parties* $\mathsf{P}_1, \ldots, \mathsf{P}_n$ *where* J_{Msg} *is the parametrisable input justifier predicate. Assume that* $\Pi_{J_{\mathsf{Msg}}}$ *specifies a designated sender* P_s *holding an input* $m \in \{0, 1\}^*$ *along with a justifier* π *such that* $J_{\mathsf{Msg}}(\mathsf{P}_s, m, \pi) = \top$ *and parties terminate upon generating output* y_i *in* P_i. *The protocol specifies an output justifier predicate* $\Pi.J_{\mathsf{Out}}$.

- **Correctness:** *Honest* P_i *outputs* $y_i = (m_i, \pi_i)$, *where* $m_i \in \{0, 1\}^* \cup \{$NoMsg$\}$ *and* $\pi_i \in \{0, 1\}^*$.
- **Justified Output:** *Outputs are justified. When honest* P_i *outputs* $y_i = (m_i, \pi_i)$ *then* $J_{\mathsf{Out}}(\mathsf{P}_i, m_i, \pi_i) = \top$.
- **Justified Message:** *Only justified inputs can appear in justified outputs. For all AJOs* $y_i = (m_i, \pi_i)$ *either* $m_i =$ NoMsg *or the justifier* π_i *is of the form* $\pi_i = (\pi_i^1, \pi_i^2)$ *and* $J_{\mathsf{Msg}}(\mathsf{P}_i, m_i, \pi_i^1) = \top$ *for all honest* P_i.
- **Validity:** *Honest senders manage to send their intended message and only that message. If* P_s *is honest and has input* (m, π), *then all honest parties* P_j *have output* $y_j = (m_j, \pi_j)$ *with* $m_j = m$. *Furthermore, for all AJOs* m' *it holds that* $m' = m$.
- **Agreement:** *All outputs are the same or* NoMsg. *For all AJOs* m^1 *and* m^2 *it holds that* $m^1 =$ NoMsg *or* $m^2 =$ NoMsg *or* $m^1 = m^2$.

We say that Π *is a send transferable message with agreement (STMA) protocol with* J_{Out}-*justified output if it has the above properties. If it lacks agreement we call it an STM protocol. If an STMA protocol has the additional property that* $m \neq$ NoMsg *for all AJOs, then we call it a justifiable broadcast. We call an output a legal STM output if it has the correctness and justified output properties.*

Remark 1. Note that justifiable broadcast ensures that all outputs are the same, so it implies the notion of broadcast in Definition 1. It additionally has input and output justifiers, which will be convenient when using it as sub-protocol. It is straight forward to see that we can create a justified broadcast protocol $\mathsf{DSC}_{\mathsf{P}_s, J_{\mathsf{Msg}}}$ by using Dolev-Strong with sender P_s and $t = n - 1$ corruptions and where parties only accept signatures from P_s on (m, π_{MSG}) where $J_{\mathsf{Msg}}(m, \pi_{\mathrm{MSG}}) = \top$. The round complexity is $\mathcal{O}(n)$. We use this protocol later.

Remark 2. Note that honest parties have input $m \neq \mathrm{NoMsG}$, so by Validity, if output $m = \mathrm{NoMsG}$ can be justified, then P_s is corrupt.

Remark 3. We have required that for all AJOs $y_i = (m_i, \pi_i)$ either $m_i = \mathrm{NoMsG}$ or the justifier π_i is of the form $\pi_i = (\pi_i^1, \pi_i^2)$ and $J_{\mathsf{Msg}}(\mathsf{P}_i, m_i, \pi_i^1) = \top$ for all honest P_i. Note that the definition does not restrict what π_i^2 is or how it affects the output of J_{Out}. Typically π_i^2 will be a protocol dependent value proving that the message m_i resulted from running Π and J_{Out} will check that this is the case. Typically π_i^2 also contains a signature on m_i from P_s to ensure validity.

4.1 Polariser Cast

We present a STM protocol PC called *polariser cast*. The protocol will proceed roughly as follows.

1. The sender signs its justified input and sends it to all parties.
2. If the sender P_s did not send a justified signed input in round 0 then each P_j accuses P_s.
3. If P_s should have been accused but a party P_j did not accuse P_s in round 1, then all parties P_k will accuse P_j in round 2, unless $\mathsf{P}_j = \mathsf{P}_s$ such that it was already accused, *et cetera*.
4. Since only corrupted parties are accused, at some point there are no more parties to accuse, and at this point an output can be computed. Either P_s sent a signed message or P_s can be moved to Corrupt along with all parties with enough accusations.
5. This gives each party an output candidate, but different honest parties might hold different signed messages m.
6. The parties exchange their output candidates, and if some P_j has different signed values in any of them, then this is used as a transferable proof that P_s is corrupt.

Before describing the protocol in detail we give some helping definitions. During the protocol each P_i will keep a set S of received well-formed *elements*.

Definition 7 (Well-formed elements). *We call an element e well-formed if it is of one of the following two forms.*

Inputs: $e = (\mathrm{IN}, m, \pi, \sigma)$, *where* $\mathsf{Ver}_{\mathsf{vk}_s}((\mathrm{IN}, m), \sigma) = \top$ *and* $J_{\mathsf{Msg}}(\mathsf{P}_s, m, \pi) = \top$.
Accusations: $e = (\mathrm{ACC}, \mathsf{P}_i, \mathsf{P}_j, \sigma_i)$, *where* $\mathsf{Ver}_{\mathsf{vk}_i}((\mathrm{ACC}, \mathsf{P}_i, \mathsf{P}_j), \sigma_i) = \top$.

Each P_i has its own version of S. When we need to distinguish it we denote it by S_i. We use S_i^r to denote the value of S_i at P_i in round r. We define some helper functions used in the protocol.

Detect corruption: The function $\mathsf{ToAccuse}^r(S) \subset \mathbb{P}$ takes as input a set of well-formed elements and a round number r and computes a set of parties $\mathcal{P} \in \mathbb{P}$, which we think of as being corrupt.

Complete: We call a set of well-formed elements S *complete* if there are no more parties to accuse, i.e., $\mathsf{Complete}(S) \equiv \exists r > 0 \, (\mathsf{ToAccuse}^r(S) = \emptyset)$.

Output: The function $\mathsf{Out}(S)$ takes as input a complete set of well-formed elements and computes a possible output of PC, i.e., if $\mathsf{Complete}(S)$ then $\mathsf{Out}(S) = (m, \pi)$ where π is a signature on m under vk_s or $\mathsf{Out}(S) = (\textsc{NoMsg}, \mathsf{Pol})$ where $\mathsf{Pol} = \overset{s}{\nrightarrow}$.

$\mathsf{PC}(\mathsf{P}_s, m, \pi)$

Input: In round 0 all P_i initialise $y_i = \bot$, $S_i = \emptyset$ and the sender P_s computes $\sigma = \mathsf{Sig}_{\mathsf{sk}_s}((\textsc{In}, m))$, sends $e = (\textsc{In}, m, \pi, \sigma)$ to all parties and adds it to S_s.

Basic Loop: For $r = 1, \dots$ party P_i does the following in round r:
1. Receive well-formed elements e sent in round $r-1$ and add them to S_i if the following holds. If e is an input, then only add e to S if there is not already an input in S_i. If e is an accusation of $(\textsc{Acc}, \mathsf{P}_i, \mathsf{P}_j, \sigma_i)$ then only add it if there is not already some $(\textsc{Acc}, \mathsf{P}_i, \mathsf{P}_j, \cdot)$ in S_i.
2. Compute $\mathcal{P}_i = \mathsf{ToAccuse}^r(S_i)$ and for each $\mathsf{P}_j \in \mathcal{P}_i$ add $e = (\textsc{Acc}, \mathsf{P}_i, \mathsf{P}_j, \mathsf{Sig}_{\mathsf{sk}_i}((\textsc{Acc}, \mathsf{P}_i, \mathsf{P}_j)))$ to S_i.
3. *Echo rule:* Send all e added to S_i above to all parties.

Produce Candidate: In the first round r where $\mathsf{Complete}(S_i)$ and $y_i = \bot$, compute $y_i = \mathsf{Out}(S_i)$ and send y_i to all other parties.

Adopt Candidate: In the first round r where $y_i = \bot$ and some P_j sent y_j with $J_{\mathsf{Out}}(\mathsf{P}_i, y_j) = \top$ let $y_i = y_j$ and send y_i to all parties.

Termination: In the first round r where $y_i \neq \bot$, run for one more round and then terminate with output y_i.

Output Justification: We define $\mathsf{PC}.J_{\mathsf{Out}}(\mathsf{P}_i, y_i)$. Parse $y_i = (m, \pi)$ and check that *either* $y_i = (\textsc{NoMsg}, \mathsf{Pol})$ and $\mathsf{P}_i \in \mathsf{Pol}.\mathsf{Honest}$ and $\mathsf{Pol} = \overset{s}{\nrightarrow}$ *or* $m \neq \textsc{NoMsg}$ and $\pi = (\pi^1, \pi^2)$ and $J_{\mathsf{Msg}}(m, \pi^1) = \top$ and $\mathsf{Ver}_{\mathsf{vk}_s}(m, \pi^2) = \top$.

Fig. 1. A Sending Transferable Message Protocol.

The protocol is given in Fig. 1. We now proceed to define $\mathsf{ToAccuse}$ and Out. We use a tree-based definition where Tree is a tree of missing accusations. What messages are missing depends on what round we are in, so the function Tree^r also depends on r. The nodes of the tree will be elements $(\mathsf{P}, \rho) \in \mathbb{P} \times \mathbb{N}$.

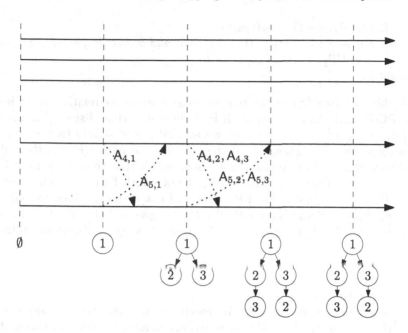

Fig. 2. Party P_1 is the sender. Parties P_1, P_2, and P_3 are corrupted. Their timelines are shown as the top three. Parties P_4 and P_5 are honest and their timelines shown at the bottom. Time runs from left to right and vertical dashed lines are round separators with the first one showing the beginning of round 0. To not clutter the figure, we do not show messages sent *to* corrupted parties. Below the timelines we show the tree built by P_5. In round 0 it is empty. In round 0 party P_1 does not send its signature σ. Therefore P_5 adds the root $(P_1, 0)$. We are then in round 1, so all parties in leafs of paths of length 1 should be accused, i.e., P_1. In round 1 party P_4 therefore accuses P_1 and P_5 also accuses P_1. The corrupted parties do not accuse P_1. Therefore P_5 adds edges from $(P_1, 0)$ to $(P_2, 1)$ and $(P_3, 1)$. We are then in round 2, so all parties in leafs of paths of length 2 should be accused, so both honest parties accuse P_2 and P_3. The corrupted parties do not accuse. Therefore P_3's missing accusation of P_2 is added as an edge and P_2's missing accusation of P_3 is added as an edge. Note that for instance P_1's missing accusation of P_2 is not added as an edge as we only add parties not already on a path. We are then in round 3 so parties in leafs on paths of length 3 should be accused, i.e., P_3 and P_2. However, no accusations are actually sent as equivalent accusations were sent already. We are then in round 4. No new nodes are added. Parties in leafs of paths of length 4 should be accused. There are no such paths, so the accusation is considered complete, and the protocol ends. We have $\mathsf{Alive} = \{P_4, P_5\}$, $\mathsf{Corrupt} = \{P_1, P_2, P_3\}$, and $\mathsf{Accuse} = \{A_{4,1}, A_{5,1}, A_{4,2}, A_{4,3}, A_{5,2}, A_{5,3}\}$, so we have a legal P_1-polariser.

Definition 8 (Tree Function). *The output of* $\mathsf{Tree}^r(S)$ *is computed as:*

1. *Let T be the empty tree.*
2. *If $\nexists (\mathrm{IN}, m, \cdot, \cdot) \in S$ then add $(P_s, 0)$ to T as the root.*
3. *For $\rho = 1, \ldots, r$:*
   (a) For all $\mathsf{path} \in T$ *with* $|\mathsf{path}| = \rho$:

      i. Let $(\mathsf{P}_j, \rho - 1) = \mathsf{leaf}(\mathsf{path})$.

     ii. For all $\mathsf{P}_k \in \mathbb{P}$ where $(\mathsf{P}_k, \cdot) \notin \mathsf{path}$ and $\nexists(\mathrm{ACC}, \mathsf{P}_k, \mathsf{P}_j, \cdot) \in S$, add the edge $((\mathsf{P}_j, \rho - 1), (\mathsf{P}_k, \rho))$ to T.

4. Output T.

We think of $\mathsf{Tree}^r(S)$ as the tree of missing elements relative to an honest run of $\mathsf{PC}(\mathsf{P}_s, \ldots)$. As an example, if P_s is honest it should send $(\mathrm{IN}, m, \cdot, \cdot)$ in round 0, so if $\nexists(\mathrm{IN}, m, \cdot, \cdot) \in S$ then we add $(\mathsf{P}_s, 0)$ to signify that P_s omitted a message in round 0. Therefore, if the tree has the path $((\mathsf{P}_s, 0))$ then all P_k should have accused P_s in round 1. If P_k does not do this, then in the iteration of the loop with $\rho = 1$ the path $\mathsf{path} = ((\mathsf{P}_s, 0))$ of length 1 will get considered and so will $(\mathsf{P}_s, 0) = \mathsf{leaf}(\mathsf{path})$. So if $\mathsf{P}_k \neq \mathsf{P}_s$ did not accuse P_s then we will have $\nexists(\mathrm{ACC}, \mathsf{P}_k, \mathsf{P}_s, \cdot) \in S$ and hence $((\mathsf{P}_s, 0), (\mathsf{P}_k, 1))$ gets added to the tree T. So we add an edge to $(\mathsf{P}_k, 1)$ to signify that in round 1 party P_k failed an obligation and then points from $(\mathsf{P}_s, 0)$ to say that the obligation was to accuse P_s because P_s failed an obligation in the previous round. The reason that Tree^r depends on r is that some accusation might be missing simply because the parties did not have a chance to send them yet.

We now define $\mathsf{ToAccuse}^r(S)$. To motivate the definition, consider a tree $\mathsf{Tree}^{r-1}(S_i)$ at P_i at the beginning of round r, i.e., after receiving the accusations $(\mathrm{ACC}, \cdot, \cdot)$ sent out in round $r - 1$. If $\mathsf{path} = (\ldots, (\mathsf{P}_j, r - 1)) \in \mathsf{Tree}^{r-1}(S_i)$ this is because P_j missed an obligation in round $r - 1$. Therefore P_i must accuse P_j. This motivate the following definition

$$\mathsf{ToAccuse}^r(S) = \left\{ \mathsf{P}_j \mid \exists(\ldots, (\mathsf{P}_j, r - 1)) \in \mathsf{Tree}^{r-1}(S) \right\} .$$

If a set S is complete then it allows to compute an output as follows.

Definition 9 (Output). *The function $\mathsf{Out}(S)$ is defined as follows.*

1. The input is a complete set S, so we can find the smallest r such that $\mathsf{ToAccuse}^r(S) = \emptyset$.

2. If $r = 1$ then pick $(\mathrm{IN}, m, \sigma, \pi) \in S$ and output $(m, (\sigma, \pi))$.

3. If $r > 1$ then output $(\mathrm{NOMSG}, \mathsf{Pol} = (\mathsf{Alive}, \mathsf{Corrupt}, \mathsf{Accuse}))$, where

$$\mathsf{Corrupt} = \left\{ \mathsf{P}_j \mid \exists(\mathsf{P}_j, \cdot) \in \mathsf{nodes}(\mathsf{Tree}^r(S)) \right\} ,$$
$$\mathsf{Accuse} = S ,$$
$$\mathsf{Alive} = \mathbb{P} \setminus \mathsf{Corrupt} .$$

We proceed to prove PC secure when using the above definitions of $\mathsf{ToAccuse}$, $\mathsf{Complete}$, and Out. Before the proof it may be instructive to consider the example runs of the protocol in Figs. 2, 3 and 4.

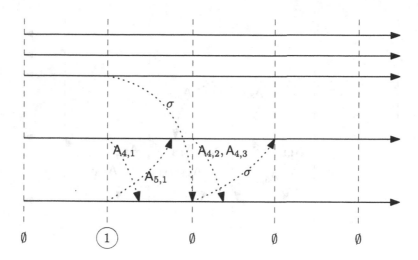

Fig. 3. For notation see Fig. 2. In round 0 party P_1 does not send its signature σ Therefore P_5 adds the root $(P_1, 0)$. We are then in round 1 and parties P_4 and P_5 accuse P_1. The corrupted parties do not accuse P_1, but P_3 forwards a signature σ by P_1 to P_5. Therefore the tree computed by P_5 in round 2 is again empty. Therefore the accusation is over for P_5. It outputs σ (it terminates one round later, not shown). Note that P_4 is in the same situation as in Fig. 2. Its tree will look like that of P_5 in round 2 in Fig. 2. So, it accuses P_2 and P_3. By the echo rule P_5 forwards σ to P_4 which will then have an empty tree by round 3 and outputs σ.

Definition 10 (equivalent sets). *Let S and T be two sets of well-formed elements. We say that $S \sqsubseteq T$ if $\exists(\text{IN}, m, \pi, \sigma_s) \in S$ implies that $\exists(\text{IN}, m', \pi', \sigma'_s) \in T$ and $\exists(\text{ACC}, P_i, P_j, \sigma_i) \in S$ implies that $\exists(\text{ACC}, P_i, P_j, \sigma'_i) \in T$. We call two sets equivalent if $S \sqsubseteq T$ and $T \sqsubseteq S$. We call two elements equivalent if $\{e_1\}$ and $\{e_2\}$ are equivalent.*

Lemma 2 (propagation lemma). *For all honest P_i and P_j and rounds $r > 0$ reached in the protocol it holds that $S_i^{r-1} \sqsubseteq S_j^r$.*

Proof. This follows from the fact that all elements s added to S_i get forwarded to P_j and if s is considered well-formed by P_i then it is also considered well-formed by P_j. Therefore s is added to S_j^r, unless S_j^r contains an equivalent element. $\square$

Lemma 3 (tree monotonicity lemma). *For all sets of well-formed elements S, T and all $r \geq 0$ its holds that*

$$S \sqsubseteq T \implies \text{Tree}^r(T) \subseteq \text{Tree}^r(S) .$$

Proof. Note that for an object o, root or edge, to be included in $\text{Tree}^r(T)$ it is required that some element is *missing* in T, i.e., $\nexists(\text{IN}, m, \cdot, \cdot) \in T$ or $\nexists(\text{ACC}, P_k, P_j, \cdot) \in T$. Since $S \sqsubseteq T$ these conditions imply that $\nexists(\text{IN}, m, \cdot, \cdot) \in S$ and $\nexists(\text{ACC}, P_k, P_j, \cdot) \in S$, so the same object o gets included in $\text{Tree}^r(S)$. $\square$

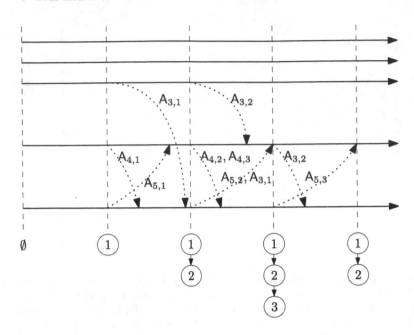

Fig. 4. For notation see Fig. 2. In round 0 party P_1 does not send its signature σ. Therefore P_5 adds the root $(P_1, 0)$. We are then in round 1 and parties P_4 and P_5 accuse P_1. Party P_3 accuses P_1 but sends the accusation only to P_5. Party P_2 does not accuse P_1. Party P_5 adds an edge representing the missing accusation of P_1 by P_2. Party P_4 being in the same situation as in Fig. 2 accuses P_2 and P_3. Party P_5 accuses all parties which are leafs on paths of length 2, i.e., party P_2. It also forwards $A_{3,1}$ because of the echo rule. Now P_3 accuses P_2 but only towards P_4. Therefore P_5 is missing the accusation of P_2 by P_3 and adds an edge to represent it. It then has a path of length 3 in round 3 and thus accuses P_3. But in the same round P_4 forwards $A_{3,2}$ because of the echo rule. Therefore by round 4 the tree computed by party P_5 is back to height 1 and the protocol ends for P_5. It outputs $\mathsf{Alive} = \{P_3, P_4, P_5\}$, $\mathsf{Corrupt} = \{P_1, P_2\}$ and $\mathsf{Accuse} = \{A_{4,1}, A_{5,1}, A_{3,1}, A_{5,2}, A_{4,2}, A_{5,3}, A_{3,2}\}$, which is a legal P_1-polariser.

The following corollary is important in showing that honest do not accuse honest parties. The tree $\mathsf{Tree}^{r-1}(S_i^{r-1})$ is the tree that P_i used in round $r-1$ to calculate who it should accuse. The tree $\mathsf{Tree}^{r-1}(S_j^r)$ is the tree that S_j uses in round r to calculate who S_i ought to have sent an accusation against—it uses the same function Tree^{r-1}, but its own set S_j^r. If $\mathsf{Tree}^{r-1}(S_j^r) \sqsubseteq \mathsf{Tree}^{r-1}(S_i^{r-1})$ then P_j does not expect to receive any accusations which are not sent.

Corollary 1. *For all honest P_i and P_j and rounds $r > 0$ reached in the protocol it holds that*

$$\mathsf{Tree}^{r-1}(S_j^r) \sqsubseteq \mathsf{Tree}^{r-1}(S_i^{r-1}) .$$

Proof. By the preceding lemmas we have that $S_i^{r-1} \sqsubseteq S_j^r$ and that $S \sqsubseteq T \implies \mathsf{Tree}^\rho(T) \subseteq \mathsf{Tree}^\rho(S)$ for all S, T and ρ. Set $S = S_i^{r-1}$, $T = S_j^r$ and $\rho = r-1$. $\square$

Lemma 4. *If P_i is honest and accuses P_j then P_j is corrupted.*

Proof. By construction, if P_i accuses P_j in round r then $\mathsf{P}_j \in \mathsf{ToAccuse}^r(S_i^r)$. By definition this means that $\exists (\ldots, (\mathsf{P}_j, r-1)) \in \mathsf{Tree}^{r-1}(S_i^r)$. If $r = 1$ then this implies that $\exists ((\mathsf{P}_j, 0)) \in \mathsf{Tree}^0(S_i^r)$, and hence $\mathsf{P}_j = \mathsf{P}_s$, as only P_s can occur in the root. Therefore $\nexists (\mathsf{IN}, m, \cdot, \cdot) \in S_i$. Hence, $\mathsf{P}_j = \mathsf{P}_s$ did not send its signed input to P_i in round 0. Therefore $\mathsf{P}_j = \mathsf{P}_s$ is corrupted. If $r > 1$ then we have that $\exists (\ldots, (\mathsf{P}_k, r-2), (\mathsf{P}_j, r-1)) \in \mathsf{Tree}^{r-1}(S_i^r)$. By construction (see Item 3(a)ii in Definition 8) this implies that $\exists (\ldots, (\mathsf{P}_k, r-2)) \in \mathsf{Tree}^{r-1}(S_i^r)$ and $\nexists (\mathsf{ACC}, \mathsf{P}_j, \mathsf{P}_k, \cdot) \in S_i^r$. If P_j is honest this implies that $\exists (\ldots, (\mathsf{P}_k, r-2)) \in \mathsf{Tree}^{r-1}(S_j^{r-1})$, as $\mathsf{Tree}^{r-1}(S_i^r) \sqsubseteq \mathsf{Tree}^{r-1}(S_j^{r-1})$. Therefore $\mathsf{P}_k \in \mathsf{ToAccuse}^{r-1}(S_j^{r-1})$. So if P_j is honest it sent $(\mathsf{ACC}, \mathsf{P}_j, \mathsf{P}_k, \cdot)$ to P_i in round $r-1$. This contradicts $\nexists (\mathsf{ACC}, \mathsf{P}_j, \mathsf{P}_k, \cdot) \in S_i^r$. □

The following lemma shows that when the set S is complete at an honest party such that it terminates, then $\mathsf{Out}(S)$ produces a correct output, i.e., if there is no signature in S, then a polariser is produced proving that P_u is corrupt.

Lemma 5 (justified output). *If S is held by an honest party P_i and $\mathsf{Complete}(S)$, such that P_i produces output $\mathsf{Out}(S)$, then $\mathsf{PC}.\mathsf{J}_{\mathsf{Out}}(\mathsf{P}_i, \mathsf{Out}(S))$.*

Proof. We want to prove that $\mathsf{PC}.\mathsf{J}_{\mathsf{Out}}(\mathsf{P}_i, \mathsf{Out}(S)) = \top$. This means that if we let $y_i = \mathsf{Out}(S)$, as defined in Definition 9, then we have to make sure that $\mathsf{PC}.\mathsf{J}_{\mathsf{Out}}(\mathsf{P}_i, y_i)$ where $\mathsf{PC}.\mathsf{J}_{\mathsf{Out}}$ is defined in **Output Justification** in Fig. 1. We write this out. First parse $y_i = (m, \pi)$. We then have to prove that *either* 1) $y_i = (\mathsf{NoMSG}, \mathsf{Pol})$ and $\mathsf{P}_i \in \mathsf{Pol}.\mathsf{Honest}$ and $\mathsf{Pol} = \overset{s}{\nrightarrow}$ *or* 2) $m \neq \mathsf{NoMSG}$ and $\pi = (\pi^1, \pi^2)$ and $\mathsf{J}_{\mathsf{Msg}}(m, \pi^1) = \top$ and $\mathsf{Ver}_{\mathsf{vk}_s}(m, \pi^2) = \top$.

By $\mathsf{Complete}(S)$ there exists r such that $\mathsf{ToAccuse}^r(S) = \emptyset$. Assume that $r = 1$. From $\mathsf{Complete}(S)$ we get that $\mathsf{ToAccuse}^1(S) = \emptyset$. This implies that $\nexists (\ldots, (\mathsf{P}_j, r-1)) \in \mathsf{Tree}^{r-1}(S)$ which for $r = 1$ means that $\nexists ((\mathsf{P}_j, 0)) \in \mathsf{Tree}^0(S)$, which by the construction of the tree T in the algorithm Tree^0 defined in Definition 8 means that it is *not* the case that $\nexists (\mathsf{IN}, m, \cdot, \cdot) \in S$. So, there is some well-formed $(\mathsf{IN}, m, \cdot, \cdot) \in S$. Therefore the output is of the form in case 2 above.

Assume then that $r > 1$. From $\mathsf{Complete}(S)$ we get that $\mathsf{ToAccuse}^r(S) = \emptyset$ and by r being minimal we have that $\mathsf{ToAccuse}^{r-1}(S) \neq \emptyset$. From $\mathsf{ToAccuse}^{r-1}(S) \neq \emptyset$, it follows that there is at least one path in $\mathsf{Tree}^{r-1}(S)$ and hence also a root. Therefore $(\mathsf{P}_s, 0) \in \mathsf{nodes}(\mathsf{Tree}^{r-1}(S))$ and hence $\mathsf{P}_s \in \mathsf{Pol}.\mathsf{Corrupt}$. We therefore just have to show that Pol is a legal polariser. Completeness follows from $\mathsf{Alive} = \mathbb{P} \setminus \mathsf{Corrupt}$. Since S contains only well-formed elements and $\mathsf{Accuse} = S$ by Definition 9, for justifiability it is sufficient to prove that for all $(\mathsf{P}_i, \mathsf{P}_j) \in \mathsf{Alive} \times \mathsf{Corrupt}$ it holds that $(\mathsf{Accuse}, \mathsf{P}_i, \mathsf{P}_j, \cdot) \in S$. So, assume that $(\mathsf{P}_i, \mathsf{P}_j) \in \mathsf{Alive} \times \mathsf{Corrupt}$. This implies that $(\mathsf{P}_j, \rho) \in \mathsf{nodes}(\mathsf{Tree}^\rho(S))$ for some $\rho < r$. We argue that this implies that S contains $(\mathsf{ACC}, \mathsf{P}_i, \mathsf{P}_j, \cdot)$. Assume to the contrary that S does not contain $(\mathsf{ACC}, \mathsf{P}_i, \mathsf{P}_j, \cdot)$. Then it would be the case that $((\mathsf{P}_j, \rho), (\mathsf{P}_i, \rho+1)) \in \mathsf{Tree}^r(S)$ by Item 3(a)ii in Definition 8 unless $(\mathsf{P}_i, \cdot)$ was already on the path in question (but $(\mathsf{P}_i, \cdot)$ being on the path contradicts $P_i \in$ Alive as we added to Corrupt all parties on all paths by construction of Definition 9). But if $((P_j, \rho), (P_i, \rho+1)) \in \mathsf{Tree}^r(S)$ then from $\rho + 1 \leq r$ and because we assume that $(\mathrm{Acc}, P_i, P_j, \cdot) \notin S$ it is not the case that $\mathsf{ToAccuse}^r(S) \neq \emptyset$, as we would have $P_i \in \mathsf{ToAccuse}^r(S)$ by construction. Since we have as premise that $\mathsf{ToAccuse}^r(S) = \emptyset$ it follows that $(\mathrm{Acc}, P_i, P_j, \cdot) \in S$, as desired.   □

Theorem 1. *The protocol* PC *is an STM protocol for* $t < n$. *Furthermore, assume that* PC *has inputs* (m, π) *with* $|(m, \pi)| \leq \ell$. *Let* λ *be the length of a signature. Then the protocol has communication complexity* $\mathcal{O}(n^2 \ell + n^4 \lambda)$ *and the size of the justified output is at most* $\mathcal{O}(\ell + n^2 \lambda)$. *The protocol uses at most* $f + 2$ *rounds.*

Proof. Correctness follows by construction of Out. Justified output follows from Lemma 5. Justified message follows by construction of J_{Out}. Validity follows by the fact that if P_s is honest then in any polariser Pol accepted by an honest party it holds that $P_s \in$ Alive by Lemma 4. We then count communication complexity. We ignore constant factors in the counting. In round 0 party P_s sends to all parties its input of lenght ℓ and a signature. This is the sending of $n(\ell + \lambda)$ bits. During the basic loop each party forwards at most one well-formed input from P_s to other parties, so this is at most $n^2(\ell + \lambda)$ bits. Besides this, each P_i might send an accusation of each P_j which will then be relayed by each other party. This is the flooding of at most $n^4 \lambda$ bits. The output consists of at most one well-formed input of P_s so is at most $\ell + n^2 \lambda$ bits. In Produce Candidate and Adopt Candidate each party sends it to at most n other parties, yielding communication at most $n^2 \ell + n^4 \lambda$. We consider round complexity. For illustration consider the easy case for $f = 0$. In the first round P_s sends its signed input to all parties and in round 2 all parties send their adopted candidate y_i. This is $2 = f + 2$ rounds. Note then that if the protocol in rounds $r \geq 1$ do not send an adopted candidate it is because $\neg\mathsf{Complete}(S)$, which implies that $\mathsf{ToAccuse}^r(S) \neq \emptyset$ which by Item 3(a)ii in Definition 8 implies that P_k for which $(P_k, \cdot) \notin$ path is added to T in Tree^r, extending path by length 1. After this path contains one more corrupted party. There are at most f corrupted parties. So this adds at most f extra rounds, for a total of at most $2 + f$.   □

The bulk for the communication of PC is the flooding of up to n^2 accusations. It turns out this can be compressed accross multiple runs of PC as each accusation needs only be sent once.

Lemma 6 (Amortized Communication Complexity). *Assume that in the life time of the system* ι *instances* $\mathsf{PC}^1, \ldots, \mathsf{PC}^\iota$ *are run and that* PC^i *has inputs* (m^i, π^i) *with* $|(m^i, \hat{\pi}^i)| \leq \ell_i$, *where* $\hat{\pi}^i$ *is* π^i *with all accusations removed. Then the communication complexity of running all* ι *copies can be compressed to* $\mathcal{O}\left(n^2 \sum_i \ell_i + n^4 \lambda\right)$ *without affecting the security of the protocol.*

Proof. If in a given system an accusation $e = (\mathrm{Acc}, P_i, P_j, \sigma_i)$ was sent as part of running one PC, then do not send it again. Also, add it to all sets S_i in all copies. Also, do not send it as part of the justifications after it was sent once. If $e = (\text{ACC}, \mathsf{P}_i, \mathsf{P}_j, \sigma_i)$ was received once then add it to all incoming justifications. This can be seen to not affect the execution of the protocol. If π justified m then it also does so after adding one more accusation. This way, overall, each of the n^2 possible $e = (\text{ACC}, \mathsf{P}_i, \mathsf{P}_j, \sigma_i)$ will be sent at most once per pair of parties for a total of $n^4\lambda$ communication. □

5   Generic Transferable Justifiers

Our second to last general tool is generic transferable justifiers. This is a short hand capturing the idea that a message can be justified by sending along all messages used to compute it and let the receiver recompute the message. In all protocols Π which follow, the protocols proceed in super rounds, where in each super round $s = 1, 2, \ldots$ the parties invoke a sub-protocol Π^s, wait for its outputs, and then run the next super round. In the first super round, we assume that each P_i has an input (x_i, π_i), where $J_{\mathsf{ln}}(\mathsf{P}_i, x_i, \pi_i) = \top$ and that this is the input to the first sub-protocol Π^1. As a sentinel, let $x_i^\cup = x_i$ and $\pi_i^\cup = \pi_i$ and define $\Pi^0.J_{\mathsf{Out}} := \Pi.J_{\mathsf{ln}}$. Consider then a super round s where in the previous $s - 1$ super rounds the parties ran protocols $\Pi^1, \ldots, \Pi^{s-1}$ and in super round s are to run Π^s. For $k = 1, \ldots, s - 1$, let y_i^k be the output of P_i from Π^k and let π_i^k be the justifier. Then the message to be input to Π^s by P_i will be computed using a function

$$x_i^s = \mathsf{NxtInp}(\{y_i^k\}_{k=0}^{s-1}) \tag{1}$$

and the accompanying justifier computed using a function

$$\pi_i^s = \mathsf{NxtJst}(\{(y_i^k, \pi_i^k)\}_{k=0}^{s-1}) \ . \tag{2}$$

Definition 11 (Generic Justifier). *When we say that we use a generic justifier predicate in a setting as described above then we mean that*

$$\mathsf{NxtJst}(\{(y_i^k, \pi_i^k)\}_{k=0}^{s-1}) = \{(y_i^k, \pi_i^k)\}_{k=0}^{s-1} \ .$$

Furthermore, the input justifier predicate for Π^s will be

$$\Pi^s.J_{\mathsf{ln}}(\mathsf{P}_j, x_i^s, \{(y_i^k, \pi_i^k)\}_{k=0}^{s-1})) \equiv$$
$$x_i^s = \mathsf{NxtInp}(\{y_i^k\}_{k=0}^{s-1}) \ \wedge \ \bigwedge_{k=0}^{s-1} \Pi^k.J_{\mathsf{Out}}(\mathsf{P}_j, y_i^k, \pi_i^k) \ .$$

We also use generic justifiers for the outputs. We simply show that the output can be computed from justified outputs of the sub-protocols.

Definition 12 (Generic Justifier for Output). *In a protocol with σ super-rounds, we give generic justified outputs by computing $x_i^{\sigma+1}$ as if it was an input for a virtual round $\sigma + 1$ (which we can also think of as the first round of the next protocol where $x_i^{\sigma+1}$ is input) and then we let the output of P_i be $y_i = x_i^{\sigma+1}$ and $\pi_i = \pi_i^{\sigma+1}$ where $x_i^{\sigma+1}$ is computed as in Eq. (1) and π_i as in Eq. (2).*

When an output is generically justified, then from the justifier one can extract a view of the protocol execution of the party producing it. We capture this in the following definition.

Definition 13 (Unfolded View). *Consider an AJO y in some σ-super-round protocol Π as described above using generic justifiers.[2] Let π' be the justifier. By the unfolded view of y we mean*

$$\mathsf{unfold}(y, \pi') := (\,(x, \pi), (y^1, \pi^1) \ldots, (y^\sigma, \pi^\sigma), y\,)\;,$$

where by construction π' contains $x = x^0$ and $\pi = \pi^0$ such that $\Pi.\mathsf{J_{In}}(x, \pi) = \top$ and outputs $y^1, \ldots, y^\sigma$ of its sub-protocols $\Pi^1, \ldots, \Pi^\sigma$ along with justifiers $\pi^1, \ldots, \pi^\sigma$ such that $\Pi^s.\mathsf{J_{Out}}(y^s, \pi^s) = \top$ and such that $y = \mathsf{NxtInp}(\{y^k\}_{k=0}^\sigma)^3$ is a correctly constructed output.

Remark 4 (Inconsistent Unfolded Views). Note that the unfolded view does not demonstrate that the input x^s to Π^s was computed according to the protocol from $(x^0, \ldots, x^{s-1})$. It only shows that the *output* y^s which is included in the justifier π' for Π^s was justified and the the final y was computed from x and these justified y^s. In particular, if we were to unfold y^s it might give an input $x^{s\prime}$ where $x^{s\prime} \neq x^s$. This is intended and seems crucial in controlling that the size of generic justifiers does not grow exponentially. It is also a desired feature that y^s might not be consistent with $x^s = \mathsf{NxtInp}(\{y^k\}_{k=0}^{s-1})$ in the view of P_i. This will soon allow us that P_i takes over a justified output y_j^s from another party P_j for some sub-protocol, i.e., it lets $y_i^s = y_j^s$ without having to recursively check consistency of the output it takes over.

6 Send Transferable Messages with Agreement and Justified Grade Cast

We now show how to add agreement to any STM protocol by giving an STMA protocol using STM as sub-protocol. The protocol is given in Fig. 5.

Theorem 2. *Protocol $\mathsf{STMA}_{\mathsf{J_{Msg}},\mathsf{P}_s}$ is an STMA protocol. Assuming that STMA has inputs (m, π) with $|m| \leq \ell$, it has communication complexity $\mathcal{O}(n^2\ell + n^4\lambda)$ and the size of the justified output is at most $\mathcal{O}(\ell + n^2\lambda)$. The amortized complexity can be optimised to be as in Lemma 6. If P_s is honest, it uses 2 rounds.*

Validity and agreement are proven below. The remaining properties are trivial. For communication, use that we run STM twice on inputs of length $\mathcal{O}(\ell)$.

Lemma 7 (Validity). *Protocol $\mathsf{STMA}_{\mathsf{J_{Msg}},\mathsf{P}_s}$ in Fig. 5 is valid.*

---

[2] Recall that this means that some honest party would accept y.

[3] Recall that we compute the output as if it was the input for a next virtual round.

$$\text{STMA}_{J_{\text{Msg}},\text{P}_s}(m, \pi_{\text{Msg}})$$

The input of P_s is (m, π_{MSG}), where $J_{\text{Msg}}(m, \pi_{\text{MSG}}) = \top$.

- P_s: On input (m, π_{MSG}) the sender inputs (m, π_{MSG}) to $\text{STM}_{J_{\text{Msg}},\text{P}_s}$.
- P_i: Let y be the output of $\text{STM}_{J_{\text{Msg}},\text{P}_s}$ and let

$$z = \begin{cases} m' & \text{if } y = (m', \pi') \text{ for } m' \neq \text{NoMsg} \\ \text{NoMsg}^{(s)} & \text{if } y = (\text{NoMsg}, \pi') . \end{cases}$$

Here, $\text{NoMsg}^{(s)} \neq \text{NoMsg}$ is a special symbol denoting that P_s sent NoMsg (and thus was corrupt). Let the justifier be $\gamma = y$ and let J denote the generic justifier predicate.
- P_i: Input (z, γ) to $\text{STM}_{J,\text{P}_i}$.
- P_i: For $j \in [n]$, let $z_j = (m_j, \gamma_j)$ be the output from $\text{STM}_{J,\text{P}_j}$ and let

$$\mathcal{A} = \{m_j\}_{j=1}^n \setminus \{\text{NoMsg}\} ,$$

$$m = \begin{cases} \text{NoMsg} & \text{if } \mathcal{A} = \{\text{NoMsg}^{(s)}\} \vee |\mathcal{A}| > 1 \\ m' & \text{if } \mathcal{A} = \{m'\} \text{ for } m' \neq \text{NoMsg}^{(s)} . \end{cases}$$

Let $\delta = \{z_j\}_{\text{P}_j \in \mathbb{P}}$ be the generic justifier and let $\text{STMA}_{J_{\text{Msg}},\text{P}_s}.J_{\text{Out}}$ be the generic justifier predicate.
- P_i: Output (m, δ).

Fig. 5. An STMA protocol.

Proof. Suppose P_s is honest and has input (m, π_{MSG}). In this case, P_s inputs (m, π_{MSG}) to $\text{STM}_{J_{\text{Msg}},\text{P}_s}$ such that $J_{\text{Msg}}(P_s, m, \pi_{\text{MSG}}) = \top$ and hence $J_{\text{Msg}}(m, \pi_{\text{MSG}}) = \top$ as P_s is honest.[4] By validity of $\text{STM}_{J_{\text{Msg}},\text{P}_s}$, every AJO is of the form $y = (m, \pi')$ with $J_{\text{Msg}}(m, \pi') = \top$ and all honest parties get an output. Hence, all honest parties P_i set $\gamma_i = (m, \pi'), z = m$ and input (z, γ) to $\text{STM}_{J,\text{P}_i}$. By validity of $\text{STM}_{J,\text{P}_j}$, every AJO (m, γ_j) has $J(m, \gamma_j) = \top$ when P_j is honest. For all dishonest P_j, the properties of the generic justifier and the justified messages property of $\text{STM}_{J,\text{P}_j}$ implies that for all AJOs z_j either $z_j = (m, \gamma_j)$ s.t. $J_{\text{Msg}}(m, \gamma_j) = \top$ or $z_j = (\text{NoMsg}, \gamma_j)$ s.t. $\text{STM}_{J,\text{P}_j}.J_{\text{Out}}(m, \gamma_j) = \top$. Hence, for all honest P_i, $m_j = m$ for all honest P_j and $m_j \in \{m, \text{NoMsg}\}$ for all dishonest P_j. Note that all AJOs must include $\delta = \{z_j\}_{\text{P}_j \in \mathbb{P}}$ and be valid with respect to the generic justifier. The properties of the generic justifier therefore imply that the unfolded view of any AJO must have $\mathcal{A} = \{m\}$ and hence be of the form (m, δ). □

Lemma 8 (Agreement). *Protocol* $\text{STMA}_{J_{\text{Msg}},\text{P}_s}$ *in Fig. 5 has agreement.*

Proof. By the properties of STM, any AJO of $\text{STM}_{J_{\text{Msg}},\text{P}_s}$ is justified by $\text{STM}_{J_{\text{Msg}},\text{P}_s}.J_{\text{Out}}$. We first show that if there exists an AJO $(m' \neq \text{NoMsg}, \pi')$

---

[4] Recall that $J(x, \pi) = \top$ denotes that $J(\text{P}_i, x, \pi) = \top$ for all honest P_i, which holds if it holds for a single P_i (cf. Definition 3).

from $\mathsf{STM}_{J_{\mathsf{Msg}},\mathsf{P}_s}$, then any AJO must be of the form (m',δ) or (NoMsg,δ), where $\delta = \{z_j\}_{P_j\in\mathbb{P}}$ s.t. the output is valid w.r.t. the generic justifier. To see this, note that by validity of $\mathsf{STM}_{J,\mathsf{P}_i}$, all its AJOs must be of the form $z_i = (m',\gamma_i)$. By the properties of the generic justifier, any party P_j must include z_i in the justifier of its output (m,δ) in order for it to be justifiable toward any honest party. Hence, the unfolded view of any AJO must form its output based on $\mathcal{A}$ which includes m'. This shows that only (m',δ) and (NoMsg,δ) can be justifiable outputs for P_j in this case. The case where there exist a justified output (NoMsg,π) from $\mathsf{STM}_{J_{\mathsf{Msg}},\mathsf{P}_s}$ is similar. Here, validity of $\mathsf{STM}_{J,\mathsf{P}_i}$ and the properties of the generic justifier together instead imply that any AJO must include $\text{NoMsg}^{(s)}$ in $\mathcal{A}$ in order for its output to be generically justifiable. Hence, all AJOs will have $m = \text{NoMsg}$. □

6.1 Justified Grade Cast

In STMA, some parties might have output NoMsg while some have $m \neq \text{NoMsg}$. We now show how to upgrade an STMA to a graded STM where the output contains a grade $g \in \{0,1,2\}$ which indicates the confidence in this output. When $g = 2$, no AJO can have $m \neq \text{NoMsg}$. Furthermore, grades are at most 1 apart and honest senders always produce grade 2. A detailed definition is given in Definition 14. Our protocol is given in Fig. 6.

Definition 14 (Graded Send Transferable Message). *Let Π be a protocol run among n parties $\mathsf{P}_1,\ldots,\mathsf{P}_n$ and let J_{Msg} be a parametrisable input justifier predicate. Assume that Π specifies a designated sender P_s holding input (m,π_{MSG}) such that $J_{\mathsf{Msg}}(\mathsf{P}_s, m, \pi_{\mathrm{MSG}}) = \top$ and parties terminate upon generating output in Π. As part of its code the protocol specifies an output justifier predicate $\Pi.J_{\mathsf{Out}}$. We say that Π is a graded send transferable message (GSTM) protocol if it has the following properties:*

- *Correctness: Honest P_i outputs $y_i = ((m_i,g_i),\pi_i)$ for $g_i \in \{1,2\}$ and $m_i \neq \text{NoMsg}$ or $y_i = ((m_i = \text{NoMsg}, g_i = 0),\pi_i)$.*
- *Justified Output: When honest P_i outputs $y_i = ((m_i,g_i),\pi_i)$ then $J_{\mathsf{Out}}(\mathsf{P}_i, (m_i,g_i),\pi_i) = \top$.*
- *Justified Message: For all AJOs $y_i = ((m_i,g_i),\pi_i)$ either $m_i = \text{NoMsg}$ and $g_i = 0$ or π_i is of the form $\pi_i = (\pi_i^1,\pi_i^2)$ and $J_{\mathsf{Msg}}(m_i,\pi_i^1) = \top$.*
- *Validity: If P_s is honest and has input (m,π_{MSG}), then all honest parties P_j have output $m_j = m$ and $g_j = 2$. Furthermore, for all AJOs (m',g') it holds that $m' = m$ and $g' = 2$.*
- *Graded Agreement: For all AJOs (m^1,g^1) and (m^2,g^2) it holds that $|g^1 - g^2| \leq 1$ and if $g^1,g^2 > 0$ then $m^1 = m^2$.*

$$\text{GSTM}_{J_{\text{Msg}},\mathsf{P}_s}(m, \pi_{\text{Msg}})$$

The input of P_s is (m, π_{Msg}), where $J_{\text{Msg}}(m, \pi_{\text{Msg}}) = \top$.

- P_s: Input (m, π_{Msg}) to $\text{STMA}_{J_{\text{Msg}},\mathsf{P}_s}$.
- P_i: Let y be the output of $\text{STMA}_{J_{\text{Msg}},\mathsf{P}_s}$ and let

$$z = \begin{cases} m' & \text{if } y = (m', \pi') \text{ for } m' \neq \text{NoMsg} \\ \text{NoMsg}^{(s)} & \text{if } y = (\text{NoMsg}, \pi') . \end{cases}$$

Let the justifier be $\gamma = y$ and let J be the generic justifier predicate.
- P_i: Input (z, γ) to $\text{STMA}_{J,\mathsf{P}_i}$.
- P_i: For $j \in [n]$, let $z_j = (m_j, \gamma_j)$ be the output from $\text{STMA}_{J,\mathsf{P}_j}$ and let

$$\mathcal{A} = \{m_j\}_{j=1}^n \setminus \{\text{NoMsg}\} ,$$

$$(m, g) = \begin{cases} (\text{NoMsg}, 0) & \text{if } \mathcal{A} = \{\text{NoMsg}^{(s)}\} \\ (m', 1) & \text{if } \mathcal{A} = \{m', \text{NoMsg}^{(s)}\} \text{ for } m' \neq \text{NoMsg}^{(s)} \\ (m', 2) & \text{if } \mathcal{A} = \{m'\} \text{ for } m' \neq \text{NoMsg}^{(s)} . \end{cases}$$

Let $\delta = \{z_j\}_{\mathsf{P}_j \in \mathbb{P}}$ be the generic justifier and let $\text{GSTM}_{J_{\text{Msg}},\mathsf{P}_s}.J_{\text{Out}}$ be the generic justifier predicate.
- P_i: Output $((m, g), \delta)$.

Fig. 6. A justified gradecast protocol.

Theorem 3. *Protocol* $\text{GSTM}_{J_{\text{Msg}},\mathsf{P}_s}$ *is a GSTM for* $t < n$. *Assume that GSTM has inputs* (m, π) *with* $|m| \leq \ell$. *Then the protocol has communication complexity* $\mathcal{O}(n^2\ell + n^4\lambda)$ *and the size of the justified output is at most* $\mathcal{O}(\ell + n^2\lambda)$. *The amortized complexity can be optimised to be as in Lemma 6.*

As for STMA, all properties but validity and agreement are trivial and so is the communication complexity.

Lemma 9 (Validity). *Protocol* $\text{GSTM}_{J_{\text{Msg}},\mathsf{P}_s}$ *in Fig. 6 is valid.*

Proof. Suppose that P_s is honest and has input m. By validity of $\text{STMA}_{J_{\text{Msg}},\mathsf{P}_s}$, every AJO y for that protocol is $y = (m', \pi')$ for $m' = m$. Now let $((m, g), \delta)$ be any AJO of $\text{GSTM}_{J_{\text{Msg}},\mathsf{P}_s}(m, \pi_{\text{Msg}})$ and assume for the sake of contradiction that $g \in \{0, 1\}$. Then the unfolded view of $((m, g), \delta)$ contains an AJO for $(\text{NoMsg}, 0)$ or $(m', 1)$ from $\text{STMA}_{J,\mathsf{P}_j}$. By definition of $\mathcal{A}$ the unfolded view of either of these AJOs will contain an AJO for $y = (\text{NoMsg}, \pi')$ from $\text{STMA}_{J_{\text{Msg}},-s}$, a contradiction. $\square$

Lemma 10 (Graded Agreement). *Protocol* $\text{GSTM}_{J_{\text{Msg}},\mathsf{P}_s}$ *in Fig. 6 has graded agreement.*

Proof. Suppose we have AJOs $((m_i, g_i), \delta_i)$ and $((m_j, g_j), \delta_j)$ with $g_i, g_j > 0$. By the properties of the generic justifier, it must be the case that the unfolded view of $((m_i, g_i), \delta_i)$ holds an AJO for $m_i \neq$ NoMsg from some $\mathsf{STMA}_{J,\mathsf{P}_k}$. By the justified message property of STMA it follows that m_i is justified using the input justifier J of $\mathsf{STMA}_{J,\mathsf{P}_k}$, which was the genetic justifier checking that m_i was an AJO of $\mathsf{STMA}_{J_{\mathrm{Msg}},\mathsf{P}_s}$. Symmetrically, we can conclude that m_j was an AJO of $\mathsf{STMA}_{J_{\mathrm{Msg}},\mathsf{P}_s}$. By the agreement property of $\mathsf{STMA}_{J_{\mathrm{Msg}},\mathsf{P}_s}$ it follows that $m_i = m_j$. It remains to show that it cannot be the case for two AJOs that $g_i = 2$ and $g_j = 0$. Assume that $g_i = 0$. Suppose then for the sake of contradiction that we have AJOs $((m_i, g_i), \delta_i)$ and $((m_j, g_j), \delta_j)$ with $g_i = 0$ and $g_j = 2$. The unfolded view of $((m_i, g_i), \delta_i)$ holds an AJO for $m_i = \mathrm{NoMsg}^{(s)}$ from all $\mathsf{STMA}_{J,\mathsf{P}_k}$ which did not output NoMsg, in particular for all honest P_k. Symmetrically, we can conclude that m_j was an AJO from $\mathsf{STMA}_{J,\mathsf{P}_k}$ for all honest P_j. Since $g_j = 2$ we have $m_j \neq \mathrm{NoMsg}^{(s)}$. Since there is at least one honest P_j we have found one $\mathsf{STMA}_{J,\mathsf{P}_k}$ where P_k is honest and it has AJO $\mathrm{NoMsg}^{(s)}$ and AJO $m_j \neq \mathrm{NoMsg}^{(s)}$. This breaks validity of $\mathsf{STMA}_{J,\mathsf{P}_k}$ as the honest P_k cannot have inputted both $\mathrm{NoMsg}^{(s)}$ and $\neq \mathrm{NoMsg}^{(s)}$. $\square$

7 Early Stopping Broadcast

We now present our main result, early stopping broadcast.

7.1 Diagonal Cast

We begin by building an early stopping protocol, called DC (for *diagonal cast*), which is early stopping, but may run up to $O(t^2)$ rounds. The protocol will be a justifiable broadcast in the sense of Definition 6, which implies that it is also a broadcast protocol. The protocol DC uses GSTM as (blackbox) sub-protocol. Since we use DC as a building block in our final protocol, we also make its output justified. During the protocol we use a helper function computing a party's next vote. In each round the parties run one GSTM to get output (m, g). Consider a party which in the previous rounds saw outputs $(m^1, g^1), \ldots, (m^r, g^r)$. Then it should use the m from the latest GSTM with $g^\rho > 0$. If no such ρ exists it should use $\mathrm{NoMsg}^{(s)}$ to indicate the sender P_s was corrupt. More formally we use this function:

$$\mathsf{NxtInp}((m^1, g^1), \ldots, (m^r, g^r)) = \begin{cases} \mathrm{NoMsg}^{(s)} & \text{if } g^1 = \cdots = g^r = 0 \\ m_{\max\{i \in [r] \mid g_i > 0\}} & \text{otherwise.} \end{cases}$$

Below we let $i^* = \max\{i \in [r] \mid g_i > 0\}$ when we are not in the case $g^1 = \cdots = g^r = 0$. At the end of the protocol we want to map $\mathrm{NoMsg}^{(s)}$ to NoMsg. For this we use a simple helper: $\mathsf{Out}(m) = \mathrm{NoMsg}$ if $m = \mathrm{NoMsg}^{(s)}$ and $\mathsf{Out}(m) = m$ otherwise. The protocol is given in Fig. 7.

Lemma 11 (Validity). DC *satisfies validity.*

Proof. Suppose that P_1 is an honest sender holding input (m, π_{Msg}). Since $J_{\mathrm{Msg}}(\mathsf{P}_1, m, \pi_{\mathrm{Msg}}) = \top$ validity of $\mathsf{GSTM}_{J_{\mathrm{Msg}},\mathsf{P}_1}$ implies that all honest parties get output $(m, 2, \pi)$. Hence, all parties terminate with output m after running for one more iteration of the loop. $\square$

Diagonal Cast $\mathsf{DC}_{J_{\mathsf{Msg}}, \mathsf{P}_s}$

Without loss of generality, assume that P_1 is the sender, i.e., $s = 1$.

- In round 1:
  - P_1: Has input (m, π_{MsG}) with $J_{\mathsf{Msg}}(\mathsf{P}_1, m, \pi_{\mathsf{MsG}}) = \top$ and inputs it to $\mathsf{GSTM}_{J_{\mathsf{Msg}}, \mathsf{P}_1}$.
  - P_i: Let $y = ((m_i^1, g_i^1), \pi_i^1)$ be the output from $\mathsf{GSTM}_{J_{\mathsf{Msg}}, \mathsf{P}_1}$.
  - P_i: If $g_i^1 = 2$ then send $(1, (m_i^1, g_i^1), \pi_i^1)$ to all other parties, output $m = \mathsf{Out}(m_i^1)$, run for one more round (to ensure that no honest party terminates until all honest gave output), and then terminate.
- For $j \in \{2, \ldots, n\}$ do as follows:
  - P_j: Compute $m_j = \mathsf{NxtInp}((m_j^1, g_j^1), \ldots, (m_j^{j-1}, g_j^{j-1}))$.
  - P_j: Compute the generic justifier $\gamma_j = \{((m_j^k, g_j^k), \pi_j^k)\}_{k=1}^{j-1}$ and let J^j be the generic justifier predicate for this round.
  - P_j: Input (m_j, γ_j) to $\mathsf{GSTM}_{J^j, \mathsf{P}_j}$.
  - P_i: Let $y = ((m_i^j, g_i^j), \pi_i^j)$ be the output from $\mathsf{GSTM}_{J^j, \mathsf{P}_j}$.
  - P_i: If $g_i^j = 2$ then send $(j, (m_i^j, g_i^j), \pi_i^j)$ to all other parties, output $m = \mathsf{Out}(m_i^j)$, run for one more round, and then terminate.
- P_i: Upon receiving a tuple $(j, (m', g'), \pi')$ (for any $j \in [n]$ and in any round) such that $\mathsf{GSTM}_{J^j, \mathsf{P}_j}.J_{\mathsf{Out}}(\mathsf{P}_i, (m', g'), \pi') = \top$ and $g' = 2$, forward it to all parties, output $m = \mathsf{Out}(m')$, run for one more round, and then terminate.
- The output justifier for the protocol is $\mathsf{DC}_{J_{\mathsf{Msg}}, \mathsf{P}_s}.J_{\mathsf{Out}}(m, \pi)$, which is true if $\pi = (j, (m', g'), \pi')$ and $j \in [n]$ and $\mathsf{GSTM}_{J^j, \mathsf{P}_j}.J_{\mathsf{Out}}(\mathsf{P}_i, (m', g'), \pi') = \top$ and $m = \mathsf{Out}(m')$.

Fig. 7. The broadcast protocol.

Lemma 12 (Stabilisation). *Let j be the minimal iteration such that for some honest P_i an AJO $((m, 2), \pi)$ satisfying $\mathsf{GSTM}_{J^j, \mathsf{P}_j}.J_{\mathsf{Out}}(\mathsf{P}_i, (m, 2), \pi) = \top$ can be produced. Then for any $j' \geq j$ and any honest $\mathsf{P}_{i'}$ and any AJO $((m', 2), \pi')$ satisfying $\mathsf{GSTM}_{J^{j'}, \mathsf{P}_{j'}}.J_{\mathsf{Out}}(\mathsf{P}_{i'}, (m', g'), \pi') = \top$ it holds that $g' = 0$ or $m' = m$. Furthermore, if $j' = j$ then $g' > 0$ and thus $m' = m$.*

Proof. We do induction in $|j' - j| = 0, 1, \ldots$. For the base case $|j' - j| = 0$ we have $j' = j$ and that $g' \in \{1, 2\}$ and $m' = m$ by graded agreement of $\mathsf{GSTM}_{J^j, \mathsf{P}_j}$. Assume then the induction hypothesis for all $|j' - j| < \ell$. We prove it for $|j' - j| = \ell$. We have to prove that $g' = 0$ or $m = m'$. So it is enough to prove that if $g' > 0$ then $m' = m$. When $g' > 0$ then by the justified message property of $\mathsf{GSTM}_{J^{j'}, \mathsf{P}_{j'}}$ we have that m' is justified by $J^{j'}$, which was the generic justifier for iteration j'. Therefore m' was computed as

$$m' = \mathsf{NxtInp}((m^1, g^1), \ldots, (m^{j'-1}, g^{j'-1}))$$

from AJOs. By induction hypothesis $g^j \geq 1$ and $m^j = m$, and for $j \leq k \leq j'-1$ it holds that $g^k = 0$ or $m^k = m$. This by construction gives

$$\mathsf{NxtInp}((m^1, g^1), \dots, (m^{j'-1}, g^{j'-1})) = m \;,$$

as desired.   □

Corollary 2. DC *has agreement.*

Proof. When an honest party P_i produces output m' then it by construction produces or receives an AJO $(m', g = 2)$ for some $\mathsf{GSTM}_{J^{j'}, \mathsf{P}_{j'}}$. Clearly there is a smallest j for which an AJO $(m, g = 2)$ can be produced for $\mathsf{GSTM}_{J^j, \mathsf{P}_j}$. By Lemma 12 it holds that $m' = m$. This holds for all honest outputs m'.   □

Lemma 13. DC *terminates in* $8(f + 1)(f + 2)$ *rounds. If* P_1 *is honest then it runs in at most* $8(f + 2)$ *rounds.*

Proof. The protocol terminates at the latest once the first honest party acts as the sender in some iteration j as this gives $g_j = 2$. This is worstcase in iteration $(f + 1)$. Each iteration runs one GSTM, which uses two STMA, which each uses two STM, which each uses $f + 2$ rounds. This gives $4(f + 2)$ rounds per GSTM, and applying the staggering compiler contributes a factor of 2.   □

7.2   Weak Early Stopping $\mathcal{O}(f)$ and Worstcase $\mathcal{O}(t)$

The protocol DC can do early stopping, but if there are $f = \omega(\sqrt{t})$ corruptions it runs for more than $\mathcal{O}(t)$ rounds, which is asymptotically sub-optimal. We solve this by capping the running time at $\mathcal{O}(t)$. Doing this safely is subtle, and we now present a protocol with weak early stopping which helps doing it safely. Weak early stopping means that the protocol achieves early stopping when the sender is honest. If the sender is corrupt it may run for $\mathcal{O}(n)$ rounds. We describe the protocol with P_1 as sender, but it can be adopted to any P_s (Fig. 8).

Theorem 4. *The protocol* $\mathsf{WES}_{J_{\mathsf{Msg}}, \mathsf{P}_1}$ *is a broadcast protocol. Parties terminate one round apart and the round complexity is* $\mathcal{O}(t)$. *If* P_1 *is honest then the round complexity is* $\mathcal{O}(f)$.

Proof. Validity is trivial: if P_1 is honest then $\mathsf{GSTM}_{J_{\mathsf{Msg}}, \mathsf{P}_1}$ outputs $((m, g), \pi)$ with $g = 2$ and all honest parties output m. This happens within one run of GSTM, so in $\mathcal{O}(f)$ rounds. We argue agreement. If all honest parties give output by receiving a tuple $((m', g'), \pi')$ which is an AJO for $\mathsf{GSTM}_{J_{\mathsf{Msg}}, \mathsf{P}_1}$ and with $g' = 2$ then agreement follows from agreement of $\mathsf{GSTM}_{J_{\mathsf{Msg}}, \mathsf{P}_1}$. If all honest parties give output by receiving $((m, g), \pi)$ from DSC then agreement follows from agreement of DSC. Assume then that some honest P_i gives output using $((m' = m_i, g' = 2), \pi')$ which is an AJO for $\mathsf{GSTM}_{J_{\mathsf{Msg}}, \mathsf{P}_1}$ and some honest P_j gives output m_j by receiving $((m, g), \pi)$ from $\mathsf{DSC}_{\mathsf{P}_1, J}$. Since $g' = 2$ and $m' = m_i$ it follows from graded agreement for $\mathsf{GSTM}_{J_{\mathsf{Msg}}, \mathsf{P}_1}$ that $m = m_i$ and $g > 0$ for all AJOs for $\mathsf{GSTM}_{J_{\mathsf{Msg}}, \mathsf{P}_1}$. Since J is the generic justifier it follows that all AJOs

---

WES$_{J_{\text{Msg}},\text{P}_1}$

- P$_1$: Has input (m, π_{MSG}) with $J_{\text{Msg}}(\text{P}_1, m, \pi_{\text{MSG}}) = \top$ and inputs it to GSTM$_{J_{\text{Msg}},\text{P}_1}$.
- P$_1$: Let $((m, g), \pi)$ be the output of GSTM$_{J_{\text{Msg}},\text{P}_1}$ and run DSC$_{\text{P}_1, J}$ with input $((m, g), \pi)$ by P$_1$, where J is the generic justifier predicate.
- P$_i$: Upon receiving a tuple $((m', g'), \pi')$ as output from GSTM$_{J_{\text{Msg}},\text{P}_1}$ or relayed by another party, where GSTM$_{J_{\text{Msg}},\text{P}_1}.J_{\text{Out}}(\text{P}_i, (m', g'), \pi') = \top$ and $g' = 2$, forward it to all parties, output $m = m'$, and terminate.
- If DSC$_{\text{P}_1, J_{\text{Msg}}}$ outputs $((m, g), \pi)$ before an output was produced using the above rule, output as follows. If GSTM$_{J_{\text{Msg}},\text{P}_1}.J_{\text{Out}}(\text{P}_i, (m, g), \pi) = \top$ and $g > 0$, output m. Otherwise, output N$_\text{O}$M$_\text{SG}$.

Fig. 8. The weak early stopping broadcast protocol.

$((m, g), \pi)$ for DSC$_{\text{P}_1, J}$ has $m'' = m_i$ and $g'' > 0$. Therefore P$_j$ has output $m_j = m = m_i$. Parties terminate one round apart as they terminate one round apart in DSC and if they terminate by the $g' = 2$ rule then they forward the AJO and then all honest parties terminate in the next round. □

7.3 Early Stopping $\mathcal{O}(f^2)$ and Worstcase $\mathcal{O}(t)$

We now give a broadcast protocol Capped Diagonal Cast which basically runs Diagonal Cast for a capped number of rounds and uses WES to have all parties report whether they saw an output from DC before the time cap. Since the reports are sent with WES parties will agree on the reports and make the same decision. Furthermore, if an honest party saw an output it will be reported with early stopping. We again describe the protocol with P$_1$ as sender, but can trivially adopt to any P$_s$ (Fig. 9).

Theorem 5. *The protocol* CDC$_{J_{\text{Msg}},\text{P}_1}$ *is a broadcast protocol. Parties terminate one round apart and the round complexity is* $\mathcal{O}(\min(f^2, t))$. *If the sender is honest output is given in* $\mathcal{O}(f)$ *rounds. From* CDC$_{J_{\text{Msg}},\text{P}_1}$ *we can get a broadcast protocol* EBC *for Definition 1 with the same communication complexity simply by dropping the input justifier predicate* J_{Msg} *and the justifier* π_{MSG}.

Proof. First note that all WES$_{\text{P}_i, \top}$ are started at most one round apart. Namely, no party starts them later then by round $8(t+1)$. So if they are to be started 2 rounds apart the first is started in round $8(t+1)-2$ or earlier. But then DC$_{\text{P}_1, J_{\text{Msg}}}$ terminated by round $8(t+1)-2$ at the first honest party. But then it terminated by round $8(t+1)-1$ at all honest. Hence all honest started WES$_{\text{P}_i, \top}$ exactly when DC$_{\text{P}_1, J_{\text{Msg}}}$ terminated, which is at most one round apart. We can then apply the staggering compiler to ensure that WES$_{\text{P}_i, \top}$ tolerates being started one round apart. This gives a $\mathcal{O}(1)$ blowup in round comlexity. We then argue validity: if P$_1$ is honest then DC$_{J_{\text{Msg}},\text{P}_1}$ outputs (m, π) within $8(f+2) \leq 8(t+2)$ rounds. Therefore an honest party P$_j$ will send (m, π) on WES$_{\text{P}_j, \top}$ which will output (m, π)

Capped Diagonal Cast $\mathsf{CDC}_{\mathsf{P}_1, J_{\mathsf{Msg}}}$

We describe the protocol from the view of party P_i.

- P_1: Has input (m, π_{Msg}) with $J_{\mathsf{Msg}}(m, \pi_{\mathsf{Msg}}) = \top$ and inputs it to $\mathsf{DC}_{\mathsf{P}_1, J_{\mathsf{Msg}}}$.
- P_i: Participate in $\mathsf{DC}_{\mathsf{P}_1, J_{\mathsf{Msg}}}$ for at most $8(t+1)$ rounds.[a]
- P_i: If $\mathsf{DC}_{\mathsf{P}_1, J_{\mathsf{Msg}}}$ produced output (m, π) in or before round $8n$ then run $\mathsf{WES}_{\mathsf{P}_i, \top}$ with input (m, π) in the round where $\mathsf{DC}_{\mathsf{P}_1, J_{\mathsf{Msg}}}$ produced output. If by round $8(t+1)$ protocol $\mathsf{DC}_{\mathsf{P}_1, J_{\mathsf{Msg}}}$ did not produce output run $\mathsf{WES}_{\mathsf{P}_i, \top}$ with input NoMsg in round $8(t+1)$.
- P_i: If and when the first $\mathsf{WES}_{\mathsf{P}_j, \top}$ outputs (m, π) such that $\mathsf{DC}_{\mathsf{P}_1, J_{\mathsf{Msg}}}.J_{\mathsf{Out}}(m, \pi) = \top$, output m.
- P_i: If $\mathsf{WES}_{\mathsf{P}_1, \top}, \ldots, \mathsf{WES}_{\mathsf{P}_n, \top}$ all terminated and none had an output (m, π) such that $\mathsf{DC}_{\mathsf{P}_1, J_{\mathsf{Msg}}}.J_{\mathsf{Out}}(m, \pi) = \top$, then output NoMsg.

---

[a] Here we count base communication rounds, not iterations of GSTM.

Fig. 9. An Early Stopping Broadcast protocol with $\mathcal{O}(\min((f+1)^2, n))$ rounds.

within $\mathcal{O}(f)$ rounds and then all honest output m. This all happens within $\mathcal{O}(f)$ rounds. Agreement is trivial from agreement of WES, as the output is computed deterministically from the outputs of $\mathsf{WES}_{\mathsf{P}_1, \top}, \ldots, \mathsf{WES}_{\mathsf{P}_n, \top}$. Consider then the round complexity. We have that all copies of WES are started after $\mathcal{O}(\min(f^2, t))$ rounds as $\mathsf{DC}_{\mathsf{P}_1, J_{\mathsf{Msg}}}$ stops after $\mathcal{O}(f^2)$ rounds and we cap after $8(t+1)$ rounds. If $\mathsf{DC}_{\mathsf{P}_1, J_{\mathsf{Msg}}}$ did give an output at all honest parties before round $8(t+1)$ then it will be input to $\mathsf{WES}_{\mathsf{P}_i, \top}$ which will output after $\mathcal{O}(f)$ rounds, and hence output is produces in $\mathcal{O}(f^2)$ rounds as $\mathsf{DC}_{\mathsf{P}_1, J_{\mathsf{Msg}}}$ terminates in $\mathcal{O}(f^2)$ rounds. If $\mathsf{DC}_{\mathsf{P}_1, J_{\mathsf{Msg}}}$ did not give output within $8(t+1)$ rounds then $8(t+1) = \mathcal{O}(f^2)$, so $\mathcal{O}(\min(f^2, t)) = \mathcal{O}(t)$. And in this case the overall protocols runs for at most $\mathcal{O}(t)$ rounds as each WES terminates in $\mathcal{O}(t)$ rounds. $\qquad\square$

Acknowledgements. We would like to thank Juan Garay for fruitful discussions in the early stages of this work. We would also like to thank Fatima Elsheimy for many detailed technical and editorial comments.

References

1. Abraham, I., et al.: Communication complexity of byzantine agreement, revisited. In: Robinson, P., Ellen, F. (eds.) 38th ACM PODC, pp. 317–326. ACM, July/August 2019
2. Abraham, I., Dolev, D.: Byzantine agreement with optimal early stopping, optimal resilience and polynomial complexity. In: Servedio, R.A., Rubinfeld, R., (eds.) 47th ACM STOC, pp. 605–614. ACM Press, June 2015
3. Alexandru, A.B., Loss, J., Papamanthou, C., Tsimos, G.: Sublinear-round broadcast without trusted setup against dishonest majority. Cryptology ePrint Archive, Report 2022/1383 (2022). https://eprint.iacr.org/2022/1383

4. Berman, P., Garay, J.A.: $n/4$-resilient distributed consensus in $t+1$ rounds. Math. Syst. Theory **26**(1), 3–19 (1993)
5. Berman, P., Garay, J.A., Perry, K.J.: Towards optimal distributed consensus (extended abstract). In: 30th FOCS, pp. 410–415. IEEE Computer Society Press, October/November 1989
6. Berman, P., Garay, J.A., Perry, K.J.: Optimal early stopping in distributed consensus (extended abstract). In: WDAG, pp. 221–237 (1992)
7. Chan, T.-H.H., Pass, R., Shi, E.: Sublinear-round byzantine agreement under corrupt majority. In: Kiayias, A., Kohlweiss, M., Wallden, P., Zikas, V. (eds.) PKC 2020. LNCS, vol. 12111, pp. 246–265. Springer, Cham (2020). https://doi.org/10.1007/978-3-030-45388-6_9
8. Chandra, T.D., Toueg, S.: Time and message efficient reliable broadcasts. In: WDAG, pp. 289–303 (1990)
9. Dolev, D., Lenzen, C.: Early-deciding consensus is expensive. In: Fatourou, P., Taubenfeld, G. (eds.) 32nd ACM PODC, pp. 270–279. ACM, July 2013
10. Dolev, D., Reischuk, R.: Bounds on information exchange for byzantine agreement. In: Probert, R.L., Fischer, M.J., Santoro, N., (eds.) 1st ACM PODC, pp. 132–140. ACM, August 1982
11. Dolev, D., Reischuk, R., Raymond Strong, H.: Early stopping in byzantine agreement. J. ACM **37**(4), 720–741 (1990)
12. Dolev, D., Raymond Strong, H.: Authenticated algorithms for Byzantine agreement. SIAM J. Comput. **12**(4), 656–666 (1983)
13. Danny Dolev and Andrew Chi-Chih Yao: On the security of public key protocols. IEEE Trans. Inf. Theory **29**(2), 198–207 (1983)
14. Feldman, P., Micali, S.: Optimal algorithms for byzantine agreement. In: 20th ACM STOC, pp. 148–161. ACM Press, May 1988
15. Fitzi, M., Nielsen, J.B.: On the number of synchronous rounds sufficient for authenticated byzantine agreement. In: DISC, pp. 449–463 (2009)
16. Garay, J.A., Katz, J., Koo, C.-Y., Ostrovsky, R.: Round complexity of authenticated broadcast with a dishonest majority. In: 48th FOCS, pp. 658–668. IEEE Computer Society Press, October 2007
17. Garay, J.A., Moses, Y.: Fully polynomial byzantine agreement in t+1 rounds. In: 25th ACM STOC, pp. 31–41. ACM Press, May 1993
18. Garay, J.A., Moses, Y.: Fully polynomial byzantine agreement for n ¿ 3t processors in t + 1 rounds. SIAM J. Comput. **27**(1), 247–290 (1998)
19. Katz, J., Koo, C.-Y.: On expected constant-round protocols for byzantine agreement. In: Dwork, C. (ed.) CRYPTO 2006. LNCS, vol. 4117, pp. 445–462. Springer, Heidelberg (2006). https://doi.org/10.1007/11818175_27
20. Keidar, I., Rajsbaum, S.: A simple proof of the uniform consensus synchronous lower bound. Inf. Process. Lett. **85**(1), 47–52 (2003)
21. Lamport, L., Shostak, R., Pease, M.: The Byzantine generals problem. ACM Trans. Programming Lang. Syst. **4**(3), 382–401 (1982)
22. Lenzen, C., Sheikholeslami, S.: A recursive early-stopping phase king protocol. In: ACM PODC, pp. 60–69. ACM (2022)
23. Lindell, Y., Lysyanskaya, A., Rabin, T.: Sequential composition of protocols without simultaneous termination. In: Ricciardi, A. (ed.) 21st ACM PODC, pp. 203–212. ACM, July 2002
24. Micali, S.: Very simple and efficient byzantine agreement. In: Papadimitriou, C.H. (ed.) ITCS 2017, vol. 4266. LIPIcs, pp. 6:1–6:1, 67, January 2017
25. Nielsen, J.B.: On Protocol Security in the Cryptographic Model. Ph.D. thesis, Aarhus University (2003)

26. Parvédy, P.R., Raynal, M.: Optimal early stopping uniform consensus in synchronous systems with process omission failures. In: SPAA, vol. 302–310 (2004)
27. Perry, K.J., Toueg, S.: An authenticated byzantine generals algoorithm with early stopping. Technical report, Cornell University (1984)
28. Srinivasan, S., Loss, J., Malavolta, G., Nayak, K., Papamanthou, C., Thyagarajan, S.A.K.: Transparent batchable time-lock puzzles and applications to byzantine consensus. In: Boldyreva, A., Kolesnikov, V. (eds.) PKC 2023, Part I. LNCS, vol. 13940, pp. 554–584. Springer, Cham (2023). https://doi.org/10.1007/978-3-031-31368-4_20
29. Wan, J., Xiao, H., Devadas, S., Shi, E.: Round-efficient Byzantine broadcast under strongly adaptive and majority corruptions. In: Pass, R., Pietrzak, K. (eds.) TCC 2020. LNCS, vol. 12550, pp. 412–456. Springer, Cham (2020). https://doi.org/10.1007/978-3-030-64375-1_15
30. Wan, J., Xiao, H., Shi, E., Devadas, S.: Expected constant round byzantine broadcast under dishonest majority. In: Pass, R., Pietrzak, K. (eds.) TCC 2020. LNCS, vol. 12550, pp. 381–411. Springer, Cham (2020). https://doi.org/10.1007/978-3-030-64375-1_14

Author Index

A

Auerbach, Benedikt 315

B

Ben-David, Shany 345
Bergamaschi, Thiago 404

C

Canales-Martínez, Isaac A. 3
Chávez-Saab, Jorge 3
Chen, Shan 251
Cremers, Cas 129

F

Fischlin, Marc 251

G

Gao, Si 221
Garay, Juan 96
Grassi, Lorenzo 188
Günther, Christoph U. 315

H

Hambitzer, Anna 3
Hiroka, Taiga 434

J

Jaeger, Joseph 283

K

Kiayias, Aggelos 34, 96
Kitagawa, Fuyuki 434
Kumar, Akshaya 283

L

Leonardos, Nikos 34
Liu-Zhang, Chen-Da 64
Loss, Julian 129, 457

M

Masure, Loïc 188
Matt, Christian 64

Méaux, Pierrick 188
Moos, Thorben 188
Morimae, Tomoyuki 434

N

Narayanan, Anand Kumar 160
Nielsen, Jesper Buus 457
Nishimaki, Ryo 434

O

Oswald, Elisabeth 221

P

Pal, Tapas 434
Pietrzak, Krzysztof 315

Q

Qiao, Youming 160

R

Rodríguez-Henríquez, Francisco 3

S

Satpute, Nitin 3
Shamir, Adi 3
Shen, Yu 34, 96
Standaert, François-Xavier 188
Steiner, Matthias Johann 375
Stepanovs, Igors 283

T

Tang, Gang 160
Thomsen, Søren Eller 64

W

Wagner, Benedikt 129

Y

Yamakawa, Takashi 434

M. Joye and G. Leander (Eds.): EUROCRYPT 2024, LNCS 14653, p. 489, 2024.
https://doi.org/10.1007/978-3-031-58734-4